THE INEVITABILITY OF TRAGEDY

THE INEVITABILITY OF TRAGEDY

HENRY KISSINGER AND HIS WORLD

BARRY GEWEN

W. W. NORTON & COMPANY

Independent Publishers Since 1923

For information about permission to reproduce selections from this book, write to
Permissions, W. W. Norton & Company, Inc., 500 Fifth Avenue, New York, NY 10110

For information about special discounts for bulk purchases, please contact
W. W. Norton Special Sales at specialsales@wwnorton.com or 800-233-4830

Manufacturing by LSC Communications, Harrisonburg
Book design by Lovedog Studio
Production manager: Anna Oler

ISBN 978-1-324-00405-9

W. W. Norton & Company, Inc., 500 Fifth Avenue, New York, N.Y. 10110
www.wwnorton.com

W. W. Norton & Company Ltd., 15 Carlisle Street, London W1D 3BS

1 2 3 4 5 6 7 8 9 0

To my colleagues, past and present, at the
New York Times Book Review

There are certain truths which the Americans can learn only from strangers or from experience.

—ALEXIS DE TOCQUEVILLE

One has to live with a sense of the inevitability of tragedy.

—HENRY KISSINGER

CONTENTS

PROLOGUE IN THE FIRST PERSON

A COUPLE OF YEARS AGO, I WAS HAVING DINNER WITH A friend when he leaned across the table and whispered to me, "Barry, Henry Kissinger is *evil*." He was in the middle of writing his own book on foreign policy, and in the course of a long friendship we had spent many mutually beneficial evenings discussing international affairs. It was not unusual for our conversations to run to 3½ or 4 hours.

We approached policy issues differently. I tended to take a Realpolitik view, which is to say that I tried to reach conclusions based on the power relationships of a given situation. I attempted to assess how American national interest would be affected by a particular decision and to measure what was possible, not simply desirable. To put it another way: I thought it was important to distinguish between what was true—Realism—and what one wished to be true. I was distrustful, even dismissive, of applying moral considerations in a field where abstract morality did not seem especially relevant. (I tended to keep in mind Justice Robert H. Jackson's admonition not to follow one's principles over a cliff: the Constitution, he once said, is not "a suicide pact.") I certainly didn't believe in moral absolutes that outweighed all other considerations, national well-being foremost among them.

My friend put more emphasis on the place of ethics in foreign policy than I did and was always ready to remind me that without a moral component international affairs would degenerate into a Hobbesian world of all against all, and that in such a world only the bullies and gangsters would prevail. Limits had to come from something other than force, and if power was the only thing restricting policy decisions, there could never be an end to warfare. This was an especially dismal prospect, he pointed out, in a nuclear age. The point of a moral code was to put an internal brake on humankind's naturally aggressive tendencies, and the hope for peace was only possible if everyone agreed to behave according to universally accepted rules. I would reply that without the authority of a transcendent power—that is, God—prescribing those rules and perhaps a belief in an afterlife where eternal punishment could be meted out to violators, no permanent agreement was possible, only temporary stopgaps devised by fallible human beings. And so we went round and round.

For all our differences, however, we were not only able to have fruitful discussions but also to find broad areas of agreement. The reason, I think, is that neither of us is an absolutist. We had our respective views, but we weren't dogmatic about them. Foreign policy, after all, is a field that doesn't lend itself to straightforward black-and-white solutions. There were too many gray areas in which one had to accept uncertainty and to some degree fall back on guesswork. It is not mathematics.

And so my friend acknowledged that, despite his moral concerns, many issues required one to think in terms of power and national interest; he could be as much a Realist as I was when he thought the situation called for it. And I had to concede that without a moral component, foreign policy could be a rotten, blood-drenched business. I confessed that I didn't much like those leaders who thought only in terms of power, with no evidence of compassion. Moral considerations had to enter the picture at some point even if they weren't the primary motivation for policy decisions. Because we were able to find so many points of overlap, our conversations didn't go round and round forever. Instead, after talking things through, we frequently found that we agreed on a number of questions, an ideal blending of Realism and morality.

But one subject where agreement proved to be impossible was on the impact of Henry Kissinger. He brought our discussions to a screeching halt. Not that we completely abandoned our flexibility: my friend was willing to recognize that Kissinger had made historic contributions (though, as I recall, he gave Richard Nixon more of the credit), and I was hardly about to argue for every decision that Kissinger ever made. What's more, I didn't like the sometimes weaselly explanations Kissinger himself offered for his own policies. At times, it seemed, he was trying to defend the indefensible—like approving of the wiretapping of his colleagues at the

National Security Council or attempting to reinvolve an exhausted United States in the fighting in Vietnam after the signing of the 1973 treaty that, largely through his own efforts, had given America a way out. But insofar as my friend and I struggled to arrive at an overall assessment of the man's career, it was as if a line had been drawn in the sand. My friend was permanently stationed on one side, I on the other. Nothing that either of us could say would persuade the other to change his mind. In one sense, therefore, this book can be seen as an extension of our discussions from my point of view.

BUT THERE IS a larger and more urgent reason for this book: Kissinger has not held public office since 1977, but I believe his time has come round again, and today we dismiss or ignore him at our peril. He is more than a figure out of history. He is a philosopher of international relations who has much to teach us about how the modern world works—and often doesn't. His arguments for his brand of Realism—thinking in terms of national interest and a balance of power—offer the possibility of rationality, coherence, and a necessary long-term perspective at a time when all three of these qualities seem to be in short supply.

Whatever else it did, the Cold War provided coherence of a kind: the United States was faced with an implacable enemy, armed with nuclear weapons and an aggressive global ideology that compelled American policymakers to devise a basic strategy for their planning. For all the mistakes made at that time, George Kennan's policy of containment worked for more than four decades. The United States won the Cold War.

For a brief moment after the collapse of the Soviet Union, it seemed that a different kind of coherence was possible: America's role had become to foster the inevitable expansion of democracy around the world, sometimes by force. Peoples with different cultures and different values would be grateful for Washington's interventions; they would greet our invading troops with flowers and candy. The United States was the "indispensable" nation, destined to lead. With the many disappointments that have occurred in the Middle East and elsewhere, this mission has obviously failed. Yet nothing has been found to replace it. How should America define its place in the world?

To be sure, there remain influential voices who believe democracy promotion must be the foundation of American foreign policy, despite the evident drawbacks. There are others who seek to replicate the readily understandable polarities of the Cold War by casting either Russia or China (and sometimes both) in the role of the Soviet Union, despite the fact that neither of those countries has a global ideology, and each is acting on the basis of what it perceives to be its national interest. And there are some, inspired by America's isolationist tradition, who wish to withdraw from any global commitments, despite the fact that two large oceans and weak or pliable neighbors no longer guarantee the kinds of protections they once did. Mainly, however, American foreign policy in the twenty-first century has bounced from crisis to crisis with uncertain aims and little or no long-range outlook. Henry Kissinger's philosophy of Realism provides both. He specializes in the long range.

In the 40 years since he left government service, Kissinger has devoted himself largely to two goals: burnishing his reputation and instructing the American people in the principles of Realpolitik. The first of these has provoked intense controversy with detractors and admirers lining up on either side, much like my friend and me across the dinner table. The second, while it has not been ignored, has hardly elicited the kind of thoughtful discussion it deserves, and the reason for this, I would say, is that Kissinger's thinking runs so counter to what Americans believe or wish to believe. He challenges people to rethink their assumptions. Kissinger's lessons about history, power, and democracy can be discomfiting, even painful, for those who insist that freedom and democracy are the aspirations of people everywhere or that America is some kind of moral beacon. To argue otherwise is to be, well, un-American.

One recent example of the more congenial "American" view is Condoleezza Rice's *Democracy: Stories from the Long Road to Freedom*, published in 2017. Both she and Kissinger have held the positions of national security adviser and secretary of state (Kissinger is the only person to have held the two positions simultaneously). Rice stands as a useful and enlightening foil to Kissinger. In *Democracy* she argues that American values like liberty have "universal appeal." She reports watching "as people in Africa, Asia, and Latin America have insisted on freedom," and says "there is no more thrilling moment than when people finally seize their rights and their liberty." The Realist's idea of balancing power is not her goal. In this book on foreign policy, Henry Kissinger is not even an entry in her index.

Rice's sentiments are in a tradition dating back to Woodrow Wilson and to a time when the United States first set foot on the world stage. But they also grow out of her personal experience as a black woman raised in the segregated South, and she presents her life story as testimony to the possibility of hope—that is, that progress in human affairs is a fact of life, that the arc of history always bends toward justice. Who could fail to be moved by her response to a skeptical colleague in 2004: "My father couldn't register to vote in Birmingham in 1952. And now Colin Powell is secretary of state and I am national security adviser. People can learn to overcome prejudices and govern themselves in democratic institutions."

Kissinger, too, learned from his personal experience, but the lessons he drew are much darker than Rice's; indeed, they are diametrically opposed. As an eyewitness to the rise of the Nazis to whom he lost many members of his family, he saw that democracy was not a universal desire and that, under certain circumstances, it could lead to the worst tyranny imaginable. Sometimes, when people "seize their rights," they do so in order to deprive other people of *their* rights. Whereas Rice understands human history as moving in a forward direction with transcendent meaning, for Kissinger history is more like one damned thing after another, unpredictable and uncontrollable; the basis of foreign policy has to be a pursuit of the national interest because, in an uncertain world, that is the anchor of stability. When correctly conceived, it contributes to rational relations among nations, giving them a shared foundation for working out their antagonisms; everyone understands where everyone else is coming from. World order is an end in its own right, and those Americans who insist on trying to impose their democratic values on others are likely to be disrupters of peace, hegemonists by another name, or in Kissinger's language, "crusaders." One can't expect too much in foreign affairs. The task for policymakers in his view is a modest, essentially negative one—namely, not to steer the world along some preordained path to universal justice but to pit power against power to rein in the assorted aggressions of human beings and to try, as best they can, to avert disaster. This is a perspective shaped by pessimism and a dim view of humanity.

Of course, Kissinger has hardly been alone in his pessimism. Other German Jews, with the Nazi example before their eyes, have paralleled his thinking, though not as many as one might imagine. The notion of progress in human affairs is very hard to resist. In particular, two writers as gloomy as Kissinger, Leo Strauss and Hannah Arendt, deserve special attention for the window they can provide into Kissinger's mind. And then there is Hans Morgenthau, who stands alone: it would be hard to overestimate the impact of Morgenthau's Realpolitik concepts on Kissinger. Nelson Rockefeller may have been the figure in public life whom Kissinger most admired, but there was no thinker who meant more to Kissinger than Morgenthau. They remained close even when they disagreed, as they did most vehemently over Vietnam.

In 1983, three years after Morgenthau's death, the National Committee on American Foreign Policy gave its annual Hans Morgenthau Memorial Award to Henry Kissinger. The speaker of the evening, Arthur Schlesinger Jr., reflected on what he saw as the similarities and differences between the two men, both of whom had been his friends. The theme of Schlesinger's talk was the relationship of the intellectual to authority, and he concluded that the country needed both the Kissingers and the Morgenthaus: one type willing to work inside government with all the necessary compromises such a role demanded, the other standing outside to preserve his integrity and speak truth to power.

That said, Morgenthau, unlike so many other oppositional intellectuals standing outside, had an appreciation of both the necessity and limitations of power and, therefore, of the difficulties of Kissinger's insider's job. Truth didn't consist of retreating to one's library to work out the most desirable position one could come up with and then sticking to it like a prophet sitting on a mountaintop (or a lemming racing toward the mountaintop's edge). For Morgenthau, it was a matter of starting with the situation at hand and adjusting one's ideas to the ever-changing facts on the ground, all for the sake of the national interest. Apparent contradictions or inconsistencies didn't bother him. Morgenthau was a Realist down to his bones. For him, it wasn't even a question of the best being the enemy of the good; the good was an enemy as well. In foreign policy, things usually come down to the bad and the less bad. Like Kissinger, Morgenthau always retained a sense of the tragic and, I would say, it was this shared German Jewish sensibility, as much as their similar ideas on national interest and balance of power, that was the foundation for the two men's decades-long friendship, whatever disagreements they may have had over the years, no matter how sharp or how strong.

In contrast to so many Americans, Kissinger has lived without hope, without expectations, and certainly without confidence in either the workings of democracy or the inevitability of progress. Policy, he has argued, must start from that grim vantage point. This is not the most inspiring or heartwarming perspective, but is there anyone looking out at the world today who would say that his pessimism is not a more sensible foundation for foreign policy than Condoleezza Rice's reassuring optimism? That is why, given the current state of international relations, it is foolish, even dangerous, to ignore him. The lessons he has been trying to teach may not be to the liking of most people, but they are more important than ever before.

BECAUSE THIS IS a book about ideas, and for readers who enjoy the interplay of ideas, it is less concerned with chronology than with intellectual problems and patterns of thought. And so it begins in medias res, as it were, with the American involvement in Chile in 1970, brought on by the prospect of the leftist Salvador Gossens Allende winning the presidency. Allende had close ties to Fidel Castro, and Nixon and Kissinger were concerned that his election would lead to an unprecedented extension of Soviet power in the Western Hemisphere. The Chile crisis remains important because it is a classic example, perhaps *the* classic example, of the potential clash between other countries' free elections and American security, an agonizing problem that is never going to go away. (A more recent and parallel example of this clash is the Army coup against the democratically elected government of the Islamist, Mohamed Morsi, in Egypt.) We can be sure that there will be more such examples in the future and that liberal democratic pieties won't be of much help to policymakers struggling to make difficult decisions about how to assure America's security.

From Chile I move back in time to Weimar Germany to understand the reasons German-Jewish intellectuals would be suspicious of democratic procedures. A key point of this chapter is to paint a picture of Adolf Hitler as a successful democratic politician with all the miserable implications that this fact presents. One friend who read the chapter complained that I was being too kind to Hitler. But I want to demonstrate not the evil of Hitler but the reason for his appeal—an appeal that extended to, yes, even Jews like Leo Strauss and Hans Morgenthau.

The discussions of Strauss, Arendt, and Morgenthau try to fill in the intellectual context for Kissinger's own Realpolitik, excavate the assumptions behind it, and explain why these German-Jewish thinkers might feel a deep ambivalence about the country that had saved their lives, the same ambivalence that is evident in Kissinger. These four were not typical immigrants to America, not even typical German-Jewish immigrants, and they certainly were not optimists. They thought more deeply than most about what they considered a serious problem of American culture and politics. They all may have felt an undeniable affection for the United States, but they also had grave doubts about the nation's health.

The Vietnam war deserves a chapter of its own, not only because of the extraordinary impact it has had on American policy ever since but also because it caused the deepest rift in the Kissinger-Morgenthau relationship, with one implementing policy and prolonging the war and the other at the forefront of those in opposition. Here was the Schlesingerian distinction between insider and outsider brought to life. The fact that the relationship of the two men survived the strain tells us a great deal about both of them, especially about their similar assumptions and the intellectual concepts they shared. In retrospect, they had more in common than seemed true at the time. The most profound opponent of the Vietnam war developed his position out of Kissingerian principles. The most prominent implementer of the war thought in Morgenthau's terms.

The final two chapters explore some broad themes of Kissinger's time in government and in the years after and try to delineate the principles that underlie Kissinger's Realpolitik. For him, there is simply no alternative to his dour perspective, and Cassandra-like, he has argued repeatedly in his waning years that any attempt to find a different path will most likely end in confusion and defeat. One doesn't have to agree with all of this, but Americans would be wise to take his warnings seriously. No one has thought more deeply about international affairs.

I do not pretend to have exhausted the topics that have preoccupied Kissinger over a lifetime of reflecting on power among nations, but I do hope that I have shed some useful light on the most central elements of his thinking, on the value of his pessimistic sensibility, and on the kinds of intellectual issues that anyone making policy at the highest level can expect to confront. Though his many critics would deny it, Henry Kissinger's life and career have an enormous amount to offer us, but only if we know where and how to look, and only if we can get beyond the distractions of his sometimes charming, sometimes annoying, always remarkable personality. I have tried in this book to point readers in the right direction.

THE INEVITABILITY OF TRAGEDY

CHAPTER ONE

CHILE

*I don't see why we have to stand by and
watch a country go Communist because of the
irresponsibility of its own people.*

—HENRY KISSINGER

HAS ANY AMERICAN PUBLIC OFFICIAL EVER UTTERED A more "un-American" statement? The time was 1970 and the occasion was the upcoming presidential election in Chile, where it appeared that the leftist Salvador Gossens Allende stood a good chance of emerging as the victor. Kissinger's remark offends American sensibilities in so many ways that astonishment and revulsion almost overwhelm any impulse to analyze it. It violates the notion that the United States does not (or at least should not) interfere in the domestic affairs of another country, especially when that country has not attacked the United States and is not considered an immediate threat to American national security. It urges preemption, calling on Washington to take action to forestall an outcome that has not taken place and may never take place. Most of all, it is a profoundly undemocratic statement. No, it is more than that: it is an *anti*-democratic statement, signaling a willingness to prevent or overturn the result of an election that is universally recognized as free and fair for some other cause—no doubt a malevolent one. The "people" will not be permitted to be the masters of their own fates. Instead, they will be subjected to the dictates of an outside force. Call this the arrogance of imperialism, even the imposition of a kind of subjection to powerful multinational corporations. It is, in any case, an assault on everything America professes to believe in and to stand for in the world.

Little wonder that Kissinger's comment—with the intervention in Chile that followed—has been a source of shame, indignation, and anger among so many Americans ever since, not to mention among millions of others around the world as well. The statement is widely viewed as indefensible, as are the policies that flowed from it. Its critics are countless, its defenders few. U.S. policy toward Chile in the early 1970s—under Presidents Nixon and Ford but with Kissinger calling the shots—has been a touchstone of outrage ever since Allende's government was toppled by the Chilean army in September 1973, initiating a bloody and repressive regime under Augusto Pinochet that lasted for 17 years. Washington's involvement in Chile leading up to Pinochet's coup is indisputable, though its precise role remains a subject of discussion and debate. And the criticism has been unceasing from that day to the present.

Peter Kornbluh, an expert on Chile and the author and editor of the acclaimed *The Pinochet File: A Declassified Dossier on Atrocity and Accountability*, writes that "after so many years, Chile remains the ultimate case study of morality—or lack of it—in the making of U.S. foreign policy." Thomas Powers, another accomplished scholar, says "the C.I.A.'s role was pervasive, it violated the spirit of the American political tradition, and it was undertaken at Nixon's explicit order, for reasons which seem shallow, cursory and off-hand at best."

Individuals in government have expressed similar sentiments. Richard Helms, who led the CIA in those years and was deeply involved in the plotting against Allende, wrote in his memoirs: "I still associate Chile with some of the most unpleasant aspects of my professional life." When he was secretary of state, Colin Powell declared: "Chile in the 1970s, and what happened with Allende . . . is not a part of U.S. history that we are proud of." Contrite officials, though not Henry Kissinger, never Henry Kissinger, have been eager to shed as much light on the Chile affair as possible within the bounds of national security. And so Chile provoked the first public accounting the U.S. Congress ever held on American covert action, conducted by a committee headed by the Idaho senator Frank Church—in effect, America's very own Truth and Reconciliation Commission. The Church committee's famous 1975 report, "Covert Action in Chile, 1963–1973," led, in Kornbluh's words, to "a widespread movement to return U.S. foreign policy to the moral precepts of American society."

When, under President Bill Clinton, the State Department announced the release of 16,000 newly declassified documents concerning Chile, it did so with a press statement that was extraordinary for its tone of apology and regret. "One goal of the project," the statement said, "is to put original documents before the public so that it may judge for itself the extent to which U.S. actions undercut the course of democracy and human rights in Chile. Actions approved by the U.S. government during this period aggravated political polarization and affected Chile's long tradition of democratic elections and respect for the constitutional order and the rule of law." This statement is a total repudiation of the policy of an earlier administration by a later one.

The State Department went on to offer what in effect constituted a public apology to the Chilean people, a conciliatory plea that despite any American wickedness in the past, the two countries should try to be friends in the future: "The Chilean people deserve our praise and respect for courageously reclaiming their proud history as one of the world's oldest democracies. Healing the painful wounds of the past, Chileans from across the political spectrum have rededicated themselves to rebuilding representative institutions and the rule of law. The United States will continue to work closely with the people of Chile—as their friend and partner—to strengthen the cause of democracy in Latin America and around the world."

Because he is widely seen as the mastermind behind the intervention, Kissinger has come in for particular opprobrium. He is branded a "war criminal" and in the movement to indict him in an international court, or some national court, Chile stands at or near the top of the list of his misdeeds. Christopher Hitchens's *The Trial of Henry Kissinger,* the most well known and most impassioned of these attacks, called for putting Kissinger in the docket "for war crimes, for crimes against humanity, and for offenses against common or customary or international law, including conspiracy to commit murder, kidnap and torture." Hitchens cited the "Nuremberg precedent" in his demand for a public trial, thus equating Kissinger with the worst of the Nazi leaders. "His own lonely impunity is rank; it smells to heaven," he exclaimed.

As with so many others, what aroused Hitchens's indignation, what branded Kissinger a war criminal, was the idea that the United States would be encouraging a coup against a democratically elected government. That is the unthinkable—it is what stirs Hitchens to the heights of rhetorical indignation—and also the undeniable. Even Kissinger himself, understanding the condemnations of his own policy, has attempted to play down America's role in any coup plot, saying that there was always less to it "than met the eye." But, of course, that's what he would say, given how bad the idea looks in the clear light of day, even without all the embarrassing mix-ups and mistakes.

Still the Chile episode has to be seen in terms more complicated than white hats and black hats. It remains an important and never-ending touchstone of debate because it represents with the utmost clarity the possible conflict that can exist between the promotion of democracy and the demands of national security, surely one of the most unnerving, most painful tensions in the conduct of foreign policy. Many Americans would prefer not to see the tension. They want to believe that support for democracy everywhere in the world and on every occasion is always desirable and, therefore, in the best interests of the United States. Democracy and morality are thought to march hand in hand, as Kornbluh suggests. But there are many instances in U.S. foreign policy—in recent times most notably in the victory of Hamas in Gaza and in the Muslim Brotherhood's triumph in Egypt—when democracy promotion has conflicted with America's national interests.

This is not to say that in the long run the virtues of democracy should not be available to everyone. The world would indeed be a far better place if it were made up of an assemblage of nation-states that all enjoyed free and fair elections, free speech, the freedoms of religion and assembly, and populations composed of citizens who were rational, tolerant, and moderate, pleased to live in peace with one another and with the citizens of other nation-states. It is a utopia much to be wished for. But so far it is just that—a utopia. It is a long way from here to there (just look at the United Nations General Assembly for a real-life image of such Kantian idealism) and until we get there, the choices confronting statesmen will be complex, sometimes contradictory, often cruel, and not inevitably supportive of democratic procedures.

Such was the case with the choices Henry Kissinger and Richard Nixon had to make with regard to Allende's Chile. Perhaps it takes individuals of a suspicious and pessimistic, even paranoid, disposition like Nixon and Kissinger to see the tension that exists between democracy promotion and national interest, or those of a resolutely anti-utopian bent to understand that in foreign policy the different goals we hope to achieve will often be in conflict with one another. Is it possible that dour neurotics make the best foreign-policy analysts?

Certainly those of an optimistic, sunny disposition do not seem to make the best implementers of foreign policy. It is easy to condemn Nixon and Kissinger if one brings to the discussion preconceptions fixated only on the virtues of democracy to the exclusion of the interplay of nations, but to anyone ready to examine the actual situation that presented itself in the early 1970s, Chile offers valuable lessons about the kind of thinking anyone making foreign policy must engage in and, as it turns out, the kind of thinking Henry Kissinger was especially well positioned to provide.

LET'S BEGIN WITH some history. Chile declared its independence from Spain in 1818, and for most of the two centuries that followed, the story of its relations with the United States consisted of a pattern of neglect that was neither benign nor malign, simply one of overwhelming indifference. There were occasional ripples in this becalmed sea, the kind of antipathies that might be expected between any two nation-states, and at one time an eruption that threatened, at least rhetorically, to turn into a stupid, unnecessary war. But any hostility invariably reverted to amity, or at least apathy, as the two countries returned to their more normal practice of facing off in different directions.

It was geography that mattered more than anything else in the relationship. Distances between Chile and the United States were simply too great for national interests to clash too seriously; pretty much all the two countries shared was the Western Hemisphere and an anticolonial birth. To most Chileans the North Americans were, in the words of one historian, "a cipher," and most North Americans would have been hard-pressed to name a Chilean writer, musician, or politician, even the capital. "Chile" would never be a category on *Jeopardy!* It was just an oddly shaped country far to the south. Little wonder that Henry Kissinger, in one of his not infrequent moments of sarcasm, explained Chile's importance to Washington's policymakers by calling it "a dagger pointed straight at the heart of Antarctica."

And yet for a brief period, Chile's connection to the United States led to one of the indelible events of the twentieth century. Even now, almost five decades later, the downfall of the democratically elected Socialist government of Salvador Allende in 1973 can arouse fierce emotions. Nathaniel Davis, the man who was the American ambassador at the time, has compared the impact of Allende's end to the impact of the Spanish civil war a generation earlier, another event that has refused to die. "The ghost of Salvador Allende will not rest." Perhaps not. But today Americans, even those who keep Allende's flame alive, have retreated to more typical attitudes toward Chile—namely, blissful ignorance. Does anyone dare to estimate the percentage of Americans who can name the current president of Chile? Five percent? Probably too high. One percent? Probably still too high. Chile was important to Washington for a few years in the 1960s and 1970s—so important that one might even say the Kennedy administration's Alliance for Progress program, intended to build bridges to Latin America, was essentially a policy directed toward Chile. Why?

IT SHOULD BE SAID at the outset that most of the story of U.S.-Chile relations is a history of nonhistory. When a wave of revolutions in the Southern Hemisphere in the early nineteenth century resulted in the independence of the Spanish colonies from the mother country, North Americans stood on the sidelines and cheered. They cheered because they were viscerally supportive of peoples who, in the cause of freedom, were liberating themselves from Old Europe. The upheavals were a validation of their own revolution, their own values.

History was moving in a single direction, and the United States was in the vanguard. During the James Madison presidency, the House of Representatives passed a resolution of support to the Latin freedom fighters: "That the House of Representatives participates with the people of the United States in the deep interest which they feel for the success of the Spanish provinces of South America which are struggling to establish their liberty and independence." The vote was a lopsided 134–12. The Monroe Doctrine itself, later a hated symbol of Yankee imperialism, was in this hopeful era of liberation an expression of hemispheric solidarity and was understood as such by the Latin revolutionaries. In Chile, the young country's first newspaper reprinted the American Declaration of Independence for the edification of its readers.

Yet for all the hopes and fine words, "stood on the sidelines" was the other core component of Washington's policy. Ideals would not be allowed to interfere with political and geographic realities, and the United States was careful to remain neutral in its dealings with Spain and the Latin Americans. North American arms were not shipped to the rebels except illegally, smuggled to them in violation of American neutrality. Emissaries were sent to the new nations as one after another was born, but as observers, not official spokesmen or partisans of independence. Events were too much in flux, outcomes too uncertain. Caution was considered the wisest policy, wait-and-see the attitude of Washington. In 1817, President James

Monroe proudly told Congress that the United States was remaining perfectly neutral, its ports open to all sides. Later in the century, when relations between the United States and Chile were in one of their slumps, a Chilean historian, complaining about the early years, wrote that "the possession of Florida was a matter a thousand times more important to the United States than the redemption of Spanish America." He was right, of course.

In 1823, five long years after Chilean independence, the situation had settled down sufficiently for Washington at last to extend recognition and to send a minister to look after its interests. That same year the United States recognized Argentinian independence as well. Then in an outburst of diplomatic activity came recognition for Brazil (1824) and Peru (1826), followed by Uruguay (1834), Venezuela (1835), Ecuador (1838), and Bolivia (1848). The people of Chile were so full of goodwill that when the American representative, Heman [sic] Allen, a farmer from Vermont, arrived in Santiago, he was treated to a 22-gun salute. Unfortunately, Allen had landed in a country still in turmoil, still in a state of upheaval that was very different from North America's calm, postrevolutionary transition to a constitutional republic. The United States was the exception among the former colonies. The warring factions competing to gain control of the Chilean government were more typical of what was to be expected in the aftermath of a revolution. In his three years in Chile, Allen had to deal with eight presidents and nine foreign ministers.

Even so, the bulk of Allen's work was tedious. Along with most of his successors, he spent his time on the frustrating, nitpicky work of negotiating tariffs and port regulations. There were also claims to be settled against rambunctious Chileans who had been seizing American vessels. If trade between Chile and the United States had been of any importance, these issues might have mattered. But it wasn't and they didn't.

Religion was another issue that, like trade and economics, had incendiary potential but never reached crisis temperature. Chile was a Catholic country, officially so its constitution declared, while the United States was unofficially Protestant, though equally committed to its beliefs. According to Allen, "A wicked and abandoned clergy still rule the country . . . and much time is devoted to their ridiculous ceremonies." Allen strongly objected to the establishment of a state religion—or maybe to the establishment of Catholicism as the state religion—arguing that it conflicted with a philosophy of republicanism. But in a country that was overwhelmingly Catholic and overwhelmingly religious, he got nowhere.

If relations with Chile didn't matter much to the people of the United States, relations with their neighbor to the north were of little concern to the Chileans. It was Europe they cared about. "The United States scarcely existed for Chile prior to 1880," writes one historian. England was Chile's major trading partner. "Our trade with Chile is trifling," Allen wrote, "but British goods have inundated the market." Even neighboring Peru was of greater commercial importance to Chile than the United States.

Politically, too, Chile was keeping its considerable distance from the United States. In the 1830s, the large landholders, known as the "Old Spanish Party," had seized control of the country, and they were no friends of American-style democracy. The same was true culturally. With its Spanish and Catholic heritage, Chile looked to the European continent. Spanish plays dominated theater. Italian opera dominated music. In literature, Chileans preferred French novels. The image that Chileans had of the United States, when they had any image at all, was of a people that was materialistic, atheistic, and crude.

Trade, tariffs, claims disputes, religious differences, cultural divergences—none of it added up to anything. In the second half of the century, the North Americans, with the Civil War and Reconstruction to occupy them, had little time or reason to think about Chile. For their part, Chileans had their own more pressing problems—for instance, the encroachments of Europeans; a nation-defining war with Peru and Bolivia; a constitutional crisis in the early 1890s that led to bloodshed and an internal upheaval. Nothing that concerned the United States concerned Chile. Nothing that mattered to Chileans mattered to North Americans. Only once in this chronicle of nonevents did "history" intervene and yet, amazingly, it brought the two countries very close to war. What created the crisis was a petty point of national pride, touched off by an event that should never have been allowed to grow into an international incident. Still, historians of U.S.-Chile relations might be inclined to celebrate this episode of jingoistic chest-thumping: it gives them something to write about

No one really knows who started a drunken brawl that broke out in 1891 in a seedy neighborhood of the port city of Valparaiso. Afterward, Chileans tended to believe Chileans and Americans believed Americans, but on the evening of October 16, sailors on leave from the U.S.S. *Baltimore* got into a lethal fight with some of the local residents. Two of the sailors ended up dead and another 17 injured; 30 were arrested, along with 10 Chileans. According to one newspaper account, the melee had begun when two Americans threw rocks at a Chilean sailor and then roughed him up; the paper said the Americans were armed and spoiling for a fight. The *Baltimore*'s captain told a different story. He reported back to Washington that his men had been assaulted without provocation by armed Chileans. Worse, the ruffians were abetted by the local police, a charge the chief of police vehemently denied. Whatever the truth, an attack on uniformed servicemen was certain to enflame nationalist passions in the north, even though Chile's representative in Washington tried to cool tempers by quite reasonably explaining that the incident was the kind that could be expected from drunken sailors on leave in a rowdy port town. The United States flexed its muscles and demanded reparation, Chile refused, and then matters escalated.

On December 8, 1891, President Benjamin Harrison delivered an indignant message to Congress in which he put the blame entirely on the Chileans and suggested the possibility of war. Early in the new year, Harrison asked Congress to authorize him to use force if necessary to obtain national satisfaction. His hawkishness was widely popular to a nation caught in the throes of expansionist exuberance. Congressmen were sure that one million men were ready to take up arms, and German and French representatives became convinced that hostilities were imminent. Harrison's belligerence paid off. The Chileans, with little choice, yielded to force majeure and agreed to indemnify the families of the dead sailors.

Chile's resentment lingered over the North American diktat long enough for it to side with Spain in its war with America at the end of the century, and even as late as World War II the Nazis used the *Baltimore* affair in their own propaganda campaign in Chile to win support for Germany. Still, there were more pressing matters closer to home, particularly a long-standing border dispute with Argentina now threatening to overflow into war. As for the North Americans, the *Baltimore* affair left not a trace. Even though the United States had never come so close to war with a South American country, and even though, when emotions were running highest, the body of one of the dead sailors was brought to Philadelphia to rest in state in Independence Hall (only two other Americans had been so honored: Henry Clay and Abraham Lincoln), the incident quickly passed into memory, and then out of memory into oblivion. Chile once again receded from sight and mind.

The history of U.S.-Chile relations in the first half of the twentieth century consists of a relatively short list of relatively uninteresting episodes.

Trade relations grew after the Panama Canal was built and more Americans made the effort to learn Spanish. Various pan-American conferences were held to negligible effect. With nothing at stake, Washington repeatedly tried to act as a mediator in disputes between Chile and its neighbors and repeatedly failed. When, in 1913, Theodore Roosevelt paid a visit to Santiago and welcomed Chile as a partner in enforcing the Monroe Doctrine, a Chilean newspaper recorded its impressions of the former president. Roosevelt, it said, "is a typical product of United States civilization: vigorous, impulsive, not heedful of the consequences of his actions, strongly susceptible to error, but at the same time possessed of the noblest of humanitarian sentiments."

During World War I, Chile remained neutral so that it could trade with all sides while increasing its economic ties to the United States. The growth of Chile's copper industry in the 1920s, replacing nitrates as the foundation of the country's economy, led to significantly deeper penetration of North American interests in Chilean affairs but to nothing that ruffled relations between the two countries as the rising value of copper benefitted everyone and Franklin Roosevelt's Good Neighbor policy set the tone for diplomacy. Chileans knew that copper miners for American companies were earning higher wages than their countrymen in other sectors of the economy and that the copper companies were paying extraordinarily high taxes for the privilege of extracting minerals from the nation's soil, as high as 70 percent according to some calculations. The taxes paid by the two major American copper companies accounted for as much as 50 percent of Chile's total tax revenues. In 1916, one Chilean newspaper referred to the Kennecott copper company as a blessing for the country.

World War II brought a mini-crisis when Chile tried to replicate its policy of neutrality and soon became a haven for fascists and spies. But after the State Department angrily accused Chile of a stab in the back, Santiago broke off relations with the Axis powers and the mood of cordiality was resumed. The 1950s resembled most of the history between Chile and the United States, which is to say that nothing happened of any consequence. A mutual assistance treaty was signed in 1951 that was long on public relations and short on substance, and there were occasional quarrels over copper pricing, as the North American companies sought to keep prices down to maintain market share while the Chilean government wanted higher prices to build up the country's revenues. But on May 22, 1960, North Americans had reason to take at least a humanitarian interest in Chile, when the largest earthquake recorded in the twentieth century devastated southern Chile, causing about 1,600 deaths and leaving two million homeless; the tsunamis that followed reached as far as Japan and the Philippines. In what has been called the "first presidential intervention in Chile," Dwight Eisenhower released funds for aid but only after Chile's president agreed to take steps toward land reform.

Then, all at once, everything changed. After almost 150 years of general neglect, Chile was turning up on Washington's maps with lights flashing. The policymakers may not have known anything about the country. Washington's near war and high-handed actions at the end of the nineteenth century may have drawn blank stares. But suddenly Chile had become of vital importance. The reason was one man: Fidel Castro.

Quite simply, after Castro triumphantly entered Havana at the start of 1959, he brought the Cold War into the Western Hemisphere. Relations between Castro's Cuba and the Soviet Union were never less than fraught, never as simple as popular accounts would have us believe, but he represented a profound problem for Washington, as well as an undeniable opportunity that the Kremlin couldn't ignore. As the KGB's Latin America expert wrote: "Cuba forced us to take a fresh look at the whole continent, which until then had traditionally occupied the last place in the Soviet leadership's system of priorities." For the first time, the Soviet Union instituted Latin American branches in its foreign ministry and the KGB. Rethinking in Moscow was necessary; to some of the Soviet planners, the Cuban revolution required nothing less than a revolution in their entire world outlook. The Cold War, they hopefully concluded, would now be won in the third world, with Cuba as the "bridgehead." In 1961, the Kremlin's Central Committee approved a plan to activate national liberation movements through the Western Hemisphere, and a year later Castro called for continental civil war. "The world was going our way," declared one KGB official, and nowhere did that seem truer than in Chile, which had the oldest and largest Communist Party in South America.

The Russians not only had close ties to Chile's Communists but also to Salvador Allende, whose Socialist Party was at once an ally and a rival of the Chilean Communists. That relationship does not lend itself to facile generalizations, but Allende's Soviet connection went back to 1953, and after the Kremlin established a trade mission in Chile in 1961, the links grew closer. The KGB began what it called "systematic contact" with Allende and, according to Soviet files, agreed to "provide any necessary assistance." It's important to say that Allende was hardly a pawn of the Kremlin. For one thing, he was a Socialist, not a Communist, a distinction that sometimes mattered and sometimes didn't. But every Socialist understood that he would not take marching orders from Moscow. Allende could be as problematic and unpredictable a friend of the Soviets as Castro was in Cuba—even more so. For example, when the Soviets marched into Hungary in 1956, he declared his opposition.

The former CIA director Richard Helms was surely wrong when he wrote that "Allende was outspoken in pushing hard-line Moscow-inspired programs." Allende took more money than inspiration from the Soviets. But Helms was certainly correct in calling Allende "an avowed Marxist," though even that label requires elaboration. Some "avowed Marxists," like many of the social democrats in Europe, were among America's best friends in the early years of the Cold War. Marxism came in many forms, a concept lost on many in Washington, though certainly not on Henry Kissinger.

More troubling and closer to the real problem was a statement of Allende's that both Helms and Kissinger quote: "Cuba in the Caribbean and a Socialist Chile in the southern cone will make the revolution in Latin America." The Kremlin had exactly the same assessment. One Moscow commentator said that Allende's electoral victory in 1970 was "second only to the victory of the Cuban Revolution in the magnitude of its significance as a revolutionary blow to the imperialist system in Latin America." Yet Allende had taken office through what everyone understood was a fair election, not like Castro through armed revolution, and he called himself not only a Marxist but a democrat as well. He was the first Marxist to take control of a country by democratic means. Did that make him part of the problem or part of the solution? The answer requires another excursion into Chile's history, this time to examine its domestic politics.

AFTER THE CHAOS of the 1820s that followed Chilean independence, the country settled into a period of political stability that was a source of pride to Chileans (the English of Latin America) and an object of admiration to many Latin Americans across the continent, as well as to many North Americans. In 1833, a constitution was agreed upon that established a presidential system with a bicameral legislature. It wasn't democratic in the modern sense (what constitution of that time was?) because literacy and property requirements restricted the vote to around only 5 percent of the population and sometimes to as little as 2 percent. The wealthy land-owners were able to maintain a tight grip on the country well into the twentieth century. But Chile had a constitution that lasted—despite the occasional failed coup attempt, insurrections, and a civil war in 1891—for almost a century until 1925. Even after that date, which marked the beginning of several years of unrest, North Americans saw much to admire about Chile's political traditions. Claude Bowers, who served as U.S. ambassador from 1939 to 1953, found the Chileans "instinctively democratic" and "tolerant in politics."

Throughout the nineteenth century, Chile was a predominantly agricultural society with a feudal, hierarchical structure. Politics was not so much an expression of issues as a game of who-do-you-know. The political was the personal. You sided with your friends to enjoy the perquisites that power brought and fought to keep your enemies out. But nothing grand was at stake, only patronage and the enjoyment that comes from flaunting your position of power over others. Everyone who ruled or wanted to rule came from the same background and the same class with the same values and the same economic interests. Chile was a decidedly provincial country, economically backward, intellectually limited, politically asleep.

Political change came as a result of Chile's ties to Europe. In the 1840s Europe was in revolutionary ferment, and the ideas that inspired the rebels began to trickle into Eurocentric Chile from across the Atlantic, modern ideas, Enlightenment ideas, ideas that at their most subversive challenged the authority of religion and the role of the Catholic Church. In Chile, as in medieval Europe, the Church authorities were the foundation of the entire feudal system, providing the nation's laws and customs with their moral and intellectual authority. Ever since independence, there had been Chileans, often looking north to the progressive example of the United States, who questioned the involvement of the Church in their country's affairs. But it was only in the 1850s, after stability had been achieved and bloodshed had been replaced by civilized negotiation and even more civilized manipulation, that liberal ideas often linked to new theories of economic development began to be broadly debated and frequently accepted. Nor, it should be said, did the aristocracy present a united front against these disruptive currents. The Church was a large landowner itself, the object of covetous yearnings by the less devout, and in the conflict between economic and religious interests, it was not always piety that prevailed.

Secular ideas presented Chile with a profound question: Did ultimate

authority rest with the State or the Church? It was a deeply unsettling
question, subversive enough to produce a politics that went beyond personal ties and friendship to matters of philosophy and belief. Indications
that the church-state sovereignty issue would dominate Chilean politics
for decades to come arrived with a seemingly insignificant quarrel—that
is, a dispute in 1856 among Church officials of the Cathedral of Santiago
known as "the affair of the sacristan." A lay employee of the cathedral
was fired for insubordination and an argument broke out over who had
the right to dismiss him. One side took the audacious step of appealing
to Chile's Supreme Court, which ruled in its favor, but the rigidly conservative archbishop of Santiago refused to recognize the court's sovereignty, setting up a clash between civil and ecclesiastical authority and
dividing the elites of Chilean society. Church or country? A compromise
was quietly hammered out, but the fears of the imperious archbishop
and his supporters had been enflamed, and out of those fears, a Conservative Party was formed to protect the interests of the Church. Modern politics had come to Chile through the backdoor of conservative
preservationism.

Then a Liberal Party emerged to oppose the Conservatives. When some
activists grew discontented because they thought the Liberal leaders were
too ready to compromise with the Conservatives, they banded together
in the Radical Party to push for a more extreme form of secularism. The
Conservatives became the steadfast voices of the large landowners in alliance with the Church. Over time, as Chile's economy grew and Chilean
society evolved, the Liberals came to represent the growing urban population, while the Radicals also had strength among the anticlerical urban
middle classes, as well as with the new business interests in mining and
elsewhere. Governments tended to be made up of coalitions with Conservatives on one side, Radicals on the other, and the Liberals shifting back
and forth between them. Other smaller parties came and went. And so the
contours of Chilean politics were fixed for the next 50 to 75 years.

What exploded this torpid political pattern were the economic and
social changes, inevitable changes, that were transforming Chile and ultimately preparing the way for the arrival of Salvador Allende, Washington's intervention, and the brutalities that followed. But it took almost a
century for those changes to work themselves out. The cities had to grow,
the old elites had to lose their feudal control, and working-class parties
had to emerge, plant roots, and finally reach the pinnacle of power.

Urban growth in Chile was dramatic. In 1885, between 34 and 42 percent of the population lived in cities. By 1940, a majority of Chileans—52.5 percent—were urbanites, and by 1960 the figure was almost 70 percent. The cities offered freedoms unavailable in the conservative, hierarchical countryside, but the fact was that most of the movement was a result of push, not pull. It wasn't so much that job opportunities had opened up in the cities as that they had dried up on the farms, where the maldistribution of land, falling productivity, increased mechanization, and population growth were leaving multitudes with little choice but to abandon their traditional ways. The newer sectors, manufacturing and mining, were expanding but not nearly fast enough to accommodate the needs of these new arrivals, and most of them found work, when they did find work, in low-paying service industries.

The result was that in the twentieth century until the 1960s, when a wave of reform demands swept the country, social conditions for those at the bottom were appalling. Malnutrition was endemic. One study in 1945 reported that 86 percent of primary school students were suffering from "long-term undernourishment." A later survey found stunted growth in 60 percent of the country's children. The average height of Chileans was actually declining because of lack of food. And in the 1950s and 1960s, at least one-third of households were without drinkable water. Diseases like tuberculosis were rife, and infant mortality rates were among the worst in the world. One midcentury estimate concluded that one out of four children born to urban low-income families would die before the age of five.

Along with malnutrition and disease, social pathologies were taking their toll on the poor. Crime had become a constant feature of urban life and illegitimacy rates reached as high as 40 percent. Worst of all, before modern opiates became widely available to numb pain and destroy the lives of the hopeless, there was the impact of alcoholism, which had started to become a serious problem as early as the 1890s, just as the cities were expanding. In the 1940s, observers claimed that 20 to 30 percent of men living in the slums were chronic alcoholics. Chilean society throughout much of the twentieth century was in serious disarray, caught between rural rigidities and urban chaos, crying out for reform.

Yet Chile's politicians, still waging their nineteenth-century battles over church-state issues, were slow to acknowledge the harsh realities. Why should they? The neediest had no voice, no organization, no expectations. The Conservatives were determined to do nothing to change things, worrying instead that medical and political advances were increasing the numbers and power of the poor. Their religious beliefs gave them all the reason they needed to avoid taking action or even showing sympathy. The leader of the Conservative Party declared in 1932 that "the suffering and the mean circumstances which beset the poor and which the sociologists say is wrong, we Christians say is proper. . . . For in our concept as Christians, poverty is the estate most rich in the means through which man realizes his eternal destiny." Groups to the left of the Conservatives were more responsive to the needs of the poor, but not much more, because intellectually they were ill-equipped to address the problems of an urbanizing, modernizing society after a century of feudal stability.

That Chile's politics were lagging badly behind its social reality became clear in the 1920s when the country's political system, ineffectual in the face of contemporary demands, collapsed. Governments came and went in rapid succession until the army, impatient with mounting instability, confusion, and incompetence, staged a coup in September 1924. It didn't help. The military itself was divided and junta followed junta until exhaustion gave way to civil rule in 1932, along with a renewed sense of stability.

Although none of the social problems had been addressed, let alone settled, the period of turmoil produced one solid accomplishment: a new constitution drafted in 1925. Among other changes, it gave the president increased authority but limited him to a six-year term and prohibited him from succeeding himself. Most important, the new constitution established once and for all the principle of the separation of church and state. The issue that had dominated Chilean politics since the 1850s had been resolved, with two major political effects.

First, it permitted the seamless merging of the religious landowners and the less religious industrialists into a unified right dedicated to social cohesiveness and stability, which in the eyes of the left consisted of safeguarding privilege. Economically, there had always been significant convergence and crossover between the rural and urban elites. In the 1960s, almost one-half of large businessmen either had major agricultural holdings or were related to someone who did. As long as the religious issue had divided these elites, free thinkers and economic liberals expended their energies in fighting the Church and its allies. But after 1925, class divisions in Chilean society emerged with a new and sharpened clarity.

Second, the new constitution cleared the way for the rise of political parties and political movements determined to represent those people the old political order had neglected: workers, the peasants, the city dwellers, the marginalized, desperate, and aggrieved. Much of the middle class, dissatisfied with Chile's complacent Conservatives for both moral and self-interested reasons, also aligned themselves with parties on the left. Three political groupings soon positioned themselves to take advantage of the new arrangements: the Communists, the Socialists, and the Christian Democrats. By the late 1950s they had attained sufficient strength and cohesion to send Chilean politics lurching to the left and for the first time drawing the attention of a nervous Washington.

It wasn't social conditions alone that gave Chile its leftward spin. The country had steadily been lifting the restrictions on voting that had traditionally made politics such a cozy affair. In 1949, women got the vote, and in 1958 the secret ballot was guaranteed, a devastating blow to the landowners in the countryside, who previously had been able to keep a close eye on cowed tenants. In 1962, voter registration was made obligatory, and in 1970 the literacy requirement was abolished and the voting age lowered to 18. From 1950 to 1973, the percentage of the population registered to vote went from 13.7 percent to 44 percent, and in 1970 the percentage of eligible voters who were registered was 82.4 percent.

Yet, ominously, at the same time that Chile was becoming a genuine democracy, economic conditions, already bad, crumbled even more. The wages of the most needy on both the farms and in the cities were falling, while unemployment and inflation were rising. In agriculture alone, workers' wages dropped 23 percent between 1953 and 1964. Chile was turning from a society in disrepair into a time bomb. Foreigners, both journalists and scholars, who visited Chile in the early 1960s returned home convinced that the country was about to explode. One of the most knowledgeable observers of Chile in those years was an American professor, an expert on Latin America, Frederick B. Pike. He wrote, "The profound consequences of the social problem have created in Chile two distinct modes of existence separated by well-nigh unbreachable barriers." He went on to warn of the possibility of "a devastating social revolution."

Enter Salvador Allende—compassionate, romantic, unbending, undisciplined, manipulative, hedonistic, naïve, theatrical—an "immaculate socialist militant," according to his friend, the left-wing French journalist Regis Debray; "all things to all men," according to Nathaniel Davis, the astute, level-headed American ambassador who was eyewitness to Allende's downfall. For all his charm, no one, even among Allende's admirers, thought he had the quickest mind in the room. Davis's predecessor, Edward Korry, who was never at a loss for words, once said of him: "Economically, he was almost an illiterate." To catalogue Allende's many mistakes once he took power is to risk being accused of "blaming the victim," but in fact Allende seemed to go out of his way to make himself a victim.

Allende's Socialist Party was the second of Chile's three major left-wing parties to be organized, and Allende was proud to say that he was there at the creation, one of the party's founders. It was formed in 1933, 13 years after the Communist Party, by intellectuals, workers, and other activists who were opposed to the dogmatism of the Communists and their obeisance to Moscow. Allende himself, a young idealistic doctor, found himself unable to ignore the dire state of his country.

The Communists were anything but idealistic. Doctrinaire and smug, they were secure in the knowledge that they had a solid base of support in Chile's mining regions, where workers in closed, tight communities were easily organized; you didn't need the writings of Marx to conclude that class conflict was the driving force of social relations. What's more, they had the guaranteed backing of the Soviet Union, a steady source of funding and direction. These facts rendered them disciplined, cautious, and unimaginative; they were bureaucrats at heart, locked in their ideology, excellent at organization but not at welcoming or embracing new ideas or responding to new conditions. They were the "suits" of the left, and though they were outlawed for 10 years between 1948 and 1958 in Chile's own version of a Red Scare, in truth they moved slowly and pragmatically, waiting for the revolution to come to them since history was on their side. Under orders from Moscow, they were disinclined to rock the boat.

Chile's Socialists were no less committed to Marxism or to the revolution than the Communists. The Leninist theme of a "dictatorship of the proletariat" was a trope that was sounded repeatedly throughout their history. But without the restrictions of Moscow's straitjacket, they were wilder, more unruly and unpredictable, capable of going off in several different directions or in several directions at once. They were more open, more inviting than the Communists, but because there was such a dilettantish quality to them, it was said that "the Communist Party was a full-time party, the Socialist Party was only a part-time one." In their Marxist house were many mansions: Trotskyists, anarchists, Titoists, Peronists, Maoists, anyone who yearned for social justice ASAP, who despised the Conservatives yet was repelled by the stolid, slow-moving, often slow-witted Communists, anyone inclined to wear a Che Guevara T-shirt. The Socialists were the perfect party for the rock-and-rolling 1960s. It appealed to freethinkers like students and teachers, to independents and iconoclasts, to anyone who surveyed the condition of Chilean society and concluded that radical reform couldn't come quickly enough. The party had another important component, however, that contributed to its character. Along with the students and intellectuals, it also attracted workers interested in reform but who retained patriotic or nationalist sentiments in opposition to the more internationalist Communists; and so, according to one scholar of the party, Chile's Socialists were not averse to exhibiting a "ferocious nationalism."

The Socialists weren't patient like the Communists. They weren't willing to wait. Because they wanted the revolution and they wanted it *now*, they were to the left of the Communists. This is a fact that must be stressed, not only to those Americans inclined to flatten important distinctions between Communism and Socialism but also to those knowledgeable students of history whose understanding is framed by the evolution of Marxism in Europe. There the Socialists were the conservatives and compromisers on the left, the Marxists who had broken with the Communists and Russia's Bolshevik Revolution for the sake of democracy and a peaceful road to progress. One of the glories of Socialist or Marxist (but not Communist) history in Europe was Leon Blum's speech at the French Socialist Party congress in Tours in 1920, where the Communists, accepting the guidance of the Bolsheviks in Moscow, split off from the Socialist leadership, taking the majority of the delegates with them (including a young Asian student who had assumed the name Ho Chi Minh). Blum spoke for the Socialist rump, defending the tradition of democratic socialism, what he called "the old house," and challenging the Communists: "For the first time in the history of socialism you are thinking of terrorism . . . as a means of government. It is this, this emphasis on dictatorial terror, on the Russian model as a grid to be applied willy-nilly to France, together with the slavish, unquestioning obedience to Moscow that it presumes, that distinguishes you from us and always will."

Chile's Socialists were not European Socialists. Leon Blum was never a guiding light or inspiration for them. They were sui generis, opposed to taking marching orders from any outsider, even refusing to join the Socialist International. They never developed a coherent ideology, and for the most part probably didn't want one. More scholarly Marxists, ensconced in their libraries and hunched over their revolutionary texts, torn apart by the agonizing divisions between Bolsheviks and Mensheviks, or Communists and Socialists, couldn't take the Chileans seriously because they were at sea philosophically, mere kibitzers, attracted to whatever ism happened to pass their way, even ones with fascist overtones. Allende lightheartedly called his socialism "con sabor a empanadas y vino tinto," that is, "with the taste of empanadas and red wine." But the ism that ultimately won his heart, and the heart of the party he led, was Castro-ism. It can be said that more than anything else, it was his devotion to Castro that sealed his fate.

Everything, it might be argued, came down to a straightforward formula: Allende = Castro = Communism = Soviet domination. That was the outlook that guided American policy in the 1960s and 1970s. It was simplistic, as all formulas must be, especially given the multilayered reality of Chilean politics it was trying to capture. But at the height of the Cold War, there was a core of truth to it, though a truth that required the kind of caveats and modifications Washington's policymakers were unwilling or unable to allow for. What cannot be denied is that Allende took power in 1970 with the support of the Communists, and what also cannot be denied are Allende's longtime ties to Castro. From the moment Fidel marched into Havana in 1959, Allende had found his idol and his inspiration.

In 1959, in the immediate aftermath of his revolution, Castro visited Chile. His guide was Salvador Allende, who became known among his countrymen as the "spokesman of the Cuban revolution." Allende declared, "The Chilean people have been aroused and deeply moved by the Cuban revolution. . . . Today Latin America is revitalized by the Cuban revolution." Different countries might use different strategies, but they were all "marching toward a common goal." There was even a family connection. In 1970 his daughter Beatriz married a Cuban who was high up in Castro's regime, and became a force pushing her father to the left, faster, faster.

But what confuses this picture, creating a vast battleground for historical interpretation, is that Allende was a Socialist, not a Communist, and it was the Communists who were intent on extending the sway of the Soviet Union in Latin America, the Socialists who were "ferocious" about maintaining their independence. Different strategies toward a common goal? That's what Allende said, but what did he mean? For that matter, what did it mean that of all the leaders of Chile's Socialist Party, Allende was the one who was closest to the Communists, perhaps the only political figure on the left who could bring the two Marxist parties together? And then how should one factor in his Kremlin connection?

Such questions will never be resolved. The lines will always remain blurry. But precisely because they are blurry what cannot be dismissed is the Nixon/Kissinger worry that Chile under Allende was a paving stone on the road to Soviet hegemony. Who could say what kind of Socialist Allende was or would become? For that matter, who could say what kind of Communist Fidel Castro was? From Washington's point of view, Castro was enough of one to risk plunging the world into nuclear holocaust during the 1962 Cuban Missile Crisis. But even in his case, the nature of his Communism was never as clear and incontrovertible as Washington pretended it was.

Castro had come to power as a revolutionary, yes, but not as a Moscow-directed Communist, and the Kremlin kept its distance at first, puzzled, as everyone else was, by the gift that had fallen into its hands, refusing to send arms to Cuba. It wasn't long before Moscow and Havana drew closer, and though it's often said that American intransigence forced Castro into Russia's embrace, what's also true is that there was a natural affinity for Castro and the Kremlin to draw upon. The United States was their common enemy, and by the end of 1959 Russian weapons were arriving in Cuba. Not long after, Khrushchev went so far as to threaten nuclear retaliation if the United States invaded Cuba.

And yet Latin American Communists with their local concerns remained suspicious of Castro. He was too impulsive for them, too "tropical." He insisted that the path to revolution was armed struggle, whereas the conservative Communists pursued more accommodationist policies. In Chile, they were prepared to work with the "bourgeois" parties, while the Socialists were not; they even evinced some sympathy for the Catholic Church.

Castro purged old-line Communists in Cuba, many of whom were friends of Chile's Communists, because they were too cautious for him, and he proceeded to support guerrilla movements throughout Latin America, a self-defeating policy in the eyes of Moscow and its Latin supporters. Che Guevara was a particularly divisive figure in this internecine dispute, and Communists across Latin America shed no tears when he was killed in 1967. Chile's Socialists, on the other hand, mourned his death as a tragedy, and in 1969, when three survivors of Guevara's ill-fated Bolivia campaign managed to find their way to Chile, it was Salvador Allende who was there to greet them and lead them to safety. Allende described Guevara as "a friend" and treasured the copy of Guevara's *The Guerrilla War* that was personally inscribed to him by its author. "The news of Che's assassination was a source of deep sadness to me," Allende told Debray. "I shared in the mourning of thousands of my compatriots."

Connoisseurs of political nuance might appreciate the complicated differences between Chilean Socialists and Chilean Communists, and Washington's policymakers might have been able to play on those differences, but few of them drew the necessary distinctions. Besides, how much difference would it have made if they had? In 1960, after Moscow had extended its nuclear protection to him, Castro, in the course of a five-hour speech, declared: "Moscow is our brain and our great leader." Was there anything else that Washington needed to know?

And since Allende was the most visible and most vocal supporter of Castro in Chile, if not in all of South America, was there anything else Washington needed to know about him? His hostility to Washington was bound up with his version of Marxism. He simply could not be allowed to take power. Whatever the ambiguities of his politics and philosophy, the risks were too great. As one State Department official wrote to McGeorge Bundy, the national security adviser, in 1964: "Another 'Castro' in the hemisphere, particularly one who achieved power through the democratic process . . . would be awfully tough to handle from both the international and domestic standpoints. This would clearly be a case where one and one totaled much more than two and the consequences throughout the hemisphere of a second Castro would be serious." Richard Helms was blunter: "The prospect of an Allende government in Chile was a clear threat to our national interest."

THE ALLENDE DANGER had been visible to Washington for years. He had first run for president in 1952 and won a negligible 5.5 percent of the vote. There was no reason to pay attention to him. But his fortunes picked up considerably in the next presidential contest in 1958. With the backing of the Communist Party, now returned to the public arena after a decade of exclusion, he came startlingly close to becoming president. Though he collected only 28.6 percent of the vote, the victor, Jorge Alessandri, was elected with a mere 31.2 percent, and only a quirk or a gimmick kept Allende out of office. To keep the left divided, the right had financed the quixotic campaign of a defrocked priest, who got 3.3 percent of the vote, a number that probably would have gone to Allende. Adding that to his actual total,

Allende would have prevailed over Alessandri by 0.7 percent. The crisis of 1970 might have arrived 12 years earlier, pre-Castro, except for a fluke.

As the 1964 presidential election approached, there was no quixotic priest to deflect Allende's growing popularity, but there was something better, a new political party that was outstripping the established left and seemed a godsend to the worried Americans. The Christian Democrats, the third of Chile's three leftist parties, formed in 1957 as an expression of liberal Catholic teachings and became a wedge between the religious conservatives on the right and the various strains of Marxism on the left. Led by the religious, buttoned-down Eduardo Frei, who liked to lecture his constituents on the virtues of neo-Thomism, the Christian Democrats were as pious as the Conservatives, but their religion had a leftward slant; they were as concerned about the suffering of the poor as the Marxists but without the atheism or the commitment to class struggle. Instead, they preached a philosophy of "communitarianism," or what Frei called "Communitarian Socialism," which taught that the individual and society were part of an organic whole and that the point of government was to find ways of healing class divisions, not exacerbating them.

Communitarianism was a foggy notion—just how foggy would become clear after Frei became president—but it sounded good, especially to voters looking for ways to reconcile economic growth with social justice or political protest with traditional values. That was a lot of people in long-suffering Chile. In 1958, a year after its founding, the Christian Democratic Party finished third, with 21 percent of the vote, a more than respectable showing. By 1963, it was the largest party in the country with particular appeal to the newly enfranchised poor, who yearned for economic reform but remained socially conservative, and to women, who tended to be more religious than men. Indeed, women were the party's secret weapon, giving Frei 63 percent of their vote in 1964 as compared to only 32 percent for Allende and putting him over the top.

But Frei's 1964 victory wasn't due simply to the preferences of Chile's voters. It wasn't a "clean" election. It was helped along by extraordinary interference on the part of the United States. Almost a decade before Nixon and Kissinger were plotting to thwart Allende, John Kennedy and Lyndon Johnson were working toward the same end. Indeed, according to the report of the Church committee "covert United States involvement in Chile in the decade between 1963 and 1973 was extensive and continuous."

American interest in the Christian Democrats began in 1962, and "nonattributable" aid started flowing into Santiago. To the Democrats of the Kennedy and Johnson administrations, Frei was understood to be a reformer opposed to both the Marxists and the oligarchs, and despite his frequent use of the word "socialism," he spoke their language. As the 1964 presidential election drew near, the secret funds turned into a flood. Washington threw its full support behind Frei, and what one scholar called "incredible sums of money" flowed into campaign materials, support for private groups like sympathetic labor unions and women's organizations, and bribes. One White House staffer told Bundy in July 1964: "We can't afford to lose this one, so I don't think there should be any economy shaving in this instance. . . . Let's pour it on and in."

More than half of the Christian Democrats' funds came from the United States. According to the Church report, the CIA, besides supporting the Christian Democrats, "mounted a massive anti-Communist propaganda campaign. Extensive use was made of the press, radio, films, pamphlets, posters, leaflets, direct mailings, paper streamers and wall painting." In the first week of the CIA's efforts, in June 1964, the agency produced 20 radio spots a day in Santiago and 12-minute news reports broadcast five times a day on three different Santiago stations. Activities in the provinces were even more extensive.

To those inclined to react with indignation or outrage at Washington's interventions, it is important to point out that Chile was hardly virgin territory whose purity was violated only by the intrusive, predatory United States. The Soviet Union and Cuba were doing their utmost to back Allende. If virtue was defined by a lack of foreign intervention, then nobody, inside Chile or out, could be said to be clothed in virtue. But even if critics are reluctant to celebrate it, the American covert effort can be seen as one of the great foreign policy success stories of the 1960s: Frei won the election with 56 percent of the vote, compared to 39 percent for Allende. Afterward, Frei thanked the Americans for their help, though almost no one, including Frei himself, knew just how extensive that help was. The CIA, which did know, congratulated itself as one of the "indispensable ingredients in Frei's success."

With all the opprobrium that has been heaped on the United States for its involvement in Chile's 1970 presidential election, it's worth remembering that the first serious intervention in Chile's politics was in the election six years earlier and was larger in scale than the one in 1970. It's also crucial to remember that the 1964 intervention was itself modeled on another of America's great postwar foreign policy triumphs, its involvement in Italy's election of 1948, which has striking parallels to the Chile example and highlights the difficulties of striking a pure noninterventionist position. Americans busily manipulating Chile's 1964 election made constant reference to Italy's election 16 years before.

In 1948, the Italian Communist Party, with considerable assistance from the Russians, was the strongest political force in the country. With the father of containment, George Kennan of the Policy Planning Staff, warning that a Communist victory was an intolerable outcome that would "send waves of panic to all surrounding areas," Washington poured in millions of lire to the Italian Christian Democrats and Socialists to assure a Communist defeat. Italy was the CIA's first major covert action and a turning point in how the United States conducted its foreign policy. Those who prefer their democratic politics pristine, disconnected from the real world, might shudder. But Washington, as Kennan said, had to "do things that very much needed to be done, but for which the government couldn't take official responsibility." In a similar fashion, Richard Helms said, with Chile in mind: "Secret intelligence has never been for the fainthearted." Henry Kissinger agreed that "covert operations have their philosophical and practical difficulties and especially for America." That doesn't mean extralegal methods haven't been employed before and won't continue to be employed. What it does mean is that every time they are exposed, there will be squeals of outrage, recriminations, and vows of change, until the next time.

Once in power, Frei moved to pursue a broad agenda of reform, what he called a "revolution in liberty." He negotiated a deal with the key American copper companies that gave the Chilean government a majority interest in the mines. He appropriated and distributed land to the peasants and, perhaps most important, allowed them to form their own unions. By 1970, union membership, with the government's encouragement, had doubled, reaching 500,000. This was indeed a revolution in liberty. Frei also established relations with the Soviet Union and the countries of eastern Europe.

But if the Christian Democrats were the centrist or center-left party in the Chilean political spectrum, and with its reformist rather than revolutionary policies the favored client of the United States, they proved to be too radical for Chile's conservatives and too moderate for Chile's radicals. Where the propertied elite was concerned, Frei's land reforms went too far while the Marxists thought his agreements with the copper companies didn't go far enough. He wanted to purchase the companies

through a policy he called "Chileanization"; they wanted outright appro-
priation. Allende attacked Frei as a right-wing "reformer." Even the newly
unionized workers turned against him through increased strikes and factory occupations, driving a wedge between Frei and his more moderate
middle-class supporters.

Assessing Frei's years in office is a glass-half-full/half-empty affair, and
historians differ in their conclusions, but about one thing they do not disagree: by 1970, everyone had found a reason either to be angry or disappointed; politically, at least, communitarianism had failed. The right was
revitalized, the left was radicalized, and the Christian Democrats were
divided among themselves in a classic case of the center being unable
to hold. Communitarianism had promised something for everyone, but
everyone, it turned out, wanted more than the promises could deliver.

In 1964, the right had supported the Christian Democrats as the only
way to prevent an Allende victory. Disenchanted with the Frei government, it refused to do the same in 1970, whatever the dangers of division,
and instead it selected the safest of safe choices, a former president and the
son of a former president, Jorge Alessandri, as its candidate. The left once
again selected its warhorse Allende, while the Christian Democrats, for-
bidden by the constitution from renominating Frei, chose instead the colorless Radomiro Tomic, who was more radical than Frei and closer to the
Marxists, at least in policy if not necessarily in philosophy. The three-way
race presented Washington with difficult choices and engendered intense
debates within the White House.

Alessandri was easily the most pro-business and pro-American candidate in 1970, and the question the instinctively pro-business Nixon
administration had to ask itself was why it shouldn't come down on the
side of the conservatives. The CIA certainly believed American interests
were best served by an Alessandri victory, and American business leaders urged support for him to whoever would listen. But the fact that there
were three candidates in 1970 instead of two and that one of the parties,
the Christian Democrats, was Washington's longtime ally greatly complicated the decision Washington had to make. "We are in a quandary as to
what action is wise," Helms said.

The confusion served to revive an old debate: Just how much of a threat
was Allende to American interests in the hemisphere anyway? Even if the
Soviet Union and Cuba were backing him with financial and organizational support, should the United States bother to get involved at all? The

Kissingers and Helmses had no doubt about the answers to those questions, but there were voices within the administration that held different views.

Yes, Allende was close to Castro, but as John Crummins, a State Department specialist on Latin America, said, "We could live with him; the election of Allende would not be the end of the world." The under-secretary of state for inter-American affairs, Charles Meyer, echoed that sentiment. All three candidates, he said, would present problems for the United States, and any gains from American involvement, either with the Christian Democrats or the conservatives, "were outweighed by the potential costs." Tomic had moved the Christian Democrats so far to the left that there was little space between him and Allende, but the problem with Alessandri was that he was backward-looking and, worse, incompe-tent, as his presidency from 1958 to 1964 had demonstrated. The Ameri-can ambassador, Edward Korry, who was never without a strong opinion, remained a self-declared social democrat and therefore a supporter of Tomic and the Christian Democrats. He worried that an Alessandri vic-tory in a country boiling over with discontent would ultimately result in an army takeover. In the months leading up to the election in Septem-ber, the State Department kept pressing the White House with its doubts about any American intervention. Finally, on June 27, Kissinger had had enough and exploded with his now-famous exclamation: "I don't see why we need to stand by and watch a country go Communist due to the irre-sponsibility of its own people."

Still, the uncertainty never went away, and rather than choosing either Tomic or Alessandri to support, Washington dithered, backing neither. Instead, it decided it had no position except the negative one of opposition to Allende, and so the American money that went into Chile's 1970 election went strictly for anti-Allende propaganda—often ham-fisted propaganda that convinced nobody—and into efforts to divide the Socialist/Commu-nist coalition. It was a strategy, as one CIA official put it, of "trying to beat somebody with nobody." According to the Church committee, the CIA spent only about one-third as much in the 1970 campaign as in the 1964 campaign, $1 million as compared to $3 million six years earlier, though the stakes were just as high, if not higher.

Whatever its impact, the outcome was as bad as the U.S. government feared it would be. Allende actually got a smaller percentage of the vote than he had received in 1964, but because he was in a three-man race, he came out on top with 36.2 percent, compared to 34.9 percent for Alessandri and 27.8 percent for Tomic. It was anything but a resounding win, though how to interpret it is open to question. Some have argued that two-thirds of the electorate chose left-wing candidates, demonstrating the leftist sympathies of the country as a whole. Others have contended that if it had been a two-man race between Allende and Alessandri, many of Tomic's supporters, especially among the women, would have rejected Marxism and gone for the conservatives. In an after-the-fact effort to cast doubt on the legitimacy of Allende's victory, Kissinger, in his memoirs, said that Allende's plurality "represented a break with Chile's long democratic history" because he would "become president not through an authentic expression of majority will but through a fluke of the Chilean political system." Nonsense. Kissinger ignores the fact that several presidents in Chile's "long democratic history" took office after receiving only a plurality of the vote, and that's not to mention those American presidents who were themselves elected with pluralities rather than majorities. Woodrow Wilson became president with under 42 percent of the vote, Abraham Lincoln with less than 40 percent.

In any case, the presidential campaign of 1970 didn't end with the September 4 vote. Because no candidate had received a majority, the congress would choose the president on October 24, just time enough for Washington to open its full bag of dirty tricks, from attempting to bribe politicians to encouraging military coups—but not time enough for it to think through the consequences of what it was doing. How could Allende have come in first? It was said that even he was surprised by the result. As for Nixon, he was beside himself, outraged, lashing out in all directions. And Kissinger was furious. Democracy or no, something, anything, had to be done. With no time for careful analysis, plans hatched like venomous snakes. The most benign of them was in effect bribes to Chile's congressmen to vote for Alessandri with the understanding that, once elected, he would step down, clearing the path for Frei to return to office legally. The idea was so convoluted, with so many pieces that had to fall into place in just the right way, that it was labeled "the Rube Goldberg plan," and it promptly went nowhere. Chile's politicians, it turned out, simply weren't corrupt enough to cooperate. The only genuine alternative was a military coup, and while the coup attempt failed ignominiously, it remains the ugliest episode in the entire history of U.S.-Chile relations.

Worse than a crime, it was a blunder, a sign of the panic that had seized the White House. Korry, the American ambassador, a loyal friend of Frei, was grimly reporting: "There is a graveyard smell to Chile, the fumes of a democracy in decomposition." Even this Kennedy-Johnson social democrat predicted a rigid, Soviet-style Communism in Chile's future. Korry's tragedy was that he saw his own position of liberal reform evaporate in front of him with the defeat of the Christian Democrats; the 1970 election left him with no ground to stand on. And the same might be said of all of America's Cold War liberals who carried on the traditions of Franklin Roosevelt, Harry Truman, and John Kennedy and who were desperate to find reformist solutions to counter the appeal of Communist totalitarianism.

It was easier for the men in power in Washington in 1970, who were not Cold War liberals but nationalistic conservatives oblivious to any need for reform. On September 15, Nixon met with Kissinger, Attorney General John Mitchell, and CIA director Richard Helms and in the strictest secrecy ordered the CIA to instigate a coup, even though no one in that room had a clue about the conditions inside Chile, the thinking of the Chilean military, or whether a coup was even remotely possible. Though he was as concerned as anyone about the consequences of an Allende presidency, Korry did know something about the facts on the ground and was convinced that it was not possible. But Kissinger dismissed him as an "unguided missile" and his advice was ignored.

However, the unguided missile was right, and when CIA operatives in Chile established contact with the military, they found themselves working with its most extremist elements, in particular a hotheaded and resentful retired general, Robert Viaux, who had almost no support among his colleagues. That is to say, the initial obstacle to a successful military coup turned out to be the military itself, so that the first step in the extremists' plot was to make war on the army by kidnapping its chief of staff, General Rene Schneider, a firm adherent to Chile's constitutional traditions.

The whole thing was crazy, something Kissinger came to realize by early October. "Viaux did not have more than one chance in 20—perhaps less—to launch a successful coup," he wrote, and on October 15 he issued an order to the CIA to call off the plot. Somehow, the CIA failed to get the message, only one in a series of comically tragic missteps, and a CIA cable went out the next day declaring "it is firm and continuing policy that Allende be overthrown by a coup," though something in Kissinger's directive must have taken hold because it advised against working with the fanatical Viaux as "counterproductive." Kissinger later said the CIA had misunderstood his orders, although he concedes that "in retrospect it is clear that I should have been more vigilant." Whatever the case, some days later Schneider was murdered. It was the first political assassination in Chile in more than 150 years, and it reeked of haste, improvisation, miscommunication, ignorance, bungling, and delusion. The right hand did not know what the far-right hand was doing. One scholar sympathetic to American policy in Chile says: "What is beyond debate is that the U.S. government, despite a lack of any operational control, was inextricably linked with the plot, to its eternal shame."

On October 24, Chile's congress, following tradition, elected the front-runner president by a vote of 153–35, with seven abstaining, and Allende became the leader of his country. Quite unsurprisingly if nonetheless disturbingly, Allende, in his first presidential address, made a point of praising Cuba, calling it an example for Chile to follow. One of his first official acts was to establish diplomatic relations with Castro.

The United States had been stymied at every turn. Its intervention in the election had failed. Its attempt to incite congress to vote against Allende had failed. Its half-baked attempt to foment a coup had failed. What now?

ON NOVEMBER 5, Kissinger sent Nixon a memo outlining the "dimensions of the problem" and a course of action for the future. It began: "The election of Allende as president of Chile poses for us one of the most serious challenges ever faced in this hemisphere." Allende, Kissinger said, was "a tough, dedicated Marxist" who would seek to eliminate U.S. influence in South America while increasing the influence of Cuba and the Soviet Union. At the same time, he posed "some very painful dilemmas for us," because he was legally elected and was Chile's legitimate leader not only to most Chileans but to most of the world as well. It was all true. But the question was whether Washington should essentially wait, in the hope that Allende would become more moderate, though at the risk that he would consolidate his power and create a Marxist dictatorship allied with the Soviet Union, or if it should take action before he became entrenched, though at the risk of turning much of the world, and Latin America in particular, against U.S. policy. "In my judgment," Kissinger concluded, "the dangers of doing nothing are greater than the risks we run in trying to do something." He recommended a policy of opposing Allende "as strongly as we can," while "taking care to package those efforts in a style that gives us the appearance of reacting to his moves."

Critics have excoriated Kissinger for choosing to do something rather than nothing, but it was a judgment call that could have gone either way, susceptible to second-guessing and Monday-morning quarterbacking. Actually, one might ask why, if Kissinger believed Allende represented so profound a threat to American national interests, the United States didn't do more—that is, why it didn't continue to instigate a coup attempt against him instead of simply seeking to hem him in through sanctions and other economic restrictions. Why, given the alternatives, was its approach so "moderate"? Indeed, the Church committee asked precisely that question: "Was the threat posed to the national security interests of the United States so grave that the government was remiss in not seeking his downfall directly during 1970–73?" It is, in fact, one of the oddities of this entire history that after Allende's installation, Washington turned its attention elsewhere. Chile had ceased to be an obsession at the very moment when the reason for the obsession had become reality. "Cambodia claimed most of my attention," Kissinger later said, and there were also the more pressing matters of the Middle East and the Soviet Union to worry about. Even he couldn't do everything at once.

The explanation for the shift from active intervention to more passive economic warfare is partly that people do sometimes learn from their mistakes, and Kissinger had learned from his. The failed coup attempt demonstrated what Korry had already told Washington: the Chilean military had no taste for overturning the constitutional order. What's more, there was America's reputation in the world to think about. It was one thing for the United States to encourage a coup to forestall an Allende presidency but quite another to foment a coup against a sitting head of state, and even Washington's allies in Latin America were making their opposition to such a policy clear. So the United States turned to less direct, more subtle ways of opposing and undermining Allende.

In effect, Washington declared economic war on Allende, following up on Nixon's now-famous declaration that the United States should make Chile's economy scream. Aid was cut off and credits denied; international organizations and other governments were pressured to sever or limit their ties to Chile. The numbers told a dramatic story. Short-term credits dropped from $300 million under Frei to $30 million under Allende. U.S. bilateral aid went from $35 million in 1969 to $1.5 million in 1971.

Still, the impact of these shifts was not as severe as the statistics might suggest and Nixon and Kissinger might have hoped. Other sources of

funds, like the Soviet Union and eastern Europe, were now available to
Allende, and Cuba was doing the best it could to shore him up. Between
1970 and 1973, the amount of credits available to Chile actually increased
by 185 percent. Spare parts were harder to come by because much of
Chile's machinery had been purchased in the United States, but Washington never did institute an embargo, and ultimately there was probably
less to its declaration of economic war than the critics claimed and the
supporters hoped. The United States, by itself, lacked the ability to make
Chile's economy scream. Nathaniel Davis, the American ambassador to
Chile after Korry, who was present during the Allende years, had written,
"If Richard Nixon and Henry Kissinger really wanted to run the Chilean economy into the ground by means of a credit squeeze, they were not
very efficient at it." Economic warfare may not have been an effective policy, but there were few choices open to Washington and none guaranteed
to work. At least Nixon and Kissinger could console themselves with the
thought that they were doing *something*—which, as Kissinger had argued,
was better than doing nothing.

The other major component of Washington's policy toward Allende
was to give support to his domestic opponents, a plan, Kissinger said, that
was designed "to preserve democracy in Chile." Money flowed to opposition parties and candidates, to newspapers and radio stations. A focal
point for this aid was Chile's largest newspaper, *El Mercurio*, an unremit-
tingly conservative publication with a circulation of 300,000 and direct
ties to the Nixon White House. It was the oldest Spanish-language newspaper in the world. Allende had declared that he would "get" the paper for
its public, often strident, stands against him, and his government forced
an increase in wages coupled with a price freeze in an effort to drive it
into bankruptcy. The United States stood by it—heavily. Out of a total of
$7 million in American covert aid in those years, as much as $1.5 million
went to *El Mercurio*. The quiet battle over *El Mercurio* was a microcosm of
the larger war going on between Chile and the United States.

In addition, if Washington was no longer ready to foment a coup against
Allende, it was certainly not going to stand in the way if the military made
a decision to overthrow him. In effect, it was walking a tightrope, maintaining ties with the army, training officers, gathering intelligence, and
cultivating relationships, while avoiding direct involvement in any internal military activity. There was little that was covert about this. With
Allende's knowledge, Americans continued to advise the Chilean military

and American arms continued to be delivered. In 1971, the United States supplied $5 million in credits for arms sales, in 1972 another $10 million, and in 1973 over $12 million. Washington was not about to abandon its friends in the military, especially now, and especially with the Soviet Union eager to step in. What kind of signal would that have sent?

Altogether the policy was a nuanced one: no support for a coup but no opposition either. It's hardly surprising that the mixed signals confused some operatives in the field. In November 1971, the CIA station in Santiago sent a message to Washington stating "that the ultimate objective of the military penetration program was a military coup." It was promptly slapped on the wrist by Washington, which responded that the CIA did not have approval to become involved in any plotting for a coup. It was the CIA's job to "report" history, not "make" history.

Yet hope springs eternal. At the same time that the Santiago station was discouraged from making history, it was instructed to be sure the United States was in a position to take advantage of the situation if the military did rise up. As a result, the CIA collected a mountain of information in preparation for a coup—arrest lists, key government installations, personnel who might need protection. But none of this information was turned over to the Chilean military and a stance of no involvement or active encouragement remained firm American policy. In a report later issued by the CIA, the agency noted that while it had maintained contact with some military plotters, it "exercised extreme care in all dealings with Chilean military officers and continued to monitor their activities but under no circumstances attempted to influence them." As rumors of a coup grew in 1973, the Santiago station questioned whether it should continue to adhere to a policy of noninvolvement and was once again reminded by Washington that "there was to be no involvement with the military in any covert action initiative." Even on September 10, 1973, the day before the actual coup, a Chilean officer approached the CIA requesting American assistance. He was turned away. As one CIA official who was in Chile at the time put it, "We had clear instructions not to foment or start coup planning." This, he said, "was gospel."

DIRECT RESPONSIBILITY FOR the coup in September 1973 that overthrew the elected government of Chile rested not with the covert war of Nixon and Kissinger but with the elected government of Chile—that is, with the policies of Salvador Allende. Or, one might say, it rested with an excess of idealism on his part. Frei, with his communitarian beliefs, came into office in 1964 declaring he was the president of all Chileans. Allende, with his Marxist philosophy of class conflict, took office declaring "I am not president of all Chileans," but only of the poor and the underdogs. Noble sentiments perhaps but not a recipe for domestic peace.

In Allende's mind, the institutions of bourgeois democracy could never achieve the transformation of society that he believed he had been elected to effect (never mind that only slightly more than one-third of the voters had supported him). "The objective," he said, "is total, scientific Marxist socialism." But he would have to move quickly because the unusual circumstances that had brought him to power would probably not be duplicated again.

Where possible, he would try to achieve his goals through democratic processes, but if that proved impossible, he had other ways. He could govern through "legal loopholes," bypassing the legislature. According to the secretary-general of the Socialist Party, Allende was prepared to follow legal rules "for now," but the Socialists were urging supporters to be ready for "the decisive confrontation with the bourgeoisie and imperialism" that was bound to come. As he put it: "The actual class struggle is irreconcilable. . . . It will come to an end only when one of the classes assumes complete power." Allende's economics minister proclaimed: "State control is designed to destroy the economic bases of imperialism and the ruling class by putting an end to the private ownership of the means of production."

As soon as he came into office, Allende unleashed a wave of nationalizations and expropriations. By the end of his first year, he had nationalized most mineral resources, which included the American copper companies, and more than 80 percent of the banks, in a way of gaining control of the credit in the country and thus of the Chilean economy overall. He nationalized the fishing and textile industries, as well as Ford and the telephone company. By 1973, the government controlled about 35 percent of the land, 30 percent of industry, and 33 percent of wholesale distribution. By one estimate, over 90 percent of Chile's GDP was under government control.

Sometimes, as in the case of the copper companies, the nationalizations were achieved through legislation that won overwhelming support. (By now, no one in Chile loved the American companies; even the head of Chile's Roman Catholic bishops declared that nationalization was right and just.) At other times the methods skirted or even overstepped the bounds of legality. The government would simply approve the seizures of farms and factories, one of those "loopholes" Allende was relying on. Perhaps the most important—and pernicious—method was by squeezing the companies economically, as he tried to do with *El Mercurio*. The government had the authority to approve price hikes and wage increases. Companies that were targets for takeovers were prohibited from raising their prices but were forced to raise their workers' pay. Moreover, as the government extended its control of the banks, credit for distressed companies dried up. Forced bankruptcies were a favorite tool of Allende's Socialists. And who was there to run these companies once they were taken over? Ambassador Davis reports: "Government-appointed managers were usually named on the basis of a political patronage system that would have put Tammany Hall to shame." Many formerly profitable companies were soon incurring heavy losses. In the countryside, where peasants—often illiterate—were seizing control of the estates, there was resistance even to the simplest methods of accounting and cost calculation.

As Allende told Debray, "We shall have real power when copper and steel are under our control, when saltpeter is genuinely under our control, when we have put far-reaching land reform measures into effect, when we control imports and exports through the state, when we have collectivized a major portion of our national production." But it wasn't just the economy that Allende was trying to control. He was also taking steps to centralize the government and restrict political freedom. He saw his most important political reform as replacing the bicameral legislature with a single chamber in order to strengthen the presidency and weaken congress's ability to block his objectives. It would also have the power to override judicial decisions. He called the proposed new body the "People's Assembly," but he never gained sufficient support from the "people" to call a plebiscite on the question.

One other important effort at centralization that went nowhere was Allende's proposal in 1973 to change Chile's education curriculum to instill "values of socialist humanism" among young people. Private and parochial schools would be required to adopt the government's curriculum, and secondary students would be compelled to work in state enterprises as part of their "instruction." The minister of education explained that the program had been modeled on the school system of East Germany. Inevitably, opposition was fierce. The Christian Democrats condemned the plan, while the archbishop of Valparaiso denounced it as one that could "lead to the control of education by a partisan ideology." Other members of the Catholic hierarchy soon joined in the protests, the first time the Church had come out against the Allende government. It was also the first time the military expressed its disagreement with an announced policy of the government. The failed education reform was a turning point of sorts.

Still another important failure was Allende's effort to seize control of Chile's only private supplier of paper, a company owned by his presidential rival Jorge Alessandri. This would have given the government the ability to control supplies to all the country's newspapers, just as the takeover of the banks was giving it control of credit. Allende's method was his tried-and-often-true one of driving the company into bankruptcy by raising wages and other costs of production while denying price increases. In this case, the strategy failed, though it was successful with another media giant, Zig Zag, the largest publishing company in Chile before 1970. Allende demanded wage increases the company could not afford, driving it out of business. The government acquired Zig Zag's property and reorganized it into a state enterprise. Meanwhile, other private media companies— newspapers, radio, and television—were coming under steady pressure and often succumbing. All of this was consistent with the Socialists' intention, announced in their 1969 platform, to use the media to create "a new culture and a new man." Frei, on the other hand, had begun calling Allende totalitarian. He had reason.

Perhaps the creeping effort to restrict civil liberties wouldn't have brought people into the streets, at least not immediately. But Allende's economic programs hit them directly. His announced policy of "first consumption, then accumulation" was an economic disaster waiting to happen. In 1971, the inflation rate was 20 percent, kept somewhat in check by the expenditure of the government's foreign reserves, but in 1972, with the government spending lavishly to support its social and economic policies, it jumped to 78 percent, and in 1973 to an unprecedented 353 percent. No country in the world had a higher rate. Then the attempt to rein in prices through government controls led to shortages of basic consumer goods and the rise of black markets. People were waiting in line to buy toothpaste.

Allende's statement that he did not consider himself president of all Chileans was coming true. It's fair to say that the most impoverished members of the population had unquestionably benefited from his policies: health services for the poor had been improved, infant mortality had been reduced, and free milk was being distributed. Unemployment had fallen to record lows and food consumption (excepting meat) had increased by about 25 percent. As one sympathetic Swedish scholar explains: "In many a modest Chilean family . . . the Allende years will be remembered as the time when the first school was built . . . or when the poorly fed children of the family suddenly began to receive medical attention and half a litre of milk a day." But just about everyone else—specifically members of the working class whose wages were failing to keep up with prices and the middle class above all—was suffering.

The first significant protest against Allende's policies, in December 1971, became known as the March of the Empty Pots. It was led by thousands of women in Santiago—the CIA estimated 30,000—carrying signs with slogans like "There is no meat; there is no nothing." Called "fascists" by Allende's supporters, they were assaulted with clubs and bottles. The violence got so bad that the government called a state of emergency and imposed a nighttime curfew.

As the inflation rate worsened and shortages became more common, the number of protests grew. In August 1972, the national confederation of shopkeepers called a one-day strike that quickly turned ugly and led to another state of emergency, along with weeks of street battles. Then in October the truckers, small businessmen generally with one or two vehicles in their possession, began to fear that the government was about to nationalize their industry. They walked out, weakening an already enfeebled economy that depended on the transport the truckers supplied. They were joined by a legion of groups and organizations—taxi drivers, shopkeepers, doctors, lawyers, architects, students, and others. In April 1973, copper miners went on strike for two months, and in July the truckers struck for a second time and once again drew support from professionals and other small businessmen.

Rumors and accusations have persisted that the United States was behind these disturbances—in effect that the strikers were pawns of imperialism—and while it seems fair to say that some American money may have filtered through to the strikers from the opposition groups Washington was backing, there is little or no evidence that America was directly involved in the stoppages. These demonstrations were widespread and spontaneous, grassroots expressions of dissatisfaction with the government's policies. The rumors of American involvement were attempts to delegitimize authentic opposition to Allende. What is evident is that the protests were by and large middle class in character led by small business-men like the truckers and abetted by professionals like doctors, lawyers, and dentists, as well as by more established workers like the copper min-ers. These were the very people who were most squeezed by the rampant inflation and the consumer shortages. Allende had brought on a class war, not of the workers against the plutocrats and oligarchs but of the middle class against the government.

If Allende needed proof that he had lost the support of the middle class, he could have found it in the evolution of the Christian Democrats and their leader Eduardo Frei. As a progressive but non-Marxist political force, the party had made efforts to work with Allende once he took office. The Communists in the government coalition were in favor of reaching out to the Christian Democrats, but the anti-accommodationist Socialists pre-vailed and pressed forward with policies that alienated ever larger num-bers of Chileans. By 1973 the party, repeatedly rebuffed by Allende, was in full retreat from any possibility of cooperation. The high point of the resis-tance came on August 22, 1973, when the Chamber of Deputies, under Christian Democratic leadership, passed a resolution by a vote of 81 to 45, which in effect said the Allende government was attempting to overturn Chile's constitution and establish a Communist dictatorship. The rights of citizens, it claimed, had been violated, private property attacked, free-dom of the press restricted, the powers of congress and the courts under-mined . . . on and on. Chile's Supreme Court was similarly up in arms at what it denounced as Allende's extraconstitutional methods.

By now, even Moscow, ever alert to the ebbs and flows of real power, was withdrawing its support from Allende and predicting he could not last. (Some, no doubt, remembered Engels's words: "The worst thing that can befall a leader of an extreme party is to be compelled to take over a government at a time when society is not yet ripe for the domination of the class it represents. . . . He who is put in this awkward position is irre-vocably lost.") In the weeks before the coup, it was clear to everyone that Allende's Chile was in a full-scale crisis, nearing an end game. The econ-omy had broken down. Street violence was out of control. The congress was in full revolt. Frei reportedly thought the choice for his country was between a dictatorship of the military and a dictatorship of the workers.

The Chilean military later used the August 22 resolution as a justification for its actions, but its antipathy to the government had been growing for a long time. Indeed, its evolution followed essentially the same path as that of the Christian Democrats, from muted, suspicious cooperation to open hostility.

Chile's generals had proved their loyalty to the constitution in 1970, at the time when Washington was plotting with the craziest among them. The military did not start out as a threat to Allende—Chile's constitutional traditions were too strong—but it became one. In mid-1972, the army had begun to worry about a breakdown of law and order and repeatedly pleaded with Allende to change his policies and curb the extremists in his party. It has been said that in February 1973, a U.S. intelligence official remarked to General Pinochet: "You are on a sinking ship. When are you going to act?" Pinochet reportedly replied, "Not until our legs are wet. If we act too soon, the people from all sides would unite against us." By June 1973 the pressures had become so great that some junior officers tried to stage a coup, hoping their superiors would join them. It was the first coup attempt in 42 years. The army, still constitutionalist, crushed the uprising.

But the mounting turmoil was taking its toll, even on the most loyal of officers. If the president himself was in violation of the constitution, what did it mean to be "constitutionalist"? And there was another factor that struck at the very heart of the military's pride and professionalism. Paramilitaries sympathetic to Allende had been organizing outside of the army's control. The right had also been forming its own paramilitary groups, and with rumors of coups in the air, the more radical elements of Allende's coalition were unwilling to put their faith in the loyalty of the military. In May 1972 the CIA reported that Allende was supplying arms to sympathizers throughout the country. One scholarly authority has argued that the rightist groups began arming themselves only after the leftists had. That was not Regis Debray's view. He said the left paramilitaries had formed to protect Allende from the right. Who knows? We should be careful about trying to determine who took the first step in the paramilitary arms race. And does it matter? What is certain is that in the early months of 1973, as civil society broke down and suspicions grew on all sides, paramilitary activity increased dramatically on both the left and the right, demonstrating the decline of legitimate authority. The government had lost control. Rumors of coups could be heard everywhere. "By August 1973," it was said, "Chile had become an armed camp." On September 11, 1973, the army had had enough. It revolted and changed Chile's history forever.

WHERE WAS THE U.S. government in all of this? Many historians and other commentators have concluded that Washington had no direct involvement in the coup, though of course one can find dissenters to this view. Ambassador Davis writes in his memoir, "I did not engage in coup plotting and am unaware of any of my U.S. colleagues having done so, including the personnel of the CIA station, the attaché offices, and the Military Advisory Group." Davis even adds: "I did not hope for Allende's downfall." The CIA's own report, released in 2000, says "there was no support for instigating a coup." The Church committee declared categorically that it "found no evidence" that the United States was directly involved. Its conclusion jibes with Kissinger's own statement in his memoirs that "our government had nothing to do with planning [Allende's] overthrow and no involvement with the plotters." Accusations to the contrary, he insisted, show "the power of political mythology."

Obviously, any comments by Kissinger carry with them the taint of self-exculpation, but in this case we can point to a smoking gun, or more precisely, two guns that weren't smoking. Following the failed coup attempt in June, Kissinger said to Nixon: "And that coup last week—we have nothing to do with it." Similarly, after the successful September coup, Kissinger told Nixon, "We didn't do it." To be sure, he then added: "I mean we helped them . . . created the conditions as great as possible." But by this he presumably meant the aid Washington was supplying to Allende's opponents and to the military. As Tanya Harmer, a student of the Chile crisis, put it: "The distinction between 'created the conditions' for a coup and 'masterminded' it is important."

Nonetheless, three things contribute to the "political mythology" of American involvement that continues to this day. First is the indisputable fact that a panicky Washington did try to foment a coup to prevent Allende from taking office in 1970. Second are the millions of dollars in covert aid that went to Allende's opponents and the overt aid that went to the military. The argument for it, as Kissinger and other officials have said, is that the money was spent to preserve Chile's democratic institutions against the threat Allende was thought to pose to them and, in the case of aid to the military, to maintain connections with American

friends in Chile. But the distinction between an effort to stabilize democracy in Chile and an effort to destabilize Allende's elected government is
vague at best.

This is especially true because of the third factor—that Nixon and
Kissinger desired nothing more than to be rid of Allende. Kissinger never
denied that he and Nixon were relieved when Allende was overthrown.
"Though we had no hand in the military coup, we thought it saved Chile
from totalitarianism." If Washington had aided and abetted the plotters,
that would only have been consistent with what it actually wanted to see
happen, so when Kissinger righteously asserted that covert action in Chile
was designed to preserve democracy, the appropriate response is, well, yes
and no. The policy might be summarized as democracy, if it is possible,
but an end to Allende even if it is not. It's easy to understand why so many
have looked at the Allende years and reached what seems an almost inevitable conclusion that the United States must have been involved, although
the reality is that critics of Nixon and Kissinger are blaming them for what
they hoped would happen, not any actions they took to make it happen.
But now we have to take a step back: Was it blameworthy or immoral, as
the critics would have it, to desire Allende's overthrow?

The real question to be asked and answered is not whether the United
States was responsible for Allende's fall—it was not—but whether the anti-
Allende policies it did pursue were justified. In short, did the freely elected
Salvador Allende represent a legitimate threat to American interests?

LITTLE IN FOREIGN POLICY is hard and fast, black and white. It's
almost always possible to find ambiguity, contingency, shades of gray,
reasons for doubt or dispute. That said, for purposes of this discussion,
there are certain outlooks that have to be considered out of bounds on
the question of Chile and Allende—two in particular held by many of
those passionately opposed to American intervention. The first outlook
is propounded by people who don't take the idea of American interests
seriously. It includes the absolute pacifists who are opposed to the use of
power in any case. More significant are those opposed to American interests as a matter of principle, who are, to put it as bluntly as possible, anti-
American. Obviously, great numbers of non-Americans belong in this
category, understandably, because the interests of the United States are
not their concern. But it includes many Americans as well. Their think-

ing goes as follows: even if the United States makes a reasoned calculation about which policy better serves its national interests, those interests are necessarily illegitimate or malevolent; Washington will always act on behalf of American imperialism or to preserve the evil of capitalism. Policy for these people is a pseudo-Marxist zero-sum game in which the maintenance or increase in American influence and power is invariably a minus in any moral calculation and a reason for opposition.

The second group practices a different kind of absolutism. It consists of those who are opposed on principle to American covert action of any kind, who certainly are opposed to covert action that contains the possibility of toppling a foreign government, and even more certainly opposed to covert action that contains the possibility of toppling a foreign government that has been democratically elected because it violates "the spirit of the American political tradition." The covert operations that preserved Italy from a Communist takeover in 1948 must be condemned even if the outcome was a desirable one. National sovereignty will be respected though the United States is weakened against the aggressive tactics of the Kremlin and Communists are allowed to make major advances in Western Europe. To be sure, many apparent national-sovereignty absolutists are not consistent: some have no problem urging intervention when they believe the cause is just from a global or international perspective, like preventing a civil war in Libya or Syria, or ending a genocide in Darfur. Washington is not to be condemned when it risks American lives on behalf of "mankind." It's only when an intervention is made on behalf of more narrow American interests without an international component that they find reason to object. They are not as directly "anti-American" as the first group. They might more properly be called "antinationalist." But for most cases, the result is the same. American interests that cannot be cast in idealistic, global terms as "global interests" are inevitably wrong.

There is no debating the Allende episode with either of these groups because there is simply no agreement on the premises of the debate. Ultimately, all that one can say to them is that their positions are deeply unrealistic. Like any nation, the United States does have legitimate national interests that it tries to protect, and no one who believes differently will ever have a voice in policy debates. Sometimes covert actions are necessary to protect those interests. In fact, sometimes covert actions are the sane, nonmilitaristic halfway house between pacifism and all-out war, diplomacy conducted by more violent means. No American president would ever think otherwise. We can put it another way: no American president is ever going to abolish the CIA. The two groups who take their stand in opposition to American self-interest, either for anti-American or antinationalist reasons, are doomed to eternal frustration.

Moving away from these absolutists, one is forced to look at the specifics of the intervention in Chile. The place to begin, perhaps the epicenter of the debate, is the Church report. "Did the perceived threat in Chile," the writers of the report ask, "justify the level of U.S. response?" That's the right question. To answer it, the Church committee examined five National Intelligence Estimates (NIEs), the syntheses of the thinking on Chile by the various intelligence agencies that were issued between 1969 and 1973. These differed greatly in their conclusions. The 1970 report warned that Allende would move to impose a Soviet-style Marxist-Leninist state, and the report a year later declared that he would try to achieve his goals through democratic means but might have to turn to methods of "dubious legality" (his "legal loopholes").

Later reports were more optimistic about the preservation of Chilean democracy because of the political obstacles that stood in Allende's way, political obstacles strengthened in large part by the aid arriving from the United States. (One might see this as a tacit endorsement of the Nixon/ Kissinger policy of giving support to Allende's opposition, though the reports don't get into that.) The 1972 report expected Allende to slow the pace of his revolution in order to consolidate the measures he had already taken in the face of growing opposition. Unfortunately for the credibility of the NIEs, the report issued just before the September 1973 coup predicted that there was only an "outside chance" that the military would try to force Allende from office.

Reading reports of agents who are out in the field is a bit of an art. So, apparently, is reading NIEs prepared in the bowels of Washington. They managed to offer something for everyone, supporters of the Nixon/ Kissinger policies and opponents as well, and the Church committee hedged its bets. It noted that "three American presidents and their senior advisers" evidently thought Allende represented enough of a danger to warrant major covert operations. The committee might have mentioned that Kennedy's Alliance for Progress was overt, not covert, but directed toward the same end of forestalling a Marxist takeover of Chile. In its summation, the committee declared: "This report does not attempt to offer a final judgment on the political propriety, the morality or even the effectiveness of American covert activity in Chile. . . . On these questions committee members may differ. So may American citizens."

Yet after all its work and with all the attention it knew its report would receive, the committee was clearly uncomfortable with so wishy-washy a conclusion. Some members obviously yearned to say more, and in the final two sentences of the report, it offered a more concrete, if still guarded, view: "Given the costs of covert action, it should be resorted to only to counter severe threats to the national security of the United States. It is far from clear that that was the case in Chile." One imagines Henry Kissinger's frizzled hair straightening out and standing on end. And while those may have been the committee's last words, they weren't its only words. Buried earlier in the report was a harsher conclusion. "As the discussion of National Intelligence Estimates . . . makes clear, the more extreme fears about the effects of Allende's election were ill-founded." By "more extreme," the committee presumably meant any fears that the Allende government would eventually lead to a Marxist dictatorship and an alliance with Cuba and the Soviet Union. The committee went on: "It appears that the Chile NIEs were either, at best, selectively used or, at worst, disregarded by policy makers when the time came to make decisions regarding U.S. covert involvement in Chile." The bottom line was the Church committee did not believe Allende represented a serious threat to American interests.

As we have seen, there had been other dissenters to the Nixon/ Kissinger policies, even before Allende became president. In August 1970, on Kissinger's request, government analysts produced a report that the Church committee called "the most direct statement concerning the threat an Allende regime would pose to the United States." It stated that "the U.S. has no vital national interests within Chile. There would, however, be tangible economic losses." It continued, "The world military balance of power would not be significantly altered by an Allende government."

Similarly, one CIA official rightly said, "Allende will be hard for the Communist Party and for Moscow to control." And an official in the State Department's intelligence unit, Wymberley Coerr, warned: "To equate an Allende victory with 'a Castro-type dictatorship' assigns insufficient weight to Chile's profound differences from Cuba." Even Kissinger's own adviser on Latin American affairs questioned the seriousness of the threat in the weeks after Allende took office. "Is Allende a mortal threat to the U.S.? It is hard to argue that."

But to prove that little is black or white, and certainly not one's reading of Allende's intentions, even the dissenters were not sure. The August 1970 report went on to note that an Allende victory "would represent a psychological setback for the U.S. as well as a definite advance for the Marxist idea." And another State Department official who had been sanguine about Allende before he took office—"he was not Fidel redux"—soon changed his mind: "I was proved wrong in the event because the Cubans got into Chile after the inauguration, in hordes. And it became much more, if you will, an extension of—with Allende, in the Chilean context—of Fidel than I had thought would be the case." Those Cubans again!

The situation was ambiguous at best—could Allende be kept out of the Soviet camp?—but deeply problematic in any case. Amid the mixed signals and the inherent complexity of the situation, Kissinger had concluded and convinced Nixon that the United States could not simply do nothing. A coup might have been out of the question, for tactical not moral reasons, but doing what could be done to weaken Allende made sense within a Cold War context. Even if Allende's intentions were unclear, providing aid to his opponents was a reasonably cautious response to a potential threat, a legitimate hedging of bets. Critics of intervention tended to argue from a position of moral clarity that wasn't available to Kissinger. Or they were willing to take a risk on Allende that Kissinger was unwilling to take.

Here was the difference: unlike so many of his critics, Kissinger saw international affairs not in terms of high moral principles like self-determination or national sovereignty (in this sense his critics are right to call him unprincipled) but from an assessment of power, and the judgment he was ineluctably drawn to was that Allende represented a diminution of American power and a corresponding increase in Soviet power. More than just U.S.-Chile relations were at stake. The rise of Allende had the potential to affect the American position throughout the world. "I don't think we should delude ourselves," Kissinger said at a press briefing, "that an Allende takeover in Chile would not present massive problems for us."

Nor, as we know, did it matter to Kissinger that Allende had been democratically elected. It's not hard to find critics for whom this single fact made all the difference (the absolutist noninterventionist view). Allende may have been a Marxist—even a Leninist—but he was not a violent revolutionary. He seemed committed to achieving his ends through peaceful, democratic means, and on this point he repeatedly emphasized his difference from Castro. The journalist Seymour Hersh, for one, found Kissinger's concerns about a second Marxist dictatorship in Latin America "ludicrous . . . in view both of Allende's graceful acceptance of defeat in the 1958 and 1964 elections and of Chile's long standing commitment to democratic government." To which any Realist would promptly respond that Allende was "graceful" only as long as he didn't hold power or as long as his opponents didn't stand in his way once he did and that his own words, his particular Marxist ideology, belied his "commitment to democratic government."

Kissinger, the Realist par excellence, pointed out in his memoirs that after Allende became president, he told Regis Debray that "as for the bourgeois state, at the present moment, we are seeking to overcome it. To overthrow it." Allende made a distinction between "popular democracy" and "bourgeois democracy," and insofar as he was forced to operate within the bounds of bourgeois rules, it was only "for the time being" out of "tactical necessity." The goal was always "total, scientific Marxist socialism."

Allende has been described as "a well-known Socialist moderate," which was true within the context of the Chilean left, though Ambassador Davis's description of him as "all things to all men" is probably closer to the mark. He was a compromiser by nature but only so long as the compromises were on the left. It is worth pausing over this question of Allende's "moderation."

Allende stood out from the more radical members of his party. He was ready to work with the Communists, who were the real moderates in the Chilean context. They sought to follow a two-step path to socialism, the first step being cooperation with the middle class to bring down the landed aristocracy. If Allende was willing to cooperate with the Communists, they were willing to cooperate with the Christian Democrats and other centrists. Allende's Socialist Party, on the other hand, proclaimed a one-step philosophy of achieving power and implementing socialism immediately. This difference produced strains within Allende's coalition; those to the left of him constantly pushed for revolution by any means, with violence always an option. Had he secured the power and the authority he wanted, could the "moderate" Allende have controlled the more violent elements within his party? Would he even have wanted to?

There is no way of knowing, but history can supply clues, and there was one historical comparison that immediately presented itself to Kissinger the European, the pessimist, the worrier who bit his fingernails down to the quick. The example of Russia in 1917 was never far from his thinking. From

February 1917 to October 1917, Russia was ruled by a moderate revolutionary and democrat, Alexander Kerensky. But in the turmoil of war and
upheaval he was unable to maintain power against the more radical Leninists with their simple answers to complex questions. He was overthrown
and Europe, not to mention the rest of the world, was upended for the next
70 years. Every revolution, in Kissinger's view, tossed up its Kerenskys—
sane, reasonable, well-meaning idealists with no grasp of the realities of
power. For them, good intentions were a substitute for weapons (whereas
hard-headed Marxists from Regis Debray to Mao Zedong believed power
came out of the barrel of a gun). Inevitably, they ended up being devoured.

Portugal went through its own revolution in 1974 and emerged with
a leftist coalition government that included Communists. Kissinger saw
no reason to believe that with their top-down Leninist ideology and their
Moscow connections, Portugal's Communists would abide by democratic
rules and compromise. Why should they if they thought they could seize
power and hold it? When the Socialist foreign minister in Portugal's new
government, Mario Soares, tried to reassure a skeptical Kissinger that
Portugal was not about to become another battlefield in the Cold War,
Kissinger told him, "You are a Kerensky. I believe your sincerity, but you
are naïve." Soares replied, "I certainly don't want to be a Kerensky." To
which Kissinger retorted, "Neither did Kerensky." In Portugal's case,
Soares turned out to be right and the gloomy Kissinger turned out to be
wrong. But was Kissinger wrong about Allende?

While others looked at Allende and saw a "moderate," what Kissinger
saw was, at best, Kerensky—that is, a well-meaning leftist who would
not survive the power struggles of the future—and so he decided to
strengthen Allende's opponents for the possible conflicts to come. But a
comparison to Kerensky was the optimistic reading of Allende's intentions. If Kissinger focused on Allende's domestic policies, what he saw
was not Kerensky but a budding Lenin, who was centralizing all political,
economic, and military power and preparing to crush any opponents who
stood in his way. Worst of all, if he listened to Allende's public statements,
what he heard was another Castro, who was determined to spread revolution across Latin America, who was prepared to install Marxist regimes
by democratic means where the conditions warranted it, but who, like his
friend Che Guevara, was ready to use violence if necessary.

Perhaps the United States could have accepted a Chilean Lenin who
was willing to limit himself to imposing his policies, however misguided,

on his own country and no others. After all, Kissinger himself has said
that "nationalization of American-owned property was not the issue," and
independent scholars—at least the non-Marxist ones—who have studied
the question have tended to agree with him.

To reinforce Kissinger's point, one might note that Washington's ally
in Chile, the Christian Democrats, had already embarked on a program
of nationalization that was greatly restricting American copper interests.
They were simply moving more slowly than the Socialists and had no links
to Castro or the Kremlin. Washington under Nixon and Kissinger might
well have accepted a domestic socialist, despite their ideological differences, much as Washington had learned to live with the Communist Tito
in Yugoslavia. What they could not accept was another Castro exporting
Marxist revolution, not with the Cold War rivalry between the United
States and the Soviet Union at full blaze. And Allende was no Tito.

But most significantly, it was not only Russia in 1917 or Cuba in 1959
that had lodged itself in Kissinger's brain. An earlier, far more emotional
memory influenced his outlook on the world and the policies he pursued. Adolf Hitler did not achieve power in Germany in the early 1930s
through revolution or a coup. What Kissinger knew and most U.S.-born
Americans did not, or chose to ignore or forget, was that Hitler was a
democrat, a democrat with quotation marks, who climbed to Germany's
highest office strictly through electoral and legal methods. As a leading
biographer, Ian Kershaw, has said, "Hitler was no tyrant imposed on Germany. Though he never attained majority support in free elections, he was
legally appointed to power as Reich Chancellor just like his predecessors
had been, and became between 1933 and 1940 arguably the most popular
head of state in the world." The historian John Lukacs shares this view:
Hitler "may have been the most popular revolutionary leader in the history of the modern world. The emphasis is on the word *popular* because
Hitler belongs to the democratic, not the aristocratic, age of history." William Shirer's enormously successful history, *The Rise and Fall of the Third
Reich*, is not much admired by scholars, but he had one crucial advantage
over the historians who came after him: he was present in Germany when
the Nazis were in charge and was able to see with his own eyes what the
majority of his countrymen preferred to ignore (his *Berlin Diaries* is one
of the invaluable documents of the period). His conclusion is echoed by
Kershaw and Lukacs: "The Germans," he said, "had imposed the Nazi tyranny on themselves."

The institutions of democracy had not prevented Hitler's rise; they had facilitated it. Most American policymakers, then or later, had no way of responding to that fact, no way even of incorporating it into their conceptual apparatus, but it was a reality Kissinger could never ignore. Hitler embodied a painful lesson of history, and one might say that lesson, even more than any lessons from the Russian revolution, underlay Kissinger's own conceptual apparatus. He had, after all, lost at least 13 close relatives to the Holocaust. As he once said, Americans had "never suffered disaster" and therefore "find it difficult to comprehend a policy conducted with a premonition of catastrophe." When Kissinger expressed concern about the irresponsibility of a people, others with narrower perspectives, or the more limited sense of history that has difficulty incorporating an idea of "catastrophe," who unquestioningly take democracy as an absolute value in international affairs, might react with shock or horror. But he knew whereof he spoke. He was thinking not only of Chile in the 1960s and early 1970s but also of Germany in the 1920s and early 1930s. As one of Kissinger's biographers has explained, "Kissinger's views of fascist and communist extremism, embodied most clearly by the figures of Hitler and Stalin, were filtered through his early years in Fürth." No, Allende was not Hitler (any more than he was Tito), but the Hitler experience could teach American policymakers something about him and something about the ambiguities of democracy.

Insofar as he understood that democratic procedures could not prevent catastrophe, Kissinger was no democrat and thus to be distinguished from the vast majority of his fellow Americans. Kissinger, always the outsider and certainly the outsider in the Nixon administration, was aware that he stood apart. He knew that the painful knowledge won through agonizing personal experience made him a Cassandra in a schoolroom of Pollyannas, the policymaker who could never allow optimism to override his sense of tragedy: "Unlike most of my contemporaries, I had experienced the fragility of the fabric of modern society. I had seen that the likely outcome of the dissolution of all social bonds and the undermining of all basic values is extremism, despair, and brutality." He could think more deeply about the Hobbesian world of international relations than the State Department bureaucrats who surrounded and annoyed him because democracy and democratic institutions did not inspire in him the kind of reverence that they did in his fellow citizens or distract him from the hard reality of the exigencies of power. And so while a democratically elected

Allende by himself may not have represented a catastrophe, the possibility of two Castros, three Castros, many Castros, in the context of the Cold War, surely did.

The Chilean people had made a mistake in electing Allende—actually only a plurality of Chileans had been mistaken. Given what he knew, what he expected, and what he feared, Henry Kissinger was not going to let the mere fact of a free election stand in his way of dealing with a potential threat to the United States.

"I don't see why we have to stand by and watch a country go Communist because of the irresponsibility of its own people." The statement looks a lot different if one has the rise of Adolf Hitler in mind.

CHAPTER TWO

HITLER

*D*IPLOMACY IS THE CLOSEST HENRY KISSINGER HAS COME to writing a historical masterpiece. Constructed on the twin pillars of Kissinger's careers as both academic and statesman, it speaks with the depth that scholarship provides and the grounding that can only come through immersion in public affairs. It carries readers along from Richelieu to Gorbachev with vivid detail and knowing evaluation, effortlessly moving backward and forward in time to draw parallels between disparate eras and demonstrate how the past is not so very different from the present. It succeeds at being both analytic and narrative history and stands as a landmark in Kissinger's efforts to impart the lessons of Realism to the American public.

At key points along the way, Kissinger pauses in his story to examine personalities, motives, possibilities, and alternative courses of action. Generally he does this with the dispassion of the scholar, peering down from the mountaintop. But there is one moment in the book when a reader can definitely feel the temperature rise, when a sense of helpless frustration explodes the cool exterior and it becomes apparent that Kissinger has a personal stake in the story he is telling. The emergence of Adolf Hitler in 1933 brings out the partisan—or perhaps the victim—in him. His language turns more heated, his judgments harsher. When he is writing about the 1930s, condemnation comes easily.

Kissinger begins this part of *Diplomacy* with the most unequivocal of declarations: "Hitler's advent to power marked one of the greatest calam-

ities in the history of the world." Few would disagree. Still, in recent years
many writers on the Nazis have tried to achieve a kind of "objective" distance by stepping away from stressing that Hitler was one of humankind's
great monsters to a more analytic posture—not, one must hasten to say, to
rehabilitate him (though some have undeniably moved in that direction)
but to be able to "historicize" the Third Reich and understand it in context.

In the preface to his expansive study *The Coming of the Third Reich*, the
historian Richard J. Evans writes, "It seems to me inappropriate for a work
of history to indulge in the luxury of moral judgment. For one thing, it is
unhistorical; for another, it is arrogant and presumptuous. I cannot know
how I would have behaved if I had lived under the Third Reich." Com-
mendably, Evans is not so self-righteous as to assume that he would have
been among the small minority of Germans who were immune to Hitler's
appeal. But unlike Evans, a Jewish German might indeed "indulge in the
luxury of moral judgment." As someone driven out of Germany, Kissinger
does not and cannot share Evans's doubts or qualms, either his well-
intentioned modesty or, as it were, his over-evenhandedness. Kissinger
belongs to the old school of moral history and lets his emotions do the
talking. His words for Hitler are "demonic" and "psychotic."

To be sure, as a rigorous analyst of power and power relations,
Kissinger cannot resist making the point that, even without Hitler, Germany was bound to take its place as the strongest nation on the continent.
Its weakness following World War I was an artificial condition that could
not last, and beginning in the Weimar years of the 1920s, before Hitler
had become a public figure, it began throwing off the restrictions of the
punitive Versailles Treaty that had hemmed it in—like the demands for
debilitating reparations and the Allied occupation of the Rhineland that
had served France as a buffer against a resurgent and resentful Germany.
In this sense, Hitler was merely continuing the policies of national restoration (rearmament among them) begun by his democratic predecessors.

Kissinger is full of praise for some of the Weimar leaders—in particular Gustav Stresemann—who were gradually bringing Germany back into
the community of nations. First as chancellor and then foreign minister,
Stresemann moved with "patience, compromise and the blessing of European consensus." In 1926 he shared the Nobel Peace Prize with the French
foreign minister, Aristide Briand. His goals were the nationalist ones any
confident German politician was likely to pursue, including the union of

Germany and Austria, but he was shrewd and moderate, proceeding one step at a time. Hitler, on the other hand, although shrewd, was anything but moderate. His initial policies built on Stresemann's accomplishments. But, as Kissinger says, his "reckless megalomania turned what could have been a peaceful evolution into a world war." As for the British and French governments that went along with him until it was no longer possible in good conscience to do so, they were "passive," "misguided," "pathetic."

Could they have known in the early 1930s that Hitler wasn't just another German nationalist in the mold of Stresemann? Probably not. His fanatical anti-Semitism was a clue, but given the widespread anti-Semitism of the time, little more than a clue. One of the most insightful of Hitler's biographers, Joachim Fest, struggling with the question of whether or not Hitler could be considered a "great man," wrote that if he "had succumbed to an assassination or an accident at the end of 1938, few would hesitate to call him one of the greatest of German statesmen, the consummator of Germany's history." Hitler had made a career of fooling everyone.

"Had the democracies forced a showdown with Hitler early in his rule," Kissinger writes, "historians would still be arguing about whether Hitler had been a misunderstood nationalist or a maniac bent on world domination." In the same vein, George Orwell remarked in 1940 that a year earlier, before the war had begun, Hitler was widely considered "respectable."

But, Kissinger insists, in the tenebrous world of international relations, it didn't matter. Statesmen can never be sure; they are always forced to act from insufficient knowledge because by the time they can be certain (if that is ever possible), it is probably too late. Reading Hitler's character and determining his intentions weren't important. What counted were configurations of power, and "the West should have spent less time assessing Hitler's motives and more time counterbalancing Germany's growing strength." One lesson that Kissinger drew from the West's trusting, optimistic, wait-and-see policy of appeasement (as we saw in his approach to Salvador Allende) is that "foreign policy builds on quicksand when it disregards actual power relationships and relies on prophecies of another's intentions." Foreign policy could not be dictated by the hope that others would do the right thing or by a simple demonstration of goodwill, as attractive as that might be on a human level. It had to be determined by a cold-blooded calculation of power relationships and an ability to project influence. That perception provided the ground for Kissinger's Realism.

The other lesson Kissinger drew from the Hitler years, of course, is that democracy by itself is no safeguard against the rise of a tyrannical fanatic prepared to shed the blood of millions to accomplish his fantastical ends. Democracy has no sure answer to the demagogue who is able to win the support of the public through fair means and foul. Minority rights are always at risk under majoritarian institutions. "My pride," Hitler declared, "is that I know no statesman in the world who with greater right than I can say that he is representative of his people." The Hitler biographer Alan Bullock has written, "despite the Gestapo and the concentration camps," his power "was founded on popular support to a degree, which few people cared, or still care, to admit." Or, as others have said, the Germans did not fear Hitler; rather, they loved him. Time and again, Hitler insisted that, compared to other political parties, "we National Socialists are the better democrats."

But what about "the Gestapo and the concentration camps," as Bullock noted, or the beatings, the torture, the book burnings, the intimidation and extirpation of civil liberties, the adoration of brute force and military might, the invasions of powerless neighbors, the oppression of minorities and murderous racism, the Holocaust? In the face of all this, is there any reason we should take Hitler at his word that he was some sort of democrat or an authentic tribune of "the people"? A long philosophical tradition warns us that there is no necessary connection between democracy and individual freedom. "Freedom has appeared in the world at different times and under different forms," Tocqueville wrote. "It is not confined to democracies." In fact, a conflict between freedom and democracy is almost certain when a mobilized majority chooses to tyrannize a powerless minority. Tocqueville also wrote, "If ever the free institutions of America are destroyed, that event may be attributed to the omnipotence of the majority." We don't, in any case, have to take Hitler at his word when he asserted his democratic credentials. A look at his rise to power shows us what we need to know: namely, that Hitler was not just a democratic politician working the hustings for votes but a brilliant and innovative one at that who, better than anyone, had learned how to make electoral processes work for him. Kissinger could draw on his classical education, on thinkers from Plato to Tocqueville, to buttress his concerns about the dangers of unfettered democracy that Hitler personified. But more than that, he could draw on his personal experience as a child of Weimar and the early years of the Third Reich. He was present at the destruction of German democracy and paid an enormous personal price.

KISSINGER HAD BEEN born into the Weimar Republic in 1923 as Heinz; his brother, Walter, was born a year later. Despite raging inflation and an increase in social tensions across Germany, it was a good time for the family. The Kissingers resided in Fürth in Bavaria, a city of about 70,000, and there was no better place for German Jews. "Growing up in Fürth during the 1920s," one scholar observes, "the Kissinger children probably had better social prospects than their counterparts in Paris, London, or even New York." Fürth was a manufacturing center, producing furniture, paint, toys, pencils, and a host of other items; about 80 factories turned out mirrors alone. Industrialization brought the usual ills—one writer called Fürth a "city of soot, of a thousand chimneys, of pounding machines and hammers." But it also brought prosperity, with 10 banking and commercial houses and trade shows that attracted buyers from across the region. In 1900 a famous department store, an opulent four stories high, opened its doors to local residents, promising merchandise that was "cheap but good."

Fürth's Jews, largely middle class and about 3,000 strong at the start of the twentieth century, shared in the city's prosperity and participated in its civic life. The community had deep roots, going back to 1523. Fürth's first synagogue was built in 1617, and by the twentieth century it was home to seven Jewish houses of worship. Around the region Fürth was known for its easygoing ways and welcoming spirit of toleration. Jews expelled from Nuremberg and Vienna found refuge in what became known as a Judenstadt, the "spiritual center" for the Jews of central Europe, the equal, some said, of metropolises like Hamburg and Frankfurt—the "Bavarian Jerusalem" no less. The community built schools, libraries, even an "artists' house." A Jewish hospital was founded in the seventeenth century, and a Jewish orphanage, the first in all Germany, in the eighteenth century. Jews had the right to vote for mayor and in later years served as magistrates and members of the district council. Some chose to marry gentiles or assimilated in other ways. "In the history of the German Jews," one scholar has written, "Fürth occupies a unique position."

Kissinger's father, Louis, arrived in this hospitable environment from a small village in 1905, when he was 18, to pursue a career as a teacher. He married Paula Stern, the daughter of a well-to-do cattle trader in 1922, and they started a family a year later. Though an observant Jew, Louis taught at a public, nonreligious school, where he exhibited some of the formality that was expected of a German professional. But he was also kindly and compassionate, far from the stereotype of the stern disciplinarian standing menacingly at the front of the classroom. He was amused when his students nicknamed him "Kissus," and he cheerfully went along when they affectionately teased him or played adolescent tricks on him. Some of the girls even developed crushes on him. When Heinz (Henry) was born, Louis's students took up a collection to buy their teacher a present. Friends described this mild-mannered, trusting soul as someone who wouldn't harm a fly. Even his wife termed him "like a child." His son Henry later said of him that "he couldn't imagine evil." And why should he have? Louis was respected, secure, and content. His world made sense—so much so that, although an Orthodox Jew who wouldn't even take pen to paper on Saturdays, he regretted the Kaiser's abdication in 1918 and during the 1920s voted for the Center Party, the political arm of Bavarian Catholics and later a progenitor of modern Germany's Christian Democrats. Marxism held no appeal for him. Those who had known him in Germany could not imagine that he would ever support the leftist Social Democrats. Revolution was the last thing on his mind. Because he was a teacher, he had the status of senior civil servant, which filled him with pride. He was on good terms with his gentile neighbors, an eager participant in civic associations, a firm believer in Germanic virtues, and a dedicated nationalist who had no reason to think that his conservative politics conflicted with his religious beliefs. He was basically an innocent, but his experience during the imperial and Weimar periods provided the space for that innocence to flourish. When he looked back on his years in Fürth from his exile in America, Louis called them the "happiest years of my professional career."

The Kissingers provided their two young boys with an upbringing appropriate to their middle-class position in society. They were assimilated Germans, but on their own Jewish terms, blurring secular and religious lines by keeping kosher and sending Heinz and Walter to synagogue every morning but hoping to enroll them in the secular Gymnasium when they were old enough. Nothing was more important in the household than German culture, *Bildung*. The boys learned the poetry of Goethe and Heine. There were amateur theatricals, piano lessons, and visits to the opera, even if Heinz would have preferred a seat at a soccer match. As a boy, he was passionate about sports, with many friends, both Jewish and gentile. He was only an average student in the schoolroom, but he was also called a "bookworm" because he always seemed to be reading something. Summers were a particularly idyllic time, when the Kissingers stayed on the farm of Paula's parents and Heinz and his brother could laze away the days swimming, bicycling, playing with the local children, happily chasing chickens. It was a life with the usual ups and downs, but on the whole one of relative ease and contentment. If a film about the Kissinger family had been made at this time, it would have been shot almost entirely in soft focus. But for Hitler, Kissinger once said, he might have spent his life as a teacher/counselor like his father.

There were grim portents of what was to come but it would have taken unusual prescience to see them for what they were, and the Kissingers were too comfortable to be on the lookout. In 1923, the year of Heinz's birth, Julius Streicher started the fanatically anti-Semitic newspaper *Der Stürmer* in neighboring Nuremberg, declaring "the Jews are our misfortune." Proto-Nazi groups were springing up, pledging rabid loyalty to the Fatherland. In September 1925 and again in March 1928 Hitler himself paid a visit to Fürth. But the Kissingers had little reason to see any danger. Late in life, Louis remembered a city where "the various faiths lived together in harmony," and his wife recalled that she never encountered anti-Semitism in the years before Hitler. When she was a girl, her closest friend was a Protestant.

Nothing in his life had equipped Louis for the shock of the Nazis. As soon as they came to power, Louis was suspended from his teaching post, and after the passage of the Nuremberg laws in 1935, he lost his job permanently. Old friends abandoned him. "We were isolated," his wife, Paula, recalled. "A few people stuck by us, but only a few." One of Louis's brothers was arrested in 1933 and sent to Dachau concentration camp, where he endured 18 months of abuse and beatings before being released in December 1934 and fleeing the country for Palestine. The hesitant, bewildered Louis wanted to remain. "This is where we belong," he told a friend. "We haven't done anything to anyone." Even in 1934, when thousands of Nazis descended on his small hometown for one of their extravagantly theatrical rallies, he stayed indoors but didn't change his mind. He certainly never gave any thought to escaping to Palestine—he was too much the

German patriot to become a Zionist. And other members of the family felt the same way. Henry's granduncle Simon was confident that because Germany had always been good for the Jews, Nazism had to be a passing phase. His life ended in a concentration camp. Of the 1,990 Jews who were living in Fürth in 1933, about 900 were murdered while hundreds more, like the Kissingers, managed to get out in time. In 1945 only about 20 to 30 Jews, according to one estimation, were left in this Judenstadt.

Paula Kissinger, more worldly-wise than her husband, was quicker to understand that there was no future for them in Nazi Germany and, with the help of a cousin in the United States, the four Kissingers managed to escape in August 1938, just weeks ahead of the terrible nation-wide pogrom known as Kristallnacht that marked the true beginning of the end for Germany's Jews. During Kristallnacht, synagogues in Fürth were looted and destroyed. One newspaper rejoiced: "Room to Breathe in the Old City." In effect, it was Paula Kissinger who saved her husband and children. "If it had been up to him, the family would never have left the country."

But though the Kissingers found safety in the United States, Louis was never the same—not even in Washington Heights in upper Manhattan, home to so large a community of German Jews that it was jokingly referred to as the "Fourth Reich." He couldn't resume his chosen profession of teaching in America, despite repeated efforts to find an opening, and the low-paying accounting job he was forced to take left him feeling impotent, emasculated. His unswerving loyalty to the Fatherland had been stolen from him, and he had nothing to fall back on. All his assumptions about himself and his life, all his expectations, had been smashed to pieces. He was a broken man. "I am the loneliest person in this big city," he told his wife. But he was not alone in his loneliness. Service organizations reported that among the new arrivals, the men had a harder time adjusting than their wives, no doubt because they had built their identities on German social and economic structures and fell farther in the New World than women whose lives had been centered on home and family. As one scholar put it, "The women often appeared to be tougher and they seemed to learn the practical elements of American life faster than their men." This was certainly the Kissingers' pattern: while Louis was floundering, the resourceful Paula used her talents as a cook to start a catering business that sustained the family through the hardest days.

Count Louis one of the millions of survivors who were nonetheless casualties of Hitler, a victim of a naïveté that his son was determined not to repeat. His father's fate taught Henry a lifelong lesson about the unpredictability of history and the danger of trusting too much. Hitler seemed to have come out of nowhere to overturn the Kissingers' secure, comfortable, coherent existence, murdering many of their extended family and sending Louis, Paula, Henry, and Walter into a void of permanent exile. How could such a disaster have happened? How could Louis Kissinger and so many other German Jews have been so mistaken? Henry Kissinger's career was his answer to those questions.

IN FACT, Adolf Hitler really did come out of nowhere and in a manner that was possible only because Germany's old regime had been overthrown and a democracy established on its ashes. A cold-blooded, cold-hearted, calculating, and opportunistic product of the post–World War I German republic, Hitler learned how to take advantage of the new freedoms set before him, and he ascended from nights spent sleeping on a park bench in Vienna to become the shaker of worlds, the destroyer of European civilization, the "psychotic" who achieved power by using democracy to eradicate democracy. Who could have predicted that history, and in particular the history of a country that had been so good to the Jews, would take such a devastating turn? History was indeed unpredictable, not a one-way avenue of perpetual progress.

As a boy, Hitler gave no evidence of what he would become. Those who knew him then were astonished that he succeeded as a politician and national leader. Born in 1889, he grew up in middle-class circumstances in the small provincial towns of Braunau am Inn, Passau, and Linz. His father was a man not far removed from the land who had labored strenuously to achieve his position as a minor Austrian civil servant. Proud of his hard-earned success and status, Alois pressed his son to follow in his footsteps. Perhaps the pressure of an insecure disciplinarian parent was too much for young Adolf, or perhaps an unhappy family life pushed him off the path that had been laid out for him. Maybe something in those unknown years ignited a spark of imagination that turned him against what he came to see as a drab, limited existence, less a future than a prison—there had to be more. Whatever the case, by the time he was an adolescent he had rejected his upbringing and collapsed in on himself, a black hole of hostility. His schoolwork suffered. He had become a temperamental loner, given to fits of rage. According to Ian Kershaw, his attitude was "scathingly negative." Hitler himself said that by age 15 he "no longer believed in anything."

Not quite. As with so many youthful misfits, he found an apparent outlet for his unfocused energies, what seemed to him—as for countless dissatisfied adolescents in the years before and after—to be a path to personal fulfillment. He told a neighbor that his goal was to become an "artist," and insofar as he applied himself at all, it was to his minor talent for drawing and painting. He also wrote poetry. At the same time, he made a point of announcing his distance from those around him, even his contempt for them, by dressing like a fop, a dandy, which included carrying an ivory-handled cane to lend an added touch of ostentatious elegance. Adolf Hitler as Oscar Wilde? (Another antisocial dandy who was two years ahead of him in school and similarly rejected convention but chose an entirely different path in life was Ludwig Wittgenstein.)

Hitler found an escape in the operas of Wagner, a passion he retained to the end of his life. Spurred on by his romantic dreams and reveries, he traveled to Vienna in 1907 to fulfill his aesthetic ambitions by taking the entrance examination for the Academy of Fine Arts. But—disaster!—he failed the exam, and when he tried to take the test a year later, he suffered the deeper humiliation of being told he wasn't even sufficiently qualified to apply. Now he was totally at sea—alienated, directionless, angry, truly a rebel without a cause. There is an old joke that if only Hitler had been a slightly better painter, he would have been accepted to the Academy, and the world would have been a much better place. It is no joke.

Hitler remained in Vienna from 1908 to 1913, from the time he was 19 until he was 24, although it was a city he had grown to hate. He described those years as ones of wrenching poverty, yet while he was without steady work and without any interest in steady work, he was able to survive on money from an orphan's pension, a family bequest, and assistance from a friendly aunt. Occasionally, he sold postcard-sized paintings of picturesque Viennese scenes. It wasn't much, and there were times when he was obliged to sleep on park benches or seek refuge in a men's shelter, but it was enough to allow him to become an idler, a flaneur, an embittered outsider hostile to everyday society and middle-class convention.

How does a dejected young aesthete with no connection to the workaday world spend those endless, meaningless days spreading out before him, a desert of emptiness for as far as his eye could see? In Hitler's case, he rose late every day so that he didn't have to deal with mornings. In the afternoons there were Vienna's museums to visit and libraries where he could educate himself; he was always reading. The city's numerous coffee houses were amiable havens where he could while away the hours perusing newspapers and thinking—thinking about his hopeless life situation and the society that had brought him to such a pass.

What he knew was that he refused to sacrifice himself, as most people had, to the tedious chore of earning a living, and his Spartan existence meant that he didn't have to, at least for a while. He survived on a spare diet of bread and butter, puddings, nut cake. He didn't smoke, he didn't drink; his beverage of choice was milk with an occasional fruit juice. Women didn't interest him; "it can be said with near certainty," Kershaw reports, "that by the time he left Vienna at the age of 24 Hitler had had no sexual experience." He filled his evenings with music, operas above all, and Wagner operas above all operas. He saw *Lohengrin* at least 10 times, *Tristan and Isolde* 30 to 40 times. He was going nowhere.

The historians and biographers who write about these years tend to speak in dismissive or derisory tones. (It is Adolf Hitler they are talking about, after all.) He is called a dilettante, a dropout, a bohemian, a nonentity, a failure. In the early 1970s, one psychologist compared him to the hippies, "content to live in filth and squalor." Sometimes these writers sound like no one so much as the uncomprehending parents who inhabit Hollywood teenager movies and don't get the adolescent angst of their sensitive offspring. Why can't Hitler just find a job, like everyone else? He's lazy, that's all, his dreamy impracticality a pose to escape having to go to work. Shape up, Adolf! But Hitler was no mere dropout, and assuredly no sixties flower child, getting high on milk and Wagner instead of pot and the Beatles.

Even at his most down-and-out, he never gave up on himself. There were artistic projects: he tried writing plays and an opera. There were business schemes, too: he would invent a new nonalcoholic drink (German Coca-Cola?) or a hair restorer; he would start a traveling orchestra. Nothing came of any of it but, still, these are not the plans of an aimless dropout or an all-you-need-is-love hippie. Joachim Fest sees more than a hostile nihilist or hedonistic bohemian in him and speaks of Hitler's "longing for middle-class respectability," but that doesn't seem right either. Hitler's discontents are philosophical, metaphysical, far beyond the bounds of middle-class respectability.

Fest quotes from a 1938 essay by Thomas Mann entitled "Brother Hitler" that comes closer to the mark. Mann, though a confirmed anti-Nazi and an exile from his own country, discerns a kindred spirit in Hitler. He perceived what he termed the character of an artist—"the vegetating like a semi-idiot in the lowest social and psychological bohemianism, the arrogant rejection of any sensible and honorable occupation because of the basic feeling that he is too good for that sort of thing." Like many successful artists (and many unsuccessful ones, for that matter), Hitler had "a vague sense of being reserved for something entirely undefinable."

Someone else who could have explained the indolence of the young Hitler with empathetic understanding was Nietzsche. Most people, he said, consider work a means, not an end—their real lives lie elsewhere. But there are occasional individuals "who would rather perish than work without any *pleasure* in their work. They are choosy, hard to satisfy, and do not care for ample rewards. Artists and contemplative men of all kinds belong to this rare breed." Nietzsche would probably have recognized one of those "contemplative men" in the young Hitler, who demanded meaning to his life whatever the cost. His Vienna years were a time of waiting, germinating, a kind of existential wager that he would find his personal mission before it was too late. He knew he was meant for something grand. He just didn't know what it was.

IN 1913, Hitler moved to Munich, a city more to his liking than Vienna. But his habits didn't change—he was still the drifter, the aimless bohemian. Only the start of World War I in 1914 gave him the direction he was missing, for now, at last, he had a cause to fight for, something to believe in. "The war was a godsend," Kershaw writes. Hitler had his own overwrought remembrance of the declaration of war. "I fell down on my knees and thanked Heaven from an overflowing heart for granting me the good fortune of being permitted to live at this time." He quickly volunteered for the Bavarian army, where he was assigned the job of courier, and he was soon promoted to corporal, the only promotion he would ever receive because of what his superiors considered a lack of leadership qualities.

As a soldier, he was, in many ways, the same old Hitler. He remained a loner who kept his distance from his comrades, priggishly upbraiding them for their unruly behavior. When he wasn't performing his duties, he spent his time reading, writing poetry, or drawing sketches. He was considered a daydreamer and nicknamed "the artist," which probably suited him just fine. "We all used to yell at him," one soldier recalled. He was no fun at all, not one to share a drink or a whore with, unable even to join in the joking banter that kept soldierly spirits up. Still, the other men hardly looked down on him as some sort of effete pansy, to be ostracized or beaten up. "Adi," as they called him, may have been eccentric, but he was undeniably courageous and respected for his "exemplary zeal." One imagines him as the company's mascot, loyal, trustworthy, and harmless. Twice wounded, he received a regimental certificate for bravery and two Iron Crosses, second class and then first class. When the war came to an end, he was in a hospital, recovering from a gas attack that had left him temporarily blinded.

But now what? As a demobilized civilian almost 30 years old, he would have faced the same bleak situation he had known before the outbreak of hostilities, except he was no longer young and could no longer hope for something, anything, turning up. Most men his age had settled into their lives, on their way to building careers and families, but, as Fest writes, "he had no training, no work, no goal, no place to stay, no friends." At least during the war his life had structure and purpose. The military may not have been the ideal solution for him, but it did provide a safety net. And so he did the only sensible thing: he clung to the army for the next two years, and the army, in turn, clung to its "exemplary" German soldier. He went to work for a reserve infantry battalion, performing guard duty, testing gas masks, reporting on subversive activities, helping to indoctrinate troops in the right-wing ideology of the military. It was this last task that resulted in his being sent to Munich University for a brief course in anti-Bolshevik "civic thinking."

Hitler's life, it could be said, had far more than its share of turning points, but this was one of the most important. The officer who sent him off to school later remarked that when he first met Hitler in May 1919, "he was like a tired stray dog looking for a master . . . ready to throw in his lot with anyone who would show him kindness." That was now about to change.

The army courses at the university, in such topics as German history, economics, and foreign policy, were held in the early weeks of June 1919, and at the end of the first lecture in history, a commotion in the classroom caught the instructor's attention. A group of students had gathered around one of their classmates, fascinated by what he was saying and by his strange intensity. According to his own account of the incident in *Mein Kampf*, Hitler had seized their attention with a furious denunciation of a fellow student who was defending the Jews. The professor reported that Hitler spoke to the other men "in a passionate, strikingly guttural tone" and with "eyes coldly glistening with fanaticism."

Those eyes were confirmations of the internal change Hitler was undergoing. No one had ever noticed them when he was a lonely, uncertain youth, but as he gained confidence they became weapons, azure lasers used to cut down opposing points of view with a burning, concentrated gaze or to freeze interlocutors in an imprisoning glare. Once he had found himself, they were impossible to ignore. One of his earliest associates, Ernst Hanfstaengl, a German-American Harvard graduate who was a member of Hitler's tight-knit entourage before breaking with him, conceded that even when Hitler was on his way to becoming a political leader, his appearance was unprepossessing—he looked like "a waiter in a railway station restaurant." But those blue eyes, with their "extraordinary luminous quality," lifted him into someone with a presence that was unforgettable.

The professor reported back that one of his students had a genuine gift for speechifying, and the army was quick to make use of that gift. Hitler was sent to a military camp to indoctrinate soldiers on the verge of returning to civilian life, and every time he spoke, denouncing the Versailles Treaty, attacking Jews and Marxists, he attracted attention. The men listened to him. They couldn't help but listen to him. He was magnetic, addressing them in easily understandable language but with a raw emotion they had never encountered before in a lecturer. Here was no rote recitation of memorized banalities by some midlevel nonentity. This man standing before them threw himself into his message with utter conviction. He meant every word. Who could not be impressed by such boundless passion? As for Hitler, the experience was no less transformative. The aspiring artist, the bohemian drifter, had at last discovered his talent, what he had been searching for all those years. "I could speak!" he exclaimed. A path had opened up. Tomorrow belonged to him.

Hitler's confidence in his newfound ability only grew when, in September 1919, the army sent him to keep tabs on one of the numerous small right-wing grouplets that were springing up all over Munich after the war.

The German Workers' Party, which had been formed at the beginning of the year, was really nothing more than a klatch of friends who gathered from time to time at one of the city's beer halls to air their grievances. This was a setting the blossoming Hitler couldn't resist, and at the meeting he attended, he crossed a line, mutating from observer to participant so that he could object to a suggestion for Bavarian independence. The group members were quick to notice what everyone else was beginning to notice. Here was someone special. "We could use him," the party's leader, Anton Drexler, a railway locksmith, declared, and Hitler was invited to join up.

Hitler began this new involvement by speaking at small, private gatherings and then to larger audiences. At the party's first public meeting in mid-October, he addressed a crowd of over one hundred. He wasn't even the featured speaker, but his effect on his listeners was astonishing. Now his rise took on a quality that was almost magical, and one catches one's breath at its inexorable rapidity. He was an overnight sensation. As word got out that someone extraordinary had emerged on Munich's political fringes, people clamored to hear him; by early 1920, the crowds were numbering in the thousands. That was when the group changed its name to the National Socialist German Workers Party and adopted the swastika as its symbol. On March 31, 1920, Hitler left the army, secure that he had finally found his vocation. The rebellious dropout had made himself indispensable, even if it was only to a tiny band of nobodies, and before long he was not only the star of the group but also its undisputed leader, exercising dictatorial control. By 1922, he was speaking at 8 to 12 rallies a day.

Quite simply, the Nazi movement was built on Hitler's oratory. There are numerous testimonies to the otherworldly spell he could weave with his words. Hanfstaengl declared, "He had the most formidable power of persuasion of any man or woman I have ever met, and it was almost impossible to avoid being enveloped by him." Others spoke of "mass hypnotism" at his rallies. Hans Frank, later the Nazi governor-general of conquered Poland who was hanged as a war criminal, was 19 when he first heard Hitler in January 1920. "He was at that time simply the grandiose popular speaker without precedent—and for me incomparable," Frank said. "From that evening onwards, though not a party member, I was convinced that if one man could do it, Hitler alone would be capable of mastering Germany's fate." Even the Austrian-Jewish literary critic George Steiner remembered Hitler's oratorical power from his radio addresses. "The voice itself was mesmeric," Steiner recalled. "The amazing thing is that the *body* comes through on the radio. I can't put it any other way. You feel you're following the gestures."

In fact, his gestures, like his eyes, were an important part of Hitler's oratorical package. The Nazis distributed photographs of Hitler's hands with the caption, "The Führer's hands organize his speech." Memorably, the philosopher Karl Jaspers asked his friend Martin Heidegger, Germany's most influential philosopher, how he could support a philistine like Hitler. "Culture is of no importance," Heidegger replied. "Just look at his marvelous hands." The friendship did not last.

The reactions of sophisticated intellectuals like Steiner and Heidegger (from opposite sides of the Hitler phenomenon) tell us we should not be misled by the ranting caricature we so often see in modern movies and documentaries, images that make it easy to reduce him to a Charlie Chaplin parody and to feel contemptuous superiority to the masses that were swayed by him. That is to make the same mistake of underestimating him that his opponents were always making. ("The history of National Socialism from beginning to end is the history of its underestimation," one historian has said.) If we cannot revise this picture of him, both sinister and comical, we will never grasp the nature of his appeal. One might even say that it was those who were susceptible to him who understood him best.

Hitler was able to hold his audiences spellbound for hours at a time, which wouldn't have been possible if his delivery had consisted simply of long harangues of raspy invective. Over time, he developed the full vocabulary of the rhetorician's art—voice, inflection, timing. His speeches were structured to build to carefully controlled crescendos. They were by turn emotional and combative and sentimental and ironic and assured and sarcastic and, yes, humorous. Hitler was quick-witted, able to deal handily with hecklers, of whom there were many in the early years. He was so attuned to his audience that he could adapt to any mood. As a speaker, he lived intensely in the moment—and what else does "presence" mean? Hanfstaengl compared him to a "tightrope walker" and "a skilled violinist." William Carr, a scholar who has examined Hitler's speaking style closely, writes: "By any objective standard Hitler must rank as one of the great orators of history, perhaps the greatest in the twentieth century."

With experience and the added resources that came with celebrity, Hitler was able to maximize the impact of his speeches through a scrupulous attention to setting and image. Before a presentation, he would check the ventilation and acoustics of the hall and would modulate his voice to fit

the conditions. His famous gestures were carefully rehearsed and choreo-
graphed, perfected through practice in front of a mirror and by studying photographs of himself. According to Carr, he may have copied some
of them from a popular Munich comedian. Once slovenly, he learned to
take special pains with his appearance. And after he had gained sufficient
renown, he could afford the pomp and circumstance that kept his audiences in a state of anticipatory excitation until his strategically delayed
arrival on stage. There were colorful banners, peppy march music, fiery
introductory speeches to warm up the crowd—and then the main event,
the attraction everyone had waited for so eagerly.

Hitler rarely if ever disappointed, rousing the assemblage to a state of
communal frenzy in which he himself was a full participant. As one fol-
lower remarked, "He actually inhaled the feelings of his audience." He
sweated profusely as he spoke, losing, he said, as much as 4 to 6 pounds
in an evening. The perspiration dyed his underwear. At the conclusion
of an address, listeners were often exhausted, satisfied yet wanting more.
Women seem to have been particularly attracted by his magnetism. Kershaw notes that, however improbably, he became a German sex symbol.
William Shirer records seeing women who, upon catching sight of him,
were "transformed into something positively inhuman." At a Nuremberg rally in 1937, Hitler spoke to an audience of 20,000 women. "Their
response," one contemporary remarked, "can only be described as orgiastic." The crowds who heard him were rendered rapturous, joyous, and
exited the halls triumphantly, chanting or singing.

Ian Kershaw writes that "it was less *what* he said than *how* he said it that
counted," which is true but only beyond a certain point. Hitler wouldn't
have won the following he did if he had been praising the Versailles Treaty
or defending the Jews. No Marxist spokesman was able to bring a crowd to
the same level of frenzy. Part of the magic was that Hitler told people what
they wanted to hear. His pronouncements were not a challenge but a confirmation of his followers' assumptions and preconceptions, an incitement
to cast off the dreary restrictions of civility and rationality and allow their
emotions full Dionysiac release, above all a permission both to maintain
hope in the face of obdurate reality and to hate anyone or anything that
was perceived to undermine that hope. Catholics, Socialists, and Communists, with intellectual structures of their own, were not as susceptible to him. He appealed to a devastated populace that, like him, had lost
everything, including their established beliefs, felt a profound sense of

grievance, and found consolation in a pan-Germanism that was part sentimentality and part utopianism, a sort of forward-looking nostalgia. The content of the speeches was important to that degree.

But after that, it was the "how" that mattered. Hitler's message was no different from that of many of the other right-wing nationalists trying to make themselves heard across Germany. He strung together bits and pieces of ideas and sentiments that he had picked up as a boy in Linz, as a drifter in Vienna, and as an enlisted man in the army. Historians still debate just when and where the different aspects of the ideology coalesced. Because he dwelled on longings instead of facts, he preferred abstractions to specifics, emphasizing honor, nation, family, loyalty. What distinguished him was the totality of his commitment, the intensity of a speaker who had stared into the abyss and drew back, once lost and now found—saved by extreme pan-Germanism and fanatical anti-Semitism and afterward devoted to spreading the message to others. He employed neither logic nor reason but sheer passion, while physically embodying the feelings of his audience like a medium. No one would ever turn to the farrago that is *Mein Kampf* for original, or even coherent, political thought, but one might profitably consult it for lessons in how to be an effective speaker and propagandist. Hitler didn't need ideas. He had the conviction of a convert.

More than one commentator has observed that Hitler rallies were like religious revivals, where the crowds went not for the articulation of policy positions but for the release of unbridled emotion. This is what was behind one contemporary's comment that "Hitler never really made a political speech." The American journalist H. R. Knickerbocker saw Hitler as "an evangelist speaking to a camp meeting, the Billy Sunday of German politics." There was indeed something religious here: "the worship of the people as a secular religion," as the historian George Mosse put it. Hitler made frequent use of religious metaphors and referred to himself as a "very small" John the Baptist before he began thinking in larger terms. One supporter called Hitler a "leader sent by God." Another claimed that after a three-hour speech, he actually saw a halo around Hitler's head.

But there was more to Nazism than the emergence of a new faith. Hitler understood that his audiences wanted not only to be saved but also to enjoy themselves in the process. His speeches were all constructed to that end, and if they were religious expressions of a kind, they were also demonstrations of the new power of popular culture in the modern age and how modern communications could be used to spread a message, however toxic. Nazi rallies may have suggested prayer meetings; they also resemble Bruce Springsteen concerts. Who ever imagined that salvation could be so much fun? Whatever else he might have been, Hitler was a performer, dealing in mass entertainment. He was no good in intimate settings, reluctant to speak even at a friend's wedding, but put him on a stage and he was in his element. He knew how to work a crowd and how to package himself as a celebrity. It didn't matter what the press said about him, he told an associate. "The main thing is that they mention us."

Now let us contemplate one simple but remarkable fact: the Nazis charged entrance fees to Hitler's speeches! Is there any other politician of the twentieth century who would be considered worth spending money to hear? Churchill at his best, perhaps, though not on so regular a basis as Hitler or with his frequency. Churchill wasn't the polished performer that Hitler was—just think of the difference in their body language. And before Donald Trump, perhaps, it's impossible to imagine any modern American candidate for office asking people to pay for the privilege of listening to him try to win their political support.

SECULAR RELIGION, YES. Mass entertainment, yes. But was this politics in any meaningful sense? Perhaps the question carries no weight in an era when politics and entertainment have merged to a degree that would have been unfathomable at an earlier time. These days we have become all too accustomed to actors, comedians, and sports figures (not to mention businessmen who became television stars)—celebrities of every kind whose only qualification for electoral office is name recognition—transforming themselves into successful politicians or at least successful vote-getters. But what about then, when the requirement for entering public life consisted of more than 15 minutes of fame? Hitler may not have been an entirely new phenomenon of democratic politics. American elections of the nineteenth century had wallowed in image-building, fantasy-mongering, and partisan vituperation. But no one had taken those procedures to such an extreme, or employed them so effectively and destructively, as Hitler did in Germany's young and fragile republic. Hitler claimed in *Mein Kampf* that it had been a difficult decision for him to abandon his earlier aesthetic aspirations for politics. It was a sacrifice for him. Max Weber, for one, would have seen the decision as something less exalted.

For Weber, politics had to be more than the unleashing of mass emotion, more than the spinning of dreams, or, to put it in the way Hitler would have put it, more than the triumph of the will. It was an occupation that required patience, dispassion, and a firm grasp both of what was real and what was possible—the virtues of Gustav Stresemann, for instance. "Politics," Weber famously declared, "is a matter of boring down strongly and slowly through hard boards with passion and judgment together." Passion was necessary to define the politician's goals; judgment provided the detachment required to guide behavior, "the ability to contemplate things as they are with inner calm and composure." Someone who possessed passion but not a "realistic sense of responsibility" was little more than a "political dilettante" consumed by "sterile excitements" or by a romanticism that, in Weber's words, "runs away to nothing." The demagogue in particular was unsuited to the vocation of politics because "he runs a constant risk of becoming a play-actor, making light of the responsibility for the consequences of his actions and asking only what 'impression' he is making." In Weber's terms, the Hitler of these years, for all his oratorical success, was not a politician but a political dilettante, with no sense of realism or responsibility. It had to end badly for him. Weber's analysis was prescient—at least it was up to 1923. For in that year, Hitler's "sterile excitements" did in fact run away to nothing.

Hitler's facility for dealing in dreams was enough to gain him a steadily growing following that was serious in its numbers yet fundamentally unserious in its ideas, substituting the lightness of desire for the concreteness of policy. By 1923, according to one police report, his movement had grown to around 150,000, including both members and sympathizers. But neither he nor they had any interest in the dull, grinding work of running for office or winning elections. Political power as they understood it and if they thought about it at all was something to be taken by force, through the brave dedication of Hitler's private army of storm troopers, the SA. Weapons were openly and proudly displayed at rallies, violence celebrated. Skirting the bounds of legality, the Nazis were constantly fighting with ideological enemies and clashing with the police. In 1922, at the head of a gang of his bully-boys, Hitler beat up the leader of a Bavarian separatist group and was sentenced to three months in jail. He was released after serving four weeks, exiting prison to a hero's welcome. The appeals to violence and the flouting of law only increased his popularity among his admirers.

By early 1923, rumors of a Nazi putsch were spreading across Munich as a hideous inflation, coupled with the occupation of the Ruhr by French and Belgian troops, undermined the fragile authority of the central government in Berlin. And if the Nazis needed anything else in the way of encouragement, there was the example of Mussolini who, in 1922, had marched on Rome at the front of his Blackshirts and took control of the Italian government. Restless supporters who looked south took to calling Hitler "Germany's Mussolini" and pressuring him to seize the moment. He didn't really need their pressure: all of his speeches had been pointing in one direction. If he was unwilling to act in this time of crisis, what was the point of his agitation? If not now, when?

On November 8, 1923, he and his storm troopers crossed their inevitable Rubicon and invaded a beer hall where Bavaria's government leaders had assembled for a public meeting. Exits were blocked, a shot fired into the air (possibly by Hitler himself). To the bewildered and frightened crowd, Hitler next did what he always did best: he gave a speech. The effect, as usual, was electric. According to one eyewitness, "There were certainly many who were not converted yet. But the sense of the majority had fully reversed itself. Hitler had turned them inside out, as one turns a glove inside out, with a few sentences." And then a familiar refrain: "It had almost something of hocus-pocus, or magic about it. Loud approval roared forth, no further opposition was to be heard."

Around the city, meanwhile, Nazis fanned out to take over key locations—government offices, communications centers, army barracks. Outside of Munich, putschists were attempting to gain control of other towns and provinces. The plan was to capture Bavaria and then march on Berlin.

It quickly turned into a total fiasco. An overreaching Hitler had come too far too fast. Among those he was able to touch directly, his captivating oratory won him the title "the king of Munich," deluding him into believing his influence was much greater than it actually was. He thought he could do anything. Megalomania trailed him like a doppelgänger. Outside of earshot, however, his following was small. Hard as it was for him to fathom, he was no more than a local hero. Most important, he had not won over the national army, not even the city police, because he didn't have the discipline to think in terms of institutions. Only the frenzy of crowds mattered. As Harold Gordon, an authority on the putsch, explained, his limited popularity had made him impatient, irrational, "incapable of weighing the odds against him carefully and coldly." How surprised should we be that a man who had risen by trafficking in irrationality should prove to be irrational himself? When armed confrontation arrived, the Nazi insurgents, for all their amateurish enthusiasm, were no match for trained professionals, and by the afternoon of November 9, the uprising had been quashed, leaving 14 Nazis and 4 policemen dead and a chastened Hitler in custody.

A trial for treason would hardly seem the ideal setting for turning someone into a national hero. But Hitler was not just someone. He had made himself news all over Germany, and that was all he needed. The circumstances couldn't have been better if he had arranged them himself. Ever the showman, he was at his best when he was on a public stage, and this was the largest stage he had ever known. With the connivance of judges sympathetic to his anti-Weimar cause, Hitler took control of the proceedings, confidently assuming full responsibility for his subversion and turning his trial into one long exercise in Nazi propaganda. "I consider myself not a traitor but a German, who desired what was best for his people," he declared. The accused had become the accuser, the criminal the victim. Let the martyrdom come, for the nation was all that mattered.

It all ended up as one of Hitler's most remarkable successes. In April 1924 the court handed down a shockingly light five-year sentence (with the prospect of a pardon after only six months), while Hitler's fame had, for the first time, spread across the entire country. To anyone ready to lend a sympathetic ear, he was now the undisputed leader of Germany's extreme right.

It was another major turning point for him, one that taught him a lasting lesson. Commitment and enthusiasm weren't enough to overcome the resistance of stony reality. There would be no triumph of the will. From this time forward, he would cease being the fantasizing demagogue promoting a violent insurrection that had little practical chance of success and would become a democratic politician dedicated to achieving power through popular support and legal means. Though the Nazis would never distance themselves from violence, they would now function mainly through persuasion and electoral calculation, not intimidation—and they had Germany's finest orator to rely on. "The putsch had transformed the old Hitler into the new," Gordon writes. It marked the end of "Hitler's political apprenticeship," Fest says. "In fact, strictly speaking, it marks

Hitler's first real entry into politics." In later years, Hitler would look back on his humiliating defeat in 1923 as "perhaps the greatest stroke of luck in my life."

IN WEBERIAN TERMS, Hitler had always had the passion, the vision. Now he developed that "sense of responsibility" that is the other part of the professional politician's vocation. One of his first acts upon leaving prison in December 1924 was to meet with Bavaria's president and acknowledge that he had learned his lesson: from that day forward, he would operate only through legal means. It wasn't entirely true—Hitler would always resort to violence when it suited his purposes. But it was largely true, true for the practical politician that Hitler had become, even though democratic procedures remained fundamentally distasteful to him. As he told an associate: "We shall have to hold our noses and enter the Reichstag."

The crucial fact was that there would be no more attempted coups, no more arrests or imprisonments for treason. Respectability replaced insurrection. Not all of his more militant followers agreed, and later he would seek to quell their passions by telling them that anyone who sought "open war against the state" was "either a fool or a criminal." Setbacks no longer ruffled him; he reacted to failure with an equanimity he had never revealed before, remaining calm and steady, his eyes coldly fixed on his distant goal. "Any lawful process," he explained, "is slow." In describing this new Hitler, historians employ words like "restraint" and "patience," hardly the qualities he had earlier displayed in Munich's beer halls. "Pragmatism," one scholar says, "had become his real strength." He was no longer Germany's Mussolini; a Swiss journalist of the time referred to him as "Prince Légalité."

Still, electoral politics is difficult, unglamorous, often frustrating work. In Hitler's absence, the Nazi movement had disintegrated into a directionless congeries of warring tribes, and once he was released from prison he had to start all over again, this time building not only an ideological movement but a political party as well. Because speeches and exhortation would no longer suffice, this immediately presented him with a problem. For he may have been able to rouse people with words, but organization was never his strong suit, not even after he became dictator of Germany. Kershaw writes that "a party leader and head of government less bureaucratically inclined, less a committee man or man of the machine than Hitler, is hard to imagine."

There are many ways to be a leader, however, and along with his oratorical skills, what Hitler possessed was an ability to spot talent and make
use of it; though he had an ego of enormous proportions, he knew enough
about his limitations to bring in a supreme organizer, a former pharmacist
from northern Germany named Gregor Strasser, to take on the arduous
chore of constructing lasting institutions. Together, they made an outstanding team, dividing responsibility according to their particular talents: Hitler would attract the crowds with his inspiring oratory; Strasser
(who could also give a capable speech when he had to) would create the
structures to bind them into a functioning political party. And because in
these "wilderness years" Hitler was often banned from public speaking,
limited to addressing the party faithful and writing articles for the party's
newspaper, Strasser's dreary, bureaucratic behind-the-scenes labors were
that much more important.

Strasser set up a party apparatus of provincial entities called *gaus*,
with *gauleiters* to lead them. He established bureaus for foreign policy,
health, justice—in effect a shadow government preparing the Nazis for
the day when they would take power. He created leagues for doctors,
lawyers, teachers, and other professionals, as well as various student and
youth groups. There were departments for veterans, farmers, civil servants, workers, along with a women's auxiliary. Everybody who sought
one could find a place in the new catchall Nazi Party (as long as they didn't
have Jewish blood). A speakers program trained cadres who memorized
speeches and practiced in front of mirrors before being sent out across
the country to discuss bread-and-butter issues like agricultural prices and
taxes. Correspondence courses and illustrated magazines were available
for those in the hinterlands.

Other Nazis at the local level collected food for the poor, ran soup
kitchens, and provided clothing and first aid. They made a point of getting to know their neighbors, demonstrating that they were just regular
folk, friendly, comfortable to be around, even churchgoing. They threw
Christmas parties. They sang in the choir. Full of youthful enthusiasm and
vigor, they were, observers said, "a genuine people's party," something the
unimaginative, bureaucratic plutocrats and Marxists who dominated the
political scene from the right and the left never could be. The Nazis paid
particular attention to converting the most respected leaders of a community, on the theory that if they could be won over, they would bring dozens
of others with them. "If he's in it, it must be all right" was the attitude.

None of the other political organizations had the personnel to match such energy and dedication, or such *Gemütlichkeit*. The Nazis were the only party in Germany to run continuous, never-ending campaigns, seeking to win backers not only during elections but also between them. They turned politics from an occasional occupation into a way of life, and in these years they remade themselves, as one German journalist put it, into "a hissing and pounding steam engine of an electoral machine, of a kind previously unknown in Germany." They were learning how to play the political game, and learning to play it better than anyone else. This was democracy in action.

As for Hitler himself, he kept busy with fundraising, charming and cajoling wealthy industrialists and landowners who were sympathetic to his cause—though as a true "people's party," the Nazis depended mainly on membership dues and contributions from thousands of small, anonymous donors to keep them afloat. He had completed the first part of *Mein Kampf* while in prison. Now he had time to finish the second part, which was published at the end of 1926. With regard to internal party matters, he devoted himself to solidifying his position as both head and figurehead of his new and growing movement. Centralization under a single, unquestioned leader was essential, because without it the party was most likely to fall apart again into self-destructive competing factions.

Grassroots activities may have been building the movement from the ground up, but direction from the top gave it cohesion. In 1926, the "Heil Hitler" salute was made compulsory, and in 1928, appointed officials replaced elected ones in the different localities. Regional leaders were instructed that "everywhere in Germany the same placards will be posted, the same leaflets distributed and the same stickers will appear." The central office even decreed the precise time placards were to be put up. Not that things always went smoothly. As with any large and growing organization, miscommunication occurred and wires got crossed. Maintaining the delicate balance between the grass roots and the central authority wasn't easy. But over time the Nazis achieved the bureaucratic flexibility a political party needed to be an effective vote-gathering operation. The Nazis prided themselves on being a leadership party, yet by 1932, when the propaganda office (RPL) was flooding localities with political material almost every day, a directive also went out saying that "it is impossible for the Propaganda Directorate to publish uniform leaflets for the whole Reich. Since the mentality of the North German is different from that of an East Prussian or a Badener, etc., the drafts composed by the RPL must be modified to conform to the mentality of the local population."

Of course, the glue that kept everything together was always Hitler, who was not shy about claiming a kind of political infallibility for himself. "Every one of my words is historic," he declared—a comical statement to anyone not caught up in the frenzy of National Socialism but simply the articulation of a basic truth to his cult-like followers. As one of them said, "Our program can be expressed in two words: 'Adolf Hitler.'"

Inevitably, there were dissidents within the movement. In the years of rebuilding they were dealt with less by force (that would come later) than by force of will. Some, most notably Gregor Strasser and his brother, the journalist Otto, took the "Socialism" in "National Socialism" seriously and wanted the movement to stand for more than pan-Germanism and anti-Semitism—and for more than the person of Adolf Hitler. (The intellectually inclined Joseph Goebbels, before he fell under Hitler's spell, was another leftist Nazi.) Hitler recognized the threat these leftists posed not only to his leadership but also to the flexibility he required as a politician hoping to win the widest possible support, and he faced them down at a historic meeting in Bamburg in February 1926 with a five-hour diatribe that squelched any socialist heresy within the movement. The ideologically committed Otto persisted. "The leader is made to serve the Idea, and it is to the Idea alone that we owe absolute allegiance," he told Hitler in 1930. "You are talking monumental idiocy," Hitler replied. "You wish to give party members the right to decide whether or not the Führer has remained faithful to the so-called Idea. It's the lowest kind of democracy, and we want nothing to do with it!" Otto left the party and eventually left Germany, while Gregor remained loyal; in 1934 his reward was to be murdered along with dozens of Hitler's other former associates during the Night of the Long Knives.

The storm troopers of the SA were another source of trouble for Hitler's democratic strategy, one that seemed never ending. They had been the spearhead behind the failed 1923 putsch, and even after Hitler committed himself to parliamentary politics, they retained an important role as the Nazis' paramilitary arm, bullying opponents and engaging in fierce street battles against the Marxists of the Communist and Social Democratic parties. Not only did the storm troopers intimidate enemies, they also served as an important recruiting tool: their testosterone-fueled marches and muscular demonstrations were useful in winning the support of those who preferred shows of strength to acts of charity. The SA was the primitive, threatening side of Nazism, a contrast to the political cadres' friendly, smiley faces (though when the storm troopers weren't beating up leftists and Jews, especially outside the battlefields of the cities, they also distributed food and sang in the choir).

But as men of action, they had no taste for the tedium of electioneering or the patience that pragmatism required. Contemptuous of all politics and politicians, they represented a constant threat to Hitler's long-term policy of legality. They were always itching for a fight, always ready for another putsch, no matter how far-fetched and unreasonable the idea was. They had learned nothing from the failure of 1923, complaining openly about their Führer's "mania of legality," his annoying moderation. At one moment of profound dissatisfaction, impatient storm troopers occupied the party's offices in Berlin and destroyed the furniture; they were turned out only with the help of the police. It was "the most serious crisis the party has had to go through," Goebbels said. Hitler may have needed the SA's muscle and swagger, but to keep on his straight and narrow path he also had to find some way of maintaining control over this unpredictable Frankenstein's monster. And a Frankenstein's monster it was: by 1932, the ranks of the SA had swollen to 400,000 troopers, four times the number of men in Germany's army. It was no easy task to contain them. Even in the days before Hitler became chancellor, storm troopers staged bloody fights with party members in Nuremberg and mutinied in Hesse. Some even defected to the Communists.

Hitler tried everything with them—quelling incipient rebellions with forceful speeches and the sheer power of his personality, shuffling and reshuffling the SA leadership, demanding that the members take an oath of personal allegiance to him. In 1926, he sidestepped the SA altogether by creating an elite corps, the SS, whose loyalty to him was unswerving. Nothing really worked, and only in 1934, when he was on the verge of becoming Germany's absolute dictator, did he arrive at his "final solution" to the problem by having his SS henchmen murder the leaders of the SA during the Night of the Long Knives.

THE WILDERNESS YEARS lasted until the election of September 1930. In two national elections for the Reichstag in 1924, the Nazis ran as part of a right-wing coalition and made little or no impact: the coalition won 6.5 percent of the vote in May, only 3 percent in December. By 1926 the

Nazis were running as a separate party in local elections and doing no better. In the national election of May 1928, with a mere 2.6 percent of the vote, they captured only 12 seats in the Reichstag out of 491. If you were a restless storm trooper twiddling your pugilistic thumbs while waiting for the party's politicians to prove their strategy of forbearance was the correct one, you had every reason to conclude that Hitler's policy of legality was a failure.

But then the hard work of the party's functionaries, together with Hitler's captivating oratory, began to pay off. Prospects first turned brighter in local and regional elections even before the onset of the Great Depression. In 1929, Nazis took control of the town council in Coburg; in the state of Thuringia, they picked up more than 10 percent of the vote and entered a governing coalition. Other local elections showed similar results. Then, as economic misery settled over the country, came the breakthrough that everyone recognized as truly historic, indeed earth-shattering. In the Reichstag election of September 1930, the party vaulted from less than 3 percent of the vote two years before to 18.3 percent and 107 seats, making it the second largest bloc in parliament, trailing only the long-established Social Democrats. In just two years, support had grown by about 800 percent. The party had become a player on the national scene and Hitler's name became recognizable around the world. It was, Kershaw says, "the most remarkable result in German parliamentary history."

The next Reichstag election was held two years later in July 1932, and for it the invigorated, confident Nazis were passionately engaged, flooding the country with leaflets, holding thousands of meetings and marches, exuberantly taking their message to every corner of the country and every sector of the society. "Voting, voting!" Goebbels exclaimed. "On to the people. We're all very happy." Politics was more to them than hammering out programs and building coalitions; it was a matter of personal identity, of life's meaning. They were rewarded with 37 percent of the vote and 230 seats, almost 100 more than the once-dominant Social Democrats. They were now Germany's largest political party. Their momentum slowed in a second election in November, when their support dropped to 33 percent, but they remained the largest bloc in parliament. More ominously, the centrist parties continued to lose ground, so that middle-of-the-road voters, without any particular ideological commitment and confronted with a choice between ineffectual, wishy-washy liberalism and vigorous, nationalistic Nazism, increasingly chose the latter.

That year, too, there was an election for president in March with a
runoff in April. For the only time in his political career, Hitler ran in a
genuine election for public office, seeking the presidency with his usual
limitless energy and even introducing the technological innovation of air
travel into German politics, which allowed him to reach larger numbers of
people than ever before. He finished behind the incumbent president and
former war hero, the doddering 85-year-old Paul von Hindenburg, but as
no candidate had received an absolute majority, an April runoff followed
in which he managed to persuade 37 percent of the voters that he was the
right man to be head of state.

Through no less than four elections in 1932, two for the Reichstag and
two for the presidency, Hitler and the Nazis had proved their broad popularity. They also continued to win wide support in state and local elections. Finally, on January 30, 1933, after much resistance and repeated,
disputatious consultations with his advisers, Hindenburg swallowed his
deep personal distaste for Hitler and named him chancellor of Germany
with the responsibility of running the government. Ecstatic Nazis celebrated with demonstrations of a size that had not been seen in Berlin since
the overthrow of the Kaiser in 1918. The French ambassador watched a
long torchlight parade that "formed a river of fire." An estimated one million took part. Similar celebrations were held across Germany. It was a
new day.

But how new? In fact, the Nazis never did win a majority of the voters—
not in 1932, not even in the election of March 1933, after Hitler had become
chancellor. It was the third Reichstag election within a year, and the last
legitimate one that Germany would see until the end of World War II.
Despite the power that Hitler's position gave them, the Nazis garnered
"only" 44 percent of the vote that March. Some scholars who insist on
viewing democratic processes as the antidote to Hitler's rise rather than its
facilitator take consolation in this fact, arguing that it was not democracy
itself that had brought Hitler to power but a circumvention of democracy—
"a backstairs political intrigue," a conspiracy, the work of "ambitious and
misguided men" who were looking "to make history," "sinister intrigues
behind the scenes." William Shirer writes of a "back-door" arrangement, a
"shabby political deal." The Nazis never became a majority party, and parliament had never voted for Hitler to become chancellor. He was imposed
on the country, it was said, by Hindenburg and his small band of cronies.
Kershaw writes, "Democracy was less surrendered than deliberately under-

mined by elite groups serving their own ends." But this perspective, as appealing as it is to liberal sensibilities, is to demand more than either the history of the Weimar Republic or the concept of democracy itself can bear.

From Weimar's very beginning, no party had ever won a majority of Germany's electorate. Parliamentary coalitions had always ruled the republic. Because the Nazis had succeeded in making themselves the largest party in the country by 1932, and because no coalition could be forged that excluded them, they had every reason—in fact, every right—to expect that they would be asked to form a government. One more election, on top of the four that had already taken place, was not going to settle anything. Indeed, by the end of 1932, with election following upon election at the national, state, and local levels, the populace was politically exhausted and voter turnout was dropping. If anything, Germany was suffering from an excess of democracy. Voters couldn't be asked to keep going to the polls until they got it right.

The problems with Germany's democracy had actually begun when the governing coalition headed by the Social Democrat Hermann Müller fell apart in March 1930, paving the way for the Nazi electoral breakthrough that September. Müller's was the last government able to construct a coalition with a majority of parliament. From that time forward, chancellors were chosen by the president as minority executives and governed only so long as parliament agreed to cooperate by refusing to push through a vote of "no confidence." This wasn't democracy in any ideal sense, as critics of the process have been quick to point out, but it was still a system that adhered to the constitution and derived its ultimate legitimacy from the people. Parliament retained the power to say no and force an election.

As makeshift as the arrangement was, it was better than no government at all, which was the alternative. There may not have been a single governing coalition after 1930, but shifting alignments in parliament permitted some semblance of functioning government for a while. That changed with the election of July 1932, when, between them, the Nazis and the Communists achieved a majority of the seats in the Reichstag. Now political rigor mortis truly set in. The two extremist parties could agree on nothing except opposition. The power to say no was all they had. This "negative majority" made government by parliamentary procedure impossible, a situation the founders of the Weimar Republic had never foreseen and democratic theorists have been unable to untangle ever since. In September 1932, the government of the archconservative Franz von Papen, which had been in power since the end of May with Hinden-burg's approval, was humiliated by a no-confidence resolution introduced by the Communists that swept parliament by 512–42, demonstrating in the most convincing way possible the isolation of the chancellor—and the president—and forcing another election. And even though the Nazis lost seats in the November polling that followed, the Communists picked up votes, so the "negative majority" held. With the extremes gaining strength, positions hardened. Everyone was digging in. The compromises that are the lifeblood of any functioning democracy and that depend on a self-sacrificing commitment to the common good were out of the question.

And yet Germany—in the midst of a depression and with near civil war raging on the streets of its cities—somehow had to be governed. How was this to be accomplished? At the end of August, before his embarrass-ing defeat in the Reichstag, Papen suggested to President Hindenburg that he dissolve parliament without scheduling new elections and rule by executive decree. This blatantly unconstitutional idea was shelved after the no-confidence vote demonstrated that it would have almost no pop-ular support. Still, it did not die. Papen's successor, Kurt von Schleicher, revived it after he too proved unable to break the legislative stalemate. On January 23, with the crisis at its height, Schleicher presented Hinden-burg with a memo prepared by the Defense Ministry that outlined three possible options: (1) dissolve parliament but postpone elections beyond the constitutionally mandated waiting period of 60 days (Papen's plan); (2) dissolve parliament with an offer to recall it if a legislative majority could be formed; and (3) maintain Schleicher as chancellor of a "care-taker government" even in the face of a no-confidence vote. The first two options were clearly unconstitutional, and the third probably so, though lawyers could be found to make the argument that, because of a gap in the constitution, a caretaker executive was not strictly illegal. That's probably not how it would have been seen on the street, however. All three options introduced a prospect of civil war. A leader of the Social Democrats called any postponement of elections an "incitement to treason."

Rumors were also flying at this time about a fourth possibility: namely, an out-and-out takeover of the government by the army. Henry Ashby Turner Jr., the historian who has studied the last days of the Weimar Republic in more detail than anyone else, concluded that "military rule offered the best available alternative to Hitler's acquisition of power." He concedes that an army dictatorship, not unlike the Third Reich, would probably have launched a war for "territorial revision" in the years to come, but he takes consolation in the expectation that it would have been nothing like the calamitous apocalypse unleashed by Hitler—and that there would have been no Holocaust. A small war was a more desirable prospect than a world war.

The problem with all four of these options is that they would have over-turned the Weimar constitution and established an authoritarian regime, but one without any popular legitimacy whatsoever. All of them were an invitation to civil war. Only with hindsight do they look like desirable courses of action. Turner writes that a violation of the constitution was the "lesser evil," but who could have known that in January 1933? Deci-sion makers could hardly conceive what a Hitler regime would bring. In the middle of the crisis an abrogation of the constitution seemed the sur-est way to make matters worse. And that is why, faced with the choice between an authoritarian government—either by the military or by a handpicked political elite—or a government headed by the leader of the most popular party in Germany, Hindenburg could be said to have exer-cised caution when he decided to obey the constitution and go with the "democratic" option instead of with his anti-Hitler instinct.

It was a gamble, but it appeared to be a reasonable one, especially if, as conservatives hoped, Hitler could be hemmed in by the other members of his cabinet, his powers contained. Under the terms of the agreement in which Hitler became chancellor, the Nazis would occupy two cabi-net posts, and not the most important ones. The majority of the execu-tive positions would be held by non-Nazi conservatives, who would be in charge of foreign policy, finance, labor, and agriculture. "We're box-ing Hitler in," said the leader of one right-wing party. "We've hired him for our act," said Papen, who was slated to become vice chancellor. Such statements reveal not only an inane optimism in the light of what was to come but also a foolish arrogance that was blind to the way power func-tioned in a mass democracy. The non-Nazi conservatives were divided among themselves and had no countervailing popular base to draw on in the face of a determined demagogue. The sad truth is that Hitler was the most legitimate choice available. His strategy of using democratic means to achieve undemocratic ends had worked. No wonder the Nazis through-out Germany celebrated with torchlight parades.

Turn to any history of the Nazis and you will almost invariably come upon the phrase "seizure of power" as the description of the events during these critical weeks and months. One major scholar even refers to "a terrorist power grab." But such language creates a misleading, if consoling, picture of what actually happened in Germany in January 1933, suggesting as it does that a small band of plotters staged a coup d'état to overturn the constitution, illegally wresting power away from the proper authorities and defying the will of the people. It may be language appropriate for what Hitler tried to do in 1923 with his putsch, but it fails to describe the path taken by Hitler the democrat. Hitler did not "seize" power. His was not a brute's hand that reached out to forcibly take hold of the governmental scepter; his was a hand that slipped smoothly into a glove. Hitler was given power because if any German politician had cause to say that he represented the will of the people, it was he.

Here is Franz von Papen, who was not only the chancellor of Germany from May to December in 1932 but also a key figure in persuading Hindenburg to name Hitler a month later. He may not be the most reliable witness for the crucial months leading up to January 1933 (later, he was only too happy to serve the Third Reich and was imprisoned for a while after the war for his work on behalf of the regime). And his many critics did not have a very high estimation of him. One said that he "combines the conscience and sense of honor of a butcher's hound with stupidity so devastating it is not an excuse but a crime." But on one essential point his testimony has to be considered accurate. "The first Hitler government," he said, "was formed in strict accordance with parliamentary procedure. He had been brought to power by the normal interplay of democratic processes."

THERE WAS NOTHING inevitable about Hitler's path to power, though neither was it obvious how he could have been stopped without violating constitutional limits or democratic ideals. As always, individuals made decisions that affected the course of history, and in late 1932 and early 1933, they could have opted for choices other than the ones they made. The most important decision was taken by Hindenburg, who was not compelled to name Hitler chancellor and who did so against his better judgment.

Another example can be cited from a month earlier. In December 1932, Hitler's closest confederate in building the Nazi Party, Gregor Strasser, was offered the vice-chancellorship by Schleicher as a way of dividing the Nazis against themselves and thwarting Hitler. The scheme had a good chance of working. The Nazis probably would have split, Hitler would have been stymied, and Germany's (and the world's) future would have been far different from the outcome we know. But Strasser, the left-wing Nazi, chose not to accept, instead resigning from the party he had been so instrumental in creating and withdrawing from politics altogether.

That is, Hindenburg could have stood his ground and refused to name Hitler. Strasser could have accepted the vice-chancellorship. Neither of the choices they made was inevitable, and yet each was reasonable in context. Hindenburg wanted to avoid a possible civil war, and Strasser preferred loyalty over backroom deals and personal ambition. There was a kind of honor in their choices (though what cannot be discounted in Strasser's case was that he feared assassination by Hitler partisans, a fate he did not escape in any event). Similarly, at every step along the way, decisions could have been made that would likely have derailed Hitler, yet all of the actual choices that paved the way to his triumph were made for entirely understandable reasons. "Undoubtedly, Hitler's way could have been blocked up to the very last moment," Fest writes. But "the real miracle would have been a decision to resist Nazism." The coming of the Third Reich was not inevitable, but it was eminently "reasonable."

After the Nazis became Germany's most popular party in July 1932, it was probably too late anyway. It would have taken extreme and dangerous measures, along with extraordinary—one might say inhuman—foresight to stop Hitler. If he was to be blocked, it surely had to have happened earlier.

No doubt the best opportunity came with Hitler's trial for treason in 1924. He was not yet a national figure, and he had no political party to lead. The judges who handed down the scandalously light five-year sentence were criticized at the time, and they have been criticized ever since, for letting Hitler literally get away with murder. But without in any way denying the all-too-evident leniency of the judges, the fact is that they were behaving the way millions of German conservatives who weren't necessarily Nazis behaved throughout the Weimar period. There was reasonableness to the unfortunate decision they made.

Jews and Marxists, as Hitler's perennial targets, didn't need to think twice about opposing the Nazis. They were his enemies, and so he was theirs. But for other Germans of the time a genuine intellectual or moral effort, backed by the strength of independent thinking, was required to stand against them—especially since anti-Semitism was not the bright red line that it became in the years after the Holocaust. The problem was particularly acute for the millions of German conservatives. The Nazis and the various conservative parties existed on a political continuum in which distinctions often blurred. All were committed nationalists, first of all, and no party could claim to be more nationalistic than the Nazis.

And so there were nationalist conservatives (or conservative nationalists) who became Nazis out of what Hermann Rauschning calls "the best of motives." Rauschning joined the party in the early 1930s and became the Nazi mayor of the city of Danzig, believing in "the eternal values of the nation" and "a political order rooted in the nation." He had a personal relationship with Hitler but soon discovered that his aims for Germany were not the Nazis' aims, and in 1934 he left the party and fled to Switzerland. National Socialism, he had concluded, was not a conservative movement but a revolutionary one, "the destroyer of all order and all the things of the mind." The only thing it understood was force and it held to no beliefs other than the acquisition of power and then more power. Rauschning was prescient enough to see that there was nothing to prevent the unscrupulous, nihilistic Hitler from forming an alliance with his supposed archenemy, Stalin. In a widely read book, *The Revolution of Nihilism*, published in 1938, he issued a warning that many did not wish to hear. The West, he said, had to prepare for "a clear, open, absolutely unflinching struggle" against the Nazis. For "nothing, not even the threat of world war, will deter them from their course."

Then there were conservatives like Papen, who took the opposite path from Rauschning. He did not start out as a Nazi but became one and ended up serving the regime throughout its existence. There were still other conservatives who kept their distance, never actually joining the party, but who thought that to a greater or lesser degree they could work with Hitler; they learned to their sorrow that Hitler worked with nobody.

There were even conservatives who, though they went along with Hitler's nationalist goals and his anti-Weimar fulminations, opposed him because they couldn't abide his populism—to them, he was *too* democratic. These individuals could be as ferocious in their opposition as any Communist. A pertinent example of the type was Friedrich Reck, a popular novelist and friend of Oswald Spengler and Gregor Strasser. He was a confirmed reactionary—a rueful monarchist and an unapologetic elitist ("increased life expectancy," he said, "is largely due to the incubation of basically unfit children"). But to him, Hitler was the plebeian embodiment of "mass man," "a deeply miscarried human being," a "poor devil sprung

out of a Strindbergian excremental Hell." Reck shared many of the premises of Hitler, but no one outdid him in his detestation of "that power-
drunk schizophrenic," the "Prince of Darkness himself."

To those conservatives who grudgingly went along, the Nazis may
have been a threat to law and order at the time of the putsch but not after.
The greater threat, the long-term threat, was Marxism. Even if Hitler was
extreme, even if he was vulgar, even if his anti-Semitism was pathologically obsessional, he remained a German nationalist of obvious talent and
a useful tool in the battle against Communism. And so he would never
lack for sympathizers in high places, like the judges at his treason trial,
even if they looked down on him and didn't take him as seriously as they
should have. Hindenburg's own dislike of Hitler had less to do with ideology than with simple snobbery—here was a revered German general
being compelled to deal on a level of equality with an anonymous German
corporal. This conservative tolerance for the Nazis (which always had the
potential, as conditions worsened, to shade over into extreme nationalism
and then into war crimes) finds an echo in Joachim Fest's observation
that down to 1938, Hitler could be considered a great German statesman, as well as in Henry Kissinger's opinion that Hitler's intentions were
ambiguous—until they weren't.

By the same token, the failure to control Hitler after he was released
from prison looks unreasonable only with the certainty of hindsight.
Through the mid-1920s, he was banned from speaking in most German
states, but as time passed and memories of the putsch receded, the bans
began to be lifted. After all, Hitler was now pledging to abide by the rules
of legality, and how, in a democracy, could a politician be denied the right
to be heard, no matter how insidious his message, if he stayed within the
bounds of the law? Who—and by what authority—had the right to silence
him? Saxony, at the start of 1927, was the first large state to lift the speaking prohibition and was followed by Bavaria and others. The last to do so
was the all important state of Prussia, by far the largest in the federation
("whoever possesses Prussia possesses the Reich," Goebbels said). It held
out until after the September 1928 elections, when the Nazis won a paltry
2.6 percent of the vote, but after that dismal showing its prohibition looked
untenable, a restriction based on bad faith and sheer partisan politics.

Such a feeble electoral result brought the question of free speech in a
democratic system into clear focus. In 1928, the Nazis seemed less a threat
to democracy than a spent force, while the Weimar Republic seemed to

have put down genuine roots. Real wages were rising. Unemployment had dropped dramatically. Industrial production had climbed 25 percent since 1925. "For the first time since the war, the German people were happy," one journalist wrote. The astute political economist Joseph Schumpeter said in early 1929 that Weimar had achieved an "impressive stability" and that "in no sense, in no area, in no direction, are eruptions, upheavals or disasters probable." The real threat to democracy during these good times appeared to be not Hitler or his party but any bans on the leaders of political organizations. Of course, two years later, after the Nazis had grown to become the second largest party in the Reichstag, it was too late to outlaw them.

Germany was confronted with a cruel paradox of democracy: the enemies of the constitution could be prohibited only so long as they were insignificant and weak, but when they were insignificant, it seemed more important to uphold democratic principles than to outlaw antidemocratic groups like the Nazi and Communist parties, yet once the Nazis had achieved the significance of broad support, a ban became impossible. It required the most refined political sensibility to say just where the tipping point was. Even loyalty oaths wouldn't have helped, since Hitler had no problem pledging his loyalty to the constitution whenever he was obliged to. After 1930, saving Weimar rested in the hands not of judges and politicians with the power to censor or ban Hitler but with the free and democratic German people and the electoral decisions they made.

The if-onlys multiply at every turn beginning with the most obvious ones: if only Hitler had been a more talented painter, if only he had been a less talented orator. The November 1932 elections, when the Nazis lost one million votes, seemed to slow their momentum. There are historians who believe that the party had reached its limit, had peaked, and if only Hindenburg had found some alternative to appointing Hitler in January 1933, the threat would have dissipated. Predictions are guesswork, of course, but it's hard not to see an enormous degree of wishful thinking in this one, which is why other historians disagree with it. Predictions of Nazi decline ignore the very potent electoral advantages the party retained even after the November setback.

To begin with, they had made themselves the most diverse, most wideranging political party in the country. The other right-wing parties were devoted to the past, enmeshed with the hated economic establishment or, worse from a popular point of view, yearning for a restoration of the mon-

archy. (They often referred to the Weimar years as the "Kaiserless time.")
Those positions would do nothing to enhance their electability in popular
elections. The left-wing parties, on the other hand, preached a Marxism
either in its hard version (Communism) or soft version (Socialism) that
alienated more people than it attracted. And the centrist parties had simply evaporated as weak alternatives with no real ideas or solutions. Gregor
Strasser explained the inherent strength of his party's political thinking:
"From the right we shall take nationalism, which has so disastrously allied
itself with capitalism, and from the left we shall take socialism, which has
made such an unhappy union with internationalism. Thus we shall form
the National Socialism which will be the motive force of a new Germany
and a new Europe." Hitler was more succinct; no one summed up the
political situation better than he did: "The nationalists on the right lacked
social awareness," he said, and "the socialists on the left lacked national
awareness." The political genius of the Nazis was to recognize an opening
that once taken advantage of became so large that a Panzer division could
drive through it.

Only the Nazis were positioned to be all things to all men and women.
They made an appeal that reached beyond narrow economic interests
and narrow religious interests. The base of their support may have been
among Germany's small-town middle-class Protestants, but they also won
important backing in the cities with Catholics and blue-collar workers. As
more research is done on Nazi support, the wider and more diverse that
support appears to have been. Indeed, anyone who had lost patience with
traditional politics and was looking for a new direction was a potential
Nazi. They were the "catchall party of protest," calling for people to put
aside social divisions and class differences for the sake of a larger ideal,
the nation, the Volk.

The message had enormous appeal to any unaffiliated (and non-Jewish)
voter, and to students and the young, who provided the party with its
bustling energy, it was a political elixir. There were no more enthusiastic Nazis than the idealistic young. Across the English Channel, George
Orwell may have disliked what he saw, but he understood its power. Hitler,
he said, "grasped the falsity of the hedonistic attitude to life." The Nazis
knew that "human beings don't only want comfort, safety, short-working
hours, hygiene, birth-control and, in general, common sense; they also,
at least intermittently, want struggle and self-sacrifice, not to mention
drums, flags and loyalty parades." Or as one anti-Nazi German journal-

ist wrote, "Hitler was able to enslave his own people because he seemed to give them something that even the traditional religions could no longer provide: the belief in a meaning to existence beyond the narrowest self-interest."

The Nazis' greatest rivals, the Social Democrats, offered none of that. Instead, their worldview—with its promise of what Orwell called "comfort, safety, short-working hours"—only restricted their popular appeal. A perennial problem of democracy was finding a way to enable voters to combine their self-interest with some overarching notion of the public good. Not even America's Founding Fathers really had a solution to the conflict: their answer, drawn from their readings in classical antiquity, was to put their faith in a gentlemanly elite inspired by the Roman ideals of integrity, virtue, and disinterestedness, a "natural aristocracy" in Jefferson's words, or the kind of leaders Madison called "proper guardians of the public weal." But even if it became clear how to determine who these natural aristocrats and proper guardians were, the larger issue was how to persuade the mass of voters to elect them.

Appeals to nationalism squared this circle for the Nazis. The Social Democrats wanted to believe that Marxism did the same for them, since the self-interest of workers was considered to be the engine of broad social progress. So when they promised to safeguard the economic concerns of their constituents, they were able to tell themselves that they were preaching a universal message. In reality, the Social Democrats' Marxist ideology turned their party into one large special-interest group with no way of reaching beyond the closed circle of the working class. If you weren't a Marxist, the Social Democrats had little or nothing to offer you, certainly not compared to the utopian allure of the Nazis. As one observer wrote, "They are incapable of issuing exciting slogans or making promises about an exciting future."

As Marxists, the Social Democrats prided themselves on their rationality, their supposed grasp of the progress of Reason in history, and they went to the voters armed with facts and data to make tightly reasoned arguments for class solidarity. Wonkery was their stock in trade. But faced with the challenge of the Nazi dream factory, they were trapped in the labyrinth of their statistics. They only began to realize that electoral success required more than limited calls for economic self-interest once the Nazis had shown them the way, and by then it was too late. Emotional appeals, especially emotional appeals based on patriotism, were anathema to them, but what did they have as an alternative? The Nazis understood long before the Social Democrats did that internationalism was a vacuous aspiration and an electoral loser. By the time of the July 1932 election, the Social Democrats' dilemma had gotten through, and they took to pandering for votes. One party leader had inadvertently offered the perfect summation of the problem's inherent contradictions: "We have to work on feelings, souls and emotions so that reason wins the victory."

And so the traditional leftist goal of educating the masses gave way to the opportunistic aim of stirring them up. Speeches became shorter or shriveled to little more than slogans. In place of the Nazis' "Heil Hitler" salute, the Social Democrats encouraged their members to raise a clenched fist and cry "freedom." In place of a swastika, they paraded under a flag with three arrows. Goebbels complained that "they are now stealing our methods from us," but he needn't have worried. Whether one calls it demagoguery or simply democratic electioneering, emotional campaigns weren't in the Social Democrats' DNA; they were Johnny-come-latelys to the game of propaganda and mass persuasion and were never able to match the Nazis in showmanship or crowd appeal. Their hearts weren't in it. And they didn't have a magnetic leader like Adolf Hitler.

One contemporary called the crucial July 1932 election "a war of symbols," but in that war, the Nazis had all the best symbols. Hitler had turned up his nose at democracy but then he learned how to use it for his own ends. His opponents, the Social Democrats above all, turned up their noses at his demagogic methods—and then they lost.

THOUGH HITLER BECAME chancellor in January 1933, he still didn't have the complete victory he wanted, and after the March election he was still forced to govern in a coalition with right-wing nationalists. His initial opportunity to consolidate his rule came with the Reichstag fire in February, when a terrified parliament gave Hitler the power to suspend civil liberties. But his real triumph came only on March 23, when the Reichstag passed an amendment to the constitution, the Enabling Act, allowing Hitler to promulgate laws without the approval of parliament or the president. The act ostensibly solved the problem of Weimar's political stalemate, but the day it passed—by a vote of 444 in favor to 94 against—was the day German democracy committed suicide. And when Hindenburg died a year later, giving Hitler the opportunity to capture the office of president as well as chancellor, his power became truly absolute, and he systematically began to eliminate his political rivals and all potential opposition to his rule.

And yet only now does one arrive at the most depressing chapter of this history. For the majority support that Hitler was never able to attain as a democratic politician he now achieved as a brutal dictator. Violence and intimidation played their part in solidifying his position, to be sure, reaching a level never seen during the Weimar years, but the sad fact for the beleaguered opponents of the Third Reich was how genuinely popular he became in these years. Repression wasn't the basis of his power. As he said, he was the true representative of the German people, the actual "democrat." The mid-1930s were the real springtime for Hitler.

Of course, not everyone agreed. From afar, it was possible to insist that Hitler ruled by terror alone. It wasn't true but it was a comforting idea, much like the idea that the Nazis had "seized power" in 1933, because it offered a kind of solace where otherwise there might have been only despair. In 1940, Otto Strasser, who had been chased across Europe by the Gestapo following his break with the party and his escape from Germany in 1933, wrote that with thousands killed and millions more in concentration camps, "the majority of the German people have since 1933 carried on a ceaseless fight against Hitler." Strasser waxed metaphorical to emphasize his message of encouragement, writing of ice on a river. The ice seemed strong and immobile, he said, but underneath the river continued to flow and "one fine day" fissures would appear; the ice would weaken enough so that "it can be smashed with a single blow of an axe." Outsiders, he insisted, should not be deceived by Nazi propaganda. The day was near when Germans would be forced to choose between Hitler and the welfare of their country, and when that day arrived, "every German workman, peasant and soldier, every German intellectual and every German officer, will not hesitate to choose Germany." It wasn't only right-wing dissidents who saw, or hoped for, a strong underground opposition to Hitler. The Marxist playwright Bertolt Brecht liked to speak of a vast army of workers and socialists engaged in subversive activity inside the Third Reich against the small capitalist elite that dominated them. "The Germans are still fighting," he said, "because the ruling classes are still ruling."

Strasser's and Brecht's mistake was understandable. Exiles like them struggled to keep optimism alive during the years of the Third Reich with claims of widespread internal opposition to Hitler. "Am I not just as much a part of the German people as Adolf Hitler?" Strasser asked those willing to listen to him—and many outside Germany, in England, France, and the United States, wanted to believe what he was saying precisely because it affirmed their democratic faith, as well as appeared to make the hard choices they had to confront a great deal easier. Henry Kissinger was right to condemn their fecklessness.

For a realistic assessment, one had to turn to those who remained inside Germany. They painted a very different, much grimmer picture. One of the most sensitive and valuable witnesses was the journalist Sebastian Haffner, who stayed in Germany until 1938. Though no one expected it when Hitler became chancellor, Haffner notes, his policies were remarkably successful at first. Within three years, Germany went from deep economic depression to full employment. Hitler also rearmed the nation, making it once again the dominant military power on the continent. And then there were the foreign policy triumphs: the reoccupation of the Rhineland, the incorporation of Austria, the acquisition of the Sudetenland from Czechoslovakia. Looking back in April 1939, Hitler could say, "I overcame chaos in Germany, restored order, enormously raised production in all fields of our national economy. . . . I have led millions of deeply unhappy Germans, who had been snatched away from us, back into the Fatherland; I have restored the thousand-year-old historical unity of German living space." To which a despondent Haffner could only reply: "Damn it, it was all true, or nearly all."

Former opponents, Communists and Social Democrats among them, were won over by Hitler's undeniable accomplishments. Haffner estimates that at his height, Hitler had the support of 90 percent of the German people, and that a majority of those who had voted against him in 1933 were now Nazi Party members or at least party sympathizers. This, Haffner says, was "perhaps his greatest achievement of all." What's more, such wide popularity made it difficult for critics to find fault, even when they weren't being hounded by the Gestapo to conform. "I don't like that business with the Jews either," Haffner would hear from acquaintances, "but look at all the things the man has achieved!" What could one say? Haffner himself was immune to Hitler's appeal in part because he had many Jewish friends and a Jewish girlfriend. But articulating a response was not easy because rejecting Hitler for his faults seemed to require rejecting his achievements as well, and few wanted to go back to the frustrating political paralysis of Weimar. Opponents of the Nazis who had the inner strength to resist the inevitable self-doubt that had to creep in when everyone around them was applauding Hitler for his all-too-obvious achievements found themselves increasingly living in a world of intellectual isolation and muted skepticism. According to Haffner, "What passive resistance there was to the wave of Hitlerism in Germany was mainly caused by his anti-Semitism," but how many wanted to stand up and be labeled defenders of the Jews?

An intense loneliness was the affliction of dissenters inside Germany. Friedrich Reck, who, like Haffner, had Jewish friends, said he felt more isolated than if he had been living at the North Pole. As Hitler went from success to success, with ever greater popular acclaim, Reck, to his horror, found himself consumed by hate and turning against Germany itself. "I have thought hate, have lain down with hate in my heart, have dreamed hate and awakened with hate. I suffocate in the knowledge that I am the prisoner of a horde of vicious apes." It was an agonizing position for a German conservative to be in. Somehow, the country he loved had gone off the rails, and unwavering courage was required to remember its "glorious past" or to hope for a better future. If the vast majority of Germans were supporting the Third Reich, what did it mean for an anti-Nazi German nationalist to love Germany? Meanwhile, the few friends who thought as Reck did were either emigrating or dying. "A light goes out, and then another. Finally, the theater is dark and the stage, where all was light and animation only a short time before, is empty." Reck was arrested at the end of December 1944 and died in Dachau in February 1945.

The loneliness was even worse for Victor Klemperer, whose diaries are an invaluable source for understanding life in the Third Reich. A Protestant convert from Judaism, Klemperer was subjected to the Nazis' racial laws and therefore endured physical suffering and deprivation that Haffner and Reck never experienced. But, like Reck, Klemperer was a German nationalist whose homeland in the 1930s was undermining everything he had once taken to be true and shaking him to his core. "I simply cannot believe that the mood of the masses is really still behind Hitler," he wrote in August 1933, when he still hoped that Hitler was only a temporary aberration. But as the months and years passed, the evidence of Hitler's popularity became inescapable. In 1935, a friend, described by Klemperer as "previously completely democratic," declared herself impressed with the Nazis' rearmament program and the reoccupation of the Rhineland. She was, Klemperer sadly remarked, "vox populi."

Like Haffner, Klemperer estimated that 90 percent of Germans were behind the Nazis and that "Hitler really does embody the soul of the German people." Deserted by his friends, ripped from the quiet, scholarly life he had taken for granted, he felt abandoned, "homeless" in his own country and always tortured by a terrible, desolating isolation—"alone, absolutely alone."

Germany in the 1930s looked very different to the dissidents like Haffner, Reck, and Klemperer who remained than it did to the ones who got away, like Otto Strasser or Bertolt Brecht. By the end of the decade, dissenters at home knew all too painfully that Germany wasn't Strasser's flowing river with ice on the surface. It was ice all the way down.

HENRY KISSINGER HAS generally resisted saying much about his life under the Nazis and with reason, as biographers are always ready to reduce the complexities of mature experience to childhood traumas. "Let me tell you," he has said, "the political persecutions of my childhood are not what control my life." Kissinger insists that, like any other young boy, he knew the joys of youth, because he didn't really understand what was happening. The restrictions were "much harder on my parents than on me."

Kissinger and his brother did have the advantage of youthful resilience to shield them, but that's not to say they didn't experience deprivation and humiliation in their own young lives. Friends from that time say Kissinger's attempts to minimize the pain—"it was not an unhappy existence," he has insisted—are a kind of "self-delusion." One remembered: "We couldn't go anywhere without seeing the sign 'Juden Verboten.'" And every time they ventured outside, they risked verbal abuse or worse.

Now the beloved public swimming pool in Leutershausen was closed to Jews, as was the public school back in Fürth, as well as its sporting events. Kissinger was a soccer enthusiast so loyal that he and his brother took the chance of sneaking into the now-forbidden games by pretending to be gentiles. They didn't always avoid being roughed up. They also were in danger when the Nazis held their annual rallies at Nuremberg with the inevitable spillover into Fürth. Gangs of storm troopers marched down the town's streets, beating any Jews they happened upon. Jewish families knew enough to hide in their homes when the Nazis came to town. The Kissinger boys were sent to their grandparents' farm to keep them out of harm's way. But the headquarters of Fürth's Hitler Youth was not far from the Kissinger apartment so danger was always near. "Every walk in the street turned into an adventure," Kissinger has recalled.

It's fair to say that no one believes Kissinger when he tries to minimize the impact of the Nazis on his psyche and says "I was not consciously unhappy during the Hitler years"—not biographers and historians who have studied his boyhood, not friends who shared his experiences in Germany, not even his own mother, who remembered how frightened her boys were when Fürth's Hitler Youth took to the streets. "There was hardly anyone for the boys to play with," she has said. No doubt closer to the truth is the comment of the Jewish-German historian Peter Gay: "More than a half century after the collapse of Hitler's Thousand Year Reich, every refugee remains to some extent one of his victims. . . . Even the most fortunate Jew who lived under Hitler has never completely shaken off their experience." On a more personal level, only the most unimaginative or insensitive biographer would deny the impact that the arc of Louis Kissinger's life had on his adolescent son's moral development, and it would be hard, even misguided, for any Kissinger biographer to resist the temptation of seeing Kissinger's attention to the realities of power as compensation for his father's powerlessness. "Weakness," he wrote in a letter at the end of World War II, was "synonymous with death."

Maybe Henry Kissinger doesn't believe his denials himself. He once told an interviewer about his memory of "being parted from our German friends," and in his memoirs he speaks of the "cruel and degrading years" when he lived under the Nazis. Most important, in sharp and self-conscious contrast to his unworldly father, Kissinger has declared: "I had seen evil in the world." There can be no question that Hitler cast a lingering shadow not only over Kissinger's moral perspective as a statesman but also over his work as a writer and teacher. He is intent on conveying a dark lesson about history and human nature to his American readers, innocent and unworldly like his father, and therefore susceptible to disaster. "Nothing is more difficult for Americans to understand than the possibility of tragedy," he has said.

And yet Louis was as much a positive as a negative inspiration for his son. How could Kissinger not feel a genuine affection for this sweet, kindhearted, utterly innocent man? After three volumes and almost 4,000 pages, Kissinger closes his memoirs with "A Personal Note," a tribute to his parents and what their example has meant to him. His mother, he says, embodied the practical in life, his father the ethical, and he quotes a letter

Louis wrote to his two boys in 1946 when he thought he was near death and after his personal disappointments had led him to place all of his aspirations in them. "Always keep in mind that we find real satisfaction only in what we are doing for others. Try always to be good, faithful, helpful, reliable, selfless." He has tried to live up to his father's moral precepts, Kissinger writes, though he then adds that readers will have to decide for themselves whether or not he succeeded.

CHAPTER THREE

LEO STRAUSS AND HANNAH ARENDT

THE AMERICANIZATION OF HENRY KISSINGER BEGAN FORTH-
with, as soon as he set foot in the United States. He embraced assimilation with an enthusiasm that distinguished him from more reticent
and ambivalent friends, claiming that he never felt homesick, though the
same could hardly be said for his parents. Within a few weeks, the sports-
obsessed adolescent had replaced his beloved soccer with baseball and was
soon attending Yankee games. Somewhere along the way he developed a
taste for Coca-Cola and began reading *Time* magazine. Nothing delighted
him more about his new country, surely, than the realization that he didn't
have to cross the street when he spotted a group of boys approaching. He
no longer needed to worry about being beaten up when he went outside.
And he had something of a head start in the crucial matter of learning
English, having acquired the fundamentals as a student in Fürth, although
his American high school noted that he suffered from "a foreign language
handicap." His parents insisted on speaking only English at home, and
"Heinz" became "Henry." Why, unlike his brother, he never succeeded in
losing his Bavarian accent has been a source of much psychological speculation and more than the occasional joke.

Unlike his years as a child in Fürth, the teenage Kissinger of Washington Heights was a highly successful high school student despite any language impediments, which remained true even after he was forced to take
a menial day job to help support the family and could attend only night
classes. The easygoing ways of small-town Bavaria, the idyllic summers on
his grandparents' farm, the security and complacency of a comfortable,

middle-class upbringing with an assured future were gone, replaced by the competitive anxieties of the upwardly striving immigrant boy who was starting out a new life in a strange land with literally nothing and with nothing to lose. America was still suffering through the Great Depression, but it did offer opportunities, especially to those willing to work as hard as the young, driven Kissinger. Because he did well in math, he entered City College with the goal, ambitious for someone in his position, of becoming an accountant. He was attending a New York Giants football game when he heard the news that Pearl Harbor had been attacked.

The Army completed Henry Kissinger's Americanization. He was drafted in 1942 and in February 1943 was sent to Spartanburg, South Carolina, for basic training. It was his first taste of an America that was completely alien to him, yet he wrote home that he found the military "exhilarating." He had been compelled to give up some of his Orthodox habits when he was employed back in New York and had to work on Saturdays. The Army completed the process—the dictates of military life left no room for Saturday Sabbaths or kosher cooking—and Kissinger abandoned whatever religious practices he may have been holding on to, though not his Jewish identity. As compensation, the Army expanded his horizons in a way that a sheltered Jewish boy from Washington Heights could never have imagined and that even his brief time at City College, with its predominantly Jewish student body, could not provide. The Army, he said, was "a tremendous education for me."

In November 1944 Private Kissinger was sent to Germany, where his natural brilliance and a command of the German language made for a rapid rise. Assigned to Army Intelligence, he was so effective at weeding out committed Nazis and breaking up sleeper cells that he was awarded the Bronze Star and promoted to staff sergeant. At the same time, he displayed what can only be called an extraordinary sensitivity toward the supporters of a regime that had killed many of his relatives and sent him and his family into exile.

Kissinger decided to stay in the Army after the war ended, and by the time he completed his military career in 1947, he was no longer the inexperienced, religiously observant young man of 1943. "When I went into the Army, I was a refugee, and when I got out, I was an immigrant." He had gained self-confidence and self-awareness. "Now I knew exactly what I want and I shall go after it," he declared. The world had opened up before him. Harvard beckoned.

Kissinger had become a U.S. citizen while in the service. The Army, he said, "made me feel like an American." But as any native-born citizen knows, there are Americans and there are Americans. Some Americans despise other Americans. Even though the only home he had known in the United States was New York City, the assimilated Kissinger didn't mean that as an American he felt like someone from the East Coast. "I hate N.Y.," he wrote to his parents in 1947. America for him was embodied in the small-town boys from Indiana and Wisconsin whom he met in his division, the infantrymen he called "heartland Americans" on one occasion, "real middle-Americans," on another. "I found that I liked these people very much," and when he entered Harvard, he requested a "Midwesterner" for a roommate. Many things distinguished Kissinger from the cosmopolitan, sophisticated, urban, and urbane friends and associates he developed through the years, but one of the most significant, certainly, was what it meant to him to be an "American."

IN THE THIRD VOLUME of his memoirs, *Years of Renewal*, Henry Kissinger praises President Gerald Ford for his strength of character, which Kissinger attributes to Ford's all-American background and upbringing. "Nowhere else is there to be found the same generosity of spirit and absence of malice," Kissinger writes, as in "small-town America."

This is an odd, even remarkable, statement coming from an East Coast intellectual and former Harvard professor, one that is likely to bring a reader up short. For it reveals nothing of the all-too-familiar, century-long indictment of the American heartland to be found in books ranging all the way from Sherwood Anderson's *Winesburg, Ohio* to Tara Westover's *Educated*. For those traveling in literary and academic circles, especially the ones Kissinger frequented at Harvard and in New York before he entered government service, "absence of malice" is not a phrase normally associated with small-town America, which more commonly has been considered a bastion of soul-deadening provincialism, to be fled at the first opportunity. Less generously, it's viewed as a fount of intolerance, repressiveness, and gun-toting violence, once the home of the Ku Klux Klan, now a potential breeding ground of right-wing militias. Grant Wood painted figures of small-town rigidity. Woody Allen imagined a landscape of serial killers. The heartland fostered suicidal desperation in Hollis Brown, the isolated South Dakota farmer who, in Bob Dylan's words, "lived on the outside of town," and who murdered his wife and five children before turning his gun on himself.

But unlike so many native artists and writers, Kissinger wasn't running away from Middle America as they were; rather, as an immigrant, he was embracing it as the real America. A common belief often expressed by new arrivals is that they love the United States more than the native-born do because they made an active choice to become part of it. Such genuine and heartfelt emotions can be witnessed at any swearing-in ceremony of new citizens, a proud occasion that is invariably joyous and tearful. And not only the unsophisticated and unlettered feel that way. In an overtly sentimental gesture, the normally hard-boiled Christopher Hitchens, himself an immigrant who chose to become an American, arranged to have his own swearing-in take place at the Jefferson Memorial, attended by a few close friends and officiated by George W. Bush's director of home-land security. "On the day that I swore my great oath," Hitchens proudly noted in his autobiography, "dozens of Afghans and Iranians and Iraqis did the same." He was delighted to be one of them.

Kissinger's love of America is the immigrant's love of America, idealis-tic, romanticized, a love of what he perceives as its core values. Even as a boy in Germany, he has said, the United States was an inspiration to him, "an incredible place where tolerance was natural and personal freedom unchallenged." Never mind the treatment of women, blacks, Native Amer-icans, Asians, Jews, homosexuals, and other groups outside the "main-stream" that has so preoccupied American intellectuals in this century and the last. He took the nation's expressed ideals seriously because as a foreign arrival he "always had a special feeling for what America means, which native-born citizens took for granted." Those native-born were too quick to see the country's flaws, while too often ignoring its many virtues (and to judge those flaws on the basis of some perfect notion of justice in be found in their imaginations but nowhere on earth). When Amer-ica made mistakes, as it did with its involvement in Vietnam, Kissinger saw not mercenary motives or imperialistic malevolence but an excess of goodwill. Such an attitude did not always endear him to his colleagues in the academic community, who were more inclined toward distanced neutrality or skepticism or even cynicism about their country. Kissinger's devotion was likely to be considered a kind of flag-waving, out of place in the cosmopolitan circles of Cambridge, Massachusetts.

For his part, Kissinger deplored "the insularity of the academic profession and the arrogance of the Harvard faculty" (though perhaps his way of connecting with people who were, after all, not only his colleagues but also his friends was to call himself "arrogant" as well). He had his own conversation-stopping response to Eastern disdain for the great fly-over between the coasts: "Having found a haven from Nazi tyranny in the United States, I had personally experienced what our nation meant to the rest of the world, especially to the persecuted and disadvantaged." The negativity he encountered among friends and associates disturbed him, because a similar negativity among Germany's sophisticates during the Weimar years had helped to undermine social institutions and individual morality, leading to catastrophe. Yes, the United States had its faults, but they should not blind native-born critics to "its greatness, its idealism, its humanity and its embodiment of mankind's hopes."

Expressions of patriotism are sprinkled throughout Kissinger's writings and interviews, though never really gathered together into a coherent declaration. In the three volumes of his massive memoirs, his Middle American sympathies emerge only fleetingly. A European exile who took the time to give more focused expression to the same kind of sentiments was the Polish Nobel Prize–winning poet Czeslaw Milosz. Born in 1911, he, like Kissinger, was an escapee from European tyranny, though in his case the tyrant was Stalin, not Hitler. Like Kissinger, he tended to look over the shoulders of the urban sophisticates who were his natural associates to the nation's heartland, discovering a worthiness that he cherished where native-born intellectuals were likely to see only humdrum provincialism.

"The United States is a land of virtue," Milosz writes, but that virtue was mainly to be found in rural America, "nourished on naïveté, ignorance and ordinary dullness." He sings the praises of unpretentious, even corny diversions like country fairs and parades down Main Street, with their garish displays of American flags, floats, high school bands, pom-pom girls, shopkeepers dressed like oriental potentates, beauty queens "of the melon growers." For America's disaffected, condescending intellectuals, such goings-on were "nothing more than the dull, insipid life of yokels and provincial boors. I, however, have a wonderful time at country fairs and applaud them." For Milosz, again like Kissinger, had seen too much of history's tragedies and knew how easily simple, life-sustaining virtue— "heavy decency" he called it—could be destroyed by irresponsible utopian illusions, the deracinated dreams of educated urban sophisticates. Ordinary people performing their ordinary tasks keep society functioning, and "there is no reason to gloat at the stupidity of average people because their horizons are narrowed by their daily work and pastimes." Milosz has no hesitation in plumping for "the so-called average man against the arrogance of the intellectuals."

And yet, this Frank Capraesque populism does not sit comfortably with him. He is too much the history-laden European, weighed down by a wider and a grimmer background than the simple folk he professes to admire. He is himself an intellectual, fully engaged in a life of ideas. And he is a pessimist too, who sees human existence "chiefly composed of pain and the fear of death." He may enjoy the virtues of small-town America, but only as an outsider looking in: he can never be part of it. "America pushes you to the wall and compels a kind of stoic virtue: to do your best and at the same time to preserve a certain detachment that derives from an awareness of the ignorance, childishness and incompleteness of all people, oneself included." Milosz knows too much. Caught between worlds, he is condemned to alienation and to irony.

Much like Henry Kissinger. There has never been a more ironic figure in American public life than the self-mocking Kissinger. When a friend had to cancel lunch because of illness, Kissinger, then secretary of state, sent him a note: "Most people go to the hospital *after* they see me, not before." But if his patriotism is deep and indisputable, it tells only half the story. The other half comprises his doubts, his fears, his insecurities, his sense of his new countrymen's blindnesses and limitations, his uneasiness about humankind in general, his dire forebodings. If he was separated from his academic colleagues by his immigrant's faith in America, he was separated from most other Americans by his sense of tragedy. His countrymen enjoyed happy endings; he didn't believe in them. He admired the political institutions of the United States, but he couldn't have full confidence in them because he had seen how the processes of democracy could go disastrously wrong. He was no populist. As early as 1939, he had written to a friend: "My personal impression of America is very two-sided: In some regards I admire it; in others I despise the approach to life here."

Before 2016, when Kissinger's fellow Americans imagined the internal destruction of the nation's liberal institutions (as opposed to destruction by America's outside enemies, whether Communists, terrorists, aliens from outer space, or a large asteroid), what they generally envisaged was a military coup or a plot by a greedy, moneyed cabal. Despite the writings of Tocqueville, the notion of a tyrannical majority had penetrated only on rare occasions—Sinclair Lewis's *It Can't Happen Here*, for instance, or Philip Roth's *The Plot Against America*. The Pentagon or CIA might represent a threat to liberty, as might Wall Street, but rarely Main Street. In the pre-Trump United States, even the elitists were populists—and if there was a contradiction between their rhetorical commitment to democracy's common man and their disdain for the actual lives of Middle Americans, it was a contradiction they were never able to resolve because it was irresolvable.

Kissinger lived the opposite contradiction: appreciation of the virtues of the Middle American common man but skepticism about democracy. He may have seemed naïve to his academic colleagues because of his love of his country, but to him they were the naïve ones because they lacked the imagination to understand how badly things could turn out, liberty and free elections notwithstanding. Democracy was admirable when the conditions were right, but it was no security blanket, no all-purpose panacea. Even when he was employed by the Council on Foreign Relations in the 1950s and 1960s, working with some of the finest minds in the foreign policy establishment, Kissinger felt a "European" superiority to the optimistic Americans, who tended to believe that peace was the normal state of affairs in the world, that the United States represented a universal prototype, that every problem had a solution, and that the solution was always the same: democracy, and then more democracy.

Kissinger was the pessimist, the temperamental outsider, prone to suspicion and paranoia. Friends remembered him as "brooding" and "melancholic," filled with a sense of imminent doom. "Life involves suffering," Kissinger had written as a young man old before his time, in an echo of his somber elder Milosz. This was not an outlook likely to engender the kind of "generosity of spirit" that Kissinger so admired in Gerald Ford and other small-town Midwesterners or the sort of joyful expectancy to be seen on the faces of the country's newest citizens at their swearing-in ceremonies. It was more like world-weary resignation. To any German Jew forced into exile by the Nazis, there could not be an unrestrained, optimistic commitment to his adopted land but only ambivalence—gratitude, even admiration, because it had been a "haven" that saved his life but also alienation, even resistance, because coming to America had not been a choice he had made for himself.

The refugees from Hitler were not like other immigrants to the United States. They had not been pulled toward America by the promise of a better life extended by a beckoning Statue of Liberty but pushed from Germany by the mortal threat of the extermination camp. For the gentiles among them, like Thomas Mann and many other artists and political dissidents of both the right and the left, they could have stayed had they wanted to, though at the cost of sacrificing their work, their beliefs, their conscience, and their personal integrity. Admittedly, it wasn't much of a choice, but it was a choice nonetheless—requiring internal exile rather than external exile. And for better or worse, many Germans made it, though some, like Friedrich Reck, still ended up losing their lives. For Germany's Jews, at least the ones who grasped what the advent of the Third Reich meant for them, there wasn't the same kind of choice. They were forced to flee, not because of what they had written or what they believed but because of who they were. They were unwilling exiles who, in Louis Kissinger's words, hadn't "done anything to anyone."

Of Germany's half million Jews, about 300,000 were able to get out in time, though they had no particular commitment to their places of destination, whether the United States, Britain, South America, or the dozens of other locations around the world where chance or luck had deposited them. Only the Communists who escaped to the Soviet Union really had a preference (though perhaps not for long once they got there). A story made the rounds about one man in a German travel agency hoping to flee his native land who was looking over a globe, his finger stopping on Australia, then South Africa, then Shanghai. Finally, he pushed the globe away and asked the clerk, "Haven't you got anything else?"

Palestine was just one stopping place among others. Zionism was not an influential motivation for the extruded Jews—back in Germany assimilationist Jews were more likely to buy a Christmas tree than to dream of next year in Jerusalem—and of the 70,000 who went to Palestine, only a minority did so out of a genuine commitment to building a Jewish state. The true Zionists turned a skeptical eye to the new arrivals and joked, "Did they come out of conviction or out of Germany?"

The 132,000 German Jews who landed in the United States were no more committed to American ideals than the Germans in Palestine were committed to Zionist ideals. Indeed, they tended to be no different in their opinion of America than the non-Jewish refugees—and that opinion was not a positive one. As one scholar of the exiles writes: "American culture seemed to the majority of émigrés both simplistic and crude." The United States may have been a land of liberty, but it was also materialistic, philistine, and coarse. The habits of civilization were in short supply. There were no proper coffeehouses. The beer was weak. Even the bread tasted bad. For a young Henry Kissinger, the problem was shallowness, a lack of serious- ness: "The American trait I dislike the most is their casual approach to life. No one thinks ahead further than the next minute, no one has the cour- age to look life squarely in the eye." The Marxists among the émigrés were particularly scornful, having been forced to take refuge in, of all places, the center of capitalism, and they self-consciously dissociated themselves from their new surroundings. If the exiles felt any patriotic loyalty at all, it was to the old, pre-Hitler Germany.

A number of refugees kept their distance by never even bothering to learn English, expecting to return to their homeland at the first opportu- nity; Hitler, after all, was "an error of history." One writer who did take the trouble to learn English nonetheless felt that by giving up German he had lost "the language of one's dreams." The future Nobel Prize–winner Elias Canetti remarked: "If, despite everything, I should survive, then I owe it to Goethe." Astoundingly, one prominent German-Jewish refugee, Franz Neumann, said there was more anti-Semitism in the United States than in Germany. And to make matters worse for the exiles, reinforcing their isolation, no one in America wanted to hear about the threat that Hitler posed to the world. They had touched down in a self-absorbed place that didn't care about anything outside itself. Those who insisted on issuing warnings were called, in Arthur Koestler's words, "fomenters of hatred." Golo Mann, Thomas's son, complained that he and his colleagues had been turned into so many Cassandras—"to know and not be listened to." They were alienated from their native land, but they were alienated from their new home as well.

The refugees were a remarkably diverse group: artists, scholars, busi- nessmen, scientists, theologians, thousands of individuals both dis- tinguished and undistinguished. In political terms, they were liberals, socialists, pacifists, conservatives, aristocrats, monarchists. Almost any generalization about them would leave some significant number out. Just about the only thing they had in common was the luck to have ended up in the United States. But by the conclusion of the war, they could roughly be divided into two broad categories—the minority who decided to return to Germany or elsewhere in Europe and the majority who decided to remain in the United States. Those who did go back had their individual reasons, not easily summarized. Jean-Michel Palmier, a scholar who has studied them closely, writes: "The decision whether to return or remain in exile is complex and difficult to analyze. In many cases it was hard to foresee." Though not so hard, perhaps, in the case of one of the most prominent of the returnees, Theodor Adorno. In his 15 years of residence in America, beginning in 1938, he never adapted to the sanctuary that was the United States, never felt the gratitude of a Henry Kissinger. Though an extreme case, he can serve as a representative of those who left America.

As an intellectual, Adorno was repelled by the shallow conformity of the United States; a thinker, he said, had to "eradicate himself as an autonomous being." As a Marxist, he rejected what he saw as America's free-wheeling capitalism, going so far as to claim that German was a better language than English for expressing the dialectical thought he and his leftist colleagues engaged in. And as a cultural elitist, he couldn't abide American popular culture; Adorno made a reputation for himself as a philosopher of modern music, assisting Thomas Mann with the musical passages of *Doctor Faustus*, but he harbored a well-known, very public detestation of jazz (which might leave any native-born American to wonder just how perceptive he was as a philosopher of music). For Adorno, it was three strikes and he was out of here. Despite his 15 years, as one of his biographers has said, he never looked back. Of course, it helped that as an eminent thinker he had a position in Frankfurt to return to (the city now has its very own Adornoplatz).

Those who stayed did so for reasons just as diverse as the reasons of those who returned. Some, like Albert Einstein, had such a degree of fame that life was easy for them under any circumstances. Others were won over by the success they achieved. The film director Otto Preminger said that every day he felt "more in love with my new country." Success came more easily for some, like engineers, scientists, and technicians, who needed only to learn a bit of the language to find work. Lawyers had a harder time, as did all those trained in the humanities, like Louis Kissinger. There may have been little reason for him to remain in America, so deep was his unhappiness, except for one thing: he had nothing to return to in Germany. And so despite the hardship and the disaffection, despite his inbred conservatism and German nationalism, he stayed, and he transferred all his hopes to Walter and Henry. As he told his two boys, "I know the different conditions in this country . . . made it impossible for me to be a guide for you both as I would have been in normal times. But I subordinated all my personal decisions to your future."

Henry was 22 when World War II ended, old enough to remain in Germany if he had wanted to, but with the rest of his family in America, that was never really an option, even after he had extended his military service; his parents had made the choice for him. In any case, the Army had turned him into an American and an American citizen, and "home" was the United States. Still, the German-Jewish refugee's complicated feelings about the United States—the gratitude combined with alienation bordering on dread—remained with him as he evolved from a teenager in Washington Heights, whose highest aspiration was to become an accountant, to the Harvard University Wunderkind, whose undergraduate dissertation became a legend in its own time, to the professorial wheeler-dealer, rising effortlessly through the American Establishment, to the powerful mover and shaker, whose imprint on foreign policy was lasting and lastingly controversial.

Kissinger never paused in the long journey of his spectacular career to work out his ideas about politics, democracy, and the American way of governance. He was a historian and a statesman, not a political thinker. One of his Harvard professors reported that he "was only average in his abilities as a political philosopher." But there was philosophy contained in his policies, and there were others, much above average, who may be said to have done his thinking for him, who reflected on the condition of the German-Jewish émigré, with all its complex and inevitable ambivalences, and thought deeply about the problems of democracy and modern society. Two in particular had an impress on political thought that has been as lasting—and as controversial—as Henry Kissinger's impact has been on international affairs.

LEO STRAUSS AND Hannah Arendt were a generation older than Henry Kissinger, and neither had any lasting ties to him. His one professional connection to Arendt seemed to have occurred in 1953, when she wrote an article for *Confluence*, the magazine he was running at the time. The experience was not a happy one; she complained about what she considered his heavy-handed editing. Strauss does not even have the connection of a bad editorial experience. What, then, is the link between Strauss and Arendt on one side and Kissinger on the other?

The fact is that the three are joined together by broad commonalities based on the similarities of their backgrounds, their life histories, and their existential situations in relation to the world they were so unwillingly thrown into. Intellectual historians speak of "family resemblances" among thinkers: Strauss and Arendt are, philosophically speaking, Kissinger's first cousins. Kissinger's "Americanism" was a complicated matter, and he never showed any inclination to try to disentangle it. But to philosophers like Strauss and Arendt, such complicated subjects were red meat to be devoured. Their writings throw Kissinger's own thinking into sharp relief, enabling us to grasp its contours and foundations, because they addressed directly themes that appear in his own publications only as subtexts, if that. Perhaps most important, Strauss, Arendt, and Kissinger all started out in America in the same place, rejecting the ideologies that provided the grounding for the vast majority of their fellow German-Jewish émigrés. They were neither Marxists nor Zionists (though all felt a deep emotional attachment to Israel), nor did they adopt the quasi-official ideology of the United States, liberal democracy. What was left for them? Arendt provided the most succinct and memorable answer: all three engaged in what she called "thinking without a banister."

In practice, what this meant was that Kissinger, Strauss, and Arendt were Germans who cherished what Germany had given them but were deprived of their identities by the Nazis; Jews who never denied their backgrounds but for whom the content of Judaism was a problem and Zionism no solution; naturalized Americans genuinely appreciative of the shelter the United States had provided to them but whose patriotism did not translate into a wholehearted identification with their adopted country; freethinking individuals who opposed tyranny but nursed a deep suspicion of democracy and its majoritarian processes; moralists whose post-Nietzschean morality, difficult to articulate at best, rested on none of the traditional ethical foundations and therefore aroused suspicions among those who weren't even aware of the banisters they themselves were leaning on; even, perhaps, religious thinkers of a kind (if the word is used in its broadest, most metaphysical sense), who could not subscribe to the antispiritual doctrines of either Marxism or liberalism—the one too materialistic, the other too hedonistic—but whose religion did not necessarily include a belief in God. They accepted the findings of modern science—indeed, sometimes relied on it in their own arguments against dogmatists, including those dogmatists who happened to be scientists—while denying that it could provide answers to life's most profound questions or unravel its deepest secrets. Science could not offer values or guidance in how to live one's life.

Nor could the quantitative methods of empiricism that were so prevalent in American society. Concerned above all with ideas, they did not believe that truth could be arrived at by counting noses in a poll, by taking a vote, or by employing the statistical procedures of contemporary social science. None of that mattered to the freethinker. Sociology, Arendt once said, has an "inherent mistrust of thought." Arendt and Strauss had an inherent mistrust of sociology. Modern social science, Strauss remarked, fostered "conformism and philistinism." (Even more comprehensively, Strauss would say, "Society will always try to tyrannize thought.") Polls and statistics were of even less help in the formulation of foreign policy. When, toward the end of his life, Kissinger made it his mission to warn of the dangers of modern technology, he echoed Strauss's and Arendt's opposition to quantification as the enemy of genuine thinking: "The internet's purpose is to ratify knowledge through the accumulation and manipulation of ever-expanding data," he wrote, but in this way "information threatens to overwhelm wisdom," leaving no room for the operation of human consciousness and its associated qualities of subjectivity, agency, responsibility, introspection, and freedom. Numbers were no substitute for thinking. The strength of Kissinger's, Strauss's, and Arendt's ideas derived from the value they placed on free, detached thought, which, all three concluded, was best achieved in their adopted country.

And yet none of them was a full-throated defender of American institutions, raising suspicions that they were hostile to democracy itself and provoking warnings about their "questionable influence." Like Kissinger, Strauss and Arendt were not liberal democrats in any way that an American would understand or—and this is the essential point—perhaps in any real way at all. They always kept their distance. "The nub of the matter is that both radiate disapproval of modern democracy," writes George Kateb, a professor of politics at Princeton and the author of a study of Arendt. "Anyone committed to modern democracy should resist the influence of both these German-American philosophers."

There's no question that neither Strauss nor Arendt was morally "committed to modern democracy" in Kateb's words, any more than Kissinger was. Their intellectual passions and moral allegiances lay elsewhere. Personal freedom, not majoritarian rule, was what claimed their loyalty and kept them in the country most likely to offer it. But like Tocqueville, they never believed that America's political institutions were the only ones that could guarantee freedom of thought. Strauss said it could be found not only in the democratic United States but also under the Kaiser in "post-Bismarckian Wilhelminian Germany." Indeed, he argued, the belief that democracy was the one valid political system could lead to Jacobin terror because "the people" would come to be identified with "the virtuous," endangering anyone who, for whatever reason, was considered an outsider to this potential mobocracy.

Like Kissinger, Strauss and Arendt have been called antidemocratic, which is not true. It would be more accurate to call them ademocratic, or nondemocratic, or at worst undemocratic (which is not the same thing as antidemocratic). The problems they wrestled with, whether in philosophy or international affairs, pushed democratic theory and values to the side. As Arendt wrote: "The politically most important yardstick for judging events in our time" was "whether they serve totalitarian domination or not." Democracy, they knew, had already failed that test. As Jews in Weimar Germany, all three had watched "modern democracy" facilitate the rise of Adolf Hitler while liberals flailed helplessly, and so they could never become the conviction democrats their American-born critics demanded they be. "Liberalism, the only ideology that ever tried to articulate and interpret the genuinely sound elements of free societies," Arendt said, "has demonstrated its inability to resist totalitarianism so often that its failure may already be counted among the historical facts of our century." Strauss said much the same thing. "All rational liberal philosophic positions have lost their significance and their power. One may deplore this, but I for one cannot bring myself to cling to philosophic positions which have been shown to be inadequate." The Weimar experience, he wrote, "presented the sorry spectacle of justice without a sword or of justice unable to use the sword." That "sorry" Weimar experience was essential to the thinking of all three of these German-Jewish refugees.

LEO STRAUSS WAS born in 1899 to a middle-class German-Jewish family in the town of Kirschhain in rural Hesse. His father was a successful grain merchant. The Strausses were Orthodox; "the 'ceremonial' laws," Strauss recalled, "were rather strictly observed," but this did not present any social problems with their neighbors because, as Strauss remembered, the Jews of the area "lived in a profound peace." Strauss was a young boy when anti-Semitism arrived on the family doorstep, not through German bigotry of any kind, but in the form of some Russian Jews, victims of a recent pogrom, who were passing through on the way to Australia. It was "an unforgettable moment," he said.

A shy, bookish, precocious boy, Strauss read the major thinkers—Plato, Schopenhauer, Nietzsche—as a teenager, but though he was absorbing big ideas he was dreaming only small dreams. At 16, he said, he had already developed a life plan: he would raise rabbits and read Plato while working as a postmaster. He also became a Zionist, if a tentative and questioning one; eventually the questions became so weighty that he shed that particular commitment (though never his loyalty to Israel). During World War I, he served the fatherland as an interpreter, and in 1919 he entered the local university at Marburg, then studied at Hamburg and Freiburg, receiving instruction from some of Germany's greatest minds—Ernst Cassirer, Edmund Husserl, and most important of all, Martin Heidegger, whom Strauss saw as opening up "the possibility of a genuine return to classical philosophy, to the philosophy of Plato and Aristotle." He earned a Ph.D. when he was 22. In 1925, he took a job with the German Academy of Jewish Research in Berlin to edit the writings of Moses Mendelsohn while working on a study of Spinoza. *Spinoza's Critique of Religion*, his first book, appeared in 1930. Two years later, with assistance from a Rockefeller Foundation grant, he was off to Paris, where he was living when Hitler came to power.

Strauss was prescient enough not to try to return to Germany and to his relatives (almost all of whom were eventually to perish), but he wasn't exactly stranded. In 1934, he moved to London to do research on Hobbes, and though he didn't have much money—his Rockefeller grant was extended but now he had a family to support—he found that the British way of life suited him. "If I had a modest income, I could be the happiest man in the world," he wrote, somewhat bizarrely, it must be said, one year after Hitler had taken power. "I like this country." He devoured Shakespeare, Thackeray, and P. G. Wodehouse, expressed a preference for Jane Austen over Dostoyevsky, and even for English cooking over French. "The hams taste too good as to consist of pork," he joked to a friend, "and therefore they are allowed by the Mosaic law according to atheistic interpretation."

His book on Hobbes was published in 1936. But while it was well received, employment was hard to find in Depression-era England, especially for a German-Jewish thinker who was wrestling with obscure topics that didn't make a whole lot of sense to his English neighbors, like what Strauss called the "theologico-political predicament," and in 1937 he accepted a temporary position at Columbia University. A year later he found a post at the New School for Social Research, known as the University in Exile because it was home to a corps of German-Jewish refugees. In 1948, he moved to the University of Chicago, where he remained until his retirement in 1967, building a name for himself as an extraordinary, life-changing teacher and laying the foundation for what would eventually become an international reputation. He continued teaching and writing up to the time of his death in 1973. His fame and influence increased exponentially after that.

Hannah Arendt's life story was more dramatic than Strauss's, as befits a personality that was more flamboyant and uninhibited. Arendt was born in Hanover in 1906 and was four years old when her family moved to the cosmopolitan port city of Königsberg. Her father was an engineer who died when she was young; her mother was a musician. Both were socialists and Reform Jews, though religion played no part in Arendt's upbringing. When she was growing up, the idea of being Jewish never arose. However, unlike so many other assimilated German Jews, the Arendts never gave any thought to converting to Christianity. That would have been a step too far. Speaking of her mother, Arendt said, "She would never have baptized me! I think she would have boxed my ears right and left if she had ever found out that I had denied being a Jew."

The young Hannah was a rebel from an early age. Her biographer, Elisabeth Young-Bruehl, writes that "her displays of independence and willfulness were ceaseless." But she was brilliant, too, reading Kant and Kierkegaard as an adolescent. During her years of university study, beginning at Marburg in 1924 and continuing at Freiburg and Heidelberg, she, like Strauss, worked with the finest minds in Germany—Edmund Husserl, Karl Jaspers, Rudolf Bultmann, and Martin Heidegger, of whom she formed the same high opinion as Strauss, though she had the advantage (if that's what it was) of sharing a bed with him. Her doctoral thesis, on the concept of love in St. Augustine, was completed in 1927 and published in 1929. She was on a path to becoming a cloistered academic and highly abstracted intellectual. As she later wrote to her friend Mary McCarthy, "I was interested neither in history nor in politics when I was young. If I can be said to 'have come from anywhere,' it was from the tradition of German philosophy."

Hitler changed all that. Arendt dates her turn toward politics to the

Reichstag fire of February 27, 1933, and she began working for a Zionist group. She had decided she could no longer be a bystander. Arrested in 1933, she was lucky to be released after eight days and luckier still to escape Germany for France, where she continued her Zionist activities until the French surrender in 1940—though she was not a Zionist as such, never believing in a Jewish state and always critical of her colleagues in the movement. Her attitude was: "If one is attacked as a Jew, one must defend oneself as a Jew." Appealing to justice and universal human rights was what the weak and powerless did.

Arendt was arrested again, this time by the French just before the Germans marched into Paris, as part of a roundup of "enemy aliens." She was lucky once again to manage an escape from the internment camp where she and thousands of others were being held; most of the women with her died at Auschwitz. She made her way south to Marseilles, then, just a step ahead of the police, to Portugal and finally in 1941 to the United States. Safe at last, she occupied herself with research into anti-Semitism, while writing columns for the German-Jewish newspaper *Aufbau* and teaching part time at Brooklyn College. She became an editor at a publishing house specializing in Jewish themes and started contributing to America's foremost intellectual magazines like *Partisan Review* and *Commentary*. The appearance of *The Origins of Totalitarianism* in 1951 brought her permanent fame. From that time on, her life as a very public intellectual was a whirligig of publishing, lecturing, teaching, travel, and recognition. The appearance of *Eichmann in Jerusalem* in 1963 caused intense controversy because she had dared to suggest that Adolf Eichmann, while undeniably a mass murderer, was less a monster than an empty-headed bureaucrat and that the Jewish leaders had played a role in the destruction of their own communities. The same year that her Eichmann book came out, she secured a position at the University of Chicago's Committee on Social Thought, staying for four years before returning to New York and a post at the New School. A nonstop smoker (in her youth, she smoked cigars), she died from a heart attack in 1975 at age 69.

Arendt and Strauss overlapped at the University of Chicago from 1963 to 1967, though they had known each other for many years before. Both had been among the most enthusiastic admirers of Heidegger in Germany, and both had benefited from the generosity and solicitousness of the Columbia University scholar Salo Baron, the first person to hold a chair in Jewish history in the United States, when they arrived in America as refu-

good. One upstate Straussian, Anne Norton, sees a "family resemblance" between Strauss and Arendt. They were, she writes, "alike in their tastes and ties, their intellectual genealogies and their historical experiences. They were alike in what they had learned, whom they had studied and how it had served them." In that both were critics of modern mass society and consumer culture, opposed the positivist and quantitative orientation common among their academic colleagues, revered classical Greek philosophy, admired America's Founding Fathers, worried about what they viewed as the threat of contemporary nihilism, affirmed the importance of a private sphere against a liberal hegemony, believed in the autonomy of thought, and perceived an intellectual decline both in the West in general and the United States in particular, Norton is surely correct.

But Strauss and Arendt were only colleagues at Chicago, not friends or allies—so much alike in ethnic and educational background, yet divided by personality, temperament, and philosophical perspective. It's said that Strauss paid court to Arendt in Germany and that her rejection left him with a legacy of enmity. When the controversy over *Eichmann in Jerusalem* erupted, Arendt reported that Strauss was "the only person here on the campus who is agitating against me." She wasn't surprised. For her part, Arendt thought Strauss had "a truly gifted intellect," but as she told her friend and mentor Karl Jaspers, "I don't like him."

The dislike each felt for the other was passed on to their legions of disciples, who exist in warring camps even today. Strauss is commonly, though not unanimously, viewed as a conservative, while Arendt, in an intellectual transformation that no doubt would have astonished her, has been turned into an icon of the left ("an untouchable authority"). The truth, however, is that neither is easily categorizable. They exist outside the normal liberal-conservative spectrum, or outside any political spectrum that can be devised. Confirmed freethinking individualists, they are political philosophers with no defined politics, much less the kind of partisan politics that would lead them into either the Democratic or Republican Party. In that, too, they are cousins of Kissinger, an expert on foreign policy whose ideas on foreign policy explode partisan categories and preconceptions. In a famous, if ill-considered, interview, Kissinger described himself as a "Lone Ranger" of international affairs. Together, Kissinger, Arendt, and Strauss form a posse of German-Jewish Lone Rangers. If a label must be attached to these three, one might call Arendt and Strauss existential political thinkers, as one might call Kissinger an existential political statesman whose refusal to engage in foundational, moralistic thinking led to his commitment to balance-of-power Realism and to a kind of detachment that critics labeled opportunism or cynicism. The truth was that there were no banisters available for any of them. But what did thinking without banisters really mean?

TREATMENTS OF Leo Strauss's ideas tend to follow the master's lead in considering his thought as it is presented in his books and articles. That is to say, they play down or even ignore the historical context in which those ideas appeared. This is in keeping with several firm Straussian tenets— namely, that serious thinkers must be taken on their own terms, not filtered through social, psychological, or historical externalities; that the problems they addressed are common to all humankind and are the same problems that exist today; and that a close analysis of the texts unencumbered by a knowledge of their background gives one a better understanding of their meaning than trying to place them in the context of their times. Trained as a Straussian, Anne Norton described how this process worked in practice: "No one could argue from authority, and a lifetime of learning was subordinated to the text. No one could refer to the latest article, or 'the literature' or an array of secondary sources for support. These, like all other arguments, had to be made through the text."

Right or wrong, this method has an undeniable virtue: it strips contemporary readers of an almost inevitable tendency to arrogance, undermining their implicit sense of superiority to the great minds of the past that comes from believing there is an intellectual advantage to living in the present. Can there be a more comical—or dispiriting—pedagogical experience than listening to a Harvard undergraduate expatiate on the intellectual shortcomings of Plato and Aristotle? Can such students be said to have learned anything from their reading of the great books? Modern readers do not, Strauss insisted, know more than the ancients did, do not, in his words, "understand the philosophy of the past better than it understood itself." The preconceptions of modernity are at odds with true knowledge. Ten pages of Herodotus, Strauss said, "introduce us immeasurably better into the mysterious unity of oneness and variety in human things than many volumes written in the spirit predominant in our age." That predominant spirit was the unquestioned belief in progress. "Modern thought is in all its forms, directly or indirectly, determined by the

idea of progress." The way to overcome this modern prejudice is to engage
the great books directly, intellectually naked. Whatever its philosophical
implications, Strauss's practice of close reading is a technique he seems to
have acquired from Heidegger, and both men were considered memorable teachers by their students because of their ability to make the classics
"come alive."

Thus, Straussians reading Strauss tend to stick to Strauss and to the ethereal, interlocking world of ideas in which he dwelled. A history of Strauss's
own thought in the Straussian manner, ignoring historical context, might
begin with his immersion in Jewish issues in the early 1920s, when he
was influenced first by the neo-Kantian Hermann Cohen and then by his
friend, the unclassifiable Jewish philosopher/theologian Franz Rosenz-
weig. Other Strauss heroes to be mentioned from this period include Max
Weber and Nietzsche, about whom Strauss confessed: "Nietzsche so dominated and charmed me between my 22nd and 30th years that I literally
believed everything I understood of him." Careers have been built trac-
ing the connections between Strauss and Nietzsche. Even more important
than Nietzsche was Heidegger, first encountered when Strauss attended
his lectures on Aristotle's "Metaphysics" in 1922.

As he matured, Strauss's youthful interest in Jewish thought broad-
ened into an interest in the relationship between religion and philosophy.
He was led to take up the study of Spinoza, the foremost thinker of Jewish origin in the Western canon, and to an examination of the tension in
Spinoza's work between revelation and reason. This came to be known,
in geographical shorthand, as the conflict between Jerusalem and Athens and also as the "theologico-political predicament," which became an
obsession for Strauss. In the 1930s, he pursued three subjects related to it:
Hobbes, as an extension of his book on Spinoza; Socrates, who became
increasingly important as Strauss grew skeptical of the notion of progress
and came to register a decided preference for ancient over modern philosophy; and medieval Jewish and Islamic thought, where revelation and reason confronted each other directly, before modern science had taken sway,
distorting pure thinking by becoming "the authority for philosophy."
Through his work on Maimonides and on Maimonides' predecessor and
teacher, the Arabic Platonist Farabi, Strauss came to see a "radical opposition between the moral-political type and the philosophic type," an opposition that would stay at the center of his thought for the rest of his life.

Out of the conflict between these two types came one of Strauss's most influential and most controversial essays, "Persecution and the Art of Writing," in which he posited the idea that many great philosophers, and in particular his beloved ancient Greeks, concealed their true meaning through a method he called "esoteric writing" in order to avoid confrontation with the political authorities. One had only to recall the fate of Socrates to see the danger of free thought. These thinkers did not simply say what they meant. They spoke obliquely. Understanding them required "reading between the lines," the kind of close textual attention that students like Anne Norton were instructed in by their Straussian professors. Packed into the notion of esoteric writing were ideas about the iconoclastically subversive role of the philosopher, the intrinsically tyrannical nature of politics and government, the extent and limits of reason, the quality and value of truth, the division between the "intelligent minority" and the "foolish majority," and similar themes that Strauss would pursue for years to come.

Viewed in this way, Strauss was an ivy-covered, book-bound scholar who vaulted from one great mind to the next as ideas impacted on ideas. He was the consummate *Luftmensch*, rarely touching down into the real world, a German Jew who, one remembers, could see the prospect of great happiness for himself even as Hitler was tightening the noose on his brethren. "Exceedingly . . . unworldly" is how he has been described by one historian. Similarly, a friend from Germany called him "an incredibly unworldly and anxious person." Entire books, knowledgeable, erudite books, have been written on Strauss's intellectual development with never a mention of Hitler, National Socialism, Weimar, the Third Reich, or the Holocaust. And it isn't only his disciples who treat him this way. One prominent critic disparaged Strauss by claiming that he "shows no interest at all in the realities of political and social life, whether ancient or modern." Strauss's ideas are seen as hermetically sealed, vacuum-packed. Socrates talks to Plato who talks to Aristotle who talks to Xenophon who talks to Thucydides, and they all talk to Leo Strauss. But no one talks to anyone outside the charmed circle.

The intellectual historian Mark Lilla has ridiculed this hermetic universe and how it functions—or fails to function. "Those who enter the Straussian orbit follow fairly predictable paths," Lilla writes. They often learn Greek to study the major figures like Plato, Aristotle, and Thucydides. The more ambitious may tackle Hebrew and Arabic. But the studies they produce "range from impenetrable exercises in esoteric analysis to solid interpretations of well-known classics." Then Lilla concludes with a sigh, "One puts most of them down thinking: just another brick in the wall."

And yet, for all the attention the unworldly Strauss has received, there is unquestionably another Strauss, an *engagé* Strauss, less the sheltered academic than the traumatized German-Jewish refugee who felt all too powerfully the impact of Hitler, both on his life and on his thought. Contrary to the claims of some of his critics, Strauss cared deeply about contemporary life. The story is told that when a friend was preparing to go to Germany after the war at the invitation of the one-time Nazi Heidegger, Strauss exclaimed: "Don't go!" Strauss "wasn't sophisticated about it," the person telling the story explained. "He *hated* Nazis. He was a political philosopher, but he was a Jew, and *he* hated Nazis!" Strauss visited Germany only once after the war, on his way to Israel, and that was to see his father's grave in Kirschhain. (By contrast, Hannah Arendt—who also hated Nazis—made several trips to Germany, including a famous, tension-filled reconnection with her former teacher and lover, Heidegger.)

Hitler is the ghost at Strauss's banquet, usually unmentioned, often unseen, but flitting grimly through the essays and books or hovering ominously over them, a menacing presence framing their approach and shaping their conclusions. "Persecution and the Art of Writing" was published in November 1941, when Europe, already in flames, had become Hitler's playground, and the United States was teetering uncertainly on the sidelines of the conflict. The essay became part of a collection that appeared in 1952, with a preface in which Strauss elliptically explained that he had started not with medieval thought but with "certain well-known political phenomena of our century." He doesn't say which phenomena; he doesn't have to. The essay itself is no less elliptical, ranging through Hobbes, Averroes, Aristotle, and Montesquieu, among others, and stating that it was fairly common for free thought to be suppressed in the past; Strauss pointed to the Spanish Inquisition as the earliest example of persecution. Never once is Hitler or modern Germany mentioned.

Still, it doesn't take training in Straussian techniques to read between the lines. The essay begins with what is for Strauss a relatively forthright declaration: "In a considerable number of countries which, for about a hundred years, have enjoyed a practically complete freedom of public discussion, that freedom is now suppressed." As Strauss had contended on other occasions, Wilhelmine Germany was a land of freedom of thought. Hitler's Germany was not. And what was more troubling, "a large section of the people, probably the great majority of the younger generation," went along with the regime willingly, without compulsion. The Germans had imposed totalitarianism on themselves, leaving the minority of independent thinkers to resort to "esoteric writing" in order to communicate with other "trustworthy and intelligent readers" who had refused to be taken in by the Nazis. Esoteric writing was required by the failure of Weimar's democracy. "Persecution and the Art of Writing" may have been molded by Strauss's studies of Maimonides and Farabi, but it was inspired by Hitler's Germany.

Elsewhere, Strauss is more direct in relating the events in Germany, "the catastrophe of 1933" as he called it, to his own thinking. The Third Reich was an unprecedented phenomenon (Hannah Arendt said the same thing), "the only regime of which I know which was based on no principle other than the negation of the Jews." And yet, with his love of the Western tradition, Strauss insistently denied that the Nazis could be traced back to Europe's Christian heritage. To believe such a thing was to grant a victory to the Third Reich and its nihilistic destruction of the past. "Only someone completely ignorant would say that anti-Jewish thugs are a matter of Christianity," he declared. "Of course not." Hannah Arendt agreed. In 1945 she wrote that Hitler and the Third Reich owed "nothing to any part of the Western tradition, be it German or not, Catholic or Protestant, Christian, Greek or Roman. Whether we like Thomas Aquinas or Machiavelli or Luther or Kant or Hegel or Nietzsche. . . . They have not the least responsibility for what is happening in the extermination camps."

The Third Reich, Strauss believed, was the Rosemary's baby of contemporary thought, not traditional Christianity, engendered out of the false but dominating notion of progress, which was responsible for the modern crisis of Western civilization. In Strauss's emphatic words, "The contemporary crisis of Western civilization may be said to be identical with the climactic crisis of the idea of progress." By substituting the alleged movement of history for fixed moral values, replacing the confident language of "good" and "bad" with the relativistic language of "progressive" and "reactionary," modern historicist thinking had eroded traditional certitudes and opened the public arena to any talented demagogue of the moment who claimed to have history on his side, that is, to "the man with the strongest will or single-mindedness, the greatest ruthlessness, daring and power over his following, and the best judgment about the strength of the various forces in the immediately relevant political field."

Resorting to facts from the real worlds of politics and history, Strauss argued that Hitler was the empirical refutation of the idea of progress. Only the classical philosophers, with their "eternal truths," could provide the bulwark against National Socialism that modern philosophy and liberal thinking had failed to offer. In this sense, contemporary events, the collapse of Weimar and the rise of the Third Reich, were fundamental to the direction of Strauss's thought and to his apparently otherworldly preference for the ancients over the moderns that has exercised such a considerable influence over his followers. Strauss didn't need Plato or Maimonides to tell him something had gone terribly wrong in Germany and in the West; he had the evidence of his own eyes. As one of the more astute Straussians has written, "One cannot downplay the impact that events from the recent historical past, like Nazi Germany and the cold war, had on Strauss's conception of philosophy." One might go further and say that Strauss's entire mission as a philosopher turned on framing an adequate intellectual response to what the Nazis represented. This was not an otherworldly aspiration. In the realm of politics, as any German intellectual would have readily confirmed, ideas mattered deeply. At a time of extreme crisis, they became a question of life and death. (And by the same token, the academic inclination to remove the great thinkers from the contemporary world—the world of ethics and morality—was to engage in a type of sterile intellectual aestheticism.)

Strauss's thinking proceeded along two tracks: one the erudite scholar's detailed analysis of the great philosophers, which was his legacy to his American students, the other the German Jew's visceral confrontation with the Third Reich, which gave Strauss his grounding in the real world of his time. The scholar's track was the more obvious one and the more influential one in the United States. The Jewish track was more occasional if more impassioned, usually put forth not in lengthy analyses but in asides or digressions or through startling eruptions breaking through the surface of the calm, scholarly flow of the arguments. So, for example, a lofty and critical discussion of Hobbes as a milestone on the misguided road to modernity would be interrupted by a condemnation of the contemporary idea of the "blond beast," allowing Strauss to pause amid his abstract speculations to present a kinder, gentler Hobbes: "No sober man could hesitate to prefer Hobbes's enlightened and humane absolute king to the contemporary tyrants." Even his most apparently arcane essays maintain an eye on the present. "How to Begin to Study

Medieval Philosophy" reiterates Strauss's familiar complaint about the "regrettable" dominance of value-free science on contemporary thought. He writes: "We are observing every day that people go so far in debasing the name of philosophy as to speak of the philosophy of vulgar imposters such as Hitler."

And in his celebrated critique of Max Weber's separation of fact and value, Strauss traces Weber's thought forward from its benign origins in neo-Kantianism to a dangerously judgment-free social science. "In following this movement toward its end we shall inevitably reach a point beyond which the scene is darkened by the shadow of Hitler." Weber's commitment to objectivity, which translated into a refusal to make value judgments, was a direct path, Strauss maintained, to Nazi nihilism. It "would lead to the consequence that we are permitted to give a strictly factual description of the overt acts that can be observed in concentration camps," without ever being allowed to speak directly of cruelty. Strauss's two tracks were separate, though they frequently intertwined—Weber and concentration camps, Hobbes and the blond beast. Where they genuinely converged, in a complex and intricate entanglement, was around the figure of Martin Heidegger.

Strauss never really lost his admiration for Heidegger after that first magical encounter in the early 1920s—"the only great thinker in our time," he told his University of Chicago students in the 1950s. Then what was Strauss to make of the Heidegger who became a Nazi Party member and a vocal supporter of Hitler during the first few years of the Third Reich, who fell out with the party leaders but never renounced his position or explained himself after the war and, worse, who as late as 1953 could speak of "the inner truth and greatness of national socialism"? Betrayal is probably too mild a term for what Strauss felt. His intellectual foundations were shaken, his very concept of philosophy and the philosophical life overturned. There was, he concluded more in anger than in sorrow, a "straight line" from Heidegger to Hitler, a "kinship." If Nazi Germany was led politically by Hitler, it was led intellectually by Heidegger, and therefore after 1933, "I ceased to take any interest in him for about two decades." Though Strauss's reaction is more than understandable, this statement is one we may feel free to doubt, as he also told his students, "The most stupid thing I could do would be to close my eyes or to reject his work." Like it or not, "Heidegger surpasses all his contemporaries by far." It was necessary to read him, to understand and absorb and take what was valuable from him. It was even more necessary to do battle against him and, if possible, to transcend him.

What, exactly, did Strauss have against Heidegger? The answer might seem obvious, but it isn't. For one thing, Heidegger's influence has extended to many undeniably liberal and humane individuals. Vaclav Havel, among others, derived strength and courage from Heidegger's teachings during his years in a Communist prison. There are some who are able to separate Heidegger's philosophy from his Nazism. There are others who are not. In his book on Strauss, Steven B. Smith has stated, "Whether Heidegger's embrace of Hitler . . . constituted a brief and unfortunate 'episode' in his career or grew out of the deepest wellsprings of his thought is a subject that is not likely to be resolved." Strauss, for one, had no trouble resolving it. For him, the linkage was "intimate" and indissoluble.

Yet Strauss's own pedagogical methods demanded that he consider Heidegger's philosophy on its own terms and not as a function of his Nazi affiliations. We must understand "the thought of a philosopher exactly as he understood himself," Strauss insisted. And what's more, in his essay on Weber, Strauss wrote, "We must avoid the fallacy that in the last decades has frequently been used as a substitute for the *reductio ad absurdum*: the *reductio ad Hitlerum*. A view is not refuted by the fact that it happens to have been shared by Hitler." Such an attitude makes severe demands on a reader and critic, but Strauss was up to the task and, true to his own intellectual dictates, offered a shrewd critique of Heidegger on philosophical, not political, grounds.

The father of existentialism drew a stark, gloomy, and unforgettable picture of the human condition. Our fundamental experience, Heidegger said, was anguish, angst, because we are "thrown" into the world condemned to knowledge of the certainty of death in a meaningless universe. To its credit, this view has given us the plays of Samuel Beckett and the sculptures of Alberto Giacometti. But it has also depressed and paralyzed more than one generation of aspiring intellectuals, resulting in thousands if not millions of European and American students dressing entirely in black while they stared into the abyss. More seriously, it enervated many of the thinkers in Weimar Germany who might have provided a roadblock on Hitler's path to power. It was only the indecent who were full of passionate intensity. "The worst have lost their fear and the best have lost their hope," Arendt wrote.

Heidegger taught that in a meaningless universe "authentic" human beings had to reject all certainties, all absolutes. There were no good or bad choices, only "resolute" ones in the face of absurdity. Heidegger's own resoluteness led him into the arms of Adolf Hitler (at least temporarily). He welcomed, Strauss wrote, "the verdict of the least wise and least moderate part of his nation while it was in the least wise and least moderate mood." He "never believed in the possibility of an ethics."

Still, it wouldn't do to criticize a philosopher for lacking ethics if part of his project was to show that all traditional ethical systems are groundless and that "ethics is impossible." It would take a "great thinker" to reestablish a firm ethical foundation, Strauss said, but the problem was that the greatest thinker of his time, really the only great thinker, was Heidegger. Strauss didn't consider himself on Heidegger's level. And so he took a different tack, perhaps even a non-Straussian one. He pointed out that there was nothing absolute about Heideggerian angst. It was not a description of the timeless human condition but very much a product of a particular moment in history, a period of extreme confusion and despair, when the culture of the West had become "uncertain of itself." Heidegger was not enunciating eternal truths in the way the ancient Greeks had; he was articulating the mood of postwar Germany.

Heidegger's philosophical vision may have been cogent and powerful, but it was time-bound and partial, and so too was his notion of humanity itself—which Strauss called "narrow." There was neither tenderness to his thought, nor a consideration of love or charity, or any of the other finer impulses in humanity. Heidegger appealed to anyone who embraced a "tragic sense of life" as the only, or at least the most sophisticated, outlook, but he had nothing to say, Strauss observed, about "laughter and the things which deserved to be laughed at." Elsewhere, Strauss suggested that Heidegger had found the perfect audience for his message in modern Germany, "the country without comedy." Lightness isn't a quality commonly associated with Leo Strauss, any more than it is with his fellow Germans (though it has been said that laughter was not uncommon in his classrooms). There is no greater fool's errand than to scour his vast corpus for wisecracks or one-liners, and an argument can certainly be made that this criticism of Heidegger is uncharacteristic of him, displaying a soft, even sentimental side to a normally austere thinker. Austerity, however, isn't everything. It could equally be said that Strauss's criticism of Heidegger showed him at his warmest and most human. "A slight bias in favor of laughing and against weeping," Strauss said in opposition to Heidegger, "seems to be essential to philosophy." Socrates laughed, Strauss observed; he did not weep. He might have added that one of his favorite authors, Shakespeare, wrote comedies as well as tragedies. (And he might have mentioned that another of his favorite authors was P. G. Wodehouse.)

But to say that Strauss's two tracks converged on Heidegger is to say that he responded to his former teacher not only as a philosopher but also personally, emotionally, as a Jew (and, if one were to universalize Strauss's subjective reaction, as a human being). Heidegger had lent his considerable prestige to a regime that declared war on the Jews, and Strauss despised him for it, even if that meant violating one of the philosopher Strauss's core principles—that "we must be willing to consider the possibility" that a thinker's teachings are "simply true." As a Jew, Strauss was unable to entertain the idea that Heidegger's teachings were simply true. How could he? Strauss didn't need to make reasoned refutations. All he needed was the fact of Adolf Hitler and a healthy, this-worldly sense of self-preservation (a greater sense of self-preservation, it would seem, than that of Louis Kissinger). The Nazis violated "the rules of decent and noble conduct as a reasonable man would understand them." As a statement of personal revulsion, nothing more need be said. Nonetheless, even as one acknowledges the legitimacy of Strauss's personal, "Jewish" response to Heidegger and the Nazis, there is no getting away entirely from philosophy in favor of raw emotion. Gnawing questions persist. What were those rules Strauss spoke of and where did they come from?

In a different context, Strauss called the reasonable man's understanding "common sense." He frequently resorted to this notion even if common sense, as Strauss put it, was "prescientific knowledge" and not susceptible to proof. Political science, Strauss said, "is nothing other than the fully conscious form of the common sense understanding of political things." The Greeks developed the discipline of political science not through pure cogitation but by looking around themselves at how people went about living their lives, which gave them an advantage over modern thinkers because their observations weren't already encrusted in political theory. They, after all, were the ones who invented political theory. Like the related concept of "decency," common sense couldn't be defined according to some abstract, disembodied principle or measured by some standard external to itself; it was "choiceworthy for its own sake," existing within a social matrix or "a kind of web" that we call "society."

Rationalists demanding rigorous thinking built on sharp definitions won't take much satisfaction from Strauss's appeals to common sense, decency, and reasonableness. "Common sense" is a notoriously squishy phrase, suited to many uses, both legitimate and illegitimate, and often the last refuge of the intellectually helpless. But Strauss had no problem with the vagueness of terms like "common sense." Political language, he said, is suggestive, subject to penumbras of meaning, and not "perfectly clear and distinct." (The same might be said of George Orwell's essential but hazy concept of "decency.") In any case, the second track of Strauss's thinking was personal, not philosophical. It was subjective and admittedly self-interested, the outcry of a Jew defending his very existence, who rightly felt no need to offer reasons for his defense. Strauss's criticism of Heidegger here was the equivalent, in a different fashion, of Shylock's soliloquy, "Hath not a Jew eyes?," in Shakespeare's *The Merchant of Venice*. When someone is trying to expel, enslave, or kill you, self-interest suffices. Strauss spoke of the necessity to pronounce concentration camps cruel without recourse to philosophical justification. They just were (and those inclined to doubt this assertive use of simple common sense were perhaps themselves devoid of it).

Strauss never commented on the far crueler phenomenon of the death camps, but a scene from one of them (which, I am told by an expert on the subject, actually took place thousands of times) sheds a sharper light on the nature of his reaction and the reason for his hostility to the disinterested thinking of the classroom. An SS guard wrenches a wailing baby from the arms of its terrified mother and smashes its head against a wall before her horrified, unbelieving eyes. (In some versions of the incident, he gives the battered corpse back to the mother to hold.) All humanity cries out against this act of unmitigated evil—all except Nazi war criminals and the modern philosopher, who, trained in value-free relativism, Strauss would say, questions the grounds for calling any action evil and sneers at the commonsense response of ordinary, unreflective people that, yes, some acts are simply evil.

Like those nonphilosophers, Strauss felt no need to demonstrate the evil of the Nazis. Reasoning had to stop somewhere, because "there are things which can only be seen as what they are if they are seen with the unarmed eye." We must simply be willing to call "a spade a spade," even though some judgments can't be proved to the satisfaction of coldly rationalist professors safe in their lecture halls and seminar rooms. Such judgments may not be entirely clear; they may even raise "theoretical doubts."

Yet they are indubitably true. Morality, Strauss said, "is a force in the soul of man." The greatest thinker of the twentieth century had joined the Nazis, and on a personal level Strauss didn't have to say anything else. As his friend explained, he "was a political philosopher, but he was a Jew and he hated Nazis."

STRAUSS RARELY ADDRESSED contemporary issues directly, and so careful readers have to extract his views on current events from his asides and digressions, those emotional eruptions. One of the few times when he did assume the role of public intellectual, and probably the most famous, was in a lecture he delivered at the New School in February 1941. Its title was "German Nihilism," and its ostensible subject was Hermann Rausch-ning's recently translated book, *The Revolution of Nihilism*. Strauss's audience consisted mainly of refugee scholars like himself who were meeting regularly for a seminar devoted to "experiences of the Second World War."

Rauschning, the reformed Nazi and one-time associate of Hitler, condemned his former colleagues for nihilism, a will to power with no aim other than power itself. But Strauss offered a twist on that criticism. The Nazis were not nihilists, if by that was meant destroyers of everything. Their target was something specific—modern civilization—and their movement was in essence a "moral" protest against open societies. In articulating the Nazi point of view, Strauss, the enemy of modernity, is surprisingly sympathetic to it: "The open society is bound to be, if not immoral, at least amoral: the meeting ground of seekers of pleasure, of gain, of irresponsible power, indeed of any kind of irresponsibility and lack of seriousness." This conviction, he said, was "not entirely unsound" because "no one could be satisfied" with the world of the Weimar Republic. "German liberal democracy of all descriptions seemed to many people to be absolutely unable to cope with the difficulties with which Germany was confronted." (Does one not hear in those words an echo of Henry Kissinger's criticisms of the United States for "a lack of seriousness"?)

These are not the words of an American liberal democrat, unthinkingly ready to celebrate open societies as an end in themselves. These are the words of a person, Jewish or non-Jewish, with a deeply conservative, or deeply skeptical, temperament, who believed that in Weimar Germany modern democracy had become part of the problem, not part of the solution. In a letter to a friend written in May 1933, when the Nazis' anti-Semitism was all too evident but their genuine crimes were only beginning—the Night of the Long Knives was a year away, Kristallnacht more than five years away—Strauss declared, "Just because the right-wing oriented German does not tolerate us, it simply does not follow that the principles of the right are therefore to be rejected." Strauss's admirers find this statement "shocking," even "infamous." Sentiments like these led Hannah Arendt to observe correctly: "Even Jews would have gone along with Hitler if they had been allowed to." When confronted with a choice between a right-wing government and a left-wing government in Germany or, even more extreme, between fascism and communism, Strauss, like so many others in his native land, Nazis and those who were merely conservatives of one stripe or another, gentiles along with Jews, instinctively faced right.

What was nihilistic about National Socialism, Strauss said in 1941, was its "rejection of the principles of civilization as such." However justified the Nazis' criticism of modern society might be, they had nothing to put in its place. For Rauschning, the conservative who believed Hitler was destroying the German nation, "all traditional spiritual standards" were being lost. But Strauss, whatever sympathy he might have felt for Rauschning's traditionalism, was not a German nationalist per se, and as a Jew (though Strauss didn't put it that way), he had deep suspicions about the word "spiritual."

"I believe it is dangerous," he said, "if the opponents of National Socialism withdraw to a mere conservatism which defines its ultimate goal by a specific *tradition*." The reason to fight Hitler and the Nazis was to defend "the eternal principles of civilization," or as he also put it, "the conscious culture of humanity" and "the conscious culture of reason." That is, Strauss was not fighting the Nazis to defend the liberal democratic principles of freedom, tolerance, and equality, as were most Americans. Unlike the fundamental value of Western civilization, the ground on which he was making his stand, all these reasons were problematic in Strauss's eyes, weak and insubstantial arguments against the Nazi juggernaut—principles of justice, perhaps, but justice without a sword.

Freedom was no end in itself because in its present form it had become an excuse for unrestrained license, divorced from any concept of virtue and social responsibility. Instructed in modern liberal ideas about the rights of man, people thought themselves entitled to pursue their greediest, ugliest, most base, and most perverse desires with no acknowledgment of limit or conscience. It was what Strauss called "the victory of the gutter." Weimar Germany was a model of this kind of freedom. But "not everything is permitted," Strauss said, and "restraint is as natural to man as is freedom." The ancients had a firmer and more nuanced understanding of freedom because they didn't think only of rights: "Premodern thought put the emphasis on duty, and rights, as far as they were mentioned at all, were understood only as derivative from duties." Western civilization was as much about limits and responsibilities as it was about liberty.

As with freedom, so with tolerance. The intolerance of the Nazis—which defined their movement and led to industrialized mass murder—was heinous. And yet leaping to the opposite position of tolerance for its own sake was hardly an adequate response to death camps. It was impossible, Strauss insisted, to be tolerant of everything and everyone. Even the most liberal of persons ran up against limits to their goodwill. Our actions are always guided by some notion of good and bad, or at least better and worse. Judgment was built into our humanity, and the necessity for choice could not be evaded by a soothing rubric of "tolerance." An ecumenical tolerance eradicated personal responsibility and denied individual will.

Strauss's favorite example for his argument was cannibalism: "If we commit ourselves to the values of civilization, our very commitment enables and compels us to take a vigorous stand against cannibalism." A relativist interlocutor could object that in certain situations—on a lifeboat in the middle of the ocean, for instance—cannibalism might be a legitimate last resort, but that hardly clinched the relativist argument. Strauss's response would seem to be that, like the classical philosophers, he was speaking about normal circumstances, not extreme conditions when exceptions had to be allowed. A crisis might precipitate a radical response or extreme measures, but once the crisis passed, a reversion to the mean was essential. Precedents could not be based on extremes. In everyday life, where the habits of civilization could be expected to prevail, moderation within the web of society was the greatest virtue.

If he were writing today, Strauss might use the example of female circumcision to underline the limits of tolerance, but in any case, the concept of tolerance, like that of freedom, had an emptiness at its core. Indeed, in its refusal to make distinctions, tolerance rejected that which Strauss valued above all—critical thinking, consciousness, reason itself. The paradox of absolute tolerance was that it demanded tolerance of the intolerant, and there was no need for Strauss to say where that led. "The relativist," he wrote, "rejects the absolutism inherent in our great Western tradition—in its belief in the possibility of a rational and universal ethics." Contrary to believers in tolerance, one had to take a firm stand in support of reason and against reason's enemies. As the liberals of Weimar demonstrated, you don't beat something (totalitarianism) with nothing (tolerance).

Finally, with regard to the principle of equality, Strauss was scarcely a believer in the American credo that all men were created equal. Society was inherently hierarchic. "Not all men strive for virtue with equal earnestness," he said, because "the accident of birth decides whether a given individual has a chance of becoming a gentleman." Object that such views are elitist, and Strauss would imperturbably embrace the label. Life was not fair. Call him antidemocratic, or at least nondemocratic, and he would snidely point out: the "salt of modern democracy" are the people who spend their time reading the sports section or the comics.

Ideally, those complacent and uninformed readers of the sports pages would be ruled by an elite that is concerned with the public good rather than its own self-interest. Strauss went further: inequalities could never be rectified, certainly not through that popular American panacea, education. "We must not expect that liberalized education can ever become universal education. It will always remain the obligation and the privilege of a minority." That democratic apostle of universal education, John Dewey, might roll over in his grave. Strauss didn't care, though he was enough of an egalitarian to believe that anyone, rich or poor, could be trained for the highest calling of philosopher. But he was stout in his conviction that "the inequality between the wise and the vulgar is a fundamental fact of human nature." Liberal education, he said, is the effort to establish "an aristocracy within democratic mass society." Western civilization, as Strauss understood it, was the property of an educated minority. But that didn't make it unworthy of defense against the nihilistic Nazis. Quite the contrary.

Yet if Western civilization wasn't to be characterized by freedom, tolerance, and equality, what was it exactly, and why was it worth defending at the cost of one's treasure and blood? Strauss made clear that when he spoke of civilization, he wasn't talking about culture, the appreciation and preservation of the West's artistic heritage. One wasn't fighting in the name of Shakespeare and Mozart. Many of the Nazis, he observed, "are

great lovers of culture as distinguished from, and opposed to, civilization." Beethoven was played in the death camps. Looked at another way,
Strauss said that "a tribal community may possess a culture i.e. produce
and enjoy hymns, songs, ornament of their clothes, of their weapons and
pottery, and enjoy fairy tales and what not; it cannot however be civilized."
For that, you needed the "conscious culture of humanity," to be found in
the works of writers like Plato and Aristotle, Spinoza and Nietzsche.

Modern readers might see in such statements an outdated Eurocen-
trism, but in fact Strauss, rare among his contemporaries, was open to
a "genuine meeting of West and East," and he regretted (though he
accepted) the intellectual provincialism that limited education to the classics of the West. In classrooms in New York, London, and Berlin, Plato
would by "unfortunate necessity" receive more attention than Confucius
and Christianity more than Islam on the principle that you had to know
where you came from before you could know where you were going.
"The Western thinker," Strauss said, had to prepare to meet the East "by
descending to the deepest root of the West." Strauss was, after all, one of
the few philosophers of his era to take Islamic thought seriously.

Where he did make his stand, however, was on his unabashed elitism.
Primitive culture couldn't and shouldn't be equated with Western civilization, despite the fact that the word "culture" had become an entirely
elastic term, allowing us to speak of such things as suburban culture and
gang culture. By this definition, everyone except lunatics is a cultivated
individual. A civilization, in contrast to a culture, was the product of its
greatest minds, whether Western or Eastern. One of Strauss's favorite
quotations was from Aquinas: "The least knowledge one can have of the
highest things is more desirable than the most certain knowledge one has
of the lowest things."

To probe more deeply into what Strauss meant by Western civilization,
one might consider an odd couple—Hermann Cohen and Adolf Hitler.
Cohen was the leading Kantian at the end of the nineteenth century, the
first Jew to hold a chair in philosophy in Germany, and "the greatest representative of German Jewry" in Strauss's words. Cohen's lifework was
his attempt to achieve a synthesis between the German philosophic tradition and Judaism, formulating an optimistic "religion of reason" that
excavated an intellectual space in which Germany's Jews could flourish as
both Jews and Germans. He was the philosopher for individuals like Louis

Kissinger, who believed and wanted to believe that they could live productive, comfortable lives as "German citizens of Jewish faith." Zionism was not an option for them. According to Cohen, Strauss observed, "There is no place for the hope that Israel will return to its own country."

Cohen died in 1918, years before Hitler had commandeered the public stage, but it was the Nazis who smashed Cohen's carefully constructed synthesis, making him look, in retrospect, like a naïf (though they did it not through the power of ideas but through the power of brute strength). "Cohen's thought belongs to the world preceding World War I," Strauss wrote. "The worst things that he experienced were the Dreyfus scandal and the pogroms instigated by Czarist Russia; he did not experience Communist Russia and Hitler [sic] Germany." These were "catastrophes and horrors of a magnitude hitherto unknown."

For Strauss, Cohen's hopeful synthesis was shattered forever by Adolf Hitler, and what was left—for all the difficulties—were the shards of an irreconcilable division between reason and religion, Athens and Jerusalem. The two traditions had many things in common, in particular a shared moral perspective. "It is as obvious to Aristotle as it is to Moses that murder, theft, adultery, etc. are unqualifiedly bad." (They also agreed, Strauss pointed out, that "the proper framework of morality is the patriarchal family," but it is probably best not to make too much of that.) Yet for all their agreement, their moral outlooks rested on different foundations—reason in the case of Athens, revelation in the case of Jerusalem—and that difference could never be bridged as Cohen had hoped to bridge it.

And yet, Strauss maintained, this permanent chasm was not a problem. On the contrary, Western civilization, he insisted, was the product of that millennia-long conflict between reason and revelation and, indeed, derived its special vitality from it. "The very life of Western civilization is the life between two codes, a fundamental tension" that was healthy and creative. No one, Strauss said, could be both a philosopher and a theologian, "but every one of us can be and ought to be either one or the other," opting for either Jerusalem or Athens, while remaining open to the claims of the other side. Strauss knew that for himself he had to choose Athens. Though he might yearn "with all his heart" for the absolutism of revelation, and though he accepted it as one form of truth, equal in every way to reason, he couldn't be religious; therefore, the aspect of Western civilization that he devoted himself to defending against the Nazis and other totalitarian enemies was philosophy, as it had been handed down by the Greeks.

What did Strauss mean by philosophy? Not what it was commonly understood to be. Philosophers were not to be found teaching in colleges and universities around the country because instructors in philosophy departments were no more likely to be true philosophers than instructors in art departments were to be true artists. Philosophy wasn't an academic discipline or the stepping-stone to a career defined by the structures and customs of higher education. It was a personal commitment, a way of life, inspired by a sense of wonder, much like a religion though without the dogma. Philosophers were devoted to wisdom but didn't propound doctrines or claim to have discovered the Truth. Their wisdom, like that of the prototype Socrates, consisted of an awareness that they knew nothing. Insofar as they could be said to possess knowledge, it was of the questions, not the answers, and philosophers ceased to be philosophers, Strauss said, when certainty replaced Socratic doubt. Monk-like, they pursued a contemplative life of reasoned discussion and disputation about that which they did not know, far from the meaningless bustle of the everyday world. Their advantage over the ignorant masses was their intellectual humility.

All that true philosophers asked from the world outside, the world of getting and spending, of violence and power, of certitude and conviction, was to be left alone on their "island of the blessed." This freedom, the freedom to philosophize, was Strauss's "highest value." But how could Strauss identify such an idealized vision of pure thought, practiced by the tiniest minority of a nation's citizens, with Western civilization itself? Because, he said, "the dignity of the mind" was the true basis of the dignity of humanity. The home of man, Strauss insisted, "is the home of the human mind. Someone who genuinely valued Western civilization admired its intellectual accomplishments, its nurturing of disembodied thought, not its material and technological successes. Widespread prosperity might be praiseworthy because it facilitated the conditions in which freethinking could thrive, but one didn't measure civilization by living standards. After all, Hitler had raised Germany's living standards.

However, dangers to freethinking lurked everywhere. Whatever the ideal, it was impossible for philosophers to withdraw entirely onto their blessed island or to be entirely self sufficient in the Straussian equivalent of monasteries. To follow their lives of quiet contemplation, philosophers required others to help with material needs. They depended on society's division of labor and had to pay for the services of ordinary people with services of their own. But what services could the deeply impractical philosophers offer? Not technical or professional expertise, to be sure, as there was no greater nonutilitarian pursuit than debates among individuals who conceded that they knew nothing. What their life of the mind could provide was "a humanizing or civilizing effect." Indeed, society "needs philosophy" for exactly that reason, Strauss said, though he was quick to add that it needed philosophy "only mediately or indirectly." The social contribution of the philosophers was immaterial, hard to define, impossible to measure, and to the uncultivated and uninformed—that is, the vast majority—they might appear to be frauds and parasites. Tensions between the down-to-earth common people and the ethereal philosophers were inevitable. "Socrates himself fell victim to the popular prejudice against philosophy."

There was worse. Philosophers needed to be able to think freely and to follow their ideas wherever they might lead. There was a kind of sociopathic madness to their endeavor. They were the ultimate iconoclasts, subversive by their very nature, because social and political activity was based on popular opinion, public dogma, and unexamined tradition, whereas philosophy existed to scrutinize all opinions, dogmas, and traditions. For those bounded by a belief in common morality, which is to say just about everyone, philosophers were immoralists or, at best, amoralists. These suspicions of the general public were not unfounded. Philosophers really were subversive! (Here, too, Strauss and Arendt shared a common—one might say Nietzschean—perspective. "Thinking," Arendt wrote, "inevitably has a destructive, undermining effect on all established criteria, values, measurements for good and evil, in short on those customs and rules of conduct we treat of in morals and ethics.") To survive in a world intrinsically hostile to freethinking, philosophers had to employ "esoteric writing" while presenting a public face of moderation and quiescence, whatever radical ideas they might be harboring. "Thought must be not moderate, but fearless, not to say shameless. But moderation is a virtue controlling the philosopher's speech." Or as Strauss also put it: "In political things it is a sound rule to let sleeping dogs lie." The best hope for the preservation of freedom of thought was to remain inconspicuous. The wise knew not to poke the beast.

Inconspicuousness was not always possible. Constantly vulnerable to tyrants and to tyrannical majorities, philosophers were in need of friends, not only other philosophers with whom they could exchange ideas but also more practical people who could mediate between the contemplative elite and the vulgar masses. The philosophers' best friends in the ordinary world were the people Strauss called "gentlemen." Philosophers were not equipped to plunge into the political world, which consisted of "very long conversations with very dull people on very dull subjects." Neither did they have the power to impose their will on the majority even if they had wanted to, which they didn't. Instead, they needed the help of gentlemen who appreciated the value of freedom of thought yet could function among the ignorant populace. Philosophers, who were disinterested by definition, could instruct these gentlemen to shun private advantage and personal gain for the common good—and it would help if the gentlemen were wealthy so that the prospect of acquiring riches at the public expense would be less enticing—but it was up to the gentlemen to act as the bridge between the pure thinking of the minority and the material self interest of the majority and to win the support of the citizenry at large. "The political problem consists in reconciling the requirement for wisdom with the requirement for consent." Gentlemen had to use their interpersonal and rhetorical skills to persuade the public to freely accept a government that stood for more than the fulfillment of base appetites or the simple will of the majority. A decent government gave the people something other than what they thought they wanted.

Strauss's notion of "gentlemen" may sound ominous, an undemocratic European import with no relevance to the boisterously egalitarian American scene, but in fact it was the equivalent of such homespun ideas as Jefferson's "natural aristocracy" and Madison's "guardians of the public weal." Strauss quoted Jefferson writing to John Adams: "That form of government is best which provides the most effectually for a pure selection of [the] natural *aristoi* into offices of the government." Gentlemen were what in another era was called "the Establishment"—another common all-American term—and stood against the force of populism. (Those who have trouble imagining any real-world application to this notion might reflect on Henry Kissinger's relationship to Nelson Rockefeller.) Gentlemen were Strauss's answer to the problem of tyrannical democracy, a problem the Founding Fathers understood but that too many modern Americans had chosen to ignore for the sake of their own self-interest. It was not a problem a German-Jewish refugee could afford to ignore. The seemingly impractical concept of "gentlemen" was very practical to a German Jew who had witnessed the rise of Hitler.

"WE ARE NOT permitted to be flatterers of democracy precisely because we are friends and allies of democracy." This is a comment Strauss's disciples like to quote to prove that their master was one of them and not antidemocratic—though careful readers have pointed out that in calling himself a friend or an ally of democracy, Strauss was steering clear of calling himself a democrat. Strauss went on to say that the advantage of democracy was that, by giving freedom to all, it allowed that small minority that cared for "human excellence" to set up outposts or cultivate their gardens. But as the triumph of the Nazis had shown, there was no guarantee that democratic institutions would permanently protect the innocent few against tyrannical majorities. In a darker comment, a wary, skeptical, and pessimistic Strauss also said, "We must realize that we must hope almost against hope." The truth was that from Strauss's perspective the philosophers—the bearers and custodians of civilization—were politically helpless. American democracy wasn't a solution to the age-old problems of democratic rule identified and analyzed by the ancient Greeks. There was no permanent solution. "We may be compelled to rest satisfied with palliatives. But we must not mistake palliatives for cures."

Like Henry Kissinger, Strauss loved the United States for the haven it had provided him, yet he was no less distanced from the popular American temperament than was Kissinger. He never took great comfort from the political instincts of his fellow citizens and in fact was deeply concerned about the decline he saw from the classical ideals of the Founding Fathers to the rude demands of modern American mass society. Tocqueville's words would have resonated with him: "If ever the free institutions of America are destroyed, that event may be attributed to the omnipotence of the majority." There was a basic vulnerability to free thought, even in democracies, and catastrophe remained forever within the realm of possibility. Persecution was a threat that could never be eradicated because philosophers lived in a condition of dependency on the powerful. In Strauss's mind, he was always dwelling on the edge, always in the Weimar Republic, with impassioned masses intent on destroying the life of the mind. One does not imagine him ever sleeping soundly at night. Intellectually speaking, the timid, anxiety-ridden Leo Strauss resorted to a kind of stoicism to survive the dangers lurking everywhere. But, helpless before the Behemoth of public opinion, he always kept his bags packed.

HANNAH ARENDT, it might be said, also kept her bags packed. Or, more precisely, that she was always unpacking them and then packing them again. She was forever admiring American institutions, then questioning their stability, praising Americans' good sense, then doubting their reliability, learning to feel at home in the United States—more comfortable than she could ever be anywhere else, including Germany and Israel—then preparing to leave it if the ominous trends she perceived grew worse. She disliked the knee-jerk anti-Americanism of educated Europeans, who projected their own ill-informed preconceptions onto a complicated country they didn't understand; at the same time, she understood why they were reluctant to embrace the United States and its ideals and why it could be so difficult to defend the country from their barbs.

The United States hopelessly whipsawed her. But hovering over all of her shifting and contradictory reactions, the reason for her deep ambivalence was the shadow of Weimar. America might be the world's greatest democracy, but as a German-Jewish refugee, she could have no abiding faith in democratic systems after personally witnessing how easily they could be overridden and destroyed by an aroused mob. The United States had strengths of its own that Weimar Germany lacked, yet even so she was haunted by a comment made by Huey Long (who, oddly, seemed to be echoing Tocqueville): "Fascism, if it ever should come to this country, will come in the guise of democracy." It was an observation that made perfect and discomfiting sense to her. Even at her most content, she never felt entirely at ease. Friends called her "catastrophe-minded," and they were right. Whatever disagreements they may have had, on this point, concerning this mood, Arendt and Kissinger were in full agreement.

The first few years after Arendt's arrival in the United States in May 1941 were spent getting settled, learning English, finding work, and tending to her elderly mother and to a husband whose adjustment to their new life was more difficult than hers was. Intellectually, she was consumed by the struggle against the Nazis and the internecine battles of the Zionists,

though once the movement coalesced around a strategy of Jewish state-
hood in Palestine, which she opposed, she found herself marginalized
and gradually withdrew from Zionist activities. She was also busy making
new friends, especially among the writers now known as the New York
Intellectuals. They were teaching her to see things from a perspective that
was both cosmopolitan and "American." She admired their freethinking
ways and their detachment from the ideological shackles that seemed to
have enchained so many of her European contemporaries. To her jaded
continental eyes, they were refreshingly idealistic and moral in an old-
fashioned way but also childlike—endearingly so.

Her friend Dwight Macdonald, Arendt said, not only felt "a total solidarity with European antifascists" but also, surprising for an American,
"responsible for their fate." She applauded his spontaneous genuineness.
"In his total naïveté," she said, he was "smarter than all the literati put
together." And after a rocky start, she was drawn to Mary McCarthy,
who became her closest friend and confidant. As with Macdonald, she
responded to what she saw as a sweet ingenuousness in McCarthy. In a
letter supporting McCarthy's 1959 application for a Guggenheim grant,
Arendt wrote, "She reports her findings from the viewpoint and with the
amazement of a child." Not many others would see a "child" in the razor-
tongued McCarthy. According to Arendt's biographer, "If there was one
quality in people that attracted Hannah Arendt above all others, it was
innocence of a special sort: innocence in combination with wide experience, innocence preserved."

Contained in Arendt's reactions to Macdonald and McCarthy was
an emotional distance that reflected her conflicted feelings about her
uprooted life, an aloofness that often has been correctly taken as arrogance. The parallels to Henry Kissinger are striking. Arendt enjoyed her
American friends and respected and leaned on them, even more than
she respected many of the European acquaintances with whom she was
temperamentally closer. Yet there is no denying that she looked down on
them, not with malice but with the affection of someone older and wiser,
a knowing parent. Cosmopolitan as they might have been, their experiences as Americans were limited, provincial compared to hers. They had
not been jailed and interrogated by the Nazis, forced to flee their native
land, imprisoned in an internment camp from which they barely escaped
alive, seen the lives of friends and relations destroyed, rendered penniless
and desperate, and forced into an exile as stateless refugees with no rights,

no protections, no guarantees about what tomorrow would bring. When Arendt first met McCarthy at a party in 1944, her future friend remarked that she felt sorry for Hitler because he persisted in trying to win the love of his victims. It was a glib, silly, mean but comment; it was meant to be clever but was only obtuse, and Arendt exploded: "How can you say such a thing to me, a victim of Hitler, a person who has been in a concentration camp."

Unlike the majority of their countrymen, Arendt's American friends possessed a sense of tragedy—necessary if one was going to be an intimate of Arendt's—but it was largely book-learned tragedy, hopelessly literary and abstract compared to the lived experience of Arendt and other German-Jewish refugees. These Americans were not philosophical, having not even "the slightest inkling of what philosophy is," as Arendt once explained, and she clung to her "European background in all its details with great tenacity." How could ambivalence not cloud her feelings toward her American friends? How could ambivalence not cloud her feelings toward America itself?

To be sure, her immediate response upon arrival was gratitude. "I'm eternally grateful that it was here I was washed ashore." She had been cut off from her revered mentor Karl Jaspers during the Hitler years, but after the war, when she resumed contact with him, she was soon communicating to a fellow European with the independence of mind to understand not only her gratitude but also her more complicated reactions. There was much to say. A letter from January 1946 contained one of her lengthiest descriptions of "lucky America" with its "basically sound political structure." There really was "such a thing as freedom here," she said. And she meant it. She felt that one could truly be an individual according to one's own lights in the United States, which was essential because, as she told Jaspers, she had become convinced that a decent human existence was possible only on society's fringes. Or as she explained years later, "What influenced me when I came to the United States was precisely the freedom of becoming a citizen without having to pay the price of assimilation." Her detached individuality was what mattered to her. She would never cease being an outsider, but she was comfortable with that. Toward the very end of her life, she was still saying that she felt "perfectly free" in America, though she added that she could be mistaken. The United States was the ideal place for one accustomed to thinking without a banister.

Arendt could find something positive to say even about the darkest episodes in American history. When Japanese Americans were forced into internment camps at the beginning of the war, she told Jaspers in 1946, the country experienced "a genuine storm of protest." She describes a New England family she had met whose lineage extended back generations. They were "thoroughly average people" who had probably never encountered a Japanese person in their lives. Yet they and their friends immediately wrote to their congressmen protesting the infringement of constitutional rights. Something similar, she said, was true with regard to the Jews. There was widespread anti-Semitism in the United States ("antipathy toward the Jews is, so to speak, a consensus omnium"). But that didn't mean Americans would stand by and allow Jews to be deprived of their political rights. America was not Germany.

The political instincts of Americans were admirable. They might not be especially thoughtful or intellectual, but they took their responsibility as citizens seriously, something Europeans didn't, or couldn't, understand. In a Rand School lecture that she gave in the late 1940s, she declared, "With the possible exception of the Scandinavians, no European citizenry has the political maturity of Americans."

Jury duty for her was a particularly inspiring experience. For two weeks in civil court, she had the chance to escape from her inbred circle of haughty intellectuals and interact directly with ordinary citizens possessed of ordinary educations. To her delight, her fellow jurors took their civic responsibility seriously, deliberating on the basis of evidence and listening respectfully to what other jurors had to say. "The objectivity and impartiality are quite astonishing, even in quite simple people." And there was that remarkable American tolerance. Puerto Rican plaintiffs who didn't speak English and required a translator were treated just like everyone else. The facts decided their cases, not prejudice or preconceptions. "The whole business is really quite wonderful." (One thinks of Henry Kissinger describing his military experience as "exhilarating.")

Arendt has been accused, much like Kissinger, of idealizing her adopted country, of "exonerating America of just about everything others might regard as dark in its history." There is truth to this charge. Her observation that everyone was happy to perform jury duty hardly rings true, and she once told Jaspers that prosperity was so widespread in the United States that even a black chauffeur whose wife worked as a maid could afford to own two or three cars. (She wasn't so sure that was a good thing, but only for the reasons a German intellectual might come up with.) She could sound as starry-eyed as the most naïve newcomer.

And yet, she always felt that ambivalence, the tug of uncertainty, the frisson of fear. Looking at Eisenhower during the 1952 presidential race, she saw Hindenburg, "a dangerous idiot," with more ominous figures like McCarthy and Nixon lurking behind him. That year she and her husband "voted again, for the first time in 20 years"—that is, since the rise of the Nazis in Germany—"and all we can do is hope that it won't be the last time." A year later, with McCarthy on the rampage, she felt "that we're looking at developments that are all too familiar." She had a personal reason to be concerned: her husband had concealed the fact that he had been a Communist in Germany and, if the truth were to come out, they stood in danger of deportation. But then the fever broke, McCarthy's hour passed, and by 1955 her American life was "pleasant and reasonable" again. The country had come through without turning fascist, "and we—thanks and jubilation be to God—were wrong."

She was wrong, too, when the Kennedy assassination left her thinking that "what is at stake is no more nor less than the existence of the republic." Worse was to come. The turmoil of the 1960s made her perpetually ill at ease, wondering if she should start packing her bags again. The Vietnam war was tearing the country apart. Racial tensions were boiling over. The campuses were exploding, the cities deteriorating. Public services like transportation and the mails were falling apart, and crime was out of control. By the start of 1968, she said, she knew of many native-born Americans, not just German-Jewish émigrés, who were thinking of leaving the country. And the nation's urban problems were having a direct impact: New York City was becoming too much for her. In 1968, she and her husband considered abandoning their Upper West Side apartment to find "more comfort than is possible in big cities," and a few years later she survived an attempted mugging, though not without psychological damage. She became fearful of venturing out onto New York's dangerous streets. "For many years now, the law-enforcement agencies have been unable to enforce the statutes against drug traffic, mugging and burglary," she said. "It looks like the end of the republic," she wrote to McCarthy.

"Crisis" became a favorite word in her vocabulary (much more than "banality"). Chapters in one book were titled "The Crisis in Education" and "The Crisis in Culture." A second book of essays on contemporary affairs was called *Crises of the Republic*. Issues that others might see as narrow policy questions to be addressed by specific, wonkish solutions registered with her as symptoms of broader social decay with grand implications. Writing about education, she said, "Certainly more is involved here than the puzzling question of why Johnny can't read." One had to take the "crisis" in education with the utmost seriousness. The failures of the schoolrooms weren't a matter of raising test scores—that could be left to the experts and professionals—but a reflection of the broadest, most dangerous trends in Western civilization: the decline of authority and tradition. Chaos threatened, and with it all the horrific political developments that had afflicted Europe in the first half of the twentieth century. "One can take it as a general rule," she gravely warned, "that whatever is possible in one country may in the foreseeable future be equally possible in almost any other." In America's ineffectual and demoralized classrooms could be heard the rumblings of totalitarianism, the footsteps of the storm troopers. Maybe the United States was Germany after all.

A kind of summa of her catastrophic concerns, written in 1975, the last year of her life, was the essay "Home to Roost." Arendt said she never received as many fan letters for anything else she wrote. It was her last word on the darkness that seemed to be enveloping America.

The mass hysteria and demagoguery of the McCarthy era were the beginnings, she said, of a decades-long decline. Though the mood of the country recovered from that "mini-crisis," the more thoughtful were left to wonder about its larger meaning and just how secure the republic really was. By the 1970s, the foundations were shaking. "The recent cataclysm of events tumbling over one another, cascading like a Niagara Falls of history," was proving the pessimists correct. The defeat in Vietnam was part of a more general failure of American foreign policy, involving NATO and the Middle East. The economy was crumbling, afflicted by the curses of inflation and unemployment. Only consumer wastefulness was sustaining it, and that was destroying the environment.

Worst of all, the release of the Pentagon Papers and the Watergate scandal had demonstrated that a cynical mentality of advertising and public relations—so central in persuading Americans to desire more and more in a nightmarish pattern of meaningless consumerism—had invaded the realm of politics like some lethal disease. For government officials, the falsity of image-making was now taking precedence over actual facts, problem solving, and a genuine attention to the public welfare, leading first to lying and then, inevitably, to criminality. Politics was becoming theater, and theater had no place in politics. Arendt reached for an analogy familiar to her. Totalitarian governments, she said, were willing to kill millions to conceal unpleasant facts. The United States was a long way from that: the manipulation of public opinion, not terror, was Washington's way of hiding the truth. But the signs were not good; the country was on a road to perdition. A "stab-in-the-back" theory, used so effectively by the Nazis to vanquish their enemies, was already developing with regard to Vietnam. And unless the docile, materialist-minded citizenry woke up to the true realities and demanded real solutions to real problems, instead of trying to escape into "images, theories and sheer follies," far greater troubles lay in store. She believed the country might be at a turning point in its history. The handwriting was on the wall. The chickens were coming home to roost.

Any republic, Arendt had written elsewhere, required "the spirit and the vigilance" of its citizens to survive. "It is the people's support that lends power to the institutions of a country." But while she could praise the political maturity of Americans in one moment, in the next she was filled with apprehension, with no great confidence in public spiritedness. In the 1946 letter to Jaspers in which she applauded the ideal of freedom to be found in the United States, she also told him of a darker side to her new homeland. America was a land of social conformity where material success was all that mattered, a place in which everyone was pressured to think like everyone else. Individualism was valued in theory, despised in practice. Here was a conundrum. "The fundamental contradiction of the country," she said, "is the co-existence of political freedom and social oppression."

The result was an uneasy, possibly unstable tension. With a nod to one of her favorite political philosophers, Montesquieu, Arendt pointed out that all societies were a combination of laws and customs. The state was the protection of the law, which guaranteed every individual in the country "his rights as man, his rights as citizen and his rights as a national." Customs were this province of society, the basis for community and tradition, the common, inherited, not-quite-rational feelings that made a nation a nation, but also a force for oppressive conformity and unreflective orthodoxy. For the sake of public health, the state and society, or law and custom, had to be in balance. But this was not always the case. At those times when the rationality of law was undermined or lost its legitimacy, society could overwhelm the state, with the voice of "the people" drowning out the authority of the law and the freedoms it protected. Laws "are always in danger of being abolished by the power of the many, and in a conflict between law and power it is seldom the law which will emerge as victor." Under such circumstances, individual rights are crushed for what is perceived to be the common good, as defined by the will of the majority. In Germany in the 1930s, Arendt pointed out, Hitler proudly declared, "Right is what is good for the German people."

In the United States, where the nation's political institutions were in conflict with the delusions of the unthinking, anti-intellectual masses, the public was always a potential threat to freedom, and in the early 1950s that threat was embodied in Joseph McCarthy. McCarthyism was, Arendt said, a movement that spread outside the law as "a kind of parallel government." It was taking over the civil service and the entertainment industry, even the colleges and universities. Its weapons were intimidation and self-censorship, and no sector of society was immune.

America's political institutions survived that particular challenge, but Arendt emerged from the McCarthy years shaken, with no assurance that the American people would necessarily do the right thing. It was the Constitution and the courts that had saved the republic, and as long as the Constitution, that "sacred document," remained intact, the republic and the individual freedoms it safeguarded were probably secure from mob passion. But the threat to America's liberal institutions was ever present: "Large numbers of people, crowded together, develop an almost irresistible inclination toward despotism, be this the despotism of a person or of majority rule." Similarly, "totalitarian movements are possible whenever there are masses who for one reason or another have acquired the appetite for political organization." What was more, "a consumers' society" like the one that had developed in the United States, with its stoking of personal pleasure and indifference to the public realm, "spells ruin to everything it touches."

In an observation whose implications would become clearer when she attended the Eichmann trial, Arendt also wrote that America was "a society of jobholders," and the Nazi experience had taught her not to trust such people, though they were commonly considered the salt of the earth. As she said about Eichmann, "What he fervently believed in up to the end was success, the chief standard of 'good society' as he knew it." In times of uncertainty, average middle-class citizens, whose attention was narrowly focused on their families and their careers, with little civic or moral awareness to speak of, "will willingly undertake any function, even that of the hangman" to preserve their self-interested positions and their unreflective tranquility. The ordinary Joe with his ordinary cares was a sleeping menace to republican freedoms. It was a mistake even to call him a "citizen." He was "mob man," and under the right (which is to say, wrong) conditions, he was "quite willing to believe—well, just anything." We are a long way from Henry Kissinger's middle Americans and Czeslaw Milosz's melon growers.

As usual, given the complexity of her feelings, this was not Arendt's last word on the subject. For her, there never was a last word. She continued to swing back and forth in her views, condemning the mass of the American people as proto-fascists at one moment, marveling at their good political sense at another. But in one way she remained consistent throughout, and that was in her refusal to embrace democratic ideals as most Americans understood them. It should be said here that there are scrupulous, knowledgeable scholars, Arendt partisans, who describe her as a champion of democracy, just as there are Strauss partisans who vigorously attest to his democratic values. But as with Strauss, Arendt's own words too often belie that claim. "A democracy ruled by majority decisions but unchecked by law is just as despotic as an autocracy," she wrote. And "a terrifying and truly tyrannical authority," she said, was "the tyranny of the majority." Mass society, she told Jaspers, seemed to be overwhelming the republic, and though the institutions of the state should constrain and limit the dictates of the people, the American republic, as the McCarthyite experience demonstrated, was "being dissolved from within by democracy."

Americans were deluded, Arendt insisted, if they thought their political institutions were meant to establish a democracy. That was never the intent of the Founding Fathers, who had read the ancient Greeks attentively and worried as much about tyrannical majorities as did German-Jewish refugees fleeing Hitler's popular and populist regime. They were kindred spirits. "What men" they were, Arendt exclaimed in breathless admiration of the Founders, and how little understood in modern times, with its ethos of democratic egalitarianism.

The recent arrival felt obliged to lecture her native-born countrymen by reminding them about their true history. "It's a great mistake if you believe that what we have here is democracy, a mistake in which many Americans share. What we have here is republican rule, and the Founding Fathers were most concerned about preserving the rights of minorities."

Such words had an oddly familiar ring at the time, though emanating from a political corner far removed from Arendt and her friends. "A republic, not a democracy" was the rallying cry of the extreme, often loony, reactionaries gathered around the John Birch Society during the 1950s and after. But though Arendt, with her stress on individual freedom, shared language and even long-term worries with the far right, she could never be mistaken for one of them—not with her contempt for bourgeois, money-obsessed self-interest, her support for trade unions, her identification with the weak and vulnerable, her anti-anti-Communism, her determined pluralism, and her praise of immigration as the means by which the United States continually revitalized itself. The "magnificence" of the country, she said, "consists in the fact that from the beginning this new order did not shut itself off from the outside world." (She also said that the attempt to equate freedom with free enterprise was a "monstrous falsehood.")

In their wisdom—which could also be called their fear of majority rule—the Founders had established a system based on the separation of powers. Arendt approved: "Only division of powers can guarantee the rule of law" because only when there were differentiated power bases would discussion, rationality, and persuasion find a place in the process of governing; no single source exercising tyrannical rule could dictate to others without any appeal to the open exchange of ideas and to the instrument of reason. At the national level, the Constitution gave us the horizontal tripartite structure of executive, legislature, and judiciary, but it also gave us a vertical construct of states' rights, and to Arendt this division was no less important for the preservation of freedom and law. Liberals, she said, were inclined to minimize the value of states' rights, which was, Arendt insisted, "a dangerous error." (She added, contrary to many on the left, that "all this has nothing to do with being a liberal or a conservative.") There had to be a balance between the states and the "Federal power." She was even prepared to cite John C. Calhoun for support: "Calhoun was certainly right when he held that in questions of great national importance the 'concurrence or acquiescence of the various portions of the community' are a prerequisite of constitutional government."

Inevitably, she was driven to discuss race and civil rights, which she did in her 1959 article "Reflections on Little Rock." Though commonly ignored today, especially by her supporters, it was a most revealing piece of work. With the exception of the Eichmann book, nothing else she wrote ever generated so much criticism and so many personal attacks. None of her friends agreed with her, she told Jaspers; some were "really angry." The article was originally intended for *Commentary* magazine, which had commissioned it and then got cold feet about running it. The socialist magazine *Dissent*, which did publish it a year later, treated it like a ticking bomb. The editors took the unusual step of including a preliminary disclaimer that distanced them from Arendt even before their readers had a chance to decide for themselves: "We publish it not because we agree with it—quite the contrary!—but because we believe in freedom of expression even for views that seem to us entirely mistaken." And they took the added precaution of following the piece with two lengthy rebuttals so that her incendiary opinions were cushioned by a pillow of comforting opposition voices. The magazine can hardly be said to have done Arendt any favors with its smothering treatment of her piece. It was almost as if they were holding it up as a specimen of how *not* to think.

Arendt wrote that she disapproved of using the powers of the federal government to force integration in the South's public schools. As a practical matter, this placed her on the side of the racists, as did her invocation of states' rights. No wonder her liberal friends reacted with fury. But there was nothing else in her article to warm the heart of a die-hard segregationist. Klan leaders would not be distributing copies of *Dissent* to their followers. As she said at the beginning, "As a Jew I take my sympathy for the cause of the Negroes as for all oppressed or underprivileged peoples for granted, and should appreciate it if the reader did likewise."

The basis of her argument was Montesquieu's distinction between society and the state, custom and the law. It was the duty of the authorities to enforce legal and political equality, not social equality. Thus, voting rights were a legitimate concern for federal officials, as was the desegregation of public facilities like buses, trains, hotels and restaurants located in business districts (a crucial detail), theaters, and museums. Most of all, Arendt was distressed by antimiscegenation laws, which were an unambiguous denial of legal equality. The state had no business interfering in what should be the most private and individual of decisions. Take that, bigots!

But the government also overstepped if it tried to eliminate discrimination as such. That was a utopian ideal that through its very lack of realism must result in tyranny because everyone made social distinctions of one kind or another that could be wiped out only by oppressive force. Prejudice was contained in our choice of friends and neighbors. "Without discrimination of some sort," Arendt declared, "society would cease to exist." And just as people should have the right to marry whom they wished, they should have the right to associate with whom they wished. She offered an example of what she called "legitimate" discrimination. Jews might prefer to spend their vacations among their own kind; gentiles, likewise, might choose to enjoy their leisure time outside of the company of Jews. Resorts should be free to cater to these private preferences, however unenlightened, and the government should not intrude so long as these establishments existed as private institutions within the social realm. But she emphasized again, "While the government has no right to interfere with the prejudices and discriminatory practices of society, it has not only the right, but the duty to make sure that these practices are not legally enforced." Government could not demand social equality of its citizens or, it goes without saying, social inequality, "but it can and indeed must enforce equality within the body politic." For "only there are we all equals."

Within Arendt's framework, schools seemed to exist in an in-between area as both political and social. But Arendt made a further distinction. She recognized that education was a necessary political function, which might seem to call for legal equality, but the public function of schools, she said, was to train future citizens, not to dictate social relations. White parents had the right to determine whom their children associated with, for that was a private question. By forcing school integration, the government was blurring important categories and piggybacking in pursuit of an ideal of social equality. And beyond these theoretical distinctions, Arendt urged caution as a practical matter. By forcing integration in the face of generations of tradition and personal belief, the federal government was inviting massive resistance and mob violence. Arendt quoted William Faulkner saying that enforced integration was no better than enforced segregation; she added, "This is perfectly true." Whatever one thinks of this view, there was prescience here: a straight—if not inevitable—line ran from school desegregation in the South to the busing in the North of unwilling school-children outside their neighborhoods for the sake of racial mixing, as well as to affirmative action policies that pitted racial groups against one another in a zero-sum numbers game refereed by government bureaucrats with little more on their minds than statistics. An even straighter line ran from broad public support for civil rights to widespread opposition to federal interference in the social lives of citizens. Forced integration has left an enduring legacy of hostility to government that soon spread beyond the South and that we have not yet overcome.

Better, and more cautious, solutions, Arendt argued, were to create black schools that were genuinely separate but equal or to establish pilot programs of integrated schools where parents, both black and white, could voluntarily send their children. And she said that if mobs or state authorities tried to shut down those schools, the federal government could legitimately intervene, based on a principle of public equality that preserved individual choice. White and black parents had the legal right to encourage their children to mingle, if that's what they wanted; they should not be prevented by government from raising their children as they saw fit. (Exactly who would finance these integrated schools, the state or the participating families, was a subsidiary issue she did not address, but one can imagine Arendt supporting public funding on the grounds that the role of the government was to back the legal equality of parents who favored integrated schools as much as it did those who valued segregation.)

Her critics pounced. Arendt had a superficial idea of federalism and a "specious idea of freedom." She claimed to be interested in justice for black Americans, but by suggesting that she knew what was good for them better than they did themselves, she demonstrated—a familiar accusation—that "she is an aristocrat, not a democrat at heart." More substantively, she had failed to indicate that the fight against segregated schools didn't compel integration; it simply removed laws that discriminated against a powerless minority of the population in favor of the bigoted majority: white parents weren't being forced to send their children to integrated schools; they were free to set up private segregated schools if they wished. (This, of course, is precisely what they did, though it also led them to question why their taxes should go to pay for integrated schools they did not want.) Her suggestion that the government would have been better advised to begin the fight against discrimination with antimiscegenation laws, not school segregation, was outrageously impractical and politically naïve; only a person far removed from the realities of American life would propose it. And she had ignored the argument made in the Supreme Court itself that segregated public schools were "inherently unequal" because they degraded and humiliated the group being discriminated against. If history is an arbiter, then Arendt lost this debate. Still, it's hard not to feel that she and her critics were talking past one another.

The critics were concerned with political outcomes and the kind of society they wanted the United States to be. Because discrimination was reprehensible, the levers of government should be employed to achieve integration with all due speed and with force if necessary. Equality was the ideal—never mind possible distinctions between political and social, between public and private. "The moral question is primary," said the philosopher Sidney Hook, and the law as a reflection of public morality could be legitimately used to combat "certain evil social practices." Arendt also considered discrimination reprehensible, even incomprehensible. "Like most people of European origin, I have difficulty in understanding, let alone sharing, the common prejudices of Americans in this area." But she was concerned with political process, measuring actions not by their immediate outcomes but by their underlying principles. Ideas mattered. Public policy had to take into consideration more than facts on the ground. It especially had to be wary about imposing a particular social ideal.

"The point at stake," she wrote in full catastrophic mode, "is not the well-being of the Negro population alone, but at least in the long run, the survival of the republic." Coming from a country where "the people" had overridden all legal processes for the sake of what was viewed as the common good, she was highly sensitive to maintaining the role of law in society. And that role, pace Hook, was definitely not to enforce some notion of morality, which was a private matter and which she knew—obviously with Nietzsche whispering in her ear—could be defined any which way, depending on the momentary mood of the public. Hook's government-enforced morality was a path on the way to the thought police and the midnight knock at the door. Against the vicissitudes of popular opinion, the law, developed through reason, persuasion, and judgment, provided stability and protection for the individual. The critics never really did understand her distinction between state and society. "Metaphysical mumbo jumbo," one of them contemptuously called it. But then he had never experienced—or couldn't even imagine—the damage that a tyranny of the majority could wreak (and he received an even more contemptuous flick of the wrist from Arendt in response).

Though he did not weigh in on the Little Rock controversy, there was one person who took Arendt's distinction between state and society as seriously as she did—Leo Strauss, of course. He insisted that any liberal society depended on a firm distinction between public and private. For liberal freedoms to survive, the private sphere had to be preserved even if that meant the perpetuation of evils like discrimination. Reformers might dream of "clean solutions," but those solutions invariably failed, or they led to still greater evils.

These two German-Jewish exiles could be accused of insensitivity to the rights of black Americans or a lack of understanding of the fundamental values of the United States, its social identity, but they were thinking from a different perspective than most of their countrymen, trying to impart the lessons of Weimar. And so they tended to view contemporary events from a great height, *sub specie aeternitatis*. A problem was never simply a problem to be solved by whatever means were at hand in the pragmatic American fashion; it had to be analyzed in terms of its deeper implications. What's more, they were decidedly anti-utopian, sniffing out unbounded idealism wherever it arose, and skeptical of those who offered solutions to what seemed to them to be part of the human condition. Neither believed that prejudice and discrimination could ever be completely eradicated. Tamp it down in one area and it would reemerge in another. The best one could hope for was to keep it confined to the social realm, to develop or degenerate as it would. People could not—and should not—be forced to be good, since everyone knows what the paving stones are on the road to Hell.

To optimistic and idealistic Americans, such views were pessimistic and cynical. Arendt and Strauss were pessimistic to be sure, cautious about the uses of power, but neither was cynical. Even on a matter that was closer to his heart than civil rights, one in which he had a personal stake, Strauss was consistent about the impossibility of dictating the ideal of a moral society. "The Jewish problem," he said, "is insoluble."

ARENDT'S MOST ELABORATE statement on the United States and its "basically sound political structure" was her 1963 book, *On Revolution*. With its celebration of the American Revolution and its denigration of the French Revolution, it has accurately been called "an act of gratitude" to her adopted country, a book-length expression of personal appreciation of America. Yet it is an extremely odd expression of appreciation. It is not a fulsome account of the establishment of democracy in the way American schoolchildren are taught about their revolution; indeed, the word "democracy" hardly enters Arendt's discussion at all, and when it does, it is with a notable lack of enthusiasm. ("The Founding Fathers tended to equate rule based on public opinion with tyranny; democracy in this sense was to them but a newfangled form of despotism.") What is more, the book has not necessarily pleased professional historians with its broadly philosophical, less than empirical treatment of events; major scholars like Bernard Bailyn and Gordon Wood feel little need to refer to it in their work on the period. Once again, Arendt was writing from a great height. She was not interested in the accumulation of facts. Historical detail took second place to the stream of ideas she was analyzing. *On Revolution* has an outsider's perspective; in its insistent abstraction, one might, if one were given to generalizations, even term it "Germanic." It is, in any case, clearly not the work of any native-born American lacking "the slightest inkling of what philosophy is." Nonetheless, it has resonated sufficiently with readers to have gone through numerous printings, and while some find it "baffling," others have labeled it "a political classic." Jaspers thought it Arendt's best work (though, admittedly, he may have been biased since the book was dedicated to him and his wife, and his knowledge of English was not perfect).

It definitely has not won praise from most readers on the left. At the time it appeared, when Marxism was a living, even dominating philosophical presence, the French Revolution was considered the model for political activists, the American Revolution a local episode with no global significance, perhaps not even a revolution at all. To Arendt, this was an intellectual tragedy of the first order, for the French Revolution had ended in "disaster" while the American Revolution has been "triumphantly successful." Not all leftists dismissed *On Revolution*; Arendt's admiration for small, radical councils throughout history won supporters in the 1960s among the members of the Students for a Democratic Society, who were happy to find parallels with their own ill-formed notions of participatory democracy in the musings of a world-famous thinker. Still, her assessment of the French Revolution was so harsh that she has been called, not inaccurately, a proponent of "a kind of Burkean Toryism."

Arendt was especially agitated by how the Marxist interpretation of the two revolutions had come to dominate historical thinking, and she met the Marxists head-on. The problem was that there was no true theorist of the American Revolution, she said, in the way that Marx was the theorist of the French Revolution—not even Tocqueville—and in a sense *On Revolution* was her attempt to fill that gap. Marx's genius could neither be denied nor his insights into modern economics ignored (here, as on so many other occasions, what Arendt offered to the political right with one hand she took back with the other). But Marx's influence, whatever his virtues, had been "pernicious" in the long run; he and the disciples who acted in his name were prepared to sacrifice the highest goods, individual freedom and unencumbered thought, for the dead weight of materialism and the stultifying dogma of the dialectic. Everywhere that Marxism took hold, economics trumped politics, and physical need dictated to spiritual freedom. Pushed to its most extreme, this was a prescription for total slavery (cf. Cambodia). With Marx serving as history's bridge, Lenin could be seen as "the last heir of the French Revolution." And Lenin, Arendt insisted, was a man with "no theoretical concept of freedom."

In 1963 these were fighting words, though not so much today. The Marxist model of revolution began to disappear in the 1970s as "the gulag" entered the common vocabulary, when countries like Spain and Portugal cast off their anachronistic fascist dictatorships, not for socialist utopias but for liberal democracy, and when, a few years after that, upheavals in Eastern Europe brought down the Soviet Empire. Influential voices in these events, like Vaclav Havel and Adam Michnik, were self-declared Arendt admirers. In his 2006 introduction to an edition of *On Revolution*, Jonathan Schell is able to speak of the revolutions of the last quarter of the twentieth century as a "wave of Arendtian democratization." Another Arendt admirer said that "it is because of her that the left in America no longer attacks the American Revolution."

THE FIRST PART of *On Revolution* is a study of why the American Revolution got it right and how the French Revolution got it wrong. Both had started in the same place, Arendt said, with calls for freedom and the rights of man. The French had even borrowed their revolutionary language from the Americans. But the demand for individual freedom in France was quickly outstripped by other more radical aims. The revolution had "changed its direction." Equality replaced freedom as the goal of revolution—and not equality as it was understood in the New World, equality before the law, but equality of social condition. The cathartic violence of rebellion held the promise of an end to poverty. In Arendtian terms, the social question had overwhelmed the political one with horrendous results. So hostile was Arendt to the dominant French model of revolution in the nineteenth and twentieth centuries that she was led to make one of the most provocative, most extreme statements to be found in any of her writings throughout her career: "We . . . know to our sorrow that freedom has been better preserved in countries where no revolution ever broke out, no matter how outrageous the circumstances of the powers that be, and that there exist more civil liberties even in countries where the revolution was defeated than in those where revolutions have been victorious." There is an echo in this statement of Goethe's famous comment, "I would rather commit an injustice than suffer disorder." But it is not hard to recognize the voice of Henry Kissinger as well. His policy toward Allende's Chile is contained in Arendt's words.

The French Revolution took a wrong turn once the impoverished "multitude" was galvanized into making its own demands, not for a government that would guarantee individual liberty but for an end to material want. This became the very definition of human happiness, just as the phrase "le peuple" became the "key words for every understanding of the French Revolution." In Arendt's mind, such a goal could only be met—if at all—by the application of technology and administrative expertise to economic problems; the question of poverty could not be answered by changing the form of government. It was not a political issue. Contra Marx, she did not believe that poverty was caused by capitalist exploitation; she seemed to be more inclined toward Jesus' position that the poor would always be with us, in good times and bad, under feudalism, under capitalism, under socialism.

Such views have opened Arendt up to an endless barrage of criticism, even from her closest friend, Mary McCarthy. One of the more telling examples came from the German philosopher Jürgen Habermas, who lamented what he called Arendt's "curious perspective." She imagined "a state," he said, "which is relieved of the administrative processing of social problems; a politics which is cleansed of socioeconomic issues; an institutionalization of public liberty which is independent of the organization of public wealth; a radical democracy which inhibits its liberating efficacy just at the boundaries where political oppression ceases and social repression begins—this path is unimaginable for any modern society." But Arendt, the witness to both the blood-stained economic successes of the Third Reich and the blood-stained economic failures of the Soviet Union, resolutely insisted that it was essential to keep economics and other social matters divorced from political ones. Freedom was not advanced by mixing them. Rather, it was endangered. And in a Leo Straussian vein, she felt obliged to remind her American readers that prosperity and private well-being were wholly possible under a tyranny. Once again can be spied the ghost of Adolf Hitler.

Once the masses had seized control of events in France, Arendt wrote, the revolution moved in a catastrophic populist direction. No longer was the goal the founding of a republic but the fulfillment of "the will of the people," as Robespierre had said. Any consideration of creating neutral governmental structures like the separation of powers that could survive the inevitable conflicts of interest in a body politic was abandoned as an obstacle to the final end, which was, as Arendt rather ungenerously put it, "a right to burst with resentment, greed and envy." Means, that is to say the rule of law, were swallowed up by unattainable ends and by the force of sheer emotion that found cruel expression in the execution of presumed enemies. With abstractions like "le peuple" beclouding their thinking, the French revolutionaries came to see themselves as actors in a struggle of good against evil, of the innocent, well-meaning populace against the predatory few. Thus their revolution was transformed into theater, not so much a drama as a melodrama, and yet a tragedy. To understand the perverse psychology of these populist incorruptibles, whose faith in their own goodwill was unquestioning, and for whom, therefore, brutality and inhumanity exercised at the expense of their enemies had become virtues, Arendt had recourse to the fictions of Dostoyevsky and Melville. "We can learn from them," she said, "that absolute goodness is hardly any less dangerous than absolute evil."

HOW HAD "LUCKY AMERICA" managed to avoid the French disaster? To begin with, it was fortunate in the enemy it faced—not the absolute king who dominated France but a constitutional monarch whose powers were already reined in by legal institutions and tradition. The American colonists had grown up with a legacy of rule by law, whereas the French had known only dictatorship, and thinking in each case reflected past political experience. "Nothing, indeed, seems more natural than that a revolution should be predetermined by the type of government it overthrows," Arendt wrote. She went on, "Nothing, therefore, appears more plausible than to explain the new absolute, the absolute revolution, by the absolute monarchy which preceded it, and to conclude that the more absolute the ruler, the more absolute the revolution will be which replaces him." It was not only the French example that lent support to this argument. Her readers had the example of the Russian Revolution right before their eyes.

But Arendt, always the eclectic thinker (indeed, with Marx as an influence), was not one to ignore material conditions. To understand why the "multitude," with its absolute demands, had succeeded in taking over the French but not the American revolution, she turned to economic factors for part of her explanation. Her aim, however, was not to glorify the poor and oppressed. The masses in France and throughout Europe knew only grinding poverty, poverty that was constant, abject, and dehumanizing, and the call to revolution awakened in them not an aspiration for freedom but a salvational, almost apocalyptic hope to end their misery. Inevitably, that hope turned to rage when promises went unkept. If desperation was not a fact of life, someone had to be blamed. This train of thought, with its cold, hard logic, sped on uninterrupted tracks in the pursuit of scapegoats and to the violence and terror that destroyed the French Revolution.

The Americans were twice blessed, both in the nature of the regime they were overthrowing and also in the condition of the citizenry who would be the foundation of the new order. Americans simply did not know European misery. A long line of recent scholarship has brought to light the deep inequalities of the colonies; the New World was not an egalitarian paradise and had never been. Arendt did not deny the divisions of rich and poor in America or the injustices of inequality, but for her it was a matter of degree, and that difference made a great difference. Poverty was not missing from the colonies, but the desperation of utter destitution was. "The laborious in America were poor but not miserable," she said, and she cited what she called the unanimity of European visitors on this point. "In a course of 1,200 miles I did not see a single object that solicited charity," said one. Contemporary historians have reached the same conclusion. "The social conditions that generically are supposed to lie behind all revolutions—poverty and economic deprivation—were not present in colonial America," Gordon Wood has written. Not only were the Americans far from being oppressed like the vast majority of Europeans, but "in fact, the colonists knew they were freer, more equal, more prosperous . . . than any other part of mankind in the eighteenth century."

By the same token, Americans who traveled to Europe were shocked at the conditions they encountered. Nothing of what they saw existed among ordinary Americans. Of the 20 million people in France, Jefferson said in 1787, "There are 19 millions more wretched, more accursed in every circumstance of human existence than the most conspicuously wretched individual of the whole United States." Benjamin Franklin contrasted the lives of the French poor to "the happiness of New England, where every man is a freeholder, has a vote in public affairs, lives in a tidy warm house, has plenty of good food and fuel." These impoverished masses, "the canaille of the cities of Europe," could scarcely be potential revolutionaries in any American sense, Jefferson insisted. Quite the contrary: they were a threat to the cause of freedom, which "would be instantly perverted to the demolition and destruction of everything private and public." No Rousseau-like appeals to "le peuple" in these words. Arendt counted the Founding Fathers' fear of these desperate multitudes as one of the key components of their "realism."

Only one group in America could be compared in its misery to Europe's wretched poor, and that group, of course, was the slaves. Arendt had almost nothing to say about them, but this was not because she lacked compassion or because she believed, in the manner of some apologists for the antebellum South, that slavery was not the terrible institution generations of historians have proved it to be. At a time when debates were still going on over whether slavery had been a blessing to blacks forcibly transported from Africa, she declared that slavery was "the primordial crime upon which the fabric of American society rested." If it had been her intention to describe the depth of human suffering in the American colonies, slavery would have taken up much more than the three pages she devotes to it in her book; it might even have been its focus. But her subject was the nature of political revolution, the causes of it and the theory behind it; wretchedness and revolution were not ineluctably intertwined. Human misery was one thing; the causes of revolution were quite another. From her abstract perch there was nothing to be said about the inhumane if anomalous institution of slavery or the slaves themselves except to point out, with Jefferson, with Tocqueville, with Lincoln, that once the banner of freedom had been raised, the question of America's enchained blacks was bound to follow.

IF DRAWING A firm distinction between the French and American revolutions to the advantage of the American was the first of Arendt's objectives in *On Revolution*, the second was to solve the intellectual problem that the experience of the United States presented to her, one that went to the heart of her political thinking. The American government rested on democracy, the will of the people, and it had been a great success. Yet the will of the people, as the French Revolution but equally the example of Hitler showed, could not be trusted. Left to their own devices, "the people" could degenerate into a mob, which, in the twentieth century, unleashed unprecedented horrors. The second half of *On Revolution* addressed itself largely to explaining how these two apparently contradictory propositions could be reconciled.

Arendt began by noting that although the two ideas of "liberation" and "freedom" were often confused and conflated, they were not the same. Liberation consisted of a rebellious breaking of shackles, the dream of political upheavals from the dawn of recorded history, and had always been the focus of historians and other intellectuals because all the drama was contained in the fight against tyranny, or what Arendt called all the good stories. Liberation was enabling, it was exhilarating, it was sexy. Adolescents were drawn to it. But by itself liberation was negation: it had no goal in sight and produced only anarchy as enabled, exhilarated rebels struggled, gun in hand, to gain power for themselves, their cohort, their tribe, their people. This was not freedom but its antithesis, one tyranny confronting another tyranny—a case of meet the new boss, same as the old boss. And it was not what Arendt meant by revolution: "The end of rebellion is liberation, while the end of revolution is the foundation of freedom." Most often, liberation crushed freedom.

Freedom, the true goal of revolution, could only be achieved in a second stage of rebellion with the writing of a constitution, the codifying of law, the imposing of limits to liberation. Law did not stand in opposition to freedom but was its very foundation and articulation. It made freedom possible. Constitution-writing, therefore, was "the foremost and the noblest of all revolutionary deeds." Those historians who, following the lead of Charles Beard, taught that the American Constitution was a "reactionary" backlash to the inspiring revolutionary rhetoric of the Declaration of Independence were borrowing their concepts from the failed French experience and simply did not know what they were talking about. Such American historians did not understand American history. Neither did the political theorists who, in a familiar tradition of American liberal thought, insisted on viewing government as the enemy of the individual and of freedom. In an idea utterly foreign to most Americans, weaned on the writings of Thoreau and others like him, Arendt insisted that individuals had no freedom without law, which the hardheaded Founding Fathers understood as the rule of reason over passion. The incorruptible Robespierre, with his distrust of reason, "made light of laws."

Admirably, in Arendt's opinion, the successfully rebellious American colonists rushed to avert liberation's potential anarchy with a flurry of constitution-writing across the newly established states. "There existed no gap, no hiatus, hardly a breathing spell between the war of liberation, the fight for independence which was the condition for freedom, and the constitution of the new states." This was the "miracle" that saved the revolution, and it culminated in the sacred federal Constitution, which established a new governing authority. "Power and freedom belonged together," Arendt said. Separating and balancing power at the federal level, or between the federal government and the states, was not intended to curtail government, she argued. Rather, it created an arena for public discourse and rational lawmaking; the point was to acknowledge and channel the reality of power, not deny it. "The true objective of the American Constitution," Arendt declared, "was not to limit power but to create more power, actually to establish and duly constitute an entirely new power center" as a replacement for the British Crown. And the Bill of Rights, which restrained power? A "supplement," in Arendt's mind, really something of an afterthought (it rates only five fleeting mentions in her book).

A problem remained, however. Other revolutions, beginning with the French, had followed up their rebellions with the promulgation of constitutions, and yet all had failed. Why? Another way of putting the question is to ask why the Americans trusted their constitution-makers in a way that the French and other revolutionaries did not trust theirs. What gave the Founders the authority to impose restraints in the form of a constitutional system on the newly liberated, centrifugally inclined, potentially lawless masses? Why should anyone accept their handiwork? Didn't one prominent historian famously sum up the Founding Fathers as an assemblage of "the well-bred, the well-fed, the well-read and the well-wed"?

Authority was a topic that had long obsessed Arendt. It was what endowed rulers with the power to govern, but she was at pains to emphasize, much like Kissinger, that authority was not the same thing as force or compulsion, which depended on violence. Authority, by definition, required the voluntary acquiescence of followers to leaders. Otherwise, it was doomed to failure, leaving only Hobbes's cruel choice between tyranny and anarchy. "Authority," she said, "implies an obedience in which men retained their freedom." It was not to be confused with authoritarianism. She also wrote that the disappearance of traditional authority "has been one of the most spectacular characteristics of the modern world," the modern world that has given us Nazism, Fascism, Communism, and now militant Islam. When a revolution overturned traditional authority, it pushed society to the edge of anarchy, requiring a new authority to restore order. "The great and fateful misfortune of the French Revolution," Arendt wrote, "was that none of the constituent assemblies could command enough authority to lay down the law of the land." This lack of authority, she said, has been "the curse of constitutional government in nearly all European countries since the abolition of absolute monarchies." America was different.

America was different because its revolution did not throw the colonists back into a Hobbesian state of nature. It did not begin at the beginning with a war of all against all. The new country may have severed its ties to the British Crown, but it hardly destroyed those institutions that stood apart from the king's authority, namely, the domestic townships, councils, and legislatures. In fact, they had been the engines of rebellion. In Arendtian terms, most modern revolutions, starting with the French, had overthrown the one legitimate authority they knew, sanctified by religion and tradition, and then collapsed in the futile search for a new, broadly acceptable authority that, under the circumstances, had to be imposed from the top down. The American Revolution, by contrast, represented a clash of authorities, with local, bottom-up popular assemblies, dating back a century and a half to the Pilgrims' Mayflower Compact, prevailing over the distant British monarch. Governing power did not have to be destroyed and then artificially recreated from scratch. It merely had to be transferred and elaborated. "Since the colonial covenants had originally been made without any reference to king or prince, it was as though the Revolution liberated the power of covenant and constitution-making as it had shown itself in the earliest days of colonization." As Arendt understood the American experience, it might be appropriate to speak less of a revolution than of a fulfillment.

Legitimacy in the colonies derived from "the people," to be sure, and not from those traditional repositories of authority, Church and Crown. But if it flowed from the bottom up, it did not do so in the way revolutionary Europeans understood, not in broad terms like "the general will" or "the nation." These were both pathways to tyranny—Napoleon, Hitler.

The Americans drew not on abstractions or theory in their understanding of legitimacy (Arendt minimized even the influence of John Locke) but on lived practical experience. For generations, they had been coming together in townships and assemblies to discuss, deliberate, and reason as a group in a condition of cooperative interdependence. They hung together. The power of the people was not the will of the mob but the expression of rational interaction by collectivities organized to withstand outside forces, cold New England winters, hostile Native Americans, and the other severities of the New World.

One salubrious result is that the colonists were spared the need to be philosophers; they didn't have to determine whether humans were good or bad, a question that would otherwise have vexed and confused them as they debated the kind of government they would establish. Nor did they have to fall back on Hobbesian theories to combat the centrifugal dangers of anarchy. Ideas didn't matter in the American context (and this was a good thing when the colonists were founding governments, not so good when Americans later had to confront the larger world). The evils of human nature were checked, Arendt said, "by virtue of common bonds and mutual promises." The governmental legitimacy of the townships, which was bequeathed to the framers of the Constitution, existed in "the worldly in-between space by which men are mutually related," and that in-between space fostered what Leo Strauss also valued so highly—simple common sense. Again like Strauss, Arendt pointed out that common sense was not the same thing as logic. Common sense assumed a lived, quotidian, shared world, what Strauss had called "a kind of web." Logic existed outside the world and the web, subject to abstract rules beyond the conflicts and contradictions of human experience. As Arendt wrote in *The Origins of Totalitarianism*, the deracinated masses of modern societies had "lost the whole sector of communal relationships in whose framework common sense makes sense." What had taken its place was logic, and logic was the weapon of the totalitarians, who began with a fundamental premise from which everything else followed. ("If you believe A, then it necessarily follows that you must believe B . . . ," and so on, down to the deaths of millions.)

Power came from the people interacting in the humane in-between space, but at the same time it was exerted institutionally through law and was limited by law. Without those institutions, the people were powerless—isolated individuals alone in the wilderness. Coming together in popularly constituted bodies is what gave them potency. In this way, power and law were successfully joined together yet kept apart. The power of the people was preserved, but so was the authority of the law. This, Arendt declared, was "an entirely new concept of power and authority," and in passages like these, one senses the authorial temperature of *On Revolution* rising markedly. Arendt has reached the center, the very essence, of her argument, and she can't hide her enthusiasm. With obvious excitement, she declares that the colonial compacts "made a new beginning in the very midst of the history of Western mankind." With her ardor mounting to its peak, she proclaims that "we are confronted with an event of the greatest magnitude and the greatest import for the future," one that "was without parallel in any other part of the world." The American Revolution, in short, told "an unforgettable story." Here, then, was Arendt's "act of gratitude" to the United States.

IF THIS CONCLUSION had signaled the end of Arendt's thinking on the subject, American readers of *On Revolution* could close the book basking in a feeling of self-satisfaction, offering a hymn of praise to their country's exceptionalism, singing a chorus of "God Bless America" and retiring to their beds secure in the conviction that theirs was a nation unlike all others. But this was not the German-Jewish immigrant's complex understanding of the United States, where gratitude was inevitably tempered by ambivalence and pessimism. Arendt was not one to close on so optimistic a note. The book's last chapter, bringing the narrative up to the present, takes a sharp turn toward the ominous. It exhibits what one commentator calls a "particularly bleak and embattled tone." It is a bucket of cold water thrown on the warm glow of the earlier exuberance.

Political freedom, Arendt insisted in the book's final pages, "means the right 'to be a participator in government,' or it means nothing." The colonial townships and assemblies, building pyramidally to the constitutional conventions, were paradigms of citizen participation, but the popular elections that Americans today consider the hallmark of their democratic republic are hardly the same thing. Voting is not what Arendt meant by participation. The individual in the privacy of the voting booth is not engaged with others in the public arena, putting one's opinions to the test against differing views and life experiences, but instead is choosing among professional politicians offering to promote and protect his or her personal interests through ready-made formulas, mindless banalities, blatant pandering, and outlandish promises cobbled together as party programs. (And heaven help the elected official who, in the manner of Edmund Burke, tries to argue against the personal interest of his or her constituents or to communicate bad news.) Leaders are selected on the basis of private, parochial concerns, not the public welfare, producing a mishmash of self-interested demands, or what Arendt called "the invasion of the public realm by society."

This was almost the opposite of genuine participation. Instead of the kind of intimate interchange of views and the deliberation that might be expected to resolve conflict, which was the practice of the townships and assemblies, isolated voters left to their own devices and with no appreciation of any larger good or of people different from themselves demand an affirmation of their particular prejudices and preconceptions. They have no opportunity, or desire, to come together with the aim of reaching mutual understanding and agreement on shared problems. Centrifugality prevails. American democracy, Arendt writes, had become a zero-sum game of "pressure groups, lobbies and other devices." It is a system in which only power can prevail, or at best the blight of mutual back-scratching to no greater end than mere political survival, lending itself to lies and demagoguery, quarrels and stalemates, cynical deal-making, not public exchange and calm deliberation. To a thinker like Joseph Schumpeter, another exile from Hitler (though not Jewish), this was the best that democracy had to offer and was not to be despised. He accepted it as the picture of "realism," as does his disciple Judge Richard Posner. Democracy, Schumpeter wrote, "does not mean and cannot mean that the people actually rule. . . . Democracy means only that the people have the opportunity of accepting or refusing the men who are to rule them." In short, "democracy is the rule of the politicians." Arendt hoped for something better.

True citizenship, Arendt wrote, requires more than merely pulling a lever; the best that could be said about America's electoral politics, she wrote, was that "it has achieved a certain control of the rulers by those who are ruled, but that it has by no means enabled the citizen to become a 'participator' in public affairs." It may have solved the problem of tyranny because the separation of powers assured that personal freedom was not endangered. But corruption, not tyranny, was the bane of such a

system, corruption springing "from the people themselves." The rotten-
ness extended all the way down. To cynics, corruption was the price to be
paid for peace and stability. But the revolutionary spirit of the Founding
Fathers—the ideal of the free citizen-participant as Arendt understood
it—had withered to the point of death. "In this republic, as it presently
turned out, there was no space reserved, no room left for the exercise of
precisely those qualities which had been instrumental in building it." The
"unforgettable story" had, by the end of the book, mutated into "a strange
and sad story."

Was there a remedy, a path back to the Founding Fathers? Arendt
looked, of all places, to the failed Hungarian revolution of 1956. Before
they were crushed by the Soviet military, the rebels of Budapest had developed a council system for public discussion that spread spontaneously
throughout the entire country. These were genuinely grassroots organizations—"spaces of freedom"—because they were "the only political organs
for people who belonged to no party." Discussion could be open, non-
partisan, independent of particular agendas, built up out of the personal
experiences and outlooks of each participating individual. In Arendt's
words, these organizations had the capability of establishing the power
not of "the many" but of "every one," much as the assemblies and townships had in early America.

Such councils, Arendt observed, had appeared many times before:
during the French Revolution in the eighteenth century, in 1870 when Paris
was under siege by the Prussian Army, in 1905 and 1917 in pre-Bolshevik
Russia, and after World War I among German soldiers and workers. They
had many names: communes, *Räte*, soviets. Jefferson himself had something similar in mind when he suggested dividing the United States into
wards where people could join in discussion of the common good apart
from the bureaucratized formalities of the electoral framework. The fact
that councils had emerged in so many different countries under such
different circumstances, sui generis, indicated to Arendt that they were
expressions of a fundamental political impulse—not "democracy" if by
that was meant mass voting and simple rule of the majority, but a more
horizontal process in which everyone got to express an opinion, exchange
ideas, and be personally involved in the decisions of the group. It's little
wonder that the sixties' theorists of "participatory democracy" thought so
highly of Hannah Arendt.

But how realistic were council systems for modern societies, and how long could they last once formal governing arrangements had been put in place? Arendt's idea has not won many followers apart from those sixties radicals, and they have disappeared into one of the more neglected dustbins of history. As one scholar has put it: "For most of Arendt's readers her views in this area are something of an embarrassment, a curiously unrealistic commitment in someone who had laid particular stress on realism in politics." Arendt herself had doubts. She acknowledged that every time councils had emerged in the past, they had been crushed, "either directly by the bureaucracy of the nation-states or by the party machines." Perhaps her idea was "a pure utopia," she said, and she conceded that it had very little chance of being implemented at the present time. Still, she wasn't willing to give up on it. A council system offered the hope of replacing the top-down sovereignty of party politics with egalitarian deliberation. "In this direction I see the possibility of forming a new concept of the state."

In the end, it has to be said, councils, communes, wards, whatever one called them, were really little more than an escape hatch for Arendt, a device to avoid the gloomy conclusion her ideas about public participation seemed to be forcing upon her. There was always something improvised and contrived about the council idea, making it easy to criticize as unworkable and irrelevant to modern America, just as Strauss's notions of apolitical philosophers advising "gentlemen" seem equally far-fetched in terms of the world we inhabit. Or as one scholar said about Strauss and Arendt, "Their ability to integrate themselves into America . . . involved inventing an America they could love rather than accepting the one they actually found." But there was a reason for that. They couldn't genuinely love the America they found. It worried them.

For this reason, even the most valid criticisms of their thought are, in a way, beside the point, because they don't grapple with the problem that was of the greatest urgency to the two German Jews as they surveyed the United States—the problem of democracy itself. Most of their American readers couldn't be worried in the same way. Quite the contrary. Democracy for them wasn't an issue to be addressed, it was a given—the life-sustaining ocean everyone swam in—and it was even more than that: a good, a virtue, an aspiration, a touchstone, a metric, a cause, a talisman, a foundation, a faith. Search long and hard and you will never find public figures in the United States ever openly declaring themselves *against* the spread of democracy at home or abroad. (This would become a problem for a Henry Kissinger trying to explain his policies to the American people.) But these two outsiders couldn't share that faith. Democracy for them was a question, not an answer, and even if the solutions they devised were unsatisfactory or inappropriate to the real world of the United States, or perhaps any world at all, at least Arendt and Strauss were struggling to produce solutions when most of their compatriots couldn't even see a problem. It was this challenge to the national orthodoxy by two foreigners that gives their writings on America such depth and richness, such salience. It is also, inevitably, what provokes the hostility each encountered from true believers in democracy and The American Way. The patriotically inclined, it's clear, don't like to think without banisters.

American democracy has been a great success for over 200 years, but why is that? Will it continue being a success? And what does the American system have to offer the rest of the world? The German-Jewish émigrés—not just Hannah Arendt and Leo Strauss but Kissinger, too—responded to those questions with complexity and ambiguity, based on their unhappy experience of Weimar Germany and the rise of Adolf Hitler. Nazism taught them harsh lessons most Americans still resist learning and left them immune to the standard platitudes and feel-good clichés about democracy that are trotted out whenever political difficulties arise. This has been especially true with regard to foreign policy. Government of the people, by the people, and for the people is a fine thing when it works. But the fact is, as Kissinger knew so well, frequently it doesn't.

HANS MORGENTHAU

W HEN THE GERMAN-JEWISH POLITICAL SCIENTIST HANS
J. Morgenthau died in 1980 at the age of 76, Henry Kissinger
wrote an affectionate and admiring tribute to him. They had known each
other since the early 1950s, when they entered into a lifelong relationship that was often close, sometimes tense, but never lacking in mutual
respect. During the years of the Vietnam war, when Kissinger was in government formulating and implementing policy and Morgenthau was the
leading academic critic of that policy, perhaps the most articulate of all
the dissenters, certainly one of the most influential, their communication
dropped off. This is hardly surprising. Both men were confident, arrogant,
proud, gruff, somewhat suspicious and slightly paranoid, accustomed to a
degree of deference to their obvious intelligence and also to winning arguments with their peers. Neither suffered fools gladly. The disagreement
between them must have been painful to both. What is surprising is that
it never boiled over, ending the relationship, which even recovered its earlier degree of intimacy after Kissinger returned to private life. "We shared
almost identical premises," Kissinger wrote. It is probably no exaggeration
to say that there was no thinker Kissinger respected more than Morgenthau. And Morgenthau considered Kissinger one of the best secretaries
of state in American history. He told a colleague that, emotionally, he felt
toward Kissinger like a brother.

Kissinger's 1980 remembrance was warmly personal. Although Morgenthau had made his reputation as a rigorous, even cold-blooded analyst of international relations, often condemned for amorality if not

immorality, the man Kissinger knew was sweet-tempered, gentle, very shy, and possessed of a winning sense of humor. Kissinger called him "a lovable man."

And "a noble man." His critics, who saw only a "Germanic" devotee of power, did not understand him, Kissinger said. Still, whatever differences critics had with him, they could not ignore his teachings. He was, in Kissinger's words, one of those rare thinkers whose ideas have so suffused modern discussion that many in the years since his death adopted his intellectual framework for international affairs without even realizing it. As Kissinger put it, teachers of international relations had to begin with Morgenthau's ideas. Anyone employing the phrase "national interest" as an analytical tool is probably a disciple, knowing or unknowing, of Hans Morgenthau.

IF A SENSE OF tragedy was something Morgenthau helped impart to Kissinger, it was because gloom came naturally to him throughout his life. As a boy Morgenthau grew up lonely, angry, and combative. An only child, he was born in 1904 in Coburg, Bavaria, to a successful doctor, Ludwig. His mother, Frieda, was the daughter of a prosperous businessman. The young Hans gravitated to military affairs; his favorite playthings were the toy soldiers with which he used to reenact famous battles like Waterloo. But his real war was with his stiff, oppressive father.

Ludwig was a dyed-in-the-wool conservative and patriot. According to his daughter-in-law, he was "a Jew who wanted to be a German and who adored the emperor." Hans was given the middle name Joachim in honor of the emperor's youngest son. In matters of religion, the Morgenthaus were Jewish in little more than name only. Instead of attending synagogue, they celebrated Christmas with presents and a tree. Every year young Hans wrote to Santa Claus. The family was one step away from conversion, but that was a step never taken, impeded, no doubt, because of a modern physician's professional training and rationalistic way of thinking. The nineteenth-century Jewish poet Heinrich Heine had said he converted to Christianity because it was the "ticket of entry into European culture." Science, not religion, was the ticket of entry into twentieth-century society.

Still, there seems to have been a quality of deep anxiety about Ludwig's German patriotism, which found expression in the treatment of his son. Hans was a dreamy child, with aspirations to be a philosopher or writer, even a poet (the hardheaded Realist continued writing poetry into his thirties). One thing that did not interest him was devoting his life simply to the pursuit of money or a career. He wanted to live "in the service of a great idea." But life to Ludwig consisted of stern, unreflective self-discipline, rigidly toeing the line, and his criticism of his wayward son was unending and suffocating. There was a right way to do things, and that's how they would be done. The Kissingers' assimilationist German household, similar to that of the Morgenthaus, if linked more tightly to Jewish tradition, was undoubtedly a healthier, happier, more hospitable environment. For better—and for worse—the impractical Louis Kissinger, though he too could be a strict disciplinarian with his boys, had a nurturing softness that Ludwig Morgenthau lacked. The young Henry Kissinger may have rejected his father's gentleness. But he never stood in rebellion against him.

By contrast, the home Ludwig created was, from his son's point of view, a prison camp of sorts, mitigated only by the comforting warmth of Frieda. "My father is totally crazy," Morgenthau wrote to his wife-to-be in 1931. And "he is as stupid as they come. Things are really pretty bad." The catalogue of complaints went on and on, and it is hard to resist interpreting young Hans's chronic sickliness as anything but psychological, his internal exile.

Yet Morgenthau took his rebellion only so far. His father's son, he too was a patriot and nationalist who, as a boy, was an ardent supporter of the German cause in World War I. In college he joined a dueling fraternity "dedicated to German patriotism, to the German Reich and to honor," and he bore the physical scars from his youthful duels for the rest of his life. Had he been allowed to, he would probably have matured into a civic-minded and loyal German conservative, just as Henry Kissinger might have matured into a teacher in Nuremberg. But there was no straight path for German-Jewish patriots after World War I, and Morgenthau can be said to have embodied all their conflicts and agonies. He wanted to belong to a club that no longer wished to have him as a member.

MORGENTHAU'S HOMETOWN of Coburg was an early hotbed of Nazism, even though Jews constituted only 1 percent of the population (or maybe *because* Jews constituted only 1 percent of the population). Hitler received an enthusiastic reception when he visited the town in 1922, the same year a Jewish cemetery was desecrated. The next year the windows of the local synagogue were smashed. At school, Morgenthau was spit on and publicly humiliated when he won academic honors. Reflecting on his situation, Morgenthau wrote at the time that his life was determined by three factors—that he was German, that he was Jewish, and that he had come of age in the postwar period. The "socially dominant groups," he said, blamed the Jews for Germany's troubles, but in his assimilationist no-man's-land, he distanced himself from the bigots' hatred in a telling way: "I am innocent of what the Jews are reproached with. The accusations that are directed against me as a Jew are totally unjustified." Did this mean that the accusations against other Jews were justified? He was not above complaining about Jews, for instance, the number of them employed in the theater, and he once wrote about a man he knew: "He is an unusually appealing person, a truly decent fellow. In our country, there are hardly any Jews like him."

Like that other German-Jewish nationalist, Leo Strauss, Morgenthau was susceptible to the appeal of fascism and similar forms of authoritarianism. Although he confided to his diary in 1929 that "in England I would be a member of the Labor Party," he went on, "in Italy I might be a Fascist and in Russia a Bolshevist." What such fluid politics came down to was his wish that "rulers and the ruled alike were prepared to accept authority."

Even Hitler had an allure. Morgenthau remembered visiting his grandparents in Munich in 1922 and hearing that one of the local "rabble rousers" was scheduled to speak. Curious, he attended the meeting, where he "had one of the most profound experiences of my life." Hitler spoke passionately and eloquently, telling the crowd "exactly what it wanted to hear." And Morgenthau himself? He said he felt a "paralysis of will" even though he didn't believe a word of Hitler's speech. Morgenthau recorded these memories in a short book review in 1973, when he took the occasion to reproach biographers and historians for giving us all the facts of Hitler's life without ever capturing the magnetism of the man or the historic phenomenon that he was. Rational categories could not contain him. Perhaps "only a poet could recreate and make plausible" Hitler's uniqueness, "the sheer force of his personality." Condemnation was what historians had in mind when they wrote about Hitler after World War II. It was important for them to keep their distance. The kind of portrait Morgenthau was calling for with its acknowledgment of the undeniable "attractiveness" of Hitler would have been considered too dangerous.

The magnetism of Hitler to millions of ordinary Germans and even to German Jews like Morgenthau reflected the fact that everything seemed to be falling apart in the Weimar Republic. "It is impossible," Morgenthau wrote, "to visualize the ignorance, confusion, meanness and general moral and intellectual degradation that dominated German public life." With the possibility of a respectable, tolerant conservatism that prized nationalism and the rule of law over militant ethnicity and recognized Jews as fellow Germans disappearing under his feet, Morgenthau was forced to explore other avenues. He briefly "experimented with Freudian concepts," but they proved unsatisfactory. Marxism enjoyed a wider and more immediately political popularity, and for a time he fell in with the Marxist thinkers of the famous Frankfurt School. But he hated Marxism's "closed intellectual system"—an independent thinker like Morgenthau was temperamentally incapable of giving his allegiance to any ideology. And before long he was complaining that the so-called politics of the Marxist intellectuals consisted of nothing but "hair-splitting" textual arguments, while "the Nazi enemy was standing at the gates."

And Zionism? Like Arendt, Morgenthau never denied his Judaism, but neither did he actively embrace it. Indeed, later in life, no doubt under the influence of his good friend and Realist ally, the Protestant theologian Reinhold Niebuhr ("Reinie" to Morgenthau and other close friends), he seems to have come very near to adopting his own version of Christianity. God was divorced from the world, he once wrote in an uncharacteristically religious frame of mind, because to live in the world was to suffer and God did not suffer. But He could choose to unite with the world, Morgenthau went on, through suffering by becoming the Son of Man, so that "the suffering of the world becomes His own suffering."

Religious thinking, however, was not Morgenthau's métier. He was no theologian, and he accepted his "fate" as a Jew; "there was no escape" from it. Renunciation or conversion under the circumstances of lethal, widespread anti-Semitism would have been undignified, ignoble. He was a battler and, like his friend Hannah Arendt, when he was attacked as a Jew, he fought back as a Jew. He would not "grovel or duck." Again like Arendt and also like Strauss, he would remain loyal to Israel throughout his life, taking an increased interest in Jewish affairs after the Six Day War of 1967. But the Promised Land held no promise for him personally.

IN HIS CHOICE of career, too, Morgenthau showed himself to be a man without a country. He entered the University of Frankfurt in 1923 and, much to the dismay of his father, gave little thought to vocational goals. Intellectually inclined, he decided to study philosophy, a choice that he quickly came to see as a "real disaster," at least at Frankfurt. The department was dominated by narrow epistemologists, and the skeptical Morgenthau couldn't abide "the rationalistic pretenses" of his professors. He wanted to discuss grander metaphysical questions and answers. He moved on to Munich with the thought of studying literature, but after his father put his foot down, Morgenthau chose the eminently practical field of law, though continuing his resistance as best he could by taking the minimal number of law courses; his preference now was for art history, though he also took more standard history courses, where he was introduced to Bismarck's Realpolitik.

After receiving his degree, he returned to Frankfurt for a doctorate, concentrating on international law because, he said, it allowed him to explore issues of politics and philosophy. Torn between the practical and the theoretical, Morgenthau managed a balancing act until the rise of the Nazis, simultaneously pursuing careers in law and academics. A question intrudes: What if he hadn't started out at Frankfurt but had attended, say, Marburg, and encountered the thought of Martin Heidegger? Based on what we know about Morgenthau, it seems likely, or at least possible, that he would have become a disciple, much like Arendt and Strauss, and that his path in life would have been very different. Even without Heidegger, there is a Heideggerian reverberation in Morgenthau's meditation on death: "the spectacle of an animal endowed with conscious intelligence coming, as it seems, from nowhere and destined to sink into the night of death as though it had never been."

Morgenthau joined the University of Frankfurt's law faculty in 1931, though with anti-Semitism on the rise and prospects for a young Jewish scholar in Germany eroding, he accepted a temporary post at the University of Geneva a year later. But with Hitler's ascension to power in January 1933, Morgenthau's life became one of rootlessness and deprivation. Returning to Germany was out of the question (his parents had managed to escape in 1933), and Geneva was proving to be no haven. Anti-Semitic students were boycotting his classes and, he wrote to a friend in 1934, "As things now stand, I will have to give up my academic career at the end of this semester, without the slightest notion of what to do next."

A position in Madrid in 1935 seemed to provide relief, and Morgenthau took the opportunity of this newfound security to marry, although in the tumultuous 1930s, any security was bound to be short-lived. After the Spanish Civil War broke out, anyone of German origin, even German Jews, fell under suspicion among Madrid's republicans and Morgenthau, now with a new wife, was back on the road—to Paris, Amsterdam, The Hague, and Geneva again. Finally, in 1937, the couple managed to obtain visas to the United States. It wasn't Morgenthau's first choice, nor his second or even his third. Christoph Frei, in his indispensable biography of Morgenthau's early years, writes that "the United States was the last place that Morgenthau considered as a possible destination." But beggars and German-Jewish exiles couldn't afford to be choosers.

Desperation in Europe was followed by desperation in the United States. Jobs in Depression-era America were hard to come by, especially for people like the Morgenthaus, with few contacts to help them and a shaky knowledge of English. His wife, Irma, found work as a salesperson at Macy's while Morgenthau was being turned down repeatedly for academic positions and even for nonacademic ones that he felt suited him like proofreader. (He rejected the chance to be an elevator operator.) At last, he landed a temporary post teaching night school at Brooklyn College, though it did little to improve the Morgenthaus' straitened circumstances. "I was hungry most of the time," Irma recalled. Meanwhile, Morgenthau was fighting new battles with his American students—not over the anti-Semitism he encountered in European classrooms but because he was now teaching young Brooklyn Stalinists. "They would shout at me, interrupt me and debate with me, and they didn't like me, particularly because of my anti-Communist position."

Another opportunity—if it can be called that—came with a 1938 appointment at the University of Kansas City. Although Morgenthau quickly found himself overworked and underpaid in an academic sweatshop that was struggling to get by on limited funds and predictably was soon in conflict with the administration in his new Midwestern setting, "Kansas City," his wife said, "was heaven after the New York curse." Only in 1943 would she get to know what heaven truly was when an offer arrived from the generously endowed University of Chicago, perhaps on the basis of Morgenthau's European writings. It was a temporary one but it became permanent in 1945. Finally, Hans J. Morgenthau could begin to become Hans J. Morgenthau. Christoph Frei reports that between 1946 and 1951, he published six books and 34 articles.

FEW SCHOLARS CAN be said to have invented an entire discipline, but Morgenthau comes close. It's true that colleges and universities were teaching political science long before he arrived on the scene. Michigan, Johns Hopkins, and especially Columbia had introduced the subject into their curriculums as early as the 1880s. But their aim was to train civil servants, much as law schools were training attorneys and medical schools were training doctors. Government departments offered courses that were essentially vocational, including instruction not only in political history and constitutional law but also in such subjects as "the best methods of supplying pure water and air," "the proper disposal of decomposing matter," and "the care of the insane and the management of asylums." The intention behind the courses was progressive, as the idea was understood at the time, but also narrow, antitheoretical, and parochial. The goal was to populate government bureaucracies with skilled professionals who would replace ad hoc amateurism with the kind of rational, problem-solving thinking considered de rigueur for the operation of a successful democracy. Large ideas were discouraged.

After World War I, the study of foreign policy as a feature of good government took a broader, more programmatic turn. According to Morgenthau, the first chair in international relations was established at the University of Wales in the early 1920s with the specific aim of supporting the League of Nations and promoting world peace. In the United States, a key figure in the field was Quincy Wright, whose formidable two-volume *A Study of War* was published in 1942. A professor of international law at the University of Chicago since 1923, Wright had, Casaubon-like, drawn on every academic field from anthropology to mathematics in order to develop a precise formula to enable policymakers to calculate the probability of war and then take steps to prevent it. The dictates of mathematics were replacing the contingencies of history.

Such overreaching rationalism had little appeal for Morgenthau. He insisted throughout his life that all politics contained both a rational element and a "contingent" element. The study of International relations could never determine with certainty what an outcome would be, and unquantifiable wisdom was more important than the predictions shaped by algorithms. "Political wisdom is the gift to grasp intuitively the quality of diverse interests and power," he said. "It is a gift of nature, like the gift of artistic creativity." It could not be learned. (Henry Kissinger also equated statesmanship with artistry.)

But the uncertainty of politics also made foreign affairs irremediably "tragic" as one could never be sure that a chosen policy would have a desired outcome, and so the era's optimistic moralism was no less foreign to Morgenthau's way of thinking. He remembered attending a meeting of the German Society of International Law in 1929, where a distinguished professor gave a talk on the Kellogg-Briand Pact, the 1928 document that defined the mood of a decade traumatized by world war. Named after the American secretary of state and the French minister of foreign affairs, it called upon nations to outlaw war and was signed by over 60 countries, including Great Britain, Germany, Italy, and Japan; the United States Senate ratified it by a vote of 85–1. In 1929 Kellogg was awarded the Nobel Peace Prize for his efforts. One Harvard instructor stopped teaching the history of war because the agreement had rendered such study "anachronistic." The professor Morgenthau heard speak in Germany insisted that anyone who could not see that the pact would put an end to war was lacking in imagination. Morgenthau recalled years later: "I was, indeed, lacking in imagination even then." As early as 1931, when Japan invaded Manchuria and the League of Nations stood helplessly by, the Kellogg-Briand Pact was revealing itself—not only to those "lacking in imagination"—as little more than a scrap of paper.

Even as a young man, Morgenthau resisted the idea that good intentions by themselves could prevail in the anarchic world of international affairs or that written documents could carry the weight of law without a credible threat of force behind them. Soothing words were never enough. Only the potential loss of blood demonstrated conviction. Or to put it another way, any attempt to end war required the possibility of going to war.

In a lifetime of teaching, Morgenthau urged students, commentators, and public officials to look beyond the hopefulness of idealism and to step back from their own individual or culturally determined notions of morality to understand the actual on-the-ground facts of particular situations requiring particular responses suited to particular circumstances.

As he later told the policymaker Paul Nitze in a statement that might be said to encapsulate the idea of an existential politics, "We cannot assume to be able to look at the world scene from a vantage point which, as it were, lies outside this world."

Appropriately, the school Morgenthau founded was called Realism, and while there is much dispute about the exact meaning of the term—one person's Realist is another's war criminal—what is indisputable was its premise: you could not formulate foreign policy based simply on how you wished the world to be or by trying to impose either an abstract theory or your own moral template on a recalcitrant reality. In the end, power was reality. "The distinctive character of Realism," Morgenthau told the journalist Max Lerner, "is a particular way of thinking about politics in general and foreign policy in particular, but not a commitment to a particular kind of foreign policy." Realism today comes in many shapes and sizes. There is "offensive" Realism and "defensive" Realism, "economic" Realism and "neo-Realism," an English school of Realism and a Munich school of Realism, all flowing out of Morgenthau's writings. The Harvard professor Stanley Hoffmann proclaimed Morgenthau the "pope of Realism." Others have said that if any single person can be called the founding father of the entire modern study of international relations, it was Morgenthau. Scholars compared his role to that of Sigmund Freud in psychology. Certainly, the discipline can be divided into two parts: before Morgenthau and after Morgenthau. And of his many students, Henry Kissinger is the most famous: "I never ceased admiring him or remembering the profound intellectual debt I owed him."

Morgenthau exists as the bridge between Kissinger on the one side and Leo Strauss and Hannah Arendt on the other. He was Kissinger's mentor, Strauss's colleague, and Arendt's friend. He is the figure bringing together the public policies of Kissinger and the Continental outlook of Strauss and Arendt. Look closely, and Martin Heidegger is fewer than six degrees of separation removed from Richard Nixon.

Before Morgenthau came to know Kissinger, there was Leo Strauss. Apparently, the first connection between them occurred in 1933, when Morgenthau read a 1932 article by Strauss on Carl Schmitt, a leading political theorist in Germany with pronounced anti-Semitic tendencies, who was soon to become a confirmed Nazi, more so even than Heidegger, and the most prominent jurist of the Third Reich. It was Schmitt who developed the intellectual rationale for the *Führerprinzip*, calling for total allegiance to Adolf Hitler. Strauss's article on Schmitt had been critical, but only because he thought Schmitt had not gone far enough in revealing the weaknesses of liberalism. In his challenge to "humanitarian-pacifist morals," Strauss said, Schmitt "remains trapped in the view that he is attacking." Strauss's commentary so impressed Schmitt that he enthusiastically recommended Strauss for a Rockefeller Foundation fellowship to study Hobbes in England. In March 1932, Strauss wrote to Schmitt that the interest Schmitt took in him "represents the most honorable and crucial validation of my scholarly work that has ever been bestowed upon me and that I could ever dream of."

But Schmitt joined the Nazi Party on May 1, 1933, the same day as Heidegger, and broke off their correspondence. Now Strauss was that "Jewish scholar," if not that "Jew scholar." Schmitt claimed that Strauss continued to write to him until 1934, but no letters have been found after July 1933. Strauss was later to complain that Schmitt had taken some of his ideas without proper acknowledgment. As one of his biographers writes, "There is no doubt that Schmitt's slight and affirmation of the new Nazi regime dealt a heavy blow to Strauss."

Morgenthau read and reread Strauss's article, finding it "excellent." He no doubt relished such passages as Strauss's criticism of pacifist thinking, in which he argued that the pacifists would be forced to make war against the nonpacifists and that such a conflict would be more terrible than the limited wars for specific ends that the Europeans were familiar with because it would be seen as an apocalyptic struggle of good against evil. "The war against war will then be undertaken as 'the definitively final war of humanity.'" After World War II, Morgenthau was still recommending the article to his American university students.

Morgenthau had his own tangled relationship with Schmitt, which moved along a similar track as Strauss's. Morgenthau admired Schmitt for exhibiting "an intellectual intensity and a sure instinct" that, he said, was "unusual in Germany." He sent Schmitt a copy of his doctoral thesis and was delighted when Schmitt took an interest in his work. But a personal meeting in 1929 did not go well, in fact went very badly indeed, and Morgenthau later recalled (albeit with hindsight) that when he left Schmitt's apartment, he stopped on the landing and said to himself: "Now I have met the most evil man alive." Like Strauss, Morgenthau accused

Schmitt of stealing his ideas, adding that he lacked moral principles (the same charge that would be leveled against Morgenthau in America). But even in the United States, Morgenthau's work, as has been pointed out more than once, showed the influence of Schmitt's thinking, what one writer has called "deep intellectual ties."

What was that thinking? Many young German political scholars just starting their careers, with the failure of Weimar as a fact of their lives, responded positively to Schmitt's teaching that politics was an autonomous realm with its own principles (in contradistinction to the Marxist belief that it was an epiphenomenon masking the more fundamental realities of economics), and his thought remains valuable for its attempt to work through just what it means for politics to be "autonomous," not reducible to economics, psychology, or any of the other departmentalized fields of social science or the humanities. Part of that analysis included a critique of liberalism, which, with its disdain of power, was a superficial philosophy that could not withstand challenges to its own unexamined and unrealistic assumptions about the benignity of mankind. As Morgenthau wrote, "Liberalism expresses its aims in the international sphere not in terms of power politics, that is, on the basis of the international reality but in accordance with the rationalist premises of its own misconception." And to repeat Strauss's charge, Weimar liberalism "presented the sorry spectacle of justice without a sword or of justice unable to use the sword." (Unlike Strauss and Morgenthau, Hannah Arendt didn't know Schmitt personally, but she was entirely sympathetic to the notion that politics was an autonomous realm, detached from economics, almost a kind of theater in her mind, and she found his ideas "ingenious" and "arresting.") Schmitt's anti-Marxist assault on the principles of the Weimar Republic led him to embrace Germany's Volk and Vaterland. Though Strauss and Morgenthau were similarly dissatisfied with Weimar's politics, and similarly immune to Marxism's appeal, that particular path was closed to them.

YEARS AFTER the crisis of Weimar, in the late 1940s, the University of Chicago organized a three-man search committee to recruit an expert on political philosophy. Morgenthau had been teaching at Chicago since 1943, and the committee consisted of Theodore Schultz, later to win the Nobel Prize in economics, Edward Shils, a sociologist whose influence was to extend far beyond his discipline and university, and Morgenthau, who at the time was serving as temporary chair of the political science department. There were three candidates for the position, but Shils and Morgenthau agreed that "by all odds, the best of the three" was Leo Strauss, who was then at the New School in New York. (Schultz, lacking expertise in the subject, deferred to the opinion of his two colleagues.) According to Shils, Morgenthau, for reasons of departmental politics, stayed in the background while Shils made the case for Strauss with the administration. Strauss got the job. Kenneth Thompson, a close associate and collaborator of Morgenthau, and the coeditor of a collection entitled *Truth and Tragedy: A Tribute to Hans J. Morgenthau*, writes that Morgenthau "played a decisive role" in bringing Strauss to Chicago, suggesting that he hardly took a backseat to Shils. Taking a backseat wasn't Morgenthau's usual modus operandi. It may be worth noting that in a collection of essays edited by Shils on 47 outstanding scholars at the University of Chicago, Strauss was included in the volume but Morgenthau was omitted. (Maybe he was number 48.) Whatever the case, Morgenthau remained an admirer and supporter of Strauss, first in Weimar Germany, then in the United States. When he had the chance to advance Strauss's career, he seized the opportunity.

The two men immediately became allies at Chicago. Thompson speaks of Morgenthau's "unbounded admiration for Strauss," and reports Morgenthau saying that "he learned more from him in a few minutes' conversation than from hours with other political scientists." Strauss reciprocated the feeling. Strauss was one of the few people mentioned by Morgenthau in the acknowledgments of the second edition of his magnum opus, *Politics Among Nations* (Shils was acknowledged in the 1948 first edition). In 1953 he sent Walter Lippmann, who he felt had "almost unfailing political judgment," a copy of the book that would establish Strauss's reputation in the United States, *Natural Right and History*, apparently in the hope that Lippmann would review it.

The Morgenthau-Strauss alliance at Chicago was unsurprising, even fated, one might say. Not only were they both German-Jewish exiles from the Third Reich who were struggling to achieve recognition and academic standing in their new country, but they also shared a common enemy— their very own department of political science. The department had been molded by Charles Edward Merriam, founder of the Chicago School, which carried forward the "good government" meliorist philosophy of the nineteenth-century political science departments and in the twentieth century, it was said, "significantly shaped the model of modern political science in the United States."

Merriam was intent on turning the study of government into what he considered a true science that was mathematical, quantitative, empirical, precise, dependent on measurement and statistics, and dedicated to the construction of frameworks and "paradigms." At his most utopian and grandiose, Merriam saw his goal as "the conscious control of human evolution toward which intelligence steadily moves in every domain of human life." One of Merriam's most prestigious colleagues was Quincy Wright, who was busily devising mathematical formulas for bringing an end to human conflict. Who needed theory in such an intellectual environment? Who even needed intellectuals? Thompson, who was a member of the department, reports that "its strongest voices were openly contemptuous of philosophy," and that Morgenthau had to battle to justify his interest in the subject.

In other words, instruction at the University of Chicago was the antithesis of the way the two Continental émigrés conceived of politics and the study of politics. Exiled to the American Midwest, they had somehow managed to find themselves deep inside an enemy camp. Their department was housed in a five-story, Gothic-inspired social science research center, the "first building on any American university campus devoted solely to the social sciences." On its front was carved the motto, "When you cannot measure, your knowledge is meager and unsatisfactory." What did Morgenthau and Strauss make of that? One can only imagine them averting their eyes when they passed by to avoid a rise in blood pressure.

The kind of work promoted by the Chicago School, Morgenthau said, was directed to the utopian goal of eliminating uncertainty from political activity, an utter impossibility in his view. Their theories "are in truth not so much theories as dogmas," dogmas that substituted "what is desirable for what is possible." For all their claims to be grounded in empirical fact, these scholars, with their models, frameworks, and paradigms, "tell us nothing we need to know about the real world" because their mathematically based methodology was deficient, offering no understanding of actual human beings. Power, the core subject of international relations, was too complex, too integrated and organic, to be quantified or broken down into its alleged component parts. It was, Morgenthau said, like love.

Strauss, for his part, did see value in what the political scientists were doing. The data they collected and the statistical analyses they performed could be "useful" (he said somewhat condescendingly) because they provided "knowledge of political things," that is, of public opinion and common prejudices. Even so, Strauss could also be deeply skeptical about exactly what it was that public opinion polls revealed, as "many answers to the questionnaires are given by unintelligent, uninformed, deceitful and irrational people," and "not a few questions are formulated by people of the same caliber."

In any case, as soon as these political scientists aspired to be more than the data collectors they were, when they donned the robes of philosophers to make the argument that only measurable knowledge was genuine knowledge, with its implicit denial of individual free will, they showed their limitations as thinkers. Morgenthau's critics disparaged his way of thinking as "pre-scientific." But this was a term Strauss embraced and championed. For him, prescientific thinking was the equivalent of common sense, and social science, he said, was "distrustful of common sense." In a typically Straussian salvo he declared, "Moral obtuseness is the necessary condition for scientific analysis."

The so-called science of the Chicago School and its adherents might be "exact," but that didn't mean, Strauss said, echoing Morgenthau, that it was relevant to public affairs. Politics could not be quantified because human beings were not rats; their political perspectives were shaped by values and goals, about which the quantifiers and statisticians had nothing to say. Or when they did try to say something about values, they attempted to measure the immeasurable, reflexively falling back on counting noses to homogenize all ethical differences for the sake of achieving the utilitarian aim of the greatest good for the greatest number. This, Strauss insisted, was not an affirmation of value but a denial of value. It reflected "the most dangerous proclivities of democracy." It was the tyranny of the majority dressed up as empirical research.

Still, if Strauss and Morgenthau were fated to be allies in their war against their Chicago colleagues, they were equally fated to be intellectual antagonists. Their interests were too different, their perspectives too divergent. Both admired the wisdom of the ancient Greeks—Morgenthau, the foreign affairs specialist, taught a course on Aristotle—but when it came to the moderns, clashes were inevitable. Morgenthau accepted "the eternal truth of Hobbes's insight into the nature of society," for example, whereas for Strauss he was one of the progenitors of everything that had gone wrong with contemporary thought. Strauss viewed Machiavelli in the same way, while Morgenthau believed he "has been misinterpreted." It was not true, Morgenthau argued, that Machiavelli thought ethics had no place in international relations. "He only saw clearly that if you want to be successful in foreign affairs, you must use the instruments by which foreign aims are achieved—that is, power politics."

Similarly, Nietzsche had been a profound influence on Strauss in his youth but a writer he turned away from once he began immersing himself in classical thought. Nietzsche was no less crucial for the young Morgenthau's intellectual development, and though he sometimes chose to remain silent before uncomprehending and antagonistic postwar American audiences about the man's significance, he always retained his early admiration. Asked in 1976 to name the 10 books that meant the most to him, Morgenthau cheated a bit by listing as one of the 10 "the collected works of Friedrich Nietzsche."

Of all the differences between Strauss and Morgenthau, however, perhaps the most unbridgeable was their disagreement over the very large question of the meaning of history. For Morgenthau, history was an invaluable weapon in his battle against the Chicago School and was no less central for the study of international relations. The models and measurements of the quantifiers had no way of encompassing lessons that could only be learned from the study of the past. "Modern theorists of international relations," he wrote, "are repelled by history, for history is the realm of the accidental, the contingent, the unpredictable." It revealed people in all their uniqueness and humanity. It was the province of individual choice, of freedom. "In history," Morgenthau said, "man meets himself." This was "Germanic" thinking indeed—and also evidenced in Strauss and Arendt—if what is meant by that is the affirmation of the role of the "will" in the conduct of human affairs.

Strauss agreed with Morgenthau, though only up to a point. The unpredictability of history, he said, was useful in the fight against the dogmatism of the statistically minded, but since the nineteenth century, history had become a doctrine in its own right, a tsunami that washed away any absolutes with the argument that all knowledge was relative, dependent on a particular time and place, and that there were no permanent truths. This was a dogma of its own, Strauss argued, one that went by the name of "historicism," and historicism was only one step away from the modern diseases of relativism and nihilism.

History, according to Strauss, was simply a "meaningless web" in which there were no eternal verities or universal principles and, therefore, no natural rights. "The unbiased historian had to confess his inability to derive any norms from history," and without norms the way was cleared for the amoral Adolf Hitlers of the world, who were always lurking, opportunistically looking for any path to power. His treasured classical philosophy, Strauss wrote, was the antidote to the dangers of history and relativism, "nonhistoricist thought in its pure form."

Morgenthau did not say that the study of history provided "norms" in Strauss's sense, but with a nod to Thucydides, he did say that history was philosophy by example—drama—and, what was more, a necessity to clear away the distortions of scientific thinking. It offered essential insights that could be learned in no other way, the most meaningful of which was that men always and everywhere strive for power. History was purgative, performing a cleansing function for the mind by stripping away all optimistic ideals and rationalist utopias. For Morgenthau it was a nightmare from which neither he nor anyone else could ever awaken, and those who did not grasp that fact could never grasp the fundamentals of international relations.

Kenneth Thompson, who witnessed the early friendship between Strauss and Morgenthau and then the falling out, explained the change from Strauss's point of view: Strauss objected that Morgenthau was giving courses in the philosophy of international relations. "It was as wrongheaded," he believed, "to speak of the philosophy of international relations as it was to speak of the philosophy of sanitation workers." Philosophy had to concern itself with universal matters. "The essential task of the philosopher was to examine fundamental issues concerning the good life and the best state."

But the differences between the two men were not only intellectual. One can't ignore the role that personality played in the relationship. These were two thinkers not easily given to making friends or courting allies. Each resolutely went his own way, incapable of dealing with the mundane interactions of the social sphere or the trivia of faculty intrigues. "My main objective in campus politics," Morgenthau said, "is to be left alone." One of his colleagues remembered that "Strauss had remarkably little contact with other teachers at the University of Chicago." He was unfailingly polite, but that politeness was a barrier, not an invitation. Uneasy around most people, including those he worked with on a regular basis, he even once confided that "he could never feel completely comfortable with a non-Jew." And Morgenthau had neither the disposition nor the temperament to try to break through Strauss's wall.

Henry Kissinger may have considered Morgenthau sweet-tempered and gentle, but that wasn't how most of his colleagues saw him. To them, he was distant and cantankerous, a loner with a fierce, take-no-enemies style of argument. "His responses to views he found unacceptable were immediate, sharp, hostile and uncompromising." One man who had the painful experience of being a target for Morgenthau's barbs was Harold D. Lasswell, a political scientist who taught at the University of Chicago from 1926 to 1938 before moving on, after a brief excursion in radio, to a distinguished career at Yale Law School. To his admirers, he "ranks among the half dozen creative innovators in the twentieth century." To Morgenthau, not so much.

In 1950, Lasswell, together with the philosopher Abraham Kaplan, published a book with the perfect Morgenthau-ian title, *Power and Society*. It was meant to be a primer on political science, at least as taught by members of the Chicago School. To Morgenthau, it represented everything that was wrong with his own academic discipline, and in an article entitled "The State of Political Science" (in tacit acknowledgment, perhaps, of Merriam's groundbreaking 1921 article, "The Present State of the Study of Politics"), he set out, all guns blazing, to destroy it. Scholarly blood would be shed.

Lasswell and Kaplan offered definitions of basic terms like "democracy," "despotism," and "republic." These, Morgenthau said, were "either platitudinous, circular or tautological, and at best convey information that Aristotle would have taken for granted." The book exhibited "a thorough misunderstanding of the nature of political theory," and its "sweeping judgments" were "barely supported by evidence." It even got simple facts wrong, like the century in which one German political philosopher lived. And sounding a familiar theme, Morgenthau said Lasswell's problem was that he was hostile or, at the least, "indifferent" to political philosophy, and as a result his book was a demonstration of "intellectual barrenness . . . logical aimlessness and diffuseness." Lasswell's attempt to enclose political science within nothing but an empirical framework was "a contradiction in terms and a monstrosity." This of a scholar about whom it was said: "Few would question that he was the most original and productive political scientist of his time."

Someone else who ran up against Morgenthau's irascibility was Norman Podhoretz, the editor of *Commentary* magazine. Morgenthau had been a regular contributor in the early 1960s, saying he found its Jewish-liberal format congenial. All that changed after the appearance of his article "Goldwater—The Romantic Regression" in September 1964. An infuriated Morgenthau counted up 37 changes in his meaning and 65 in his style. This was an "editorial attack," he said, "vulgar and barbaric," even "immoral." Morgenthau vowed never to write for the magazine again. The assault left Podhoretz bewildered. He had, he said, edited at least 15 Morgenthau pieces over the previous five years, correcting only grammar and syntax. In the last word of the exchange, Morgenthau was unforgiving, dismissing Podhoretz with a cold response: "I have written in identical style for a great number of distinguished publications." True to his word, Morgenthau never appeared in *Commentary* again.

If either the combative Morgenthau or the withdrawn Strauss had found a way of reaching out to the other to make a connection, a sympathy based on their similar life situations might have overcome their intellectual differences and produced discussions that would have benefited both of them, as was the case in the early days of their relationship. But once a deterioration set in, neither was inclined or equipped to change course.

THAT ESSENTIAL QUALITY of sympathy was never absent from Morgenthau's relationship with Hannah Arendt, colored, it should be said, by an element of the erotic. They met in the early 1950s and developed an unshakeable friendship that lasted up to her death in 1975. Hans Jonas, who had known Arendt since their student days in Germany during the 1920s and who saw her every day when they were both attending the University of Marburg, remembered that "It was almost to be taken for granted that men of high intelligence and sensibility would be enchanted by Hannah." Morgenthau was enchanted. "What struck one at first meeting Hannah Arendt," he recalled, was "the vitality of her mind, quick—sometimes too quick—sparkling, seeking and finding hidden meanings and connections beneath the surface of man and things." She had an extraordinary depth of knowledge combined with rare intellectual passion. "As others enjoy playing cards or the horses for their own sake, so Hannah Arendt enjoyed thinking."

On another occasion, he likened her manner of thinking to poetry. "If you consider the enormous suggestiveness of her insights into political matters . . . you realize that her mind worked in a way not dissimilar to the poetic mind, which creates affinities, which discovers relationships that appear obvious once they are formulated but that nobody had thought of before the poet formulated them." And in an expression of grievous sorrow at her death, he said, "I am left with an unutterable regret."

Arendt has been described as Morgenthau's "intellectual companion," and through the decades of their friendship, each supported the other in good times and bad. There was no more trying period for Arendt than the months in the mid-1960s when the Eichmann controversy was burning white-hot. Along with Mary McCarthy and Karl Jaspers, Morgenthau was unfailingly loyal. He dined with her at the University of Chicago faculty club when other faculty members were making a point of shunning her, and when she was attacked in the *New York Times*, he wrote a letter to the editor in her defense. Reporting from New York where a public meeting to discuss her ideas on Eichmann quickly deteriorated into a shouting match, Morgenthau said: "The Jewish community is up in arms." And he went on, "Reality has protruded into the protective armor of illusion and the result is psychological havoc." For her part, Arendt was there for him when he was suffering through a series of illnesses, a nurse, a sister, a mother. When he was in danger of damaging his professional reputation because of his opposition to the Vietnam war, she was by his side.

Over the years, they celebrated New Year's together, watched JFK's funeral together, even vacationed together—though on a trip to Rhodes, Morgenthau may have made a not uncommon discovery that even the dearest friends sometimes do not make good traveling companions. "She can be a real pain in the neck," he wrote in a letter home. On that list of the 10 books that mattered most to him, Morgenthau included Arendt's *The Human Condition*. Late in life, according to her biographer, Morgenthau even proposed marriage. Arendt was "disconcerted," but she was hardly unaccustomed to male attention and knew how to handle a delicate situation. A psychoanalyst who was extremely close to Morgenthau in his later years took a somewhat different view: "My hunch is that each of them thought it would solve many problems if they were able to love the other, but neither one did or could, yet each believed himself (herself) to be loved and desired by the other." The relationship survived her rejection and they continued to enjoy each other's company, as well as their wide-ranging discussions. (What if they had wed? One pictures a young

Henry Kissinger as a dinner guest, conversing animatedly with Morgenthau about the events of the day while Arendt looked on severely, mentally dissecting the arguments of both men.) Arendt had been involved in the planning of Thompson's testimonial volume to Morgenthau in the 1970s. She had been commissioned to write the concluding essay but died before she could take up the assignment.

Intellectually, they were very close. Like Morgenthau's work, Arendt's work was a rebuff to the quantifiers who dominated American political thought. The Princeton political scientist Sheldon S. Wolin said Arendt "occupies a special place in the recent history of political theory" because she understood the importance of ideas and rescued theory from "the dreary and trivial categories of academic political science," as it was taught by the adherents of the Chicago School. Philosophical works like Arendt's *The Human Condition* "came as a deliverance," Wolin said, permitting discussion once again of large and challenging concepts like freedom, action, judgment, and human happiness. And as with Morgenthau, her thinking, Wolin observed, "led toward a radical pessimism." (At Chicago, of course, the common view was that whatever it was Arendt was doing, it wasn't philosophy.)

Politically, too, Morgenthau and Arendt tended to see eye to eye. Though both were fierce anti-Communists and accused by critics of heightening Cold War tensions, they were united in their opposition to the Vietnam war. And when Arendt looked out at the world, she did so from Morgenthau's perspective, seeing a violent global environment not readily susceptible to the demands of moral imperatives. Promises of world peace through international organizations like the League of Nations and the United Nations did not seduce her. Together, they were campaigners for a hard and grim reality against overweening American optimism. To be sure, international relations as a subject did not preoccupy her, but as one scholar has put it, "Her emphasis on the anarchy of the sovereign state system and her skepticism about the regulatory capacity of international law and institutions showed marked affinities with the American Realists of her generation."

Such views only confused many of their academic colleagues, not to mention the rest of their fellow citizens. Here were Cold Warriors with no illusions about the Soviet Union, who understood the indispensable role of the United States in the reconfigured postwar world and distrusted liberal ideals of internationalism, yet who stoutly opposed McCarthyism, Washington's fixation on military power, and the Manichean anti-Communism of the American establishment. Just because the Soviets embodied evil did not mean the Americans embodied virtue. Were they liberal or conservative? The correct answer is that they were neither, because they approached political questions from a Continental, "un-American" perspective. They were not nationalistic thinkers. "What an idiocy," Morgenthau once said to Arendt, "to assume that when you write you must of necessity champion a cause."

Morgenthau once confronted Arendt directly about her politics. At a 1972 conference in Toronto organized around her work, Morgenthau challenged her: "What are you? Are you a conservative? Are you a liberal? Where is your position within the contemporary possibilities?" To which Arendt responded: "I don't know. I really don't know and I've never known. And I suppose I never had any such position. You know the left think I am conservative, and the conservatives sometimes think I am left or I am a maverick or God knows what. And I must say I couldn't care less. I don't think the real questions of this century will get any kind of illumination by this kind of thing." Her views couldn't be confined within the standard categories or with the help of "banisters," and neither could Morgenthau's. "I am nowhere," she told Mary McCarthy at the same conference. Years earlier, as a young scholar, Morgenthau had similarly declared: "You are asking where I stand politically? My answer is: nowhere." Left, right, center—these were labels to be attached to people within the American political spectrum, not to outsiders like Arendt or Morgenthau, or to Leo Strauss, or to Henry Kissinger. The many attempts that have been made over the years to pigeonhole them—was Strauss a neocon? was Arendt an "icon of the left"? was Morgenthau a "conservative liberal"? was Kissinger a war criminal?—have only created intellectual confusion.

A tribute to Arendt that Morgenthau wrote in 1977, two years after her death, provides a window on the kinds of discussions these two unclassifiable political intellectuals from "nowhere" must have had over the years (though only Morgenthau's voice is heard). He expresses admiration for her *Origins of Totalitarianism*, endorsing her view that totalitarianism was a new form of regime, unknown to the Western tradition of political philosophy that began with Aristotle. It not only gave rise to genocidal ideologies resulting in the deaths of millions, but it also incorporated thousands of ordinary citizens into operating its efficient killing machines, bureaucratizing mass murder. This was an idea Arendt was to make famous through her endlessly debated phrase "the banality of evil," from her book *Eichmann in Jerusalem*.

Much (though not all) of the controversy surrounding that book turned on Arendt's portrait of Adolf Eichmann as a thoughtless, non-descript functionary who never really understood what he was doing, and therefore not so different from the legions of clerks and secretaries, mechanics and plumbers, who were required to keep the trains running and the ovens burning. Seizing on Eichmann's own impenitent statements when he was hiding in Argentina, which are indisputably anti-Semitic and genocidal, Arendt's critics have insisted that she got it wrong, that Eichmann was anything but banal; his deeds were as heinous and intentional as his Israeli accusers claimed they were. But that criticism lost sight of Arendt's observation that Eichmann's anti-Semitism had evolved over time as he absorbed and accepted the genocidal aims of his superiors—his statements when he was a fugitive in Argentina did not reflect the changes he had undergone in the 1930s—and though he didn't think for himself, his "thoughtlessness" did not absolve him of guilt. Most important, her critics tended to ignore the larger point she was making about the nature of totalitarianism and, by implication, about our modern condition: that is, how so many normal people could be transformed into desk murderers because instead of confronting the reality of their deeds, even when reality was right in front of their eyes, they simply followed the rules of their society. It just so happened that in Nazi Germany the rules of society included the commission of hideous crimes. In the twentieth century, with the collapse of religion and traditional authority, external social norms were taking precedence over internalized, ungrounded morality, and that was a problem for everyone.

For Arendt, Eichmann was only an extreme illustration of the phenomenon, so extreme—and this proved deeply offensive to many of her readers—that his life and career as a mediocrity elevated by chance to the position of mass murderer had to be seen as in some sense "comic" because of the enormous gap that existed between his deeds and his motives. The consequences of his acts were monstrous, the intentions behind them petty. This was the stuff of silent comedy, Chaplin, Keaton, when a slip on a banana peel or a pie in the face could escalate into social chaos. As Arendt wrote, "The horrible can be not only ludicrous but outright funny." Mary McCarthy, with her refined aesthetic sensibility, understood her friend and said she found the book exhilarating, like a chorus from Mozart.

Morgenthau saw Arendt's point entirely and agreed with it. The "banality of evil," he said, suggested "there exists no correspondence between the evil done and the evildoer. The evildoer can be a minor figure in a bureaucratic machine believing in the presuppositions of the doctrine. He executes almost mechanically, bureaucratically, the mandates of that doctrine." Here again, Morgenthau grasped what Arendt's critics did not: Eichmann may have become genocidally anti-Semitic as he rose to a position of influence in the Third Reich, but *he did not have to hate Jews in order to murder them.* There were numerous other dedicated and opportunistic bureaucrats living in Nazi Germany who would have done what he did without giving it a second thought, as long as they were abiding by society's rules and advancing their own careers. And for Morgenthau, the lesson taught by totalitarianism—though many liberals had a hard time accepting it—was that "people not only strive for freedom and are willing to die for freedom, but that they also strive for order and are willing to die for order." Almost gleefully, he pointed out that this "represents a denial of the optimism of the 18th and 19th centuries."

Arendt, the more compassionate personality, struggled to retain a ray of light in the "dark times" she and Morgenthau were living through, and her celebration of voluntary council systems was her way of preserving human freedom and plurality in the face of the overwhelming forces arrayed against them, not only by totalitarianism but also by the bureaucratic mass societies of the liberal democracies that, in their own way, threatened human liberty. The dour Morgenthau would have none of it, and his arguments against her qualified optimism must have been ones Arendt heard again and again through the decades of their friendship. How, he asked, could the open, pluralistic spaces of council systems be safeguarded in a world where power dominated and evil was ubiquitous? It was the problem of the pacifists all over again—also of Strauss's blessed island of philosophers—and Arendt was never able to resolve it. About the practical difficulties of the council idea, Morgenthau went on, Arendt had nothing to say, and though he was writing in praise of his friend, he couldn't resist pointing out what he called the "romantic element in Hannah Arendt's conception of freedom."

Still, he was not wholly unsympathetic. Rather than merely criticize his "intellectual companion," he offered support of a kind by acknowledging the quality of pessimism and desperation in her thinking, which was clearly something he liked about her, the only appropriate stance for a thoughtful person living in dark times. "Perhaps one can argue that the theoretical character of Hannah Arendt's political philosophy is a symptom of this impossibility to think creatively in a hopeless political situation." Arendt tried to keep one small door open for optimism. Morgenthau insisted on slamming it shut. To think, he said, was to suffer. "Consciousness does not save man from perdition, but it makes him understand the source and end of his fate." The challenge, in his mind, was learning to live in an unpredictable, often savage world without hope. If mankind was catapulting down the road to hell, at least one could recognize the signposts.

MORGENTHAU'S INITIAL STEP onto America's public stage, and on his way to becoming a public intellectual, came in 1946 with his book *Scientific Man Versus Power Politics*. Nietzsche had once written, citing Stendhal, that men should "make their entry into society with a duel." It's a fair assumption that Morgenthau, the Nietzsche enthusiast, was familiar with the line—it appears in *Ecce Homo*, one of Nietzsche's most accessible and entertaining books (if also one of his most portentous, as he edged closer to insanity). But Morgenthau, with his argumentative temperament, didn't need Nietzsche's or Stendhal's advice to come to the same conclusion. He would enter society, that is, the intellectual society of his new country, with guns blazing.

His first book to be published in the United States was a manifesto—and a polemic. Morgenthau was drawing a line in the sand. He decried what he saw as the dominant approach of American political thinking, more particularly that of his University of Chicago colleagues (though he never mentioned them directly), which, he insisted, had fallen into a state of decay because of its "belief in the power of science to solve all problems." There was more to life than statistics and calculation, and Morgenthau found the perfect epigraph for his book in a comment by Edmund Burke: "Politics ought to be adjusted, not to human reasonings, but to human nature; of which the reason is but a part, and by no means the greatest part." Across the 245 pages that followed, Morgenthau reiterated Burke's point again and again, relentlessly, repetitiously, from every angle and with every argument at his disposal, circling like a hungry lion stalking a helpless wildebeest. Nietzsche had said that his mission was "overthrowing idols (my word for 'ideals')." Morgenthau's goal was to overthrow America's idols (ideals) and wipe the slate clean. As one scholar put it, "Morgenthau's book is nothing less than a fundamental critique of the social, political and moral philosophy of the modern West." He would be the terminator.

The dominant philosophy in the West, Morgenthau declared, was a reliance on reason. Everything he went on to say flowed from this simple assertion. Reason was thought to give man the means to understand the world because the world was inherently intelligible, governed by rational and accessible laws, graspable by the processes of human thought— and those processes, it was held, were the methods of natural science. By defining, quantifying, and measuring, we could understand everything that is, or at least everything that needed to be understood. Every effect had a cause, which itself had a cause, and so on, ad infinitum. Pushed to an extreme but not preposterous limit, this manner of thinking led to the conclusion that "a sufficiently great mathematician, given the distribution of the particles in the primitive nebula, could predict the whole future of the world." In this way, reason was conjoined with science, while the people who insisted on the connection were, in Morgenthau's language, "liberals."

For Morgenthau, his use of the term "liberal" carried no narrow political connotation, though admittedly there was a tendency for the left to emphasize reason and science in their battles against religion. Conservatives could be "liberals," too. "No political thinker can expect to be heard who would not, at least in his terminology, pay tribute to the spirit of science, and, by claiming his propositions to be 'realistic,' 'technical' or 'experimental,' assume their compliance with scientific standards." Morgenthau was casting his net across the whole of Western culture, and liberals were merely those (who, in Morgenthau's eyes, included practically everybody) who exhibited "the largely unconscious assumptions by which the age lives, its basic convictions as to the nature of man and society, which give meaning to thought and action."

This modern belief in reason, with science as its handmaiden, was inherently optimistic; it confidently adhered to the notion of progress. As humankind's understanding of the universe and its mechanisms increased, so too did its ability to gain control over nature and improve the conditions of human life. And it was not only physical laws that reason and science unraveled. Social questions were also amenable to the methods of definition and measurement. The practical and political issues that divided men could be resolved by the ministrations of rational experts and professionals trained in the scientistic tradition: economists, sociologists, psychologists, political scientists. The problems that had bedeviled politicians and statesmen since the beginning of recorded history all had technical solutions; it was only a matter of applying the appropriate knowledge gained through the techniques of social science.

There was an obvious utopianism to all this. Perfection was possible, and "the perfect world is the world in which all obey the commands of reason." As Morgenthau pointed out, it was not only liberals in the West like Jeremy Bentham and John Dewey who placed their trust in scientific reason. Marxists did so as well. "Marx simply transfers the liberal confidence in the rational powers of the individual to the class." And just as Marxists held out the eschatological promise that history would come to an end once the working class prevailed, liberals preached an eschatology of their own. The triumph of freedom and democracy throughout the world would usher in a golden age, its own end of history. As Woodrow Wilson told Congress in January 1918, "making the world safe for democracy" would culminate in the "final war for human liberty," the "war to end war." Wilson, Morgenthau wrote, "is the perfect interpreter of liberal thought." For his part, he preferred the British statesman George Canning, who in 1823 warned: "The general acquisition of free institutions is not necessarily a security for general peace." Indeed, with his experience of the democratic rise of Hitler as a lingering, unhealed wound, Morgenthau went further: the liberal, Wilsonian ideals of democracy and self-determination had the potential to undermine the prospects for peace by unleashing the anarchic tendencies of aggressive nationalism and genocidal ethnicity. Throughout his career in the United States, Morgenthau never stopped trying to explain to Americans (who persistently had difficulty understanding the point) that "modern totalitarian regimes, fascist and Communist, have not been imposed by a tyrannical minority upon an unwilling population." Rather, they "have come to power and maintained their rule with the support of populations willing to sacrifice individual freedom and self-government, actual or potential, for order and what they consider to be social justice."

Reason, Morgenthau insisted, was not the only force operative in human history. Men were not only rational beings but also, and equally, biological and spiritual ones. "By neglecting the biological impulses and spiritual aspirations of man," the philosophy of rationalism "misconstrues the function reason fulfills within the whole of human existence." Reason could never dictate; it could only coexist with the other aspects of human nature.

Contrary to what the rationalists believed, reason was limited in what it could achieve. It had no answers to those ultimate questions that have been raised since the time of the ancient Hebrews and Greeks about the meaning and purpose of life. Even though modern, scientistic thought had done its best to deny that those questions even made sense—Life has no meaning! Now get on with it!—they kept emerging and reemerging, much to the annoyance of the rationalists. One's spiritual nature, one's metaphysical, religious, artistic, poetic side, could not be suppressed. (It is worth remembering that Morgenthau was saying all this only a decade after he gave up writing poetry.)

What is more, by ignoring or denying the questions that philosophy, metaphysics, and religion sought to address, the rationalism of science had left man "impoverished in his quest for an answer to the riddle of the universe and of his existence in it." Science may have "lightened the burden of living" but it had not "lightened the burden of life." Painless dentistry did not relieve the metaphysical ache. And in their desperation for large answers that the prevailing rationalistic wisdom could not supply, multitudes of people, both educated and uneducated, had turned away from science and from reason, Morgenthau said, to find meaning in "degenerate derivations of art, religion and metaphysics, such as astrology, prophecy, belief in miracles, occultism, political religions, sectarianism, all kinds of superstitions and all the lower types of entertainment." One such "political religion" was fascism, which liberalism, in its blind commitment to its own preconceptions, had completely failed to understand. Fascism, Morgenthau said, was not a retreat into irrationality and reaction. "In its mastery of the technological attainments and potentialities of the age, it is truly progressive."

A victim of its limitations, modern rationalism was caught in a "vicious circle," doomed to repeat its mistakes over and over again. At those times when it did recognize failure, it didn't revise its philosophical approach but merely called for more facts to fit into its prefabricated framework, which was exactly the problem. Defeat brought forth only "a renewed effort with essentially the same means." The accumulation of facts was a substitute for thought. Liberals were Don Quixotes, forever tilting at unconquerable windmills.

It wasn't always so. At the dawn of the age of reason, science was opening up the prospect of exciting new discoveries, but with each undeniable triumph, it extended its domain and hardened its approach. What had started out as an empirical, pragmatic philosophy ossified into an ideology that recognized no truth outside its own purview. It claimed to stand for openness but had in fact become exclusionary and dogmatic. This was especially true with regard to human relations, where, instead of taking each problem on its own terms, in all its immediate complexity and with an acknowledgment of the inherent uncertainty contained in freedom of the will, it confronted the world by making logical deductions from its particular abstract rational principles. Answers were easier when the map of reality had already been plotted out as a rule-bound system. But no formula could eliminate the unpredictability of actual life, and too often the liberals' map pointed in the wrong direction.

That rationalistic thought couldn't see its limitations meant for Morgenthau that liberalism had decayed, fallen from its earlier heights. In the twentieth century it had entered its decadent phase, placing its faith in rules and abstractions like "human rights" or "legality." There was no better example of this than "Chamberlain's waving of a piece of paper with Hitler's peace pledge as guaranty of 'peace in our time.' " The Munich agreement was "a tragic symbol of this period of intellectual history, which believed in the miraculous power of the legal framework." Yet, as Morgenthau caustically observed, "The choice is not between legality and illegality, but between political wisdom and political stupidity."

It is important to understand precisely what Morgenthau was objecting to. It wasn't reason itself that was his enemy but the contemporary misuse of reason. Morgenthau was not championing "irrationalism," as some of his critics charged. Rationality was required for the solution or, more accurately, the management of social problems even if people were behaving irrationally. Human interactions could be understood through reason, which could encompass un-reason (just as un-reason could encompass reason), but it was a mistake to project reason as a template onto nonrational reality itself by developing mechanical equations to explain and predict behavior. Each situation was unique, to be interpreted according to its own particularity and evaluated on its own terms. Social science could describe broad possibilities but not certainties. "What can be stated scientifically in way of prediction on the basis of a 'social law' is merely that, given certain conditions, a certain social trend is more likely to mate-

rialize than are others—in other words, that the odds are in favor of one
trend as over against others." One could employ the teachings of the social
scientists as long as one remembered their unalterable contingency. But
inevitably, eager, ambitious politicians would want more from their economists, political scientists, and sociologists, and eager, ambitious economists, political scientists, and sociologists would attempt to give it to
them—though in the end, "whoever seeks more will get less."

Not surprisingly, Morgenthau, still the brooding child playing with his
toy soldiers, turned to military experience to illustrate the need for resilience and flexibility in the face of formulaic, "rational" thinking. A general
plans a campaign based upon reasoned assessments of his own strength,
the enemy's strength, and the circumstances under which the battle will
be fought. All the proper calculations will be made ahead of time. But "history abounds," Morgenthau said, with examples of intentions frustrated
by the unexpected. "Orders may be wrongly transmitted, misunderstood
or not carried out. . . . The enemy may fail to do something the other side
expected." It was the unpredictability of weather that destroyed the Spanish Armada and changed the course of history. "In modern times, a small
and incalculable difference in industrial production, technical progress or
speed and reliability of transportation may make the difference between
victory and defeat." The lesson of warfare was to expect the unexpected
and use one's intelligence, one's presence of mind, to adapt. That, not the
application of predetermined formulas, was the mark of a great general.
But accepting contingency did not mean forsaking planning or reasoned
thinking. It simply meant that rationality was no panacea, that one always
stood in the middle of life, not outside it, assessing and reassessing based
on immediate circumstances and the best knowledge that was available at
any given moment. Improvisation should be employed only when improvisation was required, and then rationally. The quality of independent,
unsupported thinking that goes by the hard-to-pin-down name of "intuition" was an important element in victory.

And what was true of generals in warfare was even more true of politicians and policymakers, because military battles came to an end whereas
political conflict never did. Policy disputes reflected the Aristotelian truth
that we are always and forever political animals. "Social problems are
never solved definitely. They must be solved every day anew" and with no
guarantee of success. "The social world is indeed a chaos of contingen-

cies. Yet it is not devoid of a measure of rationality if approached with the expectations of Macbethian cynicism." Morgenthau's aim was, Kant-like, to trace the limits of reason, not to abandon it.

Morgenthau saw the worst of rationalistic overreaching in his own field of foreign affairs. The influence of scientific thinking had steadily grown since the days of Copernicus and Galileo as it extended beyond the measurement of physical objects to the measurement of human beings. But only in the twentieth century, following World War I, did it intrude into international relations. Statesmen and scholars set about applying what they understood as the powers and the promise of reason to conflicts among nations, with the expectation that all disputes could be settled rationally, through discourse and mutual understanding, and insofar as disagreements were not resolved through discussion and compromise, failure was a problem of irrationality and unreasonableness, not of the rationalistic approach itself. "For liberalism, international relations reveal their true nature in the harmony of interests," whereas war was a product of irrational emotion, an absolute evil because it violated the natural order of things. To all right-thinking individuals it was a horror to be consigned to the past, an "atavism." Here, it might be said, Morgenthau's use of "liberal" and "liberalism" shaded into the more narrow and partisan meaning of those words, standing in for views associated with the internationalistic and pacifistic perspective of the left—though not entirely. Even nationalistic right-wingers, displaying their own brand of eschatological utopianism, held out the liberal promise of peace in our time. The difference was that their eternal peace would be achieved through military means and the total submission of the enemy. And what if the enemy refused to submit? Then unrestricted air warfare or even nuclear weapons could be used to achieve a "Carthaginian peace," which was still harmony of a kind.

From the liberal perspective, the goal of diplomacy should be to find a way to bring an end to war, which had now become a genuine possibility, whether through treaties like the Kellogg-Briand Pact or institutions like the League of Nations and the United Nations. Abstract ideals counted for more than harsh realities, and the belief in a natural harmony among nations represented, for Morgenthau, a "foreign policy without politics." He quoted the French Socialist leader Leon Blum declaring in 1932, "The more danger there is in the world, the more necessary it is to disarm."

To Morgenthau, the mistake in such thinking was to apply domestic experience to the international realm or, more precisely, to misapply it. In the successful Western democracies, people had learned to live peaceably with one another. Leaders were replaced not by revolutions or coups d'etat but through the participatory rituals of elections. The rule of law prevailed, stability was achieved, and there was a shared understanding that citizens could work together for their common advantage and mutual prosperity.

But this unspoken consensus, Morgenthau said, was not in any sense a timeless reality to be pursued as an end in itself. It was a product of history, a contingent result of middle-class hegemony in the democracies. The rule of law worked as long as one didn't look too closely at its underpinnings. "The middle classes," Morgenthau said, "developed a system of indirect domination which replaced the military method of open violence with the invisible chains of economic dependence and which hid the very existence of power relations behind a network of seemingly egalitarian liberal rules." Morgenthau didn't push this Marxist-inflected argument too far: he was less interested in the economic origins of the liberal consensus than in its misguided impact on foreign policy, and he turned to the ever-reliable Woodrow Wilson for an example of wrongheaded thinking. "We are at the beginning of an age," Wilson declared in 1917, "in which it will be insisted that the same standard of conduct and of responsibility for wrong done shall be observed among nations and their governments that are observed among the individual citizens in civilized states." With their own domestic arrangements as their model, liberal, rationalistic policy-makers were wont to ask: If a "community of rational interests and values" existed on the domestic front, then why not in the international community as well?

Because, Morgenthau answered, there was no such thing as an international community. Domestic disputes could be resolved—not solved—through discussion and negotiations, or when negotiation failed, by appeals to the sovereignty of the state and the authority of the law. In the relatively benign context of the Western democracies, even those who disagreed with particular outcomes were willing to accept them so that they could live to dispute another day. Only small, knuckle-dragging minorities resorted to violence, and they were vastly outnumbered by the overwhelming law-abiding majority. Consensus was possible because within national borders people agreed to disagree. This was the very meaning of "legitimacy." "Disputants could not fail to realize that what they had in common was more important than what they were fighting about. They met, indeed, on the common ground of liberal rationality, and their conflicts, since they arose under the conditions and within the framework of the liberal society, could all be settled through the instrumentalities of liberal rationality."

No such peaceful consensus prevailed in the international arena. Nations were the products of different values, different traditions, different beliefs. Their actions and goals had more to do with geography, history, and national character than with their forms of government. "Nations are peace-loving under certain historic conditions and are warlike under others, and it is not the form of government or domestic policies which makes them so." Discussion could take disputing parties only so far because identity was nonnegotiable and not to be governed by formal rules or agreements. Ultimately foreign affairs were "an unending struggle for survival and power."

Every attempt to bring order to the world through parliamentary mechanisms based on Western domestic models—for example, the League of Nations, the United Nations—succeeded only so long as the various governments saw it as to their advantage to abide by the agreed-upon rules. But if—or more likely when—the rules came into conflict with fundamental national interests, the apparent international consensus fell apart. Conflicts over basic interests—Morgenthau's examples were the Romans and the barbarians, the Arab world and the Christian West, Napoleonic France and the rest of Europe, the fascist regimes and the democracies (and he might have added the Cold War)—were not susceptible to rational compromise because these were existential struggles for absolute power. "To enter such a conflict with the equipment of the bargaining negotiator is to give up the struggle before it has really started."

Morgenthau's reading of history might seem to be a prescription for perpetual warfare, but that wasn't the case. He didn't address the question directly in *Scientific Man Versus Power Politics*, but he suggested that military conflict was not inevitable, that it was always better to seek solutions beneficial to all the parties than to resort to arms. He was no warmonger. But if war was not inevitable in international affairs, the preparation for war was. Governments had to be prepared unflinchingly to employ violence when violence was necessary.

Once Morgenthau had stripped away all rationalist ideals and scientistic hopes, the foundations of modern thinking, here was the way the world looked: it was one in which violence was both an ever-present threat and a sometimes necessary tool. Without utopian dreams, the power of nation-states was what remained—"violence reigns supreme." The wise statesman did not deny the reality of power politics. Neither did he use national might for idealistic ends, which in truth amounted to the same thing—a denial of politics, though one that would take place in the future, when the ideal would be attained, rather than in the present. Instead, he understood that power and the yearning for power would never disappear from human affairs and therefore he employed violence judiciously, as circumstances dictated. "Peace is subject to the conditions of time and space and must be established and maintained by different methods and under different conditions of urgency in the everyday relations of concrete nations." Viewing peace as an abstraction was a foolish delusion, an intellectual chimera. "The problem of international peace," Morgenthau said, "exists only for the philosopher."

And because there was no escape from the reality of power politics, Morgenthau concluded, the situation of the statesman was necessarily "tragic." The choices he faced were not between good and evil, though Americans were always inclined to think in such terms, but between bad and less bad. There was always the prospect that people, innocent people, would die because of decisions a statesman made. "Man cannot hope to be good but must be content with being not too evil," or "to be as good as he can be in an evil world." It was said that Morgenthau's essential objection to scientific, rationalist thinking was an aesthetic one—that it failed because it denied the permanence of tragedy. There is truth to the charge: the retired poet continued to think poetically. "No formula will give the statesman certainty, no calculation eliminate the risk, no accumulation of facts open the future." One was always, to a greater or lesser degree, in the dark. That was the inescapable human condition. And just as Morgenthau turned to Burke for the epigraph to *Scientific Man Versus Power Politics*, years later he found the perfect condensation of his tragic way of thinking in a comment by Justice Oliver Wendell Holmes: "Every year if not every day we wager our salvation upon some prophecy based upon imperfect knowledge." To operate realistically in the brutal world of social interaction required the acceptance of uncertainty, which was wisdom, not the false assurances of science. And wisdom was reserved not for those who plunged into events with the certitude of the fanatic but for those statesmen who maintained their distance, their irony, through a sense of the tragic. For Morgenthau, the ideal statesman was Abraham Lincoln, "a man of unique greatness," whose fatalistic detachment allowed him to view events and people (himself included) with objectivity, humility, and compassion. Lincoln's ironic humor was inextricably linked to his melancholy separateness. Morgenthau viewed Henry Kissinger as another statesman who possessed a sense of humor and a sense of irony, who exhibited a fatalistic detachment linked to melancholy separateness.

Habitually optimistic Americans, especially in the triumphal years immediately following World War II, were hardly prepared for such teaching. "They literally don't know what I am talking about," Morgenthau complained a year after the appearance of *Scientific Man Versus Power Politics*. But what could he do but press on? He had completed his Nietzschean act of intellectual destruction. Now his task was to build from the ground up and present international affairs as they were actually conducted, and should be conducted, by Realistic statesmen with the obligatory tragic sense. That would be the project of his next book, which would become one of the most influential of the twentieth century and the one generally accepted as Morgenthau's masterwork.

ONLY TWO YEARS separated *Scientific Man Versus Power Politics* from *Politics Among Nations*, but Morgenthau's second American book was a long time in the making. He had been thinking about the project since the 1920s and actually wrote an early draft in 1937. Once in America and settled at the University of Chicago, he incorporated themes from his lectures and honed his ideas in light of the give-and-take he had with his students, many of whom were recently returned from the war. Battle-hardened veterans, they were ready to challenge their professor on every point, practically after every sentence, and an appreciative Morgenthau took their criticisms to heart. In their maturity and seriousness, they were very different from the anti-Semites he had tried to teach in Geneva or the young Stalinists of Brooklyn. Morgenthau called them "the most engaged group of students he had ever encountered anywhere in his career."

Finding a publisher for the forbidding, ambitious manuscript wasn't easy. Despite the appearance of *Scientific Man Versus Power Politics*, Morgenthau didn't have what would be considered an attractive track record, and early readers were troubled by what would become a recurrent criticism throughout Morgenthau's career: that in his emphasis on power politics, he lacked a moral outlook, was indeed "immoral." Besides, what in fact *was* this book? In its range, comprehensiveness, and formidable 500-

page length, it seemed to be a textbook, yet it was much more opinionated than orthodox textbooks and often more aphoristic as well. Morgenthau was arguing for a firm position; he called it "a frontal assault," though it was far less polemical than his previous book. Morgenthau was simply incapable of writing neutrally, without a point of view.

Along with the textbook question was the question of the book's intended audience. Morgenthau shifted around, sometimes on the same page, from political science to history to psychology to philosophy (economics by and large was ignored). It wasn't clear if he was writing for professionals, for students, or for general readers with an interest in international affairs. Answering vaguely that the book was for anyone who cared wasn't going to assuage the doubts of publishers with their eye on the bottom line, and seven of them turned down the manuscript. As his research assistant at the time, Kenneth Thompson, wrote, "Morgenthau recognized that he had a struggle on his hands if the book was to be published."

Morgenthau finally found a sympathetic publishing house in Knopf, but even its editors wanted revisions to the initial draft, calling for less opinion and more factual detail. Though he had a great deal to lose in refusing to make the changes, an exasperated Morgenthau resisted, and only after the personal intervention of Alfred Knopf himself was the manuscript published to Morgenthau's satisfaction and, as it turned out, to that of the Knopf publishing house as well. The first edition was an instant success, going through eight printings and making Morgenthau a "household word" on campuses around the country. Within a year, it had been adopted as a textbook by Harvard, Yale, Princeton, and close to 100 other colleges and universities. During Morgenthau's lifetime, it went through four more editions and numerous printings. Morgenthau was made a full professor at Chicago in 1949 and was soon lecturing around the country. Through the auspices of the like-minded George Kennan, Morgenthau began serving as an adviser to the U.S. State Department. By the time of the second edition in 1954, he was being called "world-renowned."

What accounted for the success of *Politics Among Nations*? And why were so many publishing professionals wrong about it? It was no less pessimistic than *Scientific Man Versus Power Politics*, no less against the American grain, no less "Germanic." One early critic accused Morgenthau of trying to insinuate ugly and immoral Continental power politics into the wholesome American environment. This objection was not inaccurate as far as it went, though Morgenthau and his followers would have chalked up a plus where the critics saw a minus. But one advantage that *Politics Among Nations* had over Morgenthau's first American book consisted of the fact that it wasn't the battering ram *Scientific Man Versus Power Politics* was. Instead of an assault on its readers, it offered diagnosis and analysis. It moved with an ebb and flow as Morgenthau considered first one argument, then another, deconstructing positions, finding positives in negatives and vice versa. It gave readers, even those American readers hostile to Realpolitik thinking, something to engage with, an argument they could accept or reject but one they had to ponder. They weren't targets for Morgenthau to shoot at but collaborators and interlocutors. This was the Morgenthau of the classroom.

Then there was the crucial fact of the book's timing. *Politics Among Nations* appeared just when Americans were looking for fresh ways of thinking about foreign policy. The United States had emerged from World War II as a superpower and the undisputed leader of the West, facing off against a dangerous, expansionist foe with a world-encompassing ideology. Under such circumstances, Wilsonian idealism hardly seemed sufficient, any more than did the internationalism of organizations like the United Nations—though Washington continued to be populated by more than its share of idealists and internationalists.

Morgenthau made a point of demonstrating just how ill-equipped Americans were to shoulder their new responsibilities. Since its founding, the United States benefited from having geography on its side. Protected by two vast oceans, it could expand at will across the continent while dominating its weak neighbors to the south. As for Europe, with its age-old rivalries, resentments, and wars, Americans were content to play the role of "spectators," and smug and self-righteous ones at that. What was a lucky accident of history and geography they took to be a permanent and universal condition, and in their splendid isolation, with no threat to the national interest, they came to believe in their own moral exceptionalism, with a God-given mission to spread an antimilitaristic, antigovernment libertarianism around the world.

In Morgenthau's terms, this prevailing ideology was not politics but the negation of politics, moralism masquerading as reality, utopian aspirations misconceived as foreign policy. "When the need for an active American foreign policy became manifest in the late 1930s, there was nothing to build on but a mediocre foreign service, the condemnation of power politics and of secret diplomacy transformed into moral indignation at 'aggressor nations,' and the tradition of the big stick." With the end of World War II and the United States plunged into the complex, dark arena of international power politics, the need for thinking unburdened by Wilsonianism had become that much more urgent. Morgenthau had a warning for his readers: "Since in this world situation the United States holds a position of predominant power, and hence of foremost responsibility, the understanding of the forces that mold international politics and of the factors that determine its course has become for the United States more than an interesting intellectual occupation. It has become a vital necessity."

The men who were in the process of formulating and implementing the Marshall Plan, the North Atlantic Treaty Organization (NATO), and the containment policy had, in Morgenthau's words, "played it by ear." They were reacting to immediate problems, improvising brilliantly it had to be said, but with no theoretical coherence or overarching perspective. Morgenthau arrived on the scene to give them that perspective. Here was a thinker who was charting a path not between but beyond head-in-the-sand isolationism and crusading, big-stick militarism. With his thorough classical grounding in history and philosophy and his awe-inspiring erudition—for example, he could turn the War of the Spanish Succession into an issue of contemporary relevance—he provided the requisite intellectual framework for those coping with the new, evolving, dimly understood challenges of the Cold War. Among the readers who were ready to listen to him were George Kennan, Walter Lippmann, Reinhold Niebuhr, Raymond Aron, Arthur Schlesinger Jr., and Henry Kissinger.

POLITICS AMONG NATIONS had an elaborate structure but it rested on a simple foundation. Morgenthau said that two schools could be discerned in modern political thought. One relied on universal abstract principles, however derived, and assumed "the essential goodness and infinite malleability" of human beings, promising a future of eternal peace based on whatever general principles happened to be espoused. This was the moralistic school, so familiar to Americans. The other, Morgenthau's Nietzschean school, denied the existence of abstract principles (except in humankind's dreams and delusions) and looked to the lessons of history for "objective laws that have their roots in human nature." What it claimed to have found was a distasteful truth: "The struggle for power is universal in time and space and is an undeniable fact of experience."

Because the drive to dominate was "common to all men," it followed that to focus on kindhearted motives and well-meaning ideals was a mistake. "How often have statesmen been motivated by the desire to improve the world and ended up making it worse." Robespierre, out of the sincerest of intentions, destroyed the French Revolution. Wilson was always on hand to serve as a useful negative example.

Ideologies as such had both positive and negative aspects for foreign policy. As expressions of popular ideals, they might make the underlying struggle for power morally acceptable to the masses, who could not deal with too much reality. But they also had the potential for catastrophic inhumanity. Morgenthau quoted Tolstoy in *War and Peace* observing that in the cause of freedom and equality the French marched east and committed all manner of "crimes, murders, wars." Cynical but sophisticated political leaders might make use of ideology to garner popular support and rally the masses behind the government. The risk they ran was that they could be overwhelmed by those who genuinely subscribed to the ideology, the true believers with a sense neither of irony nor tragedy, who were unable to indulge in the kind of hypocrisy that was often a feature of skilled statesmanship. The ideologues knew no limits, and that was when all hell could break loose. It was said of Hitler (by Stalin of all people) that he was a zealot who "didn't know when to stop." Follow the logic of this thought to its bitter end and you could find yourself arguing that Hitler failed as a statesman because he lacked the kind of detachment that was revealed by a Lincolnesque sense of humor. (Morgenthau was always one to stress the importance of humor.)

The wise statesman saw through evanescent ideologies to the bedrock of reality, which was power. To penetrate "ideological disguises and grasp behind them the actual political forces" was the key to formulating a realistic (and Realistic) foreign policy. "We assume that statesmen think and act in terms of interest defined as power, and the evidence of history bears that assumption out." Grasping the truth of the struggle for power grounded policy in rationality and caution, saving it from "moral excess" and "political folly."

Morgenthau may have been the philosopher of power politics, but he was also at pains to explain what power was not. The crucial point, often forgotten even by his own Realist disciples, was that violence was not

Henry Kissinger and Condoleezza Rice share a moment, 2008. (AP Photo / Keystone, Laurent Gillieron)

Fidel Castro and his admirer Salvador Allende (Keystone Press / Alamy Stock Photo)

The Chilean Army moves on the presidential palace, 1973 (Horacio Villalobos / Contributor via Getty Images)

Fürth synagogues, 1708 (LEBRECHT MUSIC & ARTS / ALAMY STOCK PHOTO)

Hitler Youth march into Fürth, 1938. (© TOPFOTO / THE IMAGE WORKS, INC.)

Adolf Hitler and Gregor Strasser (CLASSIC IMAGE / ALAMY STOCK PHOTO)

Henry Kissinger and his parents return to Fürth, 1975. (KEYSTONE PRESS / ALAMY STOCK PHOTO)

Leo Strauss (COURTESY OF JENNY STRAUSS CLAY)

Hannah Arendt (TYRONE DUKES / THE NEW YORK TIMES / REDUX)

Hans Morgenthau opposes the Vietnam war at a teach-in, 1965. (AP Photo / HWG)

Hans Morgenthau's seventy-first birthday party, 1975. Left to right: Caroline Stoessinger, Morgenthau, Saul Bellow, Elie Wiesel, Susanna Morgenthau (daughter), Henry Kissinger

Henry Kissinger and the North Vietnamese negotiator, Le Duc Tho, talk peace in Paris, January 1, 1973. (KEYSTONE PRESS / ALAMY STOCK PHOTO)

A dejected Henry Kissinger contemplates the U.S. withdrawal from Vietnam, April 28, 1975. (DAVID HUME KENNERLY / CONTRIBUTOR VIA GETTY IMAGES)

The evacuation of Saigon, April 29, 1975 (BETTMANN / CONTRIBUTOR VIA GETTY IMAGES)

President Richard Nixon congratulates Henry Kissinger on becoming secretary of state, September 22, 1973. (BETTMANN / CONTRIBUTOR VIA GETTY IMAGES)

President Gerald Ford confers with his secretary of state, 1974.

(PHOTO 12 / ALAMY STOCK PHOTO)

With President Ronald
Reagan, 1983 (DAVID
HUME KENNERLY / CONTRIB-
UTOR VIA GETTY IMAGES)

With President Bill Clinton,
1995 (AP PHOTO / J. SCOTT
APPLEWHITE)

With President George W. Bush,
2008 (AP PHOTO / CHARLES DHARAPAK)

With President Barack Obama,
2015 (ZACH GIBSON / THE NEW
YORK TIMES / REDUX)

Many Henrys

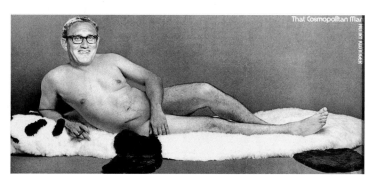

political power. The threat of force might be necessary in international relations, but its use signaled the failure of political power and its displacement by military power, which was a very different thing. In a telling statement, Morgenthau declared, "The actual exercise of physical violence substitutes for the psychological relation between two minds, which is the essence of political power, the physical relation between two bodies, one of which is strong enough to dominate the other's movements." Such domination, however, was a crude and temporary tool, unrelated to genuine political power, because "no dominion can last that is founded upon nothing but military force." Generals usually made lousy diplomats. "The armed forces are instruments of war; foreign policy is an instrument of peace."

Conquerors who thought only in material and military terms, like the Germans and Japanese of World War II, were bound to pass from the scene, no matter how much damage they might do, whereas those with a more nuanced and restrained notion of power, like the Romans and British, were able to construct successful, long-standing institutions. "Winning hearts and minds" might have become a phrase of derision in the years of the Vietnam war because of the blatant insincerity of America's military leaders, who were wont to employ the notion as propaganda only (in their own hearts and minds, they preferred body counts). But to Morgenthau, hearts and minds constituted the very essence of what he meant by political power. "All foreign policy," he declared, "is a struggle for the minds of men."

Many factors went into building political power among nations, from the most unchanging, like geography, to the most mutable and evanescent, like public opinion or morale. Population, raw materials, industrial capacity, technology, and leadership all contributed to power, but for Morgenthau no factor was more important than national character. The Germans were collectivist and authoritarian, the French rationalistic, and the English undogmatic and individualistic; the Americans were an uneasy combination of success-oriented pragmatism and "dogmatic idealism." All were products of the complicated intertwining of history, values, and circumstance. Morgenthau knew he was treading on controversial ground with these generalizations, making pronouncements that would be offensive to many Americans (which, of course, was part of their national character). Two decades later, in a survey of American foreign policy he wrote for the Council on Foreign Relations, he was even more succinct: "To put it bluntly: As there are bums and beggars, so are there bum and beggar nations."

Morgenthau's adopted countrymen preferred to believe the fiction that all people everywhere were basically the same and yearned for American-style freedom. Not only did this view encourage the counting-heads style of American social science; it also meant that Washington's policymakers were likely to make the same mistakes over and over again in the conduct of foreign policy.

Morgenthau's discussion of national character was hardly thorough. He wasn't interested in analyzing the historical, spiritual, and material forces that went into its formation—he would leave that to Max Weber and similar thinkers—but he did preach that understanding the differences among peoples, however contrary to liberal pieties, was crucial to wise statesmanship. "National character cannot fail to influence national power; for those who act for the nation in peace and war, formulate, execute and support its policies, elect and are elected, mold public opinion, produce and consume—all bear to a greater or lesser degree the imprint of those intellectual and moral qualities which make up the national character." Elusive and changeable over time it might be, but national character was a fact of life.

Morgenthau may have constructed his house on his understanding of power, but just how sturdy was the foundation? Wasn't his notion of human nature too one-sided and simplistic, perhaps too much the expression of a German Jew forced by the Nazis to give up everything, and a German Jew who was inclined toward pessimism in any case? The Holocaust was a trauma, an ineradicable scar across European history, but what lessons should be drawn from it? Was it a clue to true human nature as many German Jews tended to argue, or was it a horrifying aberration, as numerous congenitally optimistic Americans wanted to believe? Wasn't there a more positive side to humankind than the will to power, and wasn't that the more "normal" condition?

These were the toughest challenges to Morgenthau's arguments, going to the root of his thinking, and they were made no more authoritatively than by one of the most talented political journalists of the postwar era, George Lichtheim, who, as it happened, was also classically trained and extraordinarily erudite and also a Jewish refugee from Hitler's Germany. Lichtheim derived a very different lesson from history than Morgenthau. What it showed him was that, as the social animals Aristotle said they were, people everywhere were able to work together in "simple, ordinary common solidarity." (Lichtheim was influenced in his own thinking not only by Aristotle but also by Hegel and Marx; he anathematized Nietzsche and Heidegger.) The very idea of politics required consensus and cooperation, demonstrating that Morgenthau's notion of a fixed and aggressive human nature was nothing more than a "quasi-theological" prejudice. "There is something seriously deficient," Lichtheim wrote, "about a theory of politics which reduces 'the political act' to the exercise of one man's power over another." And in what he no doubt took to be the final word, the coup de grace, he put the matter directly: "To Mr. Morgenthau's rhetorical question, 'Why is it that all men lust for power?' the answer is: 'Some don't.' "

Game, set, match? Not at all. To begin with, for Morgenthau, there was power and there was power. It expressed itself in many ways. "The scholar seeking knowledge seeks power; so does the poet. . . . So do the mountain climber, the hunter, the collector of rare objects." All were forcing themselves intrusively into the world, often to the great benefit of humankind. Any kind of ambition revealed a yearning for power. "In the domestic societies of Western civilization, the possession of money has become the outstanding symbol of the possession of power. Through the competition for the acquisition of money, the power aspirations of the individual find a civilized outlet."

But the type of power that primarily concerned Morgenthau, and was also the object of Lichtheim's argument, was political power. Specifically, in Morgenthau's terms, political power was the assertion of will not over inanimate objects like books, words, mountains, objets d'art, or even money but over other human beings. Political power was a nuanced and complex interaction that took in every sort of social relationship, down to "the most subtle psychological ties by which one mind controls another." In civilized societies, this particular power drive was tamed by moral and institutional constraints, but on the world stage it was raw and "barbaric." Unfortunately, it was also ubiquitous.

Yes, as Lichtheim had observed, there were "some" who didn't strive for political power in international affairs, but they were doomed to be losers. In *Politics Among Nations* Morgenthau pointed to "certain primitive people" who exhibited no thirst for power. Their futures were not bright. "If the desire for power cannot be abolished everywhere in the world, those who might be cured would simply fall victims to the power of others." The fate of the conscientious objector was similar. In *Scientific Man Versus Power Politics*, Morgenthau wrote that "he may set an example for oth-

ers to emulate, but he does not do away with war nor does he even influence the incidence of war." Weakness might be considered a virtue but
it was still weakness. The pacifist's ostentatious moral virtue could even
be said to culminate in immorality if, like Morgenthau, you believed that
national survival was itself "a moral principle." A proto-Realist writing
about Gandhi's philosophy of nonviolence made a similar point: "If you
are not prepared to take life, you must often be prepared for lives to be lost
in some other way," George Orwell declared. "Applied to foreign politics,
pacifism either stops being pacifist or becomes appeasement."

HAVING ARTICULATED his premises to his own if not to everyone
else's satisfaction, Morgenthau proceeded to draw out the logical implications of his argument over several hundred pages. Political power was
the final determinant in international relations, but that was not the end
of the story. There did seem to be restraints on it. Three that merited Morgenthau's special attention were international law, world opinion, and
transcendent morality. All were presented as solutions to the problem
Morgenthau had set out, and all might have their place in encouraging
global stability. None, ultimately, could guarantee it.

Unlike many of his disciples, Morgenthau recognized the usefulness
of international law, "an imposing edifice," he said, "of thousands of treaties, hundreds of decisions of international tribunals and innumerable
decisions of domestic courts." Binding agreements governed territorial
jurisdiction, the law of the sea, the rights of diplomatic representatives,
and postal services, and they were overseen by a panoply of bodies, from
the International Red Cross and International Labor Organization to the
World Health Organization and the International Monetary Fund. What
distinguished these international laws from domestic laws, however, was
that enforcement was voluntary, dependent on the consent of the parties
to the agreements and not some sovereign authority beyond the individual
nation-states. Governments accepted international treaties and agreements
because it was in their interest to do so, and while a coalition of nations
might try to compel agreement from a recalcitrant country through sanctions, boycotts, and the like, where a question of national interest was at
stake no government was likely to yield short of war. As Morgenthau put it,
"International law is a law among coordinated, not subordinated, entities."

The United Nations (UN) presented a concrete manifestation of the problem. Ostensibly, it represented an effort to join nations into a rule-bound international community, but the Security Council, the enforcement arm of the UN, was scarcely able to reach agreement on issues of genuine consequence. The major powers retained their freedom of action through the veto, and even smaller powers ignored UN resolutions when they felt it necessary to do so. Morgenthau called the United Nations "a constitutional monstrosity" and "a building designed by two architects who have agreed upon the plans for the second floor but not upon those for the first." As long as sovereignty rested with individual nations and not some overarching governing body, "the threat of war, especially under the moral, political and technological conditions of our age, may be said to be unavoidable."

A second restraint on power, world opinion, did not have the force of law, but it was widely seen as a means of curbing national ambitions. The argument was hardly worth the back of Morgenthau's hand. On no issue had humankind been more united than its acknowledgment of the evil of warfare, he pointed out, yet such unanimity had scarcely prevented the loss of millions of lives in the twentieth century. People opposed war in the abstract but fervently supported it when their own country was involved. Except in the case of the ineffectual pacifists, the widespread condemnation of war was always to other people's wars. "In politics the nation and not humanity is the ultimate fact." World opinion was a fiction, Morgenthau said. "Modern history has not recorded an instance of a government having been deterred from foreign policy by the spontaneous reaction of a supranational public opinion."

If international law existed but could not prevent war and world opinion did not even exist, public morality could be said to have existed in the past and served to restrain the lust for power, but it had grown weaker over time to the point of ineffectuality. In the present age, it had become the flimsiest reed on which to conduct a foreign policy.

In the period from 1648 and the Treaty of Westphalia down to the 1930s, with one disruption during the Napoleonic era, Morgenthau discerned an international system in which moral imperatives carried genuine weight. Europe, he said, was "one great republic," with common standards of "politeness and cultivation." A "sense of honor" was not just a phrase or a deceitful pose but a quality that leaders took seriously and that imposed real limitations on their national freedom of action. Certain things were simply not done. But humankind had moved so far from this internalized moral code that many decisions made in the past had come to seem incomprehensible in the present. When it was suggested to the Austrian emperor in 1792 that he counterfeit currency in order to disrupt revolutionary France's economy, he replied, "Such an infamous project is not to be accepted." Even Bismarck, the master of Realpolitik, "rarely deviated from the rules of the game," Morgenthau said. International relations were an aristocratic pastime, the practice of a small elite community, and reputation among one's social peers mattered even more than national interest, keeping the desire for power in check.

Moral limitations that grew out of that aristocratic ethos remained recognizable in the present. Civilians are to be considered noncombatants in time of war. Prisoners of war have inviolable rights. Certain weapons, like poison gas, are outside the bounds of acceptable combat. Preventive war is to be condemned. Yet times have changed irreversibly. Hitler recognized no rules or restrictions and might nonetheless have been successful in his maniacal designs if not for self-inflicted wounds like his decision to start a two-front war by invading the Soviet Union. Even in the absence of Hitler, external developments were rendering the old restrictions obsolete. The technology of air warfare, for example, had destroyed the distinction between combatants and noncombatants. "Warsaw and Rotterdam, London and Coventry, Cologne and Nuremberg, Hiroshima and Nagasaki are stepping stones, not only in the development of the modern technology of war, but also in the development of the modern morality of warfare." The presence of nuclear weapons only raised the stakes.

Meanwhile, in the age of mass democracy, behavior based on an aristocratic code of personal honor was being replaced by loyalty to one's country and to narrow national interests. "The nation became the ultimate point of reference for the allegiance of the individual and the members of different nations all had their particular object of allegiance." The cosmopolitan moral structure prevailed down to the end of the nineteenth century, but at the present time, "only shreds and fragments survive of this system of supranational ethics," and even these are "threatened with extinction." Humanity was faced with the prospect of total war, unbounded by any common standard of morality, and with "a ferociousness and intensity not known to other ages." Because the lust for power has been a constant of human history in Morgenthau's view, and familiar restraints no longer served to restrain, he was pushed to the inevitable conclusion that the future could (would) witness "a global conflagration."

Was there any way out? One answer was to work for the establishment of a single global authority. Writing in the age of the Cold War, Morgenthau said: "The experience of two world wars within a quarter of a century and the prospects of a third to be fought with nuclear weapons have imparted to the idea of a world state an unprecedented urgency." As he watched nuclear arsenals grow in the 1960s and 1970s and the weapons themselves become ever more powerful and lethal, his sense of urgency only deepened. Soon he was arguing for "support of supranational institutions and procedures capable of performing the function that in view of modern technological developments the individual nation-states are no longer able to perform." The prospect of further nuclear proliferation left him appalled, aghast, and fearful.

Still, he had a problem. He saw no way of getting to there (a single global authority) from here (a multistate, multisovereign system). It couldn't be done through disarmament treaties, "the story of many failures and few successes." Believers in disarmament were guided by the mistaken philosophy that "men fight because they have arms," when the truth was that "they have arms because they deem it necessary to fight." The issue, as always for Morgenthau, was one of winning hearts and minds. At the present time, and for as far into the future as one could see, people gave their "highest secular loyalties" to their own countries, which constituted "an insurmountable obstacle" to world government. "Under the present moral conditions of mankind, few men would act on behalf of a world government if the interests of their own nation, as they understand them, required a different course of action." These "few men" talked only to themselves. It was simply impossible to imagine, Morgenthau said, the Americans, Russians, Chinese, and Indians all working together in some kind of parliamentary system to resolve their differences for the sake of a universal good. "There can be no world state without a world community willing to support it," and that world community did not exist.

To be sure, Morgenthau wasn't alive to witness the rise of radical Islam, when thousands and perhaps hundreds of thousands have transferred their allegiance from their nation to their faith and who hope for a world state in the form of a modern caliphate. The Islamists seem to make Morgenthau's repeated references to "nations" outmoded. But they hardly represent a refutation of what Morgenthau wrote more than half a century ago about human lust for power or the possibility of a global authority. Achieving a world state through conquest, as the jihad-minded Islamists desire, was, he said, a "false solution." It "would be a totalitarian monster resting on feet of clay, the very thought of which startles the imagination." Like all other types of militarists, the radical Islamists have no capacity for establishing long-lasting governing institutions. Outside of the Islamic world—and even within most of it—no one would be freely persuaded by the Islamists' utopian plans, and persuasion remained the sine qua non of world government.

Whatever practical steps politicians might take toward the goal of a world state, and those were bound to be uncertain at best, avoiding "global conflagration" in the here and now meant working within the system of sovereign nation-states. That left only one means of curbing humans' unalterable lust for power: namely, neutralizing it by setting off force against force through a balance of power.

Americans, Morgenthau said, tended to avoid thinking in terms of a balance of power because that meant accepting, even cooperating, with "evil," but they should be familiar with the concept because their own domestic institutions were constructed on the basis of checks and balances. The writers of *The Federalist Papers* had praised the notion of pitting interest against interest. In fact, the ideal of balance of power was "as old as political history itself." In an anarchic world, it was "necessary," an "essential stabilizing factor." To Morgenthau, it was an "inevitable" arrangement, a "universal principle." Over centuries of European history, statesmen pursued a balance of power through constantly shifting alliances. From an abstract ethical perspective (or from across the Atlantic Ocean), the process may have seemed immoral or hypocritical, but it prevented any one nation from gaining dominion over all the others, which was its purpose. It worked. In the nineteenth century, the concept extended from Europe to the world as a whole, and after World War II it changed from being a multilateral system to a bipolar game between two superpowers. Morgenthau was prescient enough to see that the Cold War bipolar balance of power might change once again as China emerged on the international stage, but the principle itself never changed, and short of a global government or world conqueror, it was the only hope of promoting a semblance of stability and a condition of peace.

There was no question that a balance of power arrangement had weaknesses, dangerous ones. Morgenthau pointed out that the price of the balance of power in Europe was almost continuous warfare, including the horrendous world wars of the twentieth century when the system broke down. The driving force of any balance of power arrangement was "constant fear," as each government tried to gauge the strength of its adversaries and the possibility of alliances with unreliable friends. Calculations were little more than a "series of guesses," and the uncertainty that was an inevitable element of the balance of power encouraged nations to try to maximize their own strength, even through preventive war. Confrontations testing relative strength were unavoidable and had to be considered the price of living among national adversaries. The inherently unstable balance of power was not a perfect arrangement by any means, and the security it provided was always precarious—something the utopian moralists never tired of pointing out. Its shortcomings were real even in those years when aristocratic statesmen shared a common moral code. But what was the alternative? According to Morgenthau, there was none. As he was later to write, the balance of power "is the very law of life."

Any balance of power system did not arise by itself or continue automatically. It required human agency to construct the right arrangement and adapt it to changing circumstances. Fallible human beings had to labor constantly to keep the system from breaking down, which they had failed to do before World War I. The people who traditionally performed this function were diplomats, and diplomacy, Morgenthau said, "is the brains of national power."

Diplomats were the antithesis of the absolutists and true believers, the moral ideologues. The balance of power could only work through accommodation, and the job of diplomats was to reach that accommodation through persuasion and compromise and also, if necessary, through the threat of force. They had to assess the power and objectives of their own country as well as those of other nations and determine the best means of obtaining their goals. They had to be able to distinguish the essential from the merely desirable and to see the world from the point of view of other governments. They required minds that were both "complicated and subtle." They needed to be true realists, "sensitive, flexible and versatile."

Diplomacy, Morgenthau wrote, "is the best means of preserving peace which a society of sovereign nations has to offer." What was more, its compromises and accommodations were the necessary building blocks to the kind of integrated world community that the nuclear age so desperately demanded. And yet in the twentieth century the role of diplomacy, as essential as it was, had been depreciated and derided. Several factors account for its diminishment, but as Morgenthau saw it, a single powerful

enemy had arisen to contest all of the assumptions and practices of traditional diplomacy, an enemy that went by the name of democracy. In short,
modern democracy was the opponent of peace.

Where diplomacy requires compromise and accommodation, Morgenthau said, democratic public opinion calls for absolutism and a crusading
spirit. Where statesmen must be flexible in pursuit of the long view, the
masses demand firmness and immediate results. Little wonder that "the
diplomat's reputation for deviousness and dishonesty is as old as diplomacy itself." The virtues of one are considered vices by the other, because
diplomats must be "horsetraders," not heroes. Their undertakings dissolve when subjected to the light of mass opinion, and Woodrow Wilson's
"open covenants . . . openly arrived at" were a prescription for confrontation and war. "Where foreign policy is conducted under the conditions
of democratic control," Morgenthau wrote, "the need to marshal popular
emotions to the support of foreign policy cannot fail to impair the rationality of foreign policy itself."

One of Morgenthau's favorite observations on the subject came from
Tocqueville. "Foreign politics demand scarcely any of those qualities
which are peculiar to a democracy; they require, on the contrary, the perfect use of almost all those in which it is deficient. . . . A democracy can
only with great difficulty regulate the details of an important undertaking, persevere in a fixed design and work out its execution in spite of serious obstacles. It cannot combine its measures with secrecy or await their
consequences with patience."

In one of his more subtle analyses, Morgenthau explained that the wish
for a universal ethic to guide behavior has remained constant even as traditional ethical systems have lost their authority. As a result, the masses,
sensing the loss of spirituality in the modern age, have translated their particular national values into moral absolutes and seek to impose them onto
other people. He called the tendency "nationalistic universalism," and he
observed that the more insecure citizens feel at home, the more "vicarious
satisfaction" they take from projecting power abroad. This thought caused
Morgenthau to wax Nietzschean: "Carrying their idols before them, the
nationalistic masses of our time meet in the international arena, each
group convinced that it executes the mandates of history, that it does for
humanity what it seems to do for itself, and that it fulfills a sacred mission
ordained by Providence, however defined. Little do they know that they
meet under an empty sky from which the gods have departed."

Leo Strauss and Hannah Arendt have been called antidemocratic though they were really nondemocratic, accepting the workings of democracy in some ways, rejecting them in others. The real antidemocrat among them was Hans Morgenthau. Not that he was calling for tearing up the Constitution and for storm troopers at the door. As much as anyone, he recognized that where a domestic consensus existed, democracy was the best means of assuring peaceful change and free expression. But in his chosen field of international relations, and in a democratic era in which legitimacy derived from "the people," democracy could only be an impediment to intelligent policy, though one that was "unavoidable."

Thinkers like Plato and Tocqueville were suspicious of democracy because of their fears of tyranny, but Morgenthau raised an additional criticism: democracy could be the enemy of world peace. The wise statesman in the modern age, according to Morgenthau, had to walk a fine line, resisting the temptation to sacrifice sound policy on "the altar of public opinion," while at the same time doing what he could to prevent the gap that existed between "good foreign policy" and unstable public opinion from widening into a chasm of destructive hostility. In open societies, statesmen were handicapped, limping along with one leg shackled to a ball and chain. A genuinely rational foreign policy was an impossibility in a democracy, an ideal that could only be approximated but never fully realized or implemented; any diplomat serving an open society had to bend to the public will, no matter how irrational or shortsighted he considered it to be. Or as Henry Kissinger might say: Welcome to my world.

With these thoughts about democracy, Morgenthau seemed to have painted himself into a corner. Even if the excesses of democracy had to be restrained, there was no authority on the international stage to restrain them. And how could the democratic United States ever hope to conduct a successful foreign policy? These were troubling questions, and so Morgenthau could not rest with the conclusions of *Politics Among Nations*. The book could not be his last word about the United States and its system of government. He had to push on.

THOUGH HERALDED AS a public lecturer and teacher for the rest of his career, Morgenthau refused to accept payment for his appearances at America's military academies. It was one way he could show his appreciation of his adopted land. "I have tried to pay back a small fraction of the debt of gratitude I owe to this country," he said. But his arguments in *Politics Among Nations* left him with a seemingly irresolvable intellectual and emotional problem. Like Leo Strauss, Hannah Arendt, and Henry Kissinger, he admired America but not for the reason so many of his patriotic fellow citizens did—not for the nation's freewheeling, undisciplined, popular democracy. Whenever he could, he reminded his American audiences that Hitler had been popular, too. As a foreign policy intellectual, Morgenthau was no democrat. Public opinion was an obstacle to rationality. What was it, then, that the United States offered to him and other outsiders like him apart from simple survival? How could he remain positive about the United States? The answer required an entire book, *The Purpose of American Politics*, which was constructed out of lectures he delivered at Johns Hopkins University in 1959 and published a year later.

At the time of its appearance, *The Purpose of American Politics* "made hardly a stir," and it remains probably Morgenthau's most neglected work today. In part, this was because it seemed to contradict *Politics Among Nations*, the book that had made Morgenthau's reputation. If you subscribed to Morgenthau's Realpolitik teaching that international affairs were a three-dimensional chess game with every government coldly pursuing the same goal of national survival and with no larger aim in mind, you were not likely to turn to a work that tried to understand what it was that made the United States special. And if you weren't persuaded by *Politics Among Nations*, you weren't going to read *The Purpose of American Politics* in any case, as its questions were not your questions. It did not help, too, that the book's argument was anything but linear, proceeding in fits and starts and taking too much pleasure in its own complexity.

It was Morgenthau's most personal book, not in the sense that it was autobiographically revealing but because it was trying to wrestle with the deep ambivalence Morgenthau, like other German-Jewish intellectuals, felt about the United States. As one scholar put it, "In many surprising ways, *The Purpose of American Politics* anticipated Hannah Arendt's *On Revolution*," which appeared three years later. Not surprising at all. Each book was "an act of gratitude." Yet each was also an attempt by its author to work through very complicated and not always positive emotions about American democracy.

When Morgenthau surveyed the contemporary United States in *The Purpose of American Politics*, what he saw wasn't pretty. Americans were materialistic, hedonistic, and apathetic, their only aim in life apparently to consume more and more in a complacent haze of unconstrained appetite. The economy was wasteful, the government paralyzed. The public sphere had virtually disappeared as individuals struggled to grab what they could for themselves and the hell with anyone else or any larger purpose. Public policy was determined by moneyed pressure groups with no concerns beyond their own parochial interests, and morality consisted of what you could get away with. Americans no longer made any distinction between freedom and license, and the consequences for the country were bound to be dire. "No society," Morgenthau warned, "can go on like this forever without decay following stagnation; the fate of Spain tells us what is in store for such a nation."

The culprit, in Morgenthau's analysis, was democracy itself, or rather what most Americans had come to understand by democracy. Authority for them was simple rule of the majority. What the people wanted, they should get, and governance was turning into decision making by opinion poll. There was an emptiness at the core. Morgenthau made a crucial distinction: public opinion, always shifting, frequently ignorant, and predisposed to emotional appeal rather than disinterested, rational consideration, was a source of legitimacy in the modern age—there was no other. But it could not be an arbiter of policy. The majority could restrain rulers but it could not rule, which left the door open for powerful private interest groups to impose their will in what Morgenthau called a "new feudalism." Worse, when the will of the majority was not restrained, when it gathered enough strength within itself to attempt to rule against the established interests, "the government, and with it the nation, continuously runs the risk that the place of leadership vacated by the government will be occupied by someone else, more likely than not a demagogue or a demagogic elite catering to popular emotions and prejudices."

The United States had so far been spared from such dangerous majoritarianism by its constitutional separation of powers, but the prospects were not good, as rule by majority seemed to be the only governing principle available. (And Morgenthau couldn't have been comforted when he considered the thought that the separation of powers didn't really operate in the realm of foreign affairs, where a demagogic president armed with nuclear weapons was free to do almost anything.) "Genuine democracy," he said, safeguarded the individual, "his integrity, happiness and self-development." What Americans had at the present time was a "perversion of the democratic process."

In all this, Morgenthau, like Hannah Arendt and Leo Strauss, spoke of a drastic decline from the nation established by the Founding Fathers. And like them, he can be accused of seeing an ideal America he wanted to see rather than the one that actually existed. He applauded what he understood as the idea of America. Contemporary reality deserved no applause. In any case, he found the solution to the country's current problems in a restoration of what he took to be its extraordinary founding principles. Like Arendt, he was a believer in American exceptionalism, although this was an odd position for the father of Realism to espouse.

The United States was "a distinct moral, social and political entity," Morgenthau declared in the introduction of *The Purpose of American Politics*. All other countries defined themselves by their "ethnic affinities and historic traditions," but the United States defined itself by an idea, with "a particular purpose in mind." That idea, that purpose, was what Morgenthau called "equality in freedom." Admittedly, this was a vague concept, even contradictory, or in Morgenthau's words "intangible, shapeless and procedural," as the principles of equality and freedom often came into conflict with each other. Pursued for its own sake, freedom became libertarianism, which necessarily undermined equality because, as Morgenthau said, there was a "natural inequality of man." And equality by itself led to a repressive "equalitarianism," or the denial of individual freedom. The two principles had to be forcibly yoked together to avoid extremes and the destruction of the American purpose. This required an "act of will." Nothing good came automatically.

The ideal of equality in freedom could never be static, frozen in time, because in truth it could never be realized; each generation had to define the concept anew. And so the American Revolution was "an endless process rather than an isolated act," and the ongoing effort to achieve the ideal constituted "a restless and dynamic search for a state of society that could at best be approximated, never fully attained." It was a Sisyphean task, but no less real or desirable for that.

But then why bother? Why continue pushing that rock up the hill if you were never going to reach the top? Throughout its history, the country has had its doubters and naysayers, particularly among pessimistic and sophisticated intellectuals and writers like Hawthorne, Poe, Melville, James, Adams, and Mencken. Repelled by the country's ambient, oppressive vulgarity, they "refused to identify themselves with America as they found it." Morgenthau, who yielded to no one in either pessimism or sophistication, was not unsympathetic to them. They were, in one sense, the best of the best. "They uncovered in America the human condition, drastically at variance with the American dream." He could admire their rejection of America's often fatuous optimism and philistine materialism, could share their "tragic sense of life." But he perceived an aura of irresponsible aestheticism in their anti-American stance. He could not go along with the rejection of the American ideal. Without it, he said, the country would lose its internal coherence and fall apart, and he was too appreciative of what his adopted land had given him to accept that.

His concept of the American purpose drove him to make one of the most personal declarations in the book. It was as personal as Morgenthau ever got. "The man who chooses the United States as his nation," he said in an obvious comment on himself, "concludes, as it were, a silent compact with himself, his fellow citizens and his government to cooperate in the achievement" of the American purpose. "This man will reconcile himself to the achievement falling short of the ideal, he will forgive sporadic violations of that purpose. What he cannot reconcile himself to and cannot forgive is the denial of the purpose itself in theory or practice. Such a denial denies his obligation to remain loyal to a government and a society that are no longer loyal to the common purpose. Thus, it is in the nature of things that the denial of the American purpose will alienate the people from America itself."

The national purpose of equality in freedom was the necessary glue that prevented social disintegration, and the survival of the United States as a meaningful entity depended on it. Americans had no choice: they had to keep pushing that rock up the hill, with no hope of ultimate success. Normally gloomy, stoical at best, Morgenthau counseled a kind of positive pessimism. Rather like Camus, he was able to picture Sisyphus happy. (And lest modern readers find this perspective too complex or tension-ridden to fathom, even too "un-American" in its denial of any kind of hopeful outlook to place one's faith in, it is worth pointing out that only a few years after the appearance of *The Purpose of American Politics*, another voice emerged to give expression to an optimism that also reposed on a bed of despair: Was Morgenthau saying anything other than that the times were changing even if a hard rain was bound to fall?)

Domestic survival was reason enough for Americans to engage in their Sisyphean task, but it was not the only one. The nebulous and contradictory purpose of equality in freedom had a crucial significance outside the United States. Building beyond what he had written in *Politics Among Nations*, Morgenthau now made a key distinction among political bodies. Looking over the entirety of human history, he said that "to be worthy of our lasting sympathy, a nation must pursue its interests for the sake of a transcendent purpose that gives meaning to the day-by-day operations of its foreign policy." Phrases like "lasting sympathy" and "transcendent purpose" were alien to the vocabulary of *Politics Among Nations*, but now Morgenthau was arguing that the Mongols and Huns, for all their undeniable success in their own time, had left nothing but Ozymandius-like ruins for future generations to contemplate, whereas ancient Greece, Rome, and Israel had bequeathed to humankind permanent legacies because they had moved across history's stage with transcendent goals.

Which would Americans be—Huns or Romans? Actually, once again, Morgenthau insisted that they had no choice. Just as the national purpose of equality in freedom was essential to domestic survival, so too it was necessary to America's survival in the larger world, and there could be no retreating from it. Like it or not, the United States "has become the Rome and Athens of the Western world, the foundation of its lawful order and the fountainhead of its culture." And not only for the West. America "addresses itself to all the nations of the world." Its ideal of equality in freedom had taken on global relevance for "if we fail, the nations of the world will look elsewhere for models of social organization and political institutions to emulate, and we will be alone in a hostile world." Uniquely, America's national interest (in the language of *Politics Among Nations*) was conjoined with transcendent goals (the language of *The Purpose of American Politics*). Survival both at home and abroad required the continuing (if ultimately futile) pursuit of the national purpose.

And yet the United States that Morgenthau had chosen to become a part of faced a crisis, unprecedented in its history. "We are no longer as sure as we used to be of what America stands for." The country had lost its way. The bulk of *The Purpose of American Politics* was taken up with analyzing that crisis as it had developed both domestically and internationally and suggesting the beginnings of solutions—or at least pointing in the direction in which solutions would necessarily be found.

THE COUNTRY HAD lost its way because in the past Americans had been able to pursue their ideal of equality in freedom under conditions that no longer existed and would never exist again. Morgenthau subscribed to the "safety valve" theory of the American past: the inevitable discontents that emerged in any society had been siphoned off in the United States by the call of the frontier. Those unable to make a go of it at home were free to move west and try again, which is what millions of Americans had done for three centuries. On the frontier they were both free and equal. There is an anachronistic ring to Morgenthau's comment that "the experience of endless opportunity was predicated upon the availability of limitless empty land." We are more aware today than he was that the opportunities of the pioneers required them to step over the bodies of countless dead Native Americans to claim that "empty land." But even if Morgenthau had demonstrated a more modern sensibility and absorbed the Indians into his account, as a Realist he no doubt would have argued that the frontier's blood-stained, even genocidal past was not about to be reversed (and might even be considered inevitable, one of history's many tragedies). This was a view likely to rattle modern humanitarians and universalists, but from Morgenthau's perspective there could be no retreating from the argument that the frontier was a major component in preserving the ideal of equality in freedom, at least for white Americans. And what about blacks? Morgenthau joined with Arendt in calling slavery "a tragic denial of the American purpose," though again, as with her, the ugly history of race relations in the United States was not central to the concepts he was analyzing. Racism demanded no intellectual effort from him. In the realm of ideas, it was not worth taking seriously; it was all too easy to refute. From his point of view, race relations were a practical matter, a question of policy, not an abstract one requiring theoretical meditation.

The special condition of the American frontier preserved the ideal of equality in freedom at home. The special condition of two huge oceans and two weak neighbors did the same internationally, and from the time of its founding down to the beginning of the twentieth century, the United States, with the exception of a few disgruntled intellectuals, had no reason to question its ideal. The nation was a petri dish, self-contained, removed from the problems that had bedeviled every other society on earth. Europe's past was a picture of unfathomable tragedy with nothing to teach Americans about human nature since the United States had wiped out history and created a new Adam. Even the murderous Civil War was a conflict over the meaning of the American ideal—did it include blacks as well as whites?—and not a challenge to it.

Then history caught up with America. As the United States grew into a modern, industrialized, urban society, all of the Old World ills emerged in the New World—and none was more significant than the problem of social stratification. The accumulation of vast fortunes and the power that went with them mocked the very notion of equality. "The man in the street could not compete on equal terms," and because modern society penetrated into every corner of the country, eliminating the freedom and equality that could once be found on the frontier, this man had, "as it were, no place to go." Equality in freedom had been an apolitical ideal to be realized apart from government and even, if necessary, apart from social contact. Morgenthau referred to Americans as "fugitives from politics." Now, for the first time, they were confronted by the inescapability of power, power in the form of great wealth. Yet the general suspicion of government left them ill-equipped to address this new affront to their ideal and to their national purpose. "The spontaneous emergence of concentrations of private power," Morgenthau said, "found the United States intellectually and politically unprepared. It brought the nation face to face with a dilemma which is inherent in all political situations and indeed in the human experience." The problem of power and how to use it could no longer be fled from or ignored. Neither could human history.

Social stratification necessitated a more public response than Americans were traditionally comfortable with, and similarly, the end of geographical isolation brought the United States into a confrontation with the rest of the world that rendered the traditional conduct of foreign policy obsolete. By the time of World War I, "the crisis of the American purpose abroad was at hand," and as at home the country had to struggle to find a conception of power appropriate to its new role in the world. The earliest response, imperialism, the conquest of subject peoples like the Filipinos, was no more than a passing phase, wholly at odds with the ideal of equality in freedom and, therefore, "an unavoidable embarrassment rather than the achievement of a national purpose." Two other responses, more deeply rooted in the American ethos, had a more lasting impact.

It was Woodrow Wilson who came up with the first of these. Instead of subjugation and annexation, so contrary to the American ideal, he urged intervention on behalf of freedom and democracy. World War I and the League of Nations were his instruments for carrying out this purpose, which in his mind amounted to nothing less than an end to power politics and the recasting of the world in the American image of antipolitical liberalism. But he learned to his sorrow that the world was not ready for his moral crusade. Wilsonianism collapsed almost as soon as it had begun. Wilson had "lifted the American purpose up to the skies," but "he could not divorce it from the experience of the world." Most countries, Morgenthau said, "are manifestly unsuited for a democratic system after the American model."

Yet instead of dying, Wilsonianism repeatedly reemerged throughout the twentieth century because it spoke to a fundamental part of the American consciousness. It answered the question of the nation's place in the world with the claim that the United States was obliged to project its values across the globe. Morgenthau was writing before the misguided efforts of the Vietnam war and the second intervention in Iraq, but in making his argument that Wilsonianism was an enduring component of the American mind, it was sufficient for him to point out the continuity of Wilson's utopian aspirations in the words of Franklin D. Roosevelt shortly before his death in 1945. Channeling Wilson, Roosevelt told Congress that the Yalta Conference "spells the end of the system of unilateral action and exclusive alliances and spheres of influence and balances of power." Roosevelt, too, hoped for a liberal end to history. And the Soviet Union demonstrated that he was as mistaken as his predecessor had been.

The other response, a reaction to Wilson's moralistic overreaching, was isolationism. If the United States could not change the world, it would withdraw from it. Isolationism was the dominant mood in the country in the 1920s and 1930s, and it assumed a virulent form in the 1950s under the name of McCarthyism, when it became not enough to raise the drawbridges to avoid foreign contamination; the United States also had to search out heretics within its midst to preserve its virtue. To vast numbers of Americans, McCarthy's purgative isolationism spoke to their fears about a nation they saw as endangered by enemies within and without. In 1954, Morgenthau noted, 50 percent of the public approved of the senator and only 29 percent disapproved, while 21 percent had no opinion. As was his habit, Morgenthau drew on a familiar analogy: "In truth, the American people were no more victimized by McCarthy than were the German people by Hitler; both followed their tempters with abandon."

Isolationism, Morgenthau said, was not a temporary aberration even in its virulent McCarthyite form. Like Wilsonianism, it was a serious expression of the American ideal, in this case the hope to return to the image of the United States as a city on the hill, a model for other nations to follow if they chose, but not a political cause to be aggressively projected in the international arena. "Isolationists appeared to themselves as the champions of the purpose of America against its American despoilers," and they have never ceased wielding influence over foreign policy with their own utopian ideal. But like Wilsonianism, isolationism collapsed whenever it had to deal with dangers in the real world—before World War II from fascist aggression, after World War II from Soviet imperialism. Neither Wilsonian crusades nor isolationist retreats offered solutions for America's new place in the world. Then what was left for American policymakers to draw on?

FOR ONE BRIEF PERIOD it seemed that the United States had found an answer. Over 15 weeks in 1947, Washington proclaimed the containment policy to restrain the Soviet Union, the Truman Doctrine to assist threatened nations, and the Marshall Plan to strengthen and firm up allies. The normally imperturbable Morgenthau described these programs with an excitement he rarely allowed himself to display. This was "a radical break," a "great reversal," a "great creative effort." For the first time in its history, the United States recognized that it had interests that extended beyond the Western Hemisphere, and it had reacted not with preconceived notions of American virtue but realistically with a calculated and shrewd understanding of the new situation. Specific solutions addressed specific problems, employing American power while understanding the limits of that power, and with no expectation of achieving a permanent peace. The new policy had not only a military component but also economic, political, and diplomatic ones as well. It was multilayered and pragmatic, adapted for the world as it existed. "A whole new system of American foreign policy was devised, derived from a radically new conception of the American purpose abroad."

Yet it was a "radically new conception" with a radically short shelf life because it was so at odds with traditional ways of thinking. Morgenthau dates its demise to the early 1950s and the confusions that enveloped Washington as it faced the crises of Asia. China and Korea "tested the ability of the United States to meet with purposeful action a foreign threat that was not of a clear-cut military nature. The United States did not pass those tests." The Korean War had begun as a clear-cut military conflict, but once Washington's aim shifted from defending South Korea from Communist aggression to attempting to "liberate" the north and

reunite the entire peninsula under an American aegis, the United States
had moved from a military goal to a political one, one that was beyond
its capabilities, even its understanding. Relatedly, it failed to comprehend
the Chinese revolution as a broad-based political movement with wide
support. "A far-sighted government would have made its peace with the
inevitable, however distasteful," Morgenthau said, but American policymakers had trouble grasping a popular uprising that wasn't democratic
and insisted instead on seeing only a narrow conspiracy of evil-minded
totalitarians, who could be fought with a military intervention that would
enable "the people" to win back their "freedom."

That is to say, what were essentially political issues requiring "subtlety and complexity" as well as patience were met with ham-fisted military actions that were inappropriate to the situation. What was more,
America's one-sided military perspective revealed a delusionary sense of
omnipotence: with its overwhelming military might, the United States
could accomplish anything it set out to do. Gone was the multilayered,
pragmatic approach of 1947. Diplomacy was disdained, history ignored.
Troops and bombs were enough to do the job. In its utopian aspirations to
remake the rest of the world, this was Wilsonianism all over again. But it
was also isolationism in its go-it-alone armed bravado. (Elsewhere, Morgenthau was to write, "Isolationism is a kind of introverted globalism, and
globalism is a kind of isolationism turned inside out.") George Kennan,
the father of the containment policy, shared Morgenthau's resistance to
this "myth of omnipotence" and the overmilitarization of American foreign policy, lamenting his country's "blind militaristic hysteria." Washington had abandoned subtlety and nuance for guns and bombs, but when
sheer force of arms did not work, as it did not in Asia, it had no answer,
no plan B, and it fell back into bewilderment. This was coupled with a
self-deception that echoed the "stab-in-the-back" complaints heard in
Germany after World War I. Traitors and a weakness of will by cowardly
government officials were to blame for the loss of American lives and prestige, not the fundamental misconceptions of what the United States could
actually accomplish in the world. Hard-line militarists faced off against
ineffectual internationalists. The American foreign policy that Morgenthau saw in 1960 had lost its sense of purpose, become "aimless and inconsistent," and faced a "crisis of perplexity."

And so Morgenthau was led to write *The Purpose of American Politics*
not only to resolve his own intellectual quandaries but also to explain how

the country could recover its laudable aspiration of equality in freedom. Besides being an act of gratitude, his book was a sermon, a call to action.

Restoration had to begin at home, he said, where the American ideal had to be updated for an urban, industrial society. The safety valve of the frontier no longer sufficed. The problem of social stratification, "the unchecked social and political power of wealth," had to be addressed in an active manner. "Millions of Americans are deprived of the middle-class security and comforts that have become the mode of life in America." Rethinking was necessary in just about every facet of national life—production, distribution, education, housing, transportation, "the very nature of public purposes and standards of thought." And no domestic issue was more urgent than securing equality for racial minorities.

Morgenthau was being radical without being specific, but for his purposes he didn't have to be. His aim was to awaken Americans from their complacency through a positive resolve, a commitment of will, to equality in freedom. Precisely how the ideal would be pursued domestically was something he was happy to leave to the policy wonks with their charts and statistics to work out. Inevitably, there would be disagreements about the best way to proceed. What mattered to him was that the policymakers were moving in the right direction, which was to "compel the public power to extend its protective hand more deeply than ever before." Of that, there could be no dispute in Morgenthau's mind. Retreating to a libertarian frontier mentality was out of the question. Political power had become a fact of life, as it had long been for Europeans, and for all of the problems it presented, all of the dangers threatened by a stronger central government, Americans were just going to have to learn to deal with them. "From this dilemma, there is no escape." There was no choice. "The survival of America and of the civilized world depends upon it."

In foreign affairs, too, Morgenthau urged a reassertion of national will, not through Wilsonian crusades for democracy abroad but in the spirit of the formulators of the containment policy. Specific problems of international relations required specific answers, not ideology or rhetoric, not a knee-jerk reliance on military arms or a hubristic conviction that the United States could achieve whatever it wanted so long as it had the determination. And for Morgenthau, the specific problem that took precedence over all others was nuclear proliferation. Left unimpeded, more and more nations would acquire nuclear weapons until a disaster eventually became unavoidable. Morgenthau saw no way of averting catastrophe under the present system of nation-states, and at his most idealistic, he called for a supranational system that would bring these weapons under international control. Morgenthau was not so idealistic, however, as to believe such a system could be created overnight. "There is no need to stress the magnitude of this task in view of the obstacles that technology and politics, domestic and international, put into the way of its accomplishment." But great challenges produced great civilizations. Taking the lead on the issue of curbing nuclear proliferation would give the United States the opportunity to reaffirm its national purpose on the global stage. "It will be as it was at the beginning: what America does for itself it also does for mankind, and political experimentation on a worldwide scale in order to save mankind will be in a direct line of succession to the political experiment as which at its inception America offered itself to the world."

There is much in *The Purpose of American Politics* that is outdated or anachronistic: Morgenthau's neglect of American Indians, for example, and also his belief that the primary social problem the country faced was too much leisure time brought about by too much abundance. We are still a long way from that. His distress about American conformity sounds very 1950s and, of course, the spread of Communism is not something we lose sleep over anymore—schoolchildren are no longer taught to hide under their desks in case of nuclear attack. (On the other hand, global warming is now something that keeps us up at night.) Nonetheless, in his focus on social stratification and nuclear proliferation Morgenthau could sound remarkably contemporary. Unlike Communism, these problems haven't gone away.

It was reasonable to assume that in the writings that followed *The Purpose of American Politics,* Morgenthau would direct much of his analytical powers to these two concerns. And in fact over the next few years, he turned increasingly to questions of domestic affairs, urging the government to support egalitarian "positions which conform most closely to the best traditions of America." In foreign affairs, he repeatedly warned that the "overriding issue" was nuclear war. Nuclear power had forever transformed the nature of foreign policy. It was "the only real revolution which has occurred in the structure of international relations since the beginning of history, because it has radically changed the relationship between violence as a means of foreign policy and the ends of foreign policy." The theorist who grasped this new reality was obliged to "prepare the ground for a new international order."

The issues of America's future seemed evident in 1960, and Morgenthau's task in the coming years seemed set out for him with a rare clarity. He even found cause for optimism, because, as he declared in *The Purpose of American Politics*, the impulse of his fellow citizens "to renew the national purpose is strong." If ever he had reason to hope for rational American policies both at home and abroad, it was at that historical moment between Dwight Eisenhower and John Kennedy, when his job appeared to be the very patriotic one of bringing Americans to a revived understanding of their national purpose, to a recasting of the nation into the image of the country he had come to love. A collection of his essays published in 1962 was even entitled *The Restoration of American Politics*. Change for the better was very much on his mind.

Then came Vietnam.

CHAPTER FIVE

VIETNAM

I N THE EARLY 1950S, HANS MORGENTHAU TOOK TIME OFF
from his duties at the University of Chicago to accept an appointment
as a visiting professor at Harvard, where he taught a graduate seminar on
international relations. Among his students were such future giants in the
field as Zbigniew Brzezinski, Samuel Huntington, and Stanley Hoffmann.
But the student who stood out above them all was Henry Kissinger, already
something of a legend on campus for his dense, gargantuan undergraduate thesis on Spengler, Kant, and Toynbee. It was said that his dissertation adviser, the formidable William Yandell Elliott, had read less than
a third of it before awarding Kissinger a summa cum laude (whether out
of admiration or frustration was not said). Morgenthau was told to make
the acquaintance of the promising young man, 19 years his junior, and he
came away from the encounter impressed enough to consider Kissinger
for a position at Chicago. But Kissinger stayed at Harvard to work on his
doctoral dissertation and so Morgenthau became Kissinger's "informal
mentor" from a distance.

The dissertation was completed in 1954 and published three years
later as *A World Restored: Metternich, Castlereagh and the Problems of
Peace, 1812–22*. It was audacious in many respects, but perhaps no more
so than in its effort to understand the present by examining the past.
Most of Kissinger's contemporaries in the political science department
were employing contemporary methodology to analyze modern issues,
in particular the impact of nuclear weapons on foreign policy (a subject
that Kissinger would later make his own), and some even suggested that

the unconventional Kissinger might think about transferring to the history department. But like Morgenthau and unlike so many political scientists of the time, Kissinger believed the study of history was essential for an understanding of international relations. The past was never past. History taught complexity and contingency, the way political and military leaders went about selecting among indeterminate options in the particular circumstances they faced and the mistakes they often committed as individuals making individual choices. There was no escaping uncertainty; tragedy was an ever-constant presence in human affairs. One obtained from the past not abstract formulas to be applied mechanically to modern-day problems but a flexible awareness of the human condition that could enrich the decision-making process. "History teaches by analogy, not identity," Kissinger wrote. "This means that the lessons of history are never automatic." Needless to say, Kissinger was no more enamored of quantitative thinking than Morgenthau.

In the case of *A World Restored*, Kissinger saw parallels between the Congress of Vienna, which concluded the Napoleonic wars, and the Paris Conference of 1919 that followed World War I—the first a measured response that resisted calls for vengeance and led to a century of relative calm, the second a self-righteous attempt to impose a punitive settlement that produced a "victors' peace" and resulted in disaster. Other diplomatic parallels Kissinger perceived related more directly to his immediate present. He was writing about Europe in the early nineteenth century, but at times he might just as well have been describing the recent alliance with the Soviet Union during World War II and its inevitable collapse into the Cold War: "Since the appearance of harmony is one of its most effective weapons, a coalition can never admit that one of its members may represent a threat almost as great as the common enemy and perhaps an increasingly greater one as victories alter the relative position of the powers. Coalitions between status quo and acquisitive powers are always a difficult matter, therefore, and tend to be based either on a misunderstanding or an evasion." Such observations could have come directly out of the Morgenthau playbook.

Indeed, Morgenthau's fingerprints were all over Kissinger's first book. At the very start, Kissinger warned against policies based on good intentions and urged the pursuit of equilibrium through a carefully constructed balance of power that might be ethically unsatisfactory but met the requirements of global stability. "Moral claims involve a quest for absolutes, a denial of nuance, a rejection of history." And like Morgenthau, Kissinger drew a distinction between force and legitimacy. Military methods were necessary in the heat of conflict, but short of extermination, they could never produce peace: "Force might conquer the world but it could never legitimize itself," especially in the mind of a defeated and resentful enemy that might surrender its immediate claims but could not abandon what it considered its long-term interests. Legitimacy was not something that could be imposed; it was a function of national character, that which is "taken for granted." States were more than mere collections of individuals. Again, history mattered.

It followed that the construction of peace could not be left to the generals. It was the work of diplomats, who practiced "the art of relating states to each other by agreement rather than by the exercise of force." While advancing his own country's interests, the statesman also had to demonstrate an understanding of his antagonists' concerns, taking them into account. This way of thinking was viewed as traitorous by moral and nationalistic absolutists, but as Morgenthau said, "It is the task of statesmanship to settle disputes in such a way as to minimize the damage to the prestige of the parties involved," all the parties. And writing at the height of Cold War tensions, he added, "Of such statesmanship there is not a trace to be found on either side." For both Morgenthau and Kissinger, the diplomat was the hero of international relations, often unsung and unappreciated, frequently reviled by his own countrymen. In *A World Restored*, the embodiment of the successful diplomat, whose triumphs were intertwined with personal failure and an unhappy end, was Lord Castlereagh, the British foreign secretary, a man who was plodding and stolid in person but whose life represented drama of the highest order.

"The most European of British statesmen," Kissinger said of Castlereagh who, more than anyone else, was responsible for the agreements that assured decades of continental peace among the great powers. He mediated between victorious and competing rivals while welcoming the enemy, France, back from the ruins of defeat. He took the long view. Yet his labors for stability and moderation met with hostility in Britain as, more and more, his work on the continent distanced him "from the spirit of his country." Britain was an insular nation, proud of its isolation and exceptionalism; it wanted no part of European political intrigues or moral ambiguities. And where Castlereagh sought international engagement to guarantee national security, the British public demanded withdrawal.

Where Castlereagh worked to achieve an enduring peace with a former enemy, the people he was supposed to represent called for vengeance and humiliation. The difference was between a pragmatic statesman who understood the necessity for often unsatisfying compromise and a public that thought in terms of absolutes. In *Politics Among Nations*, Morgenthau had painted a picture of the diplomat as a misunderstood hero, a man without a country. Kissinger put flesh and bones on the picture with his portrait of Castlereagh. The press of events had left the foreign secretary increasingly torn between conflicting demands, increasingly isolated from his shortsighted compatriots. But whom, then, was he working for? "No one after me understands the affairs of the continent," he said to the king in 1822. A few days later he committed suicide. Many of his countrymen cheered.

Yet if Kissinger wrote *A World Restored* under the influence of Morgenthau's Realpolitik, it was not only because their ideas meshed but also because they shared a sensibility. Each of these conservative German Jews was an outsider, skeptical and isolated, though eager to make a mark on American policy. "We were both in a way lonely among our associates," Kissinger wrote. They were pessimists who disdained ideas of progress. Life, each believed, was tragic, and to lose sight of that painful fact was to stumble into disaster. In foreign policy, Morgenthau said, the choice was usually between the bad and the less bad—the implication being that it was not enough to point out the flaws in a given policy: one had to consider all the alternatives and argue for "the less bad." Morgenthau would have wholeheartedly endorsed Kissinger's statement that "nothing is more difficult for Americans to understand than the possibility of tragedy."

Through the 1950s and into the 1960s, when Morgenthau had established himself as the Grand Old Man of international relations and Kissinger had produced a surprise bestseller in 1957 with *Nuclear Weapons and Foreign Policy*—a book Morgenthau said that put Kissinger "in the forefront of the new breed of political-military thinkers"—each could recognize himself in the other. Their relationship was warm and supportive. They sent each other pieces they had written. In 1956, Kissinger told Morgenthau that his articles were among "the very best things that I have read on the melancholy events of the past few months." They dined together when they could, though geographical distance and busy schedules made get-togethers less frequent than they might have wished. "It has been much too long since we have met," Kissinger said in 1962. Morgenthau wrote for Kissinger's magazine, *Confluence*, and made a guest appearance at Kissinger's seminar at Harvard. He invited Kissinger to become formally associated with his institute at Chicago, the Center for the Study of American Foreign Policy (Kissinger turned down the offer, pleading other commitments). After Kissinger became Nixon's national security adviser and then secretary of state, a sympathetic Morgenthau expressed surprise that someone he thought he knew so well could exhibit such extraordinary diplomatic skills, able to act as an "honest broker" because he "has persuaded all concerned that he seeks only the satisfaction and reconciliation of their respective interests." When Morgenthau paid a visit to the White House, Kissinger gave him a tour, carefully pointing out all the Jews whose portraits hung on the walls.

Inevitably, however, these two lonely Realists did not always see eye to eye on specific issues—Realism offered guidelines for policy but not prescriptions—and their disagreements became sharpest after Kissinger had entered government service. Nothing highlighted their divisions more than the debate over the Jackson-Vanik amendment of 1974–75. It is now nearly forgotten, except by experts in the field, but it had a lasting significance that almost no one, and neither Morgenthau nor Kissinger, understood at the time—though Kissinger later called it a "sea change" in American policy.

Henry Jackson, a Democratic senator from Washington, has been called "effectively the first prominent neoconservative politician," a liberal welfare statist in domestic affairs but so anti-Communist in his foreign policy positions that he sounded like a Republican hard-liner; in 1969 Richard Nixon asked him to become his secretary of defense (Jackson, who had higher ambitions, rejected the offer). In 1972, while Nixon and Kissinger were negotiating economic issues with the Soviet Union and seeking paths to accommodation, Jackson proposed an amendment to a trade bill to force the Russians to loosen restrictive emigration policies that were limiting the number of Jews who could leave the country. In the House the amendment was sponsored by Charles Vanik, a congressman from Ohio, and after two fraught years of controversy, it overwhelmingly passed both houses before being signed into law by a reluctant President Ford in 1975. The amendment reduced Kissinger's flexibility as a diplomat and he saw it as part of a "relentless and nearly continuous attack" on his work. Its immediate impact, however, was the very opposite of what its framers intended. Instead of liberalizing its policies, the Kremlin cracked down: emigration of Soviet Jews fell from 35,000 in 1973 to about 13,000 in 1975 and didn't total 35,000 again until 1979.

More significantly for the future of American foreign policy, the Jackson-Vanik amendment marked one of the first rebellions against Kissinger's Realpolitik and implicitly was a repudiation of Morgenthau as well. It signaled a return to the Wilsonian moral posturing that both men so disliked, with an emotionally satisfying idealistic emphasis on human rights and democracy promotion—the start of a trend that eventually blossomed into the movement known as neoconservatism. The young staffers who surrounded Jackson during the fight over the amendment constituted what has been called a neoconservative "nursery." Among the names that would become much more familiar in later years were Paul Wolfowitz and Richard Perle. Cold considerations of national interest were in the process of being overridden, or at best tempered, by American moralism, the very tendency Morgenthau had persistently deplored in *Politics Among Nations* and his other writings.

Surprisingly, given the developments that were to follow, so contrary to his own thinking, Morgenthau was a strong supporter of Jackson-Vanik, though not for the reasons advanced by the nascent neocons. In the aftermath of the 1967 war between Israel and its Arab neighbors, Morgenthau began to immerse himself in Israeli and Jewish affairs, accepting the chairmanship of the Academic Committee for Soviet Jewry in 1970. From that perch he wrote letters, signed petitions, and generally spoke out in support of Soviet Jews, and after the Jackson-Vanik amendment was introduced, he testified in favor of it at a congressional hearing.

But it wasn't enough for Morgenthau to support Jackson-Vanik on behalf of narrow Jewish interests or simple humanitarianism; his position had to be grounded in national interest and, Morgenthau being Morgenthau, national interest was defined for him in terms of power relationships and concrete policy advantage, not morality and "values." In Morgenthau's view, the Nixon-Kissinger policy of détente, which sought to find areas of accommodation and compromise as a way of relieving Cold War tensions, could only work if the Soviet Union was itself willing to compromise by adhering to certain broad moral principles that were generally accepted worldwide. Otherwise, détente was bound to fail.

"Détente in a genuine sense, real détente, real relaxation of tensions, real diminution of the main sources of conflict which might lead to war," he told Congress, required a change in Soviet behavior. And in a letter to Henry Jackson, he said that the amendment was "in the best American tradition," pointing out that the Realpolitiker Theodore Roosevelt had canceled a trade agreement with the Russians because of the pogroms then taking place.

Morgenthau was quick to add that he was not calling for regime change in the Soviet Union or for linking the emigration question to other issues of vital concern to the United States, like arms control. He was arguing about the specific issue of Jewish emigration and in effect proposing a gamble that in any cost-benefit analysis, the Kremlin would prefer to obtain American trade credits than to restrict the free movement of troublesome Soviet Jews. This was an attempted bluff in a global poker game, and indeed the Soviets bought the bluff: they were willing to make back-stage concessions by raising the annual quota of Jews allowed to emigrate. But Jackson and Congress overplayed their hand. For the Soviets, counting numbers behind the scenes was one thing, publicly acquiescing to humiliation through American congressional pressure was quite another. That was something, Kissinger wrote, to which "the Soviets would never agree." He turned out to be right. Morgenthau and Jackson lost their gamble, as of course did the Jews of the Soviet Union.

Israel was another area of disagreement between the two friends. Kissinger the statesman was famously engaged in shuttle diplomacy and step-by-step negotiations between the Israelis and the Arabs to find possibilities of agreement. Morgenthau, who doubted that the Arabs were willing to compromise on the fundamental question of Israel's existence, warned against what he saw as salami-tactics that weakened Israel's security inch by inch, negotiation by negotiation; he called instead for an overall settlement. Absent that, "the best that can be expected is a cessation of the state of war—that is, an ill-defined, precarious, intermediate stage between peace and war." In March 1974, Kissinger reached out to Morgenthau in a letter from the White House. "I have followed your recent statements on the Middle East with great interest," he said. "I attach great weight to them because of my respect for your judgment," and while he went on to say that "it is clear that we disagree on many of the issues," he added that it was possible Morgenthau had a "mistaken impression of the premises and objectives of our policy." He proposed that the two of them get together. "I would very much welcome a chance to talk about this with you." When they met a year later, Kissinger, with his trademark irony, said, "I hope you don't think it's my purpose in life to destroy Israel." To this Morgenthau replied in a more sober vein, "It's not a question of purpose, but the obvious consequences of your policy."

Finally, on Kissinger's overall policy of détente—about which the battle over the Jackson-Vanik amendment was an opening skirmish—Morgenthau was broadly skeptical without being entirely negative. He found much to praise, particularly Kissinger's steps to effect an "ideological decontamination" of the Cold War, changing the conflict from an unyielding philosophical struggle to one of national interest. As long as the dispute between the Americans and the Russians was conceived ideologically, any possibility of cooperation between the two superpowers "remained philosophically inconceivable and practically unfeasible." In the abstract, détente had produced the necessary condition for a successful foreign policy. Concretely, however, détente had failed, or in Morgenthau's softer language, "not succeeded." Arms control had not managed to curb "the dreaded proliferation of nuclear weapons," and the Soviet Union continued to exhibit aggressive intentions that damaged the possibility for a more peaceful world. Moreover, for all his "uncommon imagination, skill, and persistence," as Morgenthau put it, Kissinger's apparent preference for authoritarian stability over progressive change thwarted the chance of moderate reform in countries like Greece, and so increased the dangers of more violent upheavals.

Kissinger was clearly troubled by this assessment from "someone for whom I have always had the highest admiration and whose friendship I have valued over many years," and he expressed his disappointment in the third volume of his memoirs, though he took comfort from the fact that Morgenthau hadn't sided with those critics of détente calling for democracy promotion and a reassertion of American values but had rested his arguments on Realist balance-of-power premises. Whatever their differences, neither man provided any opening for neoconservatism and a more moral—Kissinger and Morgenthau would say more moralistic—foreign policy. Moral considerations might offer boundaries for policy: Morgenthau wrote that "morality limits the interests that power seeks and the means that power employs." Genocide, therefore, was unacceptable under all circumstances. But moral aims could not dictate policy—lest a natural inclination to view the enemy as "evil" foster genocidal tendencies of its own. Morality, Morgenthau insisted, could not provide goals.

WHATEVER AGREEMENTS or disagreements the two Realpolitikers may have had in the 1960s and 1970s, in the end everything came down, as it always did at the time, to the Vietnam war, what Kissinger called "the defining experience of the second half of the twentieth century" and Morgenthau said was "the great moral calamity of American foreign policy to that time." As one writer put it, "After 1965, there was no United States foreign policy; there was only a Vietnam policy." From a contemporary perspective, it's possible to ignore or forget Vietnam in the sense of dismissing it as a disastrous mistake without giving any further thought to context, motives, choices, or lessons. But as soon as one begins to examine the questions surrounding the war as it was seen at the time, and not with the luxury of hindsight, it becomes once again the wound that will not heal.

George Ball, the assistant secretary of state and insider's insider, who took on the role of unofficial dove in both the Kennedy and Johnson administrations, stated that Vietnam was "probably the greatest single error made by America in its history." There is no "probably" required. More Americans may have died in the Civil War than the total number of deaths from the Revolution through Korea—620,000 in all, and more than 10 times the number who fell in Vietnam—but in the end the stain of slavery was expunged from the American fabric, and so those deaths (at least in the North) might be said not to have been in vain. Surveying the conflicts of the twentieth century, there are always positives to be gleaned from America's loss of life. One can see World War I as having deterred German aggression (though undermined by a precarious peace) and World War II as having vanquished the most heinous enemy the United States, and Western civilization, had ever faced. For all the mistakes made during the Korean war, it succeeded in forestalling North Korea's attempted conquest of South Korea, and similarly the first Iraq war punished Saddam Hussein's aggression against Kuwait, along with his attempt to seize vital oil resources. For many today, the second Iraq war is seen as no less futile and inimical than the war in Vietnam, but it too had the positive consequences of eliminating a vicious dictator and possibly preventing a dangerous nuclear arms race between Iraq and Iran.

But no positives came out of Vietnam: the 58,000 Americans who lost their lives there may indeed be said to have died as John Kerry put it, for a "mistake."

But that is the conclusion of hindsight. To those who were actually immersed in the events and making the decisions that drew the country ever deeper into the quagmire, things looked very different. Each step along the way, however reluctantly taken, seemed to be the best choice available among a range of bad options. That is what Leslie Gelb and Richard Betts meant when they subtitled their Vietnam book *The System Worked*. As they wrote, "In the context of Cold War assumptions, definitions, and constraints, the leaders' choices always seemed foreordained." And that is also why Hans Morgenthau's early and vigorous opposition to the war was not only percipient but also heroic. At the start, he was, as one scholar has put it, "a lone voice within the Cold War establishment" challenging those assumptions, and by the 1970s he was being called "the single most important thinker in the debate on Vietnam." Even after he was joined in his opposition by millions of other Americans, his dissents remained the deepest, the most coherent, reaching to the very root of the question and, therefore, of continuing relevance.

IN 1970, the comedian Bob Hope told his television viewers that the future of India rested on what the United States did in Indochina, going on to warn that "before you know it, we are going to fight on Staten Island." This was self-evidently an absurd statement, but then it was Bob Hope, and what did he know? But it was possible to find almost identical statements being made by people not only in a much better position to know but also who should have known better. In 1954 President Eisenhower, in a landmark speech, declared that if Indochina fell to the Communists, eventually Japan, the Philippines, and even Australia would be threatened. In 1964, Richard Nixon asserted that the fate of all Asia rested on the outcome in Vietnam. As secretary of defense, Robert McNamara expanded the danger to include the vast continent of Africa. No place anywhere in the world was safe; everyone was threatened by the Red Menace. Americans saw themselves engaged in a zero-sum game: allow Communism to gain an inch even in a backwater like Vietnam, which in the early 1960s, 99 percent of Americans would have been unable to identify on a map, and the entire so-called free world might begin to crumble. John Kennedy gave full expression to the idea in 1963, two months before his assassination: "Every time a country, regardless of how far away it may be from our borders—every time a country passes behind the Iron Curtain, the security of the United States is thereby endangered." How outlandish was it for Bob Hope to worry about the security of Staten Island when Vice President Lyndon Johnson was telling Americans that if Vietnam fell, they would eventually be fighting "on the beaches of Waikiki"? A variant of the theme was offered to foreign citizens. Exasperated by the lack of support for the war in the United Kingdom, Dean Rusk fulminated to a British journalist: "When the Russians invade Sussex, don't expect us to come and help you."

The intellectual foundation for these concerns became known as the "Domino Theory," with every country in the world seen as a standing domino tile, ready to fall over if its neighbor fell, until the entire set, everyone, everywhere, had collapsed into a totalitarian hell. A better metaphor might have been an infectious disease and a global contagion, but the point is that it was a metaphor, the imposition of an abstract idea upon a diverse and variegated reality, with no consideration given to local conditions and history or human expectations and desires. Communism was an unalterable monolith that had erupted with the Bolshevik Revolution before beginning an inexorable expansion from its central base of operations in Moscow. To American policymakers it was unthinkable that people in some other part of the world, for example, China or Vietnam, might choose to become Communists (whatever they meant by that) out of their understanding of their immediate life situation and their own free will; the prevailing image that guided policy might well have come out of a 1950s science fiction movie, *Invasion of the Body Snatchers*, with mindless automatons marching to the demands of a totalitarian military machine.

Dean Rusk, who had been an assistant to Secretary of State Dean Acheson in the Truman administration before becoming secretary of state himself under Kennedy, said in 1951 that Communist China was not an independent nation but merely a vassal of the Soviet Union. "It is not Chinese," he declared, taking his body-snatcher image to its logical conclusion. Rusk's views, according to one historian of the Vietnam war, "remained extraordinarily consistent for nearly two decades." In 1968 he was still arguing that the North Vietnamese "took their orders from Moscow." Naturally, he could view American protests against the war only as Communist inspired. How could anyone be opposed to "freedom"?

A similar inability to look at the world from any perspective other than one's own infected Richard Helms, the director of the CIA. By 1968, much to the surprise and dismay of Washington, Vietnam's Communists had proved themselves to be dedicated, tenacious warriors for their cause, easily a match for the much-better trained and equipped Americans. "I wish they were on our side," the troops fighting them were heard to say. How could that be? Asked why the Vietnamese Communists were fighting so well, Helms didn't point to culture or local conditions or personal beliefs or what should have been a simple matter for a spymaster to understand, that is, the nationalist impulse to repel a foreign invader. It was "good brainwashing," he said. In his anguished reassessment of his own role in fomenting the war, Robert McNamara said that he had failed to understand Indochina's "history, language, culture or values." And the same, he went on, "must be said to varying degrees about President Kennedy, Secretary of State Dean Rusk, National Security Adviser McGeorge Bundy, military adviser Maxwell Taylor, and many others." All were blinded by their rigid adherence to the Domino Theory and their belief that Communism was a monolithic, dehumanizing enemy.

The theory had emerged with the Cold War. It had its origins in a 1950 National Security Council statement that the outcome of the war the French were fighting for their colonial possessions in Indochina would have an impact on neighbors like Burma and Thailand. Infinitely elastic, it was expanded in another national security memorandum of 1954 to include all of Southeast Asia, India, and much of the Middle East. And if the enormous, fathomlessly diverse subcontinent of India was in danger, what chance did Staten Island have? A line had to be drawn, and the place to draw the line was Vietnam.

Looking back at the theory in 1975, a columnist for *The New Republic* asked, "Is it possible that we once believed that? Yes we did." And the "we" meant practically everyone—not seasoned European statesmen like Winston Churchill and Charles de Gaulle, to be sure, each with his own firmly grounded sense of history, but almost every American in a position to influence policy. In the Kennedy White House the question was never whether to save Vietnam but how to save it. "Amid all the debate," McNamara recalled, Kennedy's advisers "failed to analyze the pros and cons of withdrawal." They weren't the only ones. It was not simply nationalistic and conservative anti-Communists who lined up behind American intervention but Washington's liberals too—stalwarts like Hubert Humphrey and Mike Mansfield. Brooding in the White House some years later as he tried to extricate the United States from the mess in Vietnam, President Richard Nixon self-pityingly moped that the war was a liberals' war; he was wrong—no group was more hawkish than his own Republican base, including the party's radical, saber-rattling 1964 presidential candidate, Barry Goldwater—but he was not entirely wrong.

The press was on board too. The *Washington Post, Time, Newsweek*, even that leading voice of American liberalism, *The New Republic*, supported the effort to stop Communism in Vietnam. In 1962, before it became skeptical of the war, the *New York Times* editorialized that Vietnam "is a struggle this country cannot shirk." And the *Times'* own correspondent in Vietnam, who was later to write one of the first books questioning the decisions of "the best and the brightest," warned in 1965 against a precipitous American withdrawal. The prestige of the United States "will be lowered throughout the world," David Halberstam said, and "the pressure of Communism on the rest of Southeast Asia will intensify." And not only in Asia. The war against Communism was a global struggle. "Withdrawal means that throughout the world the enemies of the West will be encouraged to try insurgencies like the one in Vietnam."

Robert McNamara noted that in the early 1960s, "the majority of journalists" felt the same way. Another reporter, Neil Sheehan, agreed. Like Halberstam, he was covering the war in the early years and was later to write his own massive critique, *A Bright Shining Lie*. He explained that correspondents like himself began questioning policy only when it became clear to them that the facts on the ground that they had seen with their own eyes conflicted with the official statements of the American military in the field and the politicians back in Washington. And were they supposed to believe the rosy predictions coming from the government or their own eyes? Before the contradictions of their experiences became too blatant to be denied, reporters in the field "shared the advisers' sense of commitment to this war." They became critics against their will. As Sheehan said, "We regarded the conflict as our war too," and in a personal testimony, he wrote, "In those years, like almost all Americans, I saw nothing wrong with shooting Communists and their 'dupes.'"

Once the costs of the war and the death counts mounted, commitment began to peel away and support turned to opposition, but Americans waded into the quagmire in near unanimity. Even later personifications of antiwar fervor were early enthusiasts. J. William Fulbright, who in a few years' time would lead the congressional opposition, was at first a "firm supporter" of involvement. Daniel Ellsberg, who did what he could to undermine American policy during the Nixon years by releasing the Pentagon Papers, was as gung-ho as anyone at the start. When he couldn't get to Vietnam to fight the Communists as a Marine, he went as a civilian to play an active part in a pacification program. It took the Tet uprising of 1968 to disillusion him. As Lyndon Johnson was making the crucial decision in 1964 to escalate the conflict, "only the fringes of opinion," Gelb and Betts write, "were challenging the administration."

Hans Morgenthau represented the greatest challenge, in part because he couldn't be dismissed as simply a fringe dissenter. His anti-Communist credentials could scarcely have been firmer, his commitment to an American presence in the world and his support for a strong American military a matter of ongoing public record. His influence on foreign policy was widespread and palpable. He was no isolationist. And neither was he a Marxist or fellow-traveling leftist ready to oppose any American action that threatened a Communist regime. Indeed, his academic critics charged him with being a "mouthpiece" for the Cold War.

Yet, unlike nearly every other expert on foreign policy, Morgenthau was never tempted to support the Vietnam adventure, a fact that surprised many of his readers, who saw "an abrupt break with his earlier theorizing." To these people Morgenthau replied that they hadn't been reading him very carefully. "I have always emphasized the importance of power in all its manifestations as an instrument of foreign policy," he wrote in 1965. "But I have as consistently been opposed to equating national power with military power, and I have warned against the improvident and foolish use of power." He saw no more "foolish use of power" in his lifetime than the American intervention in Vietnam, and that was long before more than half a million troops had become bogged down in a hopeless cause. He could see where the early, relatively insignificant interventions were heading.

Morgenthau's involvement with Vietnam went back to the mid-1950s. Wesley Fishel, a professor at Michigan State University and a former student of Morgenthau's, was an early lobbyist for an independent South Vietnam. He had long been a close friend of Ngo Dinh Diem, who became president of South Vietnam in 1954 and ruled in dictatorial fashion for nine years, until his assassination in 1963, two weeks before John Kennedy was himself assassinated. Diem was a Catholic, with little or no support among the majority Buddhist population, but that didn't stop Americans from fawning over him as an anti-Communist savior. He was called a "miracle worker," the "Winston Churchill of Asia," and a "modern political Joan of Arc." On a visit to New York in 1957 he was honored with a ticker-tape parade and awarded the city's Medal of Freedom by a doting Mayor Robert Wagner, who announced that Diem was a man "to whom freedom is the very breath of life." Obviously hoping to enlist the influential Morgenthau among Diem's crowd of supporters, Fishel arranged a trip to Vietnam in 1955, along with a personal interview with the South Vietnamese president. To say Fishel's plan misfired would be the kindest way of putting it. Shooting himself in both feet would be closer to the truth.

Morgenthau observed many of the same positive qualities in Diem that had ensorcelled so many others. His political accomplishments were indisputable. He demonstrated "extraordinary qualities," Morgenthau said, somehow managing to assert authority over a fractious country immersed in civil war. By the mid-1950s he had gained control of the army, largely eliminated police corruption, subdued the competing political factions, and crushed the Communists. It was doubtful that anyone else in South Vietnam could have achieved what he did. What was not to like?

Yet to a practitioner of Realpolitik like Morgenthau, Diem presented a classic dilemma: his strongman tactics were probably necessary to pacify the country and unite it insofar as it could be united. Morgenthau noted, "It would be ill-advised to be squeamish about some of the methods he used." But power employed to bring about stability without efforts to establish popular legitimacy was a recipe for upheaval and revolution, and Diem refused to accept any restraint on his authority. As a Catholic, he relied on the 10 percent of the population who were his coreligionists as his base of support; others, particularly city dwellers, could be bought off or incorporated into the economy with the massive quantities of American aid he was receiving. But Diem's influence did not extend to the countryside where the overwhelming majority of the people lived, and whenever he had to choose between accommodation and repression, he chose repression. When Morgenthau interviewed Diem in 1955, he saw the makings of a ruthless dictator "who is building, down to small details, a replica of the totalitarian regime which he opposes."

Morgenthau didn't know the half of it. Neil Sheehan recorded in stomach-churning detail the methods that enabled Diem to hold on to power against a recalcitrant or indifferent population. Communists or suspected sympathizers were wrapped in barbed wire, had the skin stripped off their backs, immersed in water and subjected to electroshock, and beaten around the abdomen until their stomachs collapsed and were vomited up. In the North, opponents of the Communist regime were being tortured and killed too—thousands died in an abortive land reform—but the Communists whom the peasants of South Vietnam encountered were not terrorizing them; they were assassinating the village leaders who were their oppressors and the extensions of the hated Saigon regime. According to Sheehan, the Communist Vietcong operating in the south were much more discriminating in their use of violence than Diem's minions and, as Morgenthau wrote as early as 1956, Diem was giving "his people little to choose between the totalitarianism of the north and his own." Indeed, the Communists presented themselves as fighting for a national cause. What was Diem fighting for except his own heavy-handed authority? Morgenthau said as much to Diem during his 1955 interview, warning that his policies were leading to a "bipolarization" in which Communism might seem a better choice to the peasants in the countryside. Diem was not pleased.

Perhaps the most important factor in Morgenthau's opposition to the war even before it had become a war was that his own Realpolitik focus on power relations meant that he did not demonize Communism as almost everyone else did during the Cold War years. Ideology of any kind was, for him, merely a smoke screen that clouded people's minds. When he examined the history of the Soviet Union—as he did repeatedly in his writings—he noted the inability of the official ideology to match reality and Stalin's pragmatic willingness to adjust Communist beliefs (or even abandon them when necessary) in order to deal with the facts on the ground. "If the Bolshevik Revolution and its consequence in the form of the Soviet Union teach anything," he wrote, "they teach the irrelevance of the teaching of Marx." Morgenthau's intellectual antagonist, George Lichtheim, said much the same thing in his masterly account, *Marxism: An Historical and Critical Study.* Lichtheim wrote that Soviet Communism "was identified with a set of beliefs which Marx would never have dreamed of putting forward." Chinese Communism, untethered from any theory at all, was even worse: "It only needed the extension of the Communist triumph to China for Marxism to be stood entirely on its head."

In the twentieth century, Morgenthau said, Communism had met with repeated failures that should have undermined it as a belief system but didn't. The first of these occurred on the eve of World War I, when the

Marxists abandoned the international solidarity of working people that they had insisted was the engine of history to support the national goals of their particular governments. British and French workers fought German and Austrian workers. Men died in the trenches not for Marxist ideals but for king and country—and dying was the best evidence of one's true beliefs.

The end of the war brought a second failure. Communism triumphed in Russia but according to the theory, revolution was expected to come to advanced industrial countries, not primitive, agricultural ones. And so the Russian Bolsheviks waited for the revolutions in the West. And they waited, and waited—until Stalin, in an improvisation to the theory, decreed his policy of socialism in one country. It was the best he could do to preserve his revolution, but it wasn't supposed to be that way, not if Marxism was the unerring guide to history it claimed to be. Socialism in one country, and especially if that country was Russia, was a grotesque distortion of Marxist doctrine. Trotsky said as much.

Another failure was the rise of fascism. Given the choice, the masses were as likely to embrace militant nationalism as class warfare or, as the example of Germany showed, workers who at first adhered to Communist or Socialist parties turned out to be malleable clay in the hands of a talented and nationalistic demagogue. And finally, in Morgenthau's litany of failure, the emergence of an independent, dissident Communist Yugoslavia under Tito after World War II gave the lie to the idea of a Communist monolith heedlessly obeying the orders of the infallible leader Stalin. "Polycentrism," as Morgenthau put it in a 1962 article with that name, had become "manifest," another "great refutation" of Communist theory.

Stalin wasn't a true believer in a new faith, Morgenthau explained. He was a cynic. But that was his virtue. He didn't take Communist principles seriously. He was cautious. (In Morgenthau's mind, Nikita Khrushchev was much more of an ideologue than Stalin, and the result was the Cuban Missile Crisis, which brought the world to the brink of nuclear war.) Morgenthau detested Russian Bolshevism—it was, he said, an "oriental despotism"—but that didn't preclude admiration for Stalin's abilities in foreign policy. Building on Churchill's observation that Stalin operated with "a complete absence of illusions of any sort," Morgenthau wrote that "absence of illusion is indeed one of the marks of the statesman." Stalin the pragmatist understood power, and he knew his limits. He also knew that although Communism might have a "quasi-religious" appeal to des-

perate millions around the world, it was ultimately the Red Army that
assured the spread of Bolshevik ideology, and when ideology clashed with
national interest, Stalin never had any hesitation about which option to
choose. When the situation demanded it, he acted as a moderating force
against his more extreme allies. (Kissinger held essentially the same view:
Stalin was "a monster, but in the conduct of international relations, he was
the supreme realist.")

The North Vietnamese had learned just how unreliable their Russian
comrades could be after they defeated the French at Dien Bien Phu and
seemed on the verge of uniting the country under Communist rule. Stalin
had died in 1953 but a year later, at the Geneva Conference, his Realist legacy lived on. The Russians urged the Vietnamese to compromise and later
suggested a permanent partition of the country, with both North Vietnam
and South Vietnam represented at the United Nations. The Chinese were
equally pragmatic. In 1954 Zhou Enlai told a French diplomat that "he had
come to Geneva to make peace, not to back the [Communist] Vietminh."
The North Vietnamese never forgot about the untrustworthiness of their
so-called allies; in the end, they could depend on no one but themselves.

That ideology counted for nothing at all was never Morgenthau's position. Affinities mattered, and "neither of the two major Communist powers can afford to watch the destruction of a fraternal Socialist country"
like North Vietnam. But ideological explanations took one only so far; in
fact, both Russia and China supported Hanoi for the good Realpolitik reason that they were in competition with each other for influence across the
Communist world. Perhaps the most extraordinary paradox, from Morgenthau's point of view, was that Washington took Communist ideology
more seriously than the Communists themselves did. Ever since the annus
mirabilis of 1947, Washington had abandoned the pragmatism of containment for the dogma of the "free world." In the topsy-turvy world of the Cold
War, the Americans had become the ideologues, the Russians the Realists.
This, Morgenthau remarked, was "one of the great ironies of history."

In one of the best accounts of the Vietnam war, the historian George
Herring wrote that American involvement was a "logical" outcome of the
policy of containment. Morgenthau didn't see it that way, and neither did
the father of containment, George Kennan. In Morgenthau's history of the
Cold War, containment represented a Realist response to the threat that
the Soviet Union posed to Europe. The Kremlin was pursuing traditional
Russian aims (dressed up and reinvigorated as Communist aims) and the

West reacted with a traditional balance-of-power response that it called containment. The only surprise in all this, Morgenthau noted, was that the United States had shed its isolationist instincts as smoothly as it did to become a full and necessary participant in the preservation of Western Europe.

Things began to go wrong only when Washington became mesmerized by the idea of containment, a particular solution to a particular problem, and extended the policy beyond the confines of Europe to areas of the world where it had no relevance and was never intended to be employed. The notion of "the free world" eventually encompassed every well-intentioned, idealistic, opportunistic, authoritarian, or simply creepy anti-Communist residing in every corner of the globe. The change was signaled by the rhetoric of President Harry Truman and enunciated in the so-called Truman Doctrine, which translated the confrontation in Europe into a global ideological struggle. As Morgenthau wrote, "The Truman Doctrine transformed a concrete interest of the United States in a geographically defined part of the world into a moral principle of worldwide validity, to be applied regardless of the limits of American interests and of American power."

In fact, the Truman administration, guided by its Realpolitik secretary of state, Dean Acheson, was careful not to let its rhetoric overwhelm its more pragmatic, discriminating policies. But the "sweeping generalities" of the doctrine were too hard to resist and were picked up uncritically by Truman and Acheson's successors. "Their foreign policies, especially in Asia, were judged by the standards of the Truman Doctrine and were found wanting." Thus did American pragmatism turn into its opposite, an ideology, a dogma of anti-Communism, the old, world–redeeming Wilsonianism now backed up with unprecedented American military might and a self-serving interpretation of history that promised a liberal millennium. This was a vision, Morgenthau said, that was "missionary in theory and crusading in practice." Just about everyone in Washington joined the anti-Communist crusade, though Morgenthau singled out John Kennedy for his failure to educate the public about the limits of power and the need to retreat from overextended commitments. Kennedy had introduced a few thousand Americans into Vietnam, and debate continues on what he would have done had he lived—escalate or withdraw? It was Lyndon Johnson who pushed the American commitment to a level that Kennedy, before his death, rejected as absurd. When George Ball warned

Kennedy against involvement in Vietnam, saying, "Within five years we'll have 300,000 men in the paddies" (the eventual figure was over 500,000), the president replied, "George, you're just crazier than hell. That just isn't going to happen."

In the early and mid-1960s, before Johnson's dramatic escalation, Morgenthau could already perceive a disaster in the making by the logic of the arguments being offered. Americans had been taken in by the Domino Theory, which "is unsupported by any historical evidence." They were deluded about the nature of the Soviet threat, "which conquered Eastern Europe on the bayonets of the Red Army, not by dint of its own inner persuasiveness." They were convinced that Communism was a monolithic danger when, in fact, it was a different phenomenon in different places, dependent upon local circumstances. "A Communist government may or may not be subservient to the Soviet Union or China and so may a non-Communist government. It is ideologically consistent, but politically and militarily foolish, to oppose a Communist government for no other reason than that it is Communist."

Around the same time that Kennedy was telling Charles de Gaulle that he saw no real quarrel between China and the Soviet Union, Morgenthau was calling for a policy based on "polycentrism," the recognition that national interest, even in Communist countries, would override pleas based on international solidarity. Tito's independent Communist state of Yugoslavia showed the way—"in fact, the United States encounters today less hostility from Tito, who is a Communist, than from de Gaulle, who is not." Because of the long history of rivalry between China and Vietnam, Morgenthau said, Ho Chi Minh had the potential to be an Asian Tito. He would "become the leader of a Chinese satellite only if the United States forced him to become one." By contrast, McNamara reported that Kennedy's inner circle "equated Ho Chi Minh not with Marshall Tito but with Fidel Castro," an ideologue who was attempting to spread revolution across Latin America. The difference was that Morgenthau was looking at international affairs through the lens of history and power relationships while McNamara and Kennedy's advisers were looking through the lens of ideology and anti-Communist orthodoxy.

One reads Morgenthau's articles from the early 1960s with feelings of sorrow and distress. Clear-sighted about the limits of American power, the dangers of the Domino Theory, and the necessity to examine any given issue nonideologically, through its particularities, Morgenthau urged the leaders in Washington to assess the commitment to South Vietnam in terms of national interest. How important was it to prevent Vietnam from being unified under a Communist government? If one understood the polycentric nature of Communism and the intellectual limits of Bolshevik ideology, the answer had to be—not very. Policymakers had to distinguish, first, between what was essential and what was desirable and, second, between what was desirable and what was possible. Triumphalist American policymakers preferred to believe that if something was desirable, it was possible, with no sense of tragedy to their thinking. The prevailing anti-Communist dogma, with its ignorance of Vietnamese history and culture, had failed to make the necessary distinctions and was therefore bound to dictate a course that could lead only to "humiliation and catastrophe." If we persisted with a military approach, Morgenthau wrote in 1962, when only a few thousand advisers had set foot in South Vietnam, "We are likely to be drawn ever more deeply into a Korea-type war, fought under political and military conditions much more unfavorable than those that prevailed in Korea." Morgenthau predicted a war that would last for five or ten years and would end in stalemate. He was closer to the truth than any of the confident White House officials urging intervention, and a few years later he rightly said, "If my advice had been followed, there would be no war in Vietnam today."

Morgenthau paid a price for his outspokenness. Because of his stature, he represented a genuine threat to anti-Communist orthodoxy. He had been a consultant to the Defense Department but was let go because of his views on Vietnam. The Johnson administration set up an operation called "Project Morgenthau" to discredit him, and it had the FBI keep tabs on him. It was said that he lost the presidency of the American Political Science Association because of his articles opposing the war, even that his son was drafted because of his father's views. Few of his academic colleagues came to his defense in these early years of the engagement in Vietnam, and of the professors who taught political science, Morgenthau said he was struck by the fact that many of those who opposed the war in private were unwilling to say so in public. It is hard not to believe he had Henry Kissinger in mind. Always the German-Jewish intellectual, Morgenthau saw intimations of totalitarianism in the Johnson administration's efforts to silence him and other dissenters, as well as the willing conformity of most of the nation's intellectuals.

Still, as American involvement in Vietnam mounted, and with Morgenthau as an inspiration, dissent on American campuses grew. The first significant student protest against the war occurred in March 1965 at the University of Michigan. It did not involve demonstrations in the streets or other disruptions, but in good, orderly academic fashion, took the form of a "teach-in," with professors and students engaging in discussion of "the new American arrogance." Morgenthau wasn't present, but the students who attended publicly thanked him for his guidance. The movement quickly spread to other campuses and reached Washington in May with a national teach-in that was broadcast on college stations around the country. Morgenthau was the keynote speaker. A month later, he was heard by a nationwide audience in a CBS news special in which he and the national security adviser, McGeorge Bundy, were the key participants. Bundy accused Morgenthau of opposing the Marshall Plan, which wasn't true. He also said Morgenthau exhibited "congenital pessimism," and he wasn't wrong about that. A little of his hard-earned sense of tragedy might have saved the United States from self-inflicted disaster. As Robert McNamara wrote years later, "It is very hard today to recapture the innocence and confidence with which we approached Vietnam." Neil Sheehan, who saw the hawkish McNamara firsthand, called him "a Gibraltar of optimism." The older, chastened McNamara offered a mea culpa about his earlier self: "I had always been confident that every problem could be solved, but now I found myself confronting one . . . that could not."

Morgenthau was discovering at this time that his reputation had evolved in three stages. The publication of *Politics Among Nations* in 1947 made him a figure to be reckoned with in classrooms and within foreign policy circles. His writings in the 1950s and 1960s for small-circulation magazines like *Commentary, The New Leader,* and *The New Republic,* as well as for more widely read organs like the *New York Times* and the *Washington Post,* had turned him into a "public intellectual," with his influence extending beyond the campuses to discerning, educated leaders at large. But it was through his opposition to the Vietnam war that he became, in his words, "famous overnight."

Even if his articles and speeches weren't altering the course of the war, there were obvious gratifications to his new renown. Those who took heart from his thoughtful dissents wrote to praise him. "Just a note to say how great to have men of your kind in this world," said one. In early 1965, Morgenthau addressed a group that included senators Jacob Javits and

William Fulbright and later testified before Fulbright's committee on foreign relations.

But nationwide fame also brought the kind of crude and profane responses to which an academic and intellectual was not accustomed. The ignoramuses were crawling out of their caves and for the first time encountering an intellectual who was actually giving thought to the complexities of the political problems of the time. "I don't like your looks. You look like a troublemaker to me." Or "Bah! You and your French (probably imitation) accent. . . . Why do you not go back to France, Russia or from wherever you come." And inevitably: "You lousy Jew." Or "Why is it that egghead Jews always seem to favor Communists?" Along with ignorant, bigoted letters, Morgenthau was subjected to anonymous telephone calls throughout the day and night. "This goes to show how thin the veneer of political civilization is," Morgenthau said to Walter Lippmann.

Generally, Morgenthau ignored the hate mail, though he occasionally responded to the more temperate letters. But one public attack that he chose to answer came from the influential, nationally syndicated columnist Joseph Alsop. Among the members of the press, he was the most vociferous of hawks. Even lifelong friends like Isaiah Berlin thought his views on Vietnam "a trifle mad . . . even odious." In March 1965 Alsop wrote a column directed at Morgenthau that began: "One proof of the wisdom of President Johnson's Vietnamese policy is its marked success to date." But that success had generated criticism from credulous politicians like Fulbright and "pompous" professors like Morgenthau, whom Alsop labeled an "appeaser" in the mold of "the be-nice-to-Hitler group in England before 1939." The mention of Hitler had to be especially wounding to Morgenthau, who said "the gates of the political underworld seem to have opened." Before Alsop's column appeared, Morgenthau reported, even those who disagreed with him did so respectfully, but now "I receive every day letters with xenophobic, red-baiting, and anti-Semitic attacks." Morgenthau responded to Alsop with a long letter to the editor of the *Washington Post*.

The debate, such as it was, turned on the intentions of the Communist Chinese. To Alsop, who prided himself on his knowledge and appreciation of Chinese civilization, the Chinese were historically expansionist, always bent on conquest and therefore analogous to the Nazis of the Third Reich. To which Morgenthau rejoined that "Mao Zedong is not Hitler, that the position of China in Asia is not like that of Nazi Germany in Europe," and that his opposition to the war in Vietnam could not be equated with the appeasers of the 1930s. No doubt wearily, he took up the task once again of explaining that spheres of influence were a reality of international relations, ignored only at one's peril, and that if China had managed to extend its power in Asia it was "primarily through its political and cultural superiority and not through conquest." (Years later, Kissinger would offer a similar assessment of the Chinese.)

Alsop rightly saw Morgenthau as one of the most influential leaders of the opposition to the war in Vietnam and, therefore, someone who had to be discredited with improbable charges of foolishness and appeasement. But the truth about Morgenthau's position in the antiwar movement was complicated. He wasn't really a protest leader. He stood almost alone among the dissenters. His power-oriented Realpolitik perspective was no more congenial to the student demonstrators than it was to the occupants of the White House. As a culturally sophisticated European of deep conservative instincts, Morgenthau saw the unruly students as little more than an embarrassment. "The New Left is essentially anarchistic," he told a journalist, "a still-born movement that can have no influence on American politics." He rejected the young leftists' Marxist explanations that the war was economically determined. "From an economic point of view, the Vietnam war is an absurdity," while so-called moral objections left him cold. For Morgenthau, opposition to the war could rest on one of three foundations: an economic one, an absolute moral one because "this kind of indiscriminate destruction cannot be condoned on any ground," and his own pragmatic position that "this particular war" was not one the United States should be fighting. He distanced himself from so important a protest leader as Noam Chomsky because Chomsky was basing his opposition on a combination of the first two foundations—a "vulgar economic determinism" and a "moral absolutism." He was even ready to rebuke Fulbright for being "dangerously naïve concerning the threat posed by the Soviet Union and Communist China."

In criticizing Chomsky, Morgenthau made the point that his moral absolutism was simply the mirror image of the moralism that dominated the thinking of the policymakers in Washington. Both divided the world into good and evil nations; the difference was in the countries they chose to label good and evil. For the student demonstrators, the United States now fell into the "evil" category. Kissinger said much the same thing about the students from a different position on the political map. The young protesters had passion but no analysis and were unable to formulate any responsible policy for Vietnam. They had allowed morality, or more accurately moralism, to do their thinking for them. Kissinger observed that at the start of the war, the supporters "did so in the name of morality. Before the war was over, many opposed it in the name of morality." What was once good was now evil, but even if positions had changed, the thinking had not—it never lost its Manichean quality. This, Kissinger said, was "American exceptionalism turned on itself" and had nothing in common with the Realpolitik principles of both Morgenthau and Kissinger.

But if the student protesters—called by the historian George Herring "the shock troops of the movement"—weren't Realpolitikers, what were they, and what was the basis of their opposition to the war? These are questions that require a bit of attention.

A few were Marxists or the children of Marxists, predisposed to dislike any policies promulgated by the bulwark-nation of capitalism, but economic explanations never figured prominently in the minds of most of the demonstrators. Both Johnson and Nixon were inclined to write them off as Communist dupes, but to the frustration of the FBI and other government investigators, there was little evidence of Communist influence to be found among the student leaders. The New Left considered it a point of pride to reject both Western capitalism and Soviet Communism—that, they believed, is what made them "new."

Nixon was not entirely wrong when, in his typical fashion, he attributed the opposition to straightforward self-interest and selfishness. The students simply did not want to fight for their country—and he could point out that the demonstrations fell off after he stopped sending draftees to Vietnam. But then one had to explain why previous generations had willingly, even enthusiastically, gone off to do battle in World War I, World War II, and the Korean war while the generation opposing the Vietnam war did not. Those war supporters who followed the logic of their argument through were left complaining about a coddled and spoiled generation so different from what came to be known as the "Greatest Generation," a growing decadence, an America gone soft, accompanied by Spenglerian laments about the decline of the West. Nixon thought that modern education was undermining the national spirit. "The more a person is educated, he becomes brighter in the head and weaker in the spine," and he said he thanked God that there were still "uneducated people" around to support him and the war. They were "all that's left of the character of this nation."

Abraham Lincoln would have been "ruined" if he had had more education, Nixon said.

But the facts didn't fit such anti-intellectual and sentimental blather. The students in the streets were often the same ones who were participating in the civil rights movement, risking their lives in the cause of racial equality. Idealism was strong among them, as was bravery, decadence the catchword of an uncomprehending older and hostile generation reluctant to examine its own assumptions or to learn anything new. The protesters tended to be the most well-informed among their peers. If they were ruined by their educations, it wasn't because they had gone soft but because they were unwilling to be sent to an Asian death trap for the sake of a mission that had become meaningless with the demise of the Domino Theory. As a song popular with the students of the time put it, "And it's one, two, three, what are we fighting for? Don't ask me, I don't give a damn. Next stop is Vietnam."

Robert McNamara, no anti-intellectual like Nixon, was disconcerted to discover that the level of opposition to the war rose on campuses with the level of academic prestige. (In that sense, Nixon was right.) Graduating students at Amherst silently protested when their college awarded him an honorary degree in 1966 by wearing armbands, and McNamara, always the statistics maven, crunched the numbers as he looked out at the assemblage before him: "I counted the number and calculated the percentage of protesters in each of the four groups: graduates, cum laude graduates, magna cum laude graduates and summa cum laude graduates. To my consternation," he wrote, "the percentages rose with the levels of academic distinction." His own children opposed what had come to be called "McNamara's war," as did the children of many in Lyndon Johnson's cabinet. During the Nixon years, when he had ceased to be an architect of the war effort, a distraught McGeorge Bundy telephoned Kissinger to complain that he was unable to justify the war policy to his own son. A disgusted Kissinger told Bundy that he should tell the boy it was his father who had gotten us into this mess, and he angrily hung up.

All of the self-justifying explanations by the supporters of the war—selfishness, cowardice, decadence, ignorance, Communist sympathies—were excuses that failed to confront the basic challenge that the protesters (and Morgenthau too) were raising about the war, namely that the very reasons the United States had become involved in Vietnam, the Domino Theory and the doctrine of a monolithic Communism, were fundamentally false and had no application to the world as it actually existed. The real question to be answered is how "the kids" could have been right about this and the country's political leaders and opinion makers so very wrong.

Clearly, the students didn't have more information than the White House, the Pentagon, the State Department, and the CIA. They had no more knowledge of the internal dynamics of Vietnamese society than did the war's devisers. With no genuine knowledge about Vietnam, both hawks and doves were operating out of preconceptions, grounded in generational experiences and then applied to the facts at hand. In the case of the members of the Kennedy and Johnson administrations, that experience rested on the rise of Hitler, the ill-fated Munich agreement, the purges in the Soviet Union, the grim sacrifices of World War II, the Holocaust, the Soviet takeover of Eastern Europe, the Communist victory in China, the continuing tensions over Berlin that threatened a new world war, and the North Korean invasion of South Korea. The danger of totalitarianism, first fascist, then Communist, was very real to them, shaping the visions of dominoes and the policies that followed.

The students who were out in the streets in the late 1960s and early 1970s hadn't experienced any of that, but they had come of age when one of the fundamental tenets of the older generation had been thrown into question and then wholly discredited. The idea of a monolithic Communism could no longer be squared with the facts. Polycentrism, as Morgenthau said, was a more accurate description of the Communist world that they knew than an indomitable Red Menace on the march, and that reality undermined the arguments for American involvement in Vietnam. The dominoes would not be collapsing. Saigon might fall to the Communists, but so what? Staten Island remained safe.

Not totalitarianism but the refutation of the Domino Theory and the evident meaninglessness of the Vietnam war was the sixties generation's defining experience. Exactly when the divisions in the Communist camp became public and irrevocable was a matter for debate. Morgenthau had pointed to the independence of Communist Yugoslavia beginning in the late 1940s, but even if the example of Tito could be dismissed as, in Morgenthau's words, a "minor aberration," the Sino-Soviet split was undeniably an event of world-historical significance. It was already developing in the late 1950s. In 1960 Moscow cut off aid to China and called back thousands of technicians, and by 1962 American journalists were describing a Communist camp "in ferment." By 1965 a *New York Times* columnist was declaring that "today there are many different kinds of Communism," and by 1969 the world had changed so much that Morgenthau could write that a belief in monolithic Communism and, therefore, the Domino Theory had become "intellectually untenable." The younger generation, with immature, developing minds like blank slates, were quicker to respond to the new facts than were their elders, still locked in preconceptions from the past. Henry Kissinger said that it took a North Vietnamese diplomat to suggest to him that Russia and China might be useful in ending the war in Vietnam—and that was in 1969. The Nixon trip to China three years later might be called the official coup de grace to a Domino Theory that history had rendered obsolete. Kissinger observed that the new relationship with China fundamentally changed everything. And yet Americans were still fighting in Vietnam. If you were a young person of a questioning temperament and being called upon to risk your life in Vietnam, you were bound to ask your elders why.

Morgenthau had offered his own explanations several times over, but the protesting students had little inclination to pause and consider the lessons of *Politics Among Nations* and his other writings. There was a war to be opposed, not by carefully sifting through notions of national interest, balance of power, and the distortions of ideological thinking, but by taking a firm moral stand and sticking to it. The war was evil, and nothing more need be said about it. One could be against without explaining what one was for; negativity sufficed. Passion came to dictate politics, or as one protester said in the language of the time, the students were in "the morality bag," and a "morality bag" was the only tool that was necessary to understand foreign policy. The questioning of teach-ins had quickly given way to the certainties of demonstrations. In a situation of continuing and meaningless bloodshed "shock troops" were a necessary tool of opposition.

In a profile of Robert Kennedy, Morgenthau explained how emotion, even in the best of causes, could obscure reason and rationality, and what he said about Kennedy applied to the student demonstrators as well: "Robert Kennedy was not reflective but emotional," Morgenthau remarked. When he saw evil and suffering in the world, he felt he had to do something. "But since he was unaware of the ambiguity of moral judgments, he was also unaware of the moral and pragmatic ambiguity of the political act performed in emotional response to a moral judgment. His approach was morally fundamentalist and politically simplistic." Much like the student protesters, many of whom became Kennedy followers after he came to share their passion about the war. Moral fundamentalism and perfectionism were their credo. Emotion, not reflection, determined a policy of resistance that was no-policy. Except for a shared opposition to the Vietnam war, the stern, Nietzschean, hyperintellectual Morgenthau and the idealistic, impassioned students had almost nothing in common. Their intellectual premises barely overlapped; their mind-sets functioned in different universes. As Morgenthau had written in *Politics Among Nations*, "A man who was nothing but 'moral man' would be a fool." The students were "moral men" and proud of the fact. And then in 1968, as if to pound his point home, Morgenthau took a step that would have been incomprehensible to most of them. He came out in support of Richard Nixon for president.

He had two reasons. The first was the more immediate—he was choosing the candidate he thought more likely to extricate the United States from the mire of Vietnam. Neither Hubert Humphrey nor Richard Nixon was really qualified to be president of the United States, Morgenthau said, but Humphrey had a history that Nixon did not. As a senator, Humphrey had been one of the skeptics before the United States had plunged fully into the Vietnamese quagmire but, like so many members of Congress, had muted his doubts. And after he became vice president, he fell into line behind the strong-willed Johnson. His record of support for the administration's policies was there for all to see—the students who considered him a full-fledged member of the Cold War establishment and Morgenthau, too. Humphrey's efforts to distance himself from his own hawkish history during the 1968 campaign failed to convince him. "There has only been one Humphrey, wholeheartedly and passionately supporting the war in private as well as public." Morgenthau saw no prospect for a change of policy under a President Humphrey, whatever backpedaling candidate Humphrey engaged in. The man was an emotional politician—"warm-hearted, decent, idealistic, enthusiastic, uncritical"—and he remained "emotionally committed" to the Vietnam war.

Nixon had never said anything to give solace to the doves and protesters, but to Morgenthau he had an important quality that Humphrey lacked—cynicism. Morgenthau had no doubt who was the better man, and he observed that if he had to be stuck on a desert island with one of them, he would unhesitatingly choose Humphrey. By contrast, "Nixon would be capable of having me for dinner and making me thank him for the privilege." But choosing a president was not the same thing as choosing a dinner companion. Unlike Humphrey, Nixon was not emotionally committed to the war; he was not emotionally committed to anything except his own fortunes. With no personal responsibility for America's involvement in Vietnam, he could allow sheer political calculation to determine his policy, and what Morgenthau was counting on was that Nixon's cold-eyed opportunism would lead him to conclude that his best path was to engineer an American withdrawal. Ideals, morality, even truth, would only get in the way of a settlement, and fortunately Nixon was restricted by none of them. Besides, if things went wrong, he could always blame the Democrats for the war.

It wasn't the most heartening reason for a choice, but then Morgenthau had a larger concern and another reason for supporting Nixon. Like Leo Strauss, Hannah Arendt, and Henry Kissinger, Morgenthau worried about a democratic road to fascism, an American Weimar, and in 1968 he saw that threat embodied in the presidential candidacy of George Wallace, the racist demagogue, who was drawing support not only in his native, segregationist South but also in working-class districts of the North as well. In Morgenthau's view, Nixon stood the better chance than the liberal Humphrey of combating the Wallace phenomenon by pursuing conservative policies that undermined the fascist impulses then being unleashed. "Nixon's strength is Wallace's weakness."

After the election, the Wallace movement faded, but the war in Vietnam did not. During Nixon's first year in office, Morgenthau wrote very little about Vietnam and indeed not much more after that, nothing to match his output during the 1960s or the energy he expended opposing Lyndon Johnson's policies. But he did occasionally return to the fray, expressing disappointment with the Nixon White House, which now, of course, included his friend Henry Kissinger. To be sure, much had changed with the shift from Johnson to Nixon. In early 1970, under Kissinger's guidance, the administration issued a sweeping report on U.S. foreign policy that acknowledged the polycentric character of Communism, and Morgenthau took particular delight in the official observation that "the only times the Soviet Union has used the Red Army since World War II have been against its own allies—in East Germany in 1953, in Hungary in 1956 and in Czechoslovakia in 1968." One could hear Kissinger but also Morgenthau in those words.

Yet much also apparently remained the same. Unlike Johnson, Nixon was intent on reducing the American ground presence in Vietnam in a process that came to be called "Vietnamization," in which the South Vietnamese army would bear the brunt of the fighting with American support from the air. American casualties would be drastically reduced, which would have the additional benefit of taking the wind out of the protesters' sails. But to Morgenthau's dismay, he saw no change in the rationale for the war. All of Nixon's old arguments from the 1950s and 1960s were repeated, which, to Morgenthau, were "tantamount to the indefinite continuation of the war." In the aftermath of his electoral victory, Nixon had the opportunity to arrange a rapid American withdrawal, and he blew it. And in May 1970, Morgenthau declared, "The issue that since 1954 has pitted the United States against the Communists has always been simplicity itself: Who shall govern South Vietnam?"

Simplicity itself—and yet the fact was the war Nixon and Kissinger were fighting was not the same war Lyndon Johnson had fought, even if the weapons and tactics were the same. Morgenthau was wrong. Appearances deceived. Two Realpolitikers were now in charge of American foreign policy, with ideals, and even morality, far from the center of their thinking, and with the Domino Theory a dead letter. Slowly, inexorably, often ambiguously, the White House was moving in Morgenthau's direction. The opponents of the war remained frustrated and angry for four long, bitter, and divisive years, but they failed to see what was really happening, even if it was happening in slow motion, because it was happening in slow motion.

IN OCTOBER 1968, when Henry Kissinger was serving as a foreign policy adviser to Nelson Rockefeller, he and Morgenthau had a tense exchange of letters on the subject of Vietnam. Seeking the Republican presidential nomination, Rockefeller staked out a position on the war that had been molded by Kissinger. It called for an "honorable peace" to be achieved by a mutual withdrawal of North Vietnamese and American troops, allowing the South Vietnamese to settle the conflict by themselves and determine their own destiny. By now a veteran of the protest movement, with dozens of articles and speeches behind him, Morgenthau proclaimed the Rockefeller proposal unworkable. Kissinger took the criticism personally; he thought he deserved better from his colleague and mentor. In a "Dear Hans" letter, he wrote to say that "I found the tone and the content of your article extremely painful. We have been friends for long enough," Kissinger continued, "so that one should be able to assume that in writing about each other we should avoid the crudest interpretations that can be made." The Rockefeller (and Kissinger) proposal, he asserted, "would not be inconsistent with your own views," and in a phrase that left an opening for an entire regiment of Morgenthaus to march through, he declared, "as for myself, my record is clear."

In fact, his record was anything but clear, and when Morgenthau replied two weeks later, he called Kissinger out: "You have supported the war in public and lent your considerable prestige to it." But since it had become evident by 1968 that the war could not be won, the only question that remained was how to get out. "The real issue in South Vietnam is, who shall govern, the Communists or their opponents," and since Kissinger/ Rockefeller continued to support the legitimacy of the South Vietnamese government, they were trapped in the same dilemma that had swallowed up the Johnson administration, trying to uphold an ally that had neither genuine legitimacy nor the will to fight for itself, and one that the Communist enemy was determined to overthrow. Under such circumstances, Morgenthau said, "I conclude that your proposal is as unrealistic as all the others which have been advanced by the supporters of the war."

Kissinger's own response began by thanking Morgenthau and saying, "One is always more sensitive to attacks from friends." But the real point of his letter was to set the record straight: "I have never supported the war in public." Indeed, he said, after 1965 he had worked to end the conflict, and he believed his own views were not very different from Morgenthau's "though as a practical matter I might try to drag the process for a while because of the international repercussions." This was a disingenuous response. Kissinger's true position on Vietnam before he entered government in 1969 was too complicated, or too slippery, to be summed up by straightforward words like "support" or "oppose." He said one thing in public, another in private, and different things to different people. There is no denying his multifaced opportunism. By 1968, everyone knew where Morgenthau stood on the war. The same couldn't be said about Kissinger.

Through a steady stream of books and articles in the 1950s, Kissinger had built a reputation as a public intellectual with expertise on nuclear war and European issues. It would be generous to say his knowledge of Southeast Asia was limited—almost zero would be more like it. When John Kennedy entered the White House, Kissinger was taken on as a consultant, traveling down to Washington from Cambridge to advise on defense policy. It wasn't a happy arrangement. Kennedy failed to be charmed by Kissinger, who was frustrated by his lack of influence with the administration. He resigned after less than a year, complaining to friends that he was being treated as a "kibitzer."

Like just about every other Cold War intellectual, Kissinger was sympathetic to the American effort in Vietnam in the early 1960s, though again, like just about everyone else, he wasn't paying much attention. His active involvement with Vietnam only began after Johnson had become president. Henry Cabot Lodge was the U.S. ambassador to Vietnam, and through his connections to the Lodge family in Cambridge, Kissinger was named a "special consultant" to the embassy in Saigon. Over the next two years he made three trips to Vietnam, and their impact on his thinking seems to have been much the same as that of Morgenthau's trip in the mid-1950s—disillusionment. Everything that he saw troubled him.

Disillusionment began even before he first set foot in the country in October 1965. In preparation, Kissinger talked to a wide range of people in the administration, the military, and the CIA, and the German-Jewish intellectual, for whom conceptualization served as a prelude to action, was dismayed to discover that "there was no overall plan, no central concept." The Americans didn't know what they were doing. White House officials were optimistic about the war, members of the Pentagon were pessimistic, and top CIA officers were simply clueless. The head of the agency couldn't keep the names of the Vietnamese leaders straight and he knew as much about the country's Buddhist opposition as he did about the intricacies of Buddhist philosophy. The ignorance that Robert McNamara described at the top was apparent down through every branch of the American government, seeping into the brains of almost every person who had a hand in making policy.

What he heard and saw in Vietnam did little to improve Kissinger's mood, and if anything, his mounting doubts brought him closer to the skeptical journalists on the ground whose eyewitness accounts were rousing the furor of the Johnson White House than to the facile projections of commanders like General William Westmoreland, who were assuring him that victory was just around the corner. For Kissinger, victory was nowhere in sight and probably never would be. After three weeks in Vietnam, the best that he could report to the national security adviser McGeorge Bundy was that the situation was "less encouraging" than he had expected. Actually, he was more pessimistic than that, and two additional trips in 1966 only deepened his gloom. The South Vietnamese government, such as it was, was hopeless. Washington's program of pacification was "an illusion." Despite the administration's soothing words, he could see no light at the end of the tunnel.

Kissinger said as much in private. Acquaintances and students knew full well where he stood. He told one friend that "he considered the American involvement a blunder of the first magnitude and Johnson's military escalation a disaster." At his Harvard seminars, he said the only good news was that the United States was too powerful to suffer the kind of military defeat the French had experienced at Dien Bien Phu. But that was the end of the good news, and any hope for an American victory was seriously misguided. Hans Morgenthau knew where Kissinger stood, knew that the two of them were very close in their assessment of Washington's Vietnam policy, and knew that Kissinger's chosen word for the Vietnam adventure was "disaster." Morgenthau had heard Kissinger say so directly. But he also knew that Kissinger was unwilling to declare as much in public, instead presenting himself as a firm supporter of American intervention. There was one bright spot to Kissinger's dissembling, Morgenthau concluded in hindsight. Kissinger, he said, "was smart enough to anticipate the collapse of a policy whose unsoundness he did not doubt. By not championing it too ostentatiously when it was in its heyday, he avoided the necessity to dissociate himself too visibly from it when he was called upon to liquidate the openly interventionist aspects of it, thereby earning him a Nobel Peace Prize."

In December 1965, Kissinger joined with 189 other academics in signing a letter to the *New York Times* urging support for the administration and decrying the growing protests for prolonging the war. He said the same things in public debates and lectures. And in August 1966, when Morgenthau and Kissinger both contributed articles to *Look* magazine, Morgenthau made his now familiar arguments about the futility of the war while Kissinger said Vietnam was "a crucial test of American maturity" and that withdrawal was out of the question. Although he did acknowledge that negotiations would eventually have to take place, he said they would occur only after North Vietnam had become convinced that it couldn't win the war. Morgenthau was correct: Kissinger had lent his prestige to the war effort.

Yet that was hardly all that need be said. A man of many faces,

Kissinger, inside the Johnson White House, was a closet dove. One historian has counted up 2,000 occasions when the Johnson administration tried to get negotiations started with the North Vietnamese, but the numbers are deceiving. Compromise was never on Johnson's mind. What he understood by negotiations was that Hanoi should give up its war aim of conquering South Vietnam while Washington would achieve its war aim of assuring an independent South Vietnam. For Johnson, compromise meant heads I win, tails you lose. The North Vietnamese, of course, had the opposite point of view—which is why there was a war going on in the first place, or as Morgenthau repeatedly insisted, it always came down to the question of who would rule in South Vietnam. John Kennedy too had always opposed negotiations. The American policy under both Kennedy and Johnson was victory, nothing less. The dominoes could not be allowed to fall. For Dean Rusk, to enter into talks with Hanoi was to reward aggression. Even calling the war a stalemate "was enough to get one labeled a dove" in Johnson's mind and excluded from his inner circle. The same was true for foreign leaders. "As more and more of them came to oppose his Vietnam policy he looked for ways to avoid even speaking to them." McNamara reported that Johnson "never deviated" from his goal of winning the war, even when he ordered a bombing halt, and that he was backed up by the majority of his advisers. As one historian put it, "Through his last days in office, Johnson refused to give up on accomplishing his aims in Vietnam."

Enter Henry Kissinger. He never would have been sent to Vietnam in the first place if he had been a voice of the opposition like Morgenthau— shortly before the first of his trips, he wrote to McGeorge Bundy that he supported the war effort. But he returned a changed man. The conflict, he concluded, was essentially a civil war. The Vietcong had to have some sort of role in a final settlement. The only way out was through negotiations— Rusk's rhetoric about rewarding aggression notwithstanding. And so when he saw the possibility of opening up a line of communication to Hanoi, he grabbed it.

It was called the "Pennsylvania Initiative," and it arrived in June 1967 from an unlikely direction. Kissinger was in Paris for a disarmament conference when he met a leftist French microbiologist, Herbert Marcovich, and they agreed that Marcovich would travel to North Vietnam to discuss the possibility of a bombing halt as a prelude to serious negotiations. Accompanying Marcovich would be a United Nations official,

Raymond Aubrac, a personal friend of Ho Chi Minh. The whole thing had to be strictly unofficial, conducted by a private citizen like Kissinger and cloaked in the darkest secrecy, lest it appear that the United States was willing to make unreciprocated concessions to an avowed enemy.

Rusk was deeply skeptical about the entire undertaking, but McNamara, whose doubts about the war were increasing with every ineffectual bombing sortie, gave Kissinger the green light to pursue the connection. (McNamara, Kissinger says, "was desperate to end the war.") It was Kissinger's first exercise in backdoor diplomacy. Rusk thought the odds for success were 1 in 50; McNamara placed them closer to 1 in 10. Over the next few months, messages flew back and forth between Washington, Paris, and Hanoi, but by October it was clear that the initiative was going nowhere, even though Kissinger's authorized biographer Niall Ferguson reports that he had become so emotionally invested in making a success of the effort that he was suffering from "Stockholm syndrome avant la lettre." The two sides were simply too far apart in the mid-1960s to make any progress, though one undersecretary of state called the episode "the closest thing that we have yet had to establishing a dialogue with North Vietnam." The always doubtful, instinctively vulgar Johnson had warned Kissinger that "if it doesn't work, I'm going to come up to Cambridge and cut your balls off." Though Pennsylvania failed, Kissinger survived the experience physically intact. But mentally not so much. He lost whatever confidence he may have had in the Johnson White House and was bitter. In December 1967, he told his friend, the dovish Arthur Schlesinger Jr., that "LBJ's resistance to negotiation verges on a sort of madness"; Schlesinger reported that "I h my feels that practically anyone would be better than Johnson."

Kissinger was true to his word, and during the 1968 presidential contest, after his favorite, Nelson Rockefeller, failed to win the Republican nomination, he covered all his bases. In a well-known and still controversial episode, he passed along information to the Nixon people about the Johnson administration's last, and futile, efforts at negotiations with the North Vietnamese; he also offered to provide the Hubert Humphrey camp with the Rockefeller campaign's files on Richard Nixon. "Six days a week I'm for Hubert," he told a friend, "but on the seventh day I think they're both awful." Like Morgenthau, he reluctantly voted for Nixon—or so he says. In any case, Kissinger's political double-dealing contributed to his winning the trust of the pathologically untrusting Nixon and landing the position of national security adviser with the new administration. Humphrey later said that if he had won the presidency he too would have appointed Kissinger national security adviser, suggesting two things: first, that Kissinger's deviousness had paid off; second, that America's Vietnam policy would not have been very different if Humphrey had been in the White House instead of Nixon.

WHAT WAS THAT POLICY? Like the elusive Kissinger himself, it's not easy to pin down, despite what people at the time, both supporters and opponents of the war, might have believed. Kissinger says it took about a year before the administration had developed a coherent strategy. But there can be no doubt that from the moment Nixon and Kissinger took power, they were determined to end the war. This, by itself, was a change from Johnson, who, up to the last days of his presidency, was looking for something he could call "victory." The historian Robert Dallek has described the difference as that between seeking a "victorious" peace and seeking an "honorable" one. Nixon himself declared that he was engaged in a "war for peace," hardly the same thing as a war for victory.

Like all fresh arrivals to the White House, Nixon and Kissinger started out in an optimistic frame of mind (unusual enough for both of these dour paranoics). In March 1969, H. R. Haldeman recorded in his diary that Nixon "stated flatly that war will be over by next year," but after all the hardships and sacrifices of the past several years, Nixon recognized that a certain amount of dissembling would be necessary to achieve a withdrawal. "We have to take the public position that outlook is tough, etc., while we negotiate in private." Kissinger, too, was "very optimistic." Nixon believed a deal could be reached by the end of the year. And so did Kissinger. "Give us six months," he told a visiting group of pacifist Quakers that first year, "and if we haven't ended the war by then, you can come back and tear down the White House fence."

It's possible to find statements on the White House tapes that seem to contradict this spirit of negotiation and withdrawal and to conclude that Nixon was of at least two minds on the subject. There seems little reason to doubt that if Nixon felt he could win the war, he would have tried. The taping system wasn't installed until February 16, 1971, after Nixon and Kissinger's initial wave of optimism had begun to fade, and at that time Nixon could be heard to say—in a Johnsonian vein—"we're not going to lose this war." And a year later: "There's one determination I've made: we're not going to lose out there. . . . We have to win it." But at other times, in exchanges with Kissinger, Nixon was clear that by "winning," he didn't mean what Johnson had meant, not victory and a secure South Vietnam but a reasonable, "honorable" path to withdrawal. On February 18, 1971, Kissinger proposed a "game plan" of meeting with Le Duc Tho, the North Vietnamese negotiator, and saying to him: "Look, we're willing to give you a fixed deadline of total withdrawal next year for the release of all prisoners and a cease-fire." Nixon replied, "We should be able to get it." That's not an exchange between two men determined to guarantee an independent South Vietnam.

One of the first moves Nixon and Kissinger made upon entering office was to shift the terms under which the United States was willing to negotiate a withdrawal. Johnson had always insisted that the North Vietnamese had to pull their troops out of the south before America would do the same. As a negotiating position, this was a nonstarter, a call for surrender. Hanoi would never agree. In the first step to getting talks started, Nixon declared in May 1969 that he was willing to accept a mutual withdrawal—Hanoi would not have to go first. This position was still unacceptable to the North Vietnamese, but it represented movement on the part of the Americans, a signal that Nixon's policy was not the same as Johnson's. Kissinger called the new stand "a major change in the American negotiating position."

But the most obvious difference between Johnson and Nixon concerned the policy called "Vietnamization." Johnson's policy had been one of steady escalation—200,000 troops by the end of 1965, 400,000 in 1966, 500,000 in 1967, to a level of about 550,000 in 1968, and with his generals calling for an additional 200,000 troops by mid-1968. (That was where a thoroughly demoralized Johnson drew the line.) Nixon, by contrast, chose a path of determined de-escalation: 480,000 American troops by the end of 1969, 280,000 in 1970, and 140,000 in 1971. By 1972 only 90,000 U.S. troops remained in Vietnam, and even that last figure is deceptively high. When the North Vietnamese launched a major offensive in March 1972, only 6,000 of the remaining Americans were combat ready. The overwhelming bulk of the ground fighting had been turned over to the South Vietnamese, with the United States supplying support from the air. This was Vietnamization, which had originally been called "de-Americanization" before being given a more positive spin so that it didn't appear that the

Americans were simply pulling out. As Gelb and Betts summed up Washington's position, "After March 1968 American policy on Vietnam was all a retrograde operation, to use the military euphemism for retreat, punctuated only by Nixon's temporary re-escalations in 1970 and 1972."

But there were problems with Vietnamization. Did the South Vietnamese army really have the ability to stand up to the North Vietnamese and the Vietcong, even with American bombs falling from the sky? No one in Washington could really be sure, and a great deal of wishful thinking went into Nixon's policy of de-escalation. The South Vietnamese were still proving themselves incompetent. "We've given them everything," Nixon complained in 1971. "I mean, they've fouled everything up." All that the Americans were left with was intensified bombing. "I don't know what we can do. We don't have any cards there, Henry, nothing but the damn air force." And even the "damn air force" had its limits: "Saying we'll stay another five years with air power and all the rest, it just doesn't go. It won't wash." Vietnamization consisted literally of an air force wing and a White House prayer.

But there was another problem as well—one that Kissinger grasped immediately. With his eye on public opinion polls, Nixon the politician, encouraged by his equally political secretary of defense, Melvin Laird, was pursuing de-escalation as a way of dampening domestic dissent and healing the country's wounds. His decision to stop sending draftees to Vietnam was made for the same reason. But Kissinger, the apolitical diplomat, believed Vietnamization was cutting his legs out from under him. If the aim was to achieve an American withdrawal through negotiation yet the United States was withdrawing while negotiations were going on, what was there to negotiate about? As Kissinger later wrote, "The demand for mutual withdrawal grew hollow as the unilateral withdrawal accelerated." And on the tapes one can hear him telling Nixon in early 1971 that after another year or so, any offer to withdraw troops "doesn't make any difference." Le Duc Tho, Kissinger's counterpart at the Paris peace talks and no fool, saw the same thing Kissinger did and said as much. "Before," he observed, "there were over a million U.S. and puppet troops and you failed. How can you succeed when you let the puppet troops do the fighting? Now, with only U.S. support, how can you win?" Kissinger had no answer. There was no answer.

In effect, Vietnamization put Nixon and Kissinger in a race against time ("race" was Kissinger's own word for the situation they found themselves in), giving them only so many months in which a credible American military threat might force the North Vietnamese to the negotiating table. And the race contained its own paradox: as the Americans drew down their land troops, they expanded their military efforts in other ways to bring pressure on Hanoi—or as Nixon told Haldeman, it was necessary to "escalate to accelerate our withdrawal." In April 1969, the United States began secretly bombing North Vietnamese sanctuaries in Cambodia, a step that Johnson, for all his escalatory instincts, had never taken. This was followed in the spring of 1970, when American troops were still available, by an actual invasion of Cambodia. A botched invasion of Laos, dependent on the unreliable South Vietnamese forces, followed.

To the White House, this "war for peace" may have been part of its effort to reach a negotiated settlement, but to the protesters on the outside, the Nixon-Kissinger policy looked like more of the same old thing, Lyndon Johnson redivivus. The war was simply going on and on and, worse, it was even being expanded to other countries. Vietnamization brought the administration no credit. The result was mounting protests, culminating in the deaths of four students at Kent State and two at Jackson State following the Cambodian incursion. Nixon and Kissinger may have been striking out on a new path in Vietnam, but they were operating with paradoxes and nuances impossible for people on the outside to perceive. Even many of those inside government didn't understand. After the Cambodian invasion, about 200 State Department employees, including 50 Foreign Service officers, signed a protest petition. (Nixon's impulse was to fire them all.) Discontent to expanding the war boiled up among Kissinger's own staff as well, and several of them resigned in anger.

As the personification of the paradox of withdrawal through escalation, Kissinger, the secret dove of the Johnson administration, metamorphosed into a very public hawk under Nixon, though what hadn't changed was Kissinger's long-term goal of finding an exit path for America. As he saw it, there was no reason for Hanoi to enter into talks if they could get what they wanted without concessions. Unless they felt the pain of America's military might, they could simply wait out the Vietnamization process. As desperate as ever for negotiations, Kissinger called for stepped-up activities that went beyond anything Nixon himself was willing to contemplate (at least in those early months). He proposed mining North Vietnam's harbors and the bombing of Hanoi along with other cities. He was looking for "savage, punishing blows" that would break the will of what he called "a fourth-rate power." And no one in the White House was more opposed to troop withdrawals than Kissinger. Nixon described him as "very hard-line at that point," and Haldeman said "we knew Henry as the 'hawk of hawks' in the Oval Office."

But military pressure was only one part of the new strategy. Global diplomacy, too, had an important role to play, as Nixon and Kissinger turned first to Russia and later to China for assistance in helping them out of the quagmire. Secret channels to the Kremlin that sidestepped the State Department, followed by a spectacular trip to Beijing and a widely celebrated Moscow summit, were employed alongside the American air force. "The objective of all these things," Nixon said, "is to get out." In the heyday of the Domino Theory, such moves would have been unthinkable, since all of North Vietnam's actions were understood as being directed from Moscow, and one Communist was no different from any other Communist. But by the time Nixon and Kissinger entered the White House, with the theory, in Morgenthau's words, "intellectually untenable," Nixon had his own, Nixonian way of refuting the notion of monolithic Communism. In the privacy of the Oval Office he said, "No Communist trusts another Communist." He had moved far from dominoes and the body-snatcher image of brain-dead totalitarian automatons.

And once the idea of a monolithic Communism was discarded, what sounder policy could there be for two Realpolitikers than to play the feuding Communists off against one another? The contacts with Russia and China were grounded on, or at least coincided with, Morgenthau's concept of polycentrism and the idea that even among Communists, considerations of national interest took precedence over any avowed ideology. Give the Russians and the Chinese reasons to cooperate on Vietnam and Marxist affiliations would go to hell. It was all a slow process, secret and time-consuming, with two steps forward and one step back, and because it was impossible to explain openly in a way that wasn't self-defeating, it was conducted outside the spotlight of public awareness, where the only things that could be seen were the explosions of American bombs and the lightning flashes of napalm, bringing with them more American casualties and more dead Vietnamese. Under the circumstances, how long could Nixon and Kissinger wait for their policy to take effect before it all crumbled under its own weight?

If bombing and diplomacy were aimed at putting pressure on the North Vietnamese, Nixon and Kissinger were facing their own kind of pressure.

Domestic divisions were bringing the country to the verge of a "nervous breakdown," a "near civil war." The occupants in the White House could see the same thing that the protesters saw—that the raison d'etre for the war, the Domino Theory, had evaporated, and so what was left but to get out? Yet even though Nixon and Kissinger had started out eager for a settlement, negotiations required the cooperation of both sides, and as long as the rigid Leninists of North Vietnam had a hope for a military victory and the humiliation of the United States, they were hanging tough. As the weeks became months and the months became years, the administration's initial hopefulness and optimism turned into frustration, then desperation. Kissinger indulged in pipe dreams, suggesting "a meeting" with South Vietnamese President Nguyen Van Thieu "in which Thieu asks us to end our combat role." Nixon was more inclined to temper tantrums: "we'll bomb the goddamn North like it's never been bombed," even if that meant the United States would "go up in flames."

What was particularly galling to them was that their own policy of pursuing negotiations to achieve an American withdrawal had been the doves' position in the 1960s, when Johnson was still intent on "victory." George Ball had urged talks toward a political solution; so had William Fulbright. Kissinger was right to complain that the opponents of the war were moving the goalposts. "It used to be considered the height of enlightenment to believe that negotiations were a useful way of ending the war," he said. "Today, it is considered by many the height of obtuseness to believe that negotiations can still be a means of ending the war." Now that Washington's official policy was negotiations, the protesters had upped their demand to immediate withdrawal, the same position as that of the North Vietnamese, and that was something that Nixon and Kissinger absolutely refused to entertain. "The foreign policy of the United States will not be viable if we're run out of Vietnam," Nixon said. "That's all there is to it."

Instead, along with their military and diplomatic moves, Nixon and Kissinger tried to sweeten the deal for Hanoi. Secret negotiations began in Paris in February 1970, with Washington already on record favoring a mutual withdrawal, the Rockefeller position of two years before and a step away from Johnson's demand that the North Vietnamese withdraw first. In May, Nixon declared that he was ready to accept a cease-fire in place, even without a North Vietnamese withdrawal. Militarily, the concession was almost meaningless—how do you enforce a cease-fire in what was to a very large degree a guerrilla war? But diplomatically, it was an enormous

step toward the North Vietnamese position, and it became the basis for
the settlement that was eventually arrived at in 1972–73. "It proved to be,"
Kissinger said, "a decision of profound long-term consequence." Still, the
North Vietnamese refused to deal.

One sticking point was the issue of American prisoners of war (POWs).
No American president, not even a President McGovern, would have been
able to leave Vietnam without the release of the several hundred men being
held captive by the Communists. No issue touched the American people
more emotionally than this one. No issue touched Richard Nixon more
emotionally. "If those prisoners are not back by the time of the election,"
he exclaimed in November 1971, "win, lose or draw, we will bomb the
bejesus out of them. . . . To hell with history." At first, the North Vietnamese negotiators took the position that they would not make any guarantees; the most they were willing to do was discuss the issue. The prisoners
were a useful bargaining chip: a way of getting South Vietnam to release
its political prisoners, for example, or inducing the United States to provide reparations once a settlement was reached. But in May 1971, they
told Kissinger that the prisoners would be released when the Americans
withdrew. It was another breakthrough. Inch by inch, step by step, the two
sides were moving toward each other, even as the death tolls mounted.

In truth, as they approached their endgame only one issue separated
the negotiators, but it was agonizing and seemingly insurmountable. The
Americans continued to support the South Vietnamese government of
Nguyen Van Thieu; after so many years of sacrifice and blood, they simply
could not countenance undermining an ally who had loyally fought by
their side. The North Vietnamese demanded nothing less than a callous
sellout; peace was not imaginable for them until Thieu was gone—and
if Washington was unwilling to overthrow him publicly, or rig an election to get rid of him, there was always the alternative of assassination.
The Americans, after all, had been complicit in the assassination of Diem.
Kissinger was unyielding on all of these suggestions. "We want to end
the war," he told Le Duc Tho. "We do not want to stand in the way of the
people of South Vietnam. We are not permanent enemies of Vietnam. But
you must not expect us to do impossible things." Proposals for a coalition
government were put forward but went nowhere. Someone ultimately had
to be in charge of any coalition and to Hanoi that meant the Communists,
not Thieu. From the middle of 1971 through the first months of 1972,
peace was, in Kissinger's words, "as far away as ever."

It took pain, violence, desperation, and exhaustion to move the two antagonists from stalemate in 1971 to agreement in late 1972 and early 1973. On the North Vietnamese side, Hanoi tried one more time to achieve a military victory with a spring offensive in 1972. It was, as Kissinger put it, a "last throw of the dice," and it ended ignominiously. The United States responded with massive bombing and the mining of North Vietnam's harbors, while the often hapless South Vietnamese army, with the assistance of American air support, this time managed to hold its own on the battlefield as the North Vietnamese overreached militarily. Meanwhile, Hanoi's two Communist allies, China and the Soviet Union, increasingly concerned about their expanded working relationships with Washington and warily eying each other, were pressing for a settlement. As Kissinger gleefully reported, "We were in the process of separating Hanoi from its allies." For the two major Communist powers, Vietnam was no longer a prize of the Cold War but an "irritant" (to use Kissinger's word) or "a collateral issue" (in Nixon's language), standing in the way of their true national interests. Ever more isolated and militarily drained, the North Vietnamese came to the Paris talks following their failed spring offensive in a much softer mood. Now Le Duc Tho, Kissinger said, "was all conciliation," and Hanoi's long-standing demand for an unconditional American withdrawal was abandoned. Maybe there really was light at the end of the tunnel this time.

Getting there required a change in the American outlook as well. With divisions in the country suppurating, with congressional opposition to any U.S. involvement in Vietnam rising to a crescendo, and with the American military presence on the ground reduced to a mere shadow of ineffectuality, Nixon and Kissinger had few options available. They were trapped in a vise; the noose was tightening. And added to all this was a new geopolitical reality. Just as the Russians and Chinese were pressuring their North Vietnamese allies to settle in order to enhance their own relations with the United States, similarly, the White House now had to factor into any Vietnam policy its impact on Moscow and Beijing. There was a larger picture to be taken into account that didn't fit the old Cold War paradigm. "Vietnam poisons our relations with the Soviet [sic] and it poisons our relations with the Chinese," Nixon told Kissinger. They had to ask themselves if reaching out to the Russians and Chinese mattered more than preserving a Thieu government that was irrelevant in the larger geopolitical picture.

By April 1972, Nixon had begun to think the unthinkable. "If we can find a graceful way to let Thieu down the tubes, then maybe we'll first have to die and live to fight another day." He wasn't quite there yet: "There's no graceful way to let him go. . . . How the Christ can you do it?" But the seed had been planted, and now it was taking root. In May, Nixon said, "If we could survive past the election, Henry . . . and then Vietnam goes down the tubes, it really doesn't make any difference," except for the happy result that then they would be free to "conduct a sensible foreign policy with the Russians and the Chinese." And a few months after that a Nixon who was approaching the end of his tether declared that Thieu had "to realize that this war has got to stop. I mean, that's all there is to it." According to Haldeman, Nixon was "obviously facing the very real possibility now that we have had it in Vietnam."

THE TURNING POINT for the negotiations came in September, the breakthrough a few weeks later. On September 15, Le Duc Tho suggested that he and Kissinger simply agree to a termination date for the war, and the two negotiators settled on a deadline of October 15. Bulldozing through past disagreements, they hammered out most of the details for a settlement in early October, including provisions for an American troop withdrawal, a renewal of military aid to South Vietnam, an end to North Vietnamese infiltration, and a return of U.S. prisoners of war. On the fraught issue of the future of the South Vietnamese government, they agreed to set up an "administration of national concord" in which each side, the Saigon regime and the Communist insurgents, would hold a veto, thereby preserving the authority of the Saigon government at least until all the Americans had left. What would happen in the likely event that the two parts of the new "administration" failed to agree was not specified, and it was a question that never had to be answered as the administration of national concord never actually met. Critics of the pact later called it a sellout and a fig leaf for an American defeat. It didn't matter. Kissinger had persuaded himself that his years of mental toil and psychological pain had at last paid off. During a recess in the sessions, he could barely hold back his emotions, declaring to an aide, "We have done it." No moment in his long career, he said, moved him so deeply.

When Kissinger returned to Washington on October 12, his enthusiasm could not be contained. Nixon had his doubts about reaching any kind of agreement before the November presidential election, but his national security adviser's excitement overcame his reluctance. Knowing his man, Kissinger trotted out an argument that Nixon must have found irresistible. "You got three out of three, Mr. President," meaning the opening to China, the summit with the Soviets, and now a peace agreement ending the Vietnam war. Nixon broke out the best wine in the White House for a toast.

Others also had their doubts, but there was no slowing Kissinger down. Haldeman said that Kissinger had become "obsessed," and Alexander Haig, then the deputy national security adviser, told Nixon that Kissinger was ignoring all the question marks in his personal drive for peace. "I thought he lost touch with reality." This was not the "hawk of hawks" they thought they knew but the closet dove of the 1967 Pennsylvania Initiative, pushing a skeptical president to end a war that could never be won. Nixon joked with Kissinger, saying, "You're so prejudiced to the peace camp that I can't trust you," except it was no joke. Kissinger was tripping, exhibiting Stockholm syndrome all over again. The worst came on October 26, when at his first public press conference he jubilantly declared to an equally jubilant American public, "Peace is at hand."

Peace was not at hand. Kissinger's very public statement looked foolish in retrospect, and he was never allowed to forget it. The chief roadblock to a settlement turned out to be America's South Vietnamese ally Nguyen Van Thieu, who saw betrayal in the promise of an American withdrawal and the jerry-built administration of national concord. When Kissinger traveled to Saigon in an effort to sell the deal, Thieu didn't want to hear about it; all he could think was "I wanted to punch Kissinger in the mouth." In a throwback to Lyndon Johnson, Thieu demanded that North Vietnam pull back all its forces from the south, even though Nixon and Kissinger had given up on that condition long ago. Thieu had not pressed the point before because he had never expected the Americans and North Vietnamese to reach an agreement. Now that a settlement was in sight, he balked, very publicly and very angrily.

The warning signs had been there all along, but Kissinger, caught up in a diplomatic rapture, had made the choice to ignore them, though "choice" may not be the right word for his exuberant mental state. After four agonizing years (more if you include the Johnson period), he saw the glow of peace shimmering before him, and he galloped toward it, blind to any obstacles in his path. Nixon and Haig had warned him that Thieu might be a problem, but he didn't hear them. "I was determined to do my utmost to preserve the prospect of peace against the passions that would soon descend on us."

In his published reminiscence of the war, Kissinger professed sympathy for Thieu's predicament. He claimed that he understood that while the U.S. goal at that point was withdrawal with honor, for the South Vietnamese it was sheer survival, "a matter of life and death," and "they simply could not imagine how they would be better off without America." In private, however, Kissinger was vituperative, nearly crazed as he watched his peace agreement crumble. "Thieu is an unmitigated, selfish, psychopathic son of a bitch," he raged in the Oval Office. "He has to be insane." And as Nixon began pulling back his support in the face of Thieu's intransigence, Kissinger was left feeling isolated, his paranoia erupting into spasms of suspicion and self-doubt. "I began to be nagged by the perhaps unworthy notion that I was being set up as the fall guy in case anything went wrong." The student of Morgenthau who had learned that diplomats were often unsung and unappreciated in their own time, the scholar of the Napoleonic wars who had traced Castlereagh's tragic fate as his countrymen turned against him, was coming to know the loneliness of the statesman. "I'm uniting Vietnam," he said, and "both sides are screaming at me." Meanwhile, no one in the White House had his back. "Failure in Washington requires a sacrificial offering. I was the logical candidate."

For "insane" or not, the truth was that Thieu had the White House boxed in. The United States simply could not sign a peace accord over the objections of the Saigon government without appearing to abandon an ally, a prospect that was neither acceptable nor "honorable." But neither could it give up the promise of peace now that hope had been raised around the world. Already on edge, Nixon declared himself "fed up" with Thieu and contemplated reaching a bilateral agreement with Hanoi over Thieu's head once he had won reelection. "I don't give a goddamn what he accepts." After the new year, "It is prisoners for withdrawal." Still, a possibility to square the circle remained. If the North Vietnamese could be persuaded to make a few additional concessions to save Thieu's face, that would be the best of all possible worlds. That was something, however, requiring a return to war.

There was no more cold-blooded decision taken during the entire Vietnam war than the one to use military force against North Vietnam at the end of 1972, after Nixon was overwhelmingly returned to the White

House. It has gone down in history as the "Christmas bombing." Those foreign policy journalists looking to condemn Nixon and Kissinger for cynicism and inhumanity will find just the material they want in the Oval Office conversations that took place in the days before the bombing began, as Nixon and Kissinger plotted how to make a case for a new escalation that they didn't really believe in. They could taste peace, it was so near. Their problem was how to bring Thieu on board without appearing to force him into an unwilling acceptance, which meant they needed changes, however insignificant, to the October accord so that he could say his objections had been met. "Basically, we can't just go to Saigon with nothing," Nixon said. Kissinger agreed. It would undermine Thieu.

Impatient with all the dithering in Washington and Saigon, Hanoi began hardening its negotiating position, and that was all the opening Nixon and Kissinger needed. Even though by their own calculation, Thieu represented "80 percent" of their problem, that was something "we cannot say." Instead, the onus for blocking a deal had to be directed at North Vietnam, which would be made to pay a severe price. "I had come to the reluctant conclusion that we've got to put it to them in Hanoi, painful as it is," Kissinger told Nixon on December 14.

Bombing on a scale that had not been seen since World War II began four days later, continuing until December 30 as outrage spread around the world. The columnist James Reston called it "war by tantrum." Another columnist, Anthony Lewis, said it constituted a war crime. Still others reached for analogies with the Nazis. For all that and for all of the cynicism contained in the decision to bomb, the fact is that the cold-blooded policy worked: the North Vietnamese returned to the negotiating table ready to make concessions. Victory, after all, seemed very close to them, so that the pain they were enduring was a minor matter if one was willing to think in the long term—and Hanoi was much better at thinking in the long term than Washington. Talks resumed on January 7, and a new agreement was reached less than a week later. As for Thieu, whether he was impressed with the new show of American force, swayed by Nixon's secret promises of continuing support (as well as by Nixon's threats of abandonment), or understood that he had played out his string as far as it would go, he finally went along. The changes between the October and January pacts were insignificant, little more than cosmetic. Kissinger later said he would have happily accepted the October deal without the brutal Christmas bombing. But whatever the case, peace was now truly at hand, at least for the United States—and to an exhausted American public, that was all that mattered. When South Vietnam fell to the Communists two years later, in a precise fulfillment of all Thieu's fears, almost no one in the United States cared, with the notable exception of Henry Kissinger.

THE CHRISTMAS BOMBING can be seen as a microcosm of the entire Vietnam war—incredible violence unleashed by the United States for a questionable cause. Over a 12-day period, American planes dropped over 42,000 bombs on the North Vietnamese, killing more than 1,600 civilians. The sheer weight of the bombs—more than 36,000 tons—was more than the tonnage of bombs dropped between the years 1969 and 1971. Yet, without the Domino Theory, the war lacked a raison d'etre. In effect, after 1969 the United States was fighting in Vietnam because the United States was fighting in Vietnam, hardly the most inspiring rallying cry for the men being asked to do that fighting. George Herring detailed how American troops responded once they had lost their sense of purpose. "Many GIs became much more reluctant to put their lives on the line. Discipline broke down in some units, with enlisted personnel simply refusing to obey their officer's orders." Drug use exploded, racial tensions escalated, and "fragging," the assassination of officers by their own men, was becoming almost a daily occurrence. "I need to get this Army home to save it," wailed General Creighton Abrams, the commander of U.S. forces in Vietnam.

In a "damage assessment," Kissinger biographer Walter Isaacson added up the total costs of the war: 58,022 Americans dead, with 20,552 killed during the Nixon-Kissinger years; 924,048 Communist soldiers and 185,528 South Vietnamese soldiers killed, statistics that don't include the vast, uncounted millions of civilians who lost their lives. Isaacson concludes that "it is hard to argue" that the war was worth the costs, not only the human costs but the moral and spiritual ones as well. The country has never really recovered. The scars remain to this day. "In retrospect," he writes, "a wiser alternative would have been simply to announce in 1969 that the U.S. felt it had honored its commitment, that it was now planning to withdraw by a fixed date, and that it would not try to negotiate on behalf of Saigon." The costs, as Isaacson writes, are undeniable. It's an attractive argument and one that has been made repeatedly over the years. But was this "wiser alternative" possible for Nixon and Kissinger, or indeed for anyone else who might have occupied the Oval Office? There would have been costs involved in simply pulling out, both domestic and international ones, and they could have been severe. The problem is that, unlike body counts, there is no way of measuring them. All that one can do is engage in hypothetical thinking.

Isaacson's retrospective conclusion involves stepping outside of history. Certainly, if we could go back in time, to 1964, when Lyndon Johnson was secretly planning to deepen America's involvement in Vietnam, or 1965, when the first serious escalation began, we would want to shout at him: "Don't do it! Listen to what Hans Morgenthau is saying!" But to travel back to 1969 is to encounter a very different situation. "Don't continue the war! Get out of Vietnam!" we exclaim, sounding like the protesters of that era. "That's exactly what we're trying to do," Nixon and Kissinger could legitimately reply. By the time they began formulating policy, the issue was no longer war or no war, withdrawal or no withdrawal. That question had been all but settled. Except for some unregenerate hawks (and admittedly there were many of those in the Pentagon and elsewhere, though not in the Oval Office), withdrawal was understood to be the correct, the necessary policy. The problem was *how to* withdraw. The loss of U.S. credibility, the damage to American prestige, or the possible political backlash at home were not issues that concerned the protesters, but they were considerations that no American president could ignore.

As early as 1966, Senator George Aiken of Vermont had suggested that Washington should simply "declare the United States the winner and begin de-escalation," and once the peace agreement was signed, he could say: "What we got was essentially what I recommended six years ago—we said we had won, and we got out." His was a genteel version of the students' demand for immediate withdrawal. But it wasn't a policy, only a cry of frustration. Policy involves seeing a problem in all its dimensions, examining the pros and cons of different strategies (something neither Kennedy nor Johnson did), trying to estimate the consequences of any given decision (again a point neglected by Kennedy and Johnson), standing in the immediate present with no illusions or preconceived formulas, and trying to calculate the best path to follow, while taking into account Morgenthau's admonition that in foreign policy, there are no good choices, only less bad ones. "It was rhetorically easy to speak of an abrupt unilateral withdrawal," Kissinger wrote, but as a practical matter it was "nearly impossible to accomplish." There were several reasons Nixon and Kissinger rejected an immediate withdrawal, some of greater weight than others, some of greater merit than others. They all blended together, but broadly speaking, they can be divided into four categories: the military, the political, the ethical, and the strategic.

The military reason was the least of their concerns but one that could not merely be dismissed. If the United States made too precipitous a withdrawal, there was a genuine possibility that the South Vietnamese army, feeling abandoned and betrayed, would turn its guns on the departing Americans, a spectacle that would not only cost American lives but also do serious damage to the country's image both at home and abroad. Kissinger raised the prospect shortly after Nixon took power, when Nixon had suggested, to his astonishment, that Washington wasn't "wedded" to Thieu. Without Thieu, Kissinger foresaw the irretrievable collapse of the South Vietnamese government, which "will result in South Vietnamese troops fighting us." Kissinger returned to the point three years later, when he was worried about the 60,000 Americans still remaining in Vietnam. If the United States pulled the plug too quickly, "You could get some of these commanders turning on Americans" if only to prove to the victorious Communists that they had been anti-American all along.

The notion wasn't a figment of Kissinger's imagination. In the last days of the war, as the North Vietnamese were closing in on Saigon, CIA operatives on the ground were receiving reports "indicating that the Army might turn against us," and at least one South Vietnamese major general warned of precisely that possibility. The sense of danger from a popular and military backlash was "almost palpable" among those still in Vietnam. It didn't happen. Shots may have been fired, but in the chaos and *sauve qui peut* atmosphere of South Vietnam's last days, decision makers in Washington never had to deal with a situation of departing Americans in full battle against their former allies as they made their way to the boats and helicopters. The situation would certainly have been different if the United States had precipitously tried to withdraw half a million troops over several months in 1969. But this military concern had to be an element in any plans for a withdrawal though it was not something the antiwar protesters gave any thought to.

The political aspect meant taking into account the public's response to a rapid American withdrawal, as not everyone favored a quick retreat, far from it. At the start of the war, in 1965, there was broad support for Johnson's escalation, reinforced by rally-round-the-flag enthusiasm whenever he was thought to be taking decisive action against the Communists. Nixon experienced the same bumps in popularity when he was seen as acting aggressively. The protesting students were not only a minority among Americans but also a minority among students. Through most of 1967, a majority of Americans backed the war, and less than a third favored withdrawal. Johnson, who knew nothing if not how to read polls, proclaimed that "we are doing right" in the eyes of most citizens. Continued violence, loss of life, and indecisive results eroded that support, most notably after the Tet offensive in early 1968 raised questions about the effectiveness of the U.S. effort. But even as the numbers in opposition rose, most Americans revealed themselves to be ambivalent, even incoherent, in their views. Polls could take decision makers only so far because what the American people said they believed did not add up to a policy. By the end of 1967, the war had become widely unpopular, yet an "overwhelming majority" continued to oppose any withdrawal that suggested defeat.

The New Hampshire presidential primary of March 12, 1968, seemed to mark a transformative moment in the public's opinion of the war. The dovish Minnesota senator Eugene McCarthy won 42 percent of the vote, in what was widely considered a repudiation of the war, and it pointed the way to Johnson's decision not to seek reelection. But opposition to Johnson's war policy came in two forms, those who believed the United States should reduce its role in Vietnam and those who wanted to expand it. As it turned out, a larger percentage of the McCarthy vote consisted of hawks than doves, many of whom went on to vote for George Wallace in November. Opposition was often not what it seemed, though one fact remained certain: simple withdrawal from Vietnam will never a popular position. "Even as late as the end of 1968," Gelb and Betts write, "the bulk of the American people still wanted to avoid losing in Vietnam," and the numbers didn't change much in the Nixon years. In September 1972, a Harris poll reported that a majority of Americans favored the Nixon bombing policy while a plurality (47 percent to 35 percent) opposed forming a South Vietnam government that included Communists. And in the most important poll of all, the 1972 presidential election, the voters resoundingly rejected the America-come-home message of George McGovern. The American people may have wanted to get out of Vietnam, but they wanted to get out on their own terms, however unrealistic. Even in 1990, more than a decade after the war ended, a *Time* magazine poll found that 57 percent thought the United States should never have gotten involved in Vietnam in the first place, but about the same percentage thought that once in, "America ought to have employed all its power to prevail."

In the face of such numbers, how would the public have responded if the Nixon administration had abruptly pulled back from Vietnam? There is, of course, no way of knowing, but there were good reasons for the White House to be concerned. Some sort of backlash was likely, and it would have probably landed somewhere between harsh and harsher. Nixon himself was worried about disillusionment, an isolationist reaction against American involvement overseas that would weaken the country's position in the world. "If we should lose here," he said, "the United States will never again have a foreign policy. We don't go fight anyplace." There would be a general retreat from international commitments. "Goddamn it, nobody else is going to be for defense. Who the hell is going to be for defense?" A "dramatic cop-out," Haldeman reported Nixon telling him, "would be a great way out for him [i.e., Nixon] but terrible for the country."

Given his background, Kissinger seemed less worried than Nixon about an isolationist retreat and more concerned about a stab-in-the-back myth brought on by a sudden American withdrawal that resulted in a more militaristic, even fascistic country. And Jews, he thought, would surely be blamed. One aide reported that "the tragedy of the Weimar Republic" was always on his mind. Like Morgenthau, Kissinger considered Nixon a bulwark against the more extreme right-wingers in the country. As he told Nixon, "You'll still turn out to be the protection of the students who are rioting against you, even though they'll never thank you for it, because the alternative to you in 1968 was not a liberal Democrat but a Wallace or a Reagan." When his staff objected to the 1970 Cambodian invasion, Kissinger remonstrated, "We are saving you from the right," to which one of them replied, "You *are* the right." It was a clever retort, but it wasn't true, and not just because Kissinger had Weimar on his mind.

Kissinger had been present at the 1964 Republican convention as a Rockefeller adviser when Barry Goldwater was nominated for president, and he had seen the face of American right-wing fanaticism firsthand. It was, he said, a "shattering experience . . . worse than anything the newspapers could possibly report." In his diary he wrote that he was "struck by the frenzy, the fervor, and the intensity of most delegates and practically the entire audience." Inevitably, he was reminded of "Nazi times." How would such people react to an American withdrawal from Vietnam with nothing to show for it? Was it worth the risk to find out? Or was the best option to cajole, pressure, or bomb the North Vietnamese into making the kinds of concessions that the American people could live with?

The ethical argument against a hasty withdrawal can be approached through one of the strangest, most outlandish passages in Kissinger's book *Ending the Vietnam War*. He writes, "We sought not an interval before collapse but peace with honor." By "interval" he meant what was commonly called a "decent interval," that is, a face-saving arrangement that allowed the United States to pull out gradually, while leaving the South Vietnamese to fight on, even if it meant their eventual defeat. Kissinger's statement is strange because it is so obviously contrary to the known facts. In the years when he and Nixon were formulating policy, they were basically faced with three choices. They could attempt to push on to victory as the hawks wished, perhaps by employing nuclear weapons, which was the recommendation of the Joint Chiefs of Staff, or bombing North Vietnam's dikes, which would have killed possibly hundreds of thousands of people and left Hanoi under 11 feet of water. (One lesson Robert McNamara said he learned from his Vietnam experience was that "short of genocide, it is unlikely that you can break a nation's will by bombing.") Nixon and Kissinger could have pulled out immediately as the protesters demanded, the consequences be damned. Or they could have followed the policy they did in fact pursue. Despite Kissinger's denial, the evidence is overwhelming that their chosen policy was to find a decent interval, a face-saving agreement that Washington could call "honor."

In 1972 Morgenthau observed that once victory was abandoned as the goal of the war, all that was logically left was the decent interval, and he pointed out that this had been Kissinger's position as early as 1968. The interval Kissinger was hoping for was two to three years before a Communist takeover. Once he was in power, his language may have become softer but the idea remained the same. In a secret memo to Nixon in September 1971, he called for "a healthy interval" that would, as he cagily put it, "leave the future of South Vietnam to the historic process." He said the same thing to foreign leaders. To the Soviet ambassador he spoke of "a certain period of time, not too long," and to Zhou Enlai he used the term "respectable interval." Kissinger was under no illusions. The Communists might eventually win the war after an American withdrawal, but as he said to Zhou, "If, as a result of historical evolution it should happen over a period of time, we ought to be able to accept it." To the Soviets he delicately said, "We are prepared to leave so that a Communist victory is not excluded." Such words were never spoken to America's own ally, Nguyen Van Thieu, who didn't need an explanation for what a decent interval portended for him and his government. Not surprisingly, it is practically impossible to find a reputable historian who does not believe the true, if unstated, policy of the Nixon administration was the decent interval. So why won't Kissinger fess up?

Kissinger made a distinction that was important to him and that has remained important to much of the American public down to the present between the peace of a decent interval and a peace with honor. The first was cold-blooded, callous, Realpolitik in its cruelest form. Honor, on the other hand, gave an ethical face to what the White House was doing, an impression not only to others but also to the decision makers, Nixon and Kissinger, that the U.S. government was behaving decently, humanely, and living up to its obligations. This was not mere dissembling. As the White House tapes reveal, honor was very much on the minds of Nixon and Kissinger—at least up to a point.

To withdraw abruptly in 1969 would, in their view, have been dishonorable. It would have meant that the deaths of 30,000 Americans to that date had been in vain. Their families would have been left with nothing, in effect inhumanely abandoned with an official shrug of the shoulder. And what of the South Vietnamese who had risked everything on the basis of American promises? They too would have been tossed aside as casually as if one were turning off a light switch. Great powers did not behave like that. Kissinger insisted that the United States, though weary of war, could not simply "walk away from a small ally, the commitments of a decade, 45,000 casualties and the anguish of their families whose sacrifices would be retroactively rendered meaningless." The moral position was to fight on in order to save face.

But Isaacson and others have asked if it was worth the cost of the additional 20,000 American dead and "the near unraveling of America's social fabric." And what of the hypocrisy of it all? Critics of the decent-interval policy and Kissinger's eventual agreement condemned them, much as Thieu did, as a fig leaf for abandonment. The diplomat Richard Holbrooke called the settlement "just a camouflaged bugout"; one historian termed it "a betrayal of the South" and concluded that "Vietnam constituted, ultimately, perhaps the darkest chapter in Kissinger's career." Kissinger didn't

necessarily disagree. In private he accepted the assessment of a journalist friend that the administration's policy masked "the greatest retreat in
history."

There was undeniably something hypocritical in Nixon and Kissinger's
policy. They never really did level with the American people about what
they were doing. "What you're going to have here basically," Nixon said
in August 1972, as the two sides were drawing closer, "is a secret deal."
Secrecy? Hypocrisy? Duplicity? What was moral in that? Or honorable?
Kissinger explained that the eventual agreement, even if others saw it as
a sellout, allowed the bereaved families to "take some solace that it had
not all been in vain," and that result, he insisted, was "essentially moral."
That may be so, at least from one point of view. But one can perceive
another side to this issue of morality. Insofar as Kissinger understood that
a decent-interval policy necessarily meant the sacrifice of an ally—and
at different times he did understand that—what he did not say and could
not say was that the conflicting demands and impossible dilemmas he
and Nixon had to deal with required hypocrisy and deceptions. A decent
interval may well have been the only way out for a United States that was
veering toward self-destruction, and it was in that sense that Nixon's and
Kissinger's cynicism and dissembling were the true moral position. The
paradox was one that French moralists like La Rochefoucauld and French
diplomats like Talleyrand would have appreciated.

Finally, and most important of all, was the strategic component, which
went by the name of "credibility" or "prestige." America's credibility in
the world became an inevitable factor in any consideration of withdrawal
once Lyndon Johnson had decided to escalate the war. It was probably the
most significant consideration in Nixon's and Kissinger's thinking, even
if "prestige" and "credibility" were empty words to the war's opponents
and to numerous historians afterward, who dismiss notions of credibility
as weightless abstractions, especially when measured against the palpable
reality of dead American soldiers. Johnson's decision to expand the war
was made in 1964 even as he presented himself as the peace candidate in
the presidential election against the fiercely militaristic Barry Goldwater.
After his electoral victory, Johnson took the crucial step of bombing North
Vietnam, an action that put him on a one-way street. Bombing required
air bases in South Vietnam, which then required the protection of U.S.
troops. Marines came ashore near Da Nang in early March 1965 prepared
for combat. The ground war was on, and hundreds of thousands of Amer-

ican soldiers later, Richard Nixon would be elected president on a promise
to find a way out of Vietnam. Almost every historian who has studied the
origins of the war points to Johnson's decisions in late 1964 and early 1965
as the turning point. George Herring calls the months around the start of
1965 "the pivotal period." Gelb and Betts refer to "the Rubicon." Robert
McNamara writes of a "fork in the road." In his scrupulous examination of
the 18 months from August 1963 to late February 1965, Fredrik Logevall
says that the period he calls "the long 1964" was "the most important in
the entire 30-year American involvement in Vietnam."

What unites all of these assessments is the conviction that Kennedy or
Johnson could have pulled out several thousand advisers from Vietnam
with no loss of face, but that once Johnson made his large-scale commitments, the American involvement in Vietnam took on a completely different coloration. Withdrawal was no longer a minor matter to be consigned
to the back pages of the newspapers. Now it was an issue tied to America's
global commitments. The United States had put its credibility on the line.

As early as January 1969, just as he was assuming responsibility for the
nation's Vietnam policy, Kissinger wrote in a major statement: "The commitment of 500,000 Americans has settled the issue of the importance of
Vietnam. For what is involved now is confidence in American promises.
However fashionable it is to ridicule the terms 'credibility' or 'prestige,'
they are not empty phrases." And he concluded that a simple withdrawal
"or a settlement which unintentionally amounts to the same thing" could
lead to a loss of trust among America's friends, an outburst of aggres-
siveness among its enemies, and a "more dangerous international situation." Three difficult and inconclusive years of bloodshed didn't change
that perspective or that reality. As Nixon told Kissinger in August 1972,
just before negotiations got serious, "We have suffered long and hard, and
God knows how do we get out of it. All it is, is a question of getting out in
a way that to other countries—not the Chinese or the Russians so much,
they don't give a damn how it's settled, just that we're out—but to other
countries, it does not appear that we, after four years, bugged out. That's
all we have to do." At another time, he told Kissinger, "A non-Communist
Asia without the United States is potentially more dangerous than an Asia
with the United States."

Such estimations were open to debate over the particulars of America's
involvement in the world, but most of the war's opponents weren't interested in particulars or in debate. They were thinking in terms of moral

absolutes, whereas Nixon and Kissinger were thinking geopolitically, or in what Nixon called "a great mosaic," where no action in foreign policy could be taken in isolation because everything in the world was connected to everything else—not simplistically like dominoes falling but more like the organic interdependence of a skeleton or nervous system. Credibility was an abstraction, and it was difficult for any occupant of the White House to ask young Americans to risk their lives for an abstraction. But abstractions can have a reality of their own, as Kissinger said, and even if most of the American people were ill-equipped to think in such terms, there was a foreign policy elite whose members appreciated what the idea of credibility entailed. And while the members of that elite may have been divided on the war, they generally shared Nixon and Kissinger's language and understood why a simple withdrawal was out of the question. For those who had spent their lives studying international relations, credibility was an abstraction that was very real.

Thomas Schelling, a future Nobel Prize–winning economist and major strategic thinker who had influenced Kissinger's own ideas on nuclear warfare, had stressed the vital significance of national credibility in his writings. "If the question is raised whether this kind of 'face' is worth fighting over, the answer is that this kind of face is one of the few things worth fighting for." Whether one called it face or prestige or credibility, it represented "a country's reputation for action, the expectations other countries have about its behavior." Schelling didn't advocate following an abstraction down a rathole like Vietnam. He had been an early supporter of the war but turned against it after the Cambodian invasion, traveling down to Washington from Cambridge along with other Harvard friends of Kissinger to make their opposition known. Schelling said to Kissinger: "As we see it, there are two possibilities: either the president didn't understand when he went into Cambodia that he was invading a sovereign country, or he did understand. We just don't know which is scarier." Obviously, the criticism wasn't aimed at Nixon alone, and after the encounter an agitated, always thin-skinned Kissinger remarked, "The meeting completed my transition from the academic world."

But no one made a stronger case for the importance of credibility in international affairs than the war's leading opponent, Hans Morgenthau. Nixon and Kissinger could have found all the support they needed for sticking it out in Vietnam in the pages of *Politics Among Nations*, where Morgenthau had written that face was "an indispensable element of a rational foreign policy." This was especially true for the Cold War, when the struggle for hearts and minds "has been fought primarily with the weapons of prestige." Once the United States had plunged into the mud of Vietnam with both boots and in full battle gear, Morgenthau was to write that credibility was the most plausible argument for continuing the war, "really the decisive argument," for it was "an undeniable fact" that American prestige had become tied to the outcome of the war. Not one inclined toward straightforward conclusions, however, Morgenthau complicated his argument by pointing out that the prestige of the United States had drastically declined as a result of its intervention in Vietnam; he wondered which was worse for America's reputation: continuing the war or bringing it to an end. "What will our prestige be like if hundreds of thousands of American troops become bogged down in Vietnam, unable to win and unable to retreat?" he asked in 1965. It was damned if you do and damned if you don't. As for himself, Morgenthau concluded that any loss of prestige from a withdrawal "is a matter for speculation," whereas the loss of prestige from pursuing the war "is a matter of fact."

Still, he wasn't ready to join the student demonstrators in calling for an immediate withdrawal. He always insisted that simply pulling out had never been his position. In 1966, in congressional testimony, he said, "We can't disengage.... We are too deeply involved." He said the same thing in his private correspondence. Yet as soon as he said as much, he too was faced with the same problem as the men in the White House and in danger of falling into the same trap. He needed to articulate a policy to replace Johnson's escalations and Nixon and Kissinger's apparent military persistence. That policy went by the name of the "enclave plan." Morgenthau suggested that instead of conducting search-and-destroy operations throughout the Vietnamese countryside, the U.S. military should fall back into urban enclaves that it could secure while it waited out the war. Meanwhile, on the diplomatic front, Washington should work for "the establishment of a broadly based coalition government" that would bargain with the Communists for a phased American withdrawal. Unwilling to fool either others or himself, Morgenthau admitted that his plan was little more than a "face-saving device," and he conceded, in the cold language of Realpolitik, that "the final outcome of such an experiment . . . is of no concern to the United States." The government of South Vietnam, he said, was doomed, and Americans would just have to live with all the bloodshed that would follow a Communist victory. Such hard-nosed thinking might be discomfiting to idealistic hawks and doves alike, but for those opponents of the war who could not accept a unilateral withdrawal, the enclave idea was the only game in town. It picked up prominent supporters, the cream of America's antiwar elite, like William Fulbright, George Kennan, and Walter Lippmann.

Admittedly, the plan lost much of its salience in the 1970s, once the White House began its policy of Vietnamization, which may have been one of the reasons Morgenthau wrote much less about the war after Nixon and Kissinger took office, but the idea of replacing the Thieu government with a more pliable one that was ready to negotiate with the Communists was sufficiently attractive for even the two Realpolitikers in the Oval Office to give it consideration, especially in their worst days. Unfortunately, it raised problems for them that Morgenthau had failed to address.

For a thinker as gloomy and pessimistic as Morgenthau, the enclave notion was surprisingly optimistic. American generals didn't like it because it placed the United States in a defensive crouch—"no one ever won a battle sitting on his ass"—but more important, it depended on the compliance of the Vietnamese, both friends and enemies. Thieu would show in a few years just how difficult it was to bring a supposed ally on board with a plan that seemed to go against the interests of the Saigon government. What South Vietnamese leader would be prepared to negotiate what was, in effect, a suicide pact? And what would an enclave plan mean for the morale of the South Vietnamese army? As for the Communists, Morgenthau insisted that the Vietcong would have to refrain from attacking the enclaves if the plan was to work, and that was hardly a certainty or even a probability. Morgenthau never explained how the details of the enclave theory could be implemented, and on close examination, the Realist's enclave idea looked anything but realistic. If credibility mattered, as the war's foremost critic believed, and as Nixon and Kissinger affirmed, there simply was no quick or easy way out of Vietnam.

The unhappy truth was that by 1969, once an immediate withdrawal had been deemed impractical, the only real option available was the cynical one of a phased withdrawal, a "decent interval," even though that policy could rightly be condemned as the sellout of an ally and would necessarily mean the loss of more American lives in a cause most of the public had given up on. One of the most cogent critics of Nixon and Kissinger's policy was Charles de Gaulle, who knew as much about the quicksand of Indochina as any Western leader. Shortly after Nixon and Kissinger had come into office, de Gaulle posed the fundamental question to the new foreign policy adviser: "Why not withdraw?" Kissinger responded that "a sudden withdrawal might give us a credibility problem." To which de Gaulle drily replied, "Where?" It was hardly a fair response because a unilateral American withdrawal would in fact have shaken countries across Asia from Japan to Singapore to Australia and would have raised doubts among vulnerable allies dependent on American power and reliability like South Korea, West Germany, Taiwan, and Israel. Power vacuums invariably got filled by someone or in some way. How many of those countries would have embarked on programs to develop nuclear weapons as a replacement for the American security blanket? And what was more, as Kissinger never tired of pointing out, "It had taken de Gaulle five years to extricate France from Algeria and as an act of policy, not as a collapse." The choice Nixon and Kissinger decided on was to force the North Vietnamese to the negotiating table by whatever means necessary.

There is certainly an argument to be made that Nixon and Kissinger could have sped up the Vietnamization process and withdrawn American ground forces faster than they did—though just how fast always depended on the concessions that Hanoi was willing to make, especially with regard to the POWs—but no matter how rapid a withdrawal, there was no way to avoid the loss of additional American lives in the year or two or three that the process required. (Kissinger pointed out that 60 percent of American casualties during the Nixon years occurred in the very first year, when the administration was still figuring out what to do.) Any policy of withdrawal would have required what critics—and the troops in the field—would call meaningless sacrifice and needless deaths. There was no "correct" or "just" policy, only bad choices.

AT ONE POINT in his Vietnam book, Kissinger refers to the war as "a perhaps intractable problem." Elsewhere, he terms it a "nightmare" and "my nightmare." But more often, repeatedly, almost like a mantra, he describes the war as "tragic" or a "tragedy" as, for example, in phrases like "all actors in the Indochina tragedy" and "the tragic end of two decades of American sacrifice, dedication and national division." To a friend, he said "Vietnam is like a Greek tragedy," and like any Greek tragedy it had a quality of inevitability about it and pitted not right against wrong but right against right. For Kissinger, it was also an American tragedy, in which the country's ideals ran aground against the limitations of power and the realities of history. And it was a tragedy of cultural incomprehension as well: "It would have been impossible," he said, "to find two societies less intended by fate to understand each other than the Vietnamese and the American." There was, as he pointed out, a tragic gap between the South Vietnamese, fighting for their survival, and the United States, desperate to find a way out. And there was a domestic gap too, an abyss really, between the leaders in Washington, obliged to think in strategic and geopolitical abstractions, and a generation that was being called upon to kill or be killed for no immediate reason they could fathom.

Leaving aside the hawks' unregenerate desire for escalating the war to achieve "victory," a political impossibility in 1969, there were good arguments to be made for any of the possible policies on offer—an immediate withdrawal as suggested by Senator Aiken and others, a speeded-up withdrawal faster than the one that was pursued but still unilateral, without concessions from the North Vietnamese or the acquiescence of the South Vietnamese, or the actual Nixon-Kissinger tactic of bombing the North Vietnamese into making the kind of concessions that would allow for a face-saving withdrawal. There were also good arguments to be made against all of these choices. We are in the realm of the unknowable.

No occupant of the White House could have been sure which policy offered the best outcome, measured in terms of America's national interest. Every choice contained its own drawbacks; there were no guarantees in any direction. As Morgenthau had said, "The statesman has no assurance of success in the immediate task, and not even the expectation of solving the long-range problem." Perhaps the only certainty was that every possible course of action was a bad one, which is why no one looking back on the Vietnam War can derive any sense of satisfaction. Innocent people were going to die in any case, and redemption was not in the offing for anyone involved. As Henry Kissinger might have pointed out, that is the very essence of tragedy.

CHAPTER SIX

KISSINGER
IN POWER

T HE EARLY 1970S WERE AN EXTRAORDINARY PERIOD IN Henry Kissinger's life and in the life of the country. After the China opening, the Strategic Arms Limitation Talks (SALT) agreement with the Soviet Union, and finally the termination of America's involvement in the Vietnam war, soon to be followed by his improbably successful shuttle diplomacy in the Middle East, Kissinger's popularity reached incredible heights, to levels pollsters had never seen before. Adulation bubbled up in the unlikeliest corners of public opinion. In 1972, Playboy Club bunnies voted the squat owlish professor with the kinky hair and sallow complexion the man they would most like to have a date with. This wasn't an entirely outlandish sentiment. Barbara Walters reported that he "made careers" for women who were seen with him. Two years later, the Miss Universe contestants went the bunnies one better, naming Kissinger "the greatest person in the world today." Books were written about him with no loftier ambition than to gossip about the women in his life. The "D.C. stud corps," said one, labeled him the "fastest gun in the East."

For perspective, one need only think of the other persons who have held Kissinger's position of national security adviser—his immediate predecessors, the frosty McGeorge Bundy and the colorless Walt W. Rostow, neither ever destined to become a culture hero or sex symbol, or the many forgotten figures among his successors, with names like Allen, Clarke, McFarlane, Lake, and Berger. Brent Scowcroft, who served twice in the office, worked estimably behind the scenes, winning admiration from those in the know as a dedicated public servant, but his quiet competence never brought him any real public recognition. The better-known Zbig-niow Brzezinski, Jimmy Carter's national security adviser and a public intellectual like Kissinger, came up through the foreign policy ranks at the same time as Kissinger yet was never able to escape his rival's shadow. Perhaps the most visible national security adviser to follow Kissinger was Condoleezza Rice, in the administration of George W. Bush, but she was not the skilled diplomat or infighter that Kissinger had proved to be. There were no secret trips to China, no shuttle diplomacy in the Middle East.

To be sure, Richard Nixon had something to do with the achievements of his own administration, but much of the American public didn't see it that way. A joke made the rounds that Kissinger had better not die because then Nixon would become president. Whereas Kissinger was witty and engaging, winning over audiences and even a notoriously jaded press corps with masterful stroking, the stiff, uneasy Nixon possessed all the charm of a flat tire. Both men were duplicitous manipulators, but Kissinger was successful in his seductions, whereas deviousness was too obviously written across Nixon's jowly face, voiced in his kitschy language, and displayed in his awkward, upraised, V-for-victory arms. Millions of Americans found him repellent and would never think anything different, even if he had walked on water (or established an environmental protection agency to clean up the water). This man with an enemies list had too many enemies ever to be included on any list.

And once Nixon and just about everyone around him began drowning in the Watergate scandal, Kissinger became the irreplaceable last man standing, the only source of continuity in an anxiety-ridden time of tumult and uncertainty, a rock, an anchor. Foreign governments understood just how dangerous the moment was; even the Russians and Chinese refrained from provocative actions that might invite confrontation with an embattled, unstable Nixon and thereby undermine Kissinger. In the United States Kissinger was turned into a father figure offering reassurance to a frightened child. The newscaster Ted Koppel said that he "was the best thing we've got going for us." He had become "a legend." He was "the White House genius in residence." One congressman proposed a constitutional amendment so that the foreign-born Kissinger could run for president of the United States. In 1973 he was ranked the most admired American—ahead of Billy Graham—and in January 1974, when Nixon's approval rating had dropped below 30 percent, Kissinger's soared to an astonishing 85 percent.

Kissinger probably reached the height of his popularity in the first months of 1974, as he was successfully disentangling the armies of the Middle East. Kissinger himself certainly thought so, taking note of a *Newsweek* cover that showed him in a Superman costume. But not even Superman would have been able to sustain the kind of high-flying manic esteem Kissinger enjoyed. In its irrational exuberance, it had all the permanence of a Tulip Mania or some other financial bubble. The same nation that embraced him in an emotional catharsis would soon wake up to a cold morning-after and reject him as an appeaser or an incompetent or a villain or a war criminal. Angry students would begin identifying him not with Superman but with Charles Manson. Goldwater Republicans would label him un-American. No one thought him sexy anymore. When he was at the pinnacle of his fame, the skeptical, ironic Kissinger had an intimation of fortune's transience, sensing that he was headed for a fall. This, after all, was the man who saw tragedy around every corner. After *Time* and *Newsweek* put him on their covers at the same time, Kissinger said to the presidential speechwriter William Safire, "I understand it's the kiss of death to be on both covers the same week." (To which Safire replied: "Yes, but what a way to go.")

Kissinger's rise was built up over months and years, carefully constructed through a combination of talent, humor, intelligence, and guile. "Do you lie sometimes?" an intimate asked him. "Of course," he answered with oxymoronic candor. The fall came practically overnight. "There was a time when Henry Kissinger could do no wrong," one friend wrote. "Suddenly, Kissinger was accused of doing nothing right." And he went on: "Seldom has a man been more exposed to the fickleness of popular acclaim." The turnaround was so startling, so dramatic, that it deserves close attention in its own right, apart from the particular policies Nixon/Kissinger pursued. Historians could learn a great deal about the years after World War II simply by studying the vicissitudes of Kissinger's celebrity. Even today, American foreign policy has been shaped against the contours of Kissinger's reputation, and the consequences, as we shall see, have not been healthy.

KISSINGER FIRST GAINED national attention with *Nuclear Weapons and Foreign Policy*, published in 1957, the same year as the more scholarly *A World Restored* appeared. It was the book that introduced the American public to his brand of Realist thinking. Not long before, Kissinger had failed to receive an appointment at Harvard, and after rejecting an offer from Morgenthau's University of Chicago, he left Harvard for the Council on Foreign Relations in New York, where he chaired a convocation of experts on the fraught topic of nuclear warfare. One friend called the move "the most important event in Kissinger's adult life." *Nuclear Weapons and Foreign Policy* was the result of the group's work, written by an academic who was in the process of losing interest in an academic career. The book was decidedly nonacademic in the topicality of its subject and the provocativeness of its conclusions. Its arguments were of relevance not merely to specialists but quite simply to anyone with an active interest in staying alive.

With the development of nuclear weapons in 1945, technology, not for the first or last time, had outpaced strategic thinking. Policymakers had catching up to do. How did the awesome new power fit into the conduct of war? Could the weapons ever be used? And under what circumstances? Almost by default, the prevailing doctrine as developed during the Eisenhower years—Mutual Assured Destruction (MAD)—held that a localized or limited war waged by the Soviet Union would be met with an all-out nuclear response. Knowing this, the thinking went, the Russians would be deterred from engaging in any kind of aggressive behavior. But Kissinger had the talent of someone who could look into the mind of the enemy—that is, with the empathy that comes from an absence of self-righteousness. One biographer has called "the intuitive and empathetic" Kissinger "the most psychologically minded of all foreign policy thinkers and actors," a comment that will come as no surprise to anyone who has read Kissinger's novelistically rich, incisive portraits of foreign leaders in his three volumes of memoirs. As a result, he was able to locate the weak spot in MAD. The United States was practicing all-or-nothing reasoning, he said, whereas the more subtle Russians would employ patient motion, pushing for advantage in ways that stopped short of provoking a nuclear confrontation. Washington would then be faced with the impossible choice of unleashing a cataclysm that would be disproportionate to the matter at hand or yielding to Soviet expansion step by step, crisis by crisis, until Moscow had achieved global dominance and in effect won the Cold War. In Kissinger's mind, MAD was a form of unilateral disarmament because no U.S. president would be willing to start a nuclear war for some far-off country or people most Americans had little interest in. Far from discouraging misbehavior, Mutual Assured Destruction was an invitation to Soviet aggression.

Kissinger's solution to this problem was an unsettling one: the United States had to develop the mind-set and the capacity to conduct a "limited" nuclear war, meeting Soviet challenges with tactical nuclear weapons when necessary but not in a way that unleashed total destruction on both sides. Critics, Hans Morgenthau among them, were quick to point out the flaw in Kissinger's reasoning: there was a bright line between non-nuclear war and nuclear war but no such line between tactical nuclear war and strategic nuclear war. Once the bombs started falling, there was no clear stopping point. Any use of a nuclear weapon, however limited, risked inexorable escalation and universal annihilation.

It was a telling argument, one that Kissinger came to acknowledge, but *Nuclear Weapons and Foreign Policy* nonetheless had challenged orthodox thinking, raised uncomfortable questions to which there were no easy answers, and shed light on the darkest and most frightening corners of American military policy. The book was a sensation and not just among policymakers. A Book-of-the-Month Club selection, it spent 14 weeks on the *New York Times* best-seller lists. It had a first printing of 70,000 copies. Reviewers praised it as "thoughtful" and "challenging," though Kissinger himself had no illusions about the shallowness of his surprise success. He thought his book one of those best sellers that people bought, and even discussed at cocktail parties, but didn't read. (He alluded to the popularity of the historian Arnold Toynbee, but more modern readers may reach for the names of best-selling authors like Stephen Hawking or Thomas Piketty.) There was a scrupulous ambiguity in the reviewers' word "challenging," especially since even experts in the field were calling the book "difficult." One historian has said the sentences "drift across ideas like a thick fog."

But read or unread, the book inaugurated Kissinger's public career, and he was soon giving speeches, sitting on panels, and writing for high-quality general-interest magazines. His timing could not have been better: in October 1957 the Russians launched *Sputnik*, demonstrating that they had the capacity to attack the American homeland. This new vulnerability brought questions of nuclear war to the forefront of public attention, with Americans eager to hear anyone who might provide guidance. Kissinger made his first television appearance in November on *Face the Nation*. Politicians of both parties began citing him. Kissinger went back to Harvard in 1957 to become a tenured professor two years later, but he now had his eye on larger prizes.

THROUGH KISSINGER'S YEARS at Harvard, both as a student and professor, several qualities in his sharply etched personality stood out. No one could deny his brilliance, but neither was it possible to ignore his arrogance or his ambition—even among a cohort of nakedly ambitious people. Kissinger himself commented on his "excessively intense personal style," observing with modest understatement that "the capacity to admire others is not my most fully developed trait." When he was a student, he was viewed as pompous and unfeeling. "One heard an enormous amount about him, what an extraordinarily arrogant and vain bastard he was," a contemporary remarked. And humility was hardly a trait he developed during his sojourn with the outside experts at the Council on Foreign Relations and following the success of *Nuclear Weapons and Foreign Policy*. Back in Cambridge, he was considered abrasive, "even by Harvard standards." One of his students, Leslie Gelb, who later had a distinguished and multifaceted career that included directing the Pentagon Papers project and leading the Council on Foreign Relations, was left with a bad taste in his mouth from studying under Kissinger and working for him as a teaching assistant. He was "the typical product of an authoritarian background," Gelb recalled, "devious with his peers, domineering with his subordinates, obsequious to his superiors." The sociologist David Riesman put a kinder spin on what he called Kissinger's "commanding presence." But his mentor William Yandell Elliott once said to his face: "You're the most arrogant man I've ever met."

During Kissinger's years in the White House under Nixon, associates found his arrogance difficult to take. An "egotistical maniac" was how the attorney general, John Mitchell, described him. Nixon himself could be driven to distraction by his overbearing national security adviser. "Henry is a terribly difficult individual to have around," he confided to Bob Haldeman. He was like "a child," Nixon said, who could not bear to be wrong about anything. For all his value, Kissinger was an "emotional drain" inside the White House and, even before the end of Nixon's first year in office, what was already being called "the Kissinger problem" was something requiring constant, time-consuming attention. Fatherly lectures from the president about "how we all will have problems and we must take them in stride" didn't work, and so Haldeman was given the unenviable assignment of keeping the demanding Kissinger "on an even keel." Still, Nixon was resigned to having "a continuing problem . . . and will just have to play it day by day." Kissinger, the brilliant "child," simply did not play well with others.

Kissinger's outsized ambition was equally obvious to those who encountered him on his rise to the top. Fellow students, even his friends, called his determination to succeed "fierce." An undergraduate roommate said he studied harder than anyone else, working until the early hours of the morning. Words like "drive" and "driven" were common in descriptions of the young scholar. The historian Robert Dallek called Kissinger's ambition "a ceaseless force."

Even when he was a mere Harvard graduate student, he was laying the groundwork for later achievement, though his personal goals weren't entirely clear to him at the time. He may not have known where he was going, but he was determined to get there. In 1951 he was instrumental in the creation of an international seminar to bring promising young future leaders from around the world to study for eight weeks in Cambridge. Kissinger directed the program, selecting the participants and serving as an instructor. He was developing a network of influential connections that would prove invaluable to him in his later career. Similarly, he started a magazine, *Confluence*, in 1952. Some of the most thoughtful foreign policy writers and intellectuals—Hans Morgenthau, Hannah Arendt, Raymond Aron, and Reinhold Niebuhr—wrote for it, and though the publication wasn't a success, folding in 1959, it too provided Kissinger with acquaintances who could be of use to him in the future. He had made himself the master of networking.

Associates at Harvard, although invariably struck by his energies, weren't always persuaded that he would be a reliable colleague. Especially with a best seller under his belt, he left the impression that his sights extended beyond any rewards he might garner as a university professor. That impression was correct. Because his loyalty to the academic world was in question, when he came up for tenure some of those with a vote opposed him. They argued that Kissinger's books did not meet Harvard's academic standards and were more political than scholarly. Kissinger won tenure but not without generating controversy. The chairman of his department, Samuel Beer, said the "tenure battle was a wonderful fight."

One might have thought that Kissinger's thirst for success would have been slaked when he was named national security adviser following Nixon's 1968 electoral victory and then secretary of state in 1973. Kissinger himself has said that the most he thought he could aspire to was a position as head of the policy planning staff in the State Department or as an assistant secretary of defense. But even after he had climbed as high as he possibly could without a constitutional amendment, scaling unimaginable heights, his ambition didn't fade; it simply took a different form. An urge to dominate replaced raw striving, and now, with power at his fingertips, Kissinger sought to shape events according to his own Realpolitik principles. He is reported to have told a friend: "What drives me is an awareness of the worth of my ideas and the hope of having an impact on society." Kissinger put it differently in his memoirs: "There is no more important and personally fulfilling role than public service," he said. "No task on the outside can compare in significance." In any case, he continued to be driven.

In office, he was a force unleashed. His temper tantrums became legendary. He would berate his staff mercilessly, skulk around the room in anger and frustration, throw papers against the wall, stomp on them. Why did his staff members stay? The truth is that many didn't. But those who did knew that they were close to the seat of power and if they made an intelligent argument that it would receive a hearing from someone with the capacity to understand it.

With associates inside the Oval Office, Kissinger was more subdued, even submissive, but Bob Haldeman remarked on his "obsession with total compliance and perfection." Demanding complete control, he hated being excluded from any White House meeting. And because everything coming out of his office had to pass through him, bottlenecks became a constant problem. One staff member compared the line outside his door to that at "a Moroccan whorehouse." When presidential assistant John Ehrlichman complained about the inefficiency of this one-man show, Kissinger blew up at him, bellowing that as long as he continued working for the administration, nobody was going to go around him.

The individual who got the worst of Kissinger's will to power was the secretary of state, William P. Rogers. Disputes were inevitable between the two men assigned the task of overseeing the nation's foreign policy and began as soon as Nixon took office, if not before. Here was a "team of rivals" but without the concept of "team." Nixon's relationship with Rogers went back years. Rogers was considered the president's closest friend, whereas Kissinger was the newcomer, the academic outsider with a foreign accent, and a Jew besides. It has been reported that Kissinger's own assistant, Alexander Haig, once said that Kissinger's Jewishness made him "not an American." But Nixon and Kissinger shared not only a Realist perspective on world events but also a distrust of the State Department's entrenched, sluggish bureaucracy, which Rogers, a consummate moderate with a go-slow temperament, was ill suited to oppose. Nor was it really his job to do so. Kissinger, at the behest of the president, employed back channels to the Russians, secret trips to China, and other circuitous devices to work around the ponderous State Department; Rogers necessarily had to work through it. "The result was that the State Department would often pursue a course of action that was in direct conflict with what I was doing on behalf of the president and of which the department was unaware." Kissinger has even said that he kept the British Foreign Office more closely engaged than the State Department. Two years into his first term, Nixon had concluded that Kissinger was not only more valuable to him than Rogers but also more loyal. If someone had to "fall on a sword" to protect the president, Nixon told Haldeman, "Henry would do it, but Rogers wouldn't."

And these clashes over turf were matched by clashes of personality. Kissinger was a visionary who had brought a grand conception of foreign policy to his job. Part of his brilliance—and, some would add, a source of his limitations—was to see connections everywhere. "Foreign policy is a seamless web." The long-term consequences of any decision were always on his mind. Rogers was more of a day-to-day, one-problem-at-a-time kind of guy, whose inability to think conceptually drove Kissinger the German intellectual crazy. It wasn't long before Rogers had become a personal obsession. Time and again, Kissinger would storm into the Oval Office to complain about Rogers's incompetence or to announce that Rogers had "declared war on him," a case of projection if there ever was one. Dodge wasn't big enough for both of them. Couldn't Nixon get rid of Rogers by naming him Chief Justice of the Supreme Court, Kissinger wondered. Though with hindsight he said that he was "not proud of the way"

he had helped to marginalize Rogers, at the time when their rivalry mattered most, Kissinger's rage could not be contained. "He's psychopathic
about trying to screw Rogers," Nixon said.

MANY OF THOSE who have written about Kissinger have viewed his
aggressive behavior one-dimensionally as the naked pursuit of fame,
power, and wealth with nothing behind it, Kissinger as the embodiment of
the rank opportunist. As one critic put it, "Every single policy that Henry
Kissinger advocated as being good both materially and morally for the
long-run strategic ends of the United States, also happened to be good for
the personal advancement of Henry Kissinger." According to Christopher
Hitchens, "There is a perfect congruence between Kissinger's foreign policy counsel and his own business connections." Otto von Bismarck, one of
the men in history Kissinger most admired, once said, in an obvious reference to himself, that patriotism was a less important motive for statesmen than "the desire to command, to be admired and to become famous,"
and the ancient Greeks saw nothing wrong with the pursuit of glory for
its own sake. Kissinger did not deny the role that opportunism played in
his own rise. "Anyone wishing to affect events must be opportunist [sic]
to some extent," he told an interviewer. And as he wrote in his memoirs,
personal vanity and a quest for power were not "entirely absent" from his
motives. He was, after all, only human.
    But critics who saw nothing else to him but his ambition were being
altogether too cynical. This was a man who owed his life and the lives of
his family to the United States. Kissinger felt not only appreciation but
also a debt of gratitude, a debt he would repay by service to his adopted
country. "What sustained me," he wrote, "was the belief that I was repay-
ing the country that had rescued my family from tyranny." What gave his
public career meaning, he said, was his sense that he was doing his best to
guarantee the security of the United States at a dangerous time—and that
in doing so he was also making "a contribution to a better world." As his
friend John Stoessinger explained, "His objective, above all, was to secure
a stable international order. All specific policies were subordinated by him
to this fundamental quest." Kissinger's genuine patriotism was combined
with an equally genuine desire for peaceful resolution of conflict through
compromise, which he understood to be the essential task of the diplomat. As he had written at the outset of his career, "In any negotiation it

is understood that force is the ultimate recourse. But it is the art of diplomacy to keep this threat potential . . . to commit it only as a last resort." In short, "to the statesman, negotiation is the essence of stability."

Even before he reached the top, Kissinger demonstrated that his ambition was encased in higher motives. At no time was this more evident than when Nixon first offered him the job of national security adviser. One part of the story has become famous.

Kissinger had encountered Nixon only once before he received a call to meet the president-elect at the Pierre Hotel in New York in late November 1968. The discussion of these two strangers seems to have had all the conversational gaps of a Harold Pinter play, with a puzzled Kissinger not sure what he was doing there and a diffident Nixon unable to come to the point. Kissinger thought he was being asked to give advice on the foreign policy bureaucracy and the goals of diplomacy, both subjects in which he could claim considerable expertise. He returned to Cambridge with an inkling that he would be playing a part in the new administration, though with no clear idea what that part would be. But a day later he was called back to New York by Nixon's campaign manager, John Mitchell, who asked him if he had made a decision yet about the national security position. When Kissinger said he didn't know he had been offered the job, Mitchell barked, "Jesus Christ, he has screwed it up again," and trooped off to get Nixon so that the president-elect could clarify what he had in mind. It's a story that has been played for laughs many times, but there's a telling follow-up. What happened next tends to be overlooked by those who see ambition alone as Kissinger's motivating force.

Remarkably, the man so often condemned for his cutthroat striving didn't leap at the offer. He asked for a week to think it over—not because of any doubts he may have had about himself but because of his doubts about Nixon. Kissinger dwelt in the hothouse bubble of Cambridge, where a contemptuous attitude toward all things Nixonian was the ticket of entry to polite Harvard society. Kissinger's friends, among them such Democratic stalwarts as Arthur Schlesinger Jr. and John Kenneth Galbraith, were almost all dedicated liberals and, "to a man," Kissinger said, had voted against Nixon. Kissinger himself shared their view. During the campaign, he had called Nixon "unfit to be president" and "a disaster" waiting to happen. Just before the Republican convention he had declared that "Richard Nixon is the most dangerous of all the men running to have as president." (Such opinions didn't prevent him from providing help to the Republicans during the campaign, but then nobody ever claimed that Henry Kissinger was straightforward.)

Kissinger would later call his request for a delay before making up his mind "impudent." Nixon, he said, "would have been well justified had he told me to forget the whole thing." But Nixon didn't take offense. Indeed, in a gesture Kissinger found "rather touching," he offered to provide the names of some of his old Duke professors who would vouch for his character. It was all a weird role reversal: the job applicant was making a decision about whether to hire the man who was about to become president.

Back in Cambridge, Kissinger's anti-Nixon colleagues turned out to be enthusiastic about his accepting the post, as was the person in public life whose opinion Kissinger most valued, Nixon's longtime political rival, Nelson Rockefeller. Conservatives like William F. Buckley, a product of Kissinger's networking, also approved, and despite one or two naysayers like McGeorge Bundy, "seldom has a presidential appointment elicited such widespread enthusiasm." One Harvard professor said that he would "sleep better" knowing that Kissinger was advising the president. At his last Harvard seminar before he departed to join the new administration, Kissinger received a standing ovation from his students.

AMID ALL THE excitement, almost no one was raising what were serious philosophical issues involved in Kissinger's decision to accept the appointment. Joining the Nixon administration prompted age-old questions about the uses and abuses of power. When he was offered the national security job, Kissinger's opinion of Nixon was almost entirely negative. How could he go to work for a man who, he said, promised to be a "disaster"? Wasn't this an unworthy, even objectionable use of his talents? What price was one willing to pay in the climb to power? What sacrifices of personal honesty would be involved, not to mention personal dignity? Shortly before his meetings with Nixon, Kissinger was already pondering all this, even if nobody else was. In a conversation with the journalist Gloria Steinem, he wondered if it was better for someone to try to affect policy by working inside government, however distasteful the circumstances might be, or preserving one's independence and integrity at the price of influence by standing outside and criticizing—or in Lyndon Johnson's memorable image, whether it was better to be inside the tent pissing out or outside the tent pissing in. Steinem urged Kissinger to write an article for *New York* magazine to be entitled "The Collaboration Problem." He never did write the article. Instead, much of his life from that point forward became an illustration of the problem.

In fact, Kissinger had already written just such an article in 1959, entitled "The Policymaker and the Intellectual." At that time, with public office only a distant prospect, Kissinger didn't address the question of moral compromise directly; his approach was dryer, more academic, focused on the universal human dilemmas arising from the restraints imposed by institutions. Employing a framework familiar to any student of Max Weber, he examined the tensions between the modern bureaucratic state and the independent, freethinking intellectual. Much of what he said foreshadowed his later battles with the State Department. Anyone familiar with the article should not have been surprised that Kissinger spent much of his time in office trying to work around government bureaucracies.

Societies, he wrote, had become increasingly bureaucratized with governmental departments divided into specialties and jobs stripped down to routinized tasks defined by organizational imperatives. A premium was placed on administrative and technical skills, while planning and policy were relinquished to committees of "experts" who arrived at their decisions through consensus and compromise. "In this manner, policy is fragmented into a series of ad hoc decisions which make it difficult to achieve a sense of direction." Kissinger reached for an analogy: "It is as if in commissioning a painting, a patron would ask one artist to draw the face, another the body, another the hands, and still another the feet, simply because each artist is particularly good in one category."

What got lost in the process was any vision, any sense of overall purpose, as well as any individual responsibility for defining goals and setting direction. Kissinger observed, "Neither Churchill nor Lincoln nor Roosevelt was the product of a staff." The modern bureaucracy simply rolled along according to its own predetermined rules, with no more head and no more heart than any other well-oiled machine. Kissinger called the ideal bureaucrat a "commissar," and by that he didn't mean only placeholders in the Soviet Union but bureaucrats in the United States as well. The commissar/bureaucrat was any administrator "whose world is defined by regulations, in whose making he had no part, and whose substance does not concern him, to whom reality is exhausted by the organization in which he finds himself." The mentality of the commissar could result in the deaths of thousands, "without love and without hatred." And even if the outcome was not murderous, the placeholder's "impact on national policy is pernicious."

Standing against this entrenched bureaucracy was the autonomous intellectual. Some intellectuals insisted on preserving their freedom by remaining outside the governmental apparatus, but these people Kissinger criticized for "perfectionism," or for engaging in protest that "has too often become an end in itself." Kissinger preferred the collaborators who chose public service. Intellectuals, Kissinger insisted, should "not refuse to participate in policymaking, for to do so would confirm the administrative stagnation." Still, those who did choose public service had their own problems to deal with.

Faced with the demands of the bureaucracy, freethinking intellectuals were constantly in danger of giving up their independence and becoming cogs in the machine. "In his desire to be helpful, the intellectual is too frequently compelled to sacrifice what should be his greatest contribution to society: his creativity." How could the intellectual retain his status as an independent mind thinking outside the box and still function within the government structure? "It is difficult to generalize," Kissinger concluded, but he urged the intellectual in government to try to maintain his dual role as both insider and outsider by withdrawing "from time to time to his library or his laboratory to 'recharge his batteries.' If he fails to do this, he will turn into an administrator, distinguished from some of his colleagues only by having been recruited from the intellectual community." Kissinger's was a plea for "artistry" in the making of policy, and this was a concept he retained even after his years in government. In 1978 he told the scholar Walter Laqueur, "Foreign policy is a form of art and not a precise science." This is "something," he added, "that some professors have great difficulty grasping."

When he accepted Nixon's offer to become national security adviser, Kissinger probably had in mind the model he outlined in "The Policymaker and the Intellectual." We know that he hoped to continue to be an intellectual who advised on policy inside the White House while still living in the world of ideas and dealing in theories and abstractions; he expected to be able to avoid short-term problems. That expectation, he quickly learned, was a fantasy that could be imagined only by someone who had never had the responsibility of governing. Every problem, it turned out, was short term. There was no time for thinking. "The convictions that leaders have formed before reaching high office," an older and wiser Kissinger later observed, "are the intellectual capital they will consume as long as they continue in office." And more lightly in one of his famous quips: "There cannot be a crisis next week. My schedule is already full." There would be no retreating to the library as long as Kissinger was in Washington, no recharging of batteries. People, he observed, do not grow in public office.

Kissinger sent a copy of "The Policymaker and the Intellectual" to Morgenthau, "with kind regards." Morgenthau had his own interest in the collaboration question, and not surprisingly his thinking followed lines similar to Kissinger's. Like Kissinger, he was an intellectual who had hoped to burst the bounds of the academic community and leave his imprint on American foreign policy. He may have been acclaimed on college campuses around the country, but his impact on actual decisions was negligible. He dwelt in the world of theory, which is not where he wanted to be. For all of his intellectual stature, he felt frustrated. As early as 1953, he was complaining to Walter Lippmann about his "isolation from the center of affairs." To Robert Hutchins, the president of the University of Chicago, he wrote, "There is virtually no possibility for a friendly critic of American foreign policy, such as myself, to make his voice heard by the educated American public." He stood on the outside of Lyndon Johnson's tent, though not by choice. The most influential magazine in his field, *Foreign Affairs*, was closed to him, refusing to publish his iconoclastic, Realpolitik pieces. Astoundingly, the publication's longtime editor, Hamilton Fish Armstrong, called Morgenthau an "isolationist," as well as "a propagandist and publicity seeker." Morgenthau observed on the basis of painful experience, "The writer who speaks neither for the Establishment nor for any faction opposing it has a hard time in placing what he writes."

Whereas Kissinger knew how to seduce and deceive, Morgenthau was always forthright and outspoken, which was not the way to get ahead in Washington. Once he declared his opposition to American intervention in Vietnam and aired his unorthodox views about Communism, he became persona non grata in policymaking circles. And as the war in Vietnam ground on, he was brought close to despair over his powerlessness. "For those who have made it their business in life to speak truth to power, there is nothing left but to continue so to speak," he wrote with bitterness in 1970, but "certainly with less confidence that it will in the short run make much of a difference in the affairs of man." At his lowest, he came close to doubting the importance of reason itself. "The great issues of our day are not susceptible to rational solutions within the existing system of power relations."

It would hardly have been surprising if Morgenthau, like so many others, had resented Kissinger, not only for his success but also for the fact that his success had been achieved through the kind of dissembling and calculated ambiguity that did not come naturally to Morgenthau. Yet that wasn't Morgenthau's reaction. Kissinger, he said approvingly, was a "first-rate scholar" who was able to acquire and hold "great power with the same brilliance." To be sure, Morgenthau acknowledged that Kissinger did "very little that was not oriented toward . . . his personal power," but personal advancement wasn't necessarily a bad thing in his mind, and he admired Kissinger's ability to operate successfully in the toxic, backstabbing environment that was the nation's capital. Kissinger was no ordinary intellectual, helpless in the corridors of power. He knew how to adapt to the exigencies of politics. "Inevitably," Morgenthau wrote, "if your ambition is not limited to scholarship but extends to the political sphere, you have to trim your sails to the prevailing winds." Kissinger, he said, had trimmed his sails with "sagacity and decency," and he reproached envious academics who saw nothing but opportunism and careerism. Much of the criticism of Kissinger, he insisted, was "unabashedly self-serving."

Morgenthau never forgot a comment President Kennedy had once made to him after he had written something critical about the administration. "You should sit where I do," Kennedy said to him. "He had a point," Morgenthau conceded, and he went on to write thoughtful essays on the ways in which intellectuals and politicians both overlapped and differed and about the hopeless complexities of "the collaboration problem."

Intellectuals were important to policymaking, providing concepts and perspective, but they operated on the basis of different values from politicians. Scholars engaged with ideas, their aim was to be as intelligent as they could and to present their arguments cogently. Statesmen had different goals. "The intellectual seeks truth," Morgenthau said, "the politician power." But Morgenthau was quick to add that this difference did not make the intellectual superior to the politician because power was an inescapable reality while the abstruse pursuit of truth carried burdens of its own. The politician was obliged to deal with facts, not theories, and facts had a tendency to "make mincemeat of the wrong ideas." Intellectuals could be very smart without necessarily being especially wise, or even wise at all. The politician required "practical wisdom," whereas the scholar or intellectual "may be intelligent without being wise in the ways of the world."

Unlike the intellectual, the statesman or politician could not afford to operate from a position of absolutes. The real world was contradictory, unpredictable, untamable, tragic. Morgenthau was fond of a comment of Goethe's "that the one who acts is always unjust and that nobody has justice but the one who observes." Morgenthau came to amend this bleak thought, especially after his experience with the Vietnam war, insisting that there must be at least "an element of justice" in "the one who acts," though he continued to believe that a straightforward or naïve commitment to justice in the world of facts was foolhardy at best. Ethical adjustments were always demanded by the real world. Two qualities, he said, were essential to the statesman: a sense of limits and "a commitment to a grand design," which gave his policies an overall purpose. Intellectuals did not necessarily possess either of these qualities, and the ability to combine intellectuality and power was rare indeed. Morgenthau cited two examples from American history: the Founding Fathers and Abraham Lincoln. Henry Kissinger, apparently, was a third. Morgenthau wasn't saying that Kissinger achieved the level of a Jefferson or Lincoln, but he did believe that Kissinger was a great statesman, one of the best the United States had ever known. When their mutual friend John Stoessinger wrote a book-length apologia of Kissinger's policies, Morgenthau called it "by far the best book written about Henry Kissinger."

Confronted with the intimidating realities of power, Morgenthau said, intellectuals could choose among four possible courses. They could retreat into an ivory tower to preserve their "purity" (as well as their self-righteousness). They could, as an alternative, adopt a position of "prophetic confrontation" in opposition to government policy. The first of these attained virtue of a cloistered sort but only by denying power altogether. The second performed a traditional task of the intellectual, which was to speak truth to power, but it risked the danger of impracticality ("you should sit where I do"), along with its own form of sanctimoniousness. Once the Vietnam war heated up, Morgenthau was thrust into the second position, though it wasn't what he wanted or expected for himself.

The other two courses accepted power, even cooperated with it, but in very different ways. The third path for the intellectuals was to surrender their independence and in an act of cowardice become propagandists for authority—or, to employ Kissinger's framework, to yield to bureaucratic demands by just following orders and becoming cogs in the machine. Morgenthau was all too aware of the cowardice of intellectuals, not only from his days in Weimar Germany but also from his lonely opposition to Vietnam. Some supporters of the war, he said, have been so violent in their attacks on opponents of the war that he suspected their motives were not strictly intellectual. These scholars had ceased to be intellectuals and turned themselves into ideologues, tools of mere force, and at their worst they applied their intelligence to providing rationales for the state's brute coercions.

Morgenthau's fourth course, perhaps the most difficult, was to participate in government, hoping to influence policy with the intellectual's conceptual apparatus but accepting the restrictions with which officials were obliged to operate. The result could never be entirely satisfying because compromises with one's theories were always necessary, sometimes painful ones. Policies always fell short of the theoretical constructs intellectuals came up with. The best that intellectuals in government could do to maintain their integrity was to try to put truth to the service of power, understanding that even if the achievement of perfect justice was never possible, they could still provide practical advice about the uses of power for legitimate ends. For instance, politicians could be helped to avoid yielding to the constant temptation to substitute power for reason instead of joining the two, or advised on how much power was required for the situation at hand, avoiding the excesses that came all too easily to the wielders of military might. It was the job of the intellectuals in the White House to remind the president "of the brittleness of power, of its arrogance and blindness, of its limits and pitfalls." For the intellectuals to lose sight of truth was to capitulate to power instead of serving it.

But with all the inevitable compromises and adjustments to reality, how was it possible to know if one had made so many concessions as to become a mere tool of power? It was, Morgenthau said, "only a small step to the intellectual bankruptcy of capitulation. His answer seems to have been that there is no definitive answer to this eternal question, no moral formula one could rely on. In a world without absolutes, each individual had to be judged according to the circumstances of his particular situation, and for this reason, the historian had more to teach about statesmanship than the quantifying social scientist.

In the specific case of Henry Kissinger, Morgenthau's judgment was gen-

erous. Explaining "what manner of man" he was, Morgenthau observed
Kissinger had the "ability to move, as it were, on two disparate levels of discourse." So with regard to Vietnam, for example, Kissinger implemented
a policy that most of his friends opposed but acted "decently" toward
them, much more so than many other supporters of the war. Kissinger
"never stooped to personal attacks and tried to avoid public polemics altogether." More broadly, he was able to retain his integrity as an intellectual
in government because for all of the criticisms that might legitimately be
directed against his particular policies (often leveled by Morgenthau himself), in the larger scheme of things he always acted out of "deeply rooted
convictions" as well as a coherent body of doctrine. There was substance
behind all of the showmanship and celebrity. Morgenthau's Kissinger was
no mere opportunist. "What Kissinger does is informed by that body of
doctrine, and the energy with which he does it is nourished by the depth
of his convictions." Morgenthau would have had no difficulty believing
Kissinger when he wrote: "If the moral basis of my service were lost, public life would have no meaning for me."

What did Morgenthau mean by Kissinger's "body of doctrine"? For
that matter, what did Kissinger mean by "the moral basis" of his public service? It was a quirk of Morgenthau's analytic style always to break
down a subject into components—for example, three aspects, four features, five elements—and in the case of Kissinger's doctrine he saw four
parts. First, and most important, was the goal of minimizing the risk of
nuclear war; no objective was more important than this one. The second
was creating and maintaining a balance of power that would serve the first
goal and also reduce the possibility of conventional war. The third component, related to the second, was acknowledging that, like the United
States, other nations had their own vital interests, which a rational foreign
policy was bound to respect. Finally, Kissinger's fourth goal was to seek to
intertwine the vital interests of the various nations into a peaceful status
quo so that "the institutionalization of common interests must gradually
take the sting out of surviving hostile confrontations." The eternal pessimist, Morgenthau had his doubts about the fourth component, but as
the father of Realism in America, he could only admire and applaud the
first three. The two German-Jewish Realists spoke the same language, and
Morgenthau's appreciation of Kissinger's public career was on an entirely
different level from that of most of Kissinger's detractors, or even most of

his admirers. It was as if Morgenthau and Kissinger were talking to each other alone, speaking the language of cold-blooded Realism and relegating everyone else to the sidelines as naïve kibitzers.

ALTHOUGH THEY WOULD have resisted the word, there was something "metaphysical" in how these two intellectuals from a similar Continental background looked at foreign policy, in particular the emphasis they put on the primacy of down-to-earth power over what they saw as ungrounded morality. The voice of Nietzsche can be heard in their warning about the folly of idealism in the absence of either a living God or an afterlife, and Heidegger stood in the background teaching that it was a fact of the human condition to be "thrown into" existence without the benefit of transcendent values as a guide. All ethical systems lacked foundation. Because abstractions were illusions in affairs of state as in life, all that the policymaker had to work with was the world as it actually was—the core of Realist thinking. There was no escaping it. Trying to force reality to match one's ideals was a recipe for disruption at best, calamity at worst.

Critics like Robert Dallek reproached Kissinger for his amoral "collaboration" with Nixon. "It is difficult to understand how anyone could work for someone as volatile and irrational as Nixon sometimes was." They spoke of "a Faustian bargain which should cast a long shadow over his historical reputation." But for Kissinger, who rejected the ivory tower for the sake of a public career, the only choice involved was whether it was better to be inside the tent or outside. "If I resign," he said jestingly, but not entirely in jest, "Nixon will have a heart attack and Agnew will be president." (Kissinger wasn't the only one who raised the troubling specter of a President Spiro Agnew. Nixon also worried about the presidential succession if he should fall ill or have an accident, and in July 1971 he discussed with Haldeman and Ehrlichman how they might go about getting rid of the vice president—fodder, certainly, for conspiracy theorists all too aware of Agnew's eventual fate.) Kissinger's point was that someone was going to be in the White House, someone was going to be making the life-and-death decisions. The power of the American government was not about to disappear if he retreated to a university or to some high-paying consultancy.

In such a world, where competition among states was never ending, problems could not be solved, only mitigated, and on those occasions when seemingly permanent solutions were found, new problems would inevitably arise to replace them. There was no end to it all, no cessation to the conflicts and contradictions brought on by individuals' ubiquitous will to power, no prospect for eternal peace. Policymakers exhausted by their killing workloads could be left to feel that they were little more than corks bobbing in a sea of troubles. "The public life of every political figure," Kissinger said, "is a continual struggle to rescue an element of choice from the pressure of circumstance." And what did it mean to live in this world of nonstop challenges without the comforting illusion of utopian aspirations or perfectionist hopes as road maps for decision makers? "There are no plateaus in foreign policy," Kissinger wrote. "Every achievement is purchased by new travail." Because there were no resting places for a global superpower, the conduct of foreign policy was a full-time, 24/7 job, one that could be performed only by someone prepared to offer total dedication. If you weren't ready to sacrifice your life to history's obligations, you weren't ready to be a player in the deadly game of international affairs.

HISTORIANS AND OTHER onlookers have expressed astonishment at Kissinger's grueling work schedule—it leaves them "breathless." He was at his job 14 to 16 hours a day, seven days a week. And Kissinger demanded equal commitment from his staff, working them to exhaustion—literally. Lawrence Eagleburger did not have Kissinger's Olympic stamina and, a few months after becoming his personal aide, he collapsed from overwork. The story is told that Kissinger stepped over the prostrate Eagleburger and continued shouting out orders before he realized that perhaps someone should call a doctor. (After recovering, Eagleburger returned to a less demanding job.)

The press enjoyed reporting on Kissinger's public appearances, his dates with a succession of Hollywood starlets, but the truth was that beyond his work, Kissinger's life was little more than a nullity without the compensatory, corrupting pleasures available to holders of high office. (These would come later.) Food was not a social or sybaritic satisfaction, only fuel to keep him going. "He eats in order to stay alive," a friend said. The modest residence he rented was no more than a place for sleeping (a human necessity he no doubt would have dispensed with entirely if he could have). "I go home only to spend the night," he said. One biographer reported that his home had "the décor of an early Holiday Inn," but the best descriptions of his living quarters come from a love-struck Frenchwoman who got to see them up close. His living room, Danielle Hunebelle wrote in her chatty confessional, *Dear Henry*, "had the air of a hastily assembled dentist's waiting room." His bedroom, with dirty laundry scattered all about, had "so repulsive an aspect that it was hard to imagine anyone living there." Contrary to popular impressions, this Spartan existence apparently extended to Kissinger's sex life. He understood that his image as a "swinger" was useful to him and he did his best to cultivate it, requesting that he be seated next to the most attractive woman at state dinners, confident that he was the most charming personality in a charmless administration, until Nixon put a stop to it. But one frequent date said, "I just don't think Henry was interested in sex," and a historian who has surveyed the subject concluded, "All the available evidence points away from actual consummation." As Kissinger told Hunebelle about his indifference toward material pleasures in general, "You have to live, that's all."

Working in the Nixon White House required not only Kissinger's total dedication but also the kind of patient outlook that enabled him to endure a steady stream of reverses and humiliations, all part of the collaboration problem. Like Metternich and Bismarck before him, Kissinger could be successful in pursuing his policies only if he possessed the skill to stroke the ego of the ruler who would ultimately be making the decisions. Kissinger once described himself as a "good courtier," a necessary quality in any effective statesman. The White House tapes provide example after example of Kissinger going along with a mercurial president almost to the point of self-abasement and sometimes beyond.

At times the Nixon-Kissinger exchanges read like the more barren stretches of Plato's *Dialogues*, when Socrates' interlocutors are given nothing to say except "you're right, Socrates," or "that's correct, Socrates." Nixon asks, "Do you agree, Henry?" Henry responds, "Oh, yes." From Nixon we hear, "You agree with my analysis," followed by Kissinger, "I agree completely with your analysis." And again: "Don't you agree, Henry?" "Totally," comes the reply. To retain the president's confidence, Kissinger told Nixon what he wanted to hear, and then, if he thought it necessary, found ways to work around him, because he understood that Nixon would give vent to his frequent, sometimes drunken, rages without really expecting anything to come of them. This was a talent every newcomer to the Nixon White House had to learn. Frustrated with the North Vietnamese, Nixon exploded one morning, "We will bomb the bejesus out of them. Because, then the hell with history." To which Kissinger offered, "History will think well of you then."

When Nixon went off on one of his rants, Kissinger knew better than to challenge him. The members of "the Eastern Establishment" were among Nixon's many enemies. "That's where the damn radicals are." To which Kissinger, a charter member of the Eastern Establishment, a protégé of Mr. Eastern Establishment, Nelson Rockefeller, replied: "Right. . . . yeah." To Professor Henry Kissinger, Nixon warned, "The professors are the enemy. Professors are the enemy. Write that on the blackboard a hundred times and never forget it." And about the news media, which included many Kissinger friends, among them the archest of Nixon's archenemies, Katharine Graham, the publisher of the *Washington Post*, Nixon could become almost apoplectic: "The press is the enemy. The press is the enemy." Kissinger voiced no objection: "I'm in complete agreement with you."

As Kissinger later said in expiation, "Nixon's favor depended on the readiness to fall in with the paranoid cult of the tough guy. The conspiracy of the press, the hostility of the Establishment, the flatulence of the Georgetown set, were permanent features of Nixon's conversation, which one challenged only at the cost of exclusion from the inner circle." An effective statesman needed to possess a flexible mind that was in constant, acrobatic motion, always calculating the pluses and minuses of stating one's opinions openly. How much could one protest without stepping over the line? Kissinger understood that the tapes could make his placations of Nixon sound like "obsequiousness," but he pleaded for context, for understanding the relationship between ends and means. It was, he said, a question of "balancing," since confronting Nixon directly was "almost suicidal." One had to leave one's ego at the Oval Office door and swallow countless small humiliations for the sake of the larger good. Pride was a self-destructive impulse, whereas Kissinger's natural talent for manipulation served him well.

The most painfully humiliating moments for Kissinger must surely have been when Nixon goaded him about Jews. The refugee from Hitler's Germany, who had lost several relatives in the Holocaust, had to endure ugly outbursts of anti-Semitism—or quit in an emotional huff. He once told a Jewish journalist, "You can't begin to imagine how much anti-Semitism there is at the top of this government—and I mean at the top." Nixon saw Jews everywhere, and where there were Jews, there were Jewish conspiracies. "We've been trying to run this town by avoiding the

Jews in the government." For Nixon, Kissinger may have been an exceptional Jew, or at least a Jew who was useful to him, but that didn't stop him from complaining about Jews in Kissinger's presence. "Well, Mr. President," Kissinger would meekly reply, "there are Jews and then there are Jews." But there could be no reply when Nixon called Kissinger "Jew boy" to his face. It's enough to make anyone cringe. Looked at from one angle, Kissinger's silence was cowardice; from another it was the heroism of individual sacrifice for a higher good. It's little wonder that he reserved his greatest admiration for principled survivors like Chou Enlai.

None of this is to say that there weren't times when Kissinger was ready to tender his resignation. But personal humiliation was never the issue. Nixon could make all the foul accusations against Jews that he wanted and Kissinger would swallow hard and stay on. But when he thought that matters of policy were at stake, he declared his readiness to walk out. He was forever worrying that Nixon had lost confidence in him, and any time he believed the secretary of state was winning the competition for influence, he would cast an eye toward the exit. It didn't matter that after only a few weeks others saw him prevailing in his battles with Rogers and calling him the foreign policy "czar." Kissinger never really felt at ease, convinced that Nixon (whom he considered an astute psychologist) enjoyed playing on his emotions, and the threats to leave came early and often. Haldeman, who heard these complaints more than anyone else, quickly took the measure of Kissinger. "He's really quite insecure," and "for no reason, I believe." He "tends to be all one way optimistic or pessimistic, and colors everything based on his basic reaction."

By March 1969, when others were already thinking of him as the "czar," Kissinger was talking about quitting, and again in January 1970, and in September of that year, and in January 1971, and again in March and December. Sometimes Nixon would reassure him and sometimes simply ignore him, since most of the time he didn't take Kissinger seriously. As Nixon told Haldeman, he would "be a damn fool not to stay on," though John Ehrlichman worried that one day the high-strung Kissinger would "come charging in and quit before he actually even realizes what he's doing." In any case, the continued threats, whether serious or not, took their toll on Nixon, and by the middle of 1970 he was wondering if retaining his oversensitive, obstreperous national security adviser was worth the trouble. Haldeman assured him that it was: "We have to recognize this weakness as the price we pay for his enormous assets, and it's well worth it." But as the planned presidential trip to China, with its world-changing potential, was approaching fruition, Nixon decided to "take a hard line" and call Kissinger's bluff, telling him that if he resigned, he wouldn't be able to go to China, despite all the hard diplomatic work he had put into the effort. Either Kissinger could start worrying more about the presidency and less about himself, or he could just leave. "If Henry quits, he'll just have to quit."

Kissinger quieted down, though as his national prominence grew throughout 1972, the year of the administration's greatest foreign policy accomplishments, so too did Nixon's irritation. Too much of the media spotlight was being shone on his national security adviser. At the end of 1972, Kissinger learned that *Time* magazine was planning to name Nixon and Kissinger together as its "man of the year," setting off Kissinger's self-protective alarm bells. Pleading with *Time*'s editors to give the honor to Nixon alone, Kissinger said, "This is going to complicate my life enormously." But the magazine wasn't interested in making Kissinger's life any easier, and the editor in chief threatened to remove Nixon entirely from the cover if Kissinger didn't stop whining. Kissinger's instincts were right, though. Nixon was furious when the issue appeared. By then, the idea of firing Kissinger had lodged in his mind, and he seems to have decided that once the United States was out of Vietnam, it would be time for Kissinger to go. Kissinger had reached the same conclusion, and by early 1973 he was putting out feelers for a position at Oxford. Watergate, of course, changed everything, and just as the scandal destroyed the careers of so many, it had the perverse effect of prolonging and bolstering Kissinger's. Rogers resigned as secretary of state in August 1973 as the White House was hunkering down, and Nixon reluctantly named Kissinger to replace him, not something he would have done if he felt he had complete freedom. "Both Nixon and I knew there was no other choice."

Kissinger's most public threat to resign and, therefore, the most serious one, came after he had become secretary of state and at the height of the Watergate crisis. Its polluted waters were washing up against even the near-unassailable Kissinger. Stories that the FBI, in an effort to control leaks, had been wiretapping government officials and journalists began surfacing early in 1973, and in September of that year, at Kissinger's confirmation hearing to become secretary of state, the issue dominated the two weeks of questioning. Seventeen individuals, it turned out, had been wiretapped, including several members of Kissinger's own staff. The wiretaps had begun in May 1969 and went on until February 1971. Some of the taps lasted for a few months, others for over a year, and although the justification was to control leaks, some of those targeted continued to be tapped long after they had left government service. What did Kissinger know and when did he know it? At the hearing, Kissinger claimed that "I never recommended the practice of wiretapping," though he conceded that he had given names to the FBI, leaving it up to the agency to decide whether or not to follow through. But the distinction between supplying names and requesting wiretaps seems academic in any case, because the FBI was likely to act on any name Kissinger provided. However he chose to spin it, Kissinger was as deeply involved in the wiretapping scandal as anyone in the administration. Nonetheless, the Senate was not about to reject the most popular man in America and voted its approval 78–7. Even that lopsided majority didn't reveal the extent of his support. According to Kissinger, George McGovern, the Democrats' 1972 presidential peace candidate, told him in private how much he admired Kissinger and that his "no" vote was just a sop to his antiwar supporters.

But as revelation of criminal activity inside the Nixon White House piled on revelation, the issue refused to die, and Kissinger was soon being hounded by Jesuitical distinctions between "requesting" and "initiating" the wiretaps. Suggestions of perjury were filling the air, and after months of insinuations, Kissinger had had enough. With his freedom to function at stake, passivity had ceased to be an option, especially in the nation's capital, where "the appearance of the loss of power can quickly translate itself into the reality of it." At a press conference in June 1974 in Salzburg, Austria, he threatened to resign unless his name was cleared. Kissinger called the announcement "strong medicine," a "throw of the dice," but in his view the accusations represented not only an impediment to his conduct of foreign policy but also an attack on his "personal honor," both sufficient reasons for him to relinquish his almost unprecedented power. His threat was met with a collective gasp. A stunned Congress quickly rallied behind him, with 51 senators, both liberal and conservative, cosponsoring a resolution of support and the Senate Foreign Relations Committee, led by its dovish chairman, J. William Fulbright, issuing a report that exonerated him of any wrongdoing.

This was the last time that anyone heard about the possibility of a Kissinger resignation during the few months that remained of the collapsing Nixon presidency. Though friends urged him to get out while he could, quitting had become "unthinkable." Duty called. He felt he had to isolate foreign policy from the Watergate disaster. Personal loyalty also played its part. After all that they had been through together, good times and bad, "I was determined to stick by the president," even if, as he believed, impeachment had become inevitable. Nixon, he said, "was at the heart of the Watergate scandal."

KISSINGER SURVIVED WATERGATE but he had been wounded— "my relations with the media never fully recovered," he said—and at the very moment he was winning renewed support from Congress, a perfect storm was brewing that the powerful Kissinger was powerless to deflect. It united liberals and conservatives against him, not on questions surrounding wiretapping or other issues of possible criminal behavior but on the very policies that defined his global outlook. Once Nixon had departed, the long-term strategy he and Kissinger had been busy crafting was caught in the crosshairs, the target, it seemed, of just about everyone in Washington except the occupants of Gerald Ford's White House. "The honeymoon is over for Henry Kissinger," one journalist wrote—a honeymoon that had lasted five eventful and controversial years. Individual accusations of illegality could be answered with point by point refutations against specific charges, but a shift in the public mood represented a much more ominous danger because it was something more nebulous and therefore more difficult to grapple with. The opposition to Kissinger was uniting around matters of value, and how could he respond to that except with tedious philosophical lectures on the meaning of Realpolitik? Not that he didn't try: in 1975, he embarked on a speaking tour to explain himself to middle America. Called the "heartland speeches, " they read on the page better than they played. Taking on the Zeitgeist was like trying to fight the weather. Programmatic discourses and manipulative charm could not quell the storm. Suddenly, in this new climate, Kissinger's credibility as a policymaker came under attack in ways that would have been unthinkable only a year before; even his patriotism was called into question. On the right, he was charged with being an "unassimilated outsider, a European by heritage and cultural choice." Amazingly, claims that he was a Soviet agent began to get a hearing, and not just in extremist circles. "Does he have a country?" it was asked, and there were conservatives of every stripe ready to stand up and say that the answer was no.

The left, meanwhile, was assembling its own indictment of Kissinger the war criminal. "Conservatives who hated Communists and liberals who hated Nixon," Kissinger was later to write, "came together in a rare convergence." The assaults emerged from every direction in what had turned into a multifront war.

And the center did not hold. Kissinger had become, in his words, "a lightning rod" across the political spectrum, and in 1975 he offered to resign if Ford thought that it would help his presidency survive. "Don't leave. I need you," Ford replied. As a gesture to the critics, Kissinger gave up his position of national security adviser while remaining secretary of state, and in a laughably ham-fisted reaction, Ford stopped using the word "détente" and started speaking of a policy of "peace through strength." None of it helped. An unstoppable tsunami was gathering. Ford and Kissinger went down together in 1976 in what amounted to a national referendum on the country's character and on who best embodied its values. That was a role impossible for the German-Jewish Kissinger to play (but it was perfect for a former B-movie actor turned politician). A victorious Jimmy Carter had criticized the Ford administration for cynicism and immorality, by which he meant only one person, and Kissinger was on his way to becoming one of the most reviled figures of modern life (if also, schizophrenically, one of the most respected). What had happened?

IT WAS AS IF Richard Nixon's downfall had breached the political levees, not just on matters pertaining to Watergate but on the entire thrust and direction of American foreign policy. Distracting questions of official malfeasance could be put aside after the Nixon resignation, together with the aftershock of the Nixon pardon, and with Vietnam now consigned to history, serious debates about the role of America in the world could begin. What was the United States trying to achieve as a global power? What did the nation stand for? Given all the bloodshed and domestic turmoil that the Vietnam war had produced, these were entirely legitimate questions, ones that had divided Americans ever since the United States assumed an active role in world affairs at the beginning of the twentieth century and that had become matters of genuine urgency in the 1970s when confusion over America's objectives reigned. Except the debates never really did take place, unless shouting and posturing counted as discussion.

The two Realpolitikers, Nixon and Kissinger, had a clear idea of what they were trying to do and where they were going (at least compared with their opponents). As Kissinger said, "Nixon and I viewed international relations from a nearly identical perspective." When asked, they explained that they were looking to achieve global stability. The word that summed up these endeavors was "détente," which was the effort to find a way for the two superpowers of the Cold War to live together without blowing the world up, as well as a template for international affairs in general. Détente has been called "the centerpiece of Nixon and Kissinger's foreign policy." It was, Kissinger affirmed, "not a starry-eyed quest for cooperation for its own sake, but a method for conducting the geopolitical competition," representing the unsentimental pursuit of American national interest while at the same time recognizing that there were limits to what Washington could achieve internationally. ("Limits" was a favorite word in Kissinger's vocabulary.) It was the Realists' balance-of-power strategy by another name. As Nixon put it, "We must remember the only time in the history of the world that we have had any extended period of peace is when there has been balance [*sic*] of power."

In Kissinger's understanding of the history of the Cold War (and he was hardly alone in this), until 1969 the policy of the United States had been to use its unrivaled superiority following World War II to try to dominate through steadfast and unyielding toughness. There was a reason John Wayne had become a postwar American icon. As long as the United States possessed overwhelming military might, it could feel free to assert its hegemony, pulling back, as in Hungary in 1956 or at the end of the Vietnam war, only when countervailing pressures proved too strong even for the world's foremost power. Otherwise, it was push, push, push in the name of freedom, sometimes to the brink of war. But as the Soviet Union built up its own capabilities, it was only a matter of time before unreflective brinksmanship produced a world-threatening standoff. The United States and the Soviet Union had come frighteningly close to nuclear holocaust during the Cuban Missile Crisis of 1962, when the Russians were much weaker than they had become by 1969. With no change in the superpowers' policy goals or behavior, the future promised two, three, many missile crises, and these future confrontations would involve not slow-moving ships churning across the Atlantic while Kennedy and his advisers devised their strategies but high-flying supersonic weapons requiring decisions in a matter of minutes. The need, Kissinger insisted, was to turn the two superpowers into partners to avoid nuclear confrontation, which he called "a moral, political and strategic imperative."

Demonizing the Russians would do nothing to achieve this goal. Détente was a policy that necessarily painted in unsatisfying grays, not self-righteous blacks and whites. As Kissinger explained, Nixon "did not see relations with the Soviet Union as an all-or-nothing proposition." To be sure, the point was not to "pretend friendship" as many too desirous of world peace seemed to advocate. Cold War conflicts were real and would continue. Hopes based on little more than the fatuous optimism of trusting one's fellow man were no answer, because, as Kissinger insisted, "We and the Soviets are bound to compete for the foreseeable future." But that didn't mean areas of mutual understanding couldn't be explored or agreements reached that would be of benefit to both sides and facilitate additional ties in the future. That was the purpose, after all, of diplomacy. Dealing with the Soviet enemy wasn't appeasement or surrender, as nationalist critics charged; it was a requirement for a world on a nuclear hair-trigger.

Détente, Kissinger repeatedly stressed to the more hawkish elements in the Washington community, didn't mean forsaking a policy of deterrence or weakening the U.S. militarily. It was a process, not a goal, "a pragmatic concept of coexistence." There was no finality to it as there was no finality to the conduct of foreign policy. Closure was not an option. Neither Nixon nor Kissinger "believed détente would ease our defense burden," because Washington had to continue "to draw the line against Soviet adventure." But it was also important to recognize that "there was a limit beyond which the Soviets would not let themselves be pushed" (there was that word again). Whoever was in the White House had to walk a tightrope between confrontation and coexistence, possessing the empathy to grasp the vital interests of the men in the Kremlin by putting oneself in their place, even if such psychological sensitivity was condemned as appeasement by America's blinkered jingoists. "Disagreements among sovereign states," Kissinger starkly put it, "can be settled only by negotiation or by power," and as for those whose instinctive preference in the Cold War was for the second he also said, "The nuclear age has changed both the significance and the role of power." More than ever, it was important to "be concerned with the best that can be achieved, not just the best that can be imagined." With nuclear holocaust as the backdrop, what was the alternative to détente?

Kissinger offered extended explanations of détente in the second and third volumes of his memoirs, but his most focused defense may have come in the heat of battle during testimony he delivered before the Senate Foreign Relations Committee in September 1974. It was a time when he was already witnessing a "crusade" (his preferred word for his critics' position) in opposition to his policies but just before that opposition had swelled into a flood tide. Like the university professor that he never ceased to be, Kissinger began by instructing his "students" on the committee about what was at stake in the conduct of foreign affairs in the nuclear age. History presented the depressing spectacle of continual warfare, endless enmity among nations and groups. But (as Morgenthau also insisted) the development of nuclear weapons represented a profound break with the past. Human nature had not changed and people would continue to be willful, selfish, and aggressive, but without mechanisms of some kind to rein in their natural tendencies, the inevitable result would be nuclear catastrophe. History unrestrained was destined to end not with a whimper but with a bang of cataclysmic proportions. Kissinger may have become widely perceived as a sinister Dr. Strangelove, but in his appearance before the Foreign Relations Committee all he was saying was give peace a chance. Questions of international conflict had assumed "unprecedented urgency," Kissinger explained, and he quoted Eisenhower: "There is no longer any alternative to peace."

Creating the conditions for international stability would not be easy because there were undeniable differences between the United States and the Soviet Union in values, history, ideology, and national interest. Still, the changed circumstances of the early 1970s offered an inviting prospect of managing Cold War animosities. Even as the Soviets were engaging in a disturbing military buildup, their external and internal weaknesses were piling up, presenting an opportunity for mutual understanding. Kissinger pointed to the recent "fragmentation" of the Communist world as a sign that Moscow had lost political strength; it now had to worry about the growing hostility of the Chinese and the mounting insubordination of ideological allies and satellite nations. It was no longer "the arbiter of orthodoxy" in the Communist world. A joke made the rounds in diplomatic circles that the Soviet Union was the only country in the world surrounded by hostile Communist regimes. Economically, too, the Soviet Union and the other Communist states had fallen far behind the West, with little prospect of catching up or meeting the demands of their restless populations through central planning. Suppression could go only so far in an increasingly interconnected world, and as long as the United States exercised patience, without demanding either capitulation or regime change—which would only stiffen the backs of the Communists—an opportunity existed for dealing with the Russians. (The United States, too, had been changed by the Vietnam debacle and growing divisions among the allies, a loss of American strength that also opened the way to détente, but this wasn't something Kissinger stressed in his testimony.)

Years later, Kissinger outlined the broad perspective that guided the Nixon administration: "In our view, the longer the Soviet confrontation with the West was delayed the more unmanageable would become the task of holding together the Soviet empire, especially since its political problems were compounded by economic stagnation." This was an argument to take advantage of Soviet weakness through diplomacy and negotiation, rather than military confrontation, which Kissinger disparaged as the policy of Cold War "theologians." And coming from a congenital pessimist, it was also surprisingly optimistic: "Time was on the side of the United States," he said, "not of the Communist world." Détente was not only Realpolitik by another name; it was also a continuation and extension of George Kennan's containment policy. If containment was pursued, Kissinger was certain the West would eventually win the Cold War. Kennan himself remarked that Kissinger "understands my views better than anyone at State ever has."

Kissinger recited for the committee the benefits that had already been achieved under détente, proudly pointing to the "unprecedented consultation" taking place between the two superpowers. Little noticed was cooperation in the fight against cancer, on energy conservation and other environmental protections, in research on agriculture, and the peaceful use of atomic energy, even in the training of astronauts. More headline-worthy was the 1971 agreement on Berlin; the city was located deep in East Germany, and by guaranteeing the West access to it, the pact removed a long-standing Cold War irritant that had always contained the menace of starting a third world war. Most important of all was the Strategic Arms Limitation Treaty (SALT), "the first deliberate attempt by the nuclear superpowers to bring about strategic stability through negotiation." The details of arms control were hideously complicated because of the vast differences between the military requirements of a land-based power like the Soviet Union and a sea-based power like the United States, and it was much easier to fall back on disagreement than to do the hard work of looking for accommodation. Yet in the environment nurtured by détente the two sides discovered the will to find common ground under very difficult circumstances. As Kissinger said, SALT was a crucial step toward a more peaceful world. "We face an opportunity that was not possible 25 years or even a decade ago." But he concluded with a warning: "If the opportunity is lost, its moment will not quickly come again. Indeed, it may not come at all."

Who could object to the increased contacts between the Soviet Union and the United States that Kissinger described or to the general easing of tensions represented by the policy of détente? The answer was, just about everyone. Détente, as numerous scholars have explained, flew in the face of long-standing American traditions and ingrained American prejudices. It was, one said, "almost impossible to market at home." Détente, and the larger Realpolitik principles from which it sprang, required acquiescence in the Cold War status quo for the sake of negotiation and global stability. It meant compromising with Communist dictators in Moscow and Beijing instead of trying to overthrow them through regime change. Worse, it conceded that hostile governments would remain strong because a balance of power, not American dominance, was the pathway to peaceful negotiation of conflicts. Détente accepted that even enemies had legitimate interests. Nixon stated explicitly that a "strong, healthy" Soviet Union and China served the aims of American foreign policy.

In Kissinger's way of thinking, as John Stoessinger explained, "victories and defeats merely led to other wars. Only a settlement without victory or defeat could create stability" because America's enemies would then be acting as agents in their own right, making choices that they perceived were advantageous to themselves. Critics complained that the Soviets agreed to détente only because it was in their interest to do so. Kissinger replied that the Soviets were not going to agree to anything that wasn't in their interest. Compulsions imposed by a hostile power, even when possible, could produce only festering resentment. As Kissinger was later to say, "Absolute security for one side must mean absolute insecurity for all other sides." The point was to find areas of agreement that were in the interests of both sides. These were frustrating, even "foreign" concepts that did not come naturally to the politicians in Washington.

The policy of détente asked Americans to opt for uncertainty and nuance over idealism and the pursuit of what they considered to be justice, to give up their utopian aspirations to spread democracy around the world, and to stop seeing rivals as immoral villains. As one historian observed, "When adopting détente, the Nixon administration had bargained away, consciously, the ability to explain U.S. foreign policy in the context of a struggle between good and evil." To Realists like Nixon and Kissinger notions of justice, though not to be ignored entirely, had to be subordinated to the larger goals of foreign policy and in particular to the management of the nuclear threat. If an uncomplicated morality had dominated their thinking, they would never have toasted the blood-drenched totalitarians in Beijing, which Kissinger understood as a major step toward Realism and his enemies saw as a sellout of allies and an abdication of moral responsibility. But despite the successes of the Nixon administration, Realism, as Kissinger noted, was very much "a minority view." It had "no ready constituency" among the American people, and after Watergate, Kissinger said, "American idealism reigned supreme, unfettered by any incentives for political compromise." From time to time, he cast an envious eye abroad, where he was sure his tasks as a diplomat would have been easier: "American leadership groups are not as comfortable with the concept of national interest as those of, say, Great Britain, France or China." He quoted one of the statesmen he most admired, Charles de Gaulle: "It is only in equilibrium that the world will find peace." And he said of the Chinese: "I could not have encountered a group of interlocutors more receptive to Nixon's style of diplomacy than the Chinese leaders."

The revulsion against Nixon and Kissinger's "amoral" foreign policy was a reversion to more familiar ground for the American people, a backpedaling to the only international position they genuinely felt comfortable with—one that dated back to Woodrow Wilson and was appropriately called by Kissinger "Wilsonianism." The United States, unlike other countries, required a national purpose; it had to be a force for "good" in the world. When it took the momentous step of joining the international community by entering World War I, it did so not to restore balance to the European continent but for the idealistic and aspirational reasons articulated by Wilson: to fight a war that would end all wars, to make the world safe for democracy, to erase the sins and evils of the past, to proclaim a fresh start to humankind, to bring an end to history. European statesmen faced with matters of national survival may have been dumbfounded by such hyperbolic utopianism, but Wilson understood his countrymen because he understood himself. He knew that if he was to ask them to shed their blood, he had to give them the grandest of reasons. The country may have been in the process of becoming part of world history, but intellectually and morally, it sought to remain outside of history. Narrow questions of self-interest would not suffice for the sacrifices it was being called upon to make. The United States was not like other nations. It would engage in battle for the sake of transcendent, universal values, with the confidence that God, or at least history, was on its side.

Wilson appealed to a mind-set that was fundamentally melodramatic and absolutist rather than political and pragmatic, that saw foreign policy in terms of black and white, good guys and bad guys. Implicit in this view was the notion that the peoples of the world were ready to live as an irenic global family if only the selfish and oppressive forces that denied them their freedom were overcome. What was so funny about peace, love, and understanding? Tranquility, not animosity, was the natural condition of humankind, to be assured by the spread of democracy. For peace to prevail, the whole world had to become a simulacrum of America. There were no international problems that could not be solved by openness, the ballot box, and a system of law. These concepts could be instituted even at the highest level by the creation of an international body, called by Wilson a League of Nations, which after World War II was resurrected as the United Nations.

Just about every one of these ideas, and all of the preconceptions behind them, went against Kissinger's own beliefs and his policy of détente. He was ready to concede that Wilsonianism had its good points. "Some of the finest acts of twentieth-century diplomacy," such as the Marshall Plan and the defense of Western Europe, "had their roots in the idealism of Woodrow Wilson." But "at the same time, Wilsonian idealism has produced a plethora of problems," including "such disastrous crusades as Vietnam." It seemed like Kissinger was forever being thrust into the position of reminding his countrymen that history was not some will-o'-the-wisp to be swatted away, or a burden to be rejected for the sake of transcendent ideals, but an "immutable" force in the affairs of humankind. "Tradition matters because it is not given to societies to proceed through history as if they had no past and as if every course of action were available to them. They may deviate from the previous trajectory only within a finite margin." With the Versailles Treaty of 1919, Wilson's decent intention to overcome traditional animosities with a piece of paper had been calamitous. And yet to Kissinger's consternation, "It is above all to the drumbeat of Wilsonian idealism that American foreign policy has marched since his watershed presidency." Even his partner in Realpolitik, Richard Nixon, kept a picture of Wilson in the Cabinet room.

Peace, in Kissinger's anti-Wilsonian, "amoral" view, was not the natural condition of humankind, freedom and self-determination would not necessarily lead to the resolution of differences, and conflicts could not be solved through an appeal to some sort of default moral consensus. Above all, democracy did not guarantee global peace and stability. History showed, Kissinger insisted, that, contrary to what the Wilsonian idealists wished to believe, democracies did indeed go to war against one another, and they could be as oppressive to their own minorities as any authoritarian regime, if not more so, as rival ethnic and religious groups seeking supremacy tore at each other's throats. There was no avoiding the hard work and usually incomplete successes of diplomacy and negotiation. Yet the history of American foreign policy, Kissinger wrote, "has been a triumph of faith over experience."

This was not a message that most Americans wanted to hear during the years of détente or those that followed. To his dismay, Kissinger reported that the senators on the Foreign Relations Committee were "Wilsonians to a man," and whether liberal or conservative, they had no taste for his pessimistic (and exhausting) Realism; perfectionist in their aspirations, they were demanding that the administration pursue a more "elevated" policy. At their most hostile, they viewed détente as "a form of moral disarmament," although as Kissinger retorted, "the preservation of human life and human society are moral values too." Liberals and the left were all too eager to dissociate themselves from the men responsible for implementing the Vietnam war, but perhaps because his own political instincts were conservative, Kissinger's greatest disappointment was with those he expected to be his allies: "Aroused conservatives," he said, "are notoriously difficult to placate." They had made themselves into "moral absolutists" who called for "a policy of unremitting confrontation." The nuclear balance may have changed irrevocably from the halcyon years after World

War II when U.S. dominance was unquestioned, but like the French Bourbons of old, America's conservatives had learned nothing and forgotten nothing.

As détente came under attack from all sides, Kissinger noted, a disturbing and destabilizing trend was developing in how foreign policy was being conceived. He and Nixon had engaged in negotiations with hostile foreign governments in pursuit of what they believed to be in America's interests; the domestic policies of those governments were not their concern, at least not publicly. They would deal with the devil if they thought there was some advantage to be gained—which was exactly what the critics of détente condemned them for. But by demanding a more "moral" policy, the new Wilsonians were led almost ineluctably to a more aggressive global posture in which the United States was obliged to interfere in the internal affairs of other countries. Anything less was callousness or cynicism or selfishness. It was certainly not "elevated." Kissinger accused his critics of wanting to replace diplomacy with self-righteous militancy. Looking out for the national interest, he insisted, "was not necessarily amoral." But in a country undergoing a post-Watergate moral purging, this was a tough case to make. The members of the Foreign Relations Committee, Kissinger reported, "were embarrassed by appeals to the national interest." And combined with that was an additional objection to détente's quest for international stability that created its own assertive dynamic. Now that the United States had assumed an indisputable role on the global stage, much of the public had come to believe that freedom at home was endangered unless it was promoted abroad. American democracy was fragile and, therefore, threatened by the status quo.

To be sure, mere opposition to détente, with vague appeals to morality, did not add up to a policy, but the Wilsonians found their way forward in a simple phrase with enormous resonance. America's mission in the world would be defined by its adherence to the cause of "human rights." Here was a capacious "moral purpose" that could unite the left and the right. As Senator Henry Jackson, a liberal Democrat who as much as anyone defined the opposition to Kissinger, chose to put it, détente was "a body without a soul—a policy indifferent to human rights." If Kissinger challenged his opponents by asking who could be against the easing of tensions brought about by détente, they were ready to respond: Who, except a coldhearted bastard, could be against human rights?

The cause of human rights may have been roomy enough to house

Individuals from across the political spectrum, but there were important differences in how the left and right viewed the subject. Conservatives, who retained an ideological hostility to Communism and continued to think of it as a Satanic monolith even after the Vietnam disaster, tended to employ the idea as a cudgel with which to beat up the Soviet Union. They were willing to overlook gross abuses elsewhere as distractions from the only conflict that mattered. This opened them up to charges of hypocrisy, though from a Realpolitik perspective, hypocrisy was hardly the worst of sins. Like Kissinger, conservatives recognized that the differences between the United States and the Soviet Union were deep and real, not simply matters of misunderstanding and miscommunication. Moscow posed the most dangerous threat to America's security, and human rights could be a useful weapon in the nation's Cold War arsenal. Domestically, it gave meaning to foreign policy, rallying the public behind a comprehensible and comforting objective; internationally, it put the Communists on the defensive.

For Kissinger, however, the issue was one of proportion. "How hard can we press" the Soviets, he asked, without reigniting the Cold War, especially because there was very little Washington could do to bring about internal reform. Domestic change would come through "evolution," according to the Russians' timetable, not the Americans', and he made his familiar appeal to the dictates of the past: "We cannot demand that the Soviet Union, in effect, reverse five decades of Soviet, and centuries of Russian history." He would have been among the last to expect the collapse of the Soviet Union to usher in a golden age of democracy in places where it had no roots. To his conservative critics, he said, "Simply to needle the bear" was to invite "constant crises." The effort to bring pressure on the Soviets would undermine the benefits that diplomacy could offer. It was as futile as it was dangerous. What was more, it was likely to unnerve allies and contribute to America's isolation in the world. Perversely, the conservative challenge to détente in the cause of American national interest weakened security instead of strengthening it.

Kissinger's response to his critics on the left was different and more complicated. They were the ones who charged the anti-Soviet conservatives with hypocrisy, an accusation that could not be made in their case because they universalized the cause of human rights, seeking to apply it everywhere and under all circumstances—no inconsistencies, no mealy-mouthed equivocations for them. Once again, Kissinger could argue that his critics ignored the particularities of history. Different countries had different values, different national objectives, and different security needs that the United States could do very little to change and that required particular approaches to particular situations. Liberals tended to reject a foreign policy based on national interest, calling for more "unselfish" aims, but in a world of widespread human rights violations, the concept of national interest served a purpose by enabling policymakers to prioritize their objectives, choosing among often distasteful alternatives. With no sense of national interest, all that remained was "an undifferentiated globalism and confusion about our purposes." Similarly, the use of military power made the left uncomfortable, even though it provided a concrete measure of limits, a useful calibration of what Washington could hope to accomplish in the world and probably was the closest one could come to quantifying what were ultimately judgment calls. "If we universalize our human rights policy," Kissinger said, "applying it undiscriminatingly and literally to all countries, we run the risk of becoming the world's policeman." The liberal vision of human rights promised "an unlimited agenda of global interventionism on humanitarian issues."

Even worse, although conservatives had weakened American security with their demands for military solutions in the Cold War rivalry, their rejection of diplomacy's compromises, and their acceptance of constant confrontations with the Soviet Union, the liberals' universalizing tendencies had weakened security in the opposite way. Kissinger pointed to a paradox. The liberals' calls for human rights would have little or no impact on the Soviet Union or other powerful enemies of the United States, who were often the worst offenders yet could afford to ignore humanitarian demands from Washington. But allies more dependent on the deployment of American power would be put in a difficult position if they resisted American demands to liberalize their societies, and vulnerable allies, facing immediate internal or external threats, would be in the most difficult position of all. Should America insist on human rights perfection from its friends because it was in a position to hector or pressure them? That was no way to build international coalitions against immediate enemies and would set the United States on a path to isolation for the sake of moral purity. Few were the countries that could live up to the abstract standards of the humanitarian campaigners. "The ultimate irony would be a posture of resignation toward totalitarian states and harassment of those who would be our friends."

Kissinger said he was not unmindful of the moral claims of foreign policy, but he argued that more could be done through behind-the-scenes discussions and pressures than through public and humiliating confrontations. "We have successfully used our influence to promote human rights. But we have done so quietly." Even if his critics had reason to doubt that a Realpolitiker would be the most effective advocate for human rights in the backrooms of diplomacy—Kissinger confessed that he was more inclined to see "the dangers and dilemmas along the way"—they had no genuine response to the concerns he raised and the paradoxes he pointed out, except to reassert their moralistic convictions. As Senator Jackson declared with more passion than evidence, "A moral foreign policy based on defense and the promotion of human rights represented the best way to serve U.S. national interest."

Ultimately, the clash over human rights was as much a political battle as an intellectual one. Foreign policy depended on garnering public support around broad themes and directions, and three powerful groups stood firmly in the way of implementing détente or any other policy grounded in the principles of Realpolitik. They were the liberal left among the Democrats, the nationalist-populists within the Republican Party, and a small coterie of intellectuals—the neoconservatives—that had moved from the Democratic Party to the Republican Party. The neoconservatives may have been few in number, but by the vigor of their ideas and their unique positioning in the public discussion, they came to wield enormous influence on American foreign policy for more than a generation. (Kissinger said they brought "intellectual rigor" to the debate.) It would be hard to say which of these three groups most hated Henry Kissinger.

WHEN THE LEFT looked at Kissinger, what it saw was a callous opportunist ready to kill thousands to advance his own career, a man who, whatever the human cost, was interested in nothing but himself. He was paranoid, duplicitous, autocratic, and sycophantic. Ideas didn't matter to him, morality least of all. One of the most influential critics, Seymour Hersh, wrote in 1983 that pleasing Nixon was Kissinger's most important priority. A more venomous opponent, Christopher Hitchens, made the charge, all too familiar on the left, that Kissinger was a war criminal—what else could he be if his lethal policies had no other aim but his personal advancement? Hitchens drew up a "Bill of Indictment" that charged

Kissinger with crimes in such places as Bangladesh, Chile, Cyprus, and East Timor. International relations, Hitchens wrote, were treated "as something contingent to his own needs." One Kissinger defender, his authorized biographer Niall Ferguson, has argued that every postwar administration before Nixon's—Truman's, Eisenhower's, Kennedy's, and Johnson's—"could just as easily be accused of war crimes or crimes against humanity." He pointed out that Eisenhower's policies in Guatemala had led to the deaths of about 200,000 people. Causing or condoning death, even of innocents, was the price of being a superpower with a global role. Yet perhaps with the exception of Truman (because of his decision to use atomic weapons against Japan), no one was put in the leftist dock as a war criminal so often or to the same degree as Kissinger, not John Foster Dulles, not Dean Rusk. Why, Ferguson wondered, did Kissinger's accusers subject him to a "double standard"?

The left, however, didn't see a double standard. Kissinger, alone among postwar policymakers, was charged with making decisions out of personal interest, not national or global concerns. According to his critics, he "believed in nothing," though it would be more accurate to say that what he believed in was weighing means against ends, a kind of situational, pragmatic ethics that rejected the left's moralistic strictures. What he didn't believe in were absolutes. "There is no easy and surely no final answer," he said. To be sure, valid objections could be raised against specific Kissinger policies, even in his own terms of weighing means against ends—the invasion of Cambodia, for example, or the tilt toward Pakistan during the Bangladesh crisis—and there is certainly truth to Seymour Hersh's assertion that "Nixon and Kissinger remained blind to the human costs of their actions." Callousness has always been the besetting sin of Realpolitik, and it is not difficult to find examples of almost brutal coldness in Kissinger's record. "It's none of our business how they treat their own people," he said of Moscow's policy toward Soviet Jews. "I'm Jewish myself, but who are we to complain?" Actual human beings could get lost as power was being balanced.

But once it was conceded that Kissinger operated from a Realpolitik framework with intellectual, even moral principles of its own that were larger than himself or his personal advantage, then difficult questions about which decisions best served American interests or humanitarian ends were open to debate. Judgment calls weren't the same as the perpetration of crimes (although some Realpolitikers were sure to recall

Talleyrand's words upon hearing of the murder of the Duc D'Enghien: "It was worse than a crime, it was a blunder") Because Kissinger's leftist critics didn't accept Realism as a legitimate basis for foreign policy, they didn't see any need to debate matters of judgment. What was more, locked in their partisan cocoons, they had trouble acknowledging that policymakers frequently made those judgment calls in a fog of ambiguity, in which outcomes could not be predicted and the ethics of a situation could point in several directions at once. "Statesmanship," Kissinger said, "needs to be judged by the management of ambiguities, not absolutes." But what the left craved, what they insisted on, was moral certainty in an uncertain world, or what Kissinger, in a combative mood, called "a nihilistic perfectionism."

It was the Vietnam war that had set the left on this perfectionist course. Whereas Kissinger (and Hans Morgenthau) had seen the conflict as a mistake of America's good intentions, the student protesters of the 1960s could think only in terms of black and white: the war was "evil," meaning that those who prosecuted it were evil too, and no one was identified more with the war than Henry Kissinger. "Vietnam," Bob Woodward has written, "was like a stone around his neck." Opposition to the war was a sign of righteousness, with the children of light arrayed against the children of darkness.

This was the foreign policy legacy that the antiwar protesters of the 1960s passed on to the rest of the twentieth century and the first decades of the twenty-first century. International affairs weren't a matter of selecting among often cruel choices but of simply choosing sides. One of his critics condemned Kissinger for pursuing "endless war as a matter of course," ignoring his Realist contention that there is "an irreducible element of power involved in international politics." During the years of the Cold War, he insisted, American power was employed "to prevent Soviet military and political expansion," explaining to a generation unable to see anything beyond Vietnam that "the Cold War was not a policy mistake—though some mistakes were of course made." Vietnam had turned the attention of the left away from the realities of power to the sanctimonious realms of self-righteousness. But as Kissinger was to preach again and again: "So long as the post–Cold War generation of national leaders is embarrassed to elaborate an unapologetic concept of enlightened national interest, it will achieve progressive paralysis, not moral elevation."

The accusation of "war criminal" was an easy way for the left to avoid the responsibility of arriving at a "concept of enlightened national interest." It made the conduct of foreign policy seem unambiguously easy. Everything came down to simple, emotive conclusions: peace was good, killing people was bad—even though peace was not the natural condition of humankind and killing people was something just about every postwar American president has been compelled to do.

If Kissinger was a war criminal to the pacifistically inclined anti-Vietnam left, to the nationalist-populist right he was quite possibly a traitor or, at best, simply out of his mind, and though these two groups were united in the intensity of their hostility to Kissinger, their differences were so vast, so irreconcilable, that they might as well have been living on different planets or at least in different countries. Both rejected Kissinger's Realpolitik, but the left did so for the inchoate goal of global peace, whereas the nationalist right did so for the seemingly concrete objective of victory in the Cold War and dominance in the world. The left saw foreign affairs as "social policy," Kissinger observed, the right as the opportunity for "American hegemony."

The most elaborate articulation of the nationalist right's quest for American supremacy and rejection of Kissingerian diplomacy came in the form of an 846-page tract entitled *Kissinger on the Couch*, published in 1975 by the fervent conservative Phyllis Schlafly and coauthor Chester Ward. He was a retired rear admiral who no doubt assisted her with the chapters on military hardware, though the thrust and tone of the book are clearly Schlafly's. It's a remarkable performance—there is really nothing quite like it in the extensive literature on Henry Kissinger. Schlafly, described as the "warrior queen" of social conservatism, had risen to prominence as one of the most visible and influential supporters of Barry Goldwater at the 1964 Republican convention, the author of the right-wing call to arms *A Choice, Not an Echo*. The convention had reminded Kissinger of the Nazi rallies he had witnessed as a boy in Germany. He was never comfortable with the extreme nationalists of the Republican right (even refusing to wear a flag pin in his lapel because of the memories of enforced Teutonic patriotism it engendered in him). The Schlaflys of the country responded in kind, with enduring suspicion of him as a subverter of American interests. *Kissinger on the Couch* can be read as one long attack on Realpolitik by the populist right.

Of one thing Schlafly and Ward were certain: with his policy of détente, Kissinger had dramatically weakened the United States, bringing the country to a condition of near-surrender vis-à-vis the Soviet Union. The SALT agreement gave the Russians "decisive strategic advantages," even "potentially fatal" ones. Kissinger had turned a foreign policy that was pro-NATO and anti-Communist into its exact opposite, "anti-NATO, pro-Communist." He was the tool of the "one-world ideologists and the money-power people" centered around the Council on Foreign Relations, whose tacit goal was to subordinate the United States to the United Nations. Distrusting the American people, as evidenced by his preference for secrecy, failing to understand or appreciate "typical American values," Kissinger was an unassimilated foreigner and "surrender-prone defeatist" whose loyalty was not to the American government but to a "supranational" order. The protesters against the Vietnam war were wrong to hate him. He was really a brother-in-arms. If anything, he favored surrender even more than they did.

It was all so simple and, best of all, so easy to understand. Henry Kissinger was the source of America's woes in the world, and that was that. His Realpolitik was un-American when it wasn't anti-American. To set things right, he not only had to be removed from public office but also denied any influence on international affairs ever again. Still, if the extreme nationalists like Schlafly had simplistic explanations for what they saw as Washington's failures in the world, they also had an intellectual problem they were forced to deal with. The compromises with the Russians and the Chinese, as well as the withdrawal from Vietnam, had occurred under Richard Nixon, a man who had made his career as a hard-line anti-Communist and was hated by the left for it. He had exposed Alger Hiss, supported Joe McCarthy, and backed Barry Goldwater in 1964. Kissinger called him "the classic Cold Warrior." How could such a man, all at once, go "soft on Communism" and preside over a policy Schlafly called "America last"?

The reason she gave was that in the battle of wits between the two men, Nixon was unequally matched. He was intellectually insecure, whereas Kissinger was nothing if not confident, a Svengali with near-hypnotic powers of persuasion, "a pudgy spider at the center of a web." Nixon had fallen "captive" to the "cunning" and "sophisticated" Kissinger. He had been "duped" by his national security adviser into following un-American designs.

It doesn't take much insight to see that Schlafly's language echoes classic anti-Semitism: the rootless, diabolical Jew, the "spider," manipulating the naïve, well-meaning gentile for the sake of an international, moneyed cabal. And it can hardly be doubted that there were unregenerate anti-Semites among her readers and among the adherents to her brand of populist nationalism who were delighted to have their worst suspicions confirmed by someone knowledgeable enough to produce a massive, forbiddingly dense tome. They didn't need lessons from Leo Strauss to read between the lines of Schlafly's book.

In fact, Schlafly herself didn't traffic in Jewish conspiracies, at least not in public. She would say no more than that Kissinger's experiences as a Jew in Germany contributed to his attitude of "defeatism." The words "Jew," "Jews," and "Jewishness" do not even appear in her index. Instead, she turned to two other explanations to understand Kissinger's behavior.

The most straightforward of these, the one with which she opens her book and that provides her with her title, is that Kissinger was simply "some kind of a nut." Because of his life experiences, there was a "high probability" that he had lost touch with reality. His grandiosity, his megalomania, and his incessant lying were all signs of psychological instability, causing him to pursue policies that undermined the United States. A brilliant crazy person was leading America to disaster.

Unfortunately, she went on, one could not ignore a "more sinister" alternative. The damage Kissinger had done to America, Schlafly also suggested, was "deliberately planned"; he was "affirmatively helping the bear." Schlafly stepped back from directly charging Kissinger with being a Soviet agent: "We are not, anywhere in this book, accusing anyone of being a traitor or of being guilty of treason," that is, not in a strictly legal sense. But "if the reader feels that the evidence makes a case for de facto treason, that is his conclusion." Covering all her bases, Schlafly blithely gave with one hand what she took back with the other. There was something in her encyclopedic book for every right-wing true believer.

Kissinger on the Couch exemplified some of the most extreme thinking in American politics in its time and could easily be dismissed by those who were not already members of Schlafly's populist choir. But the overall direction of its arguments was not limited only to a small band of fringe conservatives. Even mainstream voices were ready to denounce Kissinger in Schlafly's conspiratorial terms. The longtime foreign policy expert Paul Nitze, for example, a harsh critic of détente though neither a leftist nor a populist, called Kissinger "a traitor to his country." What Schlafly did, at greater length and in more exhausting detail than anyone before or after, was to articulate a strain of thought that has persisted from Barry

Goldwater through Ronald Reagan to Donald Trump. For over 40 years,
America's populist nationalists have been among Henry Kissinger's most
powerful and most persistent political enemies.

There is, however, one area of overlap between Kissinger and his populist enemies that calls for clarification. The Realist Kissinger was the advocate of national interest and was condemned by the universalizers of the
left for it. The Schlafly populists were nothing if not nationalists, intent to
advance what they saw as America's interest against the one-world mentality of the left. "Survival or self-defense is the first law of nature," Schlafly and Ward proclaimed. The hard-nosed Kissinger, a man all too aware
of "the necessities of survival," was not someone to disagree. "We cannot
abandon national security in pursuit of virtue." Yet there was almost no
common ground between the right's America First pronouncements and
Kissingerian Realism.

For the populists, international affairs were a zero-sum game in which
there could be only winners or losers. Concepts of compromise, coexistence, even empathy—détente!—were altogether alien to them; the trade-
offs of diplomacy were a pathway to surrender. Kissinger's chessboard
strategies in a contest that he conceded could never end was "defeatism"
at best, treason at worst. Only the United States had interests that had to
be respected; looking at things from the point of view of one's adversaries,
a Kissinger specialty, was the posture of weaklings because the job of the
country's leaders was to see to it that America prevailed on the international stage. "Why not victory?" was the question that Barry Goldwater
had asked and that the populist right had adopted as its credo, but it was
one that had no place in Kissinger's way of thinking. He was a nationalist,
to be sure, ready to defend the United States against its enemies, but in
his awareness that each country had vital interests of its own and that the
United States did not, in fact, have God on its side, he was—in distinction
to the populists—what might be called an international nationalist.

And so, on the issue that Kissinger had spent much of his career struggling with, trying to get his mind around, the issue of nuclear war, the
populists had simple answers antithetical to the practice of Realist statesmanship. The United States necessarily had to pursue a policy of nuclear
supremacy, they insisted, because the "firmest foundation" for world peace
was "just one nuclear superpower, not two competing powers." Kissinger,
in the opinion of Schlafly and Ward, suffered from an inordinate fear of
nuclear conflict, but "once you declare that your overriding objective is

the prevention of nuclear war, you are well on your way to surrender." What might constitute an "ordinate" fear of nuclear conflict they did not say, nor did they spell out exactly what nuclear supremacy might look like. But even many Cuban Missile Crises was not a prospect that seemed to bother the populist nationalists, though it was a cloud that hung over much of Kissinger's thinking. Disturbingly, the more religiously fundamentalist among the populists may even have welcomed the hastening of Armageddon.

By the time of the Nixon administration, populists like Schlafly had become indispensable to the Republican Party, an essential component of its political base, imbuing it with energy and conviction. But as the overwhelming defeat of their standard-bearer, Barry Goldwater, in the 1964 presidential election demonstrated even to the most zealous of them, they were a long way from reaching beyond the already converted. There were too many obstacles to wider support—like the appeals, spoken or unspoken, to racism; the taint of nativism; the almost flippant attitude toward nuclear war. It was the rise of the neoconservatives in the late 1960s and early 1970s that helped to change this political landscape, enabling the populists to find a way into the American mainstream. Serious issues divided these two groups—none greater than the question of anti-Semitism. The neoconservatives consisted largely of Jews, so much so that one of the group's historians has called neoconservatism basically a reflection of the twentieth-century Jewish immigrant experience. Urban, educated, and cosmopolitan, the neoconservatives were hardly natural allies of the old-line nationalist right, true-believing Middle Americans from Henry Ford country who retained more than a whiff of anti-Semitism. For their part, many of the Goldwater populists considered neoconservatism a "Jewish cabal" that was concerned more about Israel than the United States. As in the past, Jewish loyalties were being questioned. What brought these strange bedfellows together was their mutual detestation of détente and their shared animosity toward Henry Kissinger; both rejected the compromises of Realpolitik, arguing for American hegemony in the world. And what further helped to solidify their unlikely coalition was the fact that each delivered something the other lacked: the neoconservatives gave the populists respectability; the populists gave the neoconservatives numbers.

The neoconservatives first emerged in the mid- to late-1960s as skeptics of Lyndon Johnson's Great Society programs, raising tough questions about race, welfare, crime, education, and other domestic issues. At the time, they were criticizing from the inside: their home was the Democratic Party. Jeane Kirkpatrick, the onetime ambassador to the United Nations, who drifted in and out of their camp, said that what distinguished the neoconservatives from traditional conservatives was a "liberal past." But as academics by and large or journalists with university connections, they were shaken deeply by the student protesters' assault on the campuses at the end of the decade, which led them to question their own political affiliations and pushed them toward conservatism. The candidacy of George McGovern and the presidency of Jimmy Carter sent them further to the right with some, like Irving Kristol and Norman Podhoretz, becoming Republicans, while others, like Daniel Bell and Daniel Patrick Moynihan, remained liberals, though ambivalent ones.

It was never hard to find sharp disagreements among them on particular issues—these were, after all, freethinking intellectuals who took pride in reaching their own conclusions. The commentator David Brooks, who came to maturity under their tutelage, has accurately observed that "there is no such thing as a neoconservative 'movement.'" But by the mid-1970s, as the neoconservatives moved right and shifted their focus from domestic to foreign policy and a younger generation of sons replaced the older generation of fathers (literally, in a few cases), it was possible to describe what Podhoretz called a "neoconservative tendency" and Kristol termed a "neoconservative persuasion." What came to unite this collection of independent minds was an assertive, unapologetic internationalism. The neoconservatives insisted on the necessity of facing down the Soviet Union at a time when the Democratic Party appeared to be giving up on the Cold War and turning away from any engagement in international affairs. No less anti-Communist than the populists, they viewed the McGovernites of the early 1970s as naïve isolationists.

It is hardly surprising that at first Kissinger considered them "philosophically close," allies in his battles on Capitol Hill and against the Russians. Indeed, many of them were his friends. But they soon revealed themselves to be as hostile to Kissinger's détente as they were to his leftist critics. Like the Schlaflys of the right, they believed that America's global influence had been seriously undermined by the Nixon and Ford administrations. A "multipolar world," they contended, was "far more dangerous" than one dominated by the United States. And again like the nationalist-populists, they viewed Kissinger as the primary villain in this woeful state of affairs. Two of the most prominent neoconservatives, in a direct attack on Kissinger's principles, declared that "the United States should seek not coexistence but transformation." As one historian has put it, "'stability' and 'balance of power' and 'equilibrium' were terms of abuse in the neoconservatives' lexicon." "Limits" was not a word that passed easily across their lips. Kissinger noted that no less than the populists, the neoconservatives were demanding "total victory." With some annoyance, he pointed out that they had commonly been opponents of the Vietnam war at a time when he was under fire from the left for trying to find an "honorable" way out. And when he traced their passage across the political spectrum from New Deal Democrats to allies of the populist right, what he saw was "the passion of the convert," whose "ideological elan" was a substitute for strategic thinking. They were trying to lure policymakers away from "the need to face complexity."

Nonetheless, for all their agreement about America's role in the world, the nationalist-populists and the neoconservatives could never be more than uneasy partners. They may have muted their differences in their common battle against détente, but the divisions were deep, extending well beyond the Jewish question. The populists applauded American power and a policy based on national interest, but they lacked a conceptual framework like Kissinger's and Morgenthau's Realpolitik to provide theoretical substance to their nationalism. In truth, they were little more than naïfs, at sea when faced with the daunting complexities and multidimensional configurations of foreign affairs. With nothing but patriotic emotion to rely on, they did their thinking viscerally: as long as the country was militarily strong, global challenges would take care of themselves. Having no taste for diplomacy, they were content to sing the national anthem at football games and wave the flag on the Fourth of July, glaring suspiciously at anyone who didn't. "My country right or wrong" was the extent of their philosophy, and what became clear as their influence within the Republican Party grew and Kissinger's waned was that an intellectual vacuum had developed among the ranks of the right wing that would somehow have to be filled. Incessant calls for larger military budgets could go only so far. It was the neoconservatives, intellectuals every one, who would take on the job, and American politics would never be the same.

What the neoconservatives could offer that the nationalist-populists could not was a world outlook based on more than mere military power. In their view, Kissinger's quest for international stability was a fool's errand. As long as there were tyrannies in the world capable of challenging American democracy, there could be no global peace. That was why, contrary to Realpolitik principles, Washington had to be concerned about the internal politics of other countries, and why the proper course to pursue with the dictatorships of Russia, China, North Korea, Cuba, Iran, and Iraq was "regime change," even if the tactics to be followed differed in each case. Anything else was appeasement.

"All serious foreign policy," Kissinger declared, "begins with maintaining a balance of power," but the neoconservatives countered that balance-of-power policies left America permanently vulnerable to its enemies and that détente was an "illusion." It had to be replaced with what they called a "forward-leaning conception of the national interest." The populists, with no ideas beyond military superiority for its own sake, may have been uncertain about America's role in the world and even ready to withdraw once the Cold War ended, but there was no uncertainty among the neoconservatives. The task of the U.S. government was to maintain "America's benevolent global hegemony." The United States had to be the "custodian of the international system." Neoconservatism, the neoconservatives confidently proclaimed, provided "the most plausible basic guidance for America's role in today's world."

In the debates about foreign policy during the last quarter of the twentieth century, the neoconservatives had an intellectual advantage over both the populists and the Realists because they could appeal to the Wilsonian instincts of the American people. The Schlaflys and the Kissingers may have differed over their perception of the national interest, but in both cases they didn't allow "morality" to occupy the central place in their thinking, whereas for the neoconservatives values came before anything else. America had a historical and ethical mission to spread democracy around the world; banishing dictatorships was a moral necessity (and also, they would add, the true national interest). It was not "my country right or wrong" for them, but "my country because she is right," which meant, however, that she could also be wrong. In contrast to the populists, the allegiance of the neoconservatives was not unquestioning, not nationalistic blind faith. How could Washington sit back, they complained, while innocent people were being slaughtered, either by their own governments or by rival groups vying for power? (To which the populists were likely to answer: that isn't our concern.) The neoconservatives' sense of themselves derived not from their identity as Americans but from their belief that they were intensely moral beings upholding a universal and transcendent code of behavior. Not for them Nietzschean cautions about the pitfalls of ethical thinking. One of their number, Charles Krauthammer, argued for what he called "democratic globalism," by which he meant "a foreign policy that defines the national interest not as power but as values." And the "supreme value," he said, was what John F. Kennedy called "the success of liberty."

In this desire to make the world safe for democracy, the neoconservatives were reviving the decades-old language of Woodrow Wilson, whom they considered a "precursor." Like him, they believed democracy was the default position of humankind once the forces of oppression were overcome. The yearning for freedom was universal and to suggest otherwise, they claimed, was to engage in a form of racism in which only white people of European heritage were thought capable of sustaining democracy. When the Soviet Union fell apart, they announced with more conviction than foresight, "so did Russian aggression beyond its borders." They were entirely comfortable describing themselves as "Wilsonian idealists."

But in one respect they differed from their "precursor," and the difference was significant. Wilson advocated international institutions to promote democracy, and near the end of his career he had no more ardent ambition than the establishment of a League of Nations to assure global order through open, liberal processes. The neoconservatives considered such an aspiration naïve. For them, democracy would arrive not through international debating societies like Wilson's League of Nations or Franklin Roosevelt's United Nations but on the heels of the U.S. military. Force was a necessary component of democracy promotion, just as democracy promotion was a necessary component of American foreign policy. The neoconservatives may have been self-confessed Wilsonians, but, in their own language, they were "hard Wilsonians," or, as one of them put it, Wilsonians "on steroids."

The Realist Kissinger might warn that the neoconservatives unrealistically "believed that values could be translated directly into operating programs" and that their "denial of any limits leads to exhaustion or disaster." But in the post-Watergate era, appeals to morality in international affairs and to the concept of an American mission, those old Wilsonian ideals brought back to life, carried more weight than arguments for moderation, compromise, and coexistence. When those appeals were

linked to a call to preserve Washington's post–World War II global hegemony, as the neoconservative script demanded, the message proved irresistible to millions of Americans uncertain and confused after the debacle
of Vietnam. The nationalist-populists and the neoconservatives may have
had well-founded suspicions about each other, but they joined together
in a marriage of convenience to vanquish both the antiwar left and the
Kissingerian Realists. And after 1976 they had a charismatic champion to
lead them to victory.

CHAPTER SEVEN

KISSINGER OUT
OF POWER

RONALD REAGAN CHALLENGED GERALD FORD FOR THE
Republican Party's presidential nomination in 1976 basically by
skewering Henry Kissinger. Echoing the populist right's complaints, he
accused Kissinger of weakening the United States militarily, undermining allies like Taiwan, and generally sacrificing American interests for the
"one-way street" called détente. Kissinger, he declared, should be fired.
"He savaged me," Kissinger said about the attacks, complaining in private that Reagan "doesn't know what he's talking about." Even though
Reagan's attempted coup against his party's sitting, if unelected, president failed, he did succeed in turning the Republicans around on foreign
policy. In its platform that year, the party effectively and humiliatingly
rebuked Kissinger: "Ours will be a foreign policy which recognizes that
in international negotiations we must make no undue concessions, that in
pursuing détente we must not grant unilateral favors with only the hope
of getting future favors in return."

By 1980, there was no denying Reagan's ascendency and the advent
of a new, more assertive perception of America's place in the world that
disdained coexistence. The legatee of Goldwater, Reagan had made himself "the political and symbolic flag bearer" of the populists, who, true
to form, spent time at the Republican convention that year warning delegates about the un-American conspiracies of the Council on Foreign
Relations. The neoconservatives, with their dreams of renewed American
hegemony, viewed him exactly the same way. He was, in the words of one,
their "standard-bearer," and after he departed the political stage in 1989,

they spent years yearning for what they understood as a "neo-Reaganite" foreign policy.

Not that Kissinger disappeared entirely from the scene. He delivered an address at the 1980 convention that attacked the Democrats and had the delegates applauding. But when Ford, in backroom negotiations, urged Reagan to name Kissinger as his secretary of state, the candidate demurred. "My own people," he said, "wouldn't accept it." He also derailed Richard Nixon's suggestion that he find a way to make use of Kissinger. To worried supporters who thought the manipulative Kissinger might manage to insinuate himself back into government, Reagan insisted, "I can assure you I would not choose him as an adviser." And with rumors flying that Kissinger was secretly assisting the campaign, he became adamant: "This is absolutely not true. I have a number of well known and very capable people . . . who are helping in the field of foreign policy. Henry Kissinger is not one of them, nor will he be."

As president, Reagan remained largely true to his word, and neither the populists nor the neoconservatives had reason to worry that Henry Kissinger would stage a comeback inside the Reagan White House. Kissinger's impact on American foreign policy had manifestly diminished, and he was now on a downward slope. In the words of one scholar, his "Realist moment revealed itself as a parenthetical period in the history of the U.S." Nonetheless, despite the insults and humiliations he had endured as Reagan rose to dominance in the Republican Party, despite his distance from policymaking circles during the 1980s and his well-known thin skin, Kissinger was to offer a retrospective assessment of the Reagan presidency that was multifaceted to say the least: negative and contemptuous in many respects, positive, even admiring, in others. It was impossible to pin Kissinger down on the subject of Ronald Reagan, whom he called "an extraordinarily complex character."

Since Reagan was a Wilsonian par excellence, confident of America's historic mission in the world and famously inclined to paint adversaries as "evil"—the kind of talk to make any Realpolitiker's hair stand on end—Kissinger had nothing good to say about the president's strategic thinking: indeed, there was no strategic thinking. Reagan, he wrote, had a shallow intellect and little interest in the details of foreign policy. "He had absorbed a few basic ideas about the dangers of appeasement, the evils of Communism and the greatness of his own country, but"—as the diplomat Kissinger explained in the most diplomatic of language—"analysis of substantive issues was not his forte." The notion of balancing power was foreign to him. Global chess was not his game.

Reagan was an old-fashioned American utopian who believed that the right combination of hard-line policies and open communication among leaders would yield "a final outcome" of global understanding. Kissinger, of course, did not believe in final outcomes or, for that matter, in open communication. When Reagan said before his first meeting with Mikhail Gorbachev that "I'd dreamed of going one-on-one with a Soviet leader," Kissinger warned that Cold War tensions "cannot be removed by the personal relationships between two leaders, and it is not in our interest to create the impression that they can be." Most disconcerting, perhaps, Reagan "treated biblical references to Armageddon as operational predictions." A centerpiece of his foreign policy was to spend the Soviets into submission through vast increases in America's military budget, an idea Kissinger had rejected just a few years before as "politically intolerable" and likely to leave both sides worse off. Reagan's first term "marked the formal end of the period of détente," Kissinger said. "America's goal was no longer a relaxation of tensions but crusade and conversion." Why not victory, indeed. Communism was not to be contained but defeated, making Reagan, at first glance, the anti-Kissinger par excellence.

For all that, at the end of Reagan's first term, Kissinger said, "I have agreed with most of the policies of the Reagan administration even when I was less than ecstatic about the manner of their presentation and justification." And after Reagan had completed his second term, Kissinger allowed a little ecstasy to creep into his assessment. He wrote that "Reagan's was an astonishing performance." He pursued a "foreign policy doctrine of great coherence and considerable intellectual power." Not bad for a shallow intellect. What was going on here?

On one level, it's hard to ignore Kissinger's ingrained propensity to play the courtier. By the time of the 1980 presidential campaign, he had cast his lot with the Republicans and had nothing to gain except political isolation by breaking with a figure who was on his way to becoming a Republican icon. With the "war criminal" accusation establishing itself as the conventional wisdom of the Democratic Party, he was not about to plunge into the political wilderness by attacking his only potential allies. As he had said, there were times when it made sense to play the opportunist. For Kissinger, the 1980s were one of those times.

But, as always, "opportunist" was not a sufficient description of

Kissinger. His admiration of Reagan was genuine, particularly what he saw as Reagan's "uncanny talent" to rally the American people behind his policies. Reagan was a master democratic politician in a way that a German-born Jewish intellectual could never be. As Kissinger said, he lacked the political ability to articulate a vision that could win widespread public support. "My skills were strategic analysis and diplomacy, not the essentially political task of mobilizing popular constituencies." His intelligence, his wit, his self-deprecation were for refined tastes like those of the Washington press corps, not the millions of Americans who expressed their views at the ballot box. Irony did not play well on the hustings, and a dour sense of tragedy could scarcely compete with the sunny optimism of "morning in America." No American statesman, Kissinger said, could ignore the nation's values. Surprisingly, even so accomplished a politician as Richard Nixon failed to measure up the way that Reagan did. As a Realist like Kissinger, he spoke in abstractions about such things as a "structure of peace," not the kind of language to win hearts and minds. Nixon, Kissinger wrote, was "probably too cerebral" for the American people. "Reagan had a much surer grasp of the workings of the American soul." Nixon might inspire respect. Reagan inspired love.

Reagan's political career, Kissinger observed with admiration and not a little awe, provided valuable lessons in how to be an effective leader in a democracy. Nixon and Kissinger had relied on secret maneuvering, diplomatic back channels, top-down decision making—all widely condemned as undemocratic and un-American, even by those who might concede that secrecy was no less important to successful diplomacy than it was to the production of sausages or the writing of laws. Wilsonian to his core, Reagan spoke in simple language about easy-to-understand goals openly achieved. He may have horrified the foreign policy professionals when he seemed on the point of reaching an agreement with Gorbachev to eliminate all nuclear weapons, but his good intentions, however misguided, were obvious to all. Whatever his intellectual shortcomings, he demonstrated that "a sense of direction and having the strength of one's convictions are the key ingredients of leadership," not a complex mind or a high IQ. Millions of Americans identified on a personal level with Reagan, and none of them ever accused him of lacking decency; no one ever described Nixon as having it. Reagan's style was far more suited to an open society than was Nixon's (or Kissinger's).

Or so it seemed. In Kissinger's complicated analysis, Reagan's inspiring utopianism was sincere as far as it went, good for public relations and for winning popular support, but it was also camouflage for a deviousness that was, well, Nixonian—"a canny reassertion of the geopolitical strategies of the Nixon and Ford administrations clothed in the rhetoric of Wilsonianism," Kissinger said. Reagan engaged in "an almost Machiavellian realism," strategically seeking the collapse of the Soviet system and opposing Communist expansion around the world, tactically working with the Russians through multiple summit meetings for the cause of world peace. "Though framing the issue as a struggle between good and evil, Reagan was far from arguing that the conflict had to be fought to the finish"—although he had strong convictions, he did not allow his rhetoric to outdistance reality. Instead, he "laid the foundation," Kissinger said, "for a period of unprecedented East-West dialogue," what just a few years earlier might have been called "détente." As Kissinger wrote, "By the end of Reagan's presidency, the East-West agenda had returned to the pattern of the détente period." Every time Reagan sat down and shared a joke with Gorbachev, the neoconservative policy of regime change took a hit, and "the longer the Reagan presidency went on," one historian has reported, "the more disgruntled the neoconservatives became." But their numbers had never been large, and Reagan's populist base was not about to turn on their avatar for being soft on Communism. With ill-disguised envy, Kissinger observed that Reagan exhibited a "diplomatic flexibility that conservatives would never have forgiven in another president"— another president named Richard Nixon. Kissinger stripped Reagan of his Goldwaterite extremism, his Wilsonian utopianism, and his neoconservative evangelicalism. Historians may debate forever the meaning of the Reagan presidency, but Kissinger had reached his own conclusion: in his estimation Reagan, far from being the anti-Kissinger, was actually Henry Kissinger in wolf's clothing.

Kissinger was even ready to concede that in his desire to ease Cold War tensions, he may have taken détente too far and that Reagan's more confrontational style was a useful corrective. "As the Reagan years would demonstrate, a bolder policy toward the Soviet Union had much to recommend it," he wrote. Zbigniew Brzezinski, Jimmy Carter's national security adviser, said much the same thing: "As the experience of the Reagan administration shows, there is some real advantage to sustaining first a reputation as a hard-line ogre and then softening one's position." Two independent analysts agreed. Anatol Lieven and John Hulsman wrote that

Reagan's tough talk during his first term gave him the "political cover" to act like George Kennan in his second. But what of Kissinger's repeated warnings that the Russians could be pushed only so far without creating a crisis for superpower cooperation and global stability? How bold was too bold? Did Reagan know?

Anyone seeking precise answers to these questions is chasing up a blind alley. Even after all the data had been collected, the strategic analyses completed, and the scenarios played out, any policy depended upon the instincts of the one making the decisions. The answer to the question "Did Reagan know?" depends on the meaning of the word "know." Kissinger was charmed by Reagan's good cheer and congeniality, and he came to trust Reagan's instincts because, for all his hard-line rhetoric, he proved in actuality to be pragmatic, not ideological, a man of "common sense" and "goodwill." Indeed, the intuitive Reagan may have been more far-seeing than his highly educated advisers in perceiving the brittleness of the Soviet system and understanding that a determined push from the United States would send it over a cliff. By contrast, his vice president, George H. W. Bush, who was far more experienced in foreign affairs than Reagan, said no one saw the collapse of the Soviet Union coming. Sometimes, it seems, Kissinger thought Reagan had a deeper grasp of the U.S.-Soviet rivalry than the so-called experts around him; sometimes he wasn't sure. But "in the end, it made no difference whether Reagan was acting on instinct or on analysis. The Cold War did not continue, at least in part because of the pressures the Reagan administration had exerted."

Timing and dumb luck were also crucial to Reagan's success. If he had been president a decade earlier, Kissinger observed, when the divisions roiling the country over Vietnam were approaching a level of civil war, his right-wing words might have been sparks to a flame. By 1980, however, a certain amount of healing had occurred, while the opposition on the left was no longer mobilized and in the streets. What was more, changes in the Soviet Union had worked to Reagan's advantage. Moscow had lost its earlier confidence in the historical inevitability of Communism, and when Gorbachev assumed control of the Kremlin in March 1985, just at the start of Reagan's second term, Washington was confronted with a Soviet leader who could be an interlocutor as well as an adversary. As Gorbachev's biographer, William Taubman, has written, "In Gorbachev, Reagan found the perfect partner—he, too, was convinced that a U.S.-Soviet settlement was possible." As someone who had the experience to know, Kissinger remarked, "Statesmen need luck as much as they need good judgment."

Unlike some of Reagan's leftist critics, who are inclined to give Gorbachev the lion's share of the credit for ending the Cold War and to minimize Reagan's contribution, Kissinger was always ready to praise Reagan for his role in turning history around. The collapse of the Soviet Union was "a process hastened by his administration's policies," Kissinger said. And "Ronald Reagan and his associates deserve much credit for the denouement of the Cold War." Kissinger's implication was that the liberal East Coast elites had to get over their contempt for anyone lacking their Ivy League credentials.

Nonetheless, those plaudits came with warnings for Reagan's admirers, who are insistent that his hard-line policies were the key to ending the Cold War. It was easy to misread the impact of Reagan's arms buildup and confrontational posture, because the tough talk, Kissinger observed, was a doorway to Reagan's version of détente. Emphasizing his militancy while ignoring his "softening" was a distortion, a partial reading of the Reagan legacy. As the historian Robert Dallek put it, to say that "'Reagan won the Cold War' is more than a celebration of Reagan's presidency; it is an argument against the wisdom of détente," a Schlaflyite dismissal of diplomacy for the sake of simple "toughness." Kissinger's admonitions that the core of foreign policy lay in statesmanship and negotiation, with armed confrontation a potential threat of last resort—"that the key to successful foreign policy is a sense of proportion"—was turned on its head by many of those who claimed to be the heirs of Ronald Reagan but who showed little evidence that they possessed a sense of proportion.

The danger of such triumphalism, Kissinger warned, was not only that it encouraged a "one-sided emphasis on military power" that was "impossible to sustain," but also that it fostered a kind of national "smugness," in which "assertiveness" replaced nuance, and hegemony in the form of "freedom" along with democracy promotion became the be-all and end-all of American foreign policy. It wasn't the idea of democracy that won the Cold War, Kissinger insisted. To believe that was to indulge in "a version of escapism." Communism collapsed because of its inherent weakness, aggravated, to be sure, by the pressures of the Reagan administration, which in turn were building on the containment policies pursued by every American administration since 1947—and that, at their core, posited the eventual collapse of Communism. What waited at the conclusion of the

Cold War, however, was not "a beneficent status quo" marking the victory of democracy and the end of history, but "triumph" forms of nationalism that would confront the United States with a completely different set of problems, "a world for which little in its historical experience has prepared it." The extinction of the Soviet Union was undeniably a great step toward the easing of nuclear tensions, a world-historical event of immense and positive consequence. Worries about a nuclear confrontation between the superpowers have much diminished since the 1980s (though they have hardly been eliminated). And Ronald Reagan was in the middle of it all. Still, it was best, Kissinger advised, to see the Reagan era not as a new beginning but "more in the nature of a brilliant sunset."

IF, DURING THE REAGAN YEARS, Kissinger stood on the sidelines looking in, that is not to say that he was entirely without influence. Through his writings, his personal connections, and his public appearances, he continued to press his case for a Realist foreign policy against Washington's moralistic instincts. He had a cause to fight for. Unlike so many public figures, he was not about to go gently into that dark night that swallowed up so many retired American statesmen. Warren Christopher, anyone? Kissinger may have had enemies on every side, but he also had millions of admirers eager to hear what he had to say. The first two huge volumes of his memoirs, published in 1979 and 1982, were best sellers. In 2014, 1,615 scholars in international relations from 1,375 American colleges and universities were asked to name the most effective secretary of state of the last 50 years. Kissinger came in first with 32.21 percent of the vote. Coming in a distant second with 18.32 percent was "don't know." The mere mention of Kissinger's name may have been enough to start an intellectual civil war between its supporters and detractors, and the intensity of his enemies' hatred was enough to guarantee that after 1977 he would never again hold public office. But every American president from Jimmy Carter through Barack Obama found a reason to make use of him. It's impossible to think of another recent public figure who has played so contradictory a role. Even with critics hounding his every step, Kissinger was a frequent visitor to the White House, where his advice was heeded at the highest echelons of government. He became the backdoor man of American foreign policy.

It began as soon as he left office. Carter had won the presidency campaigning, much like Reagan, on the need for a more moral foreign policy than the one Kissinger had pursued, but shortly after taking office as Carter's national security adviser, Zbigniew Brzezinski concluded that "the anti-Kissinger mood that had developed in the course of 1976 worked to my disadvantage." Far from emphasizing human rights as his boss did, Brzezinski channeled Kissinger, declaring that "I felt that power had to come first." Though they had long been rivals for public influence, Brzezinski talked to Kissinger on the telephone, dined with him, and valued his counsel. After Kissinger warned him about criticism from the press, Brzezinski wrote, "How right he was." During the Iran crisis precipitated by the overthrow of the Shah, the two men worked together so closely that Carter accused them of conspiring against him.

Kissinger found his way back into the Reagan White House as well. Reagan could always rally his base with his anti-Kissinger rhetoric, but he was willing to consult Kissinger in private, even when he was ostensibly an anti-Kissinger candidate for president. Contrary to the promises he made to his supporters, in September 1980 he asked Kissinger to use his China contacts to reassure Beijing that he would continue the Nixon/Kissinger policy toward Taiwan. Reagan's secretary of state after 1982, George Shultz, also maintained private connections, and at one point, even suggested to Reagan that Kissinger might be brought back to succeed him at the State Department. When Reagan needed to reach out for broader national support, he knew that in many influential circles no name came with more luster than Kissinger's. Upheavals in Central America were proving to be a constant problem for him, domestically as well as internationally, and once he decided to form a special commission to come up with a bipartisan program, who better to lead it, who more likely to provide it with the mainstream support Reagan craved, than Henry Kissinger? As Reagan told New Hampshire's conservative governor, naming Kissinger was "a price for getting the support we must have for our effort in Central America." Kissinger won praise for his evenhanded guidance of the commission, but the report it produced was promptly ignored, dying with few to mourn it, and the egocentric Kissinger does not even deign to mention it in his enormous volume on the history of diplomacy. Still, although the whole exercise may have been something of a sham, it demonstrated that the Kissinger name was valuable even to the most overtly antagonistic of presidents.

Kissinger might have expected to get a warmer welcome from Reagan's successor and possibly a public position. The George H. W. Bush administration was seeded with Realpolitikers who had past associations to Kissinger. Brent Scowcroft, Bush's national security adviser, had worked under Kissinger, as had Lawrence Eagleburger, the deputy secretary of state. Even Bush's personal secretary had a Kissinger connection. And there was no administration that was philosophically closer to Kissinger's perspective. Scowcroft acknowledged that, like Kissinger, "I was a strong proponent of back channels as a means to bypass the bureaucracy." One historian has called the years of the first Bush presidency a "Realist appendix" to the Nixon-Kissinger era.

Kissinger did in fact offer private advice on Europe and China, and Bush wrote that "I respected Kissinger's special insight." He even considered appointing Kissinger as his "special emissary" to China before deciding that he was "too high profile." Kissinger was kept in the background for reasons that were as much personal as political. One Kissinger biographer, Walter Isaacson, reports that Bush "did not like Kissinger very much," and points to the maneuvering that went on after Reagan had secured the Republican Party nomination in 1980. It was said that Bush believed Kissinger and Gerald Ford had tried to dissuade Reagan from naming Bush as his vice presidential running mate. Neither is it clear that Kissinger had a particularly high opinion of Bush, at least when he was in government. In 1971 Kissinger confided privately to Nixon that he thought Bush was "too soft" (Nixon agreed), though he later praised Bush for his moderation in the handling of the Tiananmen Square crisis, which might have been vastly more complicated if the human rights absolutists had had their way. "Bush walked this tightrope with skill and elegance." Whatever the case, Bush prided himself on his own foreign policy expertise, and he knew that with Henry Kissinger in his administration, he would never have complete control. He was all too aware of the Kissinger tantrums in the Nixon White House and the last thing he needed was his own "Kissinger problem." Kissinger would continue entering the White House through the backdoor.

Inevitably, Kissinger would be more distanced from the Clinton administration. Not only was a Democrat in the White House, but as Kissinger also said, Clinton was "the first president whose formative political experience had occurred as an activist in the Vietnam protest movement." His national security adviser was Anthony Lake, who had been on Kissinger's staff but resigned with considerable fanfare over the Cambodia invasion. In his bulky memoirs, Clinton makes only scant and fleeting mention of Kissinger. He was not about to link his name to the man who criticized him for pursuing an "extreme Wilsonian foreign policy" and whom many in his party considered evil incarnate. (Years later, when his wife chose a different course by openly acknowledging her close relationship to Kissinger, the intensity of the outcry against her revived memories of the divisive Vietnam years.)

But as with every president before and after him, Clinton drew on Kissinger's advice and trotted him out when it was to his advantage to do so. On trade policy in particular, Kissinger was invited to the White House to lend his support. Along with Jimmy Carter and Gerald Ford, he helped promote a trade bill with China. He also had a key role, if an unofficial one, in the negotiations over NAFTA, which Kissinger called Clinton's "most enduring legacy" and "a crowning achievement of foreign policy." It is probably an overstatement to say, as one historian does, that Clinton "embraced" Kissinger, but he was a regular presence at state dinners during the Clinton years, called on when the heads of important countries like China and Germany came to town.

Kissinger was also present at a dinner honoring the Czech president Vaclav Havel, who requested that the proto-punk rock legend Lou Reed be asked to perform. Reed had the good sense not to include "Walk on the Wild Side" or "Heroin" among the eight songs he played before the assembled gowns and tuxedos during his 35-minute set. When he finished, President Clinton declared, "If you had as much fun as I did just now, you should give President Havel all the credit." One struggles to imagine how "much fun" Kissinger was having or to picture his face as Reed belted out "Sweet Jane" and other numbers—diplomatically impassive, no doubt, as when he was engaged in those endless negotiations over Vietnam or when, at some official dinner in a foreign land, he was obliged to eat some especially repulsive food.

Probably no administration since Gerald Ford's drew more heavily on Kissinger's expertise than that of the second Bush. He met regularly with the president. Vice President Dick Cheney said, "I probably talk to Henry Kissinger more than I talk to anyone else," at least once a month. Kissinger also served on an advisory board for Secretary of Defense Donald Rumsfeld.

Kissinger has said that he has "great respect and affection" for George W. Bush, but that did not mean that he became a mouthpiece for the administration, which was demonstrating a strong propensity for neoconservative moralism. He supported the invasions of Afghanistan and Iraq—overthrowing Saddam Hussein, he said, was "a legitimate objective"—but he was predictably skeptical about the effort to implant democracy in barren soil. That aim, he observed, constituted a "radical reinvention of Afghan history" and "imbued the American endeavor in Iraq with a Sisyphean quality." The argument was made at the time of the invasions that the United States had successfully introduced democracy into Germany and Japan after World War II, so why not Afghanistan and Iraq? The Realist Kissinger wasn't buying it. Democratization was effective in Germany and Japan, he stated, because of the "total defeat of the adversary, long occupation and sustained American investment." It could not be achieved on the cheap or based on the hope that freedom, as defined by Washington, was an aspiration of people everywhere. When Bush, in his second Inaugural, proclaimed a worldwide campaign for freedom, Kissinger told friends that he was "appalled." And after Bush, in a separate speech, declared that "freedom can be the future of every nation," Kissinger called the idea "unmoored from realities."

Approaching age 80 at the time Bush took office, Kissinger was no doubt too old to assume a permanent position in the new administration, but Bush did try to give him a highly visible role early in his presidency with predictable results. Following the 9/11 attacks, Bush named Kissinger to lead an investigative commission. The reaction was swift and fierce. "Good grief. I turn my back for a few minutes and they bring back the old war criminal," the journalist Molly Ivins exclaimed. In the same vein, the *New York Times* columnist Maureen Dowd sneered under the headline "They Bu u u ddtl : If you want to get to the bottom of something, you don't appoint Henry Kissinger. If you want to keep others from getting to the bottom of something, you appoint Henry Kissinger." Commentators from other major newspapers piled on. Bush had named Kissinger to head the commission on November 27, 2002. Little more than two weeks later, on December 13, Kissinger withdrew from consideration. Complaints had been raised because the commission, in the course of its investigations, might have been forced to question clients of Kissinger's highly profitable consulting firm, and in turning down the position Kissinger said he wanted to avoid even the appearance of a conflict of interest. But everyone knew that the passions raised by the mere mention of his name went far beyond a list of clients. "In the end," one historian has written, "it was his record in the Nixon and Ford administrations that did the job." The

columnist William Safire said the "hate-Henry industry" was having "a
hissy fit."

Of the three Democratic administrations to follow the Nixon/Ford
years, Barack Obama's was without question the one to which Kissinger
was closest. The Henry-haters within the party might have been enraged
if they had been paying attention, but the Obama-Kissinger connection
made sense to those whose job it was to know what was going on. Even
during his race against John McCain in 2008, Obama, the analyst Fareed
Zakaria declared, was "the true Realist in the race," a judgment seconded
by many others once Obama took up residence in the White House. The
Financial Times hailed "Barack Obama's Welcome Kissinger Realism,"
and the *New York Times* chose to headline a column by its foreign policy expert Thomas L. Friedman, "Barack Kissinger Obama." Similarly,
the German magazine *Der Spiegel* headlined one of its articles "Obama
Returns to Kissinger's Realpolitik." The magazine's writer observed that
much as Kissinger tended to do in places like Chile, "Obama looks the
other way when America's allies, Bahrain and Saudi Arabia, subjugate
their people, or when China harasses dissidents." *Der Spiegel*'s conclusion
was that "Kissinger probably relishes the notion that the president resem-
bles him more and more every day." And if further confirmation were
required, Obama's first secretary of state, Hillary Clinton, declared in
2014 that Kissinger's outlook "largely fits with the broad strategy behind
the Obama administration's effort over the past six years."

Kissinger himself was moderately positive about Obama, giving him,
for example, a B-plus for his China policy (not bad coming from a tough
grader like Kissinger). He liked the fact that Obama had shown himself
to be a Realist by focusing on the national interest but worried that the
president was too passive. "Obama prided himself most on the things he
prevented from happening," and he added that Obama lacked a vision for
the future—a criticism that might be leveled against almost every aspi-
rant for the White House following the end of the Cold War, particularly if one was looking for a Realpolitik framework to succeed the Reagan
"sunset." According to Kissinger, Obama's foreign policy was too static,
"operating automatically," and he distinguished his own views in a way
that most nonprofessionals would probably find too arcane or at least too
abstract. "I believe in evolutionary stability," whatever that was. "It is key
to my thinking."

One journalist who spent hours interviewing Kissinger at the end of the

Obama era came away with the impression that Kissinger was "offended" because Obama had not consulted him as often as other presidents had. Certainly, Obama did not reach out to him the way his predecessor, George W. Bush, did. But Kissinger's influence extended deep within the Obama administration, and he had little reason to complain. Samantha Power, the ambassador to the United Nations, had taken her seat as a confirmed Wilsonian moralist but came to value Kissinger's advice. They attended baseball games together, and Kissinger described her as a "good friend," even if her perspective differed somewhat from his own. "She is doing a great job at the U.N.," he said.

John Kerry, who succeeded Hillary Clinton as Obama's secretary of state, was another administration figure who started out as a Kissinger critic, first entering the public arena as an outspoken opponent of the Vietnam war. But in office, he developed a Realist's appreciation for the uses of power and met with Kissinger before important diplomatic gatherings. "I seek his advice—he's a brilliant guy," Kerry said. And noting how much Kerry had changed from his youthful protesting days, Kissinger declared, "I respect John Kerry for his courage and persistence." Obama's Defense Department also revealed its appreciation of Kissinger's contributions. In February 2016, it presented Kissinger with its highest honor for private citizens, the Distinguished Public Servant Award. The citation noted that Kissinger had implemented a policy of détente with the Soviet Union, was instrumental in opening relations with China, and negotiated an end to American involvement in the Vietnam war. Critics predictably carped about heaping praise on a war criminal.

No one in the Obama administration was closer to Kissinger than Hillary Clinton, and she was to pay a large price for the connection. They had known each other for years, and when she became secretary of state she consulted regularly with him. An examination of her emails shows frequent exchanges. He advised her on China and acted as a go-between with the Israelis. In her memoir, *Hard Choices*, she lauded his government service, and he in turn said, "She ran the State Department in the most effective way I've ever seen."

In September 2014, she reviewed Kissinger's book *World Order* for the *Washington Post*, and to anyone aware of their long-standing admiration for each other, it was hardly surprising that she found his analyses "valuable," praising his "breadth and acuity." But when she ran for president in 2016 and was locked in a surprisingly intense, increasingly bitter contest with Bernie Sanders for the Democratic nomination, Sanders supporters resurrected the review as a weapon against her. One sentence in particular ignited their fury: "Kissinger is a friend and I relied on his counsel when I served as secretary of state." *The Nation* magazine termed the relationship "inexcusable," and a writer at *Slate* called it "downright scary." During a debate in February, Sanders said, "I happen to believe that Henry Kissinger was one of the most destructive secretaries of state in the modern history of the country," and in an echo of Ronald Reagan in 1980, he declared, "I am proud to say Henry Kissinger is not my friend." It was as if all of the ambiguities of Kissinger's years as backstreet adviser had finally come to a head. As one journalist put it, "Being pro- or anti-Kissinger has become a foreign policy litmus test for Democrats." The Clinton camp was divided on whether a Kissinger endorsement would help or hurt their candidate, though Kissinger himself had no doubt that it would "unleash the radical wing—the Sanders wing—against her." He kept his distance, remaining publicly neutral throughout the race.

What was astonishing about this kerfuffle is that it occurred when Kissinger was 93 years old and had been out of government for almost 40 years. Indeed, mention of his name in 2016, if anything, had enraged his critics even more than in the past. Everyone seemed frozen in time. He was an icon to a great many foreign policy professionals; he was poison to legions of nonprofessionals. Kissinger's public reputation, it was clear, was contradictory, schizophrenic, and divisive, and that was never going to change, at least not in his lifetime. Vietnam and Watergate had guaranteed that.

THE UPHEAVAL OF WATERGATE was a turning point in Henry Kissinger's career in many ways, but two aspects in particular stand out. For the rest of his life, Kissinger insisted that the scandal had tied the administration's hands on Vietnam, limiting its ability to bring the war to a just and honorable conclusion rather than a military victory for North Vietnam and an ignominious defeat for the United States and South Vietnam. The specter of desperate people clambering aboard the last departing American helicopters was seared into the national consciousness and was something that never stopped haunting Kissinger. Almost immediately after the agreement had been signed in January 1973, resulting in an American withdrawal, the North Vietnamese began violating the terms of the settlement. To win Saigon's support, Nixon had promised that even with the Americans gone, he would never abandon his ally. But as Washington made the transition from Nixon to Ford, abandon South Vietnam it did. "Watergate undermined what was left of national cohesion," Kissinger said, and despite his persistent pleas for increased aid to keep the Saigon regime alive, by 1974 Congress had had enough. With American intervention finally at an end, the exhausted lawmakers wanted nothing more to do with Vietnam. They were certainly not about to countenance renewed American involvement even if it seemed to mean only the use of air power and not the return of troops on the ground. They had been down that road before. They were all too familiar with the risks of gradual escalation.

Whether or not Nixon and Kissinger had been pursuing a "decent interval" policy that accepted an eventual South Vietnamese defeat, the Watergate scandal allowed Kissinger to turn the blame elsewhere, arguing that it was Congress, not the White House, that had signed the death notice for Saigon. "Washington was determined to withhold funds from an ally when the knife was at its throat." According to the diplomat Richard Holbrooke, among others, Kissinger was determined to shift the responsibility to Congress for his own failed policy (though at other times Kissinger was happy to call the extrication from Vietnam a "remarkable success").

Yet what was so striking was how broad-based the opposition to continuing involvement turned out to be. It wasn't just liberals like Hubert Humphrey who resisted Kissinger's calls but even hard-line conservative senators like John Stennis of Mississippi and John McClellan of Arkansas. Henry Jackson, godfather of the neoconservatives, declared, "There has to be a limit. There has to be a ceiling. There has to be an end." Kissinger's claims that with additional assistance the South Vietnamese could have continued the war indefinitely are dubious at best, an unusual instance of wishful thinking on Kissinger's part. In any case, his use of Watergate as a means of self-justification revealed his tin ear for domestic American politics. The refusal to recommit to the Thieu regime—whatever promises Nixon and Kissinger may have made—wasn't a partisan issue. Like the fall of Nixon himself, it reflected a national consensus. There was "national cohesion" on abandoning South Vietnam. It just wasn't Kissinger's idea of cohesion.

KISSINGER WAS ON firmer ground in his thinking about a second impact of Watergate, and it was one that determined the course of his career for the rest of his life. In his view, the early 1970s were a time when the United States should have been seriously reassessing its foreign policy. The bipolar Cold War was coming to an end as China emerged as a major player on the international stage. America's overextension in Southeast Asia called for hardheaded analysis of tough questions about the nation's global posture. The reassertion of nationalism around the world demanded new perspectives. Watergate, unfortunately, forestalled the possibility of any fresh thinking. Once he was out of power, Kissinger devoted himself to instructing the American people on the "correct"— that is, the Realistic—way of conceptualizing foreign policy.

He had always stressed the importance of the statesman's role as an educator of the American public, if only because of the tension between democratic principles and the conduct of a rational foreign policy. A drawback of democracies, he had explained at the beginning of his career in *A World Restored*, was that they tended to judge international affairs according to their own domestic values. Indeed, they had "no other standard of judgment." People living in open societies had great difficulty grasping that traditional authoritarian regimes were functioning according to principles grounded in their own histories and beliefs; in fact, nothing was more difficult for them to understand than that the ordinary people of those societies shared those histories and beliefs. Even when revolution or civil war broke out over a government's injustices, it was rarely the case that the division was between freedom-loving democrats and tyrannical oppressors. The American diplomat or statesman dealing with a variety of regimes around the world couldn't afford to indulge the democratic absolutism of his countrymen. He had to be more flexible, more far-seeing. In the conclusion to *A World Restored*, the young Kissinger wrote: "The statesman must therefore be an educator; he must bridge the gap between a people's experience and his vision, between a nation's tradition and its future."

Half a century later, more experience and greater maturity had not changed Kissinger's thinking on this matter. Richard Nixon, as Kissinger saw him, seemed perfectly suited to fill the role of educator. Almost alone among the chief executives of the twentieth century, Nixon had conducted foreign policy on the basis of national interest, not out of some high-minded transcendent principle. The only precedent for this, Kissinger claimed, was Theodore Roosevelt, for whom "America was not a cause but a great power," one nation among others. But Roosevelt's Realism avant la lettre never took hold, and in the years that followed, it was Wood-

row Wilson's spirit that presided over the direction of American foreign
policy Wilsonianism, Kissinger said "touched an essential chord in the
American soul." Until Nixon, that is. In distinction to John Kennedy's
Wilsonian pledge to "pay any price, bear any burden," Nixon thought in
the more restrained terms of a balance of power. "No American president
possessed a greater knowledge of international affairs," Kissinger wrote,
and if he was to leave a legacy for what Kissinger called "America's return
to the world of Realpolitik," he would have to assume the necessary role of
educator, instructing the American people on new ways of thinking that
ran counter to their national values and natural instincts. As Kissinger
explained, global events were compelling the United States to make a
transition from "dominance to leadership." Perhaps the greatest tragedy of the Watergate scandal in Kissinger's opinion—and "tragedy" was
his word—was that the opportunity for education had been lost. Nixon,
Kissinger wrote, "had a glimpse of the promised land," but "a president
facing impeachment was not likely to be accepted as the leader of an effort
to reshape traditional thinking."

With Ford serving as little more than a placeholder with no possibility
of assuming the role of educator-statesman, Kissinger noted what he saw
as a disastrous rise in Wilsonianism across the political spectrum. He was
being attacked by both Jimmy Carter and Ronald Reagan and in the same
language. Congress, meanwhile, was involving itself in the formulation of
foreign policy and in ways that were both "unilateral and occasionally bullying." Legislators, with their parochial concerns, were possibly the worst
public officials to take account of any larger international picture, the give-
and-take of diplomacy. Conducting foreign policy through Congressional
fiat, Kissinger said, "translates into a take-it-or-leave-it prescription, the
operational equivalent of an ultimatum." As always, Kissinger warned
that "when moral principles are applied without regard to historical conditions, the result is usually an increase in suffering." He worried that the
moralistic discourse that had come to dominate American thinking in the
wake of Watergate, without the restraint that a concept of national interest
could exert, was almost certain to lead to "sweeping overextension."

In the post-Watergate climate, who was there to make the case for the
restraint and proportionality of Realism if not Henry Kissinger? Carter,
Reagan, Clinton, and the second Bush were more Wilsonian than Realist,
and even during the first Bush and the Obama administrations, Realism
had failed to gain traction with the American public. One historian has

observed that "unlike the neoconservatives, the Realists have cultivated no successor generation." But if that is true, it wasn't for want of trying on Kissinger's part. In the last stages of his career, he churned out thousands of pages attempting to rectify what he considered America's debilitating intellectual bias, arguing that in the modern world Realism was not one possibility but the only possibility.

BROADLY SPEAKING, the books Kissinger produced after leaving office, as well as many of his articles and speeches, can be divided into two categories, though with considerable overlap. The massive three volumes of memoirs were exercises in self-vindication, efforts to set the record straight according to his own lights. But that is not all they are. They are also invaluable resources for anyone wishing to understand the nitty-gritty of American foreign policy during the years Kissinger was in government, a one-of-a-kind window into decision making in the White House at a critical moment of American history (though perhaps best read with the volumes of White House tapes at one's side).

The other books—specifically *Diplomacy* (1994), *Does America Need a Foreign Policy?* (2001), and *World Order* (2014)—present Kissinger doing the necessary work of an educator, instructing his countrymen in the proper way to think about international relations. With their repetition of historical fact, similarity of themes, and consistency of prescription, they might really be considered a single volume or the reading list for a single course. Another book, *On China* (2011), combined attributes from the two categories. It offered a justification of Kissinger's own China policy along with novelistic portraits of the country's leaders, much like the sensitive descriptions of world statesmen to be found in the memoirs. It is also a graduate course explaining how the United States should go about conducting its relations with the nation destined to be America's greatest rival in the twenty-first century.

For Professor Kissinger, Western history began in effect in the seventeenth century, with the genocidal bloodletting of the Thirty Years' War, a traumatic series of religious conflicts in which Central Europe lost about 30 percent of its population as first one faith-based army and then another swept over it. What finally brought the slaughter to an end was not military victory but simple exhaustion. Treaties were signed collectively known as the Peace of Westphalia that established agreed-upon limits so that religious absolutism didn't have to result in the wholesale extermination of peoples. Each area of governance was given the right to rule as it saw fit, particularly in matters of faith, within its own boundaries, and without interference from outside parties: *cujus regio, eius religio* (whoever rules determines the religion). This modern concept of sovereignty was born to resist the absolute claims of religion, allowing the nation-state as we know it to emerge, and along with it the study of international relations as something other than the interpretation of God's will. The Peace of Westphalia did not promise an end to all hostilities. Regimes would continue vying for power, but they would do so according to a set of principles that served as a kind of lesser evil. The parties of Europe had witnessed the alternative during three decades of wanton destruction brought about by commitments to universalist dogma. Peace "had been forged in the school of hard knocks." National sovereignty promised to be the antidote to wars of extermination.

Under this new structure of nation-states, there could be no single guarantor of international peace because no one regime was powerful enough to exert its will over all the others—and if a ruler attempted to try, as Louis XIV did in the seventeenth century and Napoleon did in the nineteenth, the other governments would unite to beat back the threat to their sovereignty. Just as the nation-state resulted in the pursuit of national interest, national interest resulted in the principle of balance of power. They were inextricably linked. "The concept of the balance of power was simply an extension of conventional wisdom," Kissinger said. "Its primary goal was to prevent domination by one state and to preserve the international order; it was not designed to prevent conflicts but to limit them."

Kissinger believed that the concept of balance of power was rare in human history, emerging in Europe in the seventeenth century because of its diversity and multiple sources of authority: it was the only part of the modern world ever to operate a multistate system." Asia and the Middle East were accustomed to religious or political centralized regimes exerting absolute dominion. That other great Realist, Hans Morgenthau, who had such an enormous influence on Kissinger's thinking, took a different view. For him, a balance of power was "the only stability obtainable" in a world of diverse political systems, religions, and ideologies. It was "natural" and "as old as political theory itself."

Not that a world order constructed through a balance of power didn't have problems of its own, however "natural" it might be. Morgenthau

pointed out that any balance of power was built on anxiety, not cooperation or good intentions, its cherished equilibrium fragile and unstable. "All nations live in constant fear." Whenever one insecure ruler—and
all rulers were insecure—believed he had achieved dominant power or
believed that a rival was about to do so, he might launch a preemptive war.
A balance-of-power system was always in danger of collapsing under its
own weight. That was exactly what happened, Kissinger pointed out, in
the years preceding World War I, when the accommodations of diplomacy
failed and "the nations of Europe transformed the balance of power into
an armaments race." As international conditions change, he explained,
any balance of power needed to be "recalibrated," but by the end of the
nineteenth century, the system had become petrified with antagonistic
blocs, conditioned by decades of suspicion, facing off against one another
with mounting anxiety and hostility. Morgenthau once called diplomats
"the brains" of international affairs. By 1914, a muscle-bound Europe,
having decided, contrary to Realist teaching, that military might was the
only force that really mattered, lost its head.

Undeniably, as Kissinger acknowledged, balance of power promised no
ultimate solutions. It resembled a sword of Damocles hanging over the
capitals of all nation-states. But what other possibility was there? Visionary one-worlders might yearn for a single sovereign state, a worldwide Pax
Romana. But the only way of achieving a global state was through imperial conquest or some other assertion of brute force by the unifying power,
corralling unwilling peoples into one governing body. Writing in the age
of Hitler and Stalin, Morgenthau warned that "such a world state would be
a totalitarian monster." His friend Hannah Arendt seconded that thought:
"A supernational authority would either be ineffective or be monopolized
by the nation that happens to be the strongest, and so would lead to world
government, which could easily become the most frightful tyranny conceivable." At a different moment in history, when the United States was
the dominant superpower and both the nationalist-populists and the
neoconservatives were dreaming of transforming American power into
unrivaled hegemony, Kissinger's warnings about a single state took a different form. "Hegemony," he said, "is not in the American interest." However benevolent America's intentions might be (at least in the minds of
its own citizens), the exercise of raw power "would gradually unite the
world against the United States." Any effort to win the hearts and minds
of the unwilling, as the dismal Vietnam experience showed, was bound to

collapse in the face of clashing cultures and civilizations. Despite appearances, hegemonic aspirations were antithetical to the national interest. "Order must be cultivated," Kissinger taught. "It cannot be imposed." The diplomat would always have a more central role than the general in promoting peace.

If force was ruled out, another possibility was the creation of a single world government through a voluntary confederation of countries united by common values—for example, Woodrow Wilson's old dream of a League of Nations or a United Nations in a revitalized and more dynamic form for our time. But as Kissinger pointed out, any voluntary arrangement rested upon the agreement or goodwill of the participants, and no country, certainly no great power, had ever been willing to yield its sovereignty to a world authority. "The United Nations did provide a convenient meeting place for diplomats and a useful forum for the exchange of ideas," Kissinger wrote. "But it failed to fulfill the underlying premise of collective security—the prevention of war and collective resistance to aggression." Throughout the decades of its existence, the United Nations had never succeeded in establishing a common front. Morgenthau, writing at the dawn of the United Nations when hopes for it were at the highest, didn't have decades of ineffectual history to draw on, but his criticism, based on his own Realist precepts, was scathing. People, he said, might be willing to die for their own nation but not for a world government. The United Nations, with its General Assembly and its elitist Security Council, was "a ruin, rent asunder by the conflict between East and West" stated Morgenthau at a time when many considered the organization a beacon for world peace.

To be sure, a balance of power system wasn't *faute de mieux*, to be applauded only because of its negative virtues. There was a positive side, which made it a goal much to be desired. Even if it promoted suspicions that continually stoked war, it also could produce equilibrium and rational relations among nations as each pursued its national interest and was understood by rivals to be doing so. It encouraged the use of reason and calculation to solve problems over the passions of patriotism, presenting the opportunity for world powers to agree to disagree without forcing the issue through arms as each carefully assessed the extent of its influence and power—and with "power" understood to be much more than simple military might. Any proponent of reason in international affairs, it seemed, had to come around to balance-of-power thinking because it relied on negotiation and compromise instead of compulsion and emotion. In the absence of agreed-upon universals or absolutes, it was the only perspective capable of producing a "shared sense of values." In any case, Kissinger insisted that "an agreed alternative has yet to emerge." A balance of power was the one system that had managed to create order out of diversity, and as he explained, "our age is insistently, at times almost desperately, in pursuit of a concept of world order." There simply was no alternative. Or as Morgenthau more than a generation ago put it, if one makes the Realist assumption that "conflicts of interest will continue on the international scene," all that is possible is "peace through accommodation." A balance of power might be precarious, but it was also "inevitable."

This was an especially important lesson for Kissinger to teach in the United States. As he wrote, unlike the citizens of other nations, advancing national interest through a balance of power "has always been repugnant to Americans." To explain why, he turned, as he invariably did, to the dictates of history. The United States had grown into a great power under conditions that anywhere else in the world would have been considered artificial. But what was artificial for others was reality for Americans. In Darwinian terms, the United States faced no natural predators and so was able to expand to fill all the space available to it. Its neighbor to the south, Mexico, was too weak to resist American expansion. To the north was Canada, and after some initial disagreements over borders, the relationship between the two countries, united by a common language and cultural background, settled into one of remarkable amicability; Morgenthau taught that the only successful example of disarmament in the nineteenth century was between the United States and Canada.

The Atlantic and Pacific Oceans served as enormous protective moats against potential overseas rivals, allowing Washington to extend its influence into what Thomas Jefferson called an "empire of liberty" across the entire continent, overwhelming the peoples who already inhabited the land. Indeed, the conquest of the American Indians could serve as a textbook example of what can happen when a balance of power fails to take hold and a single regime is able to achieve domination over all others. The white European settlers were one tribe among many engaged in unending conflict for control of disputed territory. It was a mistake to think of pre-European America as an idyllic wonderland of sweet harmony. As everywhere else around the globe, warfare was a constant of the New World, with the warrior a celebrated figure in his community, at least among those tribes likely to survive the Darwinian competition. Perhaps nothing could have been done to forestall the United States' march to the Pacific, but if the various Indian tribes had been able to overcome their disagreements and unite, they might at least have been able to bargain for more advantageous treaties from Washington. Their differences, however, were so deep-seated that pan-Indianism, though occasionally proposed by visionary leaders like Tecumseh, always remained a hopeless dream. The whites divided and conquered at little cost to themselves and at enormous cost to their Native American adversaries.

The United States had the extraordinary good fortune to develop in relative isolation with no existential threats to challenge it. ("Amerika, du hast es besser," Goethe said.) This was history in a petri dish, sanitized, unreal, and it decisively shaped the country's conception of itself. Because the United States didn't have to concern itself with the rest of the world during its formative years, it could indulge the fantasy that the rest of the world didn't matter; the only thing that did was homegrown values. The exceptional circumstances of American history were turned into a concept of American exceptionalism. "What was actually the result of a passing historic constellation appeared to Americans as a permanent condition," Morgenthau had said. Unlike other countries, "America was aware of no conflict between high-minded principles and the necessities of survival," Kissinger wrote. Peace could be taken for granted as a default position, and on those occasions when war broke out, it was viewed as an aberration from a naturally harmonious state of affairs. The long-standing rivalries and hostilities of Europeans and others in the world were incomprehensible except as the evil schemes of evil men.

Kissinger summed up the American outlook as "the conviction that its domestic principles were self-evidently universal and their application at all times salutary; that the real challenge of American engagement abroad was not foreign policy in the traditional sense but a project of spreading values that it believed all other peoples aspired to replicate." Inevitably, this resulted in a posture that was at once arrogant and missionary. "I know how to deal with boy scouts and I know how to deal with bullies," a foreign diplomat is reported to have said, "but I don't know how to deal with boy scouts who are bullies." Kissinger observed that "at no time in its history has America participated in a balance of power system." The country believed that it didn't need a foreign policy, he said, that diplomacy as commonly understood was "an optional activity." Or as Morgenthau put it, American exceptionalism was an ideology of antipolitics. In the late nineteenth century, America's army was only the fourteenth largest in the world, behind Bulgaria's, with its navy smaller than Chile's.

Even after the United States was no longer able to ignore the rest of the world, it didn't give up its power-denying idealism. The imperialistic ventures that followed the Spanish-American War were carried out with the best of intentions in the eyes of the citizenry, with the pacification of the Philippines, which was achieved through torture and extermination, conveniently forgotten, and the two world wars interpreted in the grandest of terms; simple national interest wouldn't suffice. Throughout the first part of the twentieth century, the country oscillated between two extremes—intervention when it thought it could save the world and isolation when the world refused to be saved. In fact, the two extremes were part of the same self-serving perspective, with intervention justified to preserve American idealism and purity. "Isolationism is a kind of introverted globalism," Morgenthau observed, "and globalism is a kind of isolationism turned inside out." All along, the country had to assure itself that it was a nation like no other. The United States would be in the world but not of it. Or put in more religious terms, original sin applied only to others, not to Americans, who were born not only free but also pure. They were well-intentioned and innocent, and if those intentions didn't turn out well, their innocence was their excuse for self-righteousness, national amnesia the remedy for any pain.

The great exception to this history proved ultimately to be no exception. After World War II, in a burst of farsightedness and creativity, Washington decisively abandoned its isolationist tradition through such innovative policies as NATO and the Marshall Plan. Former enemies would be built up. Allies would be cultivated around the globe. Writers in the Realist camp like Morgenthau, George Kennan, Reinhold Niebuhr, and Raymond Aron cheered America's awakened internationalism and its commitment to taking a role of leadership as befitted a major power and as the threat of Communism demanded. A power vacuum had developed in war-devastated Europe, and Stalin's armies had rushed in to fill it until Washington recognized the need for a counterweight. Balance-of-power thinking demanded nothing less. "The United States had to become a European power," Morgenthau said. As Kissinger noted, one of the realities of global power is that "vacuums always get filled."

The historian Arthur Schlesinger Jr., a young Realist and Kissinger's friend, explained in 1949 that America had wisely accepted its international responsibilities. "The beginning of maturity in foreign policy lies in the understanding that a nation has certain unalterable interests which no government can abandon."

The American tradition of isolationism had been defeated by the realities of power politics, and Washington was not about to make the same mistake it made at the end of World War I. Withdrawal was not an option, even if intervention meant a dangerous standoff with the Soviet Union that would last for decades. Still, as Kissinger explained, there was a deep ambiguity, even an inherent contradiction, that ran through the history of the Cold War. Realists like George Kennan and Dean Acheson had established the contours of American foreign policy in balance-of-power terms, but it was an outlook that dared not speak its name, and Wilsonians seized and adapted the mechanism of containment for their own world-saving purposes. "Whenever America has been tested," Kissinger wrote, "it returns to Wilsonianism," so that even if containment had been established for the defined end of restraining the Soviet Union in Europe, it came to be pursued for the utopian goal of universal world peace and global democracy. "By its own lights, America was joining the Cold War struggle not as a geopolitical contest over the extent of Russian power but as a moral crusade for the Free World." Whereas containment had implicitly rested on the concept that the conduct of foreign policy was "a process of never-completed fulfillment" with limited ends, Americans demanded that it have a final destination, a harmonious end-of-time that made all the sacrifices of blood and treasure meaningful. Otherwise, what was the point? Wouldn't it have been better to retreat behind its two protective oceans as the country had done for a century and a half? Even with the Realists arguing that isolation was no longer possible, Americans were not really ready to reconceive their role in the world, to give up their devotion to exceptionalism, to climb down from their city on a hill.

And, it must be said, there were aspects of the power struggle with Russia that fed the Wilsonian impulses of the American people. As Kissinger put it, "The Cold War had been almost made to order for American preconceptions." No one grasped this better than Ronald Reagan. The conflict between Communism and capitalism was inevitably ideological (as opposed to the conflict between Russia and the United States). There was no need to attend to the limitations of power; moral aims would suffice because disputes would always be conceptualized in terms of good and evil. Americans may have been uncomfortable thinking in terms of national interest, but they had no problem conceiving of foreign policy from a Wilsonian perspective. Crusading was built into their belief system, and when Communism was defeated and the Cold War came to an end, it was the most natural of inclinations for them to see a triumph of "freedom." In fact what had occurred was a reconfiguration of the nations of the world, which meant, as Kissinger stated repeatedly, that a balance of power had become more important than ever. "For the first time in our history, we are permanently involved in international affairs," and the only way for the United States to attain a proper equilibrium, avoiding the extremes of isolation or overextension, was through "a modernization of the Westphalian system." That was why Reagan's policies represented a "sunset," a conclusion and not a new beginning. The Cold War may have ended but the need to balance power among contending states had not.

THE COLLAPSE OF the Soviet Union introduced the country to a world without ideology, in which transcendent prescriptions for democracy were no answers to the problems at hand. "In the post–Cold War world, there is no overriding ideological challenge," Kissinger explained. "Almost every situation is a special case." Nationalism, he said, "has gained a new lease on life," and a rejuvenated nationalism might seek "national or regional identity by confronting the United States." The universalizing instincts of the American people would not suffice for the twenty-first century. To ignore national interest in such a situation, to trust American exceptionalism, was to flail helplessly against a myriad of challenges. As Kissinger wrote in 1994, "The American exceptionalism that is the indispensable basis for a Wilsonian foreign policy is therefore likely to be less relevant in the coming century."

Kissinger, working first with Nixon and then with Ford, had a foretaste of this post–Cold War world aborning, and with his experience grounded in superpower rivalry he admitted to surprise followed by helplessness and defeat. There were stern lessons to be learned as the Cold War wound down. In July 1974, as the Watergate scandal was approaching a climax, Turkey invaded the island of Cyprus. In his memoirs, Kissinger called it "a seminal event," the forerunner of the kind of ethnic and communal violence that would come to unsettle and dominate much of the world down to the present. Wars, when they erupted, increasingly were likely to be intrastate rather than interstate. Kissinger, the power politician focused on nation-states and national interest, looked on this future with gloom. He knew he had no answers.

Cyprus, although it had about an 80 percent Greek majority, had been ruled by the Ottoman Turks since 1571. For centuries, Kissinger wrote, "Greeks and Turks had nursed their mutual hatreds," with divisions that were "unbridgeable." In 1878, at the Congress of Berlin, the British replaced the receding Ottoman Empire as the sovereign authority over Cyprus and spent decades attempting to act as a broker between the two sides. But Kissinger stated a grim truth: in ethnic conflicts like the one consuming Cyprus, "Solutions are much more likely to emerge from the total victory of one side or from mutual exhaustion than from the contribution of mediators." The Greeks were seeking a unified state, probably allied with Athens. The Turks wanted a federal arrangement that, in effect, partitioned the island. No Westphalian solution marking out boundaries of sovereignty was in the offing.

While of existential concern to Greeks and Turks, Cyprus had hardly registered on American radar. But after the Turkish invasion, Washington became involved because the crisis had turned into an unprecedented clash between two members of NATO, threatening the alliance's eastern flank and inviting Russian penetration. "We made every effort to keep the Soviet Union on the sidelines," Kissinger wrote, even though the dispute was not about the Cold War. Indeed on this issue the Greeks and Turks cared more about ethnic identity than they did about any potential dangers from Moscow. Kissinger, who conceded that he had no "previous experience with ethnic conflict," could initially view Cyprus only through a geopolitical lens that had nothing to do with the facts on the ground. American calls for a "bizonal federation" proved ineffectual, and a resolution of the crisis arrived only through the power of the Turkish army, which established its own form of equilibrium by seizing about 35 percent of the island.

By the time he wrote his memoirs, Kissinger had come to understand that Cyprus was an ominous vision of the future in which the United States would be faced with a contradiction between its Wilsonian principles. It could support majoritarian democracy (the Greek goal) or it could support ethnic self-determination (the Turkish one). It couldn't have both—and unfortunately it had no clear moral basis for supporting one solution over the other. "Not every problem has a definitive solution," Kissinger wrote, and when he was asked what Cyprus portended for the next half century, he replied, "I'm glad I'm not going to be running part of it. It's going to be brutal."

THE CYPRUS CRISIS foreshadowed what the end of the Soviet Union meant for the future of the world. Actually, Communism had long ceased to be a crusading faith, and by the 1990s no one was even sure what it was. The largest Communist power, China, was casting aside the teachings of Marx and Lenin (not to mention Stalin) for an improvised and pragmatic state capitalism, while other self-professed Communist regimes like Cuba, Vietnam, and North Korea were each going their own idiosyncratic way and could hardly have been gathered under any single conceivable label; their so-called Communism had become a useless atavism in the post–Cold War world, bestowing at best a kind of sham legitimacy on shaky regimes with no real foundation. The sociologist Daniel Bell had published a collection of essays under the title *The End of Ideology* in 1960. In terms of international relations, he was 31 years too early. Most countries gave up on ideology after 1991 but it hardly brought the world closer to global peace. Indeed, with nationalism and tribal identity on the rise throughout the world, conditions seemed to be spinning out of control as never before.

In this new environment, the promotion of democracy as a goal of foreign policy often had little relevance to societies divided by identity and with no connection to the values of tolerance and reason that were a product of the European Enlightenment. The multitudinous, many-layered conflicts of the Middle East, Kissinger pointed out, were not about democracy. The tragedy of Syria revolved around questions of who would govern, not how the domestic institutions of government would be arranged. And among the countries of Asia, Kissinger said, "Democracy has not been their defining national experience." America's allies, Japan and South Korea, did not formulate their foreign policies according to Wilsonian principles, and even so close a friend as Australia made its choices on the basis of national interest, not the advancement of democracy. Australia was not about to risk a confrontation with China over some question of human rights, and the same was true of the Philippines, Thailand, Indonesia, even India. Kissinger quoted Prime Minister Jawaharlal Nehru shortly after the birth of his nation in 1947: "We may talk about international goodwill and mean what we say. But in the ultimate analysis, a government functions for the good of the country it governs."

Because a concern for human rights was likely to "remain an important feature of American foreign policy," Kissinger conceded, one had to hope that "wise Asian leaders will take America's values seriously and avoid endangering a relationship on which so much of Asia's stability as well as the peace of the world depend." For its part, as Kissinger went on, "The United States had no national interest in letting itself be drawn into long-standing Asian conflicts like the border disputes between China and India as long as neither side seeks to achieve its objective by force," despite the fact that India was the largest democracy in the world and China the most populous dictatorship. So much for American values. "In Asia, far more than in Europe, not to speak of the Middle East, the maxims of the West-phalian model of international order find their contemporary expression." Or, as Kissinger advised, "America's preference should be to maintain cooperative relations with all the nations of Asia," dictatorships as well as democracies. The goal of global order trumped the goal of democracy promotion. It almost always did.

CHINA IS, of course, the Apatosaurus in the room. It requires special attention from statesmen and analysts, the only country Kissinger considered important enough to devote an entire book to. *On China*, published in 2011, benefited from Kissinger's extensive experience with the Chinese leadership. He pointed out that he had visited the country more than 50 times. The book came with advice for future diplomats and with warnings about the very real dangers in store for them.

Just as modern European history began, for Kissinger, with Westphalia, everything about contemporary China began with Mao Zedong, and without disputing the fact that millions had perished because of Mao's cruelties, Kissinger drew a portrait of a leader who was more than just a coldhearted tyrant, a complex figure weighed down by ambiguities and contradictions. Mao had brought Western ideas to China in the form of Marxism with the intention of uprooting the stagnation that had led to a century and a half of humiliation and decline. Confucius was attacked, the long-standing mandarin bureaucracy upended in the name of perpetual revolution. Mao had "declared war" on everything the Chinese had believed to be "Chinese."

Yet if Marxism, as it was understood by Mao, was the official ideology of the state, the man who ruled that state with totalitarian ruthlessness was anything but a Marxist ideologue. He was not a universalist. Unlike Lenin, who hoped for and expected a global workers revolution, Mao pursued a nationalist "China-first" policy. He was less indebted to Lenin than to Sun Tsu, and "less likely to refer to Marxist doctrine than to traditional Chinese works."

Kissinger began his book by pointing to an incident that had occurred in 1962, when China was engaged in a confrontation with India. Mao urged his generals to learn a lesson from a war that had been fought 1,300 years before, during the Tang Dynasty (618–907). "In no other country," Kissinger said, "is it conceivable that a modern leader would initiate a major national undertaking by invoking strategic principles from a millennium-old event." Mao may have seemed determined to overthrow tradition, but he was widely read in the Chinese classics, quoting them and turning to Confucian principles when it suited his purposes. Contrary to Marx's universalist perspective, Mao believed in China's "unique destiny." This was, Kissinger declared, "the Confucian tradition through the looking glass."

To prove his point, Kissinger noted that if Mao had been driven by Marxist doctrines, he would never have pursued the opening with the United States, a move that was opposed by his own hard-liners just as it was by the ideological hard-liners in America, confident in their country's mission to expand freedom. But for Mao, the Soviet Union was a greater threat to his country than the capitalist West—the two Communist giants had already come perilously close to war and continued to eye each other with grave suspicion—and when Nixon and Kissinger arrived in Beijing, they were startled to discover a leader no less Realist than they were. "I like rightists," Mao told them in candid appreciation of American nationalism, saying that he "had voted" for Nixon. "The quintessential Cold Warrior" was how Kissinger described Mao, remarking that "American conservatives would have approved of him." Power, strategy, and pragmatism, not ideology, would dictate the course of Sino-American negotiations. "Nixon was in his element," Kissinger reports.

The same devotion to Realism oriental-style underlay the diplomacy of Mao's successors. "Ideology had disappeared from the conflict." The pragmatic Chinese simply could not comprehend the Wilsonian mania

that on occasion gripped the American people in their dealings with other
nations, their strange obsession with human rights. On subsequent visits,
Kissinger was amused that the Chinese took to lecturing him, of all people, on the importance of national interest. Like Kissinger, the Chinese
approach to foreign policy was "conceptual," understanding it as a process with no final solutions since the resolution of one problem invariably
brought new problems to be managed. Because there could never be an
end to it all, thinking had to be long term and systematic. Foreign policy had no destination. The only constant was national interest. Maybe
the Chinese weren't Realists. Maybe Henry Kissinger was "Chinese." He
had concluded, after all, that he and Chou Enlai were very much alike.
He called Chou "one of the two or three most impressive men I have ever
met," and there was no figure on the global stage with whom he sensed
such a personal affinity. "When Chou died," he said, "I felt a great sadness.
The world would be less vibrant."

China and the United States faced a common adversary in the Soviet
Union, and the Realist Nixon never doubted that in a conflict between
Moscow and Beijing, Washington would take the side of the Chinese.
This, Kissinger said, though not about himself, was a "shocking thesis,"
calling it "a revolutionary moment in U.S. foreign policy: an American
president declared that we had a strategic interest in the survival of a major
Communist country." Shocking and revolutionary from a Wilsonian perspective, but all Nixon was doing was articulating traditional Realpolitik doctrine, balancing power by supporting the weaker party against a
stronger, more aggressive one. (In this, he was doing no more than replicating Franklin Roosevelt's World War II policy of supporting the totalitarian Soviet Union against totalitarian Nazi Germany.) China had not
changed its dictatorial ways, or suddenly become America's "friend," any
more than Stalin's Russia had in the fight against fascism.

At the same time Nixon and Kissinger did not view the Soviet Union
as an irredeemable enemy. It was not Nazi Germany. Their aim, as any
student of Bismarck could have explained, was to bring the two dictatorial powers into a closer relationship with the United States than each
had with the other. This triangulation was one of the great foreign policy achievements of the Nixon administration, even if it was necessarily a temporary one subject to changing conditions. The fall of the Soviet
Union disrupted this careful juggling act, forcing a reconsideration of
Sino-American relations. As far as Kissinger was concerned, the new con-

figuration introduced fresh dangers to the global stability that was always his objective. Recalibration was required after the Cold War ended, creative statesmanship a necessity.

Until (or unless) Russia reestablished itself as a great power, the United States and China risked becoming locked into an adversarial bipolar relationship rather than a triangular one, apparently replicating the Cold War arena in which two superpowers faced off against each other, with all the inevitable possibilities of misunderstanding and conflict. "What the relationship lacked," Kissinger wrote, "was a defining shared purpose, such as had united Beijing and Washington in resistance to Soviet 'hegemonism.'" Without the Soviet Union as a counterweight, disputes—over Taiwan, the South China Sea, Korea—had a greater chance of escalating out of control. "Sooner or later, one side or the other would miscalculate."

What aggravated this problem was that neither country had much experience operating on a world stage. With its weak neighbors and ocean moats, the United States was able to bask in its insularity for most of its existence, enjoying its "exceptionalism." China, too, had a history of exceptionalist insularity, one that went back millennia rather than mere centuries. As with the United States, geography separated China from competing powers—the Himalayas from India, vast deserts from the Middle Eastern empires, formidable seas from Japan. As for lesser powers around its borders like Vietnam and Laos, it was able to exert a cultural dominance that turned them into "tributary states." China was "a world unto itself," just as the United States was a city on a hill. Both countries considered themselves polestars for humankind, not so much nation-states sharing the planet with other nation-states as ineluctable forces of global civilization with universalist aspirations. The difference, Kissinger noted, was that the United States approached others with missionary zeal for its democratic values, whereas China held back. It sought no colonies abroad and did not proselytize. It relied on geopolitical gravity to do its work and waited for others to come to it through a process that Kissinger called "osmosis."

Yet whatever the differences, the histories of the two countries fed a shared delusion of national or cultural omnipotence that was bound to come undone in a modern world shrunken by technology. The Chinese received their comeuppance in the mid-nineteenth century in their encounter with militarily superior Western powers demanding to be treated as equals, an unheard of proposition in China's long history. Nothing in its experience equipped China to deal with the West, and the result was a long period of stagnation. Even today, now that it has achieved stability and strength (if on the bodies of millions of victims), it is not clear that the leaders in Beijing accept the Westphalian concept of a community of nations in which each country is left alone to pursue its own national interest as long as it does not upset the world order by threatening others.

The equivalent trauma for the United States was unquestionably Vietnam, when America "was obliged to come to grips with its limits." The country is still struggling to understand the meaning of that defeat. "What is new about the emerging world order," Kissinger has said, "is that for the first time, the United States can neither withdraw from the world nor dominate it," and it has not yet adjusted to that essential fact. Neither China nor the United States is in a position to deny the values that are bred into their systems, but neither can they simply assert them as the reflection of some kind of natural order. Thus, both countries have been "engaged in searching debates about their domestic purposes, their world roles—and ultimately their relation to each other." One way or another, either through an intellectual evolution that accepts limits and diplomatic compromise or through the wholesale shedding of blood, they will have to give up their cherished exceptionalism for a Westphalian system of international diversity and a more modest, if uncomfortable, equilibrium.

America's Cold War experience, Kissinger has declared, is irrelevant to modern conditions, and he warns against trying to replicate the post–World War II bipolar division by putting China on one side and the United States and its allies on the other. Instead, multipolarity prevails. The world now contains "perhaps five or six major powers and a multiplicity of smaller states," with the U.S.-China relationship at the forefront of the quest for global order. As Kissinger had written, a balance of power has become "inevitable." But if the Cold War no longer serves as a model for international relations, what now haunts Kissinger is the run-up to World War I, when a similar international diversity held sway and the balance-of-power system fell apart. In particular, if China and the United States, "both indispensable pillars of world order," fail to redefine themselves and their place on the global stage, the result could be catastrophic. At the end of the nineteenth century, international relations "came to be based on raw power," with brute military domination replacing the hard work of the diplomats, and foreign policy turned into "a test of strength." Marginal disputes that should have been peacefully negotiated or muddled through were turned into existential crises, with hardened, heavily armed blocs facing off against each other. There was only one way such a standoff could end.

The danger for Beijing and Washington, Kissinger explained, was that in the absence of a shared Soviet threat, the two governments would similarly move toward confrontation over what were admittedly very real differences instead of finding common ground. "The two sides need to absorb the history of the decade before World War I," and for that, "a serious joint effort" is required, an active reordering to meet the new global conditions. "Any international order comprising both the United States and China must involve a balance of power." But as World War I demonstrated, any balance of power without "a concept of partnership" risks military rigidity. "Can China and the United States develop genuine strategic trust?"

The beginning of trust, according to Kissinger, is for both countries to recognize the legitimacy and values of the other, what he views as "a common bond." That is, each has to see the other as it sees itself and accept the fact that there are differences between the two countries unlikely to be bridged in the foreseeable future. The key is to avoid turning those differences into threats that spin out of control. The Chinese need to understand, Kissinger says, that Americans will never give up their commitment to human rights. "There are abuses bound to evoke an American reaction, even at the cost of an overall relationship." And the Americans must realize that the Chinese will never cease to worry about internal stability, that democracy represents for them not so much an expansion of freedom as a recipe for domestic disorder and chaos. If the United States pushed for human rights above all other issues, "deadlock was inevitable."

But should the two countries develop the mutual respect and understanding at the heart of Kissinger's urgings, the path would be open to more positive developments—to "constructive cooperation" around "common goals." Kissinger gazed back nostalgically to the creative post–World War II period, when enlightened policies led to the establishment of an Atlantic Community. He has looked forward, hopefully, to the construction of a Pacific Community, envisioning not so much a partnership between the United States and China as a process of "co-evolution." This means for him that the United States and China would pursue their domestic aims while trying to avoid conflict internationally. He speaks of "a joint concept of world order," "shared purposes," and "mutual benefit." If these words sound surprisingly optimistic coming from a dour and ıιιןıⁱⁱⁱⁱⁱ ןʳᵒᵒᵈⁿᵗᵘᵗ, ⁱᵗ ⁱˢ ᵇ ᵃᵃᵃᵘᵘᵉ ᵗᵘᵉ ᵃⁱᵗᵉⁱ ⁿᵘᵗⁱᵛᵉ ⁱˢ ᵘⁿᵗᵘⁱⁿᵏᵃᵇⁱᵉ. Jᵗᵃᵗᵉˢⁱⁱⁱᵉⁿ like Kissinger may consider optimism in international affairs fatuous, but unleavened pessimism can become self-fulfilling and catastrophic.

Where there were undeniable differences between China and the United States and solutions not immediately available—as over the status of Taiwan—the appropriate policy for both sides was to fudge the issue. That was what wise diplomats did if they wanted to avoid the kind of rigid positions that precipitated the collapse into the wanton slaughter of World War I. "Ambiguity," Kissinger declared, "is sometimes the lifeblood of diplomacy," adding that leaders "need to be judged by the management of ambiguities, not absolutes." The demand for "solutions" could be the enemy of peace. It was the abandonment of ambiguity, Kissinger said, that "started a sequence of increasing confrontations, culminating in World War I." Europe's leaders "had become habituated to the view that risk taking was an effective diplomatic tool."

At the same time, the world did not want for problems that the United States and China could address fruitfully in a spirit of cooperation. Many areas around the globe lacked any sort of established authority and were descending into chaos, which wasn't good for either the United States or China. The situation demanded a "cooperative effort by all responsible powers." And apart from the dangers posed by failed states and regions with no governmental legitimacy whatever, there were core political and economic issues that also required the combined efforts of skilled diplomats. Kissinger pointed to "the environment, energy security and climate change." Such problems could serve as avenues for cooperation between China and the United States, much as the problem of the Soviet Union had done during the 1970s.

NO ISSUE POSED a greater threat or offered a greater opportunity for cooperation than the danger of nuclear devastation. It is a subject that was central to the Cold War and has reemerged with renewed urgency at the start of the twenty-first century. In his waning years, Kissinger has come full circle, returning again to analyzing the threat of nuclear warfare, the topic that made his name in the 1950s. "Proliferation of nuclear weapons has become an overarching strategic problem for the contemporary international order." Mutual assured destruction, the balancing act that prevailed during the Cold War when there were only two nuclear superpowers, is increasingly inoperable as more nations acquire nuclear arms. What Kissinger called "the calculus of deterrence" becomes ever more difficult when numerous nuclear states face off against one another. "Who is deterring whom?" With his eye on the tragedies of history, Kissinger has foreseen the possibility of nuclear alliances developing "comparable in their rigidity to the alliances that led to World War I," and added that "any further spread of nuclear weapons multiplies the possibilities of nuclear confrontation."

What is more, Cold War deterrence between the United States and the Soviet Union "depended in large part on the ability to affect the adversary psychologically," but if rogue states succeed in developing nuclear arms, the deterrence policies of the Cold War would no longer apply. Irresponsible leaders of small, insecure, economically stunted nations might be more inclined to use their weapons if they felt threatened. Or they might display their new power in a variety of dangerous ways. They could shield terrorists or even supply them with the ultimate terrorist bomb; they might sell their nuclear technology to other governments. But even if they didn't do any of these things, the world would be faced with an escalatory spiral as countries neighboring the new nuclear powers raced to develop their own capabilities. The North Koreans' nuclear capacity has vastly increased the possibility of a South Korean or Japanese bomb. Iran's nuclear program could spur similar aspirations in Saudi Arabia, Turkey, and Egypt. An additional grim certainty was that one could be sure that these smaller nuclear powers wouldn't institute the same safety and security measures that the United States and the Soviet Union had developed. Accidents, unauthorized launchings, and the theft of nuclear materials were much more likely to occur.

At the same time, security, even for the established nuclear powers, was becoming much more difficult in the cyberworld of computer hacking. "A laptop can produce global consequences." All of these concerns, as Kissinger has said, create "unprecedented" dangers. The major powers had "no more urgent common interest than preventing the emergence of more nuclear-armed states." We could be entering, he has warned, "a world of devastation and human loss without precedent."

Such dire thoughts led Kissinger—along with three other major strategic thinkers, George Shultz, Sam Nunn, the former head of the Senate Armed Services Committee, and William Perry, the secretary of defense in the Clinton administration—to produce "a bolt from the blue," in the form of an op-ed article in the *Wall Street Journal* on January 4, 2007. Frustrated by past ineffectual efforts to halt the spread of nuclear weapons and awakened to twenty-first-century dangers by the attacks of 9/11, they warned that "the world is now on the precipice." A tipping point had arrived, and they called for the reduction and eventual elimination of nuclear arms. Their call was seconded by an impressive collection of experienced public servants, figures including Colin Powell, James Baker, Robert McNamara, and Zbigniew Brzezinski. As Kissinger pointed out, the abolition of nuclear weapons has been a consistent American objective since the Eisenhower administration.

If Kissinger, Shultz, Nunn, and Perry were embraced by other members of the strategic establishment, it was because the four authors were anything but starry-eyed dreamers or idealistic pacifists. They were notoriously hardheaded and dedicated to pursuing the national interest of the United States. That is what made their article news around the world. The American national interest was being redefined by some of the country's most authoritative voices to feature what the article's title daringly proclaimed: "A World Free of Nuclear Weapons." But this is also what made Kissinger reluctant to leap into the cause of abolition with both feet. Of the four authors, he was the most hesitant, the one with the most questions and reservations. He saw the dangers of nuclear proliferation, he recognized the need for fresh thinking—just as he had when he criticized the concept of Mutual Assured Destruction in the 1950s—but he was not about to give the appearance of joining the ban-the-bomb camp. Its idealism was anathema to him. It took all of Shultz's powers of persuasion to get Kissinger on board, yet the others knew that without the weight of his name, their article wouldn't get nearly the attention they thought it deserved. As William Perry said, "Whatever problems we have with Henry's reluctance in some aspects of this mission, these problems are more than offset by the value that he brings to the group."

In fact, Kissinger's doubts about lending his name to the article were not so different from those of the other signatories or other serious thinkers engaged with the problem of nuclear weapons, only more pronounced. The question was always how to get from here to there, from a nuclear-armed world becoming increasingly dangerous to one that was free of nuclear arms. Campaigners for the total abolition of nuclear weapons began from "there," the goal they wished to achieve, and sought to shape the actual world to their idealistic construct, usually through the device of an international treaty. The present would be channeled according to their aspirations, much like the doomed efforts of earlier idealists who had hoped to bring an end to war with signatures on a piece of paper. They were old-fashioned Wilsonians, all dressed up for the nuclear age. They could luxuriate in their ideals but with no idea about how to implement them.

But as Kissinger observed, America's national interest included more than abolishing nuclear arms: "The United States must continue to rely on nuclear weapons to help deter certain kinds of attacks on this country and its friends and allies," at least as far as the eye could see. What was more, the goal of a zero option had a quality of fantasy about it because "nuclear weapons cannot be uninvented," as Shultz declared. "I don't know how to get to zero," Perry said. "I couldn't imagine quite how you would get there or how you would function once you were there."

Unlike the idealists, Realists like Kissinger were caught in an excruciating dilemma: the present, with nuclear proliferation gaining momentum, promised an eventual catastrophe, yet a future of world peace seemed unattainable, forever out of reach. Their analysis provided them with no answers, but that didn't make it wrong. Their only solution, though not one that would satisfy the abolitionists or anyone else who hoped an immediate answer was at hand, was to stand in the "here" and work toward the "there" by taking incremental steps that pointed in the right direction even if the ultimate goal remained remote or even unimaginable. Kissinger explained with an image borrowed from his colleague Sam Nunn. The effort to abolish nuclear weapons was "akin to climbing a mountain shrouded in clouds. We cannot describe its top nor be certain that there may not be unforeseen and perhaps insurmountable obstacles on the way." Still, that didn't mean that the task wasn't worth pursuing. This was not much of a strategy, but it was the best that could be hoped for. All the Realists could do was to point the decision makers in a certain direction—even if what lay ahead was a very steep and uncertain ascent up a mountain. There was someone else who had found a memorable way of putting it. If Kissinger was challenged to predict how long the international community could continue to exist with the threat of nuclear holocaust hanging over it, the answer, he might have said, was blowin' in the wind.

AT THE END OF *How America Meets a Foreign Policy,* after he had finished analyzing the place of the United States in the world at the start of
the twenty-first century, Kissinger took a turn toward the philosophical,
to the long-range perspective undergirding his notions of Realism, international relations, equilibrium, and power. He did the same in the last
pages of *World Order*, as well as in an article published in the *Atlantic* in
2018 with the ominous title "How the Enlightenment Ends." Now it was
not specific problems of foreign affairs that concerned him but the intellectual approach required of successful statesmen. This was his final lesson
as a self-appointed educator of the American public, and it brought him
back to the common themes of those German-Jewish exiles who shared
his anti-ideological, anti-quantitative, existential outlook.

Kissinger saw in the emergence of the computer and the birth of the
Information Age a transformation as profound as that which had occurred
with the invention of the printing press. What had been the province of
a small clique of educated specialists privileged with arcane knowledge
had been opened up to many millions around the world, anyone with a
keyboard and a desire to shape the future of mankind. Everyman (and
woman) an expert! Those with an ideological faith in democracy and egalitarianism might celebrate this dispersal of power but Kissinger, of course,
was no ideological democrat. What he perceived about cyberspace was a
growing anarchy, which he equated with a Hobbesian state of nature in
which the prospect of world order receded ever further from view. It was
not the number of people with access to information that mattered to him
but what was done with that information, and in his mind the computer-
ization of the world encouraged a kind of irresponsible thinking that was
deleterious to rational judgment at best, disastrous at worst.

Computers, the internet, and other advances in communication had
developed a momentum of their own; the thinking behind them was
actually no thinking at all, only "the mind-set of a researcher." With
unprecedented quantities of information available at the tap of a finger,
policymakers were being drawn into a world in which the accumulation
of facts was thought to solve their problems for them. Data were fetishized;
reason, judgment, and reflection diminished. If answers weren't immediately apparent from the information available, what was needed was more
information. With the rise of the internet, Kissinger said, "Human activity becomes increasingly 'datafied.'"

What happens, Kissinger asked, "if technology has become such a part of everyday life that it defines its own universe as the sole relevant one?" In this system there was little room for human will or agency or the cultivation of such human qualities as ambiguity and intuition. Hard facts bred a tyranny of their own that prioritized the immediate present over an understanding of the past or a sensitivity toward the future. Focus groups and opinion polls replaced individual decision-making and responsibility; the immediate headline-driven mood of the crowd overrode long-range perspective. Foreign policy was "in danger of turning into a subdivision of short-term domestic politics" in which "the quest is for consensus, less by the exchange of ideas than by a sharing of emotions." The United States was in danger of "careening through crises without comprehending them." This was no way for a great power to engage with the rest of the world, least of all in a world armed with nuclear weapons.

At this point, one is brought face-to-face with a subject not frequently acknowledged, what might be called Kissinger's Continental "humanism," his fervent embrace of the role of human freedom in humankind's affairs: autonomous individuals with all their experience, emotions, values, quirks, and foibles mattered more to him than the construction of models. Algorithms knew nothing of irony or tragedy. And with this, Kissinger revealed his intellectual affinity with those German-Jewish writers who similarly approached life as freethinkers without preconceived ideologies, who deliberated "without banisters"—Leo Strauss, Hannah Arendt, and Hans Morgenthau. Just as Strauss took on the quantifiers at the University of Chicago in the name of personal responsibility, Kissinger challenged the quantifiers of the foreign policy establishment in the name of individual judgment. Had Kissinger accepted the offer early in his career to take a position at the University of Chicago, there is no doubt that he would have taken a stand as an ally of the embattled Strauss against the school's headcounters, much as Morgenthau did. Kissinger joined with Strauss in condemning the view that "only 'scientific' knowledge is genuine knowledge" and agreed with him that "the sciences, both natural and political, are frankly nonphilosophical."

Likewise, when Kissinger stressed the need for individual judgment to stand in opposition to the self-propulsion of quantitative thinking, he was sounding one of Hannah Arendt's favorite themes. In *The Human Condition* she decried the contempt for thought in the scientific ethos—the "instrumentalization of the world," the "confidence in tools," the "conviction that every issue can be solved and every human motivation reduced to the principle of utility." If this was all that mattered—if consciousness, will, subjectivity, and agency were not part of the human condition—then modern men and women faced the danger of becoming "thoughtless creatures at the mercy of every gadget which is technologically possible, no matter how murderous it is." This unreflective confidence in technological progress was "leading in so many instances straight into disaster." Pondering the particular disaster that was the Vietnam war, she declared, "One sometimes has the impression that a computer, rather than decision-makers, had been let loose in Southeast Asia. The problem-solvers did not judge; they calculated." Or as Kissinger put it, "The computer supplies tools unimaginable even a decade ago. But it also shrinks perspective. . . . Manipulation of information replaces reflection as the principal policy tool." Similarly, Kissinger asked how consciousness could be defined in a world of artificial intelligence where everything was being reduced to "mathematical data." Where, he wondered, did responsibility lie?

Morgenthau, too, had taken his stand on the side of the conscious, willful individual against the automatism of science and technology. He had staked out his own position on all this in the very first book he published in the United States, *Scientific Man Versus Power Politics*, his broadside against the faith in scientific reason dominant in postwar America. He became a public figure a couple of years later with the appearance of *Politics Among Nations*, but it was the earlier book, the one that Morgenthau grumbled was never understood, that was the more passionate, a personal declaration into which he seems to have poured his heart and soul.

Solutions to life's problems, such as they were, would come, he said, only through statesmen and diplomats applying their intelligence, experience, and reason. "It is always the individual who acts," he wrote. "Scientific standards" were no substitute for "political evaluations." What was commonly called rationality devalued thought and misconceived the nature of politics (which was always and everywhere about power). "Politics must be understood through reason," Morgenthau said, "yet it is not in reason that it finds its model." It was more art than science, and like Kissinger, but long before the advent of the Information Age, he viewed the accumulation of "more facts" as an essentially rote exercise, worthy of automatons perhaps, but not living, breathing, ethically aware human beings. "Knowledge of a different order is needed." Critics ridiculed such opinions as "prescientific." Morgenthau was said to have a "Germanic way of looking at things," which wasn't really wrong.

In the twilight of his career, Morgenthau returned to the arguments of his first English-language book. *Science: Servant or Master?* appeared in 1972, though parts of it were written as far back as the 1930s. It was, appropriately, a volume in a series entitled *Perspectives in Humanism* and was dedicated to his Realist comrade-in-arms, Reinhold Niebuhr. Anyone who knew anything about Morgenthau's work was in no suspense about how he would answer the question in the book's title. "We expect everything from science," he wrote, but "technology as applied science threatens to destroy man." To break the momentum of the scientific imperative, which has given us "medicine and poison gas . . . nuclear energy and nuclear bombs," demands human intervention, human will, a sense of value. There was no escaping decisions based on man's place among others. "To be conscious of himself, of his fate in the world, is the specifically human quality in human existence." Or as Arendt put it, "The modern age, with its growing world-alienation, has led to a situation where man, wherever he goes, encounters only himself."

For Morgenthau, the statesman, in his self-aware and vulnerable humanity, stood at the center of international relations, employing modern technology and all available sources of information but not becoming a slave to them. And for Kissinger, too, "The successful conduct of foreign policy demands, above all, the intuitive ability to sense the future and thereby to master it." Great statesmen possessed sound instinct, foresight, a fingertip feel for the shifting currents of history. These were not qualities to be arrived at through statistical analyses. Facts required context and context demanded a vision "stretching into the indefinite future." Kissinger knew he would make the confirmed rationalists uncomfortable with a quotation from Bismarck: "The best a statesman can do is to listen to the footsteps of God, get hold of the hem of His cloak and walk with Him a few steps of the way." But what Kissinger took from Bismarck's words was less the invocation of a deity than the expression of metaphysical humility, an understanding that mere humans would never know all they needed to know as they engaged in the dangerous game of international affairs. These gaps in knowledge were the spaces for instinct and intuition. The quantifiers' mathematical certainties had to be rejected for the messiness and unpredictability of real life, an acceptance of what Morgenthau had called "the very existence of the unknowable."

How could statesmen develop the sensitivity to grapple with the unknown? Kissinger drew on a traditional distinction, explaining that the mind operates in three realms—information, knowledge, and wisdom—and though the computer age has seen great advances in the acquisition and retrieval of information, this realm had limited importance for the practice of diplomacy. Most great statesmen, Kissinger noted, were not especially distinguished for their grasp of detail, and conflicts, he added, have not broken out simply because of a lack of information. "They have arisen not only between societies that do not understand each other but between those that understand each other only too well." The internet has been excellent at telling us about the actual, not so much about the contingent, although policymakers necessarily operate in an arena of uncertainty and unpredictability. Still, one should be clear: Kissinger was not denying the value of facts and information. "An advanced system of technological education has become a prerequisite for a country's long-term power." It would be folly to deny that data had an impact on policy. Kissinger was not applauding ignorance, only the ignorance of believing that facts by themselves, without the intervention of the human intellect, sufficed. What he abhorred were the technocrats and bureaucrats with no vision beyond what was in front of their noses.

To move beyond the factual was to enter the realm of knowledge, which depended on conceptualization, reflection, and responsibility to sort out the significant detail from the voluminous data blinking through the computer screen. No amount of technological training could provide this. Kissinger quoted T. S. Eliot's *Choruses from the Rock*: "Where is the knowledge we have lost in information?" Knowledge, as Kissinger understood it, was not empirical, though it drew on the empirical; it came from the cultivation of the mind, developed through conversation and the free exchange of ideas as well as, and perhaps most of all, through reading and books. "Learning from books places a premium on conceptual thinking," Kissinger said, "the ability to recognize comparable data and events and project patterns into the future." This was not the kind of STEM-like learning that taught students to manipulate information through ever more complicated mathematically based models. It was nonutilitarian. It returned the conscious individual to the heart of instruction for the cultivation of ethical awareness and a perspective that extended into the infinite. As far as statesmen, diplomats, and political leaders were concerned, Kissinger was advocating for a traditional education in the humanities, what the Germans called *Bildung*. He had grown up with *Bildung* in Fürth, but it had gone out of fashion in the Information Age.

Today's leaders, Kissinger complained, lacked "cultural preparation," which could be rectified only by "the study of history and philosophy, the disciplines most relevant to perfecting the art of statesmanship." Future leaders had to engage with ideas that were "neglected elsewhere"—ultimate and transcendent questions about humankind's destiny and the meaning of life. Like Leo Strauss, Kissinger seemed to be proselytizing for a curriculum of Great Books (though his reading list would no doubt differ from Strauss's). Morgenthau, too, looked to the humanities, to art, religion, and philosophy, to deal with "those perennial problems" that science could not resolve but that provided the statesman with his context and his vision. "The questions which the ancient Greeks and Hebrews asked are still asked by us," Morgenthau said. For his part, Kissinger described "a humanity whose inherent nature and experience of reality were timeless and unchanging." Notions of progress, the certainty that a better future was at hand, were of questionable use to diplomats and likely to lead them astray. They needed to be grounded in an understanding of history and tradition. Contingency always stared them in the face.

Of the third realm, wisdom, Kissinger had little to say, except to acknowledge both its existence and its importance, and to distinguish it from information and knowledge. "Great statesmen," according to Strauss, possessed "political wisdom." Morgenthau called wisdom "the approximation to justice which true statecraft discovers." Kissinger no doubt agreed with Morgenthau that wisdom could not be taught like knowledge or accumulated like information; it probably could not even be defined with any precision, because it was, in Morgenthau's words, "the gift of intuition." Still, it could be recognized—you knew it when you saw it. But that meant you had to be willing to see it, to grant that it exists. Because it was an elitist, hierarchical concept that didn't fit comfortably into an egalitarian age (not everyone could be wise or could hope to be wise), Morgenthau lamented that the recognition of wisdom "has well-nigh disappeared from our culture." It was not something that could be identified through a public opinion poll. Kissinger added that it was a characteristic rare in the history of human affairs. "A society is fortunate," he said, "if its leaders can occasionally rise to the level of wisdom," and he left it at that.

The wise statesman, according to Kissinger, acted in the world but was shaped and guided by ideas beyond it; he relied on facts but was not captive to them. The source of his decisions, his organizing principles, came from within himself and was determined by his will, his consciousness, and his judgment. "There exists in our society," Arendt complained, "a widespread fear of judging." The genuine statesman had no choice but to judge, and judgment, Kissinger said, demanded "character and courage . . . vision and determination . . . wisdom and foresight." And where did correct judgment come from? Insofar as policy depended on nonquantifiable choices, there was no avoiding questions of morality. "All political action," Strauss said, "implies thought of the good." Kissinger wrote that "the great human achievements must be fused with enhanced powers of human, transcendent and moral judgment." If artificial intelligence came to dominate or replace human thinking, "What is the role of ethics?"

Kissinger's critics, who see only an amoral opportunist, have a hard time taking such talk seriously, and indeed they see in Realist arguments in general an unconscionable reliance on power to be rejected by all right-thinking, "moral" people. But as Morgenthau repeatedly stressed, power was a basic reality of existence, and it was much more than simple military might. It was an expression of governmental legitimacy, not force. It was what Kissinger called "an acceptance of authority without compulsion." Power was not a fixed concept; it depended on political and cultural context. "No dominion can last that is founded upon nothing but military force," Morgenthau explained. Values mattered, though opponents of the Realist school tended to ignore Morgenthau's cautions. Like Kissinger, he was condemned for amorality or worse. Neither man was understood by his critics. "You are not the harsh Realist you are painted," Walter Lippmann once told Morgenthau, "but the most moral man I know." He had to be because policy for him rested on the decisions of the individual statesman, which meant there was no escaping personal responsibility. "It is a dangerous thing to be a Machiavelli," Morgenthau once said. "It is a disastrous thing to be a Machiavelli without virtù." All political philosophy beginning with the Greeks, Morgenthau wrote, "has started with the assumption that man in the political sphere is not allowed to act as he pleases, and that his action must conform to a standard higher than the standard of success." To live outside the law, the statesman had to be honest.

Similarly, for Kissinger, questions of morality were an ongoing concern. One biographer who interviewed him on several occasions came away convinced that "morality and justice mattered deeply" to him. Kissinger didn't help his reputation for amorality and opportunism by his reluctance to talk openly about his ethical outlook. "What are your core moral principles?" he was asked. "I am not prepared to share that," he answered. He could be loquacious discussing the principles of foreign policy, but regarding the murky foundations of moral thinking, he turned sphinxlike. Such issues were best left to the philosophers, the Strausses and Arendts. Nonetheless, expressions of moral awareness run like a leitmotiv throughout his writings. "The attainment of peace is a profound moral concern," he declared. "Our goal should be to build a moral consensus which can make a pluralistic world creative rather than destructive." He said, "Calculations of power without a moral dimension will turn every disagreement into a test of strength." One of the most important addresses he gave when he was secretary of state was entitled "The Moral Foundations of Foreign Policy." Even his quixotic desire to continue aiding the South Vietnamese regime when just about everyone else in the United States was ready to abandon it was the expression of a moral posture. He felt what he called a "moral obligation" to support the South Vietnamese, who had risked everything by trusting the U.S. government, foolishly as it turned out.

But if moral concerns have been so central to Kissinger's way of thinking, why have his critics failed to see it? And why has the Realist tradition in general, formulated by Morgenthau and embodied by Kissinger, been so repeatedly condemned for immorality? Why have the Realists and the Wilsonians always seemed to be talking past each other? The answer would appear to come down to a question of philosophy, specifically to pre-Nietzschean and post-Nietzschean approaches to life.

The Wilsonians and other critics of Realism, one might say, inhabit a pre-Nietzschean world in which morality is conceived in transcendent terms as a code of behavior "out there," enunciated in principles to be imposed on the variegated give-and-take of human existence. It stands as an unfailing guide, a procrustean abstraction that dogmatically tries to flatten out every human exception and contradiction according to its own preconceptions of what is good and what is bad. It demands a universal template applicable at all times and in all places, dictates handed down from Mount Sinai—for where else could moral principles come from? To the German-Jewish exiles—Strauss, Arendt, Morgenthau, Kissinger—all under the sway of Nietzsche, such thinking was not so much moral as moralistic, ungrounded, and exhortatory, because in a godless universe all ethical abstractions lacked foundation. True morality, to these Nietzscheans, was difficult, uncertain, personal, even hidden from sight. It "concerned the individual in his singularity," Arendt wrote, unrelated to the uplifting ideals she called "banisters." One student of Morgenthau said that what he had learned in class was that "morality was too important to be left to mush-minded moralists." And, of course, the favorite banister of the "mush-minded" American moralists was democracy, a metric ready-made for the rejection of Kissinger's Realism. Or as a former Kissinger aide turned Kissinger critic put it, "The brutal truth was that, at heart," Kissinger lacked "a steadfast faith in the democratic process, least of all as applied to the conduct of foreign policy." The observation is correct. A "steadfast faith" in democracy did not shape Kissinger's policies. Post-Nietzscheans like him lacked a steadfast faith in anything.

The Realistic (and realistic) statesman, in Kissinger's view, couldn't afford to reason according to externalized moral principles. In the law-less, Hobbesian world of international affairs, the policymaker was always dealing with particulars and exceptions, specific problems situated in the immediate present. "Moral principles are universal and timeless," Kissinger said. "Foreign policy is bounded by circumstances." The precept "thou shalt not kill," for example, was of limited use in plotting a course of action in international affairs. No nation selects a pacifist to lead it. (A more relevant maxim for the statesman would be "thou shalt not kill more than is necessary.") There was something fundamentally "unprincipled" in the morality of the statesman, who was necessarily engaged with the here and now. He stood in that moment "where the past meets the future," Kissinger observed, and "must first of all make an analysis of where he finds himself." He was plunged into life, limited by the horizons of his existence. Any move the statesman might make would find a response in countermoves by others, both friends and adversaries, followed by still other moves, and so on, ad infinitum, with every player in the game mov-ing and responding all at once. Foreign affairs was calculated chaos.

Insofar as the Realist statesman could speak of any abstract principle determining his decisions, it was national survival, which was his "first and ultimate responsibility." Assessments of national interest and the need to balance power among competing countries grew out of this "ulti-mate responsibility," and whereas the one-world moralists argued that a policy based on national interest was a prescription for amoral selfishness, even imperialism and a drive toward global hegemony, Kissinger under-stood it as a force for moderation and caution. "Accepting the limits of one's capacities is one of the tests of statesmanship; it implies a judgment of the possible." It proceeded gradually, its sense of morality expressed "in the willingness to persevere through a series of steps, each of which was incomplete." It sought the achievement of "equilibrium while restraining the dogs of war." Lacking idealistic or ultimate ends, a concern for national interest did not expect too much, accepting "imperfections and partial solutions." The Wilsonian moralists and one-worlders, on the other hand, with their global aspirations for universal democracy and world peace, had difficulty setting limits to their utopian aims. They were on an endless crusade, and their dogmatism "leads to self-righteousness, fanaticism and the erosion of all restraints." No Kissingerian irony or self-deprecation for them.

Kissinger's Realism may have put him at odds with the majority of his idealistic countrymen, making him a villain or a criminal in their eyes, but that is not to say that he didn't operate with his own post-Nietzschean sense of morality. He had convictions that mattered, even if they couldn't be translated into the kind of absolute terms that would satisfy the traditionalists. There was no simple formula, no ready-made principles he could point to. Trying to enunciate a code of behavior that could serve as an ethical standard missed the point. His morality came from his being planted firmly on the ground, through interactions with others in the here and now. He put individual consciousness at the center of the world as it actually was. The way to express his convictions was not with a catalogue of unimpeachable commands but through a series of oppositions that captured the art of diplomacy as a lived, fluid experience. So, for instance, Kissinger believed in employing power for limited ends rather than absolute ends. He also believed in

- incrementalism rather than perfectionism
- continuity rather than upheaval
- pragmatism rather than idealism
- stability rather than justice
- the particular rather than the general
- the less bad rather than the unqualified good
- improvisations rather than solutions
- the hemmed-in restrictions of reason rather than the unleashed exuberance of emotion
- the possible rather than the desirable

- the imminent rather than the transcendent
- history rather than analytics
- partiality rather than completion
- process rather than goal
- the long term rather than the immediate
- the unpredictable and uncertain rather than the mechanistic and formulaic.

Above all, he believed that it was necessary to accept evil in the world rather than attempt to eradicate it, and probably no conviction got him into more trouble than this one. He insisted that statesmen couldn't afford to leap beyond messy actuality into a situation people wished were true.

Kissinger's world was not one for idealists or visionaries. Throughout his career, he had questioned the vocation of prophet, those whose visions of a better world had the potential to produce chaotic upheaval. In its way, Kissinger's world was a barren, desolate place that offered no long-term hope, only the chance to keep on keeping on. Some might see in such a prospect a prescription for pessimism, but pessimism promised only helplessness, darkness, decadence, even temptations to suicide. As someone who had committed himself to a career of action on behalf of the country that had saved his life and the lives of his immediate family, Kissinger made a choice for stoicism, not pessimism, a willingness to endure no matter what obstacles were placed in his path, though with no ultimate ends to aim for, nothing beyond the affirmation of existence itself and the perpetuation of the United States. Life might have no meaning in this godless universe, but there was still meaningful work to be done, if only to prevent humankind from blowing itself up. This apocalyptic threat was cause enough to engage with the world, even if it was impossible to answer the question, Why not let foolish humanity destroy itself and the planet? One way of looking at Kissinger's career is as a lifelong endeavor to forestall nuclear holocaust. The very first sentence of his very first book read: "It is not surprising that an age faced with the threat of thermonuclear extinction should look back nostalgically to periods when diplomacy carried with it less drastic penalties, when wars were limited and catastrophe almost inconceivable." With his conservative moderation and Realist's awareness of what could be hoped for, he can be considered the most important diplomat who has so far emerged in the nuclear age.

That said, as a student of Morgenthau, Kissinger understood that there was no way to avoid doing evil in the conduct of foreign policy, as even the most moral statesman was bound to commit inhumane acts. International relations was not a field for anyone seeking perfection or saintliness. Even the most ethically aware statesman emerged from his endeavors with dirty hands, and if there was any moral satisfaction to be gained from the occupation of diplomacy, it consisted in the possibility of choosing the lesser evil or doing the least evil possible—in Morgenthau's words being "as good as he can be in an evil world." That is what "morality" meant in the global arena. This was not much—still, it might be enough to keep humanity from blowing itself up. What was more, it allowed for a crucial distinction: there could never be an excuse for callousness, cruelty, or inhumanity, for excesses of any kind. Limits—that favorite Kissinger word—could be enunciated, even for foul deeds. If one had to kill, it should be done with reluctance, with resignation rather than pleasure, and with the understanding that even the political leader with the best of intentions always acted to some extent in the dark, without complete knowledge or certainty, and with no guarantee of success. Mistakes would be made. Lives would be lost. Choosing a particular policy—or judging it from the outside—would always be a complicated business of weighing means and ends, a process with no certain conclusion to it, no permanently upright posture.

My friend who said to me that Henry Kissinger was evil wasn't wrong. All public figures in positions like his could be considered evil. But evaluating Kissinger's career means that it isn't enough to determine that he had made bad decisions, employing violence, even violence against innocent people. The question to be asked is whether those decisions had been more evil than they needed to be, and that question can't be answered by falling back on abstract ideals or moralistic platitudes. It calls for a sense of the immediate situation and for analysis of what could be expected from any possible alternatives. What choices did Washington have when confronted with the electoral victory of Salvador Allende? How to extricate the United States from the morass of Vietnam in a way that did the least damage to American interests? To be sure, one could argue, with justification, that Kissinger didn't always pass these tests. But to quote Morgenthau one last time, "The very act of acting destroys our moral integrity. Whoever wants to retain his moral innocence must forsake action altogether." If doing good in the world is what you yearn for, you aren't cut out for foreign affairs. Maybe there is no better way of putting all this than to say that in Henry Kissinger's world, the amoral world of statesmen and diplomats, you could allow yourself few expectations. If you were to act at all what had to be accepted was the imperfectability of man, the unpredictability of consequences, the prospect of arriving at no permanent solutions, the inevitability of tragedy.

ACKNOWLEDGMENTS

Any author who spends six or seven years on a project ends up owing a debt of gratitude to a daunting number of people—in my case, everyone from the expert professionals at the Library of Congress to the accommodating wait staff at my local Starbucks, who watched indulgently as I spent hours over a single cup of coffee furiously writing on my yellow legal pads and even more furiously tearing up what I had just written and starting all over again. But I think the best way to structure my long list of thank-yous is to divide them into two groups: the people who read some or much of the manuscript and were never less than encouraging, even when they made clear that they disagreed with my arguments; and those friends and acquaintances who were not readers for one reason or another but who offered their support in a variety of gracious and subtle ways. To both groups, I hope the end result lives up to their expectations.

The readers include Steven Aschheim, Gary Bass, Leslie Blumberg, Mitchell Cohen, Howard Darmstadter, Elsa Dixler, Joseph Dorman, Hillel Fradkin, Jacob Heilbrunn, Kay Hymowitz, David Kelly, Mark Lilla, Jancis Long, Daniel Menaker, Rajan Menon, David Oshinsky, Gary Rosen, Steven Smith, Jennifer Szalai, Sam Tanenhaus, Paul Weissman, and Michael Winston.

The others who deserve my gratitude include Carole Colsell, Belinda Cooper, Jack Fuchs, Michele Jacob, Martha Kaplan, Alice Levine, Millard Long, Patricia Lydon, Robert Merry, Bruce Nichols, John Odling-Smee, Jane Oshinsky, Walter Reich, Eveline Riemen, Rob Riemen, Katy Roberts, David Rosen, James Ryerson, Jeff Seroy, Robert Tracy, Carmela Veneroso, Jaclyn Veneroso, Lewis Wurgaft, and Steven Zipperstein.

In a separate category are all those who had a hand in ensuring that the book saw the light of day: my agent, Ike Williams, who grasped immediately what I was trying to do, perhaps because of his own Kissinger connection, and was the first to help make the book happen; my outstanding editor, John Glusman, whose wise and careful reading and excellent suggestions made this a much more coherent narrative than it was at the start, and who saved me from myself on many occasions, even when I was reluctant to take his advice and be saved; his extraordinarily capable assistant, Helen Thomaides, who kept a firm and sympathetic eye on the process every grueling step of the way; Norton's publicist, Louise Brockett, with whom I go back many years and who proved as delightful to work with as she has been to know; and my permissions freelancer, Melissa Flamson, whose job I thought would be a straightforward one, but who did so much beyond the call of duty that I'm not sure the book could ever have been completed without her. Finally, I want to thank Susanna Morgenthau, who, with enormous generosity, opened up her father's files to me, lent an understanding ear, and provided me with an invaluable, one-of-a-kind photograph—pure gold. (Henry Kissinger declined to be interviewed for this book.)

At this point it's customary for authors to accept full responsibility for any errors in their books. As someone who has been reading professionally for over 30 years, I know it's the rare volume that is entirely error-free, and like any author I worry about what I may have gotten wrong, especially because part of my job description as an editor at the *New York Times Book Review* is to catch other writers' mistakes. But I beg the reader's indulgence. Misspelled names and mistaken dates, however embarrassing, can always be corrected. I would hope to be judged by the book's ideas and overall argument, which are not so easily correctable, and in this I am reminded of what Kant said in one of the prefaces to *The Critique of Pure Reason*: "A philosophical work cannot be armed at all points like a mathematical treatise, and may therefore be open to objection in this or that respect, while yet the structure of the system, taken in its unity, is not in the least endangered."

I'm with that guy!

NOTES

vii **"the inevitability of tragedy"**: Henry Kissinger, interview with James Reston, *New York Times*, October 13, 1974: 35.

PROLOGUE

xiv **"universal appeal"**: Condoleezza Rice, *Democracy: Stories from the Long Road to Freedom* (New York: Twelve, 2017), 10.

xv **"My father couldn't register"**: Rice, *Democracy*, 26.

CHAPTER ONE: CHILE

1 **"I don't see why"**: Seymour Hersh, *The Price of Power: Kissinger in the Nixon White House* (New York: Summit Books, 1983), 265.

2 **"After so many years"**: Peter Kornbluh, ed., *The Pinochet File: A Declassified Dossier on Atrocity and Accountability* (New York: The New Press, 2013), xiii.

2 **"The C.I.A.'s role"**: Thomas Powers, *The Man Who Kept the Secrets: Richard Helms and the CIA* (New York: Knopf, 1979), 220.

2 **"I still associate:"** Richard Helms, with William Hood, *A Look Over My Shoulder: A Life in the Central Intelligence Agency* (New York: Random House, 2002), 396.

2 **"a widespread movement"**: Kornbluh, *Pinochet File*, xiii.

2 **"One goal of the project"**: The White House, Office of the Press Secretary, http://foia.state.gov/press/WH11-13-00.asp.

3 **"for war crimes"**: Christopher Hitchens, *The Trial of Henry Kissinger* (London: Verso, 2001), ix, xi.

3 **"than met the eye"**: Henry Kissinger, *White House Years* (New York: Simon & Schuster, 2011), 674.

5 **"a cipher"**: Arthur P. Whitaker, *The United States and South America* (Cambridge, MA: Harvard University Press, 1948), 358.

5 **"a dagger"**: Jossi Hanhimäki, *The Flawed Architect: Henry Kissinger and American Foreign Policy* (Oxford: Oxford University Press, 2004), 92.

5 **"The ghost of Salvador Allende"**: Nathaniel Davis, *The Last Two Years of Salvador Allende* (Ithaca, NY: Cornell University Press, 1985), xi.

6 **"That the House of Representatives"**: Samuel Flagg Bemis, *The Latin American Policy of the United States: A Historical Interpretation* (New York: Harcourt Brace, 1943), 44.

6   the young country's first newspaper: Henry Clay Evans Jr., *Chile and Its Relations with the United States* (Durham, NC: Duke University Press, 1927), 16.

6–7   **President James Monroe:** Evans, *Chile and Its Relations*, 24.

7   **"the possession of Florida":** Evans, *Chile and Its Relations*, 28–29.

7   **an outburst of diplomatic activity:** Bemis, *Latin American Policy*, 46–47.

7   **A 22-gun salute:** Evans, *Chile and Its Relations*, 29.

7   **In his three years in Chile:** Evans, *Chile and Its Relations*, 30.

7   **"wicked and abandoned":** Evans, *Chile and Its Relations*, 35.

8   **"The United States scarcely existed":** Frederick B. Pike, *Chile and the United States, 1880-1962: The Emergence of Chile's Social Crisis and the Challenge to United States Diplomacy* (Notre Dame, IN: University of Notre Dame, 1963), 10.

8   **"Our trade with Chile":** Evans, *Chile and Its Relations*, 40.

8   **on the evening of October 16:** Pike, *Chile and the United States*, 73–74.

9   **President Benjamin Harrison:** Pike, *Chile and the United States*, 149.

9   **one of the dead sailors:** Evans, *Chile and Its Relations*, 152.

10   **"a typical product":** Pike, *Chile and the United States*, 145.

10   **as high as 70 percent:** Theodore H. Moran, *Copper in Chile: Multinational Corporations and the Politics of Dependence* (Princeton, NJ: Princeton University Press, 1974), 24.

10   **a blessing:** Moran, *Copper in Chile*, 23–24.

11   **the largest earthquake:** USGS, "20 Largest Earthquakes in the World," https://earthquake.usgs.gov/earthquakes/browse/largest-world.php.

11   **"first presidential intervention":** "El Embajador Edward M. Korrey en el CEP," *Estudios Publicos* 72 (Spring 1998).

11   **"Cuba forced us":** Christopher Andrew and Vasili Mitrokhin, *The World Was Going Our Way* (New York: Basic Books, 2005), 28.

11   **"bridgehead":** Andrew and Mitrokhin, 10, *World Was Going*, 8–9, 24.

11   **Allende's Soviet connection:** Kristian Gustafson, *Hostile Intent: U.S. Covert Operations in Chile, 1964-1974* (Washington, DC: Potomac Books, 2007), 31.

11   **"systematic contact":** Andrew and Mitrokhin, *World Was Going*, 69.

12   **when the Soviets marched into Hungary:** James Petras, *Politics and Social Forces in Chilean Development* (Berkeley: University of California Press, 1969), 184.

12   **"Allende was outspoken":** Helms, *A Look*, 398.

12   **"Cuba in the Caribbean":** Helms, *A Look*, 398; Kissinger, *White House Years*, 655.

12   **"second only to the victory":** Andrew and Mitrokhin, *World Was Going*, 69.

12   **around only 5 percent:** Timothy R. Scully, *Rethinking the Center: Party Politics in 19th and 20th Century Chile* (Stanford: Stanford University Press, 1992), 15–16.

13   **"instinctively democratic":** Claude G. Bowers, *Chile Through Embassy Windows, 1939-1953* (New York: Simon & Schuster, 1958), 22.

14   **"affair of the sacristan":** Petras, *Politics and Social Forces*, 89.

14   **a Conservative Party was formed:** Scully, *Rethinking the Center*, 36–38.

15   **Urban growth:** Petras, *Politics and Social Forces*, 15.

15   **One study:** Miles D. Wolpin, *Cuban Foreign Policy and Chilean Politics* (Lexington, MA: Lexington Books, 1972), 11.

15   **The average height:** Pike, *Chile and the United States*, 278.

15   **at least one-third:** Wolpin, *Cuban Foreign Policy*, 12.

15   **mortality rates:** Petras, *Politics and Social Forces*, 29–30.

15   **one out of four:** Pike, *Chile and the United States*, 279, 106, 278, 201.

16   **large businessmen:** Petras, *Politics and Social Forces*, 53.

17   **women got the vote:** Scully, *Rethinking the Center*, 126, 141.

17   **secret ballot:** Scully, *Rethinking the Center*, 124, 142, 143.

17   **In agriculture alone:** Stefan De Vylder, *Allende's Chile: The Political Economy of the Rise and Fall of the Unidad Popular* (Cambridge: Cambridge University Press, 1976), 167.

17   **"The profound consequences":** Pike, *Chile and the United States*, 292–293.

17 **"immaculate socialist militant"**: Regis Debray, *The Chilean Revolution: Conversations with Allende* (New York: Pantheon, 1971), 40.

18 **"Economically, he was"**: *Estudios Publicos*, 36.

18 **"full-time party"**: Benny Pollack, "The Chilean Socialist Party: Prolegomena to its Ideology and Organization," *Journal of Latin American Studies* 10, no. 1 (May 1978), 147, 126.

19 **"For the first time"**: Tony Judt, *The Burden of Responsibility: Blum, Camus, Aron and the French 20th Century* (Chicago: University of Chicago Press, 1998), 67.

20 **"con sabor"**: Gustafson, *Hostile Intent*, 7.

20 **"spokesman of the Cuban revolution"**: Wolpin, *Cuban Foreign Policy*, 108.

20 **"The Chilean people"**: Pollack, "Chilean Socialist Party," 149.

20 **a family connection**: Gustafson, *Hostile Intent*, 27.

21 **there to greet them**: Wolpin, *Cuban Foreign Policy*, 133.

22 **personally inscribed**: Debray, *Chilean Revolution*, 34, 75.

22 **"Moscow is our brain"**: Aleksandr Fursenko and Timothy Naftali, *One Hell of a Gamble: Khrushchev, Castro and Kennedy, 1958–1964* (New York: Norton, 1997), 71.

22 **Another "Castro"**: Robert A. Hurwich, First Secretary of the Embassy in Chile, letter to the President's Special Assistant for National Security Affairs, McGeorge Bundy (June 19, 1964), Washington National Records Center, in Gustafson, *Hostile Intent*, 30.

22 **"a clear threat"**: Helms, *A Look*, 398.

23 **"Communitarian Socialism"**: Scully, *Rethinking the Center*, 148.

23 **"covert United States involvement in Chile"**: Church Report, *Covert Action in Chile, 1963–1973* (Washington, DC: Government Printing Office, 1975), https://www.intelligence.senate.gov/sites/default/files/94chile.pdf.

24 **"nonattributable"**: Gustafson, *Hostile Intent*, 34, 37, 47–48.

24 **"We can't afford"**: U.S. State Department, "Foreign Relations of the United States, 1964–1968," vol. 31, doc. 246, in Gustafson, *Hostile Intent*, 45.

24 **More than half**: Church Report, *Covert Action*, 9, 10.

24 **"indispensable ingredients"**: U.S. Embassy Santiago, airgram to Department of State, September 3, 1964, A-187, National Archives and Record Administration, in Gustafson, *Hostile Intent*, 48.

25 **"send waves of panic"**: John Lewis Gaddis, *George F. Kennan: An American Life* (New York: Penguin, 2011), 305, 317.

25 **"Secret intelligence"**: Helms, *A Look*, vii.

25 **"covert operations"**: Kissinger, *White House Years*, 658.

25 **"reaching 500,000"**: Julio Faundez, *Marxism and Democracy in Chile: From 1932 to the Fall of Allende* (New Haven, CT: Yale University Press, 1988), 141.

26 **"We are in a quandary"**: National Security Council (NSC) Report, Chile, March 4, 1971, p. 19.

27 **"We could live with him"**: Gustafson, *Hostile Intent*, 102.

27 **echoed that sentiment**: NSC Report, p. 5.

27 **"trying to beat somebody"**: Gustafson, *Hostile Intent*, 80.

27 **the CIA spent only**: Church Report, *Covert Action*, 2, 9, 12.

28 **"represented a break"**: Kissinger, *White House Years*, 154.

29 **"graveyard smell"**: Edward M. Korry, "The Communists Take Over Chile," memorandum to State Department, September 12, 1970, in CIA, "Chile Collection," Gustafson, *Hostile Intent*, 107.

29 **"unguided missile"**: Henry Kissinger, "Memorandum for the President," September 17, 1970.

29 **"more than one chance in 20"**: http:www.gwu.edu/~nsarchiv/NSAEBB/NSAEBB8/ch06–01.htm.

29 **"firm and continuing policy"**: http:www.gwu.edu/~nsarchiv/NSAEBB/NSAEBB8/ch05–01.htm.

29 **misunderstood his orders**: Kissinger, *White House Years*, 666.

30 **"What is beyond debate":** Gustafson, *Hostile Intent*, 137.
30 **On November 5:** Henry Kissinger, "Memorandum for the President," November 5, 1970.
31 **was the threat posed** : Church Report, *Covert Action*, 29.
31 **"Cambodia claimed":** Kissinger, *White House Years*, 666.
31 **Short-term credits:** Church Report, *Covert Action*, 18.
32 **Between 1970 and 1973:** Gustafson, *Hostile Intent*, 150.
32 **"if Richard Nixon":** Davis, *Last Two Years*, 129.
32 **"to preserve democracy":** Henry Kissinger, *Years of Upheaval* (New York: Simon & Schuster, 2011), 316.
32 **he would "get" the paper:** Gustafson, *Hostile Intent*, 160.
32 **Out of a total of $7 million:** Church Report, *Covert Action*, 15–16.
33 **the United States supplied $5 million:** Gustafson, *Hostile Intent*, 155.
33 **"the ultimate objective":** Davis, *Last Two Years*, 310, 315.
33 **a mountain of information:** Church Report, *Covert Action*, 21.
33 **"exercised extreme care":** Central Intelligence Agency, "CIA activities in Chile," https://www.cia.gov/library/reports/general-reports-1/chile/.
33 **"We had clear instructions":** Gustafson, *Hostile Intent*, 175–176.
34 **"I am not president":** Paul E. Sigmund, *The Overthrow of Allende and the Politics of Chile, 1964–1976* (Pittsburgh: University of Pittsburgh Press, 1977), 147.
34 **"The objective":** Gustafson, *Hostile Intent*, 29.
34 **"Legal loopholes":** Sigmund, *Overthrow of Allende*, 279.
34 **"The decisive confrontation":** Davis, *Last Two Years*, 45.
34 **"The actual class struggle":** De Vylder, *Allende's Chile*, 86.
34 **"State control is designed":** Davis, *Last Two Years*, 80.
34 **more than 80 percent:** Faundez, *Marxism and Democracy*, 211.
34 **the government controlled:** Gustafson, *Hostile Intent*, 197; Faundez, *Overthrow of Allende*, 211.
34 **Roman Catholic bishops:** Moran, *Copper in Chile*, 215.
35 **"Tammany Hall":** Davis, *Last Two Years*, 81.
35 **"We shall have real power":** Debray, *Chilean Revolution*, 85.
35 **"People's Assembly":** Davis, *Last Two Years*, 16, 135.
36 **archbishop of Valparaiso:** Sigmund, *Overthrow of Allende*, 203.
36 **"a new culture":** Davis, *Last Two Years*, 340.
36 **"first consumption":** De Vylder, *Allende's Chile*, 105.
36 **jumped to 78 percent:** Faundez, *Marxism and Democracy*, 247–248.
36 **toothpaste:** Sigmund, *Overthrow of Allende*, 236.
37 **health services for the poor:** Faundez, *Marxism and Democracy*, 248.
37 **Unemployment had fallen:** Sigmund, *Overthrow of Allende*, 236.
37 **food consumption:** Davis, *Last Two Years*, 122.
37 **sympathetic Swedish scholar:** De Vylder, *Allende's Chile*, 111.
37 **"There is no meat":** Santiago Station, "A Massive Demonstration," cable to CIA headquarters, December 1, 1971; Gustafson, *Hostile Intent*, 163.
38 **high point of the resistance:** Davis, *Last Two Years*, 199–200.
38 **Engels's words:** Friedrich Engels, *The Peasant War in Germany, 1969*, p. 115, in De Vylder, *Allende's Chile*, 219.
38 **the choice for his country:** Gustafson, *Hostile Intent*, 207.
39 **"on a sinking ship":** Davis, *Last Two Years*, 104.
39 **One scholarly authority:** Sigmund, *Overthrow of Allende*, 288, 227.
40 **"I did not engage":** Davis, *Last Two Years*, 348, 400.
40 **"there was no support":** CIA activities in Chile.
40 **declared categorically:** Church Report, *Covert Action*, 3.
40 **Kissinger's own statement:** Kissinger, *Years of Upheaval*, 374.
40 **"that coup last week":** Telcon, July 4, 1973, https://nsarchive2.gwu.edu/NSAEBB/NSAEBB255/19730704–1100-Nixon4.pdf.

40 **"We didn't do it"**: Telcon, September 16, 1973, https://nsarchive2.gwu.edu/NSAEBB/
NSAEBB123/Box%2022,%20File%203,%20Telcon,%209-16-73%2011,50%20Mr.%20
Kissinger-The%20Pres%202.pdf.

41 **"Though we had no hand"**: Henry Kissinger, *Years of Renewal* (New York: Simon &
Schuster, 2000), 753.

43 **"Did the perceived threat"**: Church Report, *Covert Action*, 24, 27, 29, 16, 26, 25.

44 **"Allende will be hard"**: Kornbluh, *Pinochet File*, 10, 11.

45 **"a psychological setback"**: Church Report, *Covert Action*, 25.

45 **"Fidel redux"**: Gustafson, *Hostile Intent*, 173.

45 **"Massive problems for us"**: Church Report, *Covert Action*, 15.

46 **"Allende's graceful acceptance"**: Hersh, *Price of Power*, 278.

46 **As for the bourgeois state**: Regis Debray, *The Chilean Revolution*, p. 82, in Kissinger,
Years of Renewal, 750.

46 **"popular democracy"**: Gustafson, *Hostile Intent*, 29.

46 **"tactical necessity"**: Sigmund, *Overthrow of Allende*, 140.

46 **"a well-known Socialist moderate"**: Faundez, *Marxism and Democracy*, 192.

47 **"Neither did Kerensky"**: Walter Isaacson, *Kissinger: A Biography* (New York: Simon &
Schuster, 2005), 673–674.

48 **"American-owned property"**: Kissinger, *Years of Upheaval*, 656.

48 **independent scholars**: Tanya Harmer, *Allende's Chile and the Inter-American Cold War*
(Chapel Hill: University of North Carolina Press, 2011), 60, 87.

48 **"Hitler was no tyrant"**: Ian Kershaw, *Hitler: 1889–1936, Hubris* (London: Penguin,
2001), xxix.

48 **"the most popular revolutionary leader"**: John Lukacs, *The Hitler of History* (New York:
Vintage, 1998), 50–51.

48 **"imposed the Nazi tyranny"**: William L. Shirer, *The Rise and Fall of the Third Reich: A
History of Nazi Germany* (New York: Simon & Schuster, 1990), 187.

49 **"never suffered disaster"**: Isaacson, *Kissinger*, 31.

49 **"Kissinger's views"**: Jeremi Suri, *Henry Kissinger and the American Century* (Cambridge
MA: Harvard University Press, 2007), 36.

49 **"Unlike most"**: Kissinger, *White House Years*, 229.

CHAPTER TWO: HITLER

51 **"Hitler's advent to power"**: Henry Kissinger, *Diplomacy* (New York: Simon & Schuster,
1994), 288.

52 **"I cannot know"**: Richard J. Evans, *The Coming of the Third Reich* (New York: Penguin,
2005), xx.

52 **"demonic" and "psychotic"**: Kissinger, *Diplomacy*, 288, 301.

52 **"patience, compromise"**: Kissinger, *Diplomacy*, 284.

53 **"reckless megalomania"**: Kissinger, *Diplomacy*, 29, 302, 294, 296.

53 **"succumbed to an assassination"**: Joachim C. Fest, *Hitler*, trans. Richard and Clara
Winston (New York: Harcourt Brace Jovanovich, 1974), 9.

53 **"Had the democracies"**: Kissinger, *Diplomacy*, 294.

53 **"respectable"**: Sonia Orwell and Ian Angus, eds., *The Collected Essays, Journalism and
Letters of George Orwell* (Hammondsworth, Middlesex: Penguin, 1971), 2:27.

53 **"the West should"**: Kissinger, *Diplomacy*, 294, 301.

54 **"My pride"**: Alan Bullock, *Hitler: A Study in Tyranny* (New York: Harper & Row, 1962),
404.

54 **the Germans did not fear Hitler**: John Lukacs, *The Hitler of History* (New York: Vintage,
1998), 212, 94.

54 **"Freedom has appeared"**: Alexis de Tocqueville, *Democracy in America* (New York: Vintage, 1945), 2:100.

54 **"If ever the free institutions"**: Tocqueville, *Democracy*, 1:279.

55 "Growing up in Fürth" Jeremi Suri, *Henry Kissinger and the American Century* (Cambridge MA: Harvard University Press, 2007), 26.

55 **"city of soot"**: Katrin Kasparek, *The History of the Jews in Furth* (Nuremberg: Sandberg Verlag, 2010), 44.

55 **10 banking and commercial houses:** Evi Kurz, *The Kissinger Saga: Walter and Henry Kissinger, Two Brothers from Furth, Germany* (London: Weidenfeld and Nicolson, 2009), 27.

55 **"cheap but good"**: Kasparek, *History*, 28

55 **"Bavarian Jerusalem"**: Niall Ferguson, *Kissinger, Volume 1, 1923–1968: The Idealist* (New York: Penguin, 2015), 43.

55 **"artists' house"**: Kasparek, *History*, 22.

55 **"unique position"**: Kurz, *Kissinger Saga*, 27.

56 **"like a child"**: Ferguson, *Kissinger*, 50.

56 **"he couldn't imagine"**: Walter Isaacson, *Kissinger* (New York: Simon & Schuster, 2005), 22.

56 **"happiest years"**: Suri, *Henry Kissinger*, 26.

57 **"bookworm"**: Kurz, *Kissinger Saga*, 62.

57 **"A few people"**: Isaacson, *Kissinger*, 25.

57 **"We haven't done anything"**: Kurz, *Kissinger Saga*, 78.

58 **Of the 1,990 Jews:** Kasparek, *History*, 36, 13.

58 **"If it had been up to him"**: Kurz, *Kissinger Saga*, 79, 95.

58 **"The women often appeared"**: Peter Schrag, *The World of Aufbau: Hitler's Refugees in America* (Madison: University of Wisconsin Press, 2019), 43.

60 **"scathingly negative"**: Ian Kershaw, *Hitler, 1889–1936: Hubris* (London, Penguin, 2001), 17.

60 **"no longer believed"**: Brigitte Hamann, *Hitler's Vienna: A Dictator's Apprenticeship* (New York: Oxford University Press, 1999), 19.

61 **"Hitler had had no sexual experience"**: Kershaw, *Hitler*, 44.

61 **"content to live in filth"**: Walter C. Langer, *The Mind of Adolf Hitler: The Secret Wartime Report* (New York: Basic, 1972), 10–11.

61 **Fest sees more:** Joachim C. Fest, *Hitler*, 46, 49.

62 **occasional individuals:** Friedrich Nietzsche, *The Gay Science* (New York: Vintage, 1974), 108.

62 **"The war was a godsend"**: Kershaw, *Hitler*, 87.

62 **"I fell down on my knees"**: Adolf Hitler, *Mein Kampf* trans. Ralph Manheim (Boston: Houghton Mifflin, 1973), 161.

63 **"We all used to yell at him"**: Fest, *Hitler*, 69, 68, 79, 113.

63 **"show him kindness"**: Kershaw, *Hitler*, 122, 123.

64 **"eyes coldly glistening"**: Fest, *Hitler*, 113.

64 **"a waiter in a railway station"**: Ernst Hanfstaengl, *Unheard Witness* (Philadelphia: Lippincott, 1957), 34, 40.

64 **"I could speak"**: Hitler, *Mein Kampf*, 215–216.

65 "You could win him": Fest, *Hitler*, 118.

65 **"power of persuasion"**: Hanfstaengl, *Unheard Witness*, 282.

65 **"mass hypnotism"**: Sebastian Haffner, *The Meaning of Hitler* (Cambridge, MA: Harvard University Press 1979) 14

65 **"the grandiose popular speaker"**: Kershaw, *Hitler*, 148.

66 **"The amazing thing"**: Ron Rosenbaum, *Explaining Hitler: The Search for the Origins of His Evil* (Boston: Da Capo, 2014), 303.

66 **"The Führer's hands"**: Daniel Maier-Katkin, *Stranger from Abroad: Hannah Arendt, Martin Heidegger, Friendship and Forgiveness* (New York: Norton, 2010), 99.

66 **"The history of National Socialism"**: Karl Dietrich Bracher, *The German Dictatorship: The Origins, Structure and Effects of National Socialism* (New York: Holt, Rinehart and Winston, 1970), 199.

66 **"tightrope walker"**: Hanfstaengl, *Unheard Witness*, 36.

66 **"By any objective standard"**: William Carr, *Hitler: A Study in Personality and Politics* (London: Edward Arnold, 1978), 1.

67 **"He actually inhaled"**: Fest, *Hitler*, 327.

67 **"positively inhuman"**: William L. Shirer, *Berlin Diary: The Journal of a Foreign Correspondent, 1934–1941* (New York: Knopf, 1941), 17.

67 **"described as orgiastic"**: Otto Strasser, *Hitler and I* (Boston: Houghton Mifflin, 1940), 66.

67 **"It was less *what* he said"**: Kershaw, *Hitler*, 133.

68 **"Hitler never really made"**: Carr, *Hitler*, 9.

68 **"an evangelist speaking"**: Fest, *Hitler*, 327.

68 **"the worship of the people"**: George L. Mosse, *The Nationalization of the Masses: Political Symbolism and Mass Movements in Germany from the Napoleonic Wars Through the Third Reich* (New York: New American Library, 1975), 4.

68 **John the Baptist:** Fest, *Hitler*, 154.

68 **"leader sent by God"**: Bracher, *German Dictatorship*, 148.

69 **"The main thing"**: Kershaw, *Hitler*, 147.

69 **entrance fees:** Kershaw, *Hitler*, 189.

70 **"boring down strongly"**: Max Weber, "Politics as a Vocation," from W. G. Runciman, ed., "Selections in Translation," in Mitchell Cohen and Nicole Fermon (eds.), *Princeton Readings in Political Thought: Essential Texts Since Plato* (Princeton, NJ: Princeton University Press, 1996), 510, 500.

71 **"There were certainly many"**: Harold J. Gordon, Jr., *Hitler and the Beer Hall Putsch* (Princeton, NJ: Princeton University Press, 1972), 288, 388.

72 **"I consider myself"**: Fest, *Hitler*, 191.

73 **"transformed the old Hitler"**: Gordon, *Hitler*, 618.

73 **marked the end:** Fest, *Hitler*, 190, 195.

73 **"hold our noses"**: Kershaw, *Hitler*, 228, 350.

73 **"Any lawful process"**: Fest, *Hitler*, 228, 236.

73 **"patience"**: Gordon, *Hitler*, 618.

73 **"his real strength"**: Bracher, *German Dictatorship*, 128.

73 **"Prince Légalité"**: Hanfstaengl, *Unheard Witness*, 147.

74 **"a party leader"**: Ian Kershaw, *Hitler, the Germans and the Final Solution* (New Haven: Yale University Press, 2008), 31

75 **"a genuine people's party"**: Peter Fritzsche, *Germans into Nazis* (Cambridge, MA: Harvard University Press, 1998), 194.

75 **"If he's in it"**: Kershaw, *Hitler, 1889–1936*, 321.

75 **"pounding steam engine"**: Haffner, *Meaning of Hitler*, 26.

75 **"everywhere in Germany"**: Thomas Childers, *The Nazi Voter: The Social Foundations of Fascism in Germany, 1919–1933* (Chapel Hill: University of North Carolina Press, 1983), 138, 200.

76 **"Every one of my words"**: Fest, *Hitler*, 246, 285.

76 **"monumental idiocy"**: Strasser, *Hitler and I*, 104.

77 **"mania of legality"**: Henry Ashby Turner, Jr., *Hitler's Thirty Days to Power: January 1933* (Reading, MA: Addison-Wesley, 1996), 72.

77 **"the most serious crisis"**: Kershaw, *Hitler*, 333, 349, 367.

79 **"formed a river of fire"**: Fritzsche, *Germans into Nazis*, 140.

80 **"backstairs political intrigue"**: Evans, *Coming of the Third Reich*, 451.

80 **conspiracy:** Turner, *Hitler's Thirty Days*, 117.

80 **"ambitious and misguided men"**: Bracher, *German Dictatorship*, 170.

80 **"sinister intrigues"**: Volker Ullrich, *Hitler: Ascent, 1889–1939* (New York: Knopf, 2016), 349.

80 **"Democracy was less surrendered"**: Kershaw, *Hitler*, 425.

82 **"incitement to treason"**: Turner, *Hitler's Thirty Days*, 126, 171, 177.

82 **"boxing Hitler in"**: Kershaw, *Hitler*, 421.

83 **"terrorist power grab"**: Bracher, *German Dictatorship*, 170.

83 **"sense of honor"**: Friedrich Reck, *Diary of a Man in Despair* (New York: New York Review Books, 2013), 188.

83 "The first Hitler government": David Evans and Jake Jenkins, *Years of Weimar and the Third Reich* (London: Holder and Staughton, 1999), 103.

84 "the real miracle": Fest, *Hitler*, 367.

85 "the best of motives": Hermann Rauschning, *The Revolution of Nihilism: Warning to the West* (New York: Alliance Book Corporation, 1939), xvii, xii, 87, 119, 280.

86 "basically unfit children": Reck, *Diary*, 139, 20, 77, 16.

87 "whoever possesses Prussia": Martin Broszat, *Hitler and the Collapse of Weimar Germany* (New York: Berg, 1987), 28.

87 "For the first time": Konrad Heiden, *The Führer* (New York: Skyhorse, 2012), 200.

87 "In no sense": Fest, *Hitler*, 256.

88 "Kaiserless time": Fritzsche, *Germans into Nazis*, 200.

88 "From the right": Strasser, *Hitler and I*, 9.

88 "The nationalists on the right": Fritzsche, *Germans into Nazis*, 204.

88 "catchall party": Childers, *Nazi Voter*, 268.

89 "human beings don't only want comfort": Orwell and Angus, *Collected Essays* 2: 29.

89 "able to enslave": Heiden, *Führer*, 603.

89 "They are incapable": Broszat, *Hitler and the Collapse*, 16.

90 "We have to work": Evans, *Coming of the Third Reich*, 289, 291.

91 The majority of the German people": Strasser, *Hitler and I*, 223, 229, 243.

92 "The Germans are still fighting": Jean-Michel Palmier, *Weimar in Exile: The Anti-Fascist Emigration in Europe and America* (Brooklyn, NY: Verso, 2017), 605.

92 "part of the German people": Strasser, *Hitler and I*, 228.

92 "I overcame chaos": Haffner, *Meaning of Hitler*, 32, 35, 103.

93 "I have thought hate": Reck, *Diary of a Man*, 15–16, 73, 86.

94 "I simply cannot believe": Victor Klemperer, *I Will Bear Witness: A Diary of the Nazi Years, 1933–1941* (New York: The Modern Library, 1999), 30, 156, 233, 253, 354.

94 "the political persecutions": Marvin Kalb and Bernard Kalb, *Kissinger* (Boston: Little, Brown, 1974), 35.

94 "much harder": Suri, *Henry Kissinger*, 41, 42.

94 "self-delusion": Isaacson, *Kissinger*, 26.

95 "Every walk in the street": Henry Kissinger, *White House Years* (New York: Simon & Schuster, 2011), 229.

95 "not consciously unhappy": Isaacson, *Kissinger*, 26, 25.

95 More than a half century: Peter Gay, "My German Question: Growing Up in Nazi Berlin" (New Haven: Yale University Press, 1998), 21. Quoted in Steven E. Aschheim, *Beyond the Border: The German-Jewish Legacy Abroad* (Princeton, NJ: Princeton University Press, 2007), 58.

95 "Weakness": Isaacson, *Kissinger*, 52.

95 "being parted": Kurz, *Kissinger Saga*, 66.

95 "cruel and degrading years": Kissinger, *White House Years*, 229.

96 "I had seen evil": Suri, *Henry Kissinger*, 14.

96 "Nothing is more difficult": Bruce Mazlish, *Kissinger: The European Mind in American Policy* (New York: Basic, 1976), 105.

96 "A Personal Note": Henry Kissinger, *Years of Renewal* (New York: Simon & Schuster, 2000), 1078.

Chapter Three: LEO STRAUSS AND HANNAH ARENDT

97 he never felt homesick: Evi Kurz, *The Kissinger Saga: Walter and Henry Kissinger, Two Brothers from Furth, Germany* (London: Weidenfeld and Nicolson, 2009), 92.

97 "foreign language handicap": Marvin Kalb and Bernard Kalb, *Kissinger* (Boston: Little, Brown, 1974), 36.

97 "exhilarating": Stephen Graubard, *Kissinger: Portrait of a Mind* (New York: Norton, 1973), 2.

98 "tremendous education": Jeremi Suri, *Henry Kissinger and the American Century* (Cambridge, MA: Harvard University Press, 2007), 58.

98 "I was a refugee": Suri, *Henry Kissinger*, 109.

98 "Now I knew": Niall Ferguson, *Kissinger, Vol. 1, 1923–1968: The Idealist* (New York: Penguin, 2015), 203.

99 "made me feel": Walter Isaacson, *Kissinger* (New York: Simon & Schuster, 2005), 40.

99 "I hate N.Y.": Ferguson, *Kissinger*, 203.

99 "heartland Americans": Suri, *Henry Kissinger*, 58.

99 "real middle-Americans": Isaacson, *Kissinger*, 40.

99 "liked these people": Isaacson, *Kissinger*, 40.

99 "Midwesterner": Isaacson, *Kissinger*, 58.

99 "generosity of spirit": Henry Kissinger, *Years of Renewal* (New York: Simon & Schuster, 2000), 28.

100 "outside of town": Bob Dylan, "Ballad of Hollis Brown."

100 "my great oath": Christopher Hitchens, *Hitch-22: A Memoir* (New York: Twelve, 2010), 260.

100 "an incredible place": Henry Kissinger, *White House Years* (New York: Simon & Schuster, 2011), 15, 31, 229.

101 "found a haven": Kissinger, *Renewal*, 1071.

101 "its greatness": Kissinger, *White House Years*, 229.

101 "land of virtue": Czeslaw Milosz, *Visions from San Francisco Bay* (New York: Farrar, Straus, Giroux, 1982), 152, 154, 157, 158, 175, 196, 218, 219, 220.

102 "go to the hospital": Kenneth Thompson and Robert J. Myers, eds., *A Tribute to Hans Morgenthau* (Washington, DC: New Republic Book Company, 1977), 236.

102 "my personal impression": Ferguson, *Kissinger*, 106.

103 "European": Bruce Mazlish, *Kissinger: The European Mind in American Policy* (New York: Basic, 1976), 105.

103 "brooding" and "melancholic": Kalb and Kalb, *Kissinger*, 53.

103 "Life involves suffering": Graubard, *Kissinger*, 6.

104 "out of conviction": Anthony Heilbut, *Exiled in Paradise: German Refugee Artists and Intellectuals in America from the 1930s to the Present* (New York: Viking, 1983), 344.

104 "American culture": Jean-Michel Palmier, *Weimar in Exile: The Anti-Fascist Emigration in Europe and America* (Brooklyn, NY: Verso, 2017), 501.

105 "The American trait": Ferguson, *Kissinger*, 107.

105 "an error of history": Lewis A. Coser, *Refugee Scholars in America: Their Impact and Their Experiences* (New Haven, CT: Yale University Press, 1984), 11.

105 "the language of one's dreams": Heilbut, *Exiled*, 37, 50, 57.

105 "fomenters of hatred": Palmier, *Weimar*, 633, 655, 656.

106 "eradicate himself": Martin Jay, *Permanent Exiles: Essays on the Intellectual Migration from Germany to America* (New York: Columbia University Press, 1986), 120, 122.

106 "more in love": Palmier, *Weimar*, 491.

106 "all my personal decisions": Kissinger, *Renewal*, 1079.

107 "only average": Mazlish, *Kissinger*, 159.

109 "inherent mistrust": Hannah Arendt, "Philosophie und Solziologie," Die Gesellschaft, VII/2, trans. Robert and Rita Kimber, in *Essays in Understanding, 1930-1954* (NY: Harcourt, Brace, 1994), 39.

109 "conformism and philistinism": Leo Strauss, *What Is Political Philosophy and Other Studies* (Chicago: University of Chicago Press, 1988), 20.

109 "tyrannize thought": Leo Strauss, *On Tyranny* (Chicago: University of Chicago Press, 2000), 27.

109 "overwhelm wisdom": Henry Kissinger, "How the Enlightenment Ends," *The Atlantic* (June 2018).

109 "nub of the matter": Peter Graf Kielmansegg, Horst Mewes, and Elisabeth Schmidt, eds., *Hannah Arendt and Leo Strauss: German Emigres and American Political Thought After World War II* (New York: Cambridge University Press, 1997), 29, 37.

110 **"post-Bismarckian":** Leo Strauss, *Political Philosophy*, 224.

110 **"most important yardstick":** Hannah Arendt, *The Origins of Totalitarianism* (New York: Meridian, 1971), 442.

110 **"the only ideology":** Arendt, *Essays*, 282.

110 **"all rational liberal":** Leo Strauss, *The Rebirth of Classical Political Rationalism: An Introduction to the Thought of Leo Strauss* (Chicago: University of Chicago Press, 1989), 29.

110 **"the sorry spectacle":** Leo Strauss, *Spinoza's Critique of Religion* (Chicago: University of Chicago Press, 1997), 1.

110 **"'ceremonial' laws":** Leo Strauss, "A Giving of Accounts," The St. John's Review from The College 22, no. 1 (April 1970), in *Jewish Philosophy and the Crisis of Modernity: Essays and Lectures in Modern Jewish Thought* (NY: State University of NY Press, 1997), 459-460.

110 **"profound peace":** Strauss, *Jewish Philosophy*, 313, 450, 460.

111 **"the possibility":** Leo Strauss, "An Unspoken Prologue to a Public Lecture at St. John's," in *Leo Strauss and the Politics of Exile: The Making of a Political Philosopher*, Eugene R. Sheppard (Hanover, NH: University Press of New England, 2006), 38.

111 **"modest income":** Strauss, *On Tyranny*, 222, 225, 227.

112 **"never have baptized me":** Gunther Gaus, "Zur Person, Munich, 1965, trans. Joan Stambaugh, in Arendt, *Essays*, 7.

112 **"displays of independence":** Elisabeth Young-Bruehl, *Hannah Arendt: For Love of the World* (New Haven, CT: Yale University Press, 2004), 33, 104.

113 **bystander:** Arendt, *Essays*, 5.

114 **"family resemblance":** Anne Norton, *Leo Strauss and the Politics of American Empire* (New Haven, CT: Yale University Press, 2004), 54, 37.

114 **"the only person":** Hannah Arendt and Karl Jaspers, *Correspondence, 1926–1969* (New York: Harcourt Brace Jovanovich, 1992), 535, 244.

114 **"an untouchable authority":** Steven E. Aschheim, *Beyond the Border: The German-Jewish Legacy Abroad* (Princeton, NJ: Princeton University Press, 2007), 83.

115 **"No one could argue":** Norton, *Leo Strauss*, 24–25.

115 **"understand the philosophy":** Leo Strauss, "Political Philosophy and History," Journal of the History of Ideas, January 1949, in Strauss, *Political Philosophy*, 68.

115 **"introduce us":** Leo Strauss, "Liberal Education and Responsibility," in *Education: The Challenge Ahead*, ed. C. Scott Fletcher (New York: Norton, 1962), in Leo Strauss, *An Introduction to Political Philosophy: Ten Essays*, ed. Hilail Gildin (Detroit: Wayne State University Press, 1989), 343.

115 **"Modern thought":** Strauss, *Political Philosophy*, 76.

116 **"Nietzsche so dominated and charmed me":** Leo Strauss, "Correspondence of Karl Löwith and Leo Strauss," trans. George Elliott Tucker, *Independent Journal of Philosophy* 5/6 (1988): 183, in Steven B. Smith, *Reading Leo Strauss: Politics, Philosophy, Judaism* (Chicago: University of Chicago Press, 2007), 9.

116 **"authority for philosophy":** Leo Strauss, "Progress or Return? The Contemporary Crisis in Western Civilization," *Modern Judaism* 1 (Baltimore: Johns Hopkins University Press, 1981), "Introduction," in *Jewish Philosophy*, 99.

116 **"radical opposition":** Daniel Tanguay, *Leo Strauss: An Intellectual Biography* (New Haven, CT: Yale University Press, 2007), 94.

117 **"intelligent minority":** Leo Strauss, "The Literary Character of the *Guide for the Perplexed*," from Baron, Salo Wittmayer, ed. *Essays on Maimonides* (New York: Columbia University Press. 1941), 37-91, in *Persecution and the Art of Writing* (Chicago: University of Chicago Press, 1988), 59.

117 **"Exceedingly":** Aschheim, *Beyond the Border*, 82.

117 **"incredibly unworldly":** Hans Jonas, *Memoirs* (Hanover: University Press of New England, 2008), 160.

117 **"shows no interest":** Strauss, *Rebirth*, x.

117 **"those who enter"**: Mark Lilla, "The Closing of the Straussian Mind," *New York Review of Books*, November 4, 2004.

118 **"Don't go!"**: Ron Rosenbaum, *Explaining Hitler: The Search for the Origins of His Evil* (Boston: Da Capo, 2014), 395.

118 **"certain well-known"**: Strauss, *Persecution*, 5, 22, 26.

119 **"the only regime"**: Strauss, *Jewish Philosophy*, 295, 321, 335.

119 **Hitler and the Third Reich owed "nothing"**: Hannah Arendt, "Approaches to the German Problem," *Partisan Review*, XII/1, Winter 1945, in *Essays*, 108.

119 **"contemporary crisis"**: Leo Strauss, "Progress or Return? The Contemporary Crisis in Western Civilization," *Modern Judaism* 1 (Baltimore: Johns Hopkins University Press, 1981), in *Introduction*, 263.

119 **"the man with the strongest will"**: Strauss, *Spinoza*, 1.

120 **"eternal truths"**: Strauss, *Jewish Philosophy*, 79.

120 **"One cannot downplay"**: Smith, *Reading Leo Strauss*, 164.

120 **Blond beast**: Leo Strauss, "On the Basis of Hobbes's Political Philosophy," *Critique*, April 1954, in Strauss, *Political Philosophy*, 171.

121 **"We are observing"**: Strauss, *Rebirth*, 216.

121 **"In following this movement"**: Leo Strauss, *Natural Right and History* (Chicago: University of Chicago Press, 1965), 42, 52.

121 **"Only great thinker"**: Strauss, *Rebirth*, 29.

121 **"inner truth"**: Strauss, *Jewish Philosophy*, 141, 461.

121 **"kinship"**: Strauss, *Rebirth*, 30.

121 **"I ceased"**: Strauss, *Jewish Philosophy*, 461.

121 **"most stupid"**: Strauss, *Rebirth*, 30.

121 **"Heidegger surpasses"**: Leo Strauss, "Kurt Riezler," *Social Research*, Spring 1956, in Strauss, *Political Philosophy*, 246, 260.

122 **"Whether Heidegger's embrace"**: Smith, *Reading Leo Strauss*, 109, 111–112.

122 **"the thought"**: Strauss, *Political Philosophy*, 66.

122 **"We must avoid"**: Strauss, *Natural Right*, 42–43.

122 **"The worst have lost"**: Arendt, *Origins*, 446.

123 **"the least wise"**: Strauss, *Political Philosophy*, 27.

123 **"never believed"**: Strauss, *Rebirth*, 28, 36, 39.

123 **"narrow"**: Strauss, *Political Philosophy*, 260.

124 **"the rules of decent"**: Leo Strauss, "German Nihilism," *Interpretation* 26, no. 3 (Spring 1999), 365.

124 **"prescientific knowledge"**: Strauss, *Political Philosophy*, 25.

124 **"fully conscious form"**: Leo Strauss, *The City and Man* (Chicago: University of Chicago Press, 1978), 12, 26, 32.

125 **"perfectly clear"**: Leo Strauss, "An Epilogue," from *Essays in the Scientific Study of Politics*, ed. Herbert Storing (New York: Holt, Rinehart and Winston, 1962), in *Introduction*, 147.

125 **"unarmed eye"**: Strauss, *Political Philosophy*, 89.

125 **"a spade"**: Strauss, *Natural Right*, 61.

125 **"theoretical doubts"**: Strauss, *Political Philosophy*, 89.

126 **"force in the soul"**: Strauss, *Political Philosophy*, 41.

126 **"The open society"**: Strauss, "German Nihilism," 358, 359.

127 **"Just because"**: Sheppard, *Leo Strauss and the Politics of Exile*, 60–61.

127 **"Even Jews"**: Arendt and Jaspers, *Correspondence*, 592.

127 **"principles of civilization"**: Strauss, "German Nihilism," 367, 369, 373.

128 **"victory of the gutter"**: Strauss, "Epilogue," in *Introduction*, 254.

128 **"not everything"**: Strauss, *Natural Right*, 130, 132.

128 **"Premodern thought"**: Strauss, *Jewish Philosophy*, 103.

129 **"The relativist"**: Strauss, *Rebirth*, 12, 17.

129 **"Not all men"**: Strauss, *Natural Right*, 134.

129 **"accident of birth"**: Strauss, "Liberal Education and Responsibility," in *Introduction*, 314, 325, 344.

129 **"we must not expect"**: Strauss, "Liberal Education and Responsibility," in *Introduction*, 344.

129 **"salt of modern democracy"**: Strauss, "What Is Liberal Education?" from Fletcher, C. Scott, ed., *Education for Public Responsibility* (New York: W. W. Norton, 1961), in *Introduction*, 314.

129 **"the inequality"**: Tanguay, *Leo Strauss*, 77.

129 **"democratic mass society"**: Strauss, "What Is Liberal Education," in *Introduction*, 314.

130 **"lovers of culture"**: Strauss, "German Nihilism," 364–365.

130 **"genuine meeting"**: Strauss, *Rebirth*, 43.

130 **"unfortunate necessity"**: Strauss, "What Is Liberal Education?," in *Introduction*, 317.

130 **"The Western thinker"**: Strauss, *Rebirth*, 43.

130 **"greatest representative"**: Leo Strauss, "Jerusalem and Athens," from "Jerusalem and Athens: Some Preliminary Reflections, City College Papers, Number 6, 1967, in *Jewish Philosophy*, 398.

131 **"There is no place"**: Strauss, "Introductory Essay to Hermann Cohen," from Hermann Cohen, "Religion of Reason out of the Sources of Judaism," (New York: Frederick Ungar, 1972), in Strauss, *Jewish Philosophy*, 277.

131 **"The worst things"**: Strauss, *Rebirth*, xxxv.

131 **"It is as obvious"**: Strauss, *Jewish Philosophy*, 105.

131 **"the proper framework"**: Strauss, "Progress or Return? The Contemporary Crisis in Western Civilization" (*Modern Judaism*, vol. 1, no. 1, May 1981), in *Rebirth*, 247.

131 **"with all his heart"**: Leo Strauss, "The Law of Reason in the Kuzari" (Proceedings of the American Academy for Jewish Research, 1943), vol. XIII, 47-96, in Strauss, *Persecution*, 140.

132 **"Island of the blessed"**: Leo Strauss, "On Classical Political Philosophy," Social Research, February 1949, in *Introduction*, 76.

132 **"highest value"**: Smith, *Reading Leo Strauss*, 107.

132 **"the dignity of the mind"**: Strauss, "What Is Liberal Education," in *Introduction*, 319.

133 **"humanizing or civilizing"**: Strauss, "Liberal Education and Responsibility," in *Introduction*, 330.

133 **"Socrates himself"**: Strauss, "On Classical Political Philosophy," in *Introduction*, 77.

133 **"destructive, undermining"**: Hannah Arendt, *Responsibility and Judgment* (New York: Schocken, 2003), 175–176.

133 **"not moderate"**: Strauss, *Political Philosophy*, 32.

133 **"sleeping dogs"**: Strauss, "Liberal Education and Responsibility," in *Introduction*, 329.

134 **"very long conversations"**: Strauss, *Rebirth*, 74.

134 **"The political problem"**: Strauss, *Natural Right*, 111.

134 **"a pure selection"**: Strauss, "On Classical Political Philosophy," in *Introduction*, 68, 344, 345.

135 **"We are not permitted"**: Strauss, "Liberal Education and Responsibility," in *Introduction*, 344.

135 **"If ever the free institutions"**: Alexis de Tocqueville, *Democracy in America* (New York: Vintage, 1945), 1:279.

136 **"Fascism, if it ever"**: Arendt and Jaspers, *Correspondence*, 213.

136 **"catastrophe-minded"**: Young-Bruehl, *Hannah Arendt*, 299.

137 **"a total solidarity"**: Arendt and Jaspers, *Correspondence*, 38, 267.

137 **"She reports her findings"**: Young-Bruehl, *Hannah Arendt*, 197, 198.

138 **"slightest inkling"**: Arendt and Jaspers, *Correspondence*, 129.

138 **"European background"**: Arendt, *Responsibility*, 4.

138 **"eternally grateful"**: Arendt and Jaspers, *Correspondence*, 173, 30, 29.

138 **"What influenced me"**: Arendt, *Responsibility*, 4.

138 **"perfectly free"**: Hannah Arendt, interview with Roger Errera, October 1973, trans.

Andrew Brown, *The Last Interview and Other Conversations* (Brooklyn: Melville House, 2013), 121.

139 **"thoroughly average":** Arendt and Jaspers, *Correspondence*, 30, 31.

139 **"the possible exception":** Hannah Arendt, "The Aftermath of Nazi Rule: Report from Germany," *Commentary*, X/10, 1950, in *Essays*, 264.

139 **"objectivity and impartiality":** Arendt and Jaspers, *Correspondence*, 666.

139 **"exonerating America":** Seyla Benhabib, ed., *Politics in Dark Times: Encounters with Hannah Arendt* (New York: Cambridge University Press, 2010), 261.

140 **"a dangerous idiot":** Arendt and Jaspers, *Correspondence*, 203, 213, 264, 538.

140 **"more comfort":** Carol Brightman, ed., *Between Friends: The Correspondence of Hannah Arendt and Mary McCarthy, 1949–1975* (New York: Harcourt Brace, 1995), 230.

140 **"For many years now":** Hannah Arendt, *Crises of the Republic* (New York: Harcourt Brace, 1969), 70.

140 **"end of the republic":** Brightman, *Between Friends*, 235.

141 **"more is involved":** Hannah Arendt, *Between Past and Future: Six Exercises in Political Thought* (Cleveland, OH: Meridian, 1968), 174.

141 **"The recent cataclysm":** Arendt, *Responsibility*, 257–58, 259, 270, 275.

142 **"the spirit":** Arendt, *Essays*, 280.

142 **"the people's support":** Arendt, *Crises*, 140.

142 **"The fundamental contradiction":** Arendt and Jaspers, *Correspondence*, 31.

142 **"his rights as a man":** Hannah Arendt, "The Nation," *The Review of Politics*, VIII/1, Jan. 1946, in Arendt, *Essays*, 210

143 **"always in danger":** Hannah Arendt, *On Revolution* (New York: Penguin, 2006), 142.

143 **"what is good":** Arendt, *Origins*, 275.

143 **"parallel government":** Arendt and Jaspers, *Correspondence*, 210.

143 **"sacred document":** Arendt, *Last*, 112.

143 **"Large numbers of people":** Hannah Arendt, *The Human Condition* (Chicago: University of Chicago Press, 1998), 43.

143 **"totalitarian movements":** Arendt, *Origins*, 311.

143 **"spells ruin":** Arendt, *Between*, 211.

143 **"jobholders":** Arendt and Jaspers, *Correspondence*, 223.

143 **"What he fervently believed":** Hannah Arendt, *Eichmann in Jerusalem: A Report on the Banality of Evil* (New York: Viking, 1968), 126.

144 **"willingly undertake":** Hannah Arendt, "Organized Guilt and Universal Responsibility," *Jewish Frontier*, No. 12, 1945, in Arendt, *Essays*, 129, 130.

144 **"quite willing to believe":** Hannah Arendt, "Religion and the Intellectuals," *Partisan Review*, XVII/2, Feb. 1950, in Arendt, *Essays*, 230.

144 **"truly tyrannical authority":** Arendt, *Between*, 181.

144 **"being dissolved":** Arendt and Jaspers, *Correspondence*, 235, 357.

144 **"it's a great mistake":** Arendt, *Last*, 114.

145 **"consists in the fact":** Arendt, *Between*, 175.

145 **"monstrous falsehood":** Arendt, *Revolution*, 209.

145 **"division of powers":** Arendt, *Essays*, 333.

145 **"dangerous error":** Hannah Arendt, "Reflections on Little Rock," *Dissent* (Winter 1959): 45–56.

145 **"Calhoun was certainly right":** Arendt, *Crises*, 76.

146 **"really angry":** Arendt and Jaspers, *Correspondence*, 386.

146 **"We publish it":** Hannah Arendt, "Reflections."

148 **"specious idea of freedom":** David Spitz, "Politics and the Realms of Being," *Dissent* (Winter 1959): 61, 63.

149 **"The moral question":** Sidney Hook, "Democracy and Desegregation," *The New Leader*, April 21, 1958.

149 **"Like most people":** Arendt, "Reflections."

149 **"metaphysical mumbo jumbo":** Melvin Tumin, "Pie in the Sky," *Dissent* (Winter 1959): 65.

150 **"clean solutions"**: Strauss, *Jewish Philosophy*, 340.

150 **"The Jewish problem"**: Strauss, *Spinoza*, 6.

151 ꞏꞏꞏ ꞏꞏꞏꞏꞏꞏꞏꞏꞏꞏꞏ ꞏꞏꞏꞏꞏꞏꞏꞏ

151 **"Founding Fathers"**: Arendt, *Revolution*, 218.

151 **"baffling"**: Margaret Canovan, *Hannah Arendt: A Reinterpretation of Her Political Thought* (New York: Cambridge University Press, 1994), 156.

151 **"political classic"**: Robert Nisbet, "Hannah Arendt and the American Revolution," *Social Research* 4, no. 1 (Spring 1977, vol. 44, no. 1).

151 **"triumphantly successful"**: Arendt, *Revolution*, 46.

151 **"Burkean Toryism"**: Young-Bruehl, *Hannah Arendt*, 403.

152 **"pernicious"**: Arendt, *Revolution*, 51, xxvi.

152 **"because of her"**: Kielmansegg, *Hannah Arendt*, 170.

152 **"changed its direction"**: Arendt, *Revolution*, 51, 65.

153 **"which is relieved"**: Jurgen Habermas, "Hannah Arendt's Communications Concept of Power," *Social Research* (Spring 1977, vol. 44, no. 1).

154 **"burst with resentment"**: Arendt, *Revolution*, 63, 72, 146–147, 58.

155 **"The social conditions"**: Gordon S. Wood, *The Radicalism of the American Revolution* (New York: Vintage, 1993), 4.

156 **"There are 19 millions"**: Arendt, *Revolution*, 57, 58, 63, 61, 81, 132, 133, 141, 143, 145, 150.

158 **sum up:** James Macgregor Burns, *The Vineyard of Liberty* (New York: Knopf, 1982), 33.

159 **"implies an obedience"**: Arendt, *Between*, 100, 106.

159 **"fateful misfortune"**: Arendt, *Revolution*, 137, 156, 159, 166, 167.

160 **"the whole sector"**: Arendt, *Origins*, 352.

161 **"entirely new concept"**: Arendt, *Revolution*, 157, 164, 187, 206.

161 **"bleak and embattled"**: Canovan, *Hannah Arendt*, 238.

161 **"means the right"**: Arendt, *Revolution*, 210, 213, 261.

162 **"the people actually rule"**: Joseph A. Schumpeter, *Capitalism, Socialism and Democracy* (New York: Harper Colophon, 1975), 284–85.

162 **"it has achieved"**: Arendt, *Revolution*, 224, 243, 246, 247, 255, 256, 260.

164 **"most of Arendt's readers"**: Canovan, *Hannah Arendt*, 237.

164 **"either directly"**: Arendt, *Crises*, 231.

164 **"their ability to integrate"**: Kielmansegg, *Hannah Arendt*, 177.

CHAPTER FOUR: HANS MORGENTHAU

166 **"We shared"**: Henry Kissinger, "Hans Morgenthau: A Gentle Analyst of Power," *The New Republic*, August 2 and 9, 1980.

166 **like a brother:** John G. Stoessinger, *Henry Kissinger: The Anguish of Power* (New York: Norton, 1976), 37.

167 **"a Jew who wanted"**: Christoph Frei, *Hans J. Morgenthau: An Intellectual Biography* (Baton Rouge, Louisiana State University Press, 2001), 10.

168 **"a great idea"**: Kenneth Thompson and Robet J. Myers, eds., *A Tribute to Hans Morgenthau* (Washington, DC: New Republic Book Company, 1977), 3.

168 **"totally crazy"**: Frei, *Morgenthau*, 11, 32.

169 **"unusually appealing"**: Frei, *Morgenthau*, 97n.15, 155.

169 **"profound experiences"**: Hans J. Morgenthau, "The Incarnation of Demoniac Power," *Business Week*, April 21, 1973.

170 **"it is impossible"**: Thompson, *A Tribute*, 2, 7, 14, 13, 14.

170 **"the suffering of the world"**: Hans J. Morgenthau, *Science: Servant or Master?* (New York: New American Library, 1972), 68.

170 **"there was no escape"**: Frei, *Morgenthau*, 98.

170 **"grovel or duck"**: Thompson, *A Tribute*, 2, 4, 9.

171 **"the spectacle"**: Hans J. Morgenthau, *Scientific Man Versus Power Politics* (Chicago: Phoenix Books/University of Chicago Press, 1965), 208.

172   **"As things now stand"**: Frei, *Morgenthau*, 52, 58, 65, 64, 66.
173   **"the best methods"**: Hans J. Morgenthau, *The Decline of Democratic Politics* (Chicago: University of Chicago Press, 1964), 22.
174   **"contingent"**: Hans J. Morgenthau, *Truth and Power: Essays of a Decade, 1960–1970* (New York: Praeger, 1970), 254.
174   **"political wisdom"**: Morgenthau, *Science*, 45.
174   **"anachronistic"**: Edward Shils, *Remembering the University of Chicago: Teachers, Scientists, and Scholars* (Chicago: University of Chicago Press, 1991), 561.
174   **lacking in imagination**: Proceedings of the 68th Annual Meeting of the American Society of International Law, April 1974.
175   **"We cannot assume"**: Box 44, Hans J. Morgenthau Papers, Manuscript Division, Library of Congress, Washington, DC.
175   **"particular way of thinking"**: Box 36, Morgenthau Papers.
175   **"offensive" Realism**: Christian Hacke, "Power and Morality: On the Legacy of Hans J. Morgenthau," *American Foreign Policy Interests* 27 (2005).
175   **"pope of Realism"**: William E. Scheuerman, *Hans Morgenthau: Realism and Beyond* (Malden, MA: Policy, 2009), 2.
175   **"I never ceased"**: Kissinger, "Hans Morgenthau."
176   **"Remains trapped"**: Carl Schmitt, *The Concept of the Political* (Chicago: University of Chicago Press, 2007), 119.
176   **"The most honorable"**: Eugene R. Sheppard, *Leo Strauss and the Politics of Exile*, 57, 65.
176   **"excellent"**: Frei, *Morgenthau*, 171.
176   **"The war against war"**: Schmitt, *Concept*, 110.
176   **"an intellectual intensity"**: Frei, *Morgenthau*, 118.
176   **"Most evil man"**: Thompson, *A Tribute*, 16.
177   **"deep intellectual ties"**: Michael C. Williams, ed., *Realism Reconsidered: The Legacy of Hans J. Morgenthau in International Relations* (New York: Oxford University Press, 2007), 63.
177   **"Liberalism expresses"**: Morgenthau, *Scientific Man*, 71.
177   **"sorry spectacle"**: Leo Strauss, *Spinoza's Critique of Religion* (Chicago: University of Chicago Press, 1997), 1.
177   **"ingenious"**: Hannah Arendt, *The Origins of Totalitarianism* (New York: Meridian, 1971), 339n.65.
178   **"by all odds"**: Shils, *Remembering*, 192.
178   **"a decisive role"**: Thompson, *A Tribute*, 22.
178   **"almost unfailing"**: Box 36, Morgenthau Papers.
179   **"significantly shaped"**: Shils, *Remembering*, 340, 350.
179   **"its strongest voices"**: Thompson, *A Tribute*, 21.
179   **"first building"**: Shils, *Remembering*, 344.
179   **"not so much theories"**: Morgenthau, *Truth*, 242–243, 245, 246.
180   **"knowledge of political things"**: Leo Strauss, *Political Philosophy*, 15.
180   **"not a few questions"**: Leo Strauss, *Natural Right and History* (Chicago: University of Chicago Press, 1965), 53.
180   **"pre-scientific"**: Williams, *Realism*, 3.
180   **"distrustful of common sense"**: Leo Strauss, *The Rebirth of Classical Political Rationalism* (Chicago: University of Chicago Press, 1989), 4.
180   **"moral obtuseness"**: Strauss, *Political Philosophy*, 18.
180   **"dangerous proclivities"**: Leo Strauss, "An Epilogue," in *Essays in the Scientific Study of Politics*, ed. Herbert Storing (New York: Holt, Rinehart and Winston, 1962), in Strauss, *An Introduction to Political Philosophy: Ten Essays*, ed. Hilail Gilden (Detroit: Wayne State University Press, 1989), 154.
180   **"eternal truth of Hobbes's insight"**: Box 108, Morgenthau Papers.
181   **"He only saw clearly"**: "Dilemmas of U.S. Foreign Policy," University of Chicago Roundtable, No. 312, March 12, 1944.

181 **"collected works":** Frei, *Morgenthau*, 113.
181 **"modern theorists":** Morgenthau, *Truth*, 245.
181 **"man meets himself":** Morgenthau, *Decline*, 15.
182 **"meaningless web":** Strauss, *Natural*, 18.
182 **"The unbiased historian":** Strauss, *Natural*.
182 **"nonhistoricist thought":** Strauss, *Natural*, 33.
182 **"It was as wrong-headed":** Thompson, *A Tribute*, 22.
182 **"My main objective":** Frei, *Morgenthau*, 74.
182 **"remarkably little contact":** Shils, *Remembering*, 493, 497.
183 **"His responses to views":** Thompson, *A Tribute*, 26.
183 **"ranks among the half dozen":** Gabriel A. Almond, *Harold Dwight Lasswell, 1902–1978: A Biographical Memoir* (Washington, DC: National Academy of Sciences, 1987), 249.
183 **"either platitudinous":** Morgenthau, *Decline*, 29.
183 **"Few would question":** Almond, *Lasswell*, 249.
184 **"I have written in identical style":** Hans J. Morgenthau, "The Writer's Duty and His Predicament," *The Hudson Review* (Summer 1965).
184 **"to be taken for granted":** Hans Jonas, *Memoirs* (Hanover: University Press of New England, 2008), 179.
184 **"the vitality of her mind":** Hans J. Morgenthau, "Hannah Arendt, 1906–1975," *Political Theory* 4, no. 1 (February 1976).
185 **"unutterable regret":** Hans J. Morgenthau, "Hannah Arendt on Totalitarianism and Democracy," *Social Research* 44, no. 1 (Spring 1977).
185 **"intellectual companion":** Hacke, "Power and Morality."
185 **"reality has protruded":** Elisabeth Young-Bruehl, *Hannah Arendt: For Love of the World* (New Haven, CT: Yale University Press, 2004), 349.
185 **"a real pain":** G. O. Mazur, ed., *One Hundred Year Commemoration to the Life of Hans Morgenthau* (New York: Semenenko Foundation, 2004), 161.
185 **"disconcerted":** Young-Bruehl, *Hannah Arendt*, 454.
185 **"My hunch is":** Mazur, *One Hundred*, 162.
186 **"a special place":** Sheldon S. Wolin, "Hannah Arendt and the Ordinance of Time," *Social Research*, Spring 1977.
186 **"Her emphasis":** Anthony F. Lang and John Williams, *Hannah Arendt and International Relations: Reading Across the Lines* (New York: Palgrave Macmillan, 2005), 115.
187 **"What an idiocy":** Young-Bruehl, *Hannah Arendt*, 424.
187 **"What are you?":** Melvyn A. Hill, *Hannah Arendt: The Recovery of the Public World* (New York: St. Martin's, 1970), 333–334.
187 **"You are asking":** Frei, *Morgenthau*, 154, 205n.83.
188 **"The horrible can be":** Hannah Arendt, *Eichmann in Jerusalem: A Report on the Banality of Evil* (New York: Viking, 1960), 49.
189 **"no correspondence":** Morgenthau, "Hannah Arendt on Totalitarianism and Democracy," 129.
190 **"Consciousness does not save man":** Morgenthau, *Science*, 55.
190 **"make their entry":** Friedrich Nietzsche, *"The Geneology of Morals" and "Ecce Homo"* (New York: Vintage, 1967), 279–80.
190 **"belief in the power":** Morgenthau, *Scientific Man*, vi.
190 **"overthrowing idols":** Nietzsche, *"Ecce Homo,"* 218.
191 **"Morgenthau's book":** Thompson, *A Tribute*, 42.
191 **"sufficiently great":** Morgenthau, *Scientific Man*, 12, 14, 22, 31, 33, 65.
192 **"modern totalitarian regimes":** Hans J. Morgenthau, "Kennedy and Foreign Policy," *New Leader*, July 3, 1961, in Morgenthau, *Truth*, 142.
192 **"By neglecting":** Morgenthau, *Scientific Man*, 5, 125, 124, 125, 6, 39, 115, 120.
194 **"irrationalism":** Scheuerman, *Hans Morgenthau*, 43.
194 **"What can be stated":** Morgenthau, *Scientific Man*, 42, 43–44, 44, 45, 75, 138, 147, 151, 167, 215–16.

197   **"community of rational":** Morgenthau, *Scientific Man*, 42, 51, 66, 107, 108, 192, 203, 217, 221.

199   **Oliver Wendell Holmes:** Hans J. Morgenthau, *Politics Among Nations: The Struggle for Power and Peace*, 4th ed. (New York: Knopf, 1967), viii.

199   **Abraham Lincoln:** Mazur, *One Hundred*, 253.

200   **"literally don't know":** Frei, *Morgenthau*, 178.

200   **"the most engaged group":** Kenneth Thompson, "The Writing of 'Politics Among Nations': Its Sources and Origins," *International Studies Notes of the International Studies Association* 24, no. 1 (1999).

201   **"frontal assault":** Morgenthau, *Politics*, xi.

201   **"he had a struggle":** Thompson, "The Writing."

201   **"household word":** Mazur, *One Hundred*, 136.

201   **"world-renowned":** Frei, *Morgenthau*, 78.

202   **"spectators":** Morgenthau, *Politics*, 34, 529, 21.

203   **"played it by ear":** Morgenthau, *Truth*, 258.

203   **"the essential goodness":** Morgenthau, *Politics*, 3, 4, 30–31, 6, 84.

204   **"when to stop":** Hans J. Morgenthau, *A New Foreign Policy for the United States* (New York: Praeger, 1969), 59.

204   **"ideological disguises":** Morgenthau, *Politics*, 93, 5, 11, 27, 59, 546, 325, 125.

206   **"bums and beggars":** Morgenthau, *New Foreign Policy*, 96.

206   **"national character":** Morgenthau, *Politics*, 127.

206   **"simple, ordinary":** George Lichtheim, *The Concept of Ideology and Other Essays* (New York: Vintage, 1967), 150, 145, 147, 150.

207   **"The scholar seeking":** Morgenthau, *Science*, 31.

207   **"domestic societies":** Morgenthau, *Politics*, 223, 31.

207   **"set an example":** Morgenthau, *Scientific Man*, 173.

208   **"moral principle":** Morgenthau, *Politics*, 10.

208   **"Applied to foreign politics":** Sonia Orwell and Ian Angus, eds., *The Collected Essays, Journalism and Letters of George Orwell* (New York: Penguin, 1980), 4:529–30.

208   **"an imposing edifice":** Morgenthau, *Politics*, 264–65, 302, 460, 464, 316, 260.

209   **"one great republic":** Morgenthau, *Politics*, 213, 238, 226, 233, 243, 248, 232, 249, 370, 483.

211   **"supranational institutions":** Scheuerman, *Hans Morgenthau*, 155.

211   **"many failures":** Morgenthau, *Politics*, 375, 392, 493, 495, 180, 161, 4, 202, 198.

213   **"the very law of life":** Morgenthau, *Decline*, 330.

213   **"brains of national power":** Morgenthau, *Politics*, 135, 547, 531, 549, 527, 7, 141, 249, 98, 249, 242.

215   **"I have tried":** Frei, *Morgenthau*, 76, 177n.125.

216   **"anticipated Hannah":** Scheuerman, *Hans Morgenthau*, 188.

217   **"No society":** Hans J. Morgenthau, *The Purpose of American Politics* (New York: Vintage, 1964), 280, 274, 264, 252, 258.

218   **"a distinct moral":** Morgenthau, *Purpose*, introduction, n.p.

218   **"an endless process":** Morgenthau, *Purpose*, 31, 60 67, 56, 8, 5, 34, 300, 4, 25, 39, 47, 45.

222   **"fugitives":** Morgenthau, *Purpose*, 130, 81, 106, 99, 110, 180, 128, 145, 118, 33, 132, 130, 129, 136, 140.

225   **"introverted globalism":** Morgenthau, *New Foreign Policy*, 16.

225   **"blind, militaristic hysteria":** John Lewis Gaddis, *George F. Kennan: An American Life* (New York: Penguin, 2011), 651.

225   **"aimless and inconsistent":** Morgenthau, *Purpose*, 130, 89, 201, 311, 318, 300, 308–9, 310.

227   **"positions which conform":** Hans J. Morgenthau, *The Restoration of American Politics* (Chicago: University of Chicago Press, 1964), 304, 117.

227   **"the only real revolution":** Morgenthau, *Decline*, 36, 75.

228   **"to renew":** Morgenthau, *Purpose*, 293.

CHAPTER FIVE: VIETNAM

229 **Among his students:** G. O. Mazur, ed., *One Hundred Year Commemoration to the Life of Hans Morgenthau* (New York: Semenenko Foundation, 2004), 132, 134.

230 **"History teaches":** Henry Kissinger, *A World Restored: Metternich, Castlereagh and the Problems of Peace, 1812–1822* (Brattleboro, VT: Echo Point Books and Media, 2013), 331, 94, 316, 145, 326.

231 **"Of such statesmanship":** Hans J. Morgenthau, *Vietnam and the United States* (Washington, DC: Public Affairs, 1965), 78.

231 **"The most European":** Kissinger, *World*, 30, 173, 311.

232 **"We were both":** Henry Kissinger, "Hans Morgenthau: A Gentle Analyst of Power," *The New Republic*, August 2 & 9, 1980.

232 **"the possibility of tragedy":** John G. Stoessinger, *Henry Kissinger: The Anguish of Power* (New York: Norton, 1976).

232 **"in the forefront":** Hans J. Morgenthau, "Henry Kissinger, Secretary of State: An Evaluation," *Encounter* (November 1974).

232 **"It has been":** Box 33, Morgenthau Papers.

233 **"honest broker":** Morgenthau, "Henry Kissinger."

233 **gave him a tour:** Mazur, *One Hundred*, 150.

233 **"sea change":** Henry Kissinger, *Does America Need a Foreign Policy? Toward a Diplomacy for the 21st Century* (New York: Simon & Schuster, 2002), 249.

233 **"the first prominent":** Jacob Heilbrunn, *They Knew They Were Right: The Rise of the Neocons* (New York: Doubleday, 2008), 115.

233 **"relentless":** Henry Kissinger, *Years of Renewal* (New York: Simon & Schuster, 2000), 135.

234 **cracked down:** Justin Vaïsse, *Neoconservatism: The Biography of a Movement* (Cambridge, MA: Harvard University Press, 2010), 118.

234 **neoconservative "nursery":** Vaïsse, *Neoconservatism*, 118.

235 **Theodore Roosevelt:** Box 31, Morgenthau Papers.

235 **"never agree":** Kissinger, *Renewal*, 133.

235 **"the best":** Benjamin M. Mollov, *Power and Transcendence: Hans J. Morgenthau and the Jewish Experience* (Lanham, MD: Lexington Books, 2002), 187.

235 **"I attach great weight":** March 23, 1974, "Hans J. Morgenthau Collection, 1904–1980," Leo Baeck Institute, Center for Jewish History, New York.

236 **"not a question":** Mollov, *Power*, 197–198.

236 **"ideological decontamination":** Morgenthau, "Henry Kissinger."

236 **"someone for whom":** September 15, 1977, Baeck Institute.

236 **"morality limits":** Hans J. Morgenthau, *The Decline of Democratic Politics* (Chicago: University of Chicago Press, 1962), 59.

237 **"defining experience":** Henry Kissinger, *Ending the Vietnam War: A History of America's Involvement in and Extrication from the Vietnam War* (New York: Simon & Schuster, 2003), 8.

237 **"moral calamity":** Louis B. Zimmer, *The Vietnam War Debate: Hans J. Morgenthau and the Attempt to Halt the Drift into Disaster* (Lanham, MD: Lexington, 2011), 339.

237 **"After 1965":** Stephen R. Graubard, *Kissinger: Portrait of a Mind* (New York: Norton, 1973), 226.

237 **"greatest single error":** Stanley Karnow, *Vietnam: A History* (New York: Penguin, 1997), 24.

238 **"In the context":** Leslie H. Gelb and Richard K. Betts, *The Irony of Vietnam: The System Worked* (Washington, DC: The Brookings Institution, 1979), 128.

238 **"a lone voice":** Udi Greenberg, *The Weimar Century: German Emigres and the Ideological Foundations of the Cold War* (Princeton, NJ: Princeton University Press, 2014), 242, 252.

238 **"before you know it":** Zimmer, *Vietnam War*, 1, xxiv–xxv.

239 **"beaches of Waikiki":** Karnow, *Vietnam*, 267.

239 **"invade Sussex":** Fredrik Logevall, *Choosing War: The Lost Chance for Peace and the Escalation of War in Vietnam* (Berkeley: University of California Press, 1999), 133.

239 **"not Chinese":** Hans J. Morgenthau, *A New Foreign Policy for the United States* (New York: Council on Foreign Relations, 1969), 32.

239 **"extraordinarily consistent":** Karnow, *Vietnam,* 194.

239 **"took their orders":** A. J. Langguth, *Our Vietnam: The War, 1954–1975* (New York: Simon & Schuster, 2000), 525.

240 **"I wish":** Karnow, *Vietnam,* 474.

240 **"good brainwashing":** Langguth, *Our Vietnam,* 478.

240 **"history, language":** Robert S. McNamara, *In Retrospect: The Tragedy and Lessons of Vietnam* (New York: Vintage, 1996), 32.

240 **"Is it possible":** Zimmer, *Vietnam War,* xxxv.

240 **"Amid all the debate":** McNamara, *In Retrospect,* 63.

241 **"cannot shirk":** Karnow, *Vietnam,* 272.

241 **"Withdrawal means":** McNamara, *In Retrospect,* 71, 72.

241 **"We regarded the conflict":** Neil Sheehan, *A Bright Shining Lie: John Paul Vann and America in Vietnam* (New York: Vintage, 1989), 191, 271.

242 **"firm supporter":** Karnow, *Vietnam,* 266.

242 **"fringes of opinion":** Gelb and Betts, *Irony,* 213.

242 **"mouthpiece":** Michael C. Williams, ed., *Realism Reconsidered: The Legacy of Hans J. Morgenthau in International Relations* (New York: Oxford University Press, 2007), 169.

242 **"an abrupt break":** William E. Scheuerman, *Hans Morgenthau: Realism and Beyond* (Malden, MA: Policy, 2009), 9.

242 **"I have always":** Morgenthau, *Vietnam,* 5.

243 **"miracle worker":** Gelb and Betts, *Irony,* 207.

243 **"Winston Churchill":** Langguth, *Our Vietnam,* 131.

243 **"political Joan of Arc":** George C. Herring, *America's Longest War: The United States and Vietnam, 1950–1975* (New York: McGraw-Hill, 2002), 60.

243 **ticker-tape parade:** Zimmer, *Vietnam War,* 24.

243 **"extraordinary qualities":** Morgenthau, *Vietnam,* 21, 24.

243 **stomach-churning:** Sheehan, *Bright,* 102–3.

244 **"little to choose":** Morgenthau, *Vietnam,* 24, 29.

244 **"Bolshevik Revolution":** Hans J. Morgenthau, *The Impasse of American Foreign Policy* (Chicago: University of Chicago Press, 1964), 140.

244 **"a set of beliefs":** George Lichtheim, *Marxism: An Historical and Critical Study* (New York: Praeger, 1967), 364.

245 **"Polycentrism":** Hans J. Morgenthau, *The Restoration of American Politics* (Chicago: University of Chicago Press, 1964), 348, 349.

245 **"oriental despotism":** Morgenthau, *Impasse,* 142, 167, 183.

246 **"a monster":** Henry Kissinger, *Diplomacy* (New York: Simon & Schuster, 1994), 333.

246 **"come to Geneva":** Langguth, *Our Vietnam,* 79.

246 **"two major Communist powers":** Hans J. Morgenthau, *Truth and Power: Essays of a Decade, 1960–1970* (New York: Praeger, 1970), 401.

246 **"great ironies":** Morgenthau, *New Foreign Policy,* 148.

246 **"logical":** Herring, *America's Longest War,* xiii.

247 **Truman Doctrine:** Morgenthau, *New Foreign Policy,* 17, 85.

248 **"George":** Langguth, *Our Vietnam,* 152.

248 **"unsupported":** Morgenthau, *Vietnam,* 77.

248 **"conquered Eastern Europe":** Morgenthau, *New Foreign Policy,* 45.

248 **"A Communist government":** Morgenthau, *Vietnam,* 47, 67, 68.

248 **"equated Ho Chi Minh":** McNamara, *In Retrospect,* 33.

249 **"humiliation":** Morgenthau, *Vietnam,* 36, 49.

249 **"If my advice":** Morgenthau, *Truth,* 49.

249 **"Project Morgenthau":** Williams, *Realism,* 184.

250 **"American arrogance":** Greenberg, *Weimar,* 250.

250 **"congenital pessimism":** Zimmer, *Vietnam War,* 60.

250 **"very hard today"**: McNamara, *In Retrospect*, 39.

250 **"Gibraltar"**: Sheehan, *Bright*, 290.

250 **"always been confident"**: McNamara, *In Retrospect*, 207.

250 **"famous overnight"**: Zimmer, *Vietnam War*, xvii.

250–51 **"Just a note"** . . . **"This goes to show"**: Boxes 94, 95, Morgenthau Papers, Library of Congress.

251 **"a trifle mad"**: Isaiah Berlin, "The Unique Qualities of Joe Alsop," *New York Review of Books*, October 8, 2015.

251 **"One proof of the wisdom"**: *Washington Post*, March 21, 1965.

251 **"I receive every day"**: Box 36, Morgenthau Papers.

251 **"Mao Zedong is not Hitler"**: *Washington Post*, April 30, 1965.

252 **"a still-born movement"**: Zimmer, *Vietnam War*, 306.

252 **"From an economic point of view"**: University of Chicago Center for Policy Study, "Vietnam: Which Way to Peace—a Discussion," May 1970.

252 **"indiscriminate destruction"**: Hans J. Morgenthau, "At War with Asia," *New York Times Book Review*, January 17, 1971.

252 **"dangerously naïve"**: Williams, *Realism*, 192n.57.

253 **"in the name of morality"**: Kissinger, *Ending*, 13, 559.

253 **"shock troops"**: Herring, *America's Longest War*, 206.

253 **"The more a person is educated"**: H. R. Haldeman, *The Haldeman Diaries: Inside the Nixon White House* (New York: Putnam's, 1994), 231, 326.

253 **"one, two, three"**: Lyrics by Joe Allen McDonald.

253 **"I counted the number"**: McNamara, *In Retrospect*, 253–254.

253 **a distraught McGeorge Bundy**: Douglas Brinkley and Luke A. Nichter, *The Nixon Tapes, 1971–1972* (New York: Houghton Mifflin Harcourt, 2014), 726.

255 **"minor aberration"**: Morgenthau, *Restoration*, 349.

255 **"in ferment"**: Zimmer, *Vietnam War*, 83.

256 **"intellectually untenable"**: Morgenthau, *New Foreign Policy*, 8.

256 **"morality bag"**: Walter Isaacson, *Kissinger: A Biography* (New York: Simon & Schuster, 2005), 282.

256 **"morally fundamentalist"**: Hans J. Morgenthau, "Robert F. Kennedy," *New York Review of Books*, August 1, 1968, in *Truth*, 185.

257 **"A man who was nothing"**: Hans J. Morgenthau, *Politics Among Nations: The Struggle for Power and Peace* (New York: Knopf, 1967), 13.

257 **"only been one Humphrey"**: Hans J. Morgenthau, "Nixon vs. Humphrey: The Choice," *New York Review of Books*, November 7, 1968, in *Truth*, 202, 201, 203, 205.

258 **"the only times"**: Hans J. Morgenthau, "Mr. Nixon's Gamble," *The New Republic*, May 23, 1970.

259 **"I found the tone"**: Morgenthau Collection, Leo Baeck Institute, October 9, 1968, October 22, 1968; November 13, 1968.

261 **"kibitzer"**: Jeremi Suri, *Henry Kissinger and the American Century* (Cambridge, MA: Harvard University Press, 2007), 76.

261 **"there was no overall plan"**: Niall Ferguson, *Kissinger: 1923–1968: The Idealist* (New York: Penguin, 2015), 637, 659, 688.

262 **"American involvement"**: Stoessinger, *Henry Kissinger*, 43.

262 **where Kissinger stood**: Hans J. Morgenthau, "A Portrait, Albeit Incomplete, of a First-Rate Intellect," *Chicago Tribune Book World*, June 24, 1973.

262 **"was smart enough"**: Morgenthau, "Henry Kissinger."

262 **"a crucial test"**: Ferguson, *Kissinger*, 672.

263 **2,000 occasions**: Herring, *America's Longest War*, 201.

263 **"labeled a dove"**: Langguth, *Our Vietnam*, 540.

263 **"more and more"**: Logevall, *Choosing War*, 79.

263 **"never deviated"**: McNamara, *In Retrospect*, 147.

263 **"last days in office"**: Mark Atwood Lawrence, *The Vietnam War: A Concise International History* (New York: Oxford University Press, 2008), 135.

264 **"desperate to end"**: Kissinger, *Ending*, 42.
264 **"Stockholm syndrome"**: Ferguson, *Kissinger*, 763.
264 **"the closest thing"**: McNamara, *In Retrospect*, 301.
264 **"cut your balls"**: Isaacson, *Kissinger*, 122.
264 **"Henry feels"**: Ferguson, *Kissinger*, 801.
264 **"Six days a week"**: Isaacson, *Kissinger*, 131, 133.
265 **Dallek has described**: Robert Dallek, *Nixon and Kissinger: Partners in Power* (New York: HarperCollins, 2007), 68.
265 **"war for peace"**: Herring, *America's Longest War*, 274.
265 **"stated flatly"**: Haldeman, *Diaries*, 42, 139.
265 **"Give us six months"**: Isaacson, *Kissinger*, 165.
265–66 **"we're not going to lose"**: Tapes, 11, 16, 383.
266 **"a major change"**: Kissinger, *Ending*, 80.
266 **determined de-escalation**: Karnow, *Vietnam*, 696–698.
266 **only 6,000**: Jussi Hanhimäki, *The Flawed Architect: Henry Kissinger and American Foreign Policy* (New York: Oxford University Press, 2004), 203.
267 **"After March 1968"**: Gelb and Betts, *Irony*, 170.
267 **"fouled everything up"**: Tapes, 69, 355, 419.
267 **"The demand"**: Kissinger, *Ending*, 84.
267 **"any difference"**: Tapes, 50.
267 **"How can you succeed"**: Kissinger, *Ending*, 116.
268 **"escalate to accelerate"**: Haldeman, *Diaries*, 305.
268 **"savage, punishing blows"**: Herring, *America's Longest War*, 275, 280.
269 **"very hard-line"**: Isaacson, *Kissinger*, 191, 247.
269 **"The objective"**: Tapes, 11, 66.
270 **"nervous breakdown"**: Isaacson, *Kissinger*, 269.
270 **"near civil war"**: Kissinger, *Ending*, 7.
270 **"a meeting"**: Tapes, 45, 53.
270 **"the height of obtuseness"**: Kissinger, *Ending*, 208.
270 **"not be viable"**: Tapes, 479.
271 **"long-term consequence"**: Kissinger, *Ending*, 179.
271 **"To hell with history"**: Tapes, 325.
271 **"We do not want"**: Kissinger, *Ending*, 221, 234, 255, 295.
272 **"collateral issue"**: Dallek, *Nixon*, 395.
272 **"was all conciliation"**: Kissinger, *Ending*, 303.
272 **"poisons our relations"**: Tapes, 471, 472, 548, 549, 605, 622.
273 **"we have had it"**: Haldeman, *Diaries*, 450.
273 **No moment**: Kissinger, *Ending*, 329–330.
274 **"three out of three"**: Tapes, 629.
274 **"obsessed"**: Isaacson, *Kissinger*, 441.
274 **"he lost touch"**: Tapes, 629, 652.
275 **"punch Kissinger"**: Isaacson, *Kissinger*, 453.
275 **"I was determined"**: Kissinger, *Ending*, 352, 362, 370.
275 **"unmitigated, selfish"**: Tapes, 705, 712.
275 **"the fall guy"**: Kissinger, *Ending*, 357, 394.
275 **"fed up"**: Tapes, 655, 678, 679, 695.
276 **"war by tantrum"**: Isaacson, *Kissinger*, 471.
276 **happily accepted**: Stoessinger, *Henry Kissinger*, 75.
277 **Over a 12-day period**: Gregory A. Daddis, *Withdrawal: Reassessing America's Final Years in Vietnam* (New York: Oxford University Press, 2017), 194.
277 **1,600 civilians**: Herring, *America's Longest War*, 301, 316.
277 **"damage assessment"**: Isaacson, *Kissinger*, 483, 484.
278 **Senator George Aiken**: *New York Times* obituary, November 20, 1984.
278 **"rhetorically easy"**: Kissinger, *Ending*, 208.
279 **"troops fighting us"**: Haldeman, *Diaries*, 65.

279   "turning on Americans": Tapes, 555–556.

279   "might turn against us" Frank Snepp, *Decent Interval: An Insider's Account of Saigon's* Indecent End Told by the CIA's Chief Strategy Analyst in Vietnam (New York: Random House, 1977), 297, 298.

280   less than a third: Gelb and Betts, *Irony*, 160.

280   "overwhelming majority": Karnow, *Vietnam*, 502.

280   "Even as late": Gelb and Betts, *Irony*, 220.

280   a Harris poll: Kissinger, *Ending*, 317.

280   Even in 1990: Karnow, *Vietnam*, 16.

281   "go fight anyplace": Tapes, 87, 453.

281   "a great way out": Haldeman, *Diaries*, 97.

281   "Weimar Republic": Karnow, *Vietnam*, 650.

281   "You'll still turn out": Tapes, 15.

281   "We are saving you": Isaacson, *Kissinger*, 279.

281   "shattering experience": Ferguson, *Kissinger*, 606, 609, 610.

282   "peace with honor": Kissinger, *Ending*, 428.

282   hundreds of thousands: Karnow, *Vietnam*, 431.

282   11 feet of water: Langguth, *Our Vietnam*, 440.

282   "short of genocide": McNamara, *In Retrospect*, 415.

282   Kissinger's position: Hans J. Morgenthau, "Kissinger's Next Test," *The New Leader*, November 13, 1972.

282   two to three years: Isaacson, *Kissinger*, 161, 485.

282   "certain period of time": Dallek, *Nixon*, 257.

282   "respectable interval": Hanhimäki, *Flawed*, 225, 231.

283   "a small ally": Kissinger, *Ending*, 207.

283   "worth the cost": Isaacson, *Kissinger*, 483, 484.

283   "betrayal of the South": Hanhimäki, *Flawed*, 232, 383.

284   "greatest retreat in history": Dallek, *Nixon*, 210.

284   "secret deal": Tapes, 605.

284   "take some solace": Kissinger, *Ending*, 207, 430.

285   "the pivotal period": Herring, *America's Longest War*, 147.

285   "the Rubicon": Gelb and Betts, *Irony*, 123.

285   "fork in the road": McNamara, *In Retrospect*, 168.

285   "the most important:" Logevall, *Choosing War*, xiii.

285   "more dangerous": Ferguson, *Kissinger*, 840–41.

285   "We have suffered": Tapes, 231, 305, 605.

286   "the question is raised": Suri, *Henry Kissinger*, 214.

286   "As we see it": Isaacson, *Kissinger*, 280, 281.

286   "an indispensable element": Morgenthau, *Politics*, 77.

287   "The obvious argument" Morgenthau, *Truth*, 101.

287   "matter for speculation": Morgenthau, *New*, 138.

287   "We can't disengage": Zimmer, *Vietnam War*, 250.

287   "the establishment": Morgenthau, *Truth*, 105.

287   "face-saving device": Zimmer, *Vietnam War*, 60.

287   "of no concern": Morgenthau, *Truth*, 197.

288   "no one ever won": Gelb and Betts, *Irony*, 82.

289   "Why not withdraw": Isaacson, *Kissinger*, 161.

289   "extricate France": Kissinger, *Ending*, 56, 454.

289   "nightmare": Tapes, 602.

289   "my nightmare": Stoessinger, *Henry Kissinger*, 49.

289   "all actors": Kissinger, *Ending*, 531, 532.

289   "Greek tragedy": Stoessinger, *Henry Kissinger*, 77.

290   "It would have been impossible": Kissinger, *Ending*, 71.

290   "no assurance of success": Hans J. Morgenthau, *Scientific Man Versus Power Politics* (Chicago: Phoenix Books/University of Chicago Press, 1965), 221.

Chapter Six: KISSINGER IN POWER

291 **"made careers":** Walter Isaacson, *Kissinger: A Biography* (New York: Simon & Schuster, 2005), 500, 501.

291 **"fastest gun":** Charles R. Ashman, *Kissinger: The Adventures of Super-Kraut* (New York: Dell, 1973), 22.

292 **"best thing":** Greg Grandin, *Kissinger's Shadow: The Long Reach of America's Most Controversial Statesman* (New York: Metropolitan, 2015), 110.

292 **"a legend":** Isaacson, *Kissinger*, 437.

292 **"genius in residence":** Jussi Hanhimäki, *The Flawed Architect: Henry Kissinger and American Foreign Policy* (New York: Oxford University Press, 2004), 294.

293 **astonishing 85 percent:** Robert Dallek, *Nixon and Kissinger: Partners in Power* (New York: Harper/Collins, 2007), 553.

293 **"kiss of death":** Marvin Kalb and Bernard Kalb, *Kissinger* (Boston: Little, Brown, 1974), 265.

293 **"Do you lie":** Danielle Hunebelle, *Dear Henry* (New York: Berkeley Medallion, 1972), 176.

293 **"There was a time":** John G. Stoessinger, *Henry Kissinger: The Anguish of Power* (New York: Norton, 1976), ix, 223.

294 **"most important event":** Stephen R. Graubard, *Kissinger: Portrait of a Mind* (New York: Norton, 1973), 60.

294 **"intuitive and empathetic":** Bruce Mazlish, *Kissinger: The European Mind in American Policy* (New York: Basic Books, 1976), 194–95.

295 **"challenging":** Niall Ferguson, *Kissinger: 1923–1968: The Idealist* (New York: Penguin, 2015), 374.

295 **"difficult":** Graubard, *Kissinger*, 103.

295 **"drift across ideas":** Isaacson, *Kissinger*, 87.

296 **"excessively intense":** Henry Kissinger, *White House Years* (New York: Simon & Schuster, 2011), 14, 942.

296 **"an enormous amount":** Isaacson, *Kissinger*, 79, 97, 99, 100.

296 **"most arrogant man":** Grandin, *Kissinger's Shadow*, 39.

296 **"egotistical maniac":** Kalb and Kalb, *Kissinger*, 99.

296 **"terribly difficult":** Douglas Brinkley and Luke A. Nichter, *The Nixon Tapes, 1971–1972* (New York: Houghton Mifflin Harcourt, 2014), 19, 341.

296 **"emotional drain":** H. R. Haldeman, *The Haldeman Diaries: Inside the Nixon White House* (New York: Putnam's, 1994), 97, 103, 136, 137, 253.

297 **"fierce":** Stoessinger, *Henry Kissinger*, 3.

297 **"a ceaseless force":** Dallek, *Nixon*, 503.

298 **"a wonderful fight":** Isaacson, *Kissinger*, 98.

298 **"an awareness":** Hunebelle, *Dear Henry*, 62.

298 **"no more important":** Henry Kissinger, *Years of Renewal* (New York: Simon & Schuster, 2000), 1062.

298 **"total compliance":** Haldeman, *Diaries*, 97.

298 **"Moroccan whorehouse":** Isaacson, *Kissinger*, 189, 389.

299 **"The result was":** Kissinger, *Renewal*, 62.

299 **the British Foreign Office:** Henry Kissinger, *Observations: Selected Speeches and Essays, 1982–1984* (Boston: Little, Brown, 1985), 11.

299 **"fall on a sword":** Haldeman, *Diaries*, 253.

299 **"seamless web":** Kissinger, *Observations*, 63.

299 **"declared war":** Haldeman, *Diaries*, 38, 372.

299 **"not proud":** Kissinger, *Renewal*, 77.

300 **"He's psychopathic":** Tapes, 18.

300 **"Every single policy":** Grandin, *Kissinger's Shadow*, 52.

300 **"a perfect congruence":** Christopher Hitchens, *The Trial of Henry Kissinger* (New York: Verso, 2001), 120.

300 **"the desire to command"**: Isaacson, *Kissinger*, 108.
300 **"Anyone wishing"**: Jeremi Suri, *Henry Kissinger and the American Century* (Cambridge, MA: Harvard University Press, 2007), 55.
300 **"entirely absent"**: Kissinger, *White House Years*, 30.
300 **"What sustained me"**: Kissinger, *Upheaval*, 1117.
300 **"a contribution"**: Kissinger, *White House Years*, 30, 45.
300 **"In any negotiation"**: Henry Kissinger, *A World Restored: Metternich, Castlereagh and the Problems of Peace, 1812–1822* (Brattleboro, VT: Echo Point Books and Media, 2013), 169, 187.
301 **"he has screwed it up"**: Kissinger, *White House Years*, 14, 15.
301 **"unfit"**: Dallek, *Nixon*, 70.
301 **"most dangerous"**: Kalb and Kalb, *Kissinger*, 16.
302 **"impudent"**: Kissinger, *Renewal*, 1060.
302 **"well justified"**: Kissinger, *White House Years*, 15.
302 **"widespread enthusiasm"**: Ferguson, *Kissinger*, 857, 858.
302 **Steinem urged Kissinger**: Isaacson, *Kissinger*, 134.
303 **"commissioning a painting"**: Henry Kissinger, "The Policymaker and the Intellectual," *The Reporter*, March 5, 1959.
304 **"some professors"**: Henry Kissinger, *For the Record: Selected Statements, 1977–1980* (Boston: Little, Brown, 1981), 114.
304 **"The convictions"**: Henry Kissinger, *White House Years*, 54.
305 **"cannot be a crisis"**: Ferguson, *Kissinger*, 12.
305 **People . . . do not grow**: Kissinger, *White House Years*, 27.
305 **"isolation"**: Box 36, Hans J. Morgenthau Papers, Manuscript Division, Library of Congress, Washington, DC.
305 **"virtually no possibility"**: Box 28, Morgenthau Papers.
305 **"publicity seeker"**: Louis B. Zimmer, *The Vietnam War Debate: Hans J. Morgenthau and the Attempt to Halt the Drift into Disaster* (Lanham, MD: Lexington Books, 2011), 178.
305 **"The writer who speaks"**: Hans J. Morgenthau, "The Writer's Duty and His Predicament," *The Hudson Review* 18, no. 2 (Summer 1965).
305 **"For those who have"**: Hans J. Morgenthau, *Truth and Power: Essays of a Decade, 1960–1970* (New York: Praeger, 1970), 6, 8.
306 **"first-rate scholar"**: Hans J. Morgenthau, "A Portrait Albeit Incomplete of a First-Rate Intellect," *Chicago Tribune Book World*, June 24, 1973.
306 **"that was not oriented"**: Hans J. Morgenthau, "Kissinger: An Eyewitness Report," *Chicago Tribune Book World*, September 11, 1977.
306 **"trim your sails"**: Morgenthau, "A Portrait," June 24, 1973.
306 **"unabashedly self-serving"**: Hans J. Morgenthau, "Henry Kissinger, Secretary of State: An Evaluation," *Encounter* (November 1974).
306 **"He had a point"**: Box 104, Morgenthau Papers.
306 **"The intellectual seeks truth"**: Morgenthau, *Truth*, 14, 68, 143.
307 **"by far the best"**: Stoessinger, *Henry Kissinger*, cover.
307 **"prophetic confrontation"**: Morgenthau, *Truth*, 15, 16, 17, 24, 28, 17.
309 **"what manner of man"**: Morgenthau, "A Portrait," June 24, 1973.
309 **"ability to move"**: Morgenthau, "Henry Kissinger."
309 **"If the moral basis"**: Kissinger, *Upheaval*, 1117.
310 **"It is difficult"**: Dallek, *Nixon*, 316, 433.
310 **"If I resign"**: Stoessinger, *Henry Kissinger*, 58.
310 **getting rid of the vice president**: Haldeman, *Diaries*, 325.
311 **"The public life"**: Suri, *Henry Kissinger*, 13.
311 **"Every achievement"**: Kissinger, *White House Years*, 758.
311 **"breathless"**: Suri, *Henry Kissinger*, 194.
311 **"He eats"**: Hunebelle, *Dear Henry*, 51, 81.
311 **"the décor"**: Isaacson, *Kissinger*, 358.

312 **"had the air"**: Hunebelle, *Dear Henry*, 78, 102.

312 **"I just don't think"**: Isaacson, *Kissinger*, 367.

312 **"All the available evidence"**: Mazlish, *Kissinger*, 144.

312 **"You have to live"**: Hunebelle, *Dear Henry*, 44.

312 **"good courtier"**: Kissinger, *White House Years*, 302.

312 **"Do you agree"**: Tapes, 70, 156, 229, 325, 460, 703.

313 **"Nixon's favor"**: Kissinger, *Upheaval*, 94.

313 **"balancing"**: Kissinger, *Renewal*, 65.

313 **"almost suicidal"**: Isaacson, *Kissinger*, 148.

313 **"begin to imagine"**: Seymour M. Hersh, *The Price of Power: Kissinger in the Nixon White House* (New York: Summit, 1983), 603.

313 **"We've been trying"**: Suri, *Henry Kissinger*, 207.

314 **"there are Jews"**: Dallek, *Nixon*, 93, 170.

314 **"quite insecure"**: Haldeman, *Diaries*, 66, 146, 189, 232, 380, 381.

315 **"complicate my life"**: Isaacson, *Kissinger*, 479.

315 **Oxford**: Kissinger, *Renewal*, 69.

315 **"no other choice"**: Kissinger, *Upheaval*, 4.

316 **"I never recommended"**: Isaacson, *Kissinger*, 505.

316 **"loss of power"**: Kissinger, *Renewal*, 609.

316 **"throw of the dice"**: Kissinger, *Upheaval*, xx, 103, 1115, 1118, 1120, 1122, 1178, 1202.

317 **"unassimilated outsider"**: Phyllis Schlafly and Chester Ward, *Kissinger on the Couch* (New Rochelle, NY: Arlington House, 1975), 486, 785.

318 **"rare convergence"**: Kissinger, *Upheaval*, 983.

318 **"a lightning rod"**: Kissinger: *Renewal*, 48, 843, 1059.

319 **"the centerpiece"**: Stoessinger, *Henry Kissinger*, 213.

319 **"not a starry-eyed quest"**: Henry Kissinger, *Diplomacy* (New York: Simon & Schuster, 1994), 740.

319 **"We must remember"**: Henry Kissinger, *World Order* (New York: Penguin, 2014), 303.

320 **"relations with the Soviet Union"**: Kissinger, *Renewal*, 714.

320 **"pretend friendship"**: Kissinger, *Upheaval*, 469.

320 **"bound to compete"**: Henry Kissinger, *American Foreign Policy* (New York: Norton, 1977), 47, 121.

320 **"defense burden"**: Kissinger, *Upheaval*, 237, 972, 998.

320 **"Disagreements"**: Kissinger, *American Foreign Policy*, 126.

320 **"The nuclear age"**: Henry Kissinger, *Does America Need a Foreign Policy? Toward a Diplomacy for the 21st Century* (New York: Simon & Schuster, 2002), 23.

320 **"be concerned"**: Kissinger, *American Foreign Policy*, 122, 143, 148.

322 **"In our view"**: Kissinger, *Diplomacy*, 714.

322 **"understands my views"**: John Lewis Gaddis, *George Kennan: An American Life* (New York: Penguin, 2011), 622.

322 **"unprecedented consultation"**: Kissinger, *American Foreign Policy*, 154, 164, 176.

323 **"almost impossible"**: Hanhimäki, *Flawed*, 381.

323 **"strong, healthy"**: Kissinger, *World Order*, 303.

323 **"victories and defeats"**: Stoessinger, *Henry Kissinger*, 203.

323 **"Absolute security"**: Kissinger, *Record*, 115.

324 **"When adopting détente"**: Hanhimäki, *Flawed*, 381.

324 **"minority view"**: Kissinger, *Renewal*, 48.

324 **"no ready constituency"**: Kissinger, *Diplomacy*, 731, 743, 752.

324 **"only in equilibrium"**: Kissinger, *Renewal*, 618.

324 **"Chinese leaders"**: Kissinger, *Diplomacy*, 726, 808–809, 833.

326 **"finite margin"**: Kissinger, *World Order*, 255.

326 **"the drumbeat"**: Kissinger, *Diplomacy*, 18, 30.

326 **"to a man"**: Kissinger, *Renewal*, 244.

326 **"elevated"**: Kissinger, *Upheaval*, 613.

326 **"moral disarmament"**: Kissinger, *Diplomacy*, 713.

326 **the preservation**: Kissinger, *American Foreign Policy*, 55.

327 **"embarrassed"**: Kissinger, *Renewal*, 244.

327 **"body without a soul"**: Mario Del Paso, *The Eccentric Realist: Henry Kissinger and the Shaping of American Foreign Policy* (Ithaca, NY: Cornell University Press, 2006), 131.

328 **"How hard"**: Kissinger, *American Foreign Policy*, 126, 172.

328 **"needle the bear"**: Kissinger, *Upheaval*, 241.

329 **"unselfish"**: Kissinger, *Does America Need*, 29.

329 **"undifferentiated"**: Kissinger, *American Foreign Policy*, 92.

329 **"world's policeman"**: Kissinger, *Record*, 83.

329 **"unlimited agenda"**: Kissinger, *Diplomacy*, 756.

329 **"ultimate irony"**: Kissinger, *Record*, 85.

330 **"done so quietly"**: Kissinger, *American Foreign Policy*, 208.

330 **"dangers and dilemmas"**: Kissinger, *Record*, 83.

330 **"moral foreign policy"**: Del Paso, *Eccentric*, 130.

330 **"intellectual rigor"**: Kissinger, *Renewal*, 107.

330 **pleasing Nixon**: Hersh, *Price*, 44–45.

331 **"something contingent"**: Hitchens, *Trial*, 20.

331 **"just as easily"**: Ferguson, *Kissinger*, 11, 12.

331 **"believed in nothing"**: Grandin, *Kissinger's Shadow*, 11.

331 **"no final answer"**: Kissinger, *American Foreign Policy*, 302.

331 **"blind to the human costs"**: Hersh, *Price*, 640.

331 **"I'm Jewish myself"**: Tapes, 148.

332 **"Statesmanship"**: Henry Kissinger, *On China* (New York: Penguin, 2011), 451.

332 **"nihilistic"**: Kissinger, *American Foreign Policy*, 96.

332 **"a stone around"**: Bob Woodward, *State of Denial* (New York: Simon & Schuster, 2006), 407.

332 **"endless war"**: Grandin, *Kissinger's Shadow*, 11.

332 **"irreducible element"**: Kissinger, *Does America Need*, 19.

333 **flag pin in his lapel**: Isaacson, *Kissinger*, 393.

334 **"potentially fatal"**: Schlafly and Ward, *Kissinger*, 18, 107, 124, 139, 784, 785.

334 **"classic Cold Warrior"**: Kissinger, *Upheaval*, 236.

334 **"pudgy spider"**: Schlafly and Ward, *Kissinger*, 224, 125, 213, 263, 11, 93, 613, 539, 490.

335 **"traitor to his country"**: Isaacson, *Kissinger*, 610.

336 **"Survival or self-defense"**: Schlafly and Ward, *Kissinger*, 259.

336 **"necessities of survival"**: Kissinger, *Diplomacy*, 34.

336 **"We cannot abandon"**: Kissinger, *Renewal*, 1076.

336 **"just one nuclear superpower"**: Schlafly and Ward, *Kissinger*, 128, 662.

337 **"Jewish cabal"**: Jacob Heilbrunn, *They Knew They Were Right: The Rise of the Neocons* (New York: Doubleday, 2008), 6.

338 **"liberal past"**: Irwin Stelzer, ed., *The Neoconservative Reader* (New York: Grove Press, 2004), 1, 235.

338 **"philosophically close"**: Kissinger, *Renewal*, 111.

338 **"far more dangerous"**: Robert Kagan and William Kristol, *Present Dangers. Crisis and Opportunity in American Foreign and Defense Policy* (San Francisco: Encounter Books, 2000), 20, 24.

339 **terms of abuse**: Heilbrunn, *They Knew*, 127.

339 **"passion of the convert"**: Kissinger, *Upheaval*, 236.

339 **"ideological elan"**: Kissinger, *Renewal*, 108, 109.

340 **"All serious foreign policy"**: Kissinger, *Record*, 79.

340 **"illusion"**: Kagan and Kristol, *Present Dangers*, 59.

340 **"forward-leaning"**: Kagan and Kristol, *Present Dangers*, 6, 14.

340 **"custodian"**: Francis Fukuyama, *America at the Crossroads: Democracy, Power and the Neoconservative Legacy* (New Haven, CT: Yale University Press, 2006), 102.

340 **"most plausible"**: Stelzer, *Neoconservative*, 76.

341 **"democratic globalism"**: Heilbrunn, *They Knew*, 8.
341 **"precursor"**: Stelzer, *Neoconservative*, 9.
341 **"Russian aggression"**: Kagan and Kristol, *Present Dangers*, 19.
341 **"Wilsonian idealists"**: Stelzer, *Neoconservative*, 49, 216.
341 **"believed that values"**: Kissinger, *Renewal*, 111, 1074.

CHAPTER SEVEN: KISSINGER OUT OF POWER

343 **"one-way street"**: Henry Kissinger, *Years of Renewal* (New York: Simon & Schuster, 2000), 841.
343 **"he savaged me"**: Henry Kissinger, *Diplomacy* (New York: Simon & Schuster, 1994), 366.
343 **"doesn't know"**: Jussi Hanhimäki, *The Flawed Architect: Henry Kissinger and American Foreign Policy* (New York: Oxford University Press, 2004), 444, 447.
343 **"political and symbolic"**: Walter Isaacson, *Kissinger: A Biography* (New York: Simon & Schuster, 2005), 608, 722.
343 **"standard-bearer"**: Irwin Stelzer, ed., *The Neoconservative Reader* (New York: Grove Press, 2004), 46, 75.
344 **"My own people"**: Isaacson, *Kissinger*, 719, 723.
344 **"I can assure you"**: Kiron K. Skinner, Annelise Anderson, and Martin Anderson, eds., *Reagan: A Life in Letters* (New York: Free Press, 2003), 699.
344 **"Realist moment"**: Mario Del Paso, *The Eccentric Realist: Henry Kissinger and the Shaping of American Foreign Policy* (Ithaca, NY: Cornell University Press, 2006), 11.
344 **"extraordinarily complex"**: Kissinger, *Diplomacy*, 765, 766, 770, 771.
345 **"cannot be removed"**: William Taubman, *Gorbachev: His Life and Times* (New York: Norton, 2017), 294–95.
345 **"biblical references"**: Kissinger, *Diplomacy*, 267.
345 **"I have agreed"**: Henry Kissinger, *Observations: Selected Speeches and Essays* (Boston: Little, Brown, 1985), ix.
345 **"astonishing performance"**: Kissinger, *Diplomacy*, 764, 766.
346 **"My skills"**: Kissinger, *Renewal*, 1074.
346 **"structure of peace"**: Kissinger, *Diplomacy*, 731, 767, 765.
347 **"a canny reassertion"**: Kissinger, *Renewal*, 110.
347 **"Machiavellian realism"**: Kissinger, *Diplomacy*, 774, 769.
347 **"laid the foundation"**: Kissinger, *Diplomacy*, 768, 784.
347 **"the more disgruntled"**: Jacob Heilbrunn, *They Knew They Were Right: The Rise of the Neocons* (New York: Doubleday, 2008), 67, 168.
347 **"diplomatic flexibility"**: Kissinger, *Diplomacy*, 756, 802.
347 **"as the experience"**: Zbigniew Brzezinski, *Power and Principle: Memoirs of the National Security Adviser, 1977–1981* (New York: Farrar, Straus & Giroux, 1983), 542.
348 **"political cover"**: Anatol Lieven and John Hulsman, *Ethical Realism: A Vision for America's Role in the World* (New York: Pantheon, 2006), 36.
348 **"common sense:"** Kissinger, *Diplomacy*, 766.
348 **no one saw:** George Bush and Brent Scowcroft, *A World Transformed* (New York: Knopf, 1998), xiii.
348 **"in the end"**: Kissinger, *Diplomacy*, 784.
348 **"In Gorbachev"**: Taubman, *Gorbachev*, 276.
349 **"need luck"**: Kissinger, *Diplomacy*, 792, 785.
349 **"deserve much credit"**: Kissinger, *Renewal*, 109–10.
349 **"more than a celebration"**: Robert Dallek, *Nixon and Kissinger: Partners in Power* (New York: HarperCollins, 2007), 617.
349 **"successful foreign policy"**: Henry Kissinger, *For the Record: Selected Statements, 1977–1980* (Boston: Little, Brown, 1981), 86.
349 **"one-sided emphasis"**: Henry Kissinger, *Does America Need a Foreign Policy? Toward a Diplomacy for the 21st Century* (New York: Simon & Schuster, 2001), 19, 24.

349 **"version of escapism":** Kissinger, *Diplomacy*, 799.

350 "beneficent status quo": Kissinger, *Does America*, 20.

350 **"brilliant sunset":** Kissinger, *Diplomacy*, 802.

350 **Kissinger came in first:** Daniel Maliniak, Susan Peterson, Ryan Powers, and Michael J. Tierney, "The Best International Relations Schools in the World," *Foregn Policy*, February 3, 2015.

351 **"the anti-Kissinger mood":** Brzezinski, *Power*, 10, 49, 502.

351 **he asked Kissinger:** Kissinger, *China*, 380.

351 **suggested to Reagan:** George P. Shultz, *Turmoil and Triumph: Diplomacy, Power and the Victory of the American Ideal* (New York: Scribner's, 1993), 313.

351 **"getting the support":** Skinner, Anderson, and Anderson, *Reagan: A Life in Letters*, 632.

352 **"a strong proponent":** Bush and Scowcroft, *World Transformed*, 26.

352 **"Realist appendix":** Del Paso, *Eccentric*, 3.

352 **"I respected":** Bush and Scowcroft, *World Transformed*, 104, 191.

352 **"did not like Kissinger":** Isaacson, *Kissinger*, 726.

352 **"too soft":** Douglas Brinkley and Luke A. Nichter, *The Nixon Tapes, 1971–1972* (New York: Houghton Mifflin Harcourt, 2014), 106.

352 **"walked this tightrope":** Kissinger, *China*, 416.

352 **"first president":** Kissinger, *Does America*, 251, 256, 94.

353 **"embraced":** Greg Grandin, *Kissinger's Shadow: The Long Reach of America's Most Controversial Statesman* (New York: Metropolitan, 2015), 222.

353 **"as much fun":** Roxanne Roberts and Libby Ingrid Copeland, "International Velvet," *Washington Post*, September 17, 1998.

353 **"I probably talk":** Woodward, *State of Denial*, 406.

353 **"great respect":** Jeffrey Goldberg, "The Lessons of Henry Kissinger," *The Atlantic*, (December 2016).

354 **"a legitimate objective":** Juliane von Mittelstaedt and Erich Follath, "Interview with Henry Kissinger: 'Do We Achieve World Order Through Chaos or Insight?'" *Spiegel Online*, November 13, 2014.

354 **Radical reinvention:** Walter Isaacson, "Henry Kissinger Reminds Us Why Realism Matters," *Time*, September 6, 2014.

354 **"total defeat of the adversary":** Jeffrey Goldberg, "World Chaos and World Order: Conversations with Henry Kissinger," *The Atlantic*, November 10, 2016.

354 **"appalled":** Woodward, *State of Denial*, 409.

354 **"unmoored":** *Time*, September 6, 2014.

354 **"good grief":** Hanhimäki, *Flawed*, 481.

354 **"get to the bottom":** Maureen Dowd, "He's Ba-a-a-ack!" *New York Times*, December 1, 2002.

354 **"In the end":** Hanhimäki, *Flawed*, 481.

355 **"a hissy fit":** William Safire, "Well, Hello, Henry," *New York Times*, December 2, 2002.

355 "the two Realists": Del Paso, *Eccentric*, 5.

355 **"Welcome Kissinger Realism":** April 19, 2015.

355 **"Barack Kissinger Obama":** *New York Times*, October 25, 2011.

355 **"Kissinger probably relishes":** Gregor Peter Schmitz, "Obama Returns to Kissinger's Realpolitik," *Der Spiegel*, May 22, 2013.

355 **"largely fits":** Hillary Rodham Clinton, "Hillary Clinton reviews Henry Kissinger's 'World Order,'" *Washington Post*, September 4, 2014.

355 **"Obama prided himself":** Goldberg, "World Chaos."

356 **"offended":** Goldberg, "The Lessons."

356 **"doing a great job":** Goldberg, "World Chaos."

356 **"I seek his advice":** David Remnick, "Negotiating the Whirlwind," *The New Yorker*, December 21, 2015.

356 **"I respect John Kerry":** Goldberg, "The Lessons."

356 **"ran the State Department":** Daniel Strauss, "Clinton's Kissinger Praise Goes Back Years," *Politico*, February 11, 2016.

357 **"inexcusable"**: Greg Grandin, "Hillary Clinton's Embrace of Kissinger Is Inexcusable," *Nation*, Aug. 8, 2016.

357 **"downright scary"**: Isaac Chotiner, "Hillary Clinton's Troubling Soft Spot for Henry Kissinger," *Slate*, April 9, 2016.

357 **"I am proud to say"**: *Washington Post*, February 12, 2016.

357 **"pro- or anti-Kissinger"**: Michael A. Cohen, "How Democrats Can Learn to Stop Worrying and Still Hate Kissinger," *World Policy Review*, Aug. 17, 2016.

357 **"unleash the radical wing"**: Goldberg, "The Lessons."

358 **"Watergate undermined"**: Henry Kissinger, *Ending the Vietnam War: A History of America's Involvement in and Extrication from the Vietnam War* (New York: Simon & Schuster, 2003), 457, 504.

358 **"remarkable success"**: Kissinger, *Does America*, 249.

358 **"has to be a limit"**: Kissinger, *Ending*, 510.

359 **"no other standard"**: Henry Kissinger, *A World Restored: Metternich, Castlereagh and the Problem of Peace, 1812–22* (Brattleboro, VT: Echo Point Books and Media, 2013), 328, 329.

359 **"not a cause"**: Kissinger, *Diplomacy*, 40.

360 **"an essential chord"**: Henry Kissinger, *World Order* (New York: Penguin, 2014), 268.

360 **"No American president"**: Kissinger, *Diplomacy*, 704.

360 **"tragedy"**: Kissinger, *World Order*, 308.

360 **"facing impeachment"**: Kissinger, *Diplomacy*, 731.

360 **"unilateral"**: Kissinger, *Does America*, 27, 258.

361 **"no successor generation"**: Heilbrunn, *They Knew*, 274.

362 **"hard knocks"**: Kissinger, *Diplomacy*, 20, 24, 67.

362 **"only stability"**: Hans J. Morgenthau, *Politics Among Nations: The Struggle for Power and Peace* (New York: Knopf, 1967), 167, 180, 202.

363 **"armaments race"**: Kissinger, *Diplomacy*, 169.

363 **"recalibrated"**: Kissinger, *World Order*, 31.

363 **"brains"**: Morgenthau, *Politics*, 135, 496.

363 **"frightful tyranny"**: Hannah Arendt, interview with Adelbert Reif, summer 1970, in *The Last Interview and Other Conversations* (Brooklyn, NY: Melville House, 2013), 102.

363 **"Hegemony"**: Kissinger, *Does America*, 57, 287.

364 **"cultivated"**: Kissinger, *World Order*, 8.

364 **"The United Nations"**: Kissinger, *Diplomacy*, 249–50.

364 **"a ruin"**: Morgenthau, *Politics*, 480.

365 **"shared sense"**: Kissinger, *Diplomacy*, 166.

365 **"agreed alternative"**: Kissinger, *Does America*, 21.

365 **"insistently"**: Kissinger, *World Order*, 2.

365 **"conflicts of interest"**: Morgenthau, *Politics*, 161, 399, 519.

365 **"repugnant"**: Kissinger, *Diplomacy*, 810.

366 **"constellation"**: Morgenthau, *Politics*, 34.

366 **"no conflict"**: Kissinger, *Diplomacy*, 34.

366 **"the conviction"**: Kissinger, *World Order*, 234.

366 **"at no time"**: Kissinger, *Diplomacy*, 22.

367 **"optional activity"**: Kissinger, *World Order*, 237.

367 **America's army**: Kissinger, *Diplomacy*, 37–38.

367 **"introverted globalism"**: Hans J. Morgenthau, *A New Foreign Policy for the United States* (New York: Praeger, 1969), 16, 164.

367 **"vacuums"**: Kissinger, *Diplomacy*, 548.

368 **"beginning of maturity"**: Arthur M. Schlesinger, Jr., *The Vital Center: The Politics of Freedom* (New Brunswick, NJ: Transaction, 1998), 222.

368 **"has been tested"**: Kissinger, *World Order*, 268, 278, 287.

368 **"made to order"**: Kissinger, *Diplomacy*, 802.

369 **"For the first time"**: Kissinger, *Record*, 44.

369 **"modernization"**: Kissinger, *World Order*, 373.

369   "no overriding": Kissinger, *Diplomacy*, 18, 803.
369   "confronting": Kissinger, *Does America*, 84.
369   "indispensable basis": Kissinger, *Diplomacy*, 810.
369   "seminal event": Kissinger, *Renewal*, 192, 196, 202, 222, 224, 232, 235, 239.
371   "defining national experience": Kissinger, *Does America*, 116.
372   "We may talk": Kissinger, *World Order*, 201.
372   "wise Asian leaders": Kissinger, *Does America*, 118, 157–158.
372   "In Asia": Kissinger, *World Order*, 178.
372   "America's preference": Kissinger, *Does America*, 118.
374   "conceptual": Kissinger, *World Order*, 226.
374   he and Chou Enlai: John G. Stoessinger, *Henry Kissinger: The Anguish of Power* (New York: Norton, 1976), 122.
374   "one of the two or three": Henry Kissinger, *White House Years* (New York: Simon & Schuster, 2011), 745, 747.
374   "shocking thesis": Kissinger, *China*, 7, 17, 218, 470, 521.
375   "osmosis": Kissinger, *World Order*, 216.
376   "come to grips": Kissinger, *Diplomacy*, 19, 700.
376   "searching debates": Kissinger, *China*, 493.
376   "five or six": Kissinger, *Diplomacy*, 805.
376   "indispensable pillars": Kissinger, *World Order*, 226.
376   "raw power": Kissinger, *Diplomacy*, 119.
377   "The two sides": Kissinger, *World Order*, 229.
377   "serious joint effort": Kissinger, *China*, 523.
377   "Any international order": Kissinger, *World Order*, 231, 233.
377   "Can China": Kissinger, *China*, 513.
377   "common bond": Kissinger, *Diplomacy*, 211.
377   "There are abuses": Kissinger, *China*, 427, 469.
377   "constructive cooperation": Kissinger, *World Order*, 233.
377   "common goals": Kissinger, *China*, 356, 451, 487, 495, 513, 526, 528.
378   "started a sequence": Kissinger, *World Order*, 145, 229, 232.
378   "the environment": Kissinger, *China*, 522.
378   "Proliferation": Kissinger, *World Order*, 337.
379   "calculus of deterrence": Kissinger, *China*, 495.
379   "comparable in their rigidity": Kissinger, *World Order*, 333, 340.
379   "A laptop": Kissinger, *World Order*, 345.
379   "unprecedented": Henry Kissinger, "Henry Kissinger on Nuclear Proliferation," *Newsweek*, February 6, 2009.
379   "a world of devastation": Kissinger, *China*, 498.
380   "a bolt from the blue": Philip Taubman, *The Partnership: Five Cold Warriors and Their Quest to Ban the Bomb* (New York: Harper Perennial, 2012), x.
380   "Whatever problems": Taubman, *Partnership*, 19, 289, 294.
381   "akin to climbing": Kissinger, "Nuclear Proliferation."
382   "the mind-set": Kissinger, *World Order*, 330, 331, 342, 351, 359.
383   "genuine knowledge": Leo Strauss, "An Epilogue," from Storing, Herbert, ed., *Essays in the Scientific Study of Politics* (New York; Holt, Rinehart and Winston, 1962), in Strauss, *An Introduction to Political Philosophy*, 129.
383   "every issue can be solved": Hannah Arendt, *The Human Condition* (Chicago: University of Chicago Press, 1998), 3, 305.
384   "so many instances": Hannah Arendt, *Crises of the Republic* (New York: Harcourt Brace, 1972), 118.
384   "The computer supplies tools": Kissinger, *World Order*, 351.
384   "It is always the individual": Hans J. Morgenthau, *Scientific Man Versus Power Politics* (Chicago: Phoenix Books/University of Chicago Press, 1965), 10, 101, 187, 215, 219.

384 **"prescientific"**: Michael C. Williams, ed., *Realism Reconsidered: The Legacy of Hans J. Morgenthau in International Relations* (New York: Oxford University Press, 2007), 3.

384 **"Germanic way"**: Kenneth Thompson and Robert J. Myers, eds., *A Tribute to Hans J. Morgenthau* (Washington, DC: New Republic Book, 1977), 25.

385 **"We expect everything"**: Hans J. Morgenthau, *Science: Servant or Master?* (New York: New American Library, 1972), 2, 3, 28, 53.

385 **"The modern age"**: Hannah Arendt, *Between Past and Future: Six Exercises in Political Thought* (New York: Meridian Books, 1968), 89.

385 **"The successful conduct"**: Kissinger, *Does America*, 283, 285.

385 **"the very existence"**: Morgenthau, *Science*, 62.

386 **"They have arisen"**: Kissinger, *World Order*, 355.

386 **"An advanced system"**: Kissinger, *Does America*, 24.

386 **"Where is the knowledge"**: Kissinger, *World Order*, 350.

387 **"cultural preparation"**: Kissinger, *Does America*, 286.

387 **"The questions"**: Morgenthau, *Scientific Man*, 123.

387 **"inherent nature"**: Kissinger, *World Order*, 348.

387 **"Great statesmen"**: Strauss, *Political Philosophy*, 14.

387 **"the approximation"**: Morgenthau, *Scientific Man*, 121.

387 **"the gift of intuition"**: Morgenthau, *Science*, 45.

387 **"A society is fortunate"**: Kissinger, *World Order*, 350.

388 **"a widespread fear"**: Hannah Arendt, *Responsibility and Judgment* (New York: Schocken, 2003), 19.

388 **"character and courage"**: Kissinger, *World Order*, 349, 360.

388 **"All political action"**: Strauss, *Political Philosophy*, 10.

388 **"the great human achievements"**: Kissinger, *World Order*, 360.

388 **"the role of ethics"**: Kissinger, *Atlantic*, June 2018.

388 **"an acceptance of authority"**: Kissinger, *Diplomacy*, 655.

388 **"No dominion can last"**: Morgenthau, *Nations*, 59.

388 **"most moral man"**: Thompson and Myers, *Tribute*, 26.

388 **"It is a disastrous thing"**: Hans J. Morgenthau, "The Political Science of E.H. Carr," *World Politics* 1, no. 1 (October 1948).

388 **"started with the assumption"**: Morgenthau, *Scientific Man*, 176.

388 **"morality and justice"**: Jeremi Suri, *Henry Kissinger and the American Century* (Cambridge, MA: Harvard University Press, 2007), 15, 186.

389 **"The attainment of peace"**: Kissinger, *American Foreign Policy*, 84, 127.

389 **"a moral dimension"**: Kissinger, *World Order*, 367.

389 **"in his singularity"**: Arendt, *Responsibility*, 97.

390 **"mush-minded"**: Thompson and Myers, *Tribute*, 320.

390 **"The brutal truth"**: Robert Dallek, *Nixon and Kissinger: Partners in Power* (New York: HarperCollins, 2007), 110.

390 **moral principles**: Kissinger, *Does America*, 258.

390 **"where the past"**: Kissinger, *World Order*, 348.

390 **"first and ultimate responsibility"**: Kissinger, *American Foreign Policy*, 204.

390 **"Accepting the limits"**: Kissinger, *China*, 426.

391 **"the willingness to persevere"**: Kissinger, *Does America*, 286.

391 **"equilibrium"**: Kissinger, *World Order*, 374.

391 **"imperfections"**: Kissinger, *American Foreign Policy*, 122.

391 **"leads to self-righteousness"**: Kissinger, *Renewal*, 1076.

393 **"as good as he can be"**: Morgenthau, *Scientific Man*, 189, 203.

SELECTED BIBLIOGRAPHY

Arendt, Hannah. *Essays in Understanding, 1930–1954*. New York: Harcourt, Brace, 1994.
———. *On Revolution*. New York: Penguin, 2006.
———. *The Origins of Totalitarianism*. New York: Meridian, 1971.
———. "Reflections on Little Rock." *Dissent* (Winter 1959).
———. *Responsibility and Judgment*. New York: Schocken, 2003.
Arendt, Hannah, and Karl Jaspers. *Correspondence, 1926–1969*. New York: Harcourt Brace Jovanovich, 1992.
Brinkley, Douglas, and Luke A. Nichter. *The Nixon Tapes, 1971–1972*. New York: Houghton Mifflin Harcourt, 2014.
Dallek, Robert. *Nixon and Kissinger: Partners in Power*. New York: HarperCollins, 2007.
Davis, Nathaniel. *The Last Two Years of Salvador Allende*. Ithaca, NY: Cornell University Press, 1985.
De Vylder, Stefan. *Allende's Chile: The Political Economy of the Rise and Fall of the Unidad Popular*. Cambridge: Cambridge University Press, 1976.
Evans, Henry Clay, Jr. *Chile and Its Relations with the United States*. Durham, NC: Duke University Press, 1927.
Ferguson, Niall. *Kissinger, Volume 1, 1923–1968: The Idealist*. New York: Penguin, 2015.
Fest, Joachim C. *Hitler*. New York: Harcourt Brace Jovanovich, 1974.
Frei, Christoph. *Hans J. Morgenthau: An Intellectual Biography*. Baton Rouge: Louisiana State University Press, 2001.
Gelb, Leslie H., and Richard K. Betts. *The Irony of Vietnam: The System Worked*. Washington, DC: The Brookings Institution, 1979.
Goldberg, Jeffrey. "The Lessons of Henry Kissinger." *The Atlantic* (December 2016).
Gustafson, Kristian. *Hostile Intent: U.S. Covert Operations in Chile, 1964–1974*. Washington, DC: Potomac Books, 2007.
Haffner, Sebastian. *The Meaning of Hitler*. Cambridge, MA: Harvard University Press, 1979.
Haldeman, H. R. *The Haldeman Diaries: Inside the Nixon White House*. New York: Putnam's, 1994.
Hanhimäki, Jussi. *The Flawed Architect: Henry Kissinger and American Foreign Policy*. New York: Oxford University Press, 2004.
Herring, George C. *America's Longest War: The United States and Vietnam, 1950–1975*. New York: McGraw-Hill, 2002.
Hersh, Seymour, M. *The Price of Power: Kissinger in the Nixon White House*. New York: Summit, 1983.

Hitchens, Christopher. *The Trial of Henry Kissinger*. New York: Verso, 2001.

Isaacson, Walter. *Kissinger: A Biography*. New York: Simon & Schuster, 2005.

Kalb, Marvin, and Bernard Kalb. *Kissinger*. Boston: Little, Brown, 1974.

Karnow, Stanley. *Vietnam: A History*. New York: Penguin, 1997.

Kershaw, Ian. *Hitler: 1889–1936, Hubris*. London: Penguin, 2001.

Kissinger, Henry. *American Foreign Policy*. New York: Norton, 1977.

——. *Diplomacy*. New York: Simon & Schuster, 1994.

——. *Does America Need a Foreign Policy? Toward a Diplomacy for the 21st Century*. New York: Simon & Schuster, 2002.

——. *Ending the Vietnam War: A History of America's Involvement in and Extrication from the Vietnam War*. New York: Simon & Schuster, 2003.

——. "Hans Morgenthau: A Gentle Analyst of Power." *The New Republic*, August 2 & 9, 1980.

——. "How the Enlightenment Ends." *The Atlantic* (June 2018).

——. *Nuclear Weapons and Foreign Policy*. New York: Harper & Brothers, 1957.

——. *On China*. New York: Penguin, 2011.

——. "The Policymaker and the Intellectual." *The Reporter*, March 5, 1959.

——. *White House Years*. New York: Simon & Schuster, 2011.

——. *World Order*. New York: Penguin, 2014.

——. *A World Restored: Metternich, Castlereagh and the Problem of Peace, 1812–22*. Brattleboro, VT: Echo Point Books and Media: 2013.

——. *Years of Renewal*. New York: Simon & Schuster, 2000.

——. *Years of Upheaval*. New York: Simon & Schuster, 2011.

Kornbluh, Peter, ed. *The Pinochet File: A Declassified Dossier on Atrocity and Accountability*. New York: The New Press, 2013.

Kurz, Evi. *The Kissinger Saga: Walter and Henry Kissinger, Two Brothers from Fürth, Germany*. London: Weidenfeld and Nicolson, 2009

Logevall, Fredrik. *Choosing War: The Lost Chance for Peace and the Escalation of War in Vietnam*. Berkeley: University of California Press, 1999.

Mazlish, Bruce. *Kissinger: The European Mind in American Policy*. New York: Basic Books, 1976.

Mazur, G. O., ed. *One Hundred Year Commemoration to the Life of Hans Morgenthau*. New York: Semenenko Foundation, 2004.

McNamara, Robert S. *In Retrospect: The Tragedy and Lessons of Vietnam*. New York: Vintage, 1996.

Morgenthau, Hans J., "Hannah Arendt on Totalitarianism and Democracy." *Social Research* 44, no. 1 (Spring 1977).

——. "Henry Kissinger, Secretary of State: An Evaluation." *Encounter* (November 1974).

——. *Politics Among Nations. The Struggle for Power and Peace*, 4th ed. New York. Knopf, 1967.

——. *The Purpose of American Politics*. New York: Vintage, 1964.

——. *Science: Servant or Master?* New York: New American Library, 1972.

——. *Scientific Man Versus Power Politics*. Chicago: Phoenix Books/University of Chicago Press, 1965.

——. *Truth and Power: Essays of a Decade, 1960–1970*. New York: Praeger, 1970.

——. *Vietnam and the United States*. Washington, DC: Public Affairs, 1965.

Palmier, Jean-Michel. *Weimar in Exile: The Anti-Fascist Emigration in Europe and America*. Brooklyn, NY: Verso, 2017.

Pike, Frederick B., *Chile and the United States, 1880–1962: The Emergence of Chile's Social Crisis and the Challenge to United States Diplomacy*. Notre Dame, IN: University of Notre Dame Press, 1963.

Rice, Condoleezza. *Democracy: Stories from the Long Road to Freedom*. New York: Twelve, 2017.

Schlafly, Phyllis, and Chester Ward. *Kissinger on the Couch*. New Rochelle, NY: Arlington House, 1975.

Smith, Steven B. *Reading Leo Strauss: Politics, Philosophy, Judaism.* Chicago: University of Chicago Press, 2007.

Stoessinger, John G. *Henry Kissinger: The Anguish of Power.* New York: Norton, 1976.

Strauss, Leo. "German Nihilism." *Interpretation* 26, no. 3 (Spring 1999).

———. *An Introduction to Political Philosophy: Ten Essays.* Detroit: Wayne State University Press, 1989.

———. *Natural Right and History.* Chicago: University of Chicago Press, 1965.

———. *Persecution and the Art of Writing.* Chicago: University of Chicago Press, 1988.

———. *The Rebirth of Classical Political Rationalism: An Introduction to the Thought of Leo Strauss.* Chicago: University of Chicago Press, 1989.

Suri, Jeremi. *Henry Kissinger and the American Century.* Cambridge, MA: Harvard University Press, 2007.

Thompson, Kenneth, and Robert J. Myers (eds.). *A Tribute to Hans J. Morgenthau.* Washington, DC: New Republic Book, 1977.

Young-Bruehl, Elisabeth. *Hannah Arendt: For Love of the World.* New Haven, Yale University Press, 2004.

Zimmer, Louis B. *The Vietnam War Debate: Hans J. Morgenthau and the Attempt to Halt the Drift into Disaster.* Lanham, MD: Lexington, 2011.

CREDITS

INDEX